International Economic

International economic integration has been one of the most important issues of recent years. It has played a significant part in the economic policy decisions for most countries and regions throughout the world. But why has the success of integration schemes been so variable? And what are the prospects for integration in the future?

This new edition of *International Economic Integration* addresses these crucial questions, presenting new material covering developments in the 1990s. The author continues to extend traditional integration theory by developing a new model which incorporates market imperfections such as economies of scale and foreign direct investment and which reflects modern approaches to trade, competition and investment. The main types of integration – customs models, common markets and economic unions – are discussed in detail and key examples of integration schemes are assessed. These include the enlargement of the European Union, integration in North America, as well as examples of emerging schemes in the Pacific region, Latin America, South-East Asia and Africa. The concluding chapter outlines the positive and negative aspects of international economic integration.

Providing an excellent understanding of the complex issues involved with international economic integration, this volume will be extremely important for students of international economics and international business.

Miroslav N. Jovanović is Associate Economic Affairs Officer at the United Nations Economic Commission for Europe in Geneva.

International Economic Integration

Limits and Prospects

Second Edition

Miroslav N. Jovanović

Foreword by Richard G. Lipsey

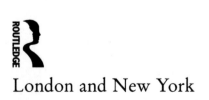

London and New York

First published 1992. This edition published 1998 by Routledge
11 New Fetter Lane, London EC4P 4EE

Simultaneously published in the USA and Canada
by Routledge
29 West 35th Street, New York, NY 10001

© 1992, 1998 Miroslav N. Jovanović

Typeset in Garamond by Pure Tech India Ltd, Pondicherry
Printed and Bound in Great Britain by
Creative Print and Design (Wales), Ebbw Vale

British Library Cataloguing in Publication Data
A catalogue record for this book is available from the British Library

Library of Congress Cataloguing in Publication Data
Jovanović Miroslav N., 1957–
International economic integration: limits and prospects /
Miroslav N. Jovanović. – 2nd ed.
Includes bibliographical reference and index.
1. International economic integration. I. Title.
HF 1418.5.J68 1998
337. 1 – dc21
97–17423
CIP
ISBN 0-415-16450-8 (hbk)
ISBN 0-415-16451-6 (pbk)

Својим синовима, Јовану и Николи-Александру
Στους υιούς μου, Γιάννη και Νικόλαο–Αλέξανδρο
To my sons, Jovan and Nikola-Aleksandar

Contents

Figures

Tables

Foreword

In this, his second edition, Miroslav Jovanović has improved and elaborated on his already comprehensive work on the economics of integration, passing from customs unions to common markets to full economic integration. The most distinctive aspect of his treatment continues to be his own creative union of theory and applied material. For him, theory is no abstract game played for the amusement of the players, but a tool for enlightening our understanding of what we see in the world around us. For him, the major interest resides always in the problems created by working out various forms of union in real situations.

Thus, theoretical and applied considerations are blended from the outset. After a brief, stage-setting, introductory chapter, Chapter 2 deals with customs unions, with an shorter concluding section on free trade areas. The chapter begins with the static, partial-equilibrium analysis of tariffs and customs unions and goes on to consider general equilibrium analyses. Even here, however, we find discussions of the European Union's Common Agricultural Policy (CAP), employment policies, national security object- ives, infant industries, bilateral and unilateral tariff reductions.

The analysis of tariffs and customs unions is followed by a brief consid- eration of subsidies. The theory is presented first, followed by a discussion which covers, among other things, the GATT (General Agreement on Tariffs and Trade) position on subsidies and countervailing duties, political issues in the choice between subsidies and tariffs, procurement policies, output and export subsidies, and the American DISC (Domic International Sales Cor- poration) policy.

In the section entitled 'Dynamic Models', we find nothing about non- linear dynamics, chaos theory, self-organizing systems or evolutionary biology. Instead, we read about competition in technological advance, intra-industry trade, the EC's competition policy, the case for state inter- vention in non-competitive markets, scale economies in various industries, predatory pricing, and pre-emptive investment. In line with the growing interest of economists in technological change at the microeconomic level the section on competition in innovation has been greatly expanded in this new edition.

In short, Chapter 2 sets the tone for the whole volume. It selects topic areas one after another; it reviews the relevant theory of each, on the assumption that the reader already has some acquaintance with it; it then goes on to consider a host of important, applied issues in the area under consideration. The reader wanting to know the relevant theory, and the main applied issues that have arisen around any topic relating to customs unions will find that this chapter provides excellent source material, as well as a valuable consideration of most of the issues.

Chapter 3 takes similar approach, this time with respect to issues surrounding a common market. It starts with the theory of factor price equalization and then goes on to consider labour mobility from the points of view of both the sending and the receiving countries in general. This is followed by a short discussion of the experience of the EU. The coverage then passes to capital mobility in general, which leads naturally to a consideration of foreign direct investment (FDI) and transnational corporations (TNCs). The experience of Canada, the US, and the EU illustrate the issues that are involved in the important question of the appropriate policy stance for national governments to adopt towards FDI of various types and in various situations. There is unlikely to be anything as simple as 'the' correct stance for all countries in all situations in anything as complex in its costs and its benefits as FDI. This is why Dr. Jovanović's pragmatic approach of looking at specific cases on their merits, rather than looking for universal theoretical presumptions, is so useful.

Chapter 4 on economic union is by far the longest chapter, around a half the book. This is as it should be, since economic union is the final goal of many of the looser associations. Sometimes this is their stated goal, and sometimes forces unleased by looser forms of integration push their members in that direction. Dr. Jovanović's treatment of these issues verges on the exhaustive.

Coordinated monetary policy is a central part of economic union. Often, as EU experience shows, it is the next step after a common market. The issues around monetary policy are studied in detail, both in terms of the traditional model and a cost-benefit analysis. This raises the well-known issues of optimal currency areas, as well as the less well known, but probably more important, issues involved in delimitating an optimal policy area. The chapter concludes with a new section on the proposed European Monetary Union. It is quite critical of the Maastricht-based EMU and is pessimistic about either of their suggested ways out of its present difficulties: relaxing the conditions of membership or delaying the timetable for the whole project.

Fiscal policy is an important aspect of any economic union. A complete unification of all spending and taxing measures in the various units of the union is not necessary – as the US economic union illustrates with its substantial variations in tax and spending patterns among individual state governments. A desirable characteristic, however, is that differences in tax policies do not exert major influences on the decisions of firms choosing locations within the union. In contrast, it does seem possible to accommodate significant differences in spending that reflect different philosophical positions on the place of the state in providing such measures as income security, welfare, environmental protection, and public goods. These spending differences call for the use of taxes that do not affect business costs to raise different sums of money in different jurisdictions, while keeping rates of taxes that do affect business costs relatively similar. These, and many other issues, arise on the fiscal side of economic integration.

Miroslav Jovanović devotes considerable space to the important topic of industrial policy, which is occupying much government attention in the 1990s, sometimes under different names. Governments are concerned about footloose, knowledge-intensive industries, both when they have them (lest they lose them), and when they do not have them (in hope of attracting them). Rightly or wrongly, new industrial policies are key issues in many countries today, and harmonizing them poses major problems for jurisdictions that belong to economic unions. In view of the vast complexity of the subject, Dr. Jovanović's treatment must be sketchy in places. He does, however, cover virtually all of the important issues that might need further, in-depth study by those seeking a detailed appreciation.

Regional policy poses even more vexing problems than does industrial policy. Over the years, and in most countries, regional policies have had much more uniformly disappointing results than industrial policies – perhaps because regional policies have so often concentrated on supporting sunset industries, and on locating isolated new enterprises with no consideration for Michael Porter's point about the need for clusters of related firms if a genuine competitive advantage is to be created. Dr. Jovanović deals with key issues of regional policy in general and then illustrates them with the experience of the EU.

The wholly new Chapter 5 provides a welcome survey of various actual integration schemes, excluding the EU which has already been dealt with inter alia in many of the previous discussions. Annex III on eastern enlargement of the EU provides an informative analysis of the transition problems, as well as those associated with the possible eventual assimilation of all of the countries of eastern Europe into the EU.

Readers who set out on these pages have a rich and varied experience awaiting them. The coverage is remarkably comprehensive, considering that it is all condensed into around 400 pages. For every reader there will be things to agree with, and things to argue with – as is to be expected in so rich a survey. In the end, however, many readers will agree with the author when he writes in the course of his summing up:

> It is hard to forecast with a high degree of accuracy when and how will the effects of integration turn out. In the short term just after the lifting of barriers to trade, production, GNP and commerce may increase while

some prices may fall....In the medium and long-term, structural adjustment takes place and economies of scale occur....Market rigidities are being eased as agents change their behaviour due to increased opportunities for business and competition. It is this context where the dynamic effects of integration are materialized. (see pp. 354–5)...International economic integration is not an economic policy choice that would frighten small and medium-sized countries. The only thing that these countries would lose while integrating is the illusion that international economic integration is a bad policy choice. (see p. 360)

This quotation comes from the concluding chapter which, if someone I had to recommend only one piece to get the flavour of the issues involved in economic integration, would be high on my short list. The conclusion is followed by a list of research topics which with any luck will be a list of realised PhD dissertations ten years from now.

R. G. Lipsey
Vancouver, B. C., Canada

Preface

The traditional theory of international economic integration is an elegant and quite convincing academic exercise. Its conclusions are straightforward and offer useful insights into the incentives for and the general consequences of integration. With that in mind, the first objective of this book is to introduce the reader to the area of international economic integration. The other objective, equally important, is to extend the traditional theory of integration by considering market imperfections, an issue put aside in the neo-classical model of integration. Analysis is supplemented by numerous examples from the real world in order to provide support for theoretical statements. A quantitative approach to analysis is kept at the minimum; thus, it is hoped that the book will be readily accessible to a wide audience, just as was the case with the first edition.

A presentation of a general theory of international economic integration is not (yet) possible. This is due primarily to the absence of a generally applicable theory of international trade. The neo-classical trade theory has looked at comparative advantages, hence, the standard theory of regional economic integration has largely been presented in such a framework. A modern theory and policy on trade cannot be separated from competition and industrial policies. New research models identified other determinants of countries' trade patterns. In a world of imperfect competition, various externalities and economies of scale, there are many reasons for trade, foreign direct investment and integration, even if countries are identical in their factor endowments, size, technologies and tastes. In such a situation, there are a number of second-best choices about economic actions. This book considers both theoretical and practical economic choices linked with international economic integration.

The analysis acknowledges the importance of the traditional, neo-classical theory of trade: countries trade because they are differently endowed with resources, technology and/or tastes. None the less, such a trade model is more appropriate to trade in simple goods such as wheat, wine or textiles, while the new theory is better suited as a theoretical tool for the analysis of trade in goods such as aircraft and pharmaceuticals, as well as services such as marketing.[1] The new theoretical model supplements the traditional one with a novel quality. This is the consideration of market imperfections: in particular, economies of scale, externalities and foreign direct investment. Being inconsistent with perfect competition, increasing returns to scale were left out of the picture in the traditional model. The new model questions the conventional argument that free trade is always an optimal economic strategy. In the case of market imperfections, integration/regionalism can make sense.

Once trade and competition take place in an imperfect economic environment, solutions to economic problems are no longer unique. The outcomes of economic games depend on assumptions about the behaviour of players. In these circumstances, economic policy (intervention in the form of integration) may simply add an adjustment mechanism to the already highly imperfect and sub-optimal market situation. It may also be abused by those who rely on certain (incomplete) economic facts in order to pursue rent-seeking goals. When the economic situation is not simple and straightforward, many outcomes become possible, but not equally desirable. Therefore, the new model of economic integration is a mix of various theoretical approaches to trade, competition and investment. It does not argue that the classical model is wrong, but rather that it is not necessarily correct. Market imperfections need not be rectified by new barriers to trade, factor mobility and foreign investment, but rather by domestic policies that assist in the easing of the problem (of competitiveness) at its source, such as the supply of certain types of labour and venture capital.

Contrary to the widespread belief, the new model does not give *carte blanche* to medium- and long-term protectionism (with the possible exception being the field of education), because retaliation and counter-retaliation makes everybody worse off. Intervention may be employed under certain conditions as a short-term tool. In addition, governments do not always have all the necessary information for intelligent intervention, but neither do free markets always bring desirable solutions. The new model argues that with a bit of astute intervention, under certain conditions, economic policy may improve a country's national and international economic position.

Treatment of the theory of international economic integration has been basically Eurocentric, because integration had its deepest meaning there. However, there are no theoretical differences between integration among industrialized and among less developed countries. The arguments in favour of integration are the same. What may differ are the intentions and ambitions of countries, as well as the starting base. In spite of the poor achievements of previous integration efforts by the developing world, those countries may still wish to employ international economic integration as their developments strategy, but perhaps by no longer following the South–South integration path as in the past, but rather trying north–south integration as exemplified in the case of Mexico.

The book is organized as follows. After the Introduction (Chapter 1), the subject matter of Chapter 2 are issues related to customs unions. That is the most rigorously developed part of the theory of international economic integration. The analysis is carried out in static and dynamic models, as well as in partial- and general-equilibrium frameworks. Increased competition, specialization and returns to scale receive special treatment as they are the most important dynamic effects. A discussion of adjustment costs suggests that they do not represent a serious barrier to integration.

Chapter 3 is devoted to common markets. Factor (labour and capital) mobility lies at the heart of the analysis. Equalization of factor prices and the prospects for increased foreign direct investment by transnational corporations are evaluated in the integration arrangements of both developed and developing countries. Analysis is supported by statistical data on foreign direct investment in the European Union.[2]

Chapter 4 examines economic unions. Monetary, fiscal, industrial and regional polices are considered in turn. The point is that all these policies in an economic union can be defended by the same arguments which are used to justify similar policies in a single country consisting of several regions. Monetary policy is the area where the effects of integration are felt first. Fiscal policy refers to taxation and budgetary problems among countries. The creation of comparative advantage and wealth is considered in the discussion of industrial policy in manufacturing and services. The distribution of wealth is stressed in regional policy which is used as a buffer against the potentially negative consequences of other economic policies.

Past, present and emerging integration schemes are examined in Chapter 5. Integration arrangements are distributed on deals in the developed and developing world. Schemes in western and eastern Europe are supplemented by the possible eastern enlargement of the European Union, integration in north America, the arrangement between Australia and New Zealand and the slowly emerging integration of the Pacific region. Integration in Latin America and the potential western hemisphere free trade area opens the discussion of deals in the developing countries. It is followed by integration arrangements in Africa and concluded by south-east Asian integration.

Chapter 6 deals with the measurement of the effects of international economic integration. There are serious methodological limits to quantification of these effects. Most importantly, it is not yet possible to create a reliable counterfactual situation which would simulate the scenarios occuring with or without integration. It is stated that the end result of estimations is an amalgam of various effects, some of which have nothing to do with integration. Hence, the theory of international economic integration is in certain cases more intuitive than conclusive.

Chapter 7 concludes the book and argues that regional economic integration is now here to stay. Even though the results of the Uruguay Round provided a major impetus to multilateral solutions in international trade, regional trade arrangements (mainly free trade areas) continue to expand. In part, that is the outcome of globalization of the economy and pressures from the business community to eliminate the remaining barriers to trade and investment. In addition, multilateral liberalization and regionalism could reinforce each other and go hand in hand, provided that the regional integration schemes adopt a relatively liberal external trade and investment policy. On those grounds, regional arrangements may be a favourable development for the world economy. It is important to keep in mind that countries grow richer in the medium and long term together (not at each others' expense).

I hope that the book will be of interest to economists specializing in international economics, international trade and integration, European studies and European integration. However, if it is also of interest to those studying economic development, international business and policy makers, then this is to be welcomed.

NOTES

1 One may even argue that both the classical and the new theory of trade are limited to a few special cases. None the less, one should not disregard the consideration of extreme cases as many useful things may be learned from the analysis of such examples.
2 The term European Union (EU) is used throughout the book as the organizational habitat for the European integration that took place over time in the European Economic Community, European Community and the EU.

Acknowledgements

My involvement in international economic integration began when I was studying European integration at the Europa Institute of the University of Amsterdam during the 1980/81 academic year. However, another event was responsible for the writing of the first edition of this book. That was my study and research programme at Queen's University, Kingston, Ontario, during the 1986/87 academic year. I continued working on it at the University of Belgrade and finalized it at the United Nations Centre on Transnational Corporations in New York. The second edition benefited from my work at the United Nations Economic Commission for Europe in Geneva.

I have benefited from human capital and discussions with many friends and colleagues. There are, however, several to whom I owe special gratitude for the assistance in the preparation of the first edition. Michael Spencer helped me the most. Oskar Kovač, Mića Panić and George Yannopoulos have read the whole manuscript of the first edition and provided valuable comments. I have also received assistance from Yngvi Hardarson, Richard G. Lipsey, Randi Moi and Ed Saperstein. Vilborg Hjartardottir entered the first version of the manuscript into a PC.

In the preparation of the second edition I had delightful and advantageous contacts with Carol Cosgrove-Sacks, Victoria Curzon Price, Persephone Economou, Cristina Giordano, Birgit Hegge, Dušan Sidjanski, Rolf Traeger, Peter Ungar and Joanna Wheeler who helped me in various ways. Slobodan Gatarić continued to solve PC-related problems. The UN library provided me with most of the sources. Finally, Alan Jarvis and Alison Kirk of Routledge encouraged this project from the outset.

I am grateful to all of them. The usual disclaimer, however, applies here: it is I who am responsible for all shortcomings and mistakes. In addition, the expressed views are my own and have nothing to do with the organization in which I work.

Miroslav N. Jovanović
Geneva, September 1997

Abbreviations

ASEAN	Association of South East Asian Nations
BAP	Biotechnologies Action Programme
BRITE	Basic Research in Industrial Technologies in Europe
CACM	Central American Common Market
CAP	Common Agricultural Policy
CEAO	Communauté Economique de l'Afrique de l'Ouest (West African Economic Community)
CEFTA	Central European Free Trade Agreement
CFA	Communauté Financière Africaine
CMEA	Council for Mutual Economic Assistance
COCOM	Coordinating Committee on Multilateral Export Controls
DISC	Domestic International Sales Corporation
DTI	Department of Trade and Industry
EAC	East African Community
ECB	European Central Bank
ECLAIR	European Collaborative Linkage of Agriculture and Industry through Research
ECOFIN	Economic and Financial Committee
ECOWAS	Economic Community of West African States
ECU	European Currency Unit
EEC	European Economic Community
EFTA	European Free Trade Association
EMI	European Monetary Institute
EMS	European Monetary System
ERDF	European Regional Development Fund
ERM	Exchange Rate Mechanism
ESPRIT	European Programme for Research in Information Technology
EU	European Union
EUREKA	European Research Cooperation Agency
FAST	Forecasting and Assessment in Science and Technology
FDI	foreign direct investment
FIRA	Foreign Investment Review Agency
GATT	General Agreement on Tariffs and Trade

GDP	gross domestic product
GNP	gross national product
GSP	Generalized System of Preferences
IBEC	International Bank for Economic Cooperation
IGC	inter-governmental conference
IIB	International Investment Bank
IIT	intra-industry trade
IMF	International Monetary Fund
LAFTA	Latin American Free Trade Area
LAIA	Latin American Integration Association
LDC	less developed country
MERCOSUR	Mercado Común del Sur (The Southern Common Market)
MFN	most-favoured nation
MITI	Ministry of International Trade and Industry
NAFTA	North American Free Trade Agreement
NAIRU	non-accelerating-inflation rate of unemployment
NATO	North Atlantic Treaty Organization
NTB	non-tariff barrier
OECD	Organization for Economic Cooperation and Development
PHARE	Poland, Hungary: Assistance for Economic Restructuring
PPS	purchasing power standard
PTA	Preferential Trade Area (for eastern and southern African states)
RACE	Research and Development in Advanced Communication for Europe
R&D	research and development
SACU	South African Customs Union
SCP	structure-conduct-performance
SITC	Standard International Trade Classification
SME	small and medium-sized enterprise
TACIS	Technical Assistance for the Commonwealth of Independent States
TNC	transnational corporation
TRIM	trade-related investment measure
UDEAC	Union Douanière et Economique de l'Afrique Centrale (Customs and Economic Union of Central Africa)
VAT	value added tax
VCR	video cassette recorder
WAMU	West African Monetary Union
WTO	World Trade Organization

Before I built a wall
I'd ask to know
What I was walling in
or walling out...

Robert L. Frost (1875–1963)

1 Introduction

I ISSUES

The importance of international economic integration is well recognized.[1] It has touched most of the countries in the world and it became an unavoidable element in most economic policy decisions. In fact, most of the countries throughout the world have attempted to integrate with other ones. The biggest achievements in integration, however, have been among the developed countries, in particular the European Union (EU), because integration both deepened and widened in that region. Countries in other areas of the world have tried to copy some of the integration achievements that took place in Europe. Policy makers usually had a favourable view of integration. They attempted to use economic integration as a means of securing access to a wider market and reinforce growth in order to attain a higher level of national welfare. The degree of success in integration, however, has varied between regions. In the EU, following the elimination of tariffs and quotas in 1968, a deepening of integration covered areas such as competition, public procurement and services, thus preceding multilateral negotiations and agreements on these issues. Developing countries have altered their past inward-looking integration strategies of 1960s towards improved economic ties with the north in the 1990s. However, because of the changed aspirations, past experiences in integration in the developing world are not very useful guides for future integration policy. None the less, international economic integration has remained an attractive economic strategy in the developing world. This is because integration can serve as a reliable 'insurance policy' against sudden changes in the trading behaviour of partner countries. 'Dividends' from such a policy include an increase in business predictability which has a potentially positive impact on domestic and foreign investment.

In spite of past experiences with integration, which may have been quite negative in certain groups that integrated the developing countries, new opportunities are still there. They have been prompted by at least four developments since the mid-1980s. First, is the deepening and widening of integration in the EU and North America; second, economic transition in the formerly centrally planned economies in central and eastern Europe and the possibility of some kind of integration with the EU; third, a change in economic policies in the developing countries towards more outward-looking models; and fourth, integration between developed countries (such as the United States and Canada) with a developing one (such as Mexico).

The founders of the General Agreement on Tariffs and Trade (GATT) recognized the importance of economic integration between countries. That process can have an identical economic rationale as integration within a single country that has different regions. Hence, regional economic integration, according to the World Trade Organization (WTO), does not pose an inherent threat to global integration. None the less, the GATT (Article XXIV) constrains the level of the common external tariff and other trade measures in customs unions. On the whole, these trade measures should not be higher or more restrictive than the ones of the member countries prior to the integration agreement. Between 1947 and 1995 a total of 98 integration agreements had been notified to the GATT (Annex I). However, only six agreements were 'cleared' by the working party through the consensus principle. For others, including the 'clearance' of the Treaty of Rome that established the European Economic Community (EEC) in 1957, the final 'clearance' was inconclusive. One of the reasons why there was no definite agreement in the working party was the ambivalent effects of integration on non-members. Therefore, this inconclusive nature of the Treaty of Rome set the pattern for nearly all future reviews of integration agreements notified under Article XXIV (World Trade Organization, 1995).

The interdependence of economic life among countries created a situation in which national economic problems increasingly become a matter of international concern. The predominant way of solving these international problems is still found at the national level where the most decisive influence is wielded by a small number of large and highly developed countries, as well as a few oil-exporting ones. While free market competition can create a situation in which large firms can absorb their small competitors, such an analogy is not possible when one deals with sovereign countries. Large and developed countries can not always behave like firms (Panić, 1988, p. 284).

Statements from prominent figures in public life, in particular from the larger nations, often make headlines and can have an impact on currency market, trade policy and the like. Therefore, such remarks need to measured with care. A statement by President Clinton of the US that each nation is 'like a big corporation competing in the global marketplace' is identical to saying that the US and Japan are competitors in the same way as Coca-Cola competes with Pepsi (Krugman, 1996a, p. 4).[2] Firms are rivals for a limited pool of potential profits. Period. What distinguishes states from firms is that one firm may absorb another, which is not possible in normal circumstances in the case of states.[3] In addition, states may introduce protectionist measures (international disintegration). Such an option is not open to firms. Countries are not firms. They can not be driven out of every business.[4]

However, countries can be driven out of some lines of business which may have permanent effects on trade. States produce goods that compete with each other, but more importantly states are each others' export markets and suppliers of useful things. David Ricardo taught us in 1817 that international trade is *not* about competition, *but* rather about mutually beneficial exchange. The purpose of trade is imports, not exports. Imports give a country the chance to get what it wants. Exports is a toll that a country must 'suffer' in order to pay for its imports. Those ideas by Ricardo were as much misunderstood two centuries ago, as they are today.

Coordination of economic policies and international economic integration may ease, and even solve the majority of international economic problems. Economic nationalism, as opposed to coordination and integration/ regionalism, has always been quite an appealing economic strategy. This is because the mechanisms for the protection from the unfavourable effects of integration/regionalism and trade liberalization, which have a basically short-term nature, are not fully developed. This book argues that:

- international economic integration is a desirable strategy, at least for small and medium-sized countries;
- the benefits of integration come in the long run; and
- the long-term benefits are greater than the possible short-run costs.

In theory, economic efficiency can be fostered by a policy of free trade which stimulates competition. It rationalizes production of goods and services and provides for a higher average standard of living and greater welfare in the future. The adjustment to free trade, at least within the integrated group, should not be traumatic at all. There is substantial evidence of this in the relatively frictionless adjustment to the successive reductions in tariffs under the GATT and the system of transparent rules for trade, as well as the smooth transition to the creation of the EU, the European Free Trade Association (EFTA) and North American Free Trade Agreement (NAFTA).

Large and developed countries depend to a lesser degree on external relations than do small countries. In theory, these countries may have a diversified economic structure which provides the opportunity for an autarchic economic policy, while such a policy for small countries in a situation of economies of scale and other externalities does not have a long-term economic rationale. Without a secure and free access to a wider market, a relatively limited domestic market and demand in small countries often prevents the employment of the most efficient technology, even if trade barriers are prohibitive. If certain production takes place, the consequences include short production runs, high prices and a lower standard of living. The efficient operation of many modern technologies requires secure access to the widest market which does not exist in small, and sometimes, medium-sized countries. Elimination of tariffs, non-tariff barriers (NTBs), restrictions on factor mobility, as well as international coordination of economic policies and integration can be solutions to this problem of country size. The goal is to increase, improve and secure access to the markets of the participating countries.

A liberal trade and flexible adjustment policy for a small country may be a superior alternative to the policy of long-term protection. The competitive position of small countries can be jeopardized if protection increases the price of inputs. Moreover, protection can provoke retaliatory measures from trading partners. It can also inhibit the adjustment incentives of the protected industry with an overall negative long-term impact on the whole economy. While having a limited influence on the events in the world economy, small countries can have leverage over their own competitive future by means of a liberal economic policy and/or international economic integration.

Global negotiations over tariff reductions were organized by the GATT/WTO with 'moderate' success. Successive rounds of negotiations have, however, significantly reduced tariffs on selected manufactured goods. Until the Uruguay Round, little was done to liberalize trade in agriculture, services, textiles and clothing, or to lower NTBs which have mushroomed as tariffs were dismantled. Due to different economic, political, climatic, cultural and other idiosyncrasies, it is unlikely that countries around the world would readily offer universal concessions in trade. One can easily imagine a case in which those concessions can be exchanged within a smaller and cosy group of countries with significantly less effort than on a universal scale. In addition, monitoring of the implementation of the arrangement and resolution of disputes is simpler within a relatively smaller group of countries, as well as there being fewer incentives and opportunities to cheat. Hence, a regional integration arrangement is more credible and the potential for cooperation within the group is improved.

Free trade and the unimpeded movement of factors is the first best policy in a world which does not have any distortions. This is only a hypothetical situation. The rationale for international economic integration may be found in the case where there are distortions. When one distortion (for example, a universal tariff of a country) is replaced by another (for example, a common external tariff of a customs union), the net welfare effect may be unchanged, positive or negative. The theory of international economic integration is the analysis of a second best situation and it is not surprising that general principles can not be found. What matters, however, is not only the prediction of theory, but rather what happens in real life. This book shows that despite the second best character of international economic integration in theory, in practice integration/regionalism may, under certain conditions, be a workable and acceptable economic strategy. A policy recommendation for small and medium-sized countries is that in a world of continuous technological and market changes, integration may expand and secure markets for the greatest variety of a country's goods and services in the future and, hence, mitigate the costs of adjustment.

II DEFINITIONS

The main objective of economic activities is an increase in welfare. The approach towards this goal is at the heart of the issue which deals with the organization of the human community because players have various and often conflicting interests and potential. The organization should allow agents to maximize their utility in the pursuit of their own ends, capabilities and expectations, subject to the limitations presented by the environment.

International economic integration is one of the means for an increase in welfare. With this arrangement, countries may increase the welfare either of the integrated group, or of some countries within the group, or of the world as a whole. Machlup (1979, p. 3) stated that the term integration in economics was first used in industrial organization to refer to combinations of firms. Horizontal integration referred to linkages of competitors, while vertical integration referred to the unification of suppliers and buyers. As a term, the integration of economies of separate states was not found anywhere in the old, chiefly historical, literature on the economic interrelationship between states, nor in the literature about customs unions (including the German *Zollverein* 1834–71), nor in the literature on international trade prior to the 1940s. Viner (1950) was the first to lay the foundation for the theory of customs unions which represented the core of the traditional theory of international economic integration.

International economic integration does not have a clear-cut meaning for all economists. One of the first definitions of integration was given by Tinbergen (1954, p. 122). He defined, on the one hand, *negative* integration as the removal of discriminatory and restrictive institutions and the introduction of freedom for economic transactions. On the other hand, the adjustment of existing and the establishment of new policies and institutions endowed with coercive powers was identified as *positive* integration. This introduced some confusion since freedom was described as 'negative', while coercion was regarded as a 'positive' move! Experience teaches us that it is easier to advance in the direction of 'negative' integration (removal of tariffs and quotas), than towards 'positive' integration (introduction of common economic policies) because the 'positive' approach deals with sensitive issues of national sovereignty.

Pinder (1969, pp. 143–145) cites the *Oxford Dictionary* which described integration as the combination of parts into a whole. Union is the outcome of the combination of these parts or members. He concluded that integration was a process towards union and defined economic integration as the removal of discrimination between the economic agents of the member countries, as well as the creation and implementation of common policies.

Kahnert *et al.* (1969, p. 11) understands integration as a process of the progressive removal of discrimination that exists along national borders. That is, however, only a part of what integration brings. Other components of integration such as a common policy in trade or factor mobility, were left out of the definition.

Balassa (1973, p. 1) defines economic integration both as a process and as a state of affairs.[5] As a process (dynamic concept), integration meant the removal of discrimination between different states, while as a state of affairs (static concept) it meant the absence of different forms of discrimination. The Achilles' heel of this definition is its restriction in concentrating only on the process or state of affairs among the countries that integrate. One can distinguish among intra-national (inter-provincial), international and world (universal, global) integration. Agreements among states about adjustment or coordination of some economic areas could be called integration, so one could deal with sectoral and general integration. Balassa's definition did not say if economic integration was the final goal or a point on the way towards some target. This ambiguity could be avoided by making a distinction between complete and partial integration.

Maksimova (1976, p. 33) argues that economic integration was a process of developing deep and stable relationships about the division of labour between national economies. That is, a process for the formation of international economic entities, within the framework of groups of countries with the same type of socio-economic system, which are consciously regulated in the interests of the ruling classes of these countries. It is true that international economic integration is a highly politicized process, but this definition excludes the possibility of integration even by means of preferential and/or cooperative agreements between countries that have different political systems. This is important in practice as there has been a whole spectrum of integration agreements between the EU and developing countries which have the widest range of political systems. None the less, the EU requests that applicant countries for the full membership of the EU have a stable democratic political system comparable to those in the current member countries.

Holzman (1976, p. 59) states that economic integration was a situation in which the prices of all similar goods and similar factors in two regions were equalized. This made the two regions in essence one region or market. This definition implies that economic integration was the realization of factor price equalization between two regions. It implicitly assumes that there are no barriers to the movements of goods, services and factors between the two regions and that there are institutions that facilitate those movements.

Marer and Montias (1988, p. 156) point out that economic integration has traditionally been equated with the division of labour in a geographical region, although it was usually not made clear what minimum level of trade would justify speaking of integration. Recently, economic integration was assumed to consist of the internationalization of markets for capital, labour, technology and entrepreneurship in addition to markets for goods and services. They argue (p. 161) that the necessary and sufficient condition for complete integration is the equality of prices of any pair of goods in every member country (adjusted for transportation costs). The same criticism as of Holzman's definition applies here too.

Panić (1988, pp. 3–5) distinguishes among openness, integration and interdependence. An economy is open if it has few barriers to international trade and factor movements. Because an economy is open does not necessarily mean that it is integrated in the international economic system. International integration has its full meaning only when it describes an active participation in the international division of labour. Two or more economies are said to be interdependent when they are linked to such a degree that economic developments in each of them are significantly influenced by the economic situation and policies in the partner country.

Molle (1991, p. 5) equates economic integration with the gradual elimination of economic frontiers between countries. As a rule, the process of elimination of 'economic frontiers' is gradual. The transition period for full adjustment to the new situation usually takes, in practice, at least five to ten years. However, following the establishment of the European Economic Area in 1994 between the EU and most of EFTA countries, the participating EFTA states had to apply the *acquis communautaire* (all existing EU laws and regulations) without delay, except in a few specified cases. There was no transition period!

Drysdale and Garnaut (1993, p. 189) look at integration only as a movement towards one single price for a good, service or factor of production. If one wants to encompass the term integration, then one needs to refer also to policies that make that movement happen. In addition, if integration refers to issues such as social policy including education, then it includes more than a 'technical' move towards equalization of prices.

Mennis and Sauvant (1976, p. 75) consider integration as a process whereby boundaries between nation-states become less discontinuous, thereby leading to the formation of more comprehensive systems. They believe economic integration consists of the linking up and merging (not the abolition) of the industrial apparatus, administration and economic policies of the participating countries.

Pelkmans (1984, p. 3) defines economic integration as the elimination of economic frontiers between two or more economies. An economic frontier is a demarcation line across which the mobility of goods, services and factors is relatively low. The potential mobility of certain factors was the criterion for economic integration according to this passive definition of integration. There is no indication that such a policy actively promotes mobility and cooperation. The mere removal of 'economic frontiers' does not necessarily offer either a carrot or a stick to factors to move. There are many non-economic obstacles to mobility which include: language, custom, the propensity to stick to place of birth and the like for labour, while political and other risks inhibit capital movements.

El-Agraa (1985a, p. 1) refers to international economic integration as the discriminatory removal of all trade impediments between participating nations and the establishment of certain elements of coordination between them. This definition implies the removal of barriers to trade in goods and services, as well as freedom of movement for factors of production. Hence, this definition only partly covers free trade areas and customs unions as types of integration. Later on, El-Agraa (1988, p. xiii) takes international economic integration to mean an act of agreement between two or more nations to pursue common goals and policies. This is an 'active' definition of integration.

Robson (1987, p. 1) notes that economic integration was concerned with efficiency in resource use, with particular reference to the spatial aspect. He defines full integration as freedom of movement of goods and factors of production and an absence of discrimination. Freedom of movement for factors is not allowed for in some types of international economic integration, hence this definition can not be applied to all arrangements.

Swann (1996, p. 3) describes economic integration as a state of affairs or a process that involves the combination of previously separate economies into larger arrangements.

All these definitions of international economic integration reveal that integration is a complex notion which must be defined with care. Definitions of international economic integration are often vague and do not offer adequate tools for the easing of the process of integration among countries. Integration means different things in different countries and at different times. In the developed market economies integration is taken to be a way of introducing the most profitable technologies, allocate them in the most efficient way and foster free and fair competition; during the period of central planning in central and eastern Europe it meant the planning of the development of certain industrial activities; while in the developing countries integration was one of the tools for economic development. At the time of the German *Zollverein* the grouping of countries meant the development of economic interdependence and self-reliance. Today, international economic integration refers to an increase in the level of welfare.

Machlup (1979, p. 24) states that one of the most obvious signs of international economic integration is the non-existence of customs posts between integrated countries. Total economic integration among countries with market economies is not achieved until these countries know the level of their mutual trade. Statistics do not exist which can show the volume of trade between Pennsylvania and Ohio. This does not apply to integration arrangements among countries with central planning. In these countries the central plan always directed flows and decided volume and structure of foreign trade.

There is an unresolved question about what is to be integrated. Is it to be citizens, markets, production, consumption, commodities, services, regions, factors, money, resources, something else altogether, or just some of these components? What are the measures for the advance, stagnation or decline of international economic integration? What is the essence of international economic integration and what are the criteria for the appraisal of this process? Machlup (1979, p. 43) argues that trade is the quintessence of economic integration and the division of labour its underlying principle. If one neglects transportation costs, then the basic principle for the appraisal of international economic integration is equality of prices for comparable goods and services in all integrated countries. Machlup's test is much easier for standardized goods and services than for differentiated ones. A meaningful comparison of the price gap of a good in different markets should take into account not only the transport costs but also, and more importantly, the consumption patterns in different countries. This is an extremely difficult exercise. Income, tastes, traditions and climate may be homogeneous in relatively small areas, sometimes even within a single country. The more homogeneous are the countries, the easier the test. None the less, what is omitted from such a view of international economic integration is any consideration of foreign direct investment (FDI) and integrated international production ('globalization'). Compared with mere trade, FDI introduces a more profound and longer-term dimension into integration among countries. However, if foreign-owned production is to take place, an integration scheme has to provide freedom of establishment.

Finally, we can conclude that international economic integration is a process and a means by which a group of countries strives to increase its level of welfare. It involves the recognition that a weak or strong partnership between countries can achieve this goal in a more efficient way than by unilateral and independent pursuance of policy in each country. Integration requires at least some division of labour and freedom of movement for goods and services within the group. Relatively 'higher' types of integration arrangements also require a free mobility of factors of production within the integrated area, as well as certain restrictions on these movements between the integrated area and countries outside of it. The essential point is that these countries together adopt a kind of inward-looking approach and take more care about what happens in the group than about what happens outside of it. In addition, at least some consultation, if not coordination of competition, monetary, fiscal and regional development policies is a necessary condition for the success and durability of integration, as is the case in federal states. This is to be supported by an effective dispute settlement system. The process of integration may be practically unlimited, just as is the continuous integration of various regions within a single country. From a 'technical' point of view, international economic integration can be a finite process, i.e. the elimination of tariffs and quantitative restrictions, as well as the introduction of rules of competition and a common external protection in a customs union. However, new dimensions of competition, NTBs, standards, new technologies, as well as changes in the market, require continuous adjustments of individual countries and the group. This all makes integration more of an evolving and continuing process than of a limited one. International economic integration is a process by which the firms and economies of separate states merge in larger entities. Such a definition of integration, incorporating the ideas in this paragraph, will be maintained throughout this book.

III   TYPES

Consumption in an integrated area is potentially higher than the sum of the consumption of individual countries which are potential partners for integration in a situation in which trade is impeded by tariffs, quotas, NTBs and barriers to factor mobility. International economic integration removes, at least partly, these and other distortions to trade, competition and, possibly, investment. In this sense, international economic integration between at least two countries can be of the following seven theoretical types:

- A *preferential tariff agreement* among countries assumes that the tariffs on trade among the signatory countries are lower in relation to tariffs charged on trade with third countries.
- A *partial customs union* is formed when the participating countries retain their initial tariffs on their mutual trade and introduce a common external tariff on trade with third countries.
- A *free trade area* is an agreement among countries about the elimination of all tariff and quantitative restrictions on mutual trade. Every country in this area retains its own tariff and other regulation of trade with third countries. The bases of this agreement are the rules of origin. These rules prevent trade deflection which is the import of goods from third countries into the area by country A (that has a relatively lower external tariff than the partner country B) in order to re-export the good to country B. None the less, production deflection is possible if the production of goods that contain imported inputs is shifted to countries that have lower tariffs if the difference in tariffs offsets the difference in production costs.
- In a *customs union*, participating countries not only remove tariff and quantitative restrictions on their internal trade, but also introduce a common external tariff on trade with third countries. The participating countries take part in international negotiations about trade and tariffs as a single entity.
- In a *common market*, apart from a customs union, there exists free mobility of factors of production. Common regulations (restrictions) on the movement of factors with third countries are introduced.
- An *economic union* among countries assumes not only a common market, but also the harmonization of fiscal, monetary, industrial, regional, transport and other economic policies.
- A *total economic union* among countries assumes union with a single economic policy and a supranational government (of this confederation)

with great economic authority. There are no administrative barriers to the movements of goods, services and factors, hence prices are equalized net of transport costs.

Table 1.1 presents select theoretical types of international economic integration arrangements. The process of integration does not necessarily have to be gradual from one type to another. The establishment of any of these types depends on the agreement among the participating countries. Spontaneous or market integration is created by actions of transnational corporations (TNCs), banks and other financial institutions, often without the involvement of their parent governments, while formal or institutional integration seeks an official agreement among governments to eliminate select or all restrictions on trade and factor movements in their economic relations (Panić, 1988, pp. 6–7). There is substantial historical evidence to support the argument that the formal (*de jure*) approach to integration seeks a spontaneous (*de facto*) way, and vice versa. The decision about entering into a customs union or any other type of integration is in fact always political. The question of abandoning part of national sovereignty regarding taxation of trade (all in a customs union, a part of that in a free trade area) is made by politicians. The EU was, after all, not established in 1957 in order to liberalize trade, but rather to exclude the possibility of war between France and Germany. Economic integration was just a means for the achievement of that political goal.

An interesting case occurred following the establishment of a free trade area between Canada and the United States in 1988. There were moves to include Mexico in the NAFTA, only if the US entered into a bilateral free trade deal with Mexico and, then, concluded similar arrangements with other (Latin American) countries, that would create the hub-and-spoke model of integration (which was undesirable for Canada and other countries involved). The US, as the regional hub, would have a separate agreement with each spoke country. As such, the US would have advantages of

Table 1.1 Types of international economic integration

Policy action	*Type*				
	Free trade area	*Customs union*	*Common market*	*Economic union*	*Total economic union*
Removal of tariffs and quotas	Yes	Yes	Yes	Yes	Yes
Common external tariff	No	Yes	Yes	Yes	Yes
Factor mobility	No	No	Yes	Yes	Yes
Harmonization of economic policies	No	No	No	Yes	Yes
Total unification of economic policies	No	No	No	No	Yes

negotiating individually with each partner country, as well as being the only country with a tariff-free access to the markets of all participants, and with locational advantages for FDI. Therefore, Canada decided to be involved in the free trade deal with Mexico in order to avoid the negative consequences of the hub-and-spoke model of integration.

IV SOVEREIGNTY

International economic integration is popularly criticized on the grounds that it reduces a country's national sovereignty (undisputed political power). When two or more sovereign countries sign a treaty, they agree to do and/or not to do specified things. Therefore, it is not a valid criticism of any international treaty to say that it entails a loss of national sovereignty. All treaties do so in one way or another. The real issue is: do the countries' concessions constitute a mutually beneficial deal? Is the surrender of sovereignty justified by the results? Consider, for example, the Canadian debate leading up to the Canada–US Free Trade Agreement in Lipsey and York (1988).

Canada is a relatively small (in economic terms) and open economy. The competitive future of this country has been seriously jeopardized by the uncertain future of the relatively liberal international trading system. So, Canada negotiated and subsequently signed a Free Trade Agreement with the US in 1988. Negotiations and the pre-election period at that time were subject to one of the greatest debates in Canadian history. The opponents of the Agreement tried, with initial success, to persuade a majority of Canadians that the deal would significantly reduce Canadian sovereignty and distinctiveness. The fuss created by the opponents was perhaps one of the greatest in the history of international economic integration. Giving their vote to the Conservatives, the Canadians, however, supported the Agreement.

There was a fear that Canada would need to harmonize a range of economic policies with the US. If experience is a reliable guide, then this fear is not relevant. The Netherlands has a developed and costly social policy while Belgium spends relatively less in this area. Yet, these two countries have been in a free trade area for more than a half a century without harmonizing their social policies! As for other economic policies, pressures for harmonization do exist. If tax rates differ among countries and if factors are allowed to move, then, other things being equal, factors will move to countries where the tax burden is lower. But note: these harmonizing pressures exist even in a situation without integration! Within, for example, a common market, apart from the agreed matters, countries will have to give each other national treatment. It means that countries can have any policy they wish, even those which are completely different from policies in the partner countries with just one important condition. The country should not use these policies to discriminate between partner countries on the basis of their nationality. International economic integration is not the enemy of diversity in many economic policies. In others, such as EU fiscal policy, integration reduces the diversity of the main policy instruments. This issue raises all sorts of problems when economies at various levels of development, facing different problems, become integrated. They ought to coordinate, even harmonize, such policies.

If a small country (such as Albania or Cuba) accepts a long-term policy of protection, as opposed to liberalization, openness or international economic integration, it chooses a long-term deterioration in its international economic position. This is coupled with a reduction in living standards in relation to countries which do not employ protectionism as their economic strategy. Can a country preserve its sovereignty and the welfare of its citizens with a long-term declining trend in the standard of living?

The expectation of a net economic gain compared with the situation without integration is the most fundamental incentive for international economic integration. Anticipated gains from secure access to a larger market include an increase in the efficiency in the use of factors due to increased competition, specialization, economies of scale, increases in investment (domestic and foreign), improvements in terms of trade, reduced risk and equalization of factor prices. Integration will be beneficial when cooperation and coordination of policies takes place instead of the disintegrated exercise of sovereign economic power through conflicting policies. National sovereignty is pooled, rather than given up. Small and medium-sized open countries need to realize that it is much less a choice between national sovereignty and international economic integration, and much more a choice between one form of interdependence and another. If one's goal is to increase the competitiveness of goods and services produced in a small country and secure the widest markets for its output in the future, then international economic integration is a serious alternative to the national freedom to implement and continue with bad economic policies.

NOTES

1 'We live in the age of integration' (Haberler, 1964, p. 1).
2 Even though international trade is larger than ever before, national living standards are chiefly determined by *domestic* economic factors, rather than by competition for world markets. After all, the 'globalized' US economy trades only around 13 per cent of its GDP, roughly the same as at the turn of the twentieth century. In addition, at least 70 per cent of employment and value added in the US is in 'non-tradable' industries that do not compete on world markets!

The rate of growth in the standard of living in large developed countries depends on national productivity growth. Period. A comparison of the productivity growth in other countries does not matter for domestic living standard. If domestic productivity growth is 1 per cent a year, the national income of that country grows roughly 1 per cent a year, even though productivity growth elsewhere is 0 or 4 per cent (Krugman, 1996b).

There is always rivalry for status and power between states. Hence, it is interesting to compare them. But asserting that Japanese growth diminishes US status is far different from saying that it reduces the US standard of living. 'So let's start telling the truth: competitiveness is a meaningless word when applied to national economies' (Krugman, 1996a, p. 22).

3 There are, however, unfortunate examples as when the US absorbed Hawaii or Turkey northern Cyprus.

4 There are strong equilibrating forces that can assure that a country sells goods in world markets. David Hume pointed out two centuries ago that in the case with the gold standard a country that imports more than it exports has a drain on gold and a fall in the money supply. Prices and wages fall, hence the goods and labour in that country become cheap so that they grow attractive to foreign buyers. The deficit in trade is corrected. In the modern world without the gold standard, deficits are not usually corrected by the depreciation of prices and wages, but rather through the depreciation of national currencies.

5 He kept the same definition of economic integration in *The New Palgrave Dictionary of Economics* (1987), p. 43.

2 Customs Union

I INTRODUCTION

All types of international economic integration provoke interest because they, both promote and restrict trade at the same time. Trade is liberalized, at least partly, among the participating countries, while it is also distorted with third countries as there are various barriers between the integrated group and the rest of the world. On those grounds the analysis of international economic integration is delicate, complex and speculative. A customs union is the type of integration that has received the most attention in research and is the most rigorously developed branch of the neo-classical theory. This chapter is limited to an analysis of the basics of the static and dynamic models of customs unions.

The tariff system may discriminate between commodities and/or countries. Commodity discrimination takes place when different rates of import duty are charged on different commodities. Country discrimination is found when the same commodity is subject to different rates of duty on the basis of country of origin. Lipsey (1960, p. 496) defined the theory of customs unions as a branch of tariff theory which deals with the effect of geographically discriminatory changes in trade barriers. While this is true in the static sense, however, in a dynamic setting a customs union may be, among other things, a means for economic development.

The efficiency criterion used most often in economics is that of Pareto optimality. An allocation of resources is said to be Pareto-optimal if there does not exist another feasible allocation in which some agents would be better off (in a welfare sense) and no agents worse off. By a judicious definition of welfare, the Pareto-optimal allocation is that allocation which best satisfies social objectives. Pareto optimality is achieved exclusively in the state of free trade and free factor mobility (the first best solution), so that other states, in which there are distortions (tariffs, subsidies, taxes, monopolies, externalities, minimum wages, local content requirements, to mention just a few), are sub-optimal. It may happen that the Pareto-optimal allocation can not be achieved because of one or several distortions. Can a second best position be attained by satisfying the remaining Pareto conditions? The theory of the second best answered in the negative (Lipsey and Lancaster, 1956–57). In the presence of distortions, if all the conditions for Pareto optimality can not be satisfied, then the removal of some of the distortions does not necessarily increase welfare, nor does the addition of other distortions necessarily decrease it! One sub-optimal situation is replaced by another sub-optimal situation. Welfare may remain unaffected, increased or decreased.[1] This implies that there can be no reliable expectation about the welfare effect of a change in the current situation. The theory of the second best has a disastrous effect on welfare economics. However, Lipsey (1960) was not discouraged enough to be prevented from writing a seminal article on the theory of customs unions.

The intuition behind the classical theory of customs unions is the proposition that the potential consumption of goods and services in a customs union is higher than the sum of individual consumptions of the potential member countries in the situation in which trade among these countries is distorted by tariffs and quotas. In this situation one should, at least partly, remove these impediments.

II   STATIC MODEL

A static model of the theory of customs unions considers the impact of the formation of a customs union on trade flows and consumption in the integrated countries. The classical (orthodox or static) theory of customs unions relies on a number of explicit and implicit assumptions. This model makes theoretical consideration easier, but it also simplifies reality to the extent that the policy recommendations are to be considered with great care. None the less, many things can be learned from the consideration of extreme cases.

1   Assumptions

Assume that there are only three countries. Country A, a relatively small country in relation to the other two, forms a customs union with country B. Country C (which may represent all other countries in the world), is discriminated against by the customs union by means of a common external tariff. A relatively small number of states provides the possibility of a relatively higher analytical power in the theoretical model. Tariffs are levied on an *ad valorem* basis in all countries. Rates of tariffs are the same both for final commodities and inputs, so that the rate of nominal protection equals the rate of effective protection. The assumption of equal rates of tariffs prior to integration removes the possible dispute about the initial level of the common external tariff. Tariffs are the only instrument of trade policy and there are no NTBs. The price of imported goods for home consumers (P_{mt}) is composed of the price of an imported good (P_m) and tariff (t):

$$P_{mt} = (1 + t)P_m \qquad\qquad (2.1)$$

where $t \geq 0$. State intervention exists only at the border and trade is balanced. Free or perfect competition, exists both in markets for goods and services, as well as in markets for factors. Perfect competition (or complete equality of opportunity) exists in all economies, but for the existence of tariffs.

Production costs per unit of output are constant over all levels of output. To put it more formally, production functions are homogeneous of degree one, i.e. to produce one more unit of good X, inputs must be increased by a constant proportion. Costs of production determine the retail prices of goods. Producers in an industry operate at the minimum efficient scale at the production possibility frontier. Countries embark upon the production of certain goods on the basis of the prices (relative abundance or scarcity) of home factors.

The theory of customs unions refers to the manufacturing sector: a fixed quantity of factors of production is fully employed. There are no sector-specific factors such as special human and physical capital, entrepreneurship and the like. In a dynamic model these specific factors can be transformed in the medium and long run, but this would require adjustment costs which are ruled out in the static model. Mobility of factors is perfect within their home country, while commodities are perfectly mobile between the integrated countries. This means that TNCs are ignored. There are no transport, insurance or banking costs.

All countries have access to the same technology and differ only in their endowments of factors. Economies are static with constant expectations. This is to say that rates of growth; technologies; tastes; propensities to consume, save, import and invest are given and unchangeable. There are no new goods, no innovation and no depreciation of the capital stock. All goods and services are homogeneous, i.e. consumers do not have a preference for the consumption of goods and services from any particular supplier. They decide upon their purchases exclusively on the basis of differences in price. All goods and services have unit income elasticities of demand, i.e. every increase or decrease in income has a proportional change in demand for all goods and services in the same direction. This means that demand is 'well behaved'. Non-tradable commodities do not exist. There is no intra-industry trade or 'cross-hauling', i.e. a country can not both export and import identical goods or close substitutes. There are no inventories. All markets clear simultaneously. Such equilibrium must be both sustainable and feasible, i.e. firms can neither profitably undercut market price nor make losses.

In this model there is no uncertainty. Firms and resource owners are perfectly informed about all markets while consumers are fully familiar with goods and services. This assumption was relevant in the past, but the existence of the Internet put the economies close to a situation of full, timely and perfect information. Fiscal (taxes and subsidies) and monetary (rates of exchange, interest, inflation and balance-of-payments) operations are ruled out. Finally, a country which is not included in a customs union is assumed not to retaliate against the integrated countries.

The above assumptions are highly restrictive, but greatly simplify the analysis so that the essential properties of the model can be highlighted. The objective of the following analysis is to make a point, rather than to be realistic.

2   Partial equilibrium model

International trade can be a response to factors that include differences in the availability of resources (factor proportions), differences in technology and efficiency in production (production functions), economies of scale, differences in tastes, differences in market structure, increase in the national income and differences in output or factor taxes. The partial equilibrium model of trade deals with the market for a single good. Suppose that three countries produce the same commodity, but with varying levels of efficiency: their production functions differ. This model, is described in Table 2.1.

Table 2.1   Unit cost of production of a commodity in dollars

Country	A	B	C
Unit cost of production	60	50	35

Country C has the lowest unit cost of production, hence this country will become the world supplier of this commodity in the free trade situation. Suppose now, that country A wants to protect its inefficient domestic producers from foreign competition for whatever reason. This intention of country A can be criticized from the outset. Tariffs are an available means of protection which have distortionary effects.[2] The most important effect is that they move the country away from free trade towards autarky. Gains from specialization are sacrificed because resources are diverted away from the pattern of comparative advantage. In addition to reducing potential consumption, tariffs redistribute income in favour of factors which are used in production in the protected industry and decrease the possibility of their more efficient employment elsewhere in the economy. If country A wants to protect its home production of this good it must levy a tariff. This tariff of, for example, 100 per cent, not only increases the price of the imported commodity to country A's consumers, but more importantly, it shifts consumption away from imports towards country A's domestic production. In these circumstances, country A could increase domestic consumption of this good if it enters into a customs union with either of the

Table 2.2 Price of an imported commodity in dollars with
the tariff in country A's market

Import duty (%)	Price of a commodity from	
	Country B	Country C
100	100	70
50	75	52.5

countries in this model. Table 2.2 presents prices of the imported commodity with the tariff on country A's market.

If country A forms a customs union with country B, then consumers in country A could import the good from country B at a cost of 50 dollars per unit, rather than buy it from domestic suppliers at the cost of 60 dollars as before. Hence, they are better off than with a non-discriminatory tariff. If country A creates a customs union with country C, then country A's consumers are in an even better position compared to a customs union with country B. Now, they purchase the good at a unit price of 35 dollars. In both cases, consumers in country A are better off than in the situation in which they were buying the domestically produced good. The final effect in both cases is welfare-increasing trade creation as the cost of trade is reduced.

The formation of a customs union encourages *trade creation* as the result of a shift from a dearer to a cheaper source of supply. Other things being equal, this is a potential move towards free trade because a less efficient protected domestic supplier is replaced by a more efficient foreign one. Country A gives up the production of a good in which it has a comparative disadvantage in order to acquire it more cheaply by importing it from a partner country, so trade is created. This welfare-improving effect depends crucially on the assumption that the freed domestic resources can find alternative employment elsewhere in the economy. If in addition to trade creation 'internal' to the customs union there appears an increase in imports from third countries ('external' to the customs union) due to increased growth, as was the case in the EU, the situation is described as *double trade creation*.

Suppose now that prior to the formation of the customs union, the duty on imports was 50 per cent in country A. Table 2.2 shows that in this case the supplier of country A would be country C. Country A's domestic industry offers this good at a unit price of 60 dollars, country B at price of 75 dollars, while country C is the cheapest source of supply at 52.5 dollars. If, instead, country A enters into a customs union with country B and if the common external tariff for the commodity in question is 50 per cent, then country A would purchase this good from country B. In this case country A pays 50 dollars per unit to country B, while at the same time, a unit of the good from country C costs 52.5 dollars. The outcome in this case is *trade diversion*. Trade creation and trade diversion are often called Vinerian effects owing to Viner (1950) who first introduced those terms and provoked discussion and research into the issues of customs unions and international economic integration.

Trade diversion works in the opposite way from trade creation. The cheapest foreign supplier is changed in favour of a relatively dearer customs union supplier. Due to the common external tariff, business is taken away from the most efficient world producer and trade in this commodity is reduced. This creates a global welfare loss. Trade within a customs union takes place at a protected (higher) level of prices. A higher union level of prices relative to the international one brings benefits to internal exporters. Importers lose as they pay the partner country suppliers a higher price per unit of import and their country forgoes tariff revenue which is not levied on intra-union imports.

The net static impact on world efficiency of a move to a customs union depends on which of the two Vinerian effects dominates. It may be positive, negative or neutral. Hence, according to this theory, the favourable attitude of the GATT (Article XXIV) towards customs unions and free trade areas as trade liberalizing moves can not be accepted without reservation.

Major economic policies in the EU such as the Common Commercial Policy (customs union) or the Common Agricultural Policy (CAP) are mostly shaped according to the interests of the domestic producers. The interests of consumers are largely neglected. Hence, the possibility of a potentially trade-diverting bias in the EU should not come as a surprise. None the less, the expanding role of the European Parliament may increase the influence of consumers in the EU decision-making structure.

Trade diversion may be more beneficial than trade creation for the consumption in the country A that gives preferential treatment to certain suppliers. That is because this country does not sacrifice home production. The source of benefits is anticipated trade creation since, by assumption, bilateral trade flows must balance. The comparison here is between trade creation and the autarkic volume of domestic production. An integrating country will not benefit from trade creation unless it increases its exports to the partners (as compared to the pre-union level) which from a partner's point of view can represent trade diversion (Robson, 1987, p. 52).

Suppose that country A and country B form a customs union and that trade flows among countries A, B and C may have the following patterns:

- If country A alone produces this good, but does so inefficiently, then the choice between domestic production and imports from country C depends on the level of the common external tariff.
- If both countries in the customs union produce the good, but inefficiently, then the least inefficient country will supply the customs union market subject to the protection of the common external tariff.
- If neither country in the customs union produces the good, then there is no trade diversion. The customs union is supplied by the cheapest foreign supplier.

- If only one country in the customs union produces the good in question, but in the most efficient way, then this country will supply the market even without a common external trade protection.

By offering a joint level of protection, the common external tariff may promote a more efficient allocation of resources within the customs union.

The influence of international economic integration on trade flows is illustrated here by two examples. When Britain joined the EU in 1973, the share of its imports from other EU partner countries significantly increased over a decade. Trade between Mexico and the US doubled over the five years that preceded the creation of NAFTA in 1994. Even the announcement and preliminary negotiations about a serious integration deal had an impact on the volume and direction of trade in the region. Figure 2.1 shows flows of imports of a commodity to country A prior to and after the creation of a customs union with country B.

Figure 2.2 illustrates the effects of a tariff and a customs union on economic efficiency for a single good in country A's market. SS represents country A's domestic supply curve, similarly, DD shows the domestic demand curve. Country B's supply curve is BB, while country C's supply curve for the same good is CC. Both foreign countries can supply unconditionally any quantity of the demanded good at fixed prices. Both foreign supply curves are flat (perfectly elastic). It is a consequence of the smallness of the country in our example. This country can not exert influence on its terms of trade, but in a customs union with other countries this is likely to change. Prior to the imposition of a tariff, at price OC home demand for the good is OQ_6. Domestic producers supply OQ_1 while country C supplies Q_1Q_6.

Suppose that country A introduces a tariff on imports such that the price for domestic consumers is OT. Now, country A can expand domestic production from OQ_1 to OQ_3 and curtail home consumption of the good from OQ_6 to OQ_4. The government collects tariff revenue equal to

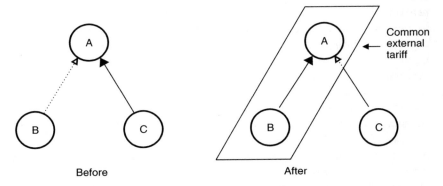

Figure 2.1 Flows of imports of a commodity to country A, before and after the creation of a customs union with country B

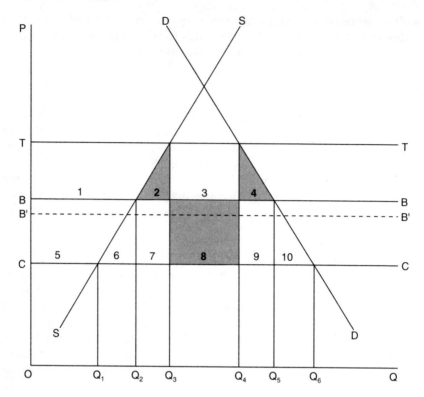

Figure 2.2 Effect of a tariff and a customs union on production and consumption in country A

CT × Q_3Q_4. This choice by country A may be questioned. There are at least two good reasons to object to trade restrictions in the medium and long term. First, new barriers to trade can provoke retaliation from foreign countries where domestic exporters already have an interest or intend to penetrate.[3] Second, and more subtle, if intermediate goods exist, all trade barriers raise the price of imported inputs. Therefore, they act as a tax on exports.[4] With the tariff, country A employs more resources in an industry in which it does not have a comparative advantage. Keeping in mind the assumption that the amount of resources is fixed and stepping out shortly from the partial equilibrium model, the fact is that resources are diverted away from business activities in which this country may have a comparative advantage. If a home industry is not competitive, a tariff may save jobs in this business in the short term. This may, however, lead to reduced activity in other home industries. If the uncompetitively produced home good is an input in other industries, their export performance may be at risk and investment reduced with the overall consequence of increased unemployment and a lower standard of living in the longer term.

Policy makers can easily identify jobs that are saved by various forms of protection, but do not easily recognize the adverse consequences of this protection, hence the need for a general equilibrium model. Through protection in the long term, resources are wasted on inefficient production. Everybody loses except the government (because of increased revenues) and the protected industry in the short term. The problem in the short run is that the general equilibrium consequences of a given policy can not be easily quantified. This policy of import substitution as opposed to a policy of export promotion and openness may be substantiated only on the grounds that foreign markets for country A's exports are closed.

The national security argument for tariffs can also be questioned. Trade-affected industries lobby for protection. This plea does not take into account the fact that industrial decline rarely, if ever, implies the actual demise of an industry. Possible nuclear warfare, long-range missiles and 'smart' bombs remove the classical national security argument for protection. Risk averse governments may consider stockpiling and/or guaranteeing supplies of goods and services from allies before imposing a tariff (Tyson and Zysman, 1987a, p. 41). Apart from security of supply, there are other reasons why a country may wish to preserve at least a part of (a declining) domestic industry which is exposed to international competition. The opportunities for domestic production increases bargaining power in negotiations about the long-term supply contracts with foreigners. In addition, if the cost situation changes in the future, some domestic research and development (R&D), as well as production capacity, may be a good starting point for regaining competitiveness.

The infant industry and similar arguments of learning-by-doing for protection state that entrants to an industry suffer losses while they acquire know-how, suppliers, customers, trained labour and the like in the period of infancy, so they need protection. It takes time for a firm to become profitable. Everybody knows it. If bankers, investors and entrepreneurs are not prepared to accept short-term losses as their investment towards long-term gains without government intervention, that is a clear indication that the market does not consider the enterprise to be viable, and so does not deserve tariff protection.

A free trader would argue that every firm profitable by market criteria does not need to be protected. If the infant industry argument is to make sense then, there must be some evidence of market failure, either in capital markets (entrepreneurs can not obtain adequate loans), or labour markets (such as inadequate training or fluctuations in the labour force) or some evidence that the production structure warrants protection. For example, these may be increasing returns to scale or other positive externalities that require a certain level of protection. These market failures may be corrected by economic policy (intervention). However, there are many old infants. What starts as an infant industry argument for protection turns into an employment protection argument. Finally, old infants are often nationalized at continuous cost to the country (Brander, 1987, p. 19). If a government bails out a declining sector and/or firm and creates a precedent, this produces expectations that the cost of poor management of business will be socialized. This may be one of the main sources of the adjustment difficulties in the 'problem' sectors in industrialized countries.

Returning to Figure 2.2, let us assume that country A, which imposed a non-discriminatory *ad valorem* tariff on imports, enters into a customs union with country B. The price of imports from country C with a common external tariff of CT is OT. Country B will supply country A's market. Country A's inefficient production contracts from OQ_3 to OQ_2 while consumption increases from OQ_4 to OQ_5. *Trade expansion* due to the creation of the customs union equals the sum of the reduction in home production Q_2Q_3 and the increase in home consumption Q_4Q_5. Country A's government does not earn any tariff proceeds from imports of the good from the customs union partner, country B. Trade expansion inevitably effects rationalization in production. This takes place through an improved deployment of existing factors, increased size of production units (reallocation of resources within sectors). One of the responses of firms in the EU to the market opening 1992 Programme was a big wave of mergers and acquisitions. The consequences of these rationalizations are in theory decreased unit costs of goods and services, as well as increased standards of living on average.

Trade expansion effects, however, should not be over emphasized. The downward adjustment of domestic tariffs to the common external tariff need not result in an increased trade expansion effect in a customs union. This alignment will first lead to a reduction to 'normal' levels of the profit margins of the protected domestic producers. If there is excess capacity in the protected industries, a possible increase in the domestic demand which comes as a consequence of the fall in price, will be met first by the country's own production (if it exists), rather than through imports. Thus the trade expansion effects due to the creation of a customs union will not be as large as would be suggested by the difference in tariffs before the creation of a customs union and after it. Therefore, the scope for trade diversion is, indeed, smaller than it may first appear. It is simply the potential for an expansion in trade and competition that does this good work for consumers, as well as producers, in the long term.

Consumers' surplus is defined as the difference between the consumers' total valuation of the goods consumed and the total cost of obtaining them. It is represented by the area under the demand curve and above the price that consumers face. Any decrease in price, other things being equal, increases consumers' surplus. Country A's consumers benefit when their country enters into a customs union with country B in relation to the situation with an initial non-discriminatory tariff. Their gain is given by the area $1 + 2 + 3 + 4$. These consumers are, however, worse off in comparison to the free trade situation in which country C is the supplier. This loss is given by the area $5 + 6 + 7 + 8 + 9 + 10$. Domestic producers lose a part of their surplus in a customs union compared to the situation with a non-discriminatory *ad valorem* tariff (area above SS up to the price OB which they receive). This is represented by area 1. From the national standpoint, area 1 nets out as part of both the consumers' gain and the producers' loss. Country A loses tariff revenue (area 3) which it collects in the initial situation. Hence, the net gain for country A is area $2 + 4$.

The formation of a customs union has increased trade and consumption in country A in comparison to the initial situation with a non-discriminatory tariff. In the situation prior to the formation of a customs union, country A imports the good from country C, pays for it an amount equal to $Q_3Q_4 \times OC$ and collects revenue equal to the area $3 + 8$. After the formation of a customs union, area 3 is returned to consumers in the form of lower prices for the good, while area 8 represents a higher price charged by the customs union partner country. The return of the area 3 to the consumers may be regarded as Hicksian compensation. When tariffs change, compensation is seldom paid. Hence, demand curve DD may be regarded simply as an approximation to the compensated Hicksian demand curve. It is important to note that country A pays, for the same amount of imports Q_3Q_4, a higher price to the customs union partner ($Q_3Q_4 \times OB$) than was paid to the country C suppliers prior to the customs union formation. The country has a greater outflow of foreign exchange and does not collect revenue which it had done when it had imposed a non-discriminatory tariff on imports from country C. The outflow of foreign exchange from country A was equal to $Q_3Q_4 \times OC$, while area $3 + 4$ illustrates the transfer from consumers to producers within the home country.

The net welfare effect of the creation of a customs union in country A depends on the relative size of the Vinerian effects; trade creation (area $2 + 4$) minus trade diversion (area 8). Instead of a *revenue generating* obstacle to trade (tariff) a government may introduce *cost increasing* barriers (various standards and tests) whose effect may be a reduction in trade. (Let the effect of the NTBs be BT in trade with country B.) If the set of NTBs is removed, the effect on domestic consumers and producers would be the same as in the situation when the tariff was removed. The government which has never earned direct revenue from the set of non-tariff regulations, would lose nothing. The social gain from reducing these barriers is area $2 + 3 + 4$. This was the case with the internal market-opening plan of the EU known as the 1992 Programme.

If one introduces dynamics into this model, in the form of increasing returns to scale, country B, as the customs union supplier of the good, faces an increased demand. Production would become more efficient and the price might fall from OB to OB'. This enhances trade creation and decreases the size of the trade diversion effect.

Figure 2.2 belongs to the family of standard microeconomic partial-equilibrium analytical tools. Unfortunately, they all deal with only a part of the business cycle, that is, with the first third of the cycle when demand rises. Other cases, such as stagnation or reduction in demand, are seldom considered.

Patterns of consumption would change following the creation of a customs union. Inter-country substitution occurs when one country replaces the other as the source of supply for some good. Inter-commodity substitution happens when one commodity is substituted, at least at the margin, for another commodity as a result of a shift in relative prices (Lipsey, 1960, p. 504). The latter occurs, for example, when country A imports from the customs union partner country B relatively cheaper veal which replaces at least some of the pork produced in country A and at least some of the chicken which is imported from country C, and when consumers in a customs union replace a part of demand for theatre and opera by relatively 'cheaper' stereo, video and other entertainment equipment.

One can ask if there are superior alternative policies to the creation of a customs union? Unilateral, non-discriminatory reductions in import tariffs may look to be a better policy than the formation of a customs union. It seems preferable to obtain exclusively trade creation as a result of unilateral tariff reductions, than to create a customs union which causes both trade creation and trade diversion (Cooper and Massel, 1965a, pp. 745–746). Such an argument can not be accepted without serious reservations. A customs union offers something which is not offered by a unilateral reduction in tariffs. That is, an elimination of tariffs in customs union partner countries. A unilateral reduction in tariffs exaggerates the price reduction effects on consumption, while it eliminates the possibility of penetration into the markets of customs union partners.

The necessity of tariff bargaining with foreigners, so important to domestic exporters, was left out of the picture in the earlier analysis. In addition, various barriers to trade with the non-union member countries were neglected (e.g. transport costs). If such barriers are present, then a redirection of trade towards customs union partners may not introduce (large extra) costs. On the contrary, it may bring certain savings in the form of lowered transport charges. Hence, this model questions, from an efficiency viewpoint, the desirability of a wide preferential-trading system such as the old British Commonwealth, where transport costs downgraded the commercial opportunities that were offered by preferential trade. Given the elimination of tariffs in the markets of customs union partner countries and obstacles to trade such as transport costs, the gains that come from the non-preferential unilateral tariff reduction need not be greater than the beneficial effects that arise from the creation of a customs union (Wonnacott and Wonnacott, 1981).

Bilateral deals can offer returns that might not be realistically expected through multilateral negotiations. In the case of free trade deal between Canada and the US, these gains include (Lipsey and Smith, 1989, pp. 319–321):

- The complete elimination of tariffs on goods that meet the stipulated rules of origin.
- A number of NTBs are eliminated, while the use of the rest is seriously restricted.
- Most commercial services are covered by the agreement.
- A number of specific trade disputes were settled.
- There is a liberal and stable bilateral FDI regime.
- Any US legislation that concerns Canada must be discussed bilaterally before it is passed.
- If there is a dispute, the complaining country may elect to use either the GATT or the bilateral mechanism.

The likelihood that Canada would obtain such pathbreaking and powerful trade liberalizing measures through multilateral negotiations in the foreseeable future is very slim.

In spite of trade diversion costs of a customs union, the terms of trade of member countries might turn in their favour, so that, on balance, each member country may be better off than in the unilateral tariff reduction case. The classical approach to the theory of tariffs is mistaken. This approach, on the one hand, finds gains in the replacement of domestic goods for cheaper foreign goods, while on the other hand, the expansion of domestic exports does not bring gains in this model to the exporting country (except possible improvement of the terms of trade), but rather to the foreigners (Johnson, 1973, p. 80).

Suppose that transfer payments between countries are allowed for. Then any customs union is potentially favourable for all countries considering participation, since they can be compensated for losses when they join. This means that customs union among countries can be extended to $n + 1$ countries. By expansion, this implies that there is an incentive to extend the customs union until the whole world is included, until free trade prevails throughout the world (Kemp and Wan, 1976). A 'deeper' integration in the EU caused 'wider' integration in Europe. A market deepening 1992 Programme triggered membership requests from European countries that were previously happy to be outside the EU. Once a group enlarges, the cost to non-members of staying out of the club increases (Baldwin, 1995a, p. 46).

Such reasoning may lead to the classical proposition that a customs union is a step towards free trade. This conclusion depends on the existence of inter-country transfers within the customs union. This is a severe restriction and the greatest weakness of this approach. The more countries there are in a customs union, the greater will be the potential need for compensation. If compensation schemes are adopted in reality, they are often the products of political bargaining and not purely of the economic impact of integration. These schemes are too complicated and they never compensate in full (compensation schemes are never perfect) which limits the actual size of customs union. This leads to the conclusion that non-economic reasons may also play a prominent role in economic integration. The experience of the EU illustrates that political considerations play a major part in integration, in particular regarding an expansion in the number of member countries.

Consideration of the impact of tariffs on imports would be incomplete without comparing them to production subsidies. The effect of a tariff on imports of a commodity is equivalent to a combination of a tax on domestic consumption and a subsidy on home production of the same good. Tariffs and subsidies are close substitutes. A reduction in one of them may be compensated for by an increase in the other. The existence of tariffs permits the domestic producers to charge higher prices on the local market than would otherwise have been the case. Unlike the 'direct' payment from consumers to producers in the case of tariffs, a subsidy goes from taxpayers to the government, and then to the protected industry. The transfer technique is different, but the policy goal is the same.

A domestic tariff increases prices both of imported goods and home-produced protected goods (at least in the short run). This distortion has as its cost the losses both of gains from exchange and gains from specialization, as well as a loss in domestic consumption. One cost of subsidies is a loss of gains from specialization, however domestic prices and consumption remain unchanged.[5] Thus, at least in the long run, a restriction of imports is equal to a reduction in potential exports when a fixed amount of resources is fully employed prior to the introduction of distortions. Resources are being shifted out of exports into import-substituting industries. However, in the short run (before elections), authorities might be more concerned about the level of (un)employment than about income transfers which both tariffs and production subsidies imply.

Tariffs are more readily 'supplied' by governments because of at least two internal factors. First, they do not pose any shot-term burden on tight budgets and, second, tariffs may be introduced in such a way that they can not be easily labelled as firm-specific, which is not always the case with subsidies. Although subsidies may be a preferred trade instrument in theory, they are not without flaws. Subsidies provide certain opportunities for a fast aggregation of skills within an industry (firm), but they lower the level of competition and ease the market pressure to create a bond between learning, doing, expanding and competing.

If country A is subject to subsidized supplies of good X from country B, country A should consider the consequences of such circumstances. Subsidies are based on the potential to earn economic rents from foreign consumers and producers (beggar-thy-neighbour). These rents refer to the proceeds of the exporters which are in excess of what is necessary to cover the costs of production and to yield an average return on investment. Such subsidies will improve the social welfare of the exporting country only if profits of the exporting industry on exports exceed the cost of the subsidy to the taxpayers. If country A obtains the good X at a lower price from country B than from its domestic producers, then domestic consumers are better off, although its home producers of good X are worse off. All this is at the expense of country B's taxpayers. If country B is willing to supply country A with the subsidized good X indefinitely, then a wise policy for country A is to accept these supplies and shift domestic resources to business activities where the return is higher in relation to the return on the home production of the good X. If country B, however, subsidizes its exports of good X in order to discharge cyclical surpluses or in order to prevent the entry of country A's firms into the market of good X or to drive them out of it in the long run, and intends later to charge monopoly prices, then country A need not accept this offer as the only source of supply.

Although tariffs and subsidies have similar effects on trade and production, the GATT does not prohibit tariffs while its Code on Subsidies and Countervailing Duties (1979) prohibits export subsidies (with the exception of certain primary products) if such subsidies cause material injury to the importing country's firms.[6] The injury must be proven prior to the introduction of a countervailing duty and its objective has to be to offset the effect of foreign subsidies on domestic business. Of course, the maximum countervailing duty permitted by the GATT is limited by the amount of subsidy embodied in imports of the country that introduces the duty. The effects of such a policy are restricted only to the competitive situation in the home market of the country that introduces the countervailing duty. Similarly, in the situation of a balance-of-payments deficit, the International Monetary Fund (IMF) recommends a tariff, but does not advise the use of export subsidies.[7]

Foreign subsidies may induce countervailing duties by the 'injured' countries. If these countries do not either produce or have some potential for the production of a good, then there are no grounds for the imposition of these duties. The relative size of trading partners and their relative openness to trade plays a crucial role. Relatively small countries are more reliant on external trade than larger ones. A small subsidy to an import-competing industry in a large country may have a more distorting impact than a large subsidy applied to a small country's exports.

Preferences for tariffs are often due to compelling political realities. People are used to tariffs, while subsidies personify unfair competition. One country can not force foreigners to eliminate tariffs on exports, but it may, if it identifies their subsidies, make them remove these by the threat of imposing countervailing duties.[8] An international abolition of tariffs would be ignored, while a prohibition of export subsidies legitimates retaliation by means of countervailing duties (Wonnacott, 1987, pp. 86–87). This flexible system of instant unilateral retaliation may result in an informal system of international cooperation in the settlement of disputes in trade. This situation was, however, due to the shortcomings of the formal settlement of disputes in trade under the auspices of the GATT. Time will tell if the WTO will fare any better. There are, of course, other incentives for the introduction of subsidies. Let us consider them in turn.

Firms invest because of the anticipation of profits in the future. Investments are undertaken because markets are foreseen, costs of production make profits possible and funds, at acceptable rates, are available. If profit opportunities are fading away, then unemployment may rise. Governments are reluctant to accept such a state of affairs, so they offer subsidies (investment, employment, R&D, production and/or export), among other things, to firms, in order to alter unfavourable trends. If a country wants to protect all the firms in an industry, then an outright subsidy may be a better alternative to reduced tax rates. A subsidy may help all firms in an industry, while reduced tax rates may help only those that are profitable. Reduced taxes may be preferred if the policy goal is to remove the lame ducks.

A valid case for subsidies can be made if there are market imperfections. Unemployment was a cyclical phenomenon in the past. Nowadays, its nature is different. In many cases labour needs retraining in order to be hired, and constant upgrading of skills in order to be kept employed. Vocational training is a valid case for subsidies. In addition, there are no countervailing duties for grants to students to study engineering (that will shape the comparative advantage and competitiveness of a country in the future).

A special type of subsidy may be present in government procurement policies. By discriminating in the award of public contracts, a government may sharpen the competitive edge of an economy. That is very important during the first fragile steps in the development of an industry, commodity or service. A firm's shareholders thus receive income transfers from home taxpayers. If the industry is successful and if sunk costs are high, then latecomers may not enter the market. This strategic pre-emption of the market may provide the firm and the country with super-normal profits from sales on foreign markets. One example is the purchase of defence equipment as a subsidy to high-technology firms. This is the case in the US aircraft industry which has been receiving indirect subsidies. In Europe, the Airbus industry is directly subsidized by participating governments. It is very hard, even impossible, for potential investors in other regions of the world to compete with firms that combine forces with national governments in this industry.

If one neglects the possibility of retaliation, intervention can make a country better off. When super-normal profits (rents) from export to foreign countries exceed the cost of subsidies (production and/or export), the exporting country obviously increases its wealth. National 'profits' from subsidies need not only be measured in pecuniary terms. By the supply of energy to the countries in the former eastern bloc at prices that were below those on the international market, the former Soviet Union was able to wrest many political advantages from the region.

A special type of subsidy may also be present in goods and services supplied to firms and citizens by the government. These goods and services are offered in certain cases at lower prices by public enterprises than would be the case if such output were provided by private firms (which must pay taxes). When managers of companies start spending more time lobbying for government grants than worrying about the actual operation of their companies, taxpayers and consumers should start geting nervous (Brander, 1987, p. 28). The long-term prosperity of a country can not be promoted by subsidies to rent-seeking inefficient firms. By doing so, new wealth is not created, but an extra tax is imposed on the prosperous. In services that are provided by the government and not by private firms, there can easily be some subsidy element. For example, in Brussels, the seat of the Commission of the EU and a number of other international organizations, there were around 3,000 interest (pressure) groups in the mid-1990s. Those rent-seekers employed around 10,000 lobbyists (Sidjanski, 1997).

An output subsidy may be 'preferable' to an export subsidy. The rationale is that an output subsidy does not necessarily lead to higher domestic prices of differentiated products as is the case with a tariff or an export subsidy (Flam and Helpman, 1987, pp. 94–95). Output subsidies are often tacitly accepted, while export subsidies are often subject to countervailing duties. An R&D subsidy always expands these activities: more varieties appear on the market and more firms enter the industry. The price of differentiated goods may increase or decline, as an enlarged number of firms may result in lower output per firm. This R&D subsidy may, therefore, improve or reduce welfare, or leave it unchanged.

One of the most obvious expressions of subsidies was the US Domestic International Sales Corporation (DISC) which supplied tax benefits to American exporters. Initially, the DISC allowed exporters an indefinite postponement of the payment of about a quarter of the income tax on their export profits. This acted as a direct subsidy to capital used in the production of exports. The GATT Council in 1976 found the DISC to be a direct export subsidy programme in conflict with the GATT rules. The subsequent legal embodiment of the DISC, with a similar effect, is the Federal Sales Corporation.

The new theory of strategic[9] trade and industrial policy (a refined variant of the optimum-tariff theory) has identified areas where government intervention can 'correct' certain market imperfections.[10] Among the available policy instruments for 'massaging markets' (intervention) are subsidies. This policy instrument, however, must be financed either by taxes or by borrowing. Taxes produce distortions because they affect the supply of labour, wage costs and/or discourage consumption. Government borrowing increases interest rates and tends to crowd out private investment. These welfare losses are not necessarily larger than the welfare gains obtained from the same subsidies. Governments often prefer to subsidize inputs. This may cause X-inefficiency problems such as a wasteful use of the subsidized resources and protection of firms from competition, which reduces pressure on firms to minimize costs. None the less, there is no presumption that the reduced costs from learning by doing and economies of scale are more important than the increased costs resulting from the X-inefficiency induced by subsidies. The new trade theorists have chosen to ignore these problems and biased their conclusions in favour of activist industrial and trade policies (de Grauwe, 1989, pp. 70–71).

To complete the discussion of subsidies, reference has to be made to the reasons why administrations tend to avoid them. Governments dislike direct subsidies because they place the cost within the government's budget, while regulatory measures transfer the cost to the private sector. If a government subsidizes then it must tax, borrow and/or reduce current expenditure. Subsidies are readily measurable and receivers identifiable. Costs incurred by a tariff are spread over numerous consumers and its effects can hardly be measured with accuracy. A subsidy may be offered on a 'one-off' basis, but often it becomes an ongoing commitment which often ends up in the nationalization of a bankrupt firm because of various 'strategic' or employment considerations. In addition, with budget deficits, governments can not easily find the necessary funds for subsidies. Therefore, one of the choices for the subsidization of exports may be a depreciation of the exchange rate.

The costs of financing and disbursing subsidies may be quite high, whereas the administrative costs of the implementation of tariffs are relatively low and the proceeds are easy to collect. Administering the distribution of subsidies may be formidable and quite difficult to handle (Robson, 1984, p. 53). Sometimes these subsidies are not necessary. If the handling of this instrument is easy, then too many marginal firms will receive support. If a private investment would have been done in any case, then a subsidy for it would be regarded as no more than the replacement of private money by public.

Research and development in the EU information technology industry was undertaken both by firms on their own and was subsidized by the public. That industry is interesting, as over 40 per cent of all strategic technology alliances took place there during the 1980s. Apart from those private cooperative deals, there developed cost-sharing technology partnerships with the involvement of governments and the EU. The two networks operated side by side. R&D that was subsidized by the EU was found to resemble the 'private' one and simply reproduced the basic 'private' network of cooperation of large EU firms. Strong oligopolistic lobbies were able to lure the EU into giving subsidies. One now wonders if the EU-funded R&D network was necessary at all (Hagedoorn and Schakenraad, 1993).

Yet another reason which prevents the introduction of subsidies is international commitment such as membership of the GATT/WTO. Subsidies may lead to foreign retaliation which would make the trade balance even worse. Some countries may enter into a subsidy warfare in order to attract FDI. This action may induce greater distortions than arise with tariffs.

Both tariffs and subsidies, as policy instruments, introduce distortions. Therefore, any policy which involves either instrument should be carefully considered and crafted. In comparison with free trade, the situation involving imperfections in either of these instruments, is sub-optimal. If a country subsidizes, then it might gain an advantage, but only temporarily. Anything that provides a country with a disadvantage in exporting in the short run, will cause the adjustment of the exchange rate or factor prices in the long run (Johnson and Krauss, 1973, p. 240). The new theory of trade and strategic industrial policy questioned such a view. It stated that intervention matters a lot as there are certain irreversibilities that can perpetuate themselves (clustering of related firms with economies of scale). Examples include chemical and pharmaceutical firms in Basle (Switzerland); financial services in London and New York; the film industry in California; aircraft-related production in Seattle, WA; and optics-related firms (Kodak, Xerox and Bausch & Lomb) in Rochester, NY. Protection distorts market signals. However, even though protection is a second best strategy by economic criteria relative to a liberal trade regime, it is a workable and often superior political strategy.

3 General equilibrium model

A partial equilibrium model considers the market for a single good. It assumes that all prices other than that of the good in question are fixed. A general equilibrium model considers all markets. All prices are variable and competitive equilibrium requires that all markets clear. All markets are connected by a chain of inputs and substitutes, information, technology, mobility of factors and goods, income (if one spends more on something, less will remain for other things), etc.

Consideration of the general equilibrium model will start with the 3×2 model. In this case there are three countries, A, B and C, as well as two goods (markets) X and Y. Lipsey (1957 and 1960) was the first to study these cases in a customs union framework. The model included full specialization and constant costs. A small country A imports good X from country C which is the foreign supplier with the lowest price.

Consider a case illustrated in Figure 2.3, where substitution in consumption is allowed for by smooth and convex indifference curves. There are three countries, A, B and C, and two goods, X and Y, respectively. In the free trade case, country A trades with country C and achieves indifference curve II. Suppose now that country A introduces a non-discriminatory tariff on imports. The relative price in country A is now AT.

Suppose that this tariff does not give enough incentive to home entrepreneurs to embark upon production of good X. Country A achieves the indifference curve I_1I_1 with equilibrium at point G. If the government either returns all tariff proceeds to consumers or spends the entire amount in the same fashion as the consumers would have otherwise done, then the equilibrium should be on line AC (as country C is the best foreign supplier). The equilibrium point is at point K, which is the point where the line T_2 (parallel to AT which illustrates compensation of consumers) intersects with terms-of-trade line AC. The extent of the rightward shift in the terms of trade line depends on how much people are willing to import at these prices and, hence, the volume of tariff revenue to be returned to them. T_2 is deliberately

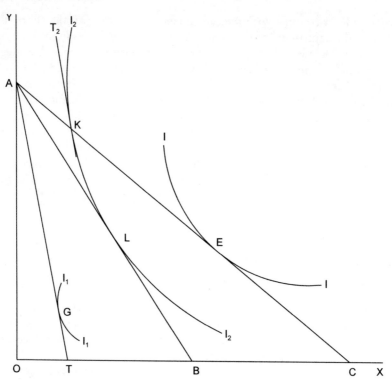

Figure 2.3 Welfare in a trade diverting customs union

drawn in such a way that K and L lie on the same indifference curve. The tariff has changed the structure of production and relative prices. Consumption of the home good increases, while imports and exports decrease.

Suppose that country A forms a trade-diverting customs union with country B. The terms of trade line with country B is illustrated by line AB. Suppose that K and L lie on the same indifference curve I_2I_2. The formation of a customs union has not changed country A's welfare, although the structure of consumption has changed. If the best situation is at point E, then the formation of a customs union for country A is a move from one sub-optimal position, K, to another sub-optimal position, L. Country A is indifferent. If country A obtains in a customs union terms of trade which are worse than OB/OA, then country A is worse off than in the situation with a non-discriminatory tariff. If country A, however, obtains terms of trade which are better than OB/OA, then a trade-diverting customs union can be welfare improving for this country. Hence, the classical statement that trade diversion is always a bad thing, is rejected.

Lipsey's model may be further developed to a case in which a country produces both goods. This case is closer to reality because substitution in production is allowed. This is done in Figure 2.4. QQ is country A's

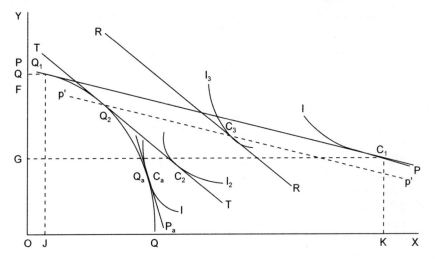

Figure 2.4 Production and consumption in country A before and after a tariff

production possibility frontier. In autarky, country A produces at point Q_a and consumes at point C_a. There is a double tangency of the autarky price line P_a with the production possibility curve QQ and indifference curve I at a single point. Suppose now that this country opens up for international trade. It is a small country, so it faces a given price ratio PP between good X and good Y. Country A then produces at point Q_1 and consumes at point C_1. The double tangency of production point Q_1 and consumption point C_1 is not required to be at one point. Country A exports quantity FG of good Y and imports quantity JK of good X from country C.

Suppose, now, that country A imposes a non-discriminatory tariff on imports. With the new price line, TT, country A's production is at Q_2 and consumption is at point C_2. Both production and consumption points are closer to the autarkic levels. If home consumers are compensated (all tariff proceeds are returned to them), then there will be additional imports. This is shown by the line RR which is parallel to line TT (the distance between the two lines equals tariff revenue) and consumption is at C_3. Now, suppose that country A enters into a trade diverting customs union with country B which is a less efficient supplier than country C. If country A achieves a lower indifference curve in this customs union than I_3, then country A is worse off than in the pre-customs union situation. If country A, however, achieves in the customs union a higher indifference curve than I_3, then this trade-diverting customs union is increasing its welfare and is beneficial to this country.

In order to be closer to reality, higher dimensional models are necessary. Consider a 3 × 3 model in which country A produces commodity X, while it imports commodity Y from country B and commodity Z from country C. Table 2.3 states three optimality conditions between country A's domestic($_d$)

Table 2.3 Prices in country A and their relationship to prices on
the international market

Free trade	Non-preferential ad valorem *tariff*	Customs union with country B
$\frac{PA_d}{PB_d} = \frac{PA_i}{PB_i}$	$\frac{PA_d}{PB_d} < \frac{PA_i}{PB_i}$	$\frac{PA_d}{PB_d} = \frac{PA_i}{PB_i}$
$\frac{PA_d}{PC_d} = \frac{PA_i}{PC_i}$	$\frac{PA_d}{PC_d} < \frac{PA_i}{PC_i}$	$\frac{PA_d}{PC_d} < \frac{PA_i}{PC_i}$
$\frac{PB_d}{PC_d} = \frac{PB_i}{PC_i}$	$\frac{PB_d}{PC_d} = \frac{PB_i}{PC_i}$	$\frac{PB_d}{PC_d} < \frac{PB_i}{PC_i}$

Source: Lipsey (1960)

and international($_i$) prices for this model. In free trade all three conditions
are fulfilled. Price ratios for the same commodities in country A and abroad
are equal. If country A imposes a non-preferential tariff on all imports, then
optimality will be achieved only in the price ratio between the imported
commodities. A customs union with country B shifts country A from one
sub-optimal position to another, since optimality is satisfied only in one case
(between country A's commodity X and country B's commodity Y).

Apart from Lipsey (1970), 3 × 3 models of customs union were studied by
Meade (1968), Berglas (1979), Riezman (1979) and Lloyd (1982). In the
model by Meade, each country exports one commodity while it imports
the other two from other countries. Riezman's model permits each country
to export two commodities and import only one commodity. The model by
Berglas is more complicated. Country A and country B have only one
export commodity each. Both countries import two commodities. Country
A exports its commodity X to both country B and country C and imports
commodity Y from country B and commodity Z from country C. Country
B exports commodity Y only to country A and imports commodity X from
country A and commodity Z from country C. Figure 2.5 illustrates trade
flows in these three models.

The models by Meade and Riezman have very different trade flows, but
the two are symmetric as opposed to Berglas's model which is asymmetric
(Lloyd, 1982, p. 49). Patterns of trade may be different and more complicated than those illustrated in Figure 2.5. Asymmetry in trade patterns prior

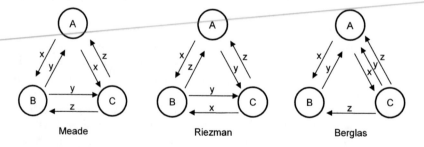

Figure 2.5 Trade flows among countries in models by Meade, Riezman and Berglas

to the formation of a customs union has an important impact on the welfare between the countries that form a customs union. The extension from three- to n-commodity models ($n > 3$) permits introduction of a greater number of trade patterns, but it does not significantly affect the results (Berglas, 1979, p. 317).

Higher dimensional models of trade such as the 3×3 model, even the more complex ones, are necessary because they offer an important advant- age: substitution effects. In a two-commodity model, one must be an export and the other an import commodity in each country. Higher dimensional models permit various restrictions on trade among different countries. The weakness of the models is that they assume that the commodities are final goods. Any reduction in impediments to trade on semi-processed goods may have a different impact on national production than a reduction of barriers to trade on final goods. A relatively high tariff on imports of final goods encourages this kind of production domestically. However, a relatively high tariff on imports of final goods in country B induces country A to expand the production and export of semi-processed goods.

4 Conditions for a welfare improving customs union

In a world with many distortions in trade, any customs union is just a second best solution. On these grounds, a prescription, along the neo-classical lines, for a welfare improvement is not possible. None the less, foreigners would find it harder to compete in an integrated area. That is not because common trade barriers are increased relative to the individual trade barriers prior to integration. In fact, these barriers may be lowered on average. However, major difficulties in penetration may come from the enhanced competitive- ness of the firms in the integrated area.

Trade creation in a customs union and welfare improvement of the group will predominate if the following ten conditions are met in full or in part:

- The lower the demand for country C's exports and the greater the demand for goods produced by partner countries in a customs union, the greater the likelihood of an improvement in welfare due to trade creation.
- The higher the trade barriers in third countries, the higher the trade creation in the customs union.
- The level of tariffs (as well as other impediments to trade) personifies a country's lack of competitiveness. In an extreme situation when country A has a prohibitive tariff and if domestic production is impossible, then there will be no home consumption of the good in question. Any reduction in this tariff has a potentially beneficial welfare effect on consumers in country A. Figure 2.2 illustrates the case in which the higher is the pre-customs union tariff in country A, the higher is the trade creation in a customs union with country B. Of course, the common external tariff must be lower than the pre-customs union tariff.

The lower the tariffs in country C on exports from country A, the lower will be export diversion towards country B. The lower the common external tariff, the smaller is the probability that the union partner will replace the most efficient supplier, which is country C. A relatively low common external tariff permits some competition from countries which are outside the customs union. A partial reduction in tariffs potentially brings greater benefits than the creation of a customs union, because it inhibits trade diversion. The lower the pre-customs union tariffs the lower the potential benefits from a customs union. All these effects, however, depend on the elasticity of trade flows to the change in tariffs.

- The 'flatter' the demand and supply curves in relation to the quantity axis in Figure 2.2 (elasticity must be greater than unity), the greater the areas 2 and 4 which embody trade creation.

- The larger the number of countries that participate in a customs union, the smaller the probability of trade diversion. An incentive to form and enlarge a customs union persists until the entire world becomes a customs union, that is, until the introduction of universally accepted free trade. A customs union among all countries of the world would have only trade creation as a consequence.

- If integration takes place between the neighbouring countries, the lower the transportation costs and the greater the gains from integration. That is why a free trade deals between the US and Israel (1985) or Canada and Israel (1997) had only a very limited impact on integrating the economies of the concerned countries.

- The more inelastic the supply from third countries, the more these countries lose, while the customs union partner countries gain. Trade diversion is preferable to trade creation for the preference-granting country, for it does not entail any sacrifice of domestic industrial production (Johnson, 1973, p. 89).[11]

- Commodities of different countries are competitive if these countries have similar costs of production for the same commodity. Integration of countries with such a production structure produces, potentially, the greatest gains. If the same countries have different costs of production for the same commodity, they have a complementary economic structure. Integration in this case may also produce gains, but perhaps not as big as in the former instance.

- The larger the number of (small) firms in the same industry, the smaller the potential resistance of vested interests that can oppose integration and a 'painful' adjustment to the new situation, with more competition on an integrated market.

- The less developed the economies prior to integration, the higher the potential opportunities for benefits from planned specialization.

Trade among countries with different costs of production for similar commodities and different factor endowments, may often be characterized by inter-industry trade, while trade among countries with similar costs of production for similar commodities, with similar factor endowments and similar consumer preferences (tastes) may be characterized by intra-industry trade. Competition between countries with complementary economic structures in a customs union will ensure that the most efficient producer supplies the customs union market, which secures a welfare gain. In a multi-country and multi-commodity case, however, country A may be the most efficient producer of good X, while country B is the least efficient producer of the same good. In addition, country B may be the most efficient producer of good Y, while country A is the least efficient producer of this good. So, regarding goods X and Y, these two countries have complementary production structures. A customs union between these two countries, which covers just two industries that produce commodities X and Y, may be only welfare improving.

If countries that contemplate the creation of a customs union have competitive structures prior to integration, but achieve complementarity after entry into the customs union, then an increase in welfare might be the outcome. All these (im)possibilities represent another reinforcement of the second best character of the theory of customs unions.

The introduction of terms such as complementarity and competitiveness are not necessary. The most important condition for a welfare-improving outcome from the creation of a customs union is that a customs union stimulates competition within its boundaries and that the common external tariff is not erected primarily for protection against imports from outside countries (Lundgren, 1969, p. 38).

III DYNAMIC MODEL

1 Introduction

The classical theory of customs unions assumed that the static effects of resource reallocation occurred in a timeless framework. If one wants to move the theory of customs unions towards reality one must consider dynamic, i.e. restructuring, effects. It is widely (?) accepted that markets are imperfect and that there are externalities such as economies of scale and product differentiation that make competition imperfect. When market structure is like this, regionalism/integration may be justified, because the market may be extended and because the market power of firms may be reduced, which may have a positive impact on competition, productivity, innovation and a reduction in prices.

The old static neo-classical rules of economics need to be significantly modified. Information technology and the pace of innovation distinguish the modern economy from the old one. A fast information flow has reduced many of the past barriers to business. In addition, innovative activity has significantly changed. The Middle Ages offered only a few important inventions, such as horseshoes and windmills. The only constant feature in the modern dynamic economy is an ever accelerating pace of innovation.

Instead of considering only the possibility of trade in commodities, dynamic models analyse the possibility of resource allocation across time. The static effects of international economic integration have their most obvious and profound influence in the period immediately following the creation of, for example, a customs union. Gradually, after several years of adjustment, the dynamic effects will increase in importance and become dominant. These effects push further technological constraints and provide the group with an additional integration-induced 'growth bonus'.

Trade flows do not remain constant. In fact, they evolve and alter over time. Changes in the equilibrium points in, for example, Figure 2.2 are described as instantaneous. Such shifts in equilibrium points, however, may not always be possible. Delays in reaction on the part of countries and consumers in a customs union could be caused by their recourse to stocks. Hence, they do not immediately need to purchase those goods whose price has decreased as a consequence of the formation of a customs union. They also may have some contractual commitments that can not be abandoned overnight. Finally, buyers may not be aware of all the changes. Up to the nineteenth century state intervention was negligible, but markets remained disconnected because of imperfect information and relatively high transport costs. The Internet has, however, eliminated the constraint of the lack of timely information. A time lapse between the implementation of a policy change (the creation of a customs union) and its favourable effects may include an initial period of economic deterioration in certain industries which may be followed by improvements due to the J-curve effect.

2   Change in the efficiency in the use of factors due to increased competition

2.1   Introduction

Free market competition provides everyone with the widest opportunities for business and produces the best allocation of resources (in theory). By so doing, competition improves efficiency in the use of factors of production. That conclusion has been accepted by the neo-classical economic theory as a truth. It has provided the intellectual backing for the competition (anti-trust) policy. Regional integration arrangements widen markets for the participating countries, hence one of its first dynamic effects is in the field of competition. Therefore, the EU has its own rules for market behaviour. They refer to the restriction of competition, abuse of the dominant position and state aids. The importance of the competition policy was enhanced by the single market programme, completed in 1992.

Competition policy is a mixture of two irreconcilable impulses. On the one hand, there is an argument for the concentration of business, which rationalizes production and which benefits from economies of scale. On the other hand, there is a case for an anti-trust policy,[12] which prevents monopolization, protects individual freedom and rights and, through increased competition, increases welfare. The challenge for a government is to balance these two tendencies. It needs to keep the best parts of each of the two opposing tendencies, profit from the harmonious equilibrium between the two and employ competition policy as a tool for the increase in the standard of living.

2.2   Monopoly

In a perfectly competitive market, the marginal revenue (MR) curve of a firm is straight (Figure 2.6). No firm can influence the market price. Each firm is a price taker.[13] Hence, the MR curve of every firm equals the market price. In a simple model with linear demand, cost and revenue curves respectively, the MR curve cuts the horizontal axis OQ (representing the quantity produced) at point E. At that point MR is zero. To the left of E on the horizontal axis, MR is positive, and moving from O to E, total revenue is increasing. To the

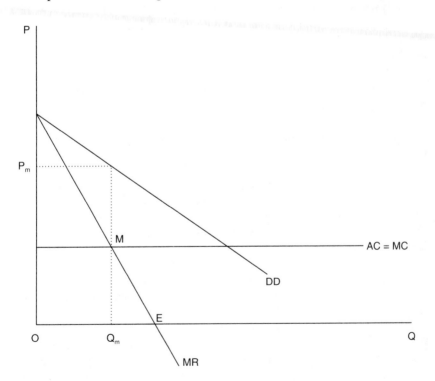

Figure 2.6 Welfare effects of a monopoly

right of E on the same axis, MR is negative, and moving from E to Q, total revenue is decreasing. At E, total revenue is at maximum.

The market structure of a monopoly is at the opposite end from perfect competition. Entry into such an industry is costly, risky, time consuming, although potentially highly profitable. While in perfect competition no firm has any power whatever over the market price, a monopoly (an exclusive supplier) has the power to influence the market price of a good or a service if there are no substitutes. To counter such behaviour, there are governments that may choose to intervene and prevent/rectify such non-competitive behaviour. That can be done by regulation of the behaviour of monopolies and/or by liberalization of imports.[14] If the monopolist wanted to maximize total revenue, he would never supply a quantity that is bigger than OE.

With constant returns to scale, average costs are constant, hence the average cost (AC) curve is horizontal. The consequence of this simplification is that marginal costs (MC) equal AC. That permits the finding of the point where profit is at the maximum if demand curve is DD. It is maximized at point M, where $MR = MC$. At that point, a monopolist produces OQ_m and charges price OP_m. The quantity produced is smaller and the price charged by the monopoly is higher than in the case with perfect competition.

This is an obvious, although very simple, example of how a monopoly (or a cartel) undermines the welfare of consumers and allocates resources in a sub-optimal way from the social standpoint. In addition, if left alone, a monopoly is not pressed to do anything about it. Such a safe and secure life does not encourage the monopoly to innovate and increase efficiency as would be the case with free competition. A secure life could make a monopoly innovation-sluggish in the longer term. None the less, there is a potentially inverted effect in the short run. If a firm thinks that an innovation may bring it a monopoly power, in the short run, such firm would venture into a process that may lead to innovation. If successful, this may bring inertia, less flexibility and reluctance to adjust in the longer term. However, such rigidities may not be found only on the side of firms. Labour, in particular labour unions, may pose obstacles and slow down the innovation process. Machines, it can be argued, may destroy jobs.[15] If this were ever true, it may be correct only in the short run. Technological progress, increased productivity and alternative employment, often requiring a superior labour profile, more than compensate for the alleged short-term social loss. Only those who are reluctant to adjust to the new situation suffer. Although technology has advanced rapidly over the past centuries, unemployment has not risen with it. Increases in productivity, output and job openings have risen together over the long term.

If a monopoly exists, one should not rush to the conclusion that its presence *per se* leads to economic inefficiency. It is possible that in industries with high entry barriers, sunk costs and economies of scale (for example, aerospace), a single efficient producer may have a lower monopoly price for the good than would be the price of many inefficient producers in the same industry. In such cases it may not be efficient to break up a concentrated industry. The authorities would be better taxing the excessive profits of firms in such industries and/or make sure that they are reinvested. If the market grows sufficiently, then the authorities need to encourage other, potentially efficient, producers to enter the same kind of business.

Policies that were intended to increase competitiveness have sometimes produced unexpected results. During the 1950s the US wanted to break up large and powerful corporations. So, the government broke up AT&T. Little attention was paid during the debate to the place of Bell Labs and the fact that it had played the major part in innovation in telecommunications over the preceding century. Deregulation of the industry prohibited the US telephone operating companies from manufacturing phones or switching equipment. As a result, US exports grew moderately, while imports exploded (Lipsey, 1992a, p. 295).

From these examples stem convincing arguments in favour of a competition policy. The intention of this policy is to improve efficiency in the use of factors with the objective of increasing welfare. However, in a real market situation that is full of imperfections (economies of scale, externalities, sunk costs, innovation, asymmetric information, etc.) one may easily find arguments in favour of a certain concentration of production (mergers) and protection of intellectual property rights. It may be sometimes argued that it is quite costly to trade intangible technology assets at arm's length. That is because 'it is a combination of skills, equipment and organization embodied in people and institutions as much as in machinery and equipment' (Sharp and Pavitt, 1993, p. 147). If an inventor fears that his patent rights[16] are not sufficiently protected (enforcement, length of the patent right, level of penalties), he would keep the innovation as a secret for himself or have disincentives for R&D in the future. A part of the innovation process may lean towards outcomes that may not be easily imitated. A conflict between static and dynamic efficiency in production, as well as between the welfare of producers and consumers, is obvious. Once technology becomes older and is no longer in the core of the business activities of the innovator, the higher the chances that the innovator will spread technology through licensing.

The appropriation of returns from innovation does not create a big problem if the innovator is a non-profit institution such as a research institute, university or a government. Non-profit sources of innovation have the biggest public profile in their work. The results of their work may directly enter the distribution phase of the process. It is estimated that around a half of total investment in R&D is financed by the business community and between a half and two-thirds of R&D is carried out by private firms (Dosi, 1988, pp. 1123–1124). The appropriability problem arises when there is a conflict between the public interest in the spread of information and knowledge, and the private interest in holding and employing that knowledge for lucrative purposes. If the private knowledge that was acquired through risky investment of resources is not protected, at least for a certain period of time, an unprotected spread of it may oust valuable incentives for innovation that propel efficiency and, hence, contribute to growth in the future.

An analysis of alternative ways of protecting the competitive (monopolistic) advantages of new and improved processes and products by Levin *et al.* (1987) found that patents are the least effective means for appropriating returns. Lead time over competitors, moving fast down the learning curve (unit costs of production fall as output increases over time) and sales/service effort were regarded among the surveyed firms as superior means of the appropriation of returns than patents. Firms may sometimes refrain from patenting products or processes to avoid revealing the facts or details of innovation, because of the possible disclosure of information to competitors and imitators. At the same time, firms have every incentive to advertise the benefits of new or improved products and disseminate them to consumers. Therefore, secrecy about innovation is both difficult and undesirable. Additional profits can be made by the production of complementary assets. Therefore, not only innovation and manufacturing (technological leadership), but also and equally important, distribution and aftersales service (commercial leadership) are of great advantage in capturing markets and profits. Japanese companies that produce cameras, audio and video goods (and some segments of the passenger-car market) have virtually ousted most of their international competitors through an uninterrupted tide of technical improvements and distribution/service network.

The benefits of increased competition will materialize only if firms compete and do not collude to avoid competition. Competition stimulates innovation. It may, in turn, bring new technologies with large sunk costs, concentration of production and other entry barriers. If this is the case, then neither markets, nor monopolies (oligopolies) need to be let alone. Otherwise, consumer welfare would be distorted and allocation of resources may take place in a sub-optimal way from a social standpoint. Hence, there is a need for a competition policy, not only in the market of a single country, but also in the widest possible area. The rule of law, based in part on economic theory, may modify market distortions both in single countries and in integration groups.

2.3 Concept

One of the most obvious initial effects of international economic integration is the improvement in efficiency in the use of factors due to increased competition in the enlarged market. Competitiveness of firms has two aspects: national and international. In both cases, a competitive firm is the one that is able to make a profit without being protected and/or subsidized. The goods and services of a country are internationally competitive if they are able to withstand competition on the world market, while, at the same time, the domestic residents keep and increase their standard of living on average.

There are three concepts related to competitiveness. *Cost competitiveness* addresses the difference (i.e. profit) between the price at which a good is sold and the cost of its production. If a firm is able to reduce the costs of production by cutting down input prices, innovate and/or organize production and marketing in a more efficient way that is not available to its competitors, it may improve its relative profit margin. A firm has a *price competitive* product if it matches other firms' products in all characteristics, including price. This type of competitiveness can be improved if the firm unilaterally reduces the price of its good (other things being equal) and/or upgrades its attributes and provides a better service. *Relative profitability* exists when there is the possibility of price discrimination (e.g. domestic and foreign markets). Then the different profit margins in these respective markets indicate relative profitability.

The measurement of the competitiveness of an integrated group of countries includes the intra-group trade ratio (intra-group export/intra-group import) and extra-group trade ratio (extra-group export/extra-group import). In addition, the competitiveness of an integrated *country's* economic sector (or industries within it) may be measured in the following two ways.

- *Trade specialization index* (TSI). This provides details about the integrated country j's specialization in exports in relation to other partner countries in the group. If this index for good i is greater than one, country j is specialized in export of good i within the group. TSI (2.2) reveals country j's comparative advantage within the group.

$$\text{TSI} = \frac{\frac{X_{i,j}}{X_{\text{ind},j}}}{\frac{X_{i,g}}{X_{\text{ind},g}}} \qquad (3.2)$$

$X_{i,j}$ = export of *good i* from country j to the partner countries in the integration group
$X_{\text{ind},j}$ = total *industry* exports to the group from country i
$X_{i,g}$ = intra-group exports of *good i*
$X_{\text{ind},g}$ = total *industry* exports within the group

- *Production specialization index* (PSI). This is identical to the TSI, except for the fact that export (X) variables are replaced by production (P) ones. PSI shows where country j is more specialized in production than its integration partners. This index reveals country j's production advantage, as well as domestic consumption pattern. Interpretation of both the TSI and the PSI may be distorted if the production and export of the good i in country j is protected/subsidized. The revealed 'advantage' would be misleading, as is the case of exports of farm goods from the EU due to the CAP.

Goods that are produced and traded by a country may be categorized by their economic idiosyncrasies. There are five, sometimes overlapping, types of goods (Audretsch, 1993, pp. 94–95):

- The Ricardo goods have a high natural-resource content. These commodities include minerals, fuels, wood, paper, fibres and food.
- Product-cycle goods include the ones that rely on high technology and where information serves as a crucial input.[17] This group includes chemicals, pharmaceuticals, plastics, dyes, fertilizers, explosives, machinery, aircraft and instruments.
- R&D-intensive goods include industries where R&D expenditure is at least 5 per cent of the sales value. These are pharmaceuticals, office machinery, aircraft and telecom goods.
- High-advertising goods are the ones where advertising expenditures are at least 5 per cent of the sales value. These include drinks, cereals, soaps, perfumes and watches.
- Goods that are produced by high-concentration industries include tobacco, liquid fuels, edible oils, tubes, home appliances, motor vehicles and railway equipment.

These five types of goods were compared among the rich western countries (mainly the OECD), poor western countries (mainly the north Mediterranean countries) and now the transition countries of central and eastern Europe in 1975 and 1983. The findings were as follows. First, in 1975 the western countries had a comparative disadvantage in the Ricardo goods while the other two groups had a comparative advantage. In 1983, the central and east European countries exhibited a comparative disadvantage in Ricardo goods together with the rich western countries, reflecting their inability to compete with resource-rich developing countries. Second, the rich western countries have a constant comparative advantage in product-cycle, R&D-intensive and advertising-intensive goods over the other two groups of countries. Third, rich western, as well as central and east European, countries have a competitive advantage in highly concentrated industries over the poor western nations (Audretsch, 1993, pp. 95–96).

   While competition in goods is more or less global, competition in many services is localized. A big part of competitive activity in manufactured goods has a price component, competition in many services has, predominantly, a non-price dimension. Reputation and past experience with services often plays a crucial role, while deciding about the choice of the supplier of certain type of service. Local providers of certain types of services, as well as the ones with a high (international) reputation have a specific market power. This kind of local market influence on producers of goods is in most cases non existent as goods may be (easily) traded. Because of a generally lower degree of competitiveness in the service industries than in the manufacturing ones, as well as because of the protection of consumers, administrative regulation in the services sector is quite high.

The competitiveness of a country's goods and services may be increased through depreciation of a home currency and/or reduction in wages. The healthiest way to increase competitiveness, however, is to increase productivity. Developing, intermediate and advanced countries trade more or less successfully all over the world. The level of living standard, however, depends on each country's productivity. But the ability to trade depends only on the ability to produce something that is wanted, while the rate of exchange ensures that exports can be sold. This was the message of David Ricardo in the early nineteenth century and is as important (and as little understood) today as it was in Ricardo's time (Lipsey, 1993a, p. 21).

The new theory of trade and strategic industrial policy argues that with imperfect competition, there are no unique solutions to economic problems.[18] The outcome depends on the assumptions about the conduct of economic agents. There is a strong possibility that in a situation of imperfect competition, firms are able to make above-average profits (rents). Intervention in trade, competition and industry may, under certain conditions, secure these rents for domestic firms. This trade policy of beggar-thy-neighbour or 'war' over economic rents may look like a zero-sum game, where everybody loses in the long term through a chain of retaliations and counter retaliations. However, there is, potentially, at least one good reason for intervention. With externalities and spillovers, the governments may find reasons to protect some growing, high-technology industries. These are the industries where the accumulated knowledge is the prime source of competitiveness. As such, the expenditure of these industries on R&D, and the employment of engineers and scientists is (well) above the average for the economy. Sunk costs and R&D may be supported by the governments, since the positive effects of introducing new technology are felt throughout the economy and beyond the confines of the firm that introduces it. The whole world may benefit, in some cases, from new technology whose development was supported by government intervention. For example, spaceships had to be equipped with computers. They needed to be small and light. A spillover from the development of this kind of equipment was the creation of personal computers. Therefore, the new theory says, with externalities and under certain conditions (no retaliation), intervention may be a positive-sum game where everyone potentially gains in the long run. The critics of the new theory did not show that this theory was wrong, but rather that it was not necessarily correct. In fact, what was not understood was that the new theory provided only a programme for research, rather than a prescription for policy (Krugman, 1993, p. 164).

2.4   Market structure

In a situation without trade and where a monopoly in country A produces good X while there is free competition in country B in the market for the same good, one can expect that prices for good X would be lower in country B. If free trade is permitted, country B would export good X to country A. This example showed that the difference in market structure between countries may explain trade, even though the countries may have identical production technologies and factor endowments.

Competition policies may be classified according to the structure–conduct–performance (SCP) paradigm. The thrust of the SCP paradigm is that performance in a defined market depends on the interaction between the structure of the market and the conduct of buyers and sellers in it.

- *Structure* refers to the organization of production and distribution, i.e. which enterprises are permitted to enter into which business activities. It structures the number and size of buyers and sellers; product differentiation; and relationship (horizontal and vertical integration) between buyers and sellers.
- *Conduct* sets how firms behave in their business. This refers to the competitive strategy of suppliers such as (predatory) pricing, innovation, advertising and investment.
- *Performance* refers to the goals of economic organization such as efficiency, technological progress, availability of goods and full employment of resources.

The most common indicator of market structure or the degree of competition is the proportion of industry output, sales, investment or employment attributable to a sub-set (usually three to ten) of all firms in the industry. It shows the intensity of the competitive pressure on the incumbents. If this ratio is relatively high, then it illustrates that market power is concentrated in relatively few firms.

It is, however, important to be cautious in dealing with these ratios. While an employment concentration ratio may show a monopoly situation, a sales concentration ratio may not. Competitiveness is not only linked to market shares, but as a dynamic phenomenon, to the relative growth of productivity, innovation, R&D, size and quality of the capital stock, mobility of resources, operational control, success in shifting out of ailing lines of business, education of management, training of labour, incentives and the like. Therefore, it is false to fear that a potential exodus of jobs from the EU to the transition countries of central and eastern Europe or to the south Mediterranean countries (because of the relatively low labour costs there) would undermine the global competitiveness of the economies of the EU. If it were true, the EU would be flooded by goods from those countries. That is, however, not the case. There are many factors other than the relative labour costs that influence competitiveness. In most of the 'other factors' (mentioned above) the EU fares much better than the competitors from the respective two regions. Anyway, this ratio is a useful second best barometer of the oligopolistic restriction of competition.

The Hirschman–Herfindahl index (HHI) is an alternative and more complete measure of market structure than the concentration ratio. It is being increasingly used in the public fight against oligopolies.

$$\text{HHI} = \sum_i S_i^2 \times 100 \qquad (2.3)$$

The HHI (2.3) is the sum of squared market shares of each firm in the defined market. It is between 0 and 100. The index is 100 when there is a monopoly, while it is relatively small in competitive industries. The HHI accounts for all the firms (i.e. both their absolute number and relative difference in size) in the defined market, while the concentration ratio accounts only for a select number of firms in the same market.

Integration may provoke several scenarios regarding competition. On the one hand, an increase in industrial concentration may be the consequence of the choice of firms to take advantage of economies of scale. Economies of scope[19] may increase concentration because they favour diversified firms which are often large. On the other hand, smaller firms may benefit, as in Japan or in Italy, because they may be included in the network of large ones. In addition, reduced cross-border transaction costs make it easier for smaller firms to penetrate into the markets of partner countries. This may reduce concentration.

Firms compete by product differentiation, quality, R&D and advertising, as well as by price. The exceptions are, of course, raw materials and semi-finished goods. Major changes in the capacity of a firm that are linked to big sunk costs do not happen frequently. It is, however, more difficult to test the impact of non-price rivalry such as competitor's R&D, design activities and non-technical matters such as management and marketing, than their prices. It also takes longer to retaliate along these dimensions than to change prices (Schmalensee, 1988, p. 670).

2.5 Innovation

The process of technological change is driven by the existence of unexploited opportunities for the solution of problems such as the transformation of electricity into sound, or light into electricity. The process has three distinct, but inter-related phases: invention (discovery of something new), innovation (putting invention into commercial use) and spread. If firms innovate (i.e. realize their technological capabilities to develop, produce and sell goods and services) and introduce new technologies and new goods/services, due to the new circumstances (integration), in order to preserve or improve their market position, then efficiency may increase. From a given set of resources one may expect to get either more and/or better quality output. That directly increases national welfare on average. In fact, integration for a small (or medium-sized country) enables economic development and progress at a lower cost than does autarky. There is, however, an opposing force. When there are imperfections, such as economies of scale and externalities, firms make rents.[20] Free competition leads to concentration that may reduce competition in the future. The new theory of trade and strategic industrial policy advocates that there may be fierce competition even among a few firms, such as in the aircraft industry, or in the US long-distance telephone call market, or in the Japanese market for electronic goods (although largely reserved for a half a dozen home conglomerates).

An innovation changes the mix of factors that are used in the production and/or consumption of goods and services. Usually, an innovation brings a reduction in the necessary quantity of factors in the production of a good or service as shown in Figure 2.7 with an arrow. That makes output cheaper and, consequently, more competitive. Suppose that the production of a good requires two factors, f_1 and f_2, respectively. If one needs to use per unit of output OA of factor f_1 and OB of factor f_2, then one gets rectangle OACB. An innovation reduces the area of rectangle OACB (note the direction of the arrow). In certain cases, when a factor such as oil or some other raw material becomes scarce, an innovation may reduce the consumption of such a factor, but disproportionally increase (at least temporarily) the use of the other factor. Hence, in such special case, the area of the rectangle OACB may increase as the result of innovation.

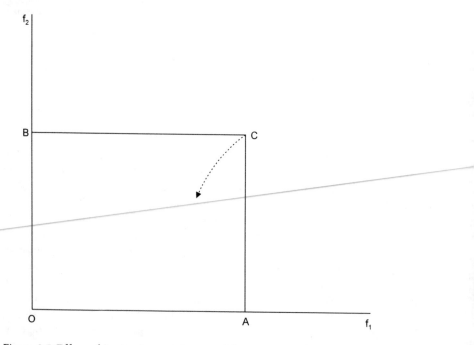

Figure 2.7 Effect of innovation on the use of factors

Economic integration opens up the markets of the integrated countries for the local firms. One can reasonably expect that competition may have a positive effect on innovation, but what are the effects of such a process in the long run? If innovation decentralizes and if it increases competition, then competition and innovation reinforce each other. If, however, innovation centralizes over time and larger firms are necessary for the kind of costly and risky innovation that can be undertaken by only a few firms, then the extension of markets for firms would have a positive effect on innovation only in the short run. Therefore, one needs to ensure that short-run positive effects do continue in the long run (Geroski, 1988, pp. 377–379). In order to maintain the 'necessary' level of competition within the integrated area, the countries involved may wish to proceed in an elegant way. That is, to reduce the level of common external tariff and non-tariff protection.

The impact of competition is not restricted only to prices and costs. Competition also yields other favourable effects. It stimulates technical progress, widens consumer choices, improves the quality of goods and services and rationalizes the organization of firms. It is important to remember that firms seldom lose out to competition because their output is priced in a non-optimal way or because their production capacity is insufficient, rather, they lose because they fail to develop new products and new production processes as well or as quickly as their competitors (Lipsey, 1993a, p. 13). If a firm does not make its own product obsolete through innovation, some other entrepreneur will do just that.

Innovations are constantly changing the way of combination of factors in the production process, i.e., technologies.[21] These changes can be from minor to revolutionary. They could have four levels (Lipsey, 1993b, p. 3) as follows:

- *incremental innovations*, each one is small, but their cumulative effect is large;
- *radical innovations*, these are discontinuous events such as the development of a new material (e.g. plastic) or a new source of power;
- *changes in the technology system* affect an economic sector and industries within it, such as the changes in and around the chemical industry in the nineteenth century; and
- *technological revolution changes* the whole technoeconomic paradigm.[22]

Innovation is an important economic impulse. There is, however, no simple answer to the question of whether international economic integration stimulates or prevents innovation by firms. There are two opposing views. First, a monopolist faces a secure market for its output. It can anticipate normal or super-normal profits (rents) from an innovation and can also reap all of the profits from its implementation. So, it is easier for such firm to innovate than for a firm that does not have such a market foresight, influence and market security. On the other hand, without the pressure from competition, the monopolist may not feel the need to innovate. The impression of long-term stability fosters a conservative way of thinking which may restrict innovative activity. Monopolists may not wish to 'rock the boat' and can prevent or delay the implementation of innovations either in their own production or in the production activity of others.

The group of countries that generate the greatest number of innovations has been relatively small and stable over time. Britain was the leader in innovative activities during the industrial revolution. It was joined in the second half of the nineteenth century by Germany, the US, France, Switzerland and Sweden. Membership of this select band of countries has been stable for over a century. The only major newcomer to the group was Japan in the post-Second World War period. Towards the end of the twentieth century, a few newly industrialized countries, in particular South Korea, might join this still exclusive club of countries.[23]

The general evidence about why some countries innovate more than the others is still imperfect. None the less, there are several factors that combine to give part of the answer. Differences in the size of the local market (remember that integration increases the size of the market),[24] competition and supply of skills provide important ingredients in the complex links between technological opportunities and entrepreneurial decisions. R&D plays a crucial role in the innovation process as it sustains a supply of knowledge. However, the most important explanation for the relative stability in the number of countries that, in general, innovate most, is that innovation reflects the *cumulative* and inter-related nature of the acquired knowledge, change in technological capabilities and economic incentives.[25] It does not only relate to the creation and absorption of new knowledge, but also to its adaptation and extension within an innovation-friendly environment. Put together, that establishes strong grounds for the creation of dynamic comparative advantages, certain irreversibilities[26] and economic growth[27] of firms and nations as success breeds the potential for further success. The higher the level of accumulation of knowledge and capital stock, the higher are the benefits of technological progress[28] and vice versa. The law of diminishing returns does not apply to the accumulation of knowledge (Lipsey, 1994). This is also reflected in the export performance of those countries measured by the share of world exports in industries where innovations take place, as well as in differences in labour productivity. Innovation is concentrated in a few firms in industries with heavy entry barriers such as aerospace, chemicals, automobiles, electric and electronic industries, while it is spread among many firms in machinery and the production of instruments (Dosi, *et al.* 1990).

Empirical studies draw attention to the fact that monopolization or concentration is not the main factor for explaining innovation. Cumulative knowledge made Germany excel at chemicals and high-quality engineering; Britain at pop music and publishing; Italy at fashion and design; and the US at computers, software and cinema. Innovations are also numerous in industries that are less concentrated and where there are no serious barriers to entry. New entrants may have greater motivation to test and develop new products and technologies than the already established firms. In many industrialized countries, the average size of firms is becoming smaller, not bigger. This reflects demand for more custom-made goods, produced in smaller batches, with factors that may be smoothly moved across various alternative uses. But that is only on average. The industries with the most advanced technology are often the most concentrated, highly profitable and the largest. Modern technology is augmenting capital, in particular, human capital.[29] Krugman (1996a, pp. 13–14) found statistical evidence for the US economy that 'really highvalue-added' industries per worker are cigarettes and petrol refining, while 'high-technology industries' such as aircraft and electronics turned to be roughly around average. However, Krugman forgot important externalities and linkages that high-technology industries have for the whole economy. Although, it is not relevant how many computers a national economy has, but rather how they are used: for example, whether it is for playing Tetris and Solitaire, or for the organization of inventories.

It is one thing is to invent, find new or improved goods or services (product differentiation) and/or uncover a new way to produce or market already existing goods and services, and quite another to commercialize that success. The basic VCR technology was the result of the invention by Ampex in the US in the 1950s. The first VCR aimed at the consumer market was launched in 1971 by Philips, a Dutch producer, several years before Sony appeared with its own model. Other Japanese manufacturers followed, after a short time lapse. After that, the Japanese began to dominate the international market for (home) video equipment.[30] A different approach was chosen by Philips after they invented compact discs. To avoid repeating their 'experience' with VCRs, Philips developed the final technology for compact discs jointly with Sony.

Similarly, commercial jet technology was a British invention. Rolls-Royce was a first producer. This led to the production of the first jet transport aircraft. Later on, the US took over the lead (with Boeing and McDonnell-Douglas) which was, subsequently, seriously challenged by the European Airbus (a consortium of government-supported British, German, French and Spanish firms). Government support of the Airbus provoked a sharp reaction from the US (who ignored the fact that US aircraft producers were generously subsidized through defence contracts). This led to the GATT Agreement on Trade in Civil Aircraft (1979). While 'supporting' the civil aircraft programmes, the signatories 'shall seek to avoid adverse effects on trade in civil aircraft' (Article 6.1). This is a statement that offers a number of different interpretations.[31] As such, it was insufficient to calm down tensions in aircraft trade. A Bilateral Agreement (1992) between the US and the EU was supposed to introduce a framework for all government 'involvement' in the development of commercial aircraft with 100 seats or more. However, it did not take account of past damage. The deal did not eliminate, but merely constrained subsidies (for innovation and R&D). It set quantitative limits on both direct and indirect (military) subsidies for the development of new aircraft. The permitted limit for the direct subsidy for the development cost of a new aircraft was set at 33 per cent. Identifiable benefits from indirect subsidies were limited to 4 per cent of each firm's annual sales (Tyson, 1992, p. 207).

A positive effect on innovation (creation of technology) in the EU was expected to come from the completion of the 1992 Programme. An enlarged market would stimulate competition and would provide an incentive to innovation which would promote competition for the benefit of the consumers. If corrective measures (in support of trade, competition or industrial policy) were added, they would not necessarily violate a free trade system in the long term. They would simply add an adjustment mechanism to the already highly imperfect and sub-optimal market situation.

Perfect competition eliminates inefficient firms from a market, but at the same time rewards the efficient ones; in the words of Schumpeter, this process is called 'creative destruction'. If inter-country factor mobility is allowed for, the supply of factors (labour, capital, land, technology, organization and entrepreneurship) increases. Competition probably operates best when a firm believes that it is in a process that is leading it towards becoming a monopolist (at best), or an oligopolist (at least). However, consumers may be made worse off if the equilibrium in the industry structure is monopolistic or oligopolistic. This can be redressed somewhat if oligopolistic firms introduce the most efficient innovations as rapidly as perfectly competitive firms would, and if governments prevent such a market structure from behaving in a non-competitive way.

Reliance on various foreign technologies is an inevitable fact for small open economies. Such countries often do not have the necessary resources to develop basic technologies for all lines of production. If this situation is regarded as detrimental, then economic integration may increase the pool of resources (human, technological and financial) for innovation and the development of new technologies, products and inputs, which may mitigate the potential disadvantage of smallness. Such pooling started in the EU in the mid-1980s with a series of R&D programmes.

In a relatively well-integrated area such as the EU, one would expect prices of similar goods in different countries to be similar, due to competition and trade. The stronger the competition and the larger the volume of trade, other things being equal, the smaller the price variation. Pre-tax prices for the same good may differ only for the cost of transportation, handling, insurance and, to an extent, marketing. However, the evidence has not substantiated this expectation. The EU was aware of the barriers to competition other than tariffs and quotas (NTBs), so it implemented an ambitious programme to create a genuine internal market at the end of 1992. There are, however, various regional factors that prevent full equalization of prices. In some regions there may be small markets for certain goods and services. So, in order to do business there, firms may price their goods relatively higher. For example, due to special requirements about the requisite ingredients in some countries, the same basic good (for instance, chocolate) may be priced differently. If there are local substitutes, then foreign suppliers may modify the price of their goods. Some goods (such as wine) may be regarded as luxuries in one country and be taxed accordingly, while in another country they may be regarded as basic necessities. This widens the price gap for the same good in different countries, even different regions of the same country. In a perfectly competitive market (together with free entry and exit) for a good, free competition ensures equality of prices and drives profits to zero. In imperfectly competitive markets there is scope for price variation and, therefore, for greater profits.

A special problem regarding innovation and new technology on the one hand, and a lack of an obvious and measurable boost in output, on the other, is known as the 'productivity paradox'. Some may argue that there is no technological revolution and that computers are not productive. If an average personal computer is 100 times more powerful than that of a decade ago, it does not mean that it is proportionately more productive. Others argue that decades must pass before one can enjoy the fruits of technological breakthroughs. Others insist that the benefits are there, but that our standard statistical tools are inadequate to measure them. This is most obvious in the services sector. How to can the output of a bank be measured? Has the economy become so complex and fast changing that it has become unmeasurable? If that is so, it is harder and harder to regulate it and tax it.

2.6 Intra-industry trade

While increased competition offers potential gains regarding the efficient allocation of resources in production and in increased consumption, there is nothing to ensure that these gains can be realized in practice. If a government takes this pessimistic view and believes that domestic production will be wiped out by foreign competition, then it may pursue a policy of protection on the grounds that it is better to produce something inefficiently at home than to produce nothing at all. This disastrous scenario has not been identified in reality. The very existence of the EU, deepening in integration and continuous enlargements is the best example of a positive scenario. Most firms in different EU countries have not been thrown out of business by competition from firms in partner countries. Instead, many of them have continuously increased their business over the long run. They have specialized in certain lines of production that are supposed to satisfy distinct demand segments throughout the EU. Trade takes place in these differentiated products. This phenomenon is known in theory as intra-industry trade.[32] Generally, product differentiation tends to dominate product specialization in the internal trade of the EU.

There are also other examples that support the thesis of a smooth intra-industry adjustment in trade. Successive rounds of negotiations within the

GATT reduced tariffs. The ensuing intra-industry adjustment in trade and specialization among developed countries occurred relatively smoothly. Contrary to the expectation of the factor-endowment theory, intra-industry adjustment prevailed and carried fewer costs than would have been the case with inter-industry adjustment. Even if there were fears that foreigners would eliminate domestic firms through competition, exchange rates can act as an important safety valve to prevent this happening and ease the process of adjustment to the new situation.

With an increase in income, consumers are no longer satisfied with identical or standardized goods. They demand and pay for varieties of the same basic good, often tailored to their individual needs. The larger the variety of available goods and services, the smaller the importance of economies of scale. Intra-industry trade refers to trade in differentiated commodities. It happens when a country simultaneously exports and imports goods (final or semi-finished) that are close substitutes in consumption. Differentiation of goods begins when various characteristics are added to the basic good or component. All that is amplified by strong R&D and advertising campaigns. Thus, gains from trade in differentiated goods may materialize through an increase in consumer choice.

The variety of goods produced in a country, as the new theory suggests, is limited by the existence of scale economies in production. Thus, similar countries have an incentive to trade. Their trade may often be in goods that are produced with similar factor proportions. Such trade does not involve the big adjustment problems common for more conventional trade patterns (Krugman, 1990a, pp. 50–51). In fact, one of the most distinctive properties of the liberalization of trade in the EU was an increase in intra-industry trade coupled with modest adjustment costs (Sapir, 1992, pp. 1496–1497).

The core of the neo-classical international trade and customs union theory refers to two goods. Therefore, it can not consider preference diversity and intra-industry trade in a satisfactory way. The neo-classical theory's 'clean' model of perfect competition can not be applied there. The potential for intra-industry trade increases with the level of economic development, similarity in preferences (tastes), openness to trade and geographical proximity which reduces costs of transport, marketing and after-sales service. A significant portion of trade among developed countries is intra-industry. Preferences may be such that variety is preferred to quantity, so a part of the volume of trade is not only due to a different factor endowment, but also to different national preferences (tastes). This is the case in the EU. The response of successful firms to such business challenges is to find a specialist market niche and to employ economies of scope, rather than scale.

Certain research shows that incentives for intra-industry trade come from the relative level of per capita income and country size, product differentiation, participation in regional integration schemes, common borders, as well as similar language and culture. A negative influence on this type of trade comes from standardization (reduction in consumer choice), distance between countries (increases the cost of information/service necessary for trade in differentiated goods) and trade barriers that reduce all trade flows (Balassa and Bauwens, 1988, p. 1436).

Intra-industry trade is relatively high among developed countries. It refers to trade within the same trade classification group. One may, therefore, wonder if intra-industry trade is a statistical, rather than an authentic phenomenon. In addition, it may be argued that two varieties of the same product are not always two distinct goods. The criteria for data aggregation in international trade statistics (SITC) are similarity in inputs and substitutability in consumption. They often contradict each other. Many of the three digit groups in SITC include heterogeneous commodities. SITC 751 (office machines) includes typewriters, wordprocessing machines, cash registers and photocopying machines, while SITC 895 (office and stationery supplies) includes filing cabinets, paper clips, fountain pens, chalk and typewriter ribbons. On these grounds one could conclude that intra-industry trade is a pure statistical fabrication. However, this is not so in reality. If one studied trade groups with more than three digits, differences could and would appear. The index of intra-industry trade (IIT) in a country is represented by the ratio of the absolute difference between exports and imports in a trade classification group to the sum of exports and imports in the same classification group.

$$\text{IIT} = 1 - \frac{|X_j - M_j|}{X_j + M_j} \tag{2.4}$$

The IIT index (2.4) equals 1 for complete intra-industry specialization (a country imports and exports goods in a group in the same quantity) and is 0 for complete inter-industry specialization. The *ex ante* expectation that trade liberalization would shift the IIT index closer to 1 in the case of developed countries has been substantiated in numerous studies. Among the EU countries, the IIT index was the highest in 1987 for France (0.83), Britain (0.77), Belgium (0.77), Germany (0.76) and the Netherlands (0.76), while the lowest in Portugal (0.37) and Greece (0.31) implying that these two countries had a high inter-industry specialization (European Economy, 1990, pp. 40–41).

Some goods belonging to the same classification group may be perfect substitutes, and have identical end uses (e.g. plates). However, goods such as plates can be made of china, glass, paper, plastic, wood, metal or ceramic. Every type of this end product requires totally different and unrelated factor inputs and technology. Similar examples may be found in tableware, furniture, clothing, etc. These differences among goods that enter a single SITC group may not be important for statistical records, but they are often of crucial importance to consumers. Demand for a variety of products increases with a rise in income. Higher income gives consumers the opportunity to express variety in taste through, for example, purchasing different styles of clothing. A customs union may change consumers' preference ordering since the choice of goods in the situation prior to a customs union or reduction in tariffs may be quite different.

Integration in the EU increased intra-industry trade within this group of countries, while integration in the former Council for Mutual Economic Assistance (CMEA) had as its consequence greater inter-industry trade (Drabek and Greenaway, 1984, pp. 463–464). Preferences in the centrally planned economies were revealed through plan targets. They were different in comparison with economies in which market forces demonstrate consumer preferences. In market economies competition takes place among firms, while competition in centrally planned economies occurred among different plans that were offered to the central planning body. A free trade area between the US and Canada (1987) was not expected to alter crucially the pattern of trade between these two countries. One reason was that the last step in the reduction in tariffs agreed during the Tokyo Round of the GATT negotiations took place in 1987. After this reduction, trade between the US and Canada became largely free, 80 per cent of all trade was duty-free while a further 15 per cent was subject to a tariff that was 5 per cent or less. Another reason was that there is greater similarity in consumer tastes in North America than in the EU.

Since a large part of trade among developed countries has an intra-industry character, this may lead to the conclusion that the Heckscher–Ohlin (factor proportions) theory of trade is not valid. Intra-industry trade (a relatively large share of total trade among the developed countries) is not based on differences in factor endowments among countries.[33] Countries tend to specialize and export goods that are demanded by the majority of domestic consumers. It is this demand that induces production, rather than domestic factor endowment. Countries have a competitive edge in the production of these goods and thus gain an advantage in foreign markets, while they import goods demanded by a minority of the home population (Linder, 1961). The US, Japan and Germany have the greatest comparative advantage in goods for which their home market is relatively big. These are standardized goods for mass consumption.[34] Because of the larger and more homogenized market that made production runs large, labour productivity in the manufacturing industries was some 50 per cent higher in the US than in Germany in 1986. Such an estimate might have exaggerated the difference in productivity as there was little allowance for the high quality of German manufactured products (Pratten, 1988, pp. 126–127). For example: being preoccupied with large quantities of output and economies of scale rendered the taste of American chocolate, for a European, absolutely appalling!

Intra-industry trade may be described in terms of monopolistic competition and product differentiation. Perfect competition is not a realistic market

Table 2.4 Intra-industry trade in major OECD countries: share in total trade (%)

Country	1964	1967	1973	1979	1985
Belgium/Luxembourg	62	66	69	73	74
France	64	67	70	70	72
Germany	44	51	60	60	65
Italy	49	45	54	48	55
Netherlands	65	66	63	65	67
UK	46	55	71	80	76
Australia	18	18	29	22	25
Canada	37	49	57	56	68
Japan	23	22	24	21	24
US	48	52	48	52	72
Mean of major OECD countries	46	49	55	55	60

Source: *Structural Adjustment and Economic Performance* (OECD, 1987, p. 273)

structure, so perfect monopolistic competition is the most perfect market structure in a situation with differentiated goods (Lancaster, 1980). Armington's assumption states that products in the same industry, but from different countries, are imperfect substitutes (Armington, 1969, p. 160). In other words, buyers' preferences for different(iated) goods are independent. Armington's assumption overestimated the degree of market power of a particular producer.

Table 2.4 provides data on the share of intra-industry trade in total trade in major OECD countries. Data show that the share of intra-industry grew, on average, from the mid-1960s for the following two decades. During that period intra-industry trade was more important for EU countries and North America (high intra-industry specialization reveals imperfect competition) than for Japan or Australia which had a relatively high inter-industry specialization.

Instead of taking goods themselves as the basis for analysis, 'address models' of goods differentiation take characteristics that are embodied in commodities as their starting point (Lipsey, 1987b). A computer is a good that can be considered as a collection of different attributes, such as memory, speed, printing, graphics and the like. Figure 2.8 illustrates two characteristics of a set of goods (computers).

Each good (computer) A, B and C, respectively, has a certain combination of characteristic S (speed) and characteristic M (memory). Each good is defined by its location in the continuous space of characteristics, hence it has a certain 'address'. Consumer preferences are defined over characteristics, not goods. Some consumers prefer memory over speed, while others have opposite tastes. Under the assumption that all three goods have the same price in Figure 2.8, let a consumer have tastes embodied in the indifference curve II. This consumer maximizes utility with the purchase of good B. Each good in this model has close and distant neighbours. There are many

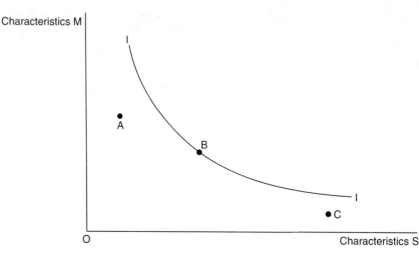

Figure 2.8 Characteristics of computers

goods and many consumers. Everyone attempts to attain one's own highest indifference curve. That gives rise to intra-industry trade. Address models of localized (monopolistic) competition can be an important factor in explaining intra-industry trade.

All general explanations of trade in differentiated goods refer only to final goods in trade among developed countries. In addition, intra-industry trade is linked with imperfect product markets (monopolization) and consumer demand for a variety of goods. Economies of scale can be the other important factor in explaining trade in differentiated goods. Countries with a similar endowment of factors will still trade. Imperfect information on the part of consumers about goods might have had an impact on intra-industry trade, but its effect has disappeared because of the Internet, advertising and other methods of disseminating information.

The Heckscher–Ohlin theory gives students the impression that the factor proportions theory of trade is orthodox. Linder's theory tends to be less rigorous and thus has not made the same impression on students. None the less, Leamer (1984) found evidence which supports the classical theory. Linder's research does not reject the factor proportion theory, it only explains that factor proportion is not the only cause of trade. One may conclude that the factor proportions theory determines trade and specialization *among* different SITC classification groups, while economies of scale and diversity in tastes determine production and trade *within* SITC classification groups. As most changes in demand take place *within* certain clusters of goods, that is a sign that changes in technology are important driving forces of trade.

2.7   European Union

2.7.1   Introduction

The EU Commission has a special responsibility for the proper operation of competition in the EU because it 'handles' a much larger number of firms than any member country. Basic rules (including exceptions) in EU competition policy can be found in the Treaty of Rome and rulings of the Court of Justice. In essence, there should be no barriers to internal trade. Freedom of movement for goods, services, people and capital (four freedoms) are contained in Article 3 of the Treaty of Rome. The EU does not tolerate any discrimination on the grounds of nationality[35] (Article 6). 'The internal market shall comprise an area without internal frontiers in which the free movement of goods, persons, services and capital is ensured' (Article 7a). This provision was supposed to oust NTBs on internal trade and ensure the most liberal competition rules for the EU residents. Freedom of movement of goods is elaborated in Articles 9–37.[36] Free movement (and establishment) of persons, services and capital is regulated by Articles 48–73. In addition, national tax provisions must not discriminate against goods that originate from other member states of the EU (Articles 95–99). In addition, Article 130 requests both the EU and its member states to ensure the necessary conditions for competitiveness of the EU industry.

Competition rules are founded on the assumption that the concentration of (private) economic power within monopolies, oligopolies, cartels or other market structures that have similar negative effects on consumers, need to be outlawed and/or regulated and monitored. Individual economic freedom needs to be fostered through the rules of market competition. The objective of this approach is to allocate factors according to the criteria of efficiency and, hence, contribute to an increase in the average standard of living.

In 1985 the EU accepted a technical blueprint, known as Programme 1992,[37] with 282 measures for the attainment of the genuine single internal market in the EU by the end of 1992. Its major thrust was the removal of NTBs to internal trade in the EU. This was supposed to increase competition and improve the competitiveness of the EU goods and services relative to exporters in the US, Japan and newly industrialized countries. The Programme removed border controls, introduced mutual recognition of standards, established a single licence and home country autonomy over financial services and opened the national public procurement contracts to suppliers from other EU member countries.[38] The principal gains from the Programme will not come from the reduction in the costs of internal-EU trade, which is a result of the removal of NTBs, but rather from the longer-term dynamic benefits of increased competition on the expanded internal market. The anti-competitive market behaviour of various local monopolies will be checked. Competition in the EU will, however, be furthered when EU internal liberalization is coupled with external liberalization. There are at least two reasons for the external opening of the EU to deepen competition. First, intra-EU trade is mostly in differentiated products (intra-industry). Second, an element of intra-EU trade takes place between subsidiaries of a single TNC. Extra-EU competitive pressure is necessary to ease such an oligopolistic structure and increase the competitiveness of both traditional and new-growth industries (Jacquemin and Sapir, 1991).

The consideration would concentrate here on rules that regulate the actions of firms and governments that can reduce competition on the EU market. Two articles of the Treaty of Rome govern actions of *firms*. Article 85 refers to restrictions on competition, while Article 86 prohibits the abuse of a dominant position. *Governments* may also jeopardize the process of competition. This is the case with state aids (subsidies). Article 92 regulates this issue. Aid above a certain level must be notified to the Commission for the examination of its legality and compatibility with the goals of the EU.

In order to execute its duties as the guardian of the Treaty of Rome, the Council of Ministers issued Regulation 17/62 (1962). The Commission has the right to request relevant information from all enterprises, their associations and member states. If the information is not provided, the Commission may impose a daily fine of up to ECU 1,000 until the information is provided. The Commission is also empowered to investigate the case. This includes 'dawn raids' (surprise visits) to the premises of the parties involved in a case. Inspectors may examine books, accounts, business records, take copies and ask questions. This happened, for example, in 1995 when the inspectors raided the offices of Volkswagen and Audi in Germany, as well as the premises of their Italian distributor Autogerma. However, all this must be with the approval of the visited party since the investigators are not permitted to use force. As the information obtained may disclose business secrets, the Commission must use it exclusively for the purpose of the case in question. If an infringement of the rules is found, the Commission may fine the culpable party/parties. The maximum fine equals 10 per cent of the total annual turnover of the enterprise concerned. While setting the fine, the Commission considers both the weight and the duration of the violation of the Treaty of Rome. A review of the fines imposed by the Commission showed that these have been increasing over time. The guilty parties may appeal against decisions of the Commission to the Court of First Instance. A further appeal may be brought before the Court of Justice.

2.7.2   Restriction of competition

Article 85 of the Treaty of Rome prohibits 'as incompatible with the common market' all explicit or implicit, as well as horizontal or vertical agreements (collusion) among firms that may have a negative impact on internal EU trade 'and which have as their object or effect the prevention, restriction or distortion of competition within the common market', unless authorized by the Commission of the EU. Private practices that restrict competition according to this Article include:

- direct or indirect fixing of prices and other trading conditions;
- limitation or control of production, markets, technical development, or investment;
- sharing of markets;
- application of dissimilar conditions to equivalent transactions with different clients; and
- tying unconnected transactions into contracts.

It has been recognized for quite some time, at least in the smaller countries on the European continent, that there is a certain need for some concentration of business. Hence, Article 85 (3) states exemptions from the general rules of competition. Its application is often based on political compromises. Hence the potential danger (uncertainty) that comes from the lack of transparency. An agreement, decision or practice may be declared as compatible with the common market if it contributes to an improvement in production or distribution of goods, or to the promotion of economic or technical progress, 'while allowing consumers a fair share of the resulting benefit'. In addition, to be exempt from the rules of competition, the restrictive agreement must be necessary for the accomplishment of the desired business end (the appropriateness principle). If certain kinds of business practices occur frequently and if they are compatible with the rules of competition, the Commission may grant a block exemption. For example, in 1985 Regulation 418/85 granted a block exemption, until the end of 1997, to agreements among firms on joint R&D and joint exploitation of those results (manufacturing or licensing to third parties).[39] The Commission also recognized the importance of cooperation for technical progress.

Manufactures in the EU wield a powerful lobbying influence on economic policy. One of the examples (Article 85 (3) of the Treaty of Rome) has been the block exemption of car producers from the full rigour of competition since 1985 (Regulation 123/85), on the grounds that cars are a very special kind of consumer good: they are specialized items that require unique attention and aftersale service. Producers have been able to request for tightly controlled exclusive dealerships and also demand that garages use original spare parts (consumers can also benefit from the better knowledge of specialist dealers, service and safety). In addition, producers can control the geographical market segmentation, as well as regulate the quantity and prices of cars sold. Although there is little competition between the retailers of the same type of the car, there is still solid competition among different producers of cars. Car manufacturers have received such favours from the Commission; however, they have failed to fulfil their part of the bargain, i.e. to let consumers shop around the EU for the best deals. There are still significant differences in prices for the same car among the member countries of the EU and guarantees are not honoured throughout the region. The cost of this uncompetitive behaviour is paid by the consumers in higher car prices and reduced choice. For example, prospective car buyers from Austria wanted to purchase vehicles in Italy because the identical models were cheaper by as much as 30 per cent in 1995 (this was in part due to the depreciation of the lira). The Italian car dealers refused to sell cars to non-nationals. In other countries dealers also often refuse to sell cars to the non-nationals or discourage them from purchasing cars through excessively long delivery times, various surcharges or warnings that aftersales service would not be honoured abroad. In spite of all these problems, the block exemption was extended in 1995 for a period of seven years (Regulation 1475/95). The new terms allow multi-dealership as a means for the avoidance of 'exclusive' dealership. This is, however, an insignificant gesture as the second franchise has to be on different premises, under different management and in the form of a distinct legal entity. If the Commission is really keen on increasing competition and efficiency in the EU car industry, then it needs to abandon limits on imports of cars from Japan.

Although there has been a certain reduction in price differential for the same model of car in the EU over the past decade, these still remain and are not likely do disappear in the medium term (at least). The car market remains a 'black hole' in the EU single market that formally started in 1993. The 'normal' rules of competition do not apply in this important market. Although the gap is narrowing, it is still as much as 20 per cent across the EU. For the best-selling models in the small and medium market segments (Lancia Y, Opel Corsa and VW Polo) price differentials are more than 30 per cent, which is more than the gap in the large car segment.[40]

Under the Uruguay Round deal on safeguards each signatory must transform all voluntary export restraint measures into GATT compatible measures, but with the exception of cars until 2000. However, if there is an evidence of injury, or threat of injury, measures must be terminated after four years in the case of discriminatory quotas, but non-discriminatory measures on cars may be extended for another four years if the circumstances justify it. Hence, it would be possible for the EU to introduce new safeguard measures against Japan for eight years after 2000 provided that the quotas were allocated in a manner that could be said to be non-discriminatory. A surge in one month's trade figures following the removal of quotas could initiate a safeguard action (Holmes and Smith, 1995, p. 151).

Examples of uncompetitive behaviour may be found elsewhere. Fragrance producers have a similar right to licence only upmarket shops to sell their products. After all, could and should competition laws force Burger King to sell McDonald's hamburgers and vice versa?

The merger/acquisition-control procedure of the EU has seven, often overlapping, steps. They are pre-notification discussions, notification, investigation, negotiation, decision, political evaluation and judicial scrutiny. The strength of the EU procedure in comparison with the past and with other jurisdictions is that it is:

- fast (a majority of the cases are resolved within a month);
- flexible (as the pre-notification discussions resolve the question of the necessary background information for the decision); and
- it has a 'one-stop shop' (the Commission is the single body in charge of receiving notifications, investigation and decision).

The Commission may approve a merger, clear it with conditions or block it. Although the EU procedure is made simpler, it has at least one weakness: the lack of transparency. The Commission has considerable discretionary room for manoeuvre in the decision-making process.[41]

Exemptions from the competition rules of the EU are possible under Article 85(3) of the Treaty of Rome. To obtain an exemption, the firms involved need to demonstrate that the benefits of the deal outweigh the anti-competitive effects. The firms need to prove to the Commission that the deal improves production and/or distribution of goods and that it promotes technological progress. In addition, the deal needs to pass on a 'fair share' of the resulting benefits to consumers. The procedure for the clearance has been quite long. It used to take up to two years to obtain an exception. Since 1993, if a deal (principally, but not exclusively, joint ventures) between firms has implications for the structure of an industry, the parties are to receive a consenting or a warning letter within two months after the mandatory notification of the Commission about such an agreement. The first examples included an approved joint venture between Olivetti and Canon for the development and production of printers and fax machines. The reason for this exception was the avoidance of duplication of development costs and the transfer of technology from Canon (Japan) to Olivetti (Italy). The joint venture by Asea Brown Bovery for the development and production of high-performance batteries was also approved on the grounds that it brings innovation, reduces dependence on imported oil and, indirectly, improves the quality of life of consumers. The merger between Aérospatiale–Alenia/de Havilland was, however, prohibited in 1991 on the grounds that it would create a dominant position in the worldwide market for medium-sized (40–59 seats) turbopropelled aeroplanes. In addition, there are a few mergers in the information and media industry that have also been blocked.

Competition rules apply not only to the written and enforceable deals among undertakings, but also to tacit ones (such as concerted practices). The *Dyestuffs* case (1969) was one of them. The biggest EU producers of aniline dyes increased their supply prices by identical margins with a time lag of only a few days. That happened on three occasions (in 1964, 1965 and 1967). Professional organizations from the textile and leather industries complained to the Commission. The parties charged denied the existence of any gentlemen's agreement and argued that in a closely-knit industry each producer follows the price leader. None the less, the Commission had enough circumstantial evidence of collusion to fine the ten guilty parties for price fixing. The total fine was ECU 0.5 million. The firms involved in this case were BASF,

Bayer, Hoechst and Cassella Farbwerke Mainkur (from Germany); Francolor (France); ACNA (Italy); ICI (Britain); and Ciba, Sandoz and Geigy (Switzerland). The Court of Justice upheld the decision of the Commission on the grounds that the national markets for dyestuffs were fragmented and that synchronized price rises did not correspond to the normal conditions of the market. One of the important issues that came out of this anti-cartel case was that the Commission and Court applied the EU competition rules on an extra-territorial basis. British and Swiss enterprises were part of the aniline dye gentlemen's agreement. Even though they came from the outside world, they were fined by the EU for the non-competitive market behaviour. The principle that was established in this case was that each firm must independently determine its business policy in the common market.

In order to avoid a potential problem regarding competition on the EU market, two Swiss companies, Ciba-Geigy and Sandoz, approached the EU Commission with a request that it 'clear' their merger into Novartis. The Commission considered over 100 affected markets. As this extraterritorial merger was predominantly of a complementary nature, it was approved in 1996. This case provided further proof that there is a need for an internationally accepted common set of minimum rules in the area of competition policy. These rules would oust, or reduce, the implementation of unilateral and extraterritorial competition-policy instruments. There was a big fuss in the EU about a purely American acquisition when Boeing bought McDonnell-Douglas in 1997. However, the deal was accepted by the EU Commission subject to (some minor) concessions by Boeing.

Competition policy requires skilful handling in a scheme that integrates countries. Breaking up a price-fixing cartel is obviously a competition issue. Deciding, however, how many big chemical or car companies the EU should have is a political question. There should be certain control over mergers with an EU dimension. All industries in the EU were using mergers and acquisitions in their business strategy.[42] That was pronounced in the second half of the 1980s when firms were facing the possibility of a genuine internal market that was supposed to come from the completion of the 1992 Programme.[43] One tool of the Programme was the elimination of unnecessary regulation (NTBs) that was splintering national markets for goods, services and factors in the EU. Mergers, acquisitions, strategic alliances, joint ventures and networking were used by the business community to respond to this challenge. All that was supposed to consolidate positions of firms in the new, frontier-free and highly competitive market. Such a business policy had an indirect positive effect on standardization. It was tolerated by the Commission because of efficiency considerations.

After an acceleration in the second half of 1980s and the peak in almost all types of concentration deals in 1989/90 (restructing was taking place), concentration activity has continued to decelerate ever since (Table 2.5). Firms adjusted their business structure and operation several years before the final implementation of the 1992 Programme took place.

Table 2.5 Mergers and majority acquisitions, 1987–1993

Year	National mergers[a]	EU internal[b]	EU international[c]	International EU[d]	Outside EU[e]
1987–8	2,110	252	499	160	114
1988–9	3,187	761	659	447	310
1989–90	3,853	1,122	655	768	356
1990–1	3,638	947	550	729	376
1991–2	3,720	760	497	605	326
1992–3	3,004	634	537	656	381

Source: XXIIIrd Report on Competition Policy 1993 (Brussels: European Commission, 1994)

Notes: [a] Deals among firms of the same country. [b] Deals involving firms from at least two different member states of the EU. [c] Deals in which EU firms acquire firms of non-EU origin. [d] Deals in which the bidder is from outside of the EU and acquires one or several EU firms. [e] Deals in which there was not any involvement of EU firms.

Table 2.6 Mergers and majority acquisitions by major economic activities in the EU 1987–1993

Economic activity	1987–8	1988–9	1989–90	1990–1	1991–2	1992–3
Agriculture	16	22	45	45	37	22
Energy and water	53	77	75	88	102	81
Minerals and chemicals	215	452	594	589	489	452
Metal, engineering and cars	588	975	1,229	1,137	1,154	941
Manufacturing	560	1,090	1,307	1,306	1,230	1,061
Distribution and hotels	547	863	1,173	899	1,025	797
Transport and telecommunications	95	178	253	257	238	224
Banks, finance and insurance	748	1,046	1,309	1,194	968	918

Source: XXIIIrd Report on Competition Policy 1993 (Brussels: European Commission, 1994)

The greatest number of concentration deals was in the manufacturing industry and within it, in paper manufacturing (Table 2.6). It was followed by food and drink,[44] sugar-based production and chemicals. That is explained by the expected removal of NTBs in internal trade. The metal-based production (mechanical and electro-based engineering and vehicles) also had a relatively high concentration activity. The suppliers of public procurement goods concentrated with the intention of withstanding potentially strong competition. Larger business units are able to share R&D costs in these two industries. Wholesale distributors reacted to the elimination of NTBs by concentration of their activities. The same was true for the providers of financial services.

The major motive for mergers and acquisitions throughout the period of observation was a strengthening of market position. It was followed by the development of commercial activities (market expansion) and rationalization of business (European Economy, 1994, p. 20). The objective was the preparation for intensive competition on an enlarged market. Companies in

Britain, Germany[45] and France were the most favoured targets for intra-EU mergers. At the same time, firms from these three countries were the most active buyers of companies in the EU. None the less, the EU concentration in manufacturing was still 12 per cent below the US one in 1993 (European Economy, 1996. p. 119). Parent companies from Britain, Germany and France (the 'trio') were also active in purchasing non-EU firms. While the British firms preferred to purchase companies in North America, the German and French parent firms have more evenly distributed their non-EU purchases among North America, western (non-EU) and eastern Europe. As for the non-EU acquirers of EU firms, North American buyers were most active in the EU 'trio'. They were followed by firms from Switzerland, Sweden and Japan.

A new trend in relations among firms was that firms in low and medium technologies use mergers and acquisitions in their business strategy, while those in high technology employ cooperation and collaboration (joint ventures). That is a breach from a historical pattern of relations among firms, as they have traditionally relied on the protection of their knowledge and experience in manufacturing and marketing. High costs of developing new and upgrading existing technologies made them share high costs in R&D.

If the structure of the market remains competitive, mergers and acquisitions are supposed to bring at least two efficiency gains. One is related to management, while the other is linked to a reduction in transaction costs. These benefits need to be weighed against the possible costs that come from the potential inefficiencies that may be the consequence of concentration. If the initial expectations about efficiency gains are not fulfilled and do not predominate, a new merged enterprise may suffer from differences in corporate cultures, inflexibility and poor coordination of business. The findings of a number of studies that examined full legal mergers in various countries in the EU was the absence of substantial efficiency gains. Economies of scale were not significant either. Mergers had little or no effect on the post-merger profitability. There was no significant difference in the returns per share three years after the merger.[46] The costs of changes in business organization were often greater than the benefits claimed by the promoters of takeovers. The main reasons for these disappointments include the high prices paid for target firms, overestimation of the business potential of the acquired firm and mismanagement of the integration process with the acquired firm (Jacquemin, 1990a, pp. 13–14; 1990b, p. 541; Jacquemin and Wright, 1993, p. 528). This is most obvious in the cases of mergers of firms in the production of steel or cars, as well as in airlines. Hence, mergers were used as defensive business policy instruments. A large wave of mergers in the US (and Britain) during the 1960s and 1970s proved to be a myopic way out of business trouble. Instead of supporting adjustment, mergers obstructed it by protecting firms from competitive pressure. That was reflected in the relatively slow response of US firms to oil crises and Japanese competition. Firms in the EU would be wise to avoid any repetition of the US experience. The presence of

Japanese TNCs with their top technology and business organization in EU may be the best motivation to EU-domestic firms to restructure their business and become more competitive.

Given the substantial number of mergers and acquisitions, the degree of concentration in the EU has risen. That may *increase* price competition on the internal EU market and abroad through rationalization of production and economies of scale. At the same time, an increased concentration of business may *restrict* competition. Therefore, the EU introduced an important legal instrument for the *ex ante* control of mergers in 1990.[47]

The EU needed a sound competition policy to prevent the creation of pan-EU oligopolies (corporate fortresses) that would replace the national ones and counter the competitive pressure that comes from open markets. According to the Merger Control Regulation 4064/89 of 1989 that came into effect in September 1990, the Commission has a say if a bid has an EU dimension,[48] i.e. if it crosses each of the following three thresholds:

- if annual world-wide turnover of the new (merged) company is above ECU 5 billion (the general threshold);
- if sales in the EU of each party are more than ECU 250 million (the *de minimis* threshold); and
- if each party achieves more than 66 per cent of sales in any EU country.

The decisive determinant according to these thresholds is *turnover*, not domicile/nationality of the parent enterprise.[49] If the proposed merger has a dominant position that may restrict competition (if the new firm can increase prices by, for example, 10 per cent without losing market share), the Commission has the authority to stop the deal. Anyhow, the Commission has not blocked a deal with a post-merger/acquisition market share below 40 per cent. Therefore, the purpose of the Merger Control Regulation is to prevent *ex ante* the creation of unwanted market behaviour that comes from the abuse of dominant position in the EU market.

2.7.3 Dominant position

If a firm has or reaches the dominant position in the market, it may significantly affect competition. This market position may be secured in several ways. They include the following five:

- Firms may have innovative skills not only for products (goods/services), but also for management and planning. They may enter risky investments in R&D, production and/or marketing that the competitors do not dare entering. Such first-mover advantages may result in dominance at the market and super-normal profits (Microsoft's MS-DOS and Windows, as well as Nintendo's Game Boy are obvious examples). The lifecycle of a product is shortening. Hence the importance of innovating. In fact, most firms compete through a perpetual creation of quasi-monopolistic positions that are based on innovation of various kind.[50] A classical view that firms are only an input-conversion mechanism does not correspond to the contemporary world. In addition to their input-conversion and value-adding functions, firms are also involved in learning-by-doing and innovation activities. Concentration in industries with various entry barriers may occur as a direct consequence of a firm behaving efficiently. A policy that promotes R&D among firms in the EU may provide them with an improved footing for oligopolistic competition at home and abroad with foreign rivals that come mainly from Japan and the US.

- The dominant position in the market could be reached through mergers and acquisitions. That is the typical way of securing this status in English-speaking countries.

- A firm may obtain or shelter its dominant position through anti-Examples of this include exclusive dealership and predatory pricing. Exclusive dealership might not always reduce welfare. For example, compared to the situation with free entry and exit among dealers/retailers, permanent and exclusive dealership (including aftersale service) might be a superior and welfare-increasing solution.

- The dominant position can be captured through a competitive and risky pricing policy. If there are important scale and learning economies with a significant fall in prices as output increases over time, a risk-loving firm (for example, Texas Instruments in the 1960s and 1970s) may choose to set current prices on the basis of the expected (low) costs of production in the future, or on the average cost of production over the lifecycle of the select output.

- Yet another way by which firms come to dominate a market may be when the public authorities grant them such a licence. Examples can be found in 'natural' monopolies such as public utilities (supply of water, gas, electricity, rail transport, mail and the local telephone service). In these industries the minimum efficient scale is so large that a single firm is necessary to serve the entire national market.

Article 86 of the Treaty of Rome refers to the issue of the dominant position on the market. It does not prohibit the possession of a dominant position (monopoly or monopsony) *ex ante*, but rather the *abuse* of it. This Article has only an *ex post* effect. In order to determine whether an infringement of the EU market took place, the Commission looks at three factors:

- the existence of the dominant position;
- its abuse (in pricing or control of production or distribution); and
- the negative effect on trade among the member countries.

Big firms are permitted by the Treaty of Rome to have market dominance, but they are forbidden to exercise it. This is quite naive! Whoever gets the power will behave as a monopolist. This temptation is hardly avoidable.

Anyway, the legal formulation recognizes that there is a need for a certain level of concentration[51] in some industries for reasons of efficiency. It is inevitable for the attainment of the efficient scale of production, both for home and foreign markets. Otherwise, protected and inefficient national firms, which have higher production costs than foreign competitors, would continue to impose welfare losses on consumers. That is why many/most European countries have relaxed their anti-trust policies. Otherwise, small domestic firms could be protected only at a high cost and a loss in production efficiency. Concentration of production is a potential barrier against foreign competition on the home market and a springboard for penetration into foreign ones.[52]

2.7.4 State aids

Perfect competition in the neo-classical economic model can be undermined by protection and subsidization. The distinction between the two distortions is subtle. On the one hand, tariff and non-tariff *protection* allow the protected suppliers to charge higher prices on the local market than would be the case with free imports. Such protection provides an 'implicit subsidy' paid directly from consumers to producers. On the other hand, *subsidies* go to the domestic producers, not directly from consumers, but rather from taxpayers to the government and, then, to producers. The two types of 'support' have the same objective. Where they differ is in transparency and the way of supply of funds to the select industries or firms within them.

Those that accept that the market functions efficiently use this argument as a case against subsidies (state aids). Although there are many instances where such an argument applies, there are others where the neo-classical theory does not always hold. In a situation of imperfections such as externalities (R&D or pollution), economies of scale, imperfect mobility of factors and sunk costs, intervention may be justified. Therefore, industrial and regional policies may be used as justification for the existence of state aids. Article 92 of the Treaty of Rome recognizes this issue and regulates it.[53] It prohibits any aid that distorts or threatens to distort competition among the member countries. This means that Article 92 does not apply to aid given as a support to firms or for the production of goods and services that do not enter intra-EU trade (local consumption), as well as aid for exports outside the EU (regulated by Article 112).

There are, however, a few exceptions to the general rule of incompatibility of state aids. Article 92 also states that aid, compatible with the Treaty, *is* of the kind given on a non-discriminatory basis to individuals for social purposes, as well as aid to the regions affected by disasters. Aid that *can be* considered compatible with the Treaty is the kind given to projects that are in the EU's interest and aid for regional development in the 'areas where the standard of living is abnormally low' (for the purpose of social cohesion in the EU). The Council of Ministers (based on the proposal from the

Commission) has the discretionary right to decide that other aid may be compatible with the EU rules. This includes aid to small and medium-sized enterprises,[54] conservation of energy, protection of environment, promotion of national culture or alleviation of serious disturbances in a national economy. If an industry comes under competitive and/or restructuring pressure, the Commission considers the social and other impact of such an adjustment according to the Guidelines of 1979. The Commission may permit aid under conditions that are based on principles that include:

- *temporariness* (a clear time limit);
- *transparency* (the amount of aid has to be measurable);
- *selectivity* (aid is supposed to be given to firms and industries that have a reasonable chance of standing on their own after the restructuring period); and
- *appropriateness* (aid has to match the basic needs of the assisted firm/industry to operate during the restructuring period,[55] after which the assisted firm/industry needs to become economically viable on its own).

In order to ease the workload and concentrate on the large and potentially the most damaging cases, the Commission introduced a *de minimis* rule in 1992. According to this rule, governments are not requested to notify aid that does not exceed ECU 100,000 over a period of three years. The Commission reckons that such aid does not distort competition. In addition, aid linked to environment issues may be allowed if it enables the improvement in conditions that go beyond the required environmental standards.

Article 92, as well as Court practice provide the Commission with a wide discretionary margin in the decision-making process. None the less, the Commission employs two criteria. First is compensatory justification. To 'clear' aid as compatible with the rules, aid has to conform with goals set in Article 92 and it needs to be proven that without state aid, free markets would not be capable of accomplishing the same end. Second is transparency. Each aid has to be justified and measurable. Member states must notify the Commission about form, volume, duration and objectives of aid. If two months after the notification the Commission does not take any explicit decision, aid is regarded as tacitly accepted. The Commission may decide 'not to raise objections', that means that the application is preliminarily approved, but the Commission needs further information in order to reach a final decision. The Commission can open the procedure (Article 93) and request the concerned parties to submit their comments. Following that, the Commission takes a final decision on the compatibility of aid with the EU rules.

Article 92 does not define state aid. None the less, the Commission and the Court of Justice interpret aid in a broad sense. They take it to mean any favour given by a government in a form that includes subsidies, special public guarantees, supply of goods or services at preferential conditions and favours regarding credit terms, that are offered to one or more firms or their associations. Loans and guarantees given by the state or its agency does not necessarily constitute aid. The aid element exists only when such injections of funds are offered on conditions that are superior to the ones prevailing on the market.

Governments can still try to disguise industrial aid as regional aid. It is difficult to trace such support if companies make losses. R&D aid can similarly be abused. The 'support' to the manufacturing and services sectors needs to be in the R&D stage. Otherwise, foreign competitors, mainly from the US, would complain that EU subsidies distort international competition. Any EU member state can finance basic and applied research in the private sector according to the agreed sliding scales.[56] The Commission's Framework on state aid for R&D of 1995 has several criteria for the compatibility of such aid with the common market. They include the following:

- There is a distinction between 'industrial research' and 'pre-competitive development activity'. As one gets closer to the marketplace for final goods, the potential distortion of competition of aid increase.
- State aid for R&D should create an incentive for the recipient firm to carry out R&D in addition to what it would undertake in the normal course of its business operation.
- Aid for 'industrial research' may be up to 50 per cent of the cost, while aid for 'pre-competitive development' may be up to 25 per cent of the cost. None the less, there are special additional bonuses of 10 per cent for projects that involve SMEs, of 15 per cent if the project is a priority under the EU R&D programme and up to 10 per cent if R&D is undertaken in regions eligible for regional aid.
- Maximum aid for R&D in the EU (allowable under the GATT Agreement on Subsidies and Countervailing Measures) is 75 per cent for 'industrial research' and 50 per cent for 'pre-competitive development activity'.
- Member states have to notify the Commission about all individual aid packages for projects exceeding ECU 25 million where aid exceeds ECU 5 million.

The State-aid Department of the EU Commission has a staff of fifty officials responsible for monitoring state aid and carrying out other tasks in the field. They can not be expected to examine every instance of state aid, especially if one has in mind that every region in each member country has staff (often significantly more numerous than the Commission's) to dispense aid. Therefore, the Commission's priority is the prevention of the biggest and most competition distorting examples of aid.[57] The Commission has to make sure that aid is given to the most disadvantaged regions and that it is compatible with the Treaty rules. All these formidable issues linked to competition are increasingly becoming a paradise for lawyers.

The EU Commission has approved aid for many purposes when there is a common interest for the EU. Such derogations from Article 92 include support to regional development, R&D, small and medium-sized enterprises, training, savings in energy and protection of the environment. The

Table 2.7 Overall state aid in member states, 1990–1992 and 1992–1994, as % of
GDP, per person employed, and relative to government expenditure

	% of GDP		ECU per person employed		% of total government expenditure	
	1990–2	1992–4	1990–2[a]	1992–4	1990–2	1992–4
Belgium	2.9	2.0	1.369	958	5.2	3.5
Denmark	1.0	1.0	435	492	1.7	1.7
Germany	2.4	2.6	1.273	1.476	5.1	5.4
Greece[b]	1.9	1.7	366	318	4.0	3.5
Spain[b]	1.3	1.2	407	379	2.9	2.4
France[b]	1.7	1.4	806	664	3.3	2.5
Ireland[b]	1.2	1.5	411	530	3.1	3.6
Italy[b]	2.4	2.3	867	844	4.5	4.1
Luxembourg[b]	2.4	2.1	1.220	1.087	4.8	4.0
Netherlands[b]	0.9	0.8	458	401	1.7	1.4
Portugal[b]	1.5	1.2	220	185	3.6	2.6
United Kingdom	0.5	0.4	162	142	1.3	1.0
EUR 12	1.8	1.7	714	713	3.6	3.3

Source: *Fifth Survey on State Aid in the European Union in the Manufacturing and Certain
other Sectors* (1997) (Brussels: Commission of the European Communities)

Notes: [a] 1990–1992 averages in 1993 prices. [b] These countries supplied no or incomplete data
on aid in agriculture

overall level of state aid in the EU(12) showed a slow downward trend from
1.8 per cent of GDP in 1990–92 to 1.7 per cent in 1992–94 (Table 2.7).
Average aid per person employed also declined from ECU 714 to ECU
713 during the same period. However, aid increased in Germany from ECU
1,273 to 1,476 (mainly because of the 'support' to eastern *Länder*)[58] and in
Ireland. Germany was the most interventionist state, while Britain was the
most liberal. Overall, national aid also declined as a share of pubic expenditure throughout the EU from 3.6 to 3.3 per cent, but remained massive,
ECU 95 billion in 1992–94.

A general downward trend in state aid reflects not only the application of
competition policy in the EU, but also a reduction in public expenditure
'forced' by the Maastricht criteria for the creation of a monetary union. That
is an encouraging development when one keeps in mind that the economies
of the EU countries were in recession during 1992–94. Those were, however,
certain trends in average numbers. Aid to the manufacturing sector in the
EU had a steady downward trend in the previous period. That came to an
end during 1992–94 which may be a cause for concern.

2.8   Conclusion

Relatively small countries that are in the process of development employ
industrial policies that may not always be competition friendly. Relatively

large and developed countries value competition quite highly. As concentration of business in certain industries increases, there is a trend to tighten anti-trust policy and keep a certain level of competition in the internal market. Increased competition would in most cases, without doubt, put a downward pressure on prices and costs. This outcome would enable economic growth with a reduced inflationary pressure. It is, however, not clear how this would happen in practice. Competition may reduce the prices of goods and services. It may increase output, but keep prices constant. In this case a reduction in prices would be offset by an increase in demand. The most likely outcome in practice would be that competition would produce a blend of benefits which accrue from increase in output and decrease in prices.

Programme 1992 enhanced the dynamic process of competition through an easing of the market segmentation and, somewhat haradoxically, increasing concentration in business. This concentration permitted the employment of economies of scale and an increase in technical efficiency in production. In addition, it enhanced R&D through a joint sharing of high costs.

A change in global competition and the relative loss of competitiveness by the EU in comparison with the US in the computer and aerospace industries, Japan in cars and consumer electronics, and developing countries in textiles and clothing, as well as a potential loss in a number of other industries, were among the driving forces that brought about the 1992 Programme. Businesses reacted to the single market programme by consolidations through mergers and acquisitions, as well as joint ventures. An increase in internal EU competition that came through the elimination of internal barriers gave the EU the chance of benefiting from the so far unexploited economies of scale that would reduce, over time, costs of production and increase the global competitiveness, not only of manufacturing, but also of services. This all would provide an additional bonus to investment and the growth of the EU's economy. Hence, not only innovating firms and those that use state-of-the-art technologies, but consumers too are able to reap rewards in the opportunities provided by increased competition. The dynamic segment (at least) of labour might gain from the integration process, as trade and competition would not determine if there were jobs; but what kind of jobs are available.

3 Specialization and returns to scale

Returns to scale refer to the relation between input requirements and output response with its impact on costs. Economies of scale comprise a number of things, from simple technical scale, to phenomena such as processing complex information; direction, control and improvement of independent activities; and experience. If a firm's output increases in the same proportion as its inputs, then that firm's technology exhibits constant returns to scale, or, one may say, a firm has constant marginal costs. If a firm's output increases by a greater proportion than inputs, then this firm's technology has increasing returns to scale or it enjoys decreasing marginal costs (or increasing marginal product).[59] If a firm's output decreases by a smaller proportion than input requirements, then the firm suffers from decreasing returns to scale or increasing marginal costs.

Suppose that a firm uses a set of inputs X in the production of a good Y. Constant, increasing and decreasing returns to scale may be defined for homogeneous production functions. A function is homogeneous of degree k if:

$$f(tx_1, tx_2) = t^k f(x_1, x_2) \qquad (2.5)$$

$t > 0$ and k is constant. If the set of inputs X is increased by t, output is increased by t^k : $k = 1$ implying constant returns to scale; $k > 1$ increasing returns to scale; and $0 < k < 1$ results in decreasing returns to scale. These can also be presented graphically.

Figure 2.9 illustrates technologies with various returns to scale. A firm's technology has constant returns to scale in case (a) where isoquants for output of quantities 1, 2 and 3, respectively, intersect the path from the origin at equal distances, making OA = AB = BC. In the increasing returns to scale (case b), isoquants are closer together, OA > AB > BC. The third case (c) describes decreasing returns to scale. Isoquants are farther away from each other, OA < AB < BC.

Figure 2.10 illustrates the cost behaviour of different technologies. With constant returns to scale marginal cost per unit of output Y is unchanged. With increasing returns to scale, as output increases, costs per unit of output are decreasing; while with decreasing returns to scale as output increases, costs per unit of output are also increasing. Decreasing returns to scale describe a situation in which there are some inputs (such as land) in fixed supply. With increasing returns to scale in industry Y, the ratio at which the two commodities exchange in the market differs from the ratio in which they can be converted into one another through production. When factors are shifted to the increasing returns to scale industry, the gain in production

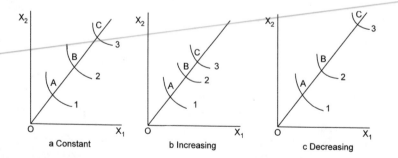

Figure 2.9 Technologies with constant, increasing and decreasing returns to scale

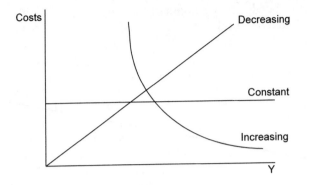

Figure 2.10 Cost curves with constant, increasing and decreasing returns to scale

in that industry is greater than the loss of output in the other, so there is a net increase in output. This increases real wages, average standards of living and GDP.

The pure theory of international trade is concerned mostly with perfect competition. In a situation in which the minimum efficient scale is relatively large, only a few firms can survive simultaneously. Competition in such markets is not perfect. When markets are enlarged by international economic integration or opened up by projects such as the EU's 1992 Programme which increase competition, firms might expand their production and specialize in order to achieve lower production costs (economies of scale).

The existence of internal NTBs to trade was in many cases the cause of unexploited economies of scale in the EU. An empirical study of potential economies of scale in the EU industry reported that in more than a half of all manufacturing industries, twenty firms of efficient size could co-exist in the EU, whereas the largest national markets can support only four each. The EU internal market offers the potential for efficiency and competition. Twenty efficient firms are more likely to ensure effective competition than only four firms (Emerson *et al.*, 1988, p. 18). That finding ignored the logic behind the role of concentration in modern industries and the contribution which a few oligopolies, exploiting economies of scale and carefully monitored by appropriate regulatory authorities, can and do make to economic welfare. Besides, there may be fierce competition even among these four firms. Just take a look at competition in the US long-distance telephone-call business or the fierce competition among a few Japanese electronic conglomerates both in the domestic and international market. In addition, relatively high diversity of tastes in EU countries can make the achievement of output in large production runs unnecessary and unprofitable, contrary to the US where the internal market is quite homogenized.

The approach to economies of scale does not have to be mechanical. Successful managers of firms must know where to find economies of scale so that a firm may lower its minimum efficient scale of production by buying certain components from outside. Take, for example, the car production and assume that each car consists of three equally important components (X, Y and Z, respectively) plus the assembly. In addition, the annual production of the following quantities of components is necessary to achieve the minimum efficient scale: $X = 800,000$; $Y = 500,000$; $Z = 250,000$; and assembly 100,000. If all inputs are produced internally, then the firm must produce 800,000 cars in order to reach the minimum efficient scale in production in X. However, if the firm buys X and Y from other firms that are specialized in the production of these components and that are sold to various car manufacturers, then it only needs to produce 250,000 cars to achieve the minimum efficient scale in the production of Z. Technological change has reduced the minimum efficient scale of production, but the firms tend to increase the value of just in time operation and minimization in stocks. Although the example is rather simplistic, in reality, Volvo could be an example of a car producer that fits such a category. Even though the production run of Volvo is significantly smaller than, for example, Toyota or Volkswagen, Volvo has often been a highly profitable car manufacturer.

The US economic system is created in such a way that it is open to internal competition. Anti-trust legislation is very strong. None the less, the President's Commission on Industrial Competitiveness (1985, vol. 2, pp. 192–193) recognized the potential efficiency gains which may come from the concentration of business in certain industries. Without the prospective reward of temporary monopoly, firms may not have big incentives to innovate. A temporary departure from free competition may be desirable, in the sense that it is better to allow the establishment of temporary monopolies as a way of inducing innovation, than to seek static efficiency at the cost of technological progress (Krugman, 1990a, p. 173). If the American firms fail to withstand international competition over a wide range of industries, then the US approach to competition in a state of market imperfections, rapidly changing technology and expanding exchange of information (both by volume and by speed) could consign the American example to the history books.

Changes in technology exert a continuous pressure on plant efficiency. Hence, the minimum efficient size of plant changes over time. Large-scale production is profitable only if there is secure access to a wide market. It is reasonable, therefore, to assume that firms which operate on a wide market are more likely to be closer to the minimum efficient plant size than those which act within a more restricted framework. However, recent developments in technology are diminishing the classic scale economies associated with mass production in large plants. Modern technology increases the role of smaller, but highly specialized or flexible, plants.

Economies of scale are largest in transport equipment, electronics, office machines, chemicals and other manufactured products. These are the industries in which demand has the highest growth and where technology changes fast. The common element in these industries is the vast investment required to produce even a small amount of output. Advanced technology is not necessary for increasing returns to scale, but such returns to scale are frequently found in high-technology industries. In addition, these industries are under continuous pressure from international competition. Industries with relatively smaller returns to scale are those with a stagnant demand and a relatively low technology content. They include food, textile, clothing and footwear industries. The problem with the EU's manufacturing sector is that a significant part of its export specialization has for a long time been in industries with relatively stagnant or declining demand and relatively weak economies of scale, while the US and Japanese producers and exporters have specialized in goods produced by industries with strong economies of scale.

Adam Smith pointed out that specialization is limited by the extent of the market. A customs union increases the market area for firms in the participating countries, hence it opens up opportunities for specialization. A country may gain from economies of scale which form an independent source for trade. If countries trade, they may gain not only from the exchange of goods and services, but also from specialization and a wider choice of goods. Trade increases the bundle of available goods and services in relation to what is available in autarky. Specialization and alteration in the output mix in a country may take full advantage of its factor endowment. That does not hold only for economic integration, but also for strategies to open up the internal market, as with the EU's 1992 Programme. It is hoped that the long-term impact of the Programme will rectify the EU's comparative advantage in comparison with both Japan and the US.

Economies of scale may be internal to individual firms. They may also be external to these firms when the whole industry grows and when all the firms in that industry enjoy the fruits of such growth. For example, networking (phones or cyberspace exchange of data) is the consequence of economies of scale. The peculiarity of economies of scale is that they are not consistent with perfect competition. With imperfect market structure many welfare outcomes are possible. A perfectly competitive firm takes the price for its output as given. A firm with increasing returns to scale in such a market will find it profitable to produce one more unit of output since it can do so at less than the prevailing price. Thus, it would tend to increase output until it dominates the market, while efficiency may set the price for its output.

Consider the case in Figure 2.11 which illustrates the impact of economies of scale on price in the exporting country A. The vertical axis shows the price in country A for good X. Increasing returns to scale are implied by the downward-sloping AC_a curve. The producer of this commodity has a monopoly position in the domestic market. There is no producer in country B, but this country has a tariff on imports of good X for fiscal reasons. Domestic demand in country A is represented by the curve D_a and the demand for the product in country B is represented by the curves D_b and

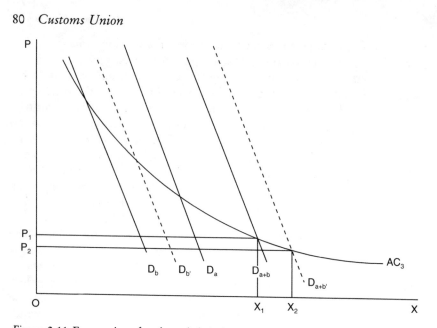

Figure 2.11 Economies of scale and their impact on price in exporting country A

$D_{b'}$. The former is the demand curve incorporating a tariff in country B on imports of good X, while the latter reflects demand for this good if no tariffs were levied.

The initial equilibrium in this market is represented by the intersection of the joint demand curve D_{a+b} and the AC_a curve as implied by the monopoly position of the country A producer. If countries A and B enter into a customs union, then the tariff on imports of good X into country B will be eliminated, increasing the demand for this good. Thus, the curve representing demand in country B is $D_{b'}$ and the joint demand in the customs union is $D_{a+b'}$. Faced with this increased demand the producer in country A will expand output. With increasing returns to scale this output expansion lowers the marginal and average costs of production and leads to a fall in the equilibrium price from P_1 to P_2. The elimination of the tariff has an unambiguously positive effect: all consumers can purchase a greater quantity of good X at a lower price and profit to the producer has increased.

The above result is called the *cost-reduction effect* (Corden, 1984, p. 123). It is distinct from trade creation since the existing supplier reduces price for the good X. There is an additional effect: suppose that there was an initial tariff on imports of good X but it was insufficient to induce domestic production of X in country A. After the creation of a customs union with country B, the market area for country A is increased. Costs of production may fall, hence production of good X may begin in country A replacing imports into both customs union partners from country C. For country A this is *trade suppression*, while for country B this represents trade diversion. While learning by doing, country A may become a more efficient producer of good X than country C, so in the longer run, this policy may pay off. The country in which production with increasing returns to scale occurs gets double gains (employment and increased production). Governments in the customs union may cooperate in order to evenly distribute the industries with increasing returns to scale, otherwise they may end up in an investment subsidy war to attract such industries.

At the start of the 1992 Programme the estimate was that the opening up of public procurement contracts in the EU would save the local taxpayers ECU 20 billion. Bids that come from third countries could be rejected if the non-EU content is more than 50 per cent (unless there is a reciprocity treaty with the third country) and if the non-EU bid is up to 3 per cent cheaper than the best bid coming from the EU. For example, such a system could cause losses to taxpayers as they would have to pay higher prices for Greek or Portuguese supplies of canned food consumed by different armies than would be the case if they were purchased in a third country. In addition, prior to the 1990s, Greece and Portugal were buying electrical turbines from Switzerland as there was no domestic production, following the 1992 Programme, the supplies would come from relatively less efficient (more expensive) suppliers in the EU. Those extra outlays could add to the budget deficits the governments want to curb. As the Swiss and other non-EU producers are subject to economies of scale, a reduction of sales/output in the EU will tend to increase their prices. The post-1992 system benefits Greek or Spanish ship builders and ship repairers relative to Japan and the developing world (Tovias, 1990).

In perfectly contestable markets price equals marginal cost (firms just cover production costs of the last unit and profits are zero). Economies of scale introduce imperfection into the market system, since firms set prices at average cost and make profits. Therefore, economies of scale lead to more specialization compared with the situation with constant returns to scale. The existence of these firms is protected by barriers to entry which increase risk, costs and delays to a newcomer relative to the incumbent. Barriers to entry include:

- sunk costs necessary to achieve minimum efficient scale of output;
- product differentiation;
- R&D;
- regulation (product quality);
- marketing (distribution network, exclusive dealership) and advertising costs;
- predatory pricing policies of incumbents;
- trade and industrial policies (tariffs, quotas, NTBs, domestic content requirements); and
- externalities (linkages).

Predatory pricing means charging unprofitably low prices in order to eliminate an existing or potential competitor from a market. This strategy is backed either by the home government's support or by charging the domestic consumers high prices in a protected market. In addition, a risk-loving firm may price its output on the bases of the expected future lower costs of production, rather than on the current costs that may be quite higher. This was the practice of Texas Instruments during the 1960s and early 1970s in order to build volume of production, gain market share and move down the learning curve. It was Texas Instruments and not the Japanese producers of semiconductors that pioneered this strategy of 'pre-emptive price cutting' (Tyson, 1992, p. 89).

Sometimes it may be hard to distinguish predatory pricing from vigorous price competition. This strategy may, in fact, be unprofitable in the long run. The predator's losses may exceed the prey's since the prey can shut down temporarily and 'mothball' output potential while the predator must make substantial sales to keep prices low. If the prey goes bankrupt, the predator may need to acquire its assets in order to prevent a new rival from buying them up. It will often be less costly to merge with the prey at the outset than to drive it out of business by a predatory strategy (Schmalensee, 1988, p. 665). In addition, 'price wars' may have negative consequences for productivity growth in the longer term. This is because firms will have to reallocate resources from investment to cover the expenses of a 'price war'.

Retaliation against predatory pricing can be done by the means of anti-dumping duties. The existence of this kind of dumping is not that easily proven in practice. Even the GATT/WTO rules do not take into account volatile exchange rates, continuous shortening in the lifecycle of high-technology goods and the complexity of modern marketing arrangements.

Investments in market penetration and some of the investments in plant and R&D are not recoverable. They also often have little market value. Large sunk costs make firms reluctant to enter an industry if long-term access to wide markets is not secure. Expectations about the future play a key role. This restricted or blocked entry results in a smaller number of firms in the industry than would be the case under free entry. Sunk costs provide advantages to the first entrants. Substantial rents may be earned from being at the forefront of technological change, where standards are set for future products and processes, and where, once standards are established and industries matured, new entry becomes difficult (Tyson, 1987, p. 74). A defensive strategy to counteract such developments would be to respond to the competitor's action in order to retain market share, while an offensive strategy would be the development of new goods or services in order to enter new market segments and/or weaken the competitor.

Market pre-emption places potential competitors at a disadvantage. It increases the possibilities for rents, but also presents great risk of failure. New technologies might not remain clandestine forever. If a monopolist makes a profit, other firms will try to enter the industry. Imitators could appear so that the firm's advantage and rents will be eroded. This is why IBM, with an 'open' PC system, had a greater longer-term success than

Macintosh with its 'closed' system. The longer the time lag for imitation, the greater the possibility for the firm to reap rents as the reward for risk and the right choice of investment.

A mature technology often means that factories for standardized goods are often similar in size, hence countries may differ in the number of plants because of variations in the size of the market. This is a lesson for small and medium-sized countries, as well as for the developing ones. They ought to pool their markets and resources in order to overcome these barriers to entry and to reap the benefits of economies of scale.

After a certain level of output some costs, such as depreciation of equipment, can increase disproportionally in relation to output, but can be partly offset by a reduction in costs that accrues from increasing returns to scale. For example, the ends of the blades on a very large turbine move at the speed that can be close to that of sound. At such a speed, 'metal fatigue' increases disproportionally in relation to a turbine's capacity. Beyond a certain level of rotation speed, the costs in all engines based on revolution increase more than the returns. A strike in a firm with an increasing returns to scale technology may have a profound impact on the profitability of a firm. The threat, however, of competition or of removing barriers to trade and imports may mitigate the distortion imposed by trade unions.

If one takes a look from the vantage point of production, it can be noted that economies of scale might require some level of standardization which could restrict product variety and consumer choice. Standards are technical regulations which specify the characteristics of goods. They can be quite different among countries. To harmonize them in a customs union for trade and competition purposes would be a difficult task. Mutual recognition of standards can be an attractive strategy in the short term. This places traders in different countries on an equal footing and eliminates disadvantages to some of them which accrue from NTBs. However, trade in general, and intra-industry trade in particular, could increase product variety in relation to autarky. Product differentiation could reduce export opportunities for small open economies such as Austria, Belgium or Switzerland. These countries have little influence on foreign tastes and tend to enjoy comparative advantages in semi-manufactured goods (Gleiser, Jacquemin and Petit, 1980, p. 521).

The US and Japan, for example, have the market for consumer durable goods dominated by a single (or so) brand which takes advantage of economies of scale. The situation in EU countries is different. Almost every country has its domestic producer. But the American or Japanese formula can not easily be replicated in Europe. This is due to diverse and deeply rooted national preferences. While the Britons want to load their washing machines from the front, the French prefer to do so from the top. The Dutch prefer high-powered machines which can spin most of the moisture out of the washing, the Italians like better slower spinning machines and let the southern sun do the drying. This situation has its impact on the protectionist pressure against third country suppliers, but also against suppliers from within the EU as they are prevented from following a pan-European production strategy. Yet, there are other (relatively new) goods where preferences among countries are identical. It is likely that French cheese producers are going to look for the same qualities in a photocopier or a fax machine as would Italian wine exporters. Common accounting, company or banking laws, therefore, could be quite useful in the EU.

If the EU approximation of standards takes place in an upward way, the overall level of regulation and costs of production will increase, south European countries will find it increasingly difficult to withstand international competition and will grow at a slower pace then the rest of the EU. As growth falls, protectionism increases. If, however, various types of, for instance, labour regulation are left to member states and the framework of mutual recognition is kept, then the northern EU countries could get rid of certain laws and south European countries would grow rapidly. The EU would expand at a substantial rate which would permit the implementation of a liberal trade policy. The ultimate irony is that only the latter course would allow northern EU countries to pay high wages and sustain a heavy social expenditure (Curzon Price, 1991, p. 124).

Although the 1992 Programme removed many NTBs to internal trade in the EU, there are others that still persist which makes the single internal market imperfect. Prior to the period when the single-market initiative was implemented (1985–92), major obstacles to internal trade included physical border controls, technical barriers (standards and product/service regulations), public procurement, different intellectual and industrial property laws, state aids, fiscal barriers, as well as obstacles to the mobility of labour and capital. The 1992 Programme made a distinction between what was essential to harmonize, and what could be left to mutual recognition. During the period when EU standards are being developed, the guiding principle should be mutual recognition of national standards. EU standards are being developed on a large scale, of around 1,000 a year. However, too many national regulations are still being produced, making it as hard as ever to reach a truly homogeneous single market (Curzon Price, 1996).

Various attempts to harmonize diverse goods at EU level created a public furore in many countries. Examples include fuss about prawn cocktail crisps in Britain; the permissible level of bacteria in cheese in France; small-size apples in Denmark; the use of other than durum (hard) wheat for pasta in Italy; the application of other than *Reinheitsgebot* (of 1516) purity rule for brewing beer in Germany; or the removal of the tilde (~) from computer keyboards in Spain. Each year every EU country produces thousands of new regulations on new technologies and products. Every one that relates to the smooth operation of the internal market must be submitted to the Commission. As each one carries a possible seed of conflict, it must be treated with caution. Otherwise, if not maintained constantly and carefully, the genuine single internal market of the EU may disappear following several years of neglect. Therefore, the Decision 3052/95 (adopted in 1995 and implemented in 1997) provides an improved procedure to deal with the remaining obstacles to the free movement of goods in the single market. The Decision obliges member states to notify the Commission of individual measures preventing the free movement of a model, type or category of a product that has been made or sold legally in another country. The purpose of the measure is to encourage member states to think twice before making any exceptions to the EU system of mutual recognition.[60]

The neo-classical theory of international trade argues that countries should specialize in the production of those goods for which they have a comparative advantage. Modern theories are questioning this line of reasoning. International specialization and trade are due to other factors as well. Economies of scale stimulate specialization in production for a narrow market niche, but on a wide international market. This may entail only the reallocation of resources within the same industry or sometimes within a single company. Modern footloose industries are not linked to any particular region by inputs such as iron ore or power. So, a country's comparative advantage can be created by deliberate actions of firms, banks and/or governments.

Any consideration of returns to scale would be incomplete without mentioning services. The impact of returns to scale on costs in the manufacturing sector is obvious indeed. It is less capable of significantly reducing costs in the services sector, although experience and competition can increase productivity in this sector too. Banking, insurance, advertising, transport and forwarding are those industries which are most affected by international competition. However, there are serious methodological limitations in the quantification of returns to scale in the services sector (for example, how does one measure the output of an insurance company?).

Returns to scale have not been thoroughly studied in the theory of customs unions because it is difficult to model them. Therefore, one should be very careful about using classical theory either as a description of what is likely to happen in a customs union or as a guide to policies that will ensure that such an union fulfils its expectations. Another important fact is that a substantial part of production is linked with economies of scope rather than scale. While economies of scale imply a certain level of standardization in tastes and production, economies of scope deal with product or process diversity. Economies of scope allow firms such as Benetton to respond swiftly to changes in the supply of inputs and shifts in demand because they come from the common control of distinct, but inter-related production activities. For example, the same kind of fabric can be used in the production of various goods.

Economies of scale are coupled with market imperfections which allow various welfare outcomes. Distortions, such as deviations from marginal cost pricing or the existence of barriers to entry mean that the creation of a customs union (or for that matter any other type of international economic integration) does not necessarily either improve or worsen welfare. With economies of scale and other distortions, the welfare effects of customs union creation and pattern of trade are much more affected by government policy than they are in the neo-classical theorists' world of comparative advantage and factor proportions.

4　Terms of trade

The terms of trade is the ratio of the quantity of imports that may be obtained in trade for a certain quantity of exports or, alternatively, it is the relative price of imports to exports.[61] Although terms of trade provide an intellectually 'justified' basis for intervention, it has not featured high in many of the arrangements to integrate countries. If home demand for good X is elastic, then the home country's tariff on imports may reduce both consumption and imports of this good. If this country can act as a monopsonist it may turn prices on the international market in its favour which improves its terms of trade (at least in the short term). The same powers may be wielded by a customs union. Third countries may not only lose exports by this possible trade diversion, but also have to increase their effort in exports to the customs union in order to mitigate the impact of adverse terms-of-trade changes.

If a customs union is large enough to influence its terms of trade on both the export and import side (externalization of integration), then the customs union sets the international prices for these goods. Other countries, supposedly small ones, which are price takers for the standardized goods, must accept prices which prevail in the customs union less the common external tariff and less the cost of transport if they want to sell in the customs union market. A big customs union may exercise its monopoly and monopsony powers at the expense of third countries' consumers who pay domestic tariffs and producers who pay the customs union's external tariff if they want to export there.

Monopoly power is not without its disadvantages. If a customs union is large enough to influence prices on international markets, then in the absence of offsetting changes in the rest of the world, an increase in the customs union's supply of good X will simply decrease the price of that good. On the side of the customs union's demand for good Y from abroad, an increase in demand will increase the price of good Y. The greater the demand in the customs union for good Y and the greater the supply of good X and the greater the trade of the customs union, the greater will be the deterioration of the customs union's terms of trade. With both monopoly and monopsony powers, as well as without changes in the outside world, the customs union is made worse off by its desire to increase trade. This situation may be called an 'immiserizing' customs union.

The terms-of-trade effects of a customs union do not only have an external dimension. There is also an internal significance. Trade flows among the member countries are affected too. The integrated partners are not only allies in their relations with third countries, but also competitors in the customs union internal market. The elimination of tariffs and quotas on trade in a customs union has a direct impact on internal trade and prices. A union member country may gain from an improvement of customs union terms of trade with third countries, but this gain may be reduced by worsened terms of trade with the customs union partner countries.

The countries which are in a customs union may experience a shift in productivity due to increased competition and the rapid introduction of new technologies. If one excludes all demographic changes, then any increase in labour productivity has the direct effect of increasing real income under the assumption of unchanged quantity and velocity of money. This has a direct impact on the terms of trade because prices of home goods fall.

The bargaining power of those countries that have entered into a customs union is greater than the power they exert as individuals prior to entering the customs union. The EU countries use this 'weapon' in trade relations with both the US and Japan. The Association of South-East Asian Nations (ASEAN) is another example of an 'integrated' group that is able to extract concessions in trade from foreign partners that are superior to the ones that would be available to the individual member countries. What matters however, is not the absolute, but rather the relative size of the union against its trading partners. The improvement of the terms of trade is not only the principal effect, but also one of the major goals of the integration of trade in manufactures in Western Europe. The reason for the official silence on the issue is the possible charges by the injured trading partners (Petith, 1977, p. 272). The statement that improvement in terms of trade (beggar-thy-neighbour) is the major goal of integration in trade in manufactures in western Europe is difficult to reconcile with what is happening in practice. Neither firms nor governments think in these terms, although the potential for the employment of a 'fortress' mentality as a bargaining chip are there.

The EU is often advised by third countries, especially the US, to adopt more liberal trade policies and to resist the temptation to create 'Fortress Europe'. The capacity and willingness of the EU to accept such advice depends, at least in part, on similar actions by its major trading partners: the US, Japan and, increasingly, by newly industrialized countries such as South Korea and Taiwan.

5 Other effects

5.1 Increase in earnings from exports

Suppose that countries A and B, respectively, form a customs union and that country B imports good X from country A. Country A exporters may expect an increase in export earnings from trade with the customs union partner because tariffs are no longer applied to their internal trade. Under similar assumptions country B firms may expect an increase in their export earnings from trade with country A. The assumption made is that the adjustment is cost free. Whether this short-term increase in export earnings will be sustained in the long run depends on the shift in the pattern of consumption in both countries. If one introduces costs of adjustment, then in the long run both countries have to generate income and production that will continue the short-run pattern of trade. It also depends on the development of substitutes and the level of the common external tariff which may (not) prevent imports from the outside world.

5.2   Public goods and services

Consideration so far referred to the effects of the formation of a customs union on final private goods. Let us introduce public goods which are consumed by everybody in a country, and which enhance welfare just as the consumption of private goods does. Those who want to consume many of these goods may not be prevented from their consumption, nor will they be forced to pay the full price for these goods or services. There are many free riders.

Without government support free markets would provide few public goods and services such as: defence; flood, fire and police protection; R&D (without the protection of the private appropriation of benefits); a system of contract law and a mechanism for its enforcement; arts; parks; statistics; airforce acrobats; weather forecasting and the like. Many countries feel public pride because they develop production of something that they have previously imported, but without mentioning either the price for this or the final good's import content. In doing so they create a 'psychological income' of a nation. Income maintenance and the provision of private goods and services at prices below costs, such as education and health care, still constitute a significant part of the activity and expenditure of every state.

Exact direct and indirect prices of every public good and service are not readily available to each consumer. If the consumers and taxpayers were informed, as well as being aware of the full cost of these goods and services they may not be very keen on supporting their massive production. If there are similar propensities for the production and consumption of these goods in the countries in a customs union, then the cost per unit of the public good or service may be reduced by integration if countries can produce and consume these goods and services jointly.

In a situation where there exists a preference for public goods (for example, a kind of industrial and/or agricultural production) the creation of a customs union may be a more efficient way of satisfying this preference than a country's individual non-discriminatory tariff protection. The classical theory suggests that a direct production subsidy, rather than a customs union, is the most efficient protective means. The rationale for this suggestion is that this policy avoids the consumption costs which are the consequence of a tariff. On these grounds, the economic rationale for a customs union can be established on a public goods basis, only if political or other constraints rule out the use of direct production subsidies (Robson, 1987, p. 53).

A country's international commitments (e.g. membership of the GATT/ WTO) rule out or severely restrict the use of subsidies or discriminatory tariff treatment, and expenditure from the national budgets is frequently curtailed. In this case the formation of a customs union seems to be the only feasible way of reaping the benefits of increased economic freedom. In most cases, international schemes that integrate countries occur among countries whose preferences for public goods are similar (Robson, 1987, p. 54). However, the fact remains that non-economic reasons play a prominent role during the creation of customs unions, as was the case in the EU.

5.3. Reallocation of resources and adjustment costs

Attention hitherto has mostly been directed to the welfare effects of a customs union due to increases in product variety and consumption. It was assumed, along the lines of a neo-classical model, that adjustment of production (shifts from unprofitable into profitable activities) is instantaneous and costless. That is a significant weakness of that model. External shocks such as changes in technology, trade liberalization and economic integration have their immediate impact on increases in efficiency and income. The employment of labour may be generated at a later stage. Adjustment to these shocks may require both time and government intervention. Gains from shifts in trade and production in a customs union should be reduced by the cost of adjustment to get a full picture of the welfare effects of a customs union.

Adjustment costs (the social price for change) may be quite high in the uncompetitive economies. Think of the 'pain' and length of time needed for the transition economies of central and eastern Europe to change to a market-type economic system! However, if they protect themselves from external trade for a long time, such a policy can become an additional obstacle to adjustment. Adjustment costs are borne both by individuals and by society. Private adjustment costs include a reduction in wages, losses in the value of housing and a depreciation of the value of firms' capital. Social costs include lost output from unemployed capital and labour.

The common external tariff may discriminate against imports from third countries in such a way that these external economies may adjust swifter than would otherwise be the case. In order to avoid the common external tariff, the governments of those countries may, among other things, respond by shaping their comparative advantage in higher lines of production to gain a competitive edge in advanced products and export them to the customs union. The dynamic models are not as simple, smooth and straightforward as classical models of trade and investment, but they are much closer to real life.

Experience in the EU, EFTA and successive rounds of tariff reductions under the GATT/WTO have shown that adjustment takes place relatively smoothly. In the case of the EU these cost were so much smaller than expected, that the elimination of tariffs has advanced at a faster pace than anticipated in the Treaty of Rome. There were intra-industry adjustments, rather than inter-industry ones. The disastrous scenario of throwing home firms out of business on a large scale has not materialized at all. The buffer against such a scenario, as well as the means for the mitigation of adjustment costs may be found in increased capital mobility and flexible rates of exchange. However, one has to add that the period of the 1960s was characterized by relatively high growth rates and near full employment, which helped the adjustment process.

If freeing trade does not produce pain in the form of pressure and adjustment costs, it probably produces no gain either. The 'compulsory' reallocation of resources is a source of gains. The adjustment cost is a finite, one-time investment. The gains from improved resource allocation present a continuous flow over time. Therefore, there are reasons to believe that the 'pain' is much exaggerated (Curzon Price, 1987, p. 16). Trade liberalization accelerates competition in participating countries. For this reason, the expectation that international economic integration is beneficial in the long run can be accepted with considerable confidence. Economic adjustment is a necessary condition if countries want to keep the growth of the economy in circumstances of high risk choices where technology and the situation in the market changes fast. They will have to learn how to live with change in order to reap gains from such a strategy.

Adjustment costs associated with shifts among economic activities, include a need for a reallocatiation of labour. Positions will be lost in some business activities, while they will be created in others. Structural funds for social, regional and industrial issues can act as built-in stabilizers which help the initial losers to recover.

An economic policy of non-interference with market forces has obvious advantages because competition and efficiency are stimulated, consumers' tastes are satisfied and there is a reduction in the costs of government administration and intervention. On the other side of the coin, government intervention may be required because markets are imperfect, firms seldom take into account social costs of production (externalities) and adjustment, and market forces may increase inequality in the regional distribution of income. However, intervention meant for the smoothing of the adjustment problems can develop into a deeply rooted protectionism which through time increases costs to everybody. Hence, neither a pure market system nor a paramount government intervention can take account of all private and social costs and benefits of adjustment. While intervention may solve major economic issues, market forces may be more successful in the fine tuning of the economy.

A country's comparative advantage is a dynamic concept. It may shift over time. Countries may not be sure that their comparative advantage will remain unchanged in the future. International economic integration may be a reliable way for a country to secure wide markets for home goods/services and to obtain sources of supply in the future. Geographical proximity of the partner countries ensures that gains from trade, specialization and a wider choice of goods are not wasted on transport costs. This leads us to the issue of optimum partners for a customs union.

IV 'OPTIMUM' PARTNERS FOR A CUSTOMS UNION

International economic integration has been exercised in all parts of the world. Since the end of the Second World War most of these attempts have failed or achieved very little. The reasons for this include a great dependence on countries outside the grouping (the case in all schemes that integrate developing countries, even the EFTA), a small internal market to support no more than a modest industrialization (the Central American Common Market), high costs of transportation and poor communications (the Latin American Free Trade Association; schemes in Africa) and the central planning system of economic integration in the CMEA which avoided market signals and prevented spontaneous integration (Panic, 1988, p. 6).

A large volume of trade between countries is a condition which may induce countries to contemplate integration. If trade is of minor importance for country A, this country may not have a serious economic interest in entering a discriminatory trade arrangement with another country. The US and Canada entered into a free trade deal with Mexico (NAFTA) primarily for political reasons. Once the eastern enlargement of the EU takes place it will also be primarily motivated by political reasons. While it is obvious what the EU may contribute to the transition countries in economic terms, it is much less obvious what the transition countries may contribute to the EU!

Common technical standards in areas of transport, telecommunications, data processing and electronics produce a relatively efficient operation of international grids without any form of economic integration. So, if this operates smoothly, then the potential partner countries may look for some other economic fields which may operate as well, but which require a customs union or other type of formal international economic integration arrangement.

Consider two countries, A and B, respectively. Country A is big and country B is small. Assume next that country A is diversified in production. If both countries are at the same level of economic development measured by income per capita, then it is likely that the structure of imports of country

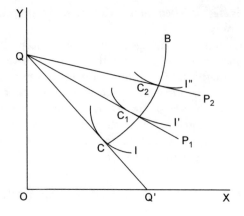

Figure 2.12 Offer curve in country B with a linear production possibility frontier

B consists of a larger number of items than the structure of imports in country A. Country A may satisfy most or all of her demands from domestic sources and this may influence its terms of trade. Country B has to accept the world market prices (country A's) for all goods and services other than those in which it efficiently specializes. Country A sets most of the international prices. If small country B wants to sell a standardized good in country A's market, then country B has to accept country A's domestic price less the tariff and cost of transport. Hence, big country A's tariff may bring greater welfare cost to small country B, than are the benefits from country B's own tariff on imports.

In Figure 2.12, QQ' illustrates country B's linear production possibility frontier. The price line coincides with the production possibility frontier in autarky. With the indifference curve I, home production and consumption is at point C. If the price line changes to P_1 due to trade, one gets the corner solution. Country B becomes completely specialized in the production of good Y at point Q. With the indifference curve I' consumption is at point C_1, that is the point where the indifference curve is tangent to the price line. If the price line changes and if one joins production and consumption points one gets the offer curve QCB for country B with a kink. The construction of the offer curve for country A is similar, but the production possibility frontier for this country is shifted outwards from QQ' and it also has a different (flatter) slope.

Consider the situation in Figure 2.13 with trade in two commodities X and Y and two countries, A and B, where country A is big and country B is small. OA represents big country A's offer curve, while OB represents small country B's offer curve. The offer curves for both countries are constructed in the manner described in Figure 2.12. The longer linear portion of OA relative to OB is due to the longer production possibility frontier of big country A. The equilibrium point between the two offer curves is where they intersect, point E. Between the origin of the Figure 2.13 and the

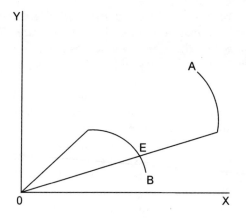

Figure 2.13 Terms of trade between a big and a small country

equilibrium point may be pencilled in the equilibrium price line. The equilibrium point is on the straight portion of big country's offer curve. The price line coincides with offer curve OA. The small country B must accept country A's price if it wants to trade. The small country can not change this situation at all. If one keeps in mind that the offer curves are concave towards the import axis, one finds that at price line OE, country B is specialized in good Y and imports good X, while country A produces both goods and is indifferent to trade.

Suppose that there is another case with many countries and where a large country A and a small country B form a customs union. An increase in country B's demand for country A's good may be relatively easily satisfied by country A, either from stocks or from a marginal increase in the use of existing resources. An increase in country A's demand for country B's product may not be satisfied immediately if country B does not have free capacity or stocks. Country B's capacity may be limited by non-specialized, short production runs. If some reallocation of resources in the economies of these two countries is necessary, the assumption is that due to its less specialized technologies the rate of transformation in country B is smaller than in country A, so country B can more easily shift its resources and direct them to the production aimed at country A's market, than the other way around. If small country B can not reallocate resources towards the production of goods which are in demand in country A, then trade can not take place between these two countries, unless country A transfers a part of its income to country B which the recipient country then spends on imports from country A.

To operate in a large market, a small country should undertake substantial investment in production and marketing. Failure in the customs union market for a small country will mean the loss of most of its external market. Investment expenses will not be recovered. The failure of a big country's exports to a small country's market will mean relatively smaller losses than those experienced by a small country in the same situation. The creation of a customs union in such a situation is a much riskier enterprise for the small country than for the large country, although there is potential for a larger marginal gain.

Government intervention in the form of subsidies is often needed for the capitalization and operation of some industries. When a small country subsidizes an economic activity, it most often has exports in mind. When a big country subsidizes home production it has in mind import substitution and employment. On these grounds part of the small country's exports may be subject to countervailing duties by country A. Due to the asymmetric size of their respective markets, the big country may not regard the opening of small country's market as an 'adequate compensation' for the opening of its own larger market. If there are many countries and if country B trades heavily with country A, then trade relations with the external world for country B are almost bilateral. The trade relations of country A may be more evenly distributed among various countries. On these grounds, country A would request further concessions from country B.

A sad example of 'integration' between a small and a large country is the US annexation of Hawaii. It all started with sugar. Very sweetly. Sugar was grown in Hawaii and exported to California as early as 1827. Exports were growing continuously. Hawaii initiated a Treaty on reciprocal trade with the US in 1848. The Treaty was signed in 1855, but the US Senate has not ratified it. The same happened with another Treaty of 1867. Finally, a new Treaty of 1875 was signed and approved by the US Senate. It provided reciprocal duty-free trade. The Treaty was supposed to be an economic success for Hawaii, in particular, for its exports of sugar. In 1890 the US passed a Tariff Bill which removed the US duties on sugar from all other countries. Thus Hawaii lost its privileged position in the US market. In this situation, annexation could have been the solution for Hawaii. In addition, Hawaii had political problems. The taxation system was inequitable and the government was not fully representing the will of the people. Various machinations, including a small revolution, ensued, with the objective of annexation. However, these efforts failed. Nevertheless, by a resolution of the US Congress in 1898, Hawaii became part of the US. The Hawaiians were, however, given no vote in the matter. This change caused little disturbance in Hawaii. After all, this country was so dependent on the US that annexation seemed to be the best way to have continued free access to the US market (Wilkinson, 1985). This unpleasant example belongs to the past century. Following the break-up of the former Soviet Union (1992), some newly independent states (Belarus) find it hard for both internal and external matters to 'go it alone' and explore ways to re-establish at least some of the broken ties, mostly with Russia.

The position of small countries in negotiations about a customs union has disadvantages, but it is not hopeless. Of course, there are other factors apart from the relative size of countries that influence negotiations. If it is to choose, a small country has its own trump cards. This country may look for partners elsewhere and/or leave the customs union if it thinks that the arrangement with the big country brings losses. If a small country has a genuine resource, geographic location and/or if it specializes in certain production niches, this country may influence negotiations and its terms of trade with a big country. The small Benelux and Scandinavian countries, as well as Greece and Portugal, found grounds for integration with the rest of the EU. Canada and Mexico have done the same in integration with the US.

The greater the similarity between the countries which contemplate integration, the easier the negotiations and the smoother the adjustment and operation of the final arrangement. Optimum partners for the creation of a customs union are those of equal economic size as France, Germany and possibly Italy were at the time of the establishment of the European Economic Community (1957). This condition of optimum partnership (political conditions aside) does not offer any country the chance to blackmail other countries on economic grounds and creates a more egalitarian relationship. Integration of partners of unequal size such as Switzerland and Liechtenstein, Belgium and Luxembourg or any enlargement of the EU made the smaller country accept *acquis helvétique*, *acquis belge* or *acquis communautaire* (around 11,000 items of EU legislation in the late 1990s), respectively in full. Major negotiations were about the length of the transition period, not the substance of the *acquis*.

The (intra-industry) adjustment to the new circumstances is easier and smoother in countries which are similar regarding income levels and factor endowments. Inter-industry adjustment in different economies is relatively hard. The existence, however, of relatively small and backward countries in the EU is evidence that there are various possibilities for countries to participate in a customs union and other types of international economic integration.

Medium-size countries such as Canada (wheat), Saudi Arabia (oil) and Brazil (coffee) may influence the price of their primary products. While income elasticities of demand for manufactured goods (traded on the oligopolistic markets of developed countries) are relatively high, the elasticities for primary goods (traded on competitive markets) are relatively low. Hence, smaller countries' exporters of primary goods generally have weaker bargaining positions than countries whose products are sold in oligopolistic markets.

The removal of tariffs on trade among countries may have substantive effects only if the integrated countries have or can create a base for the production of various goods and services which are demanded in the partner countries. This is of particular importance for developing countries. These countries are at relatively low levels of income, many of them have a similar production structure (often goods and services for subsistence which do not enter into international trade) and relatively high concentrations of one or a few commodities in their production and in exports. These countries do not have much to integrate in such a situation. Their current economic structure does not permit them to trade even on a modest scale. The level of internal trade within the groups that integrate developing countries seldom exceeds 10 per cent of total trade, as is obvious from Table 2.8. These countries compete on the same international markets with primary goods and do not have many goods and services to offer each other. As such, the developing countries have a structural bias against trade and, hence, benefit less from integration (Brada and Méndez, 1985, p. 551).

Table 2.8 Intra-group trade of select integration groups

Group	Share of intra-area trade in total group export (%)					
	1970	*1980*	*1985*	*1990*	*1993*	*1994*
Developed countries						
APEC[a]	57.1	57.5	68.8	69.0	67.2	69.9
EFTA[b](6)	18.1	14.7	13.6	13.5	11.4	11.6
EU[c](12)	53.2	55.7	54.4	60.6	56.0	56.5
EU[c](15)	59.5	61.0	59.3	66.0	61.2	61.7
NAFTA[d]	36.0	33.6	43.9	41.4	45.4	47.6
Developing countries						
America						
Andean Group	1.8	3.8	3.2	4.1	9.2	8.9
CACM[e]	26.0	24.4	14.5	15.4	14.2	14.4
CARICOM[f]	4.6	4.3	5.8	7.8	8.5	9.1
LAIA[g]	9.9	13.7	8.3	10.8	16.5	15.9
MERCOSUR[h]	9.4	11.6	5.5	8.9	17.5	18.2
Africa						
ECOWAS[i]	3.0	10.2	5.3	7.9	8.6	10.7
MRU[j]	0.2	0.8	0.4	0.1	0.0	0.0
PTA[k]	9.6	12.1	5.5	7.6	7.0	..
SADC[l]	5.2	5.1	4.7	5.2	7.0	8.0
UDEAC[m]	4.9	1.8	1.9	2.3	2.3	2.4
UEMOA[n]	6.4	9.9	8.7	12.0	10.4	12.0
UMA[o]	1.4	0.3	1.0	2.8	3.2	3.3
Asia						
ASEAN[p]	21.1	16.9	18.4	18.7	20.0	21.2
GCC[r]	6.0	3.0	4.9	7.9	5.8	5.6

Source: UNCTAD (1995) *Handbook of International Trade and Development Statistics*. New York: United Nations and UNCTAD (1997).

Notes: [a] Asia Pacific Economic Co-operation.   [b] European Free Trade Association.   [c] European Union.   [d] North American Free Trade Area.   [e] Central American Common Market.   [f] Caribbean Community.   [g] Latin American Integration Association.   [h] Southern Cone Common Market.   [i] Economic Community of West African States.   [j] Mano River Union.   [k] Preferential Trade Area for Eastern and Southern African States.   [l] Southern African Development Community.   [m] Central African Customs and Economic Union.   [n] West African Economic and Monetary Union.   [o] Arab Maghreb Union.   [p] Association of South East Asian Nations.   [r] Gulf Co-operation Council.

Reallocation of home resources in these countries, together with the discovery and commercial use of raw materials coupled with foreign aid and loans, may help the developing countries to produce differentiated output and offer a variety of goods to partners in trade. A simple liberalization of trade alone, within a group of developing countries, as the neoclassical school suggests, has not been enough. A more interventionist approach in the shaping of comparative advantage, imports of technology and capital from outside the group will be needed.

For successful international economic integration the necessary condition is a certain minimal level of economic development. With an increase in development, the presumption is that product variety in the national output mix of developing countries would increase. This may give an impetus to trade. What that minimum level of economic development is, depends on the ambitions of the countries involved. Do these countries intend to increase their bargaining power by the formation of a customs union or do they wish to use it as a means to increase or foster economic prosperity? In the second case, the required level of economic development is relatively higher than the level required in the first potential case.

An important role is played by the timing of the creation of a customs union. During periods of economic prosperity it is easier to find gains for the participants than during a recession. The prosperity makes negotiations easier because every participant may expect to obtain gains. The highest rates of growth, however, are not necessarily optimal for international economic integration. On the one hand, entry into a customs union introduces changes which do not necessarily have to be efficient because there is not sufficient capacity in the economy to accept them. The economy may be 'overheated' and the creation of a customs union may increase production (marginally), but it may also increase inflation. On the other hand, during recession an entry into a customs union may mitigate the effect of economic crisis.

In conclusion, a customs union and other types of international economic integration are not suitable for all countries at all times. This is because for different countries some types of integration are more becoming than others. There are several conditions for the success of a customs union: its size, level of tariffs, NTBs, proximity of countries, stage of development, market structure, achievement of the dynamic effects, distribution of costs and benefits, the system for the settlement of disputes and the like. The potential partners for a customs union should check if they meet these conditions or if they can achieve them by means of international economic integration.

V FREE TRADE AREA

Both free trade areas and customs unions yield similar results to an economy and the integrated group with differences only in detail. Free trade areas tend to produce more trade creation and less trade diversion than a tariff-averaging customs union. This detail has often been forgotten in discussions about international economic integration (Curzon Price, 1997, p. 182). A tariff-averaging customs union increases the level of protection of those countries which previously did not have tariffs or whose tariffs were below the level of the common external tariff as was the case when relatively liberal-trading EFTA countries joined the EU. As such, free trade areas place a much lower cost on third countries than tariff-averaging customs unions.

If one assumes that the level of the common external tariff is equal to the lowest tariff of a member country in a customs union, then there is no theoretical difference between a free trade area and a customs union. Effects of both types of integration arrangements are identical. Of course, countries in a free trade area still negotiate in international negotiations about trade and tariffs on their own, while countries in a customs union negotiate as a single unit. As there is no common commercial policy relative to third countries in a free trade area, countries (such as Canada or Switzerland) that value their sovereignty highly have the formal chance to go it alone in trade matters. Free trade areas in practice usually include manufactured goods, but exclude agricultural ones. This is because many countries want to preserve independence in national agricultural policies. It is quite another matter how wise this policy choice is.

Rules of origin are the bases of a free trade agreement. These rules prevent trade deflection. This effect of free trade area refers to the import of goods from third countries into the area by country A (which has a relatively lower tariff than the partner country B) in order to re-export the goods in question to country B. These speculations do not depend only on the difference in the level of tariffs, but also depend on transport, storage and insurance costs, as well as on the quality (perishability) of goods. Without rules of origin in a free trade area, only the lowest tariffs will be effective. Trade deflection problems do not exist in customs unions due to the existence of the common external tariff.

The proliferation of discriminatory, i.e. preferential trading agreements, increased the importance of the rules of origin. Foreign exporters seek to avoid the payment of customs duties, while the protection-seeking domestic competitors endeavour to prevent them from avoiding those requirements. Rules of origin are required especially in free trade areas in order to determine which goods are entitled to enjoy those trade preferences.[62] There are four different methods for the determination of these rules (Palmeter, 1993).

- *Substantial transformation*: the origin is determined by the country in which the good underwent the last substantial transformation (the one that gave the good a new name, a new character and a new use). Critics say that this is an imprecise and subjective method.
- *Change in the tariff heading*: even if the good made/assembled in country A has imported components, that good can be regarded by foreign countries as a good that originated in country A if that was sufficient to

change the tariff classification of the imported materials. Opponents of this system say that the flaw is that the existing tariff schedules were not designed to determine the origin of the goods and that the system may be abused by strong industrial lobbies.

- *Value-added method*: a certain minimum amount of value added must be incorporated in the good in country A in order to enable foreigners to regard the good as originating in country A. The trouble is that the method depends on controversial accounting systems and even a slight change in the exchange rate may produce a different result. The minimum area content requirement can be also criticized on the grounds that it shifts the production-factor mix away from the optimal, it reduces rationalization in production and can reinforce market rigidities.
- *Specified technological processes*: a good must pass through a certain technological transformation in country A in order to be regarded by foreign countries as having been produced in county A. The problems here are that technology changes rapidly and that it is impossible to draft and keep updated records on processes for all goods that enter into international trade.

The trade-diverting effects of the rules of origin could be mitigated by the elimination of quotas and multilateral tariff reductions.

The Kyoto Customs Convention (1973) states that unless a good is wholly produced in a country, what determines the origin of a good is the country where the 'last' substantial process took place.[63]

Rules of origin can be restrictive or liberal. If the required value added within the area is, for example, 90 per cent, then very few commodities would qualify for duty-free treatment. Liberal rules of origin require that only a minor part of the value of goods should be added within the area. Commonly, rules of origin require that 50 per cent of value added should be within the area in order that goods receive a tariff-free status (for example, EFTA, Canada–US Free Trade Agreement). As for the NAFTA, Mexico and Canada were in favour of relatively liberal rules of origin because of the positive impact of such rules on the Japanese FDI in the two countries and the potential exports of goods to the US. Initially, the required local content of goods for liberal treatment in the NAFTA was 50 per cent, but that would gradually increase to and stay at 62.5 per cent from the year 2002.

An important issue is the basis for the application of, for example, a 50 per cent value-added rule. The choice is between the application of this rule to direct manufacturing costs or to invoice values that include overheads. Consider the following example. The direct cost of manufacturing good X in country A is 75 dollars, while overheads and profits are 25 dollars, making a total invoice value of 100 dollars. For good X to be exported without tariffs to the free trade area partner country B, the 50 per cent direct-cost rule allows 37.50 dollars worth of imported components, while the 50 per cent of invoice-value rule allows 50 dollars worth. The former rule offers a higher protection against the use of out-of-area inputs than does the latter rule. The Canada–United States Free Trade Agreement uses the direct-cost rule (the same is true for the free trade deal between Australia and New Zealand). However, the EFTA uses the invoice-value rule (Lipsey and York, 1988, pp. 31–33).

Rules of origin can be criticized on the grounds that they are open to much abuse (for example, a simple change of packing), can be avoided by unscrupulous traders (for example, fake origin statements and marks on the goods) or that the costs of monitoring the system are too high. The experience of the British Imperial preference scheme offered evidence that the operation of the system may be smooth. But in this case the parties were geographically separated, while it would be difficult to prevent smuggling along a reasonably open continuous land frontier (Curzon Price, 1987, pp. 22–23).

Free trade in manufactured goods between the EU and EFTA countries operated easily. This was due to similar and low tariff rates between the parties. None the less, the implementation of the rules of origin were quite costly. The cost of formalities to determine the origin of a good was between 3 and 5 per cent of the value of shipment. Many exporters did not find it worthwhile making use of the origin rules at all and opted for paying tariffs on their exports (Herin, 1986, p. 16).

Hitherto, the analysis dealt with tariffs on final goods. If tariffs are introduced on raw materials and semi-manufactured goods and if one supposes that production functions are identical in all members of a free trade area, all other things being equal, production will be located in the member country which has the lowest tariffs on inputs. Such a situation where 'tariff factories' are created distorts investment decisions and introduces deflection in production. All this increases both the prices paid by consumers and the possibility of retaliation from abroad. A solution to the problem may be found in the liberal rules of origin which encourage trade creation and reduce misallocation of resources, rather than restrictive rules which generate trade diversion.

VI DISTRIBUTION OF COSTS AND BENEFITS

After the establishment of a customs union the welfare of the participating countries may change. Market forces will not necessarily result in acceptable results in the distribution of costs and benefits of integration. Some member countries may reap more benefits than others. The most efficient producers in some member countries may increase sales, employ more factors, introduce large-scale production and generate government revenue. Other countries in the customs union purchase from their partners who may not be the most efficient suppliers in the world, but who are protected by the common external tariff. These importing countries lose tariff revenue and they pay a higher price for the goods which their customs union partners produce less efficiently than the third countries' suppliers. These countries, whose destiny would be to lose in a customs union without being compensated in one way or another, would never enter into this arrangement. Although the establishment of a customs union can make some countries worse off than in the situation prior to integration, if compensation from gainers to losers is possible, a customs union may potentially make everybody better off. For a successful integration scheme, member countries must all remain satisfied with the distribution of the costs and benefits.

There are three possible theoretical cases of spatial distribution of costs and benefits of integration:

- all countries in a customs union reap equal benefits which accrue from integration;
- all countries gain from a customs union, but benefits are distributed disproportionately among them; and
- some countries gain, while others lose.

If the criterion for the distribution of benefits in a customs union is the equality of income per capita, then there are the following possibilities. The first case may not require any action because everybody increases their income in proportion. The second case is harder. Is compensation necessary? Countries may wish to assess before the creation of a customs union whether some of them might gain more than others, and under which conditions. In the third case, if gains are larger than losses, compensation is necessary in order to convince the losers to take part in a customs union. One must always keep in mind that one country's gains from integration does not imply similar losses for other countries in the arrangement. The question is up to which point should one compensate? Should one compensate only up to the point where losses are removed and give the rest of the benefits to the gainers? Should one compensate only up to the point where one may convince the losers to participate?

If a move increases welfare then those who gain from this move may compensate those who lose. This is the compensation test. The second, the bribery test, is one in which the potential losers remain better off by bribing the potential gainers not to make the move. If the gainers are allowed to make the change, the move will take place, unless the potential losers are able to persuade the potential gainers to stay where they are. Any change which passes the compensation test increases the size of the economic pie. If these moves are continuous, the pie grows continuously. With compensation, it is unlikely that a player's share will always go on falling. On the other hand, changes which do not pass the compensation test lower the size of the economic pie, so in the long run everyone is made worse off.

Compensation to the losers may be *ex ante* and *ex post*. In the former case the uneven results of international economic integration for the member countries are foreseen in advance, while the latter way of compensation is necessary if compensation is to be in full. There is always a danger of systematic losses. The losers may blame integration for their troubles and seek compensation. The successful entrepreneurs may be discouraged from carrying along their successful lines as their fortunes may be taxed by endless transfers to the losers.

Compensation to the losers may be paid in different ways. It may be a mere transfer of funds. If unconditional, this transfer may destroy the recipient's incentives to adjust. Compensation may be given in the form of development of infrastructure, education and training of labour, and marketing studies which help the development of the local spirit of enterprise culture.

One criterion for fiscal compensation is stated often in the case of integration deals among the developing countries. It is the loss of a part of customs revenue which is the consequence of the creation of a customs union and the purchase of goods from the partner countries. This problem may be solved by direct transfers of funds from supplier countries' treasuries to buyer countries' budgets. A country which receives full compensation of the customs revenue losses has not changed the volume of government proceeds in relation to the pre-integration situation. This country can shift its resources to the profitable production of goods which are demanded in partner countries and obtain production gains. However, full and exclusively fiscal compensation has not been accepted as the sole means of compensation to the countries which appear to lose in any type of international economic integration.

Proceeds from the common external tariff are expected to belong to the customs union. They depend not only on the relative height of the common external tariffs, type of traded goods, their volume and value, but also on the preferential trade arrangements of the customs union with the external countries. The distribution of these proceeds may be a complex problem. Countries which traded with many partners and which obtained a significant part of their revenue from tariff proceeds, do not have the right to dispose of these funds freely in the customs union framework. This was the situation with Britain prior to joining the EU in 1973. In the developing countries, tariff revenues are an important element of public finances. If integration reduces them in an important way, then there may be internal pressures to increase the level of common external tariff. In any case, there are several keys for the distribution of common proceeds. The revenue may be spent on the common activities of the customs union, distributed to the member countries, given to third countries as a compensation for trade diversion, saved as a reserve or distributed among all these choices.

Manipulating the level of the common external tariff may also be of interest. The height of the common external tariff may be set as the average rate of tariffs of the customs union member countries prior to integration. If a customs union wants to eliminate some internal monopolies it may set the common external tariff at a lower level in order to allow a certain degree of foreign competition. If the height of the common external tariff does not reduce trade with the rest of the world, then there will be no trade diversion.

The system for the distribution of costs and benefits of integration is often controversial. One must, however, remember that economic integration is not about clear balances and *juste retour* from the common budget, but rather about the enhancement of opportunities for business and growth in the group in the medium and longer run. However, certain politicians do not readily accept this argument.

A reduction in the level of the common external tariff and NTBs may be not only the most elegant, but also the least harmful way of compensating those who are felt to be losers from trade diversion in a customs union. If fiscal transfers are required between the countries which are in a common market or economic union, these transfers may be implemented through regional, social and cohesion policies. Economics is the academic field which (among other things) studies the reasons for differences in efficiency among various agents. The distribution of the results among (un)equal players is a matter to be studied in politics.

VII NON-TARIFF BARRIERS

The GATT was quite successful in the continuous reduction of tariffs on industrial goods during the post-war period. Unfortunately, on the reverse side of these achievements, NTBs have mushroomed and eroded the beneficial liberalizing effects of tariff cuts. NTBs are all measures other than tariffs that reduce international trade. Some of them are overt (quotas), while others fall into a grey area such as the application of technical standards or rules of origin. Although they are costlier in terms of resource efficiency and they do not create customs revenue, they expanded because the GATT does not permit a unilateral introduction of new tariffs, while at the same time domestic pressure groups may be quite successful in eliciting protection. NTBs are the strongest in the 'sensitive' commodity groups; in fact, the use of NTBs may determine which commodity groups are sensitive. The implementation of the Treaty of Rome eliminated tariffs and quotas on internal trade in the EU in 1968. As for NTBs, that was the task of the 1992 Programme.

While tariffs add to the costs of goods such as transport costs, NTBs act like import quotas, but do not generate revenue for the government. Currently, NTBs present the most important and dangerous barriers to trade that fragment markets more severely than tariffs have ever done. Tariffs were reduced under the auspices of the GATT/WTO to relatively low levels, of course on the average, so that they are no more than a fig leaf on the economic inefficiency of a country. None the less, national administrations try to obtain short-term political gains through protectionism at the expense of long-term economic benefits. Hence, NTBs are and will be high on the agenda for all international moves to liberalize trade.

Consideration of NTBs has always been difficult. One reason is the creativity of their authors, but also, and more importantly, the lack of data. Administrations either do not record the use of NTBs or if they do, this is done only partly. It comes as no surprise that the reported impact of NTBs can lead to considerable underestimations. Our classification of NTBs is presented in Table 2.9.

The greatest concern which stems from a growing use of NTBs is a lack in their transparency; hence, they are prone to much abuse which increases uncertainty about the access to foreign markets. Tariffs are economic policy

Table 2.9 Non-tariff barriers

Major group	Type
• Government involvement in international trade	Subsidies (production, exports, credit, R&D, below the cost government services) Public procurement (local, regional, central) State monopoly trading Exchange rate restrictions Embargoes Tied aid
• Customs and administrative entry procedures	Customs classification Customs valuation Monitoring measures (antidumping and countervailing duties) Rules of origin Consular formalities Trade licensing Deposits Calendar of import Administrative controls
• Standards	Technical Health Environment ('green standards') Testing and certification Packing, labelling, weight
• Others	Quotas (tariff-free ceilings) Local content and equity rules Tax remission rules Variable levies Bilateral agreements Buy-domestic campaigns Voluntary export restriction agreements Self-limitation agreements Orderly marketing agreements Multi-fibre agreement Ambiguous laws Cartel practices Permissions to advertise

instruments that are obvious. Market forces can thus react to this economic-policy tool through adjustment measures. The operation of NTBs asks for monitoring measures as they do not operate through markets. This proce-dure requires increased 'policing' which increases both costs to firms and uncertainty because of administrative discretion. In relation to tariffs, NTBs are less desirable as they circumvent market forces and, hence, introduce greater distortions and uncertainty and prevent efficient specialization.

A government at all its levels (local, regional and central) is an important consumer of goods and services. It can use its procurement policies either to protect home business (SMEs in particular) and employment or to support young industries during the first fragile steps in order to help the creation of a country's comparative advantage. *Public procurement* can also be employed as an instrument for the implementation of regional policy and/ or aid to the disadvantage of certain population groups (for instance women and minorities).

An open public procurement market in the EU is seen to be one of the major potential benefits that EU firms may exploit. The EU-wide compe-titive tendering directives require the publication of all tender notices above a certain (rather low) financial threshold in the *Official Journal of the European Community*. This is supposed to avoid the underestimation of the value of the contract in order to evade an open tendering. Coupled with compliance with the EU technical standards and an allowance for a reasonable time for the submission of the offer, this may increase the fairness of the bidding procedure. The Commission may exclude foreign firms from the public procurement market if the EU enterprises do not have a recipro-cal access to public contracts in the countries from which these firms originate. In spite of this, there is a chance of inertia (read: buy domestic). A public authority has the chance to split a large public contract into a series of small ones that follow each other and avoid the obligation to advertise in order to award the business locally.

Public procurement accounted for 11.5 per cent of the EU GDP or ECU 721 billion in 1994. That is the combined size of the Belgian, Danish and Spanish economies or ECU 2,000 per citizen. As a consequence of the 1992 Programme, the number of tender notices published in the *Official Journal of the European Community* increased from 12,000 in 1987 to 95,000 in 1995 (European Commission, 1997, p. 21).

The eligible goods for tariff-and quota-free trade in all integration arrangements are those goods produced within the group. The exceptions are any that jeopardize public morality, public security and order, as well as human, animal or plant life or health. An important NTB can be found in *technical standards* (set of specifications for the production and/or operation of a good). The intention of this hidden barrier to trade is in many cases to protect the national producer despite the long-term costs in the form of higher prices that come from lower economies of scale and reduced competi-tion.

One of the most famous illustrations of NTBs within an integrated group was the case of a fruit-based liqueur, *Cassis de Dijon*, from 1979. Germany forbade the importation of this French drink on the grounds that liqueurs consumed in Germany should have more than 25 per cent of alcohol, while *Cassis de Dijon* had 5 per cent less than Germany's threshold. The case was considered by the EU Court of Justice which ruled that the ban on imports of this liqueur was not legitimate. The importance of this ruling is paramount. It created a precedent in the EU for all goods that are legally produced and traded in one member country. These goods cannot be banned for import to other partner countries on the grounds that national standards differ. The gate for competition in all goods manufactured in the EU was open. The exception is the case in which the imports of a good can jeopardize an important national interest. If differences in the national standards do exist, then consumers can be protected by a warning on the good which states this difference. None the less, this case is insufficient for the creation of a uniform EU market and increase in competitiveness which goes with it. Harmonization may remove such shortcomings even though it can be criticized on the grounds of its over-regulation, reduction in choice and relatively long time being implemented. The *Cassis de Dijon* precedent was also used in the case when the EU forced Germany in 1987 to open its market for beers from other EU countries in spite of the fact that those beers do not comply with the German beer purity law (*Reinheitsgebot*) of 1516 which specified that beer must be composed only of water, barley, hops and yeast. This decision has not, in spite of fears, jeopardized Germany's beer production. There are many other national laws that define, for example, what can be sold as chocolate, pasta, sausage or lemonade.

Another imaginative NTB is illustrated by the *Poitiers* case. The French government wanted to protect the home market from imports of Japanese VCRs. There was, however, no indigenous production of VCRs. The domestic manufacturer Thomson was importing Japanese VCRs and distributing them under its own name. The government requested, just before Christmas 1982, that all Japanese VCRs must pass through customs inspection in the town of Poitiers in order to make sure that they all have instruction manuals in French. This town is in the centre of France, far from all main ports of entry for these goods, its customs post had only eight officers and was not well equipped. This action increased costs (transport, insurance, interest, delays) and reduced the quantity of imported and sold VCRs to 3,000 units a month. This measure, perhaps, would make some sense in a situation where the government wanted to restrain rising consumer expenditure that caused a short-term drain on the balance of payments. In such instances, however, a more appropriate measure might be an excise duty or high sales tax. The lesson that should be learned from this case is when imports of goods whose efficient manufacturing depends on scale economies and learning curve effects, the time to protect is before external suppliers have captured most of the domestic market. The attention which this case attracted in the media was considerable, so the French government had 'no other choice' than to revoke this measure. After Christmas, of course![64]

The importation of *Japanese cars* into Italy was subject to a quota. That arrangement was initiated by Japan in 1952. The Japanese feared, at that time, the penetration of small Italian cars into their market. The quota allowed for the annual importation of 2,800 passenger cars and 800 all-terrain vehicles directly from Japan. When the situation changed and once the Japanese became highly competitive in the production of cars, this NTB hit back at Japan.[65] From 1987 the Commission has not been supporting Italy's claim to use Article 115 and block indirect imports of Japanese cars through other EU countries. Hence, the imports of Japanese cars soared.[66] Other EU countries have annual 'caps' on the imports of Japanese cars. For example, the 'cap' for the Japanese cars in the French market is around 3 per cent, while in Britain, the same limit is around 10 per cent of the domestic sales. A tacit limit for the share of Japanese car producers in the German market is around 15 per cent. All these measures have negative effects. On the one hand, consumers lose as they pay more for both the domestic and imported cars, while on the other hand, the EU car industry is postponing its inevitable structural adjustment and potentially losing its competitive edge relative to the Japanese. The governments of the EU countries simply bow to the short-term interests of powerful domestic manufacturing lobbies.

The EU and Japan concluded a 'car deal' in 1991. The EU offered to the Japanese an increase in market share from 11 per cent in 1991 up to 17 per cent till 2000, when all quotas are, in principle, supposed to disappear. The problem is that the EU wants to include in the quota the Japanese cars manufactured in the EU. The deal is, however, subject to different inter-pretations. The EU argues that the maximum number of imported Japanese cars and those produced in Japanese subsidiaries in the EU is based on forecasts of market growth. This assumes that if the market grows less than forecast, the EU may renegotiate the deal. The Japanese interpretation of the deal is that the EU has comitted itself not to restrict the sale of Japanese cars in the EU. Another accord between the EU and Japan of 1995 is supposed to simplify EU exports of cars and commercial vehicles to Japan through the mutual recognition of vehicle standards, as well as the possibility that the Japanese inspectors who issue certificates to imported cars do their job in Europe.

There are, also, many cases of NTBs that deal with standards. Belgium allows the sale of margarine only in oval containers, while square ones are reserved for butter. The standard width of consumer durables in the EU countries is 60 centimetres, while in Switzerland this standard is a few centimetres less. The City of London stipulates that cabs must enable gentle-men to sit comfortably in an upright position with their hats on. While the stop button in elevators in Britain is forbidden, the same button is obligatory in Belgium. Beer can be sold in the Netherlands only in returnable bottles, the German standard for the same thing being non-returnable bottles. All these technical specifications do not have a crucial impact on the protection of life and health. Their final effect is to reduce competition and increase price to the consumers. Trade policy is one of details which easily escape the scrutiny of voters. Small and well-organized groups of producers may wield a strong influence on government attitude in trade policy.

Harmonized standards for some matters such as safety, health or the environment are essential, while mutual recognition (an agreement to acknowledge diversity) may be a solution for the traded goods while being in the waiting room for harmonization. The long-term effect of such a policy is that the firms would face one set of rules instead of up to fifteen different ones. This may increase the gains that come from economies of scale. However, this can only make sense when the market for a good or a service exceeds one member state. For example, consumer preferences for relatively new goods such as VCRs, fax and xerox machines, CD ROMs, mobile phones or computers may be similar throughout the EU,[67] but there are a number of differences regarding foodstuffs and beverages, where more preferences are strictly local. In those cases a potential EU standard that does not embrace these distinctions may do more harm than good. The member states of the EU are, however, obliged to notify the Commission in advance about all draft regulations and standards. If the Commission or other member states find that a new standard contains elements of NTB to trade, they may start the kind of remedial action allowed in Articles 30 or 100 of the Treaty of Rome.

Liberalization of trade and FDI with third countries potentially increases both trade with those countries and the share of foreign inputs in domestically produced 'hybrid' goods.[68] *Rules of origin* in general and the minimum local content requirement in particular, are used as NTBs in order to prevent goods with a high external content receiving preferential treatment in the internal trade of the EU. However, it is increasingly difficult to determine the 'nationality' of a car. Countries throughout the world are free to use rules of origin as policy measures, since the WTO does not yet regulate them. As a result, there has been a variety of practices which creates trouble for producers and traders.

A survey of *trade-related investment measures* (TRIMs) (UNCTC, 1991) found that local content requirements are relatively more frequent than those regarding exports or employment. Although TRIMs exist in both the developed and developing countries, they are more common in the developed world. TRIMs are usually concentrated in specific industries such as the automotive, chemicals and computers. During an examination of 682 investment projects, the finding was that in 83 per cent of cases in which firms were required to realize TRIM objectives (such as local sourcing, exporting) the investors planned to do those operations anyway. Not only that, the TRIMs were intruding in the mix of inputs in the production process and they were also redundant!

The EU rules of origin are based on the Regulation 802/68 which states four criteria for the determination of the origin of a good. Origin is obtained in the country:

- where the last substantial operation is performed
- that is economically justified
- in an undertaking equipped for the purpose and
- resulting in the manufacture of a new product or representing an important stage of manufacture.

The WTO is supposed to draft new standards for the determination of origin that would be universally applicable. Until then, the EU will continue to follow the Kyoto Convention with one important difference. The EU will determine the origin of the good according to the country where the last 'economically justified' operation took place. This allows considerable scope for arbitrary interpretations of the origin rules and introduction of NTBs.

Once a government spots a good that is or may be suddenly imported into its country, it often introduces an antidumping tariff. Foreign exporters can circumvent this barrier by locating the final, often screwdriver stage of production, in the tariff-imposing country. To counter this action, the home authorities may request that the goods produced domestically must have a certain local content in order to obtain the preferential treatment. Once the original supplier of the good meets this requirement, the local authorities may go further, as was the case with the EU control of imports of Japanese integrated circuits (microchips). Chips just assembled in the EU would not qualify for domestic treatment. The EU rules of 1989 link the origin of microchips to the place where the diffusion process takes place. Assembly and testing follow the diffusion process and they add to the final value of the chip approximately as much as diffusion. There are two reasons for such a choice by the Commission regarding rules of origin for integrated circuits. First, these rules demand that a part of the manufacturing process takes place in the EU. That requires an inflow of foreign investment and the creation of high-quality local jobs. Second, the intention was to support EU producers of microchips, as some of them performed diffusion in the EU, while assembly and testing took place in external countries where labour costs are lower. In this case, the EU defined the origin of the good by the place where the 'most' (rather than the 'last') substantial production process took place. Origin is determined by the R&D stage and the capital equipment that is used in the production of such goods, rather than by the place of transformation of goods. Such rules do not regard Ricoh photocopiers made, in fact assembled, in California as goods that originate in the US. Rather, the EU looks at the (Japanese) origin of essential parts such as drums, rollers, side plates and other working equipment. Once the origin of these machines is determined to be Japanese, the EU has an arsenal of other NTBs to curtail imports of these goods from the US. This has provoked tensions in EU trade with the US.

Yet another complication in the calculation of value added and the shares of different countries in the final origin of a good is presented by fluctuations in the rates of exchange. What rate of exchange should be used for the calculation of value added: the one on the date of importation of inputs or the one on the date when the final good is exported into the EU, for example? A case in question arose when Switzerland exported ball-point pens (made from American components) to France in 1983. The EU Court of Justice decided in favour of the date of importation.

Controversies about origin were confined for a long time to trade in goods. Nowadays, they become relevant for trade in services too. What determines the 'nationality' of traded services? Many are based on wide international networks. None the less, certain criteria are emerging. They include place of incorporation, location of headquarters, nationality of ownership and control, and the principal place of operation and intellectual input.

Rules of origin have introduced controversies, heated debates and tensions in international trade. In a supposedly 'globalized' international economy where TNCs are increasingly involved in foreign production, rules of origin make less and less sense. They may bring distortions in investment decisions, reduce international trade and bring more bad than good things.

Non-tariff barriers contribute to the costs that accrue from the non-competitive segmentation of the market. They encourage import substitution and discourage rationalizing investment. The anticipated benefits that would come from the elimination of NTBs include increased competition with its effects on the improved efficiency, economies of scale and the consequent reduction in unit costs of production for an enlarged market, as well as increased specialization. The outcome of this process would be an increased average living standard.

A study by Emerson *et al.* (1988) illustrated the possible benefits that could accrue, under certain conditions, from the completion of the EU Programme 1992. The total EU gross domestic product in 1985 (the base year for most estimates) was ECU 3,300 billion for the 12 member states. The direct cost of frontier formalities for the private and public sector may be 1.8 per cent of the value of goods traded in the EU or around ECU 9 billion. The cost for industry of identifiable barriers, such as technical regulations, may be 2 per cent of the surveyed companies' total costs, which made around ECU 40 billion. Liberalization of the public procurement would bring gains of ECU 20 billion, while the liberalization of the supply of financial services would save a further ECU 20 billion. Gains due to the economies of scale would reduce costs between 1 and 7 per cent yielding an aggregate cost saving of ECU 60 billion. A downward convergence of presently disparate price levels could bring gains of about ECU 40 billion under the assumption of a much more competitive and integrated EU market. The estimates offered a range of gains starting from ECU 70 billion or 2.5 per cent of the EU GNP, to ECU 190 billion or 6.5 per cent of the EU

GNP. The same, one-time gains, for the 1988 GNP would give a range of ECU 175 to 255 billion. At the time, these figures seemed underestimates as they excluded important dynamic effects on economic performance such as technological innovation and the introduction of new goods and services which is difficult to predict. There was no general opposition to the completion of the EU internal market by the end of 1992, for the opponents to the plan could not offer an alternative strategy that would make up for the forgone losses from preserving the *status quo*.

The analysis of Emerson was based, in part, on shaky assumptions. Hence, there were those who disagreed with Emerson's conclusions because of their *underestimation* of the effects of the 1992 Programme. Baldwin (1989) thought that the one-time gains would be translated into a substantial 'medium-term growth bonus'. The others disputed Emerson's conclusions because they thought that the expected results were *overestimates* by a factor of two or three (Peck, 1989, p. 289). A Communication from the EU Commission gave an *ex post* assessment of the impact of the 1992 Programme (European Commission, 1997, pp. 5–6). It was found that there was:

- solid evidence of the positive effects of the Single Market Programme;
- growing competition between firms in both manufacturing and services;
- an accelerated pace of industrial restructuring;
- a wider range of products and services available to the public sector, industrial and domestic consumers at lower prices, particularly in newly liberalized services such as transport, financial services, telecommunications and broadcasting;
- faster and cheaper cross-frontier deliveries resulting from the absence of cross border-controls on goods;
- greater inter-state mobility of workers, as well as students and retired people;
- between 300,000 and 900,000 more new jobs created than would have been the case without the 1992 Programme;
- an extra increase in EU income of 1.1–1.5 per cent over the period 1987–93;
- inflation rates 1.0–1.5 per cent lower than would have been the case in the absence of the 1992 Programme;
- an increase in economic convergence and cohesion between different EU regions.

The above quantitative findings are (for whatever reasons) more in accord with the expectations by Peck (1989) than in line with any other *ex ante* estimation.

VIII CONCLUSION

The traditional (static) model of customs union considered the effect of a reduction in tariffs on welfare. It concluded that the lowering or elimination of tariffs increased competition which could lead to an improvement in welfare. The new theory pays attention to the dynamic effects of integration. With economies of scale and imperfect competition, there are no unconditional expectations that all countries will gain from integration, even less that they will gain equally. In the absence of adjustment policies, such as industrial, regional and social policies, integration may impose costs on some countries, rather than give them benefits. Therefore, cooperation among countries regarding the distribution of gains and losses is a necessary condition for successful integration. In any case, integration profoundly changes the economic structure of participating countries which must modify, and even abandon, the established domestic monopolies and autarkic traditions.

The theory of a customs union is based on a large number of restrictive assumptions, so the technical modelling may be far from realistic. Various restrictions in a customs union, such as the prohibition on factor movements or coordinated fiscal and monetary policies, can be overcome in common markets and economic unions. They will be discussed in the chapters that follow.

The theory of customs unions studies extreme cases and is intuitive in nature. All analyses are suggestive rather than definitive. Yet another difficulty stems from the fact that this theory includes simultaneously both free trade within a customs union and protection against third countries in the form of the common external tariff (and NTBs). A customs union reduces tariffs on trade among some countries, so it may seem beneficial in relation to a situation where each country applies its own system of tariffs. Tariffs are removed in a customs union on the internal trade, but a common external tariff is erected. One distortion is replaced by another, so regarding the final effect on welfare, all outcomes are possible. If free trade is the first best policy, then a customs union is, at best, a second best situation. Hence a universal prescription for the success of a customs union may not be found. None the less, our effort was not in vain, as many things may be learned from the analysis of extreme and second best cases. Dynamic effects are extremely hard to model and quantify rigorously. It is, for example, difficult to predict the exact impact of competition on technological innovation. These are intuitive issues, but important for economic integration.

Still there is a question of why integration takes place in reality. Estimates of trade creation and trade diversion that could contribute to the explanation of why integration takes place have been disappointingly small in many studies. In addition, there has been slow progress in the quantification of dynamic effects of integration. Hence, the quantitative explanations for economic integration were missing. Therefore, the rationale for the creation of integration schemes in real life was found in non-economic motives. One has to recall that the important wave of theoretical contributions to the theory of international economic integration came only after the signature of the Treaty of Rome (1957) and that the major goal of European integration was the preservation of peace, and making war between France and Germany impossible through economic means.

In searching for the missing explanations for why economic integration takes place, Pomfret (1986a) directed exploration towards higher dimensional models of integration, elimination of tariffs in the rest of the world, terms of trade and economies of scale. In the end, there were three elements in the answer offered to the question of why integration and regional arrangements take place. Firstly, preferential trading arrangements exist because trade barriers can be adapted according to preferences of the involved countries. Secondly, these agreements can be employed as a bargaining tool. Thirdly, terms of trade effects and gains to exporters provide benefits from preferential trading agreements that are not available from unilateral trade liberalization policies. Given these three motives, it is not necessary to resort exclusively to non-economic reasons for economic integration.

There are also other reasons for economic integration among countries. They include the trust among the participating countries. A relatively small number of participants may create cosy relationships, make monitoring of the deal easier, and friendly positive cooperation within the group may potentially help the exchange of favours, mutual agreement and (perhaps) settle disputes in a faster and more efficient (?) way than is the case in multilateral institutions.

International economic integration increases the potential for significant international improvement in economic welfare. The countries have to organize themselves, that is, adjust individually and collectively to reap these gains. Specialization and increase in the export potentials in order to pay for the imports are necessary conditions for success. In addition, adjustment policies must be well thought out. Incorrect policies can sink all the beneficial effects which accrue from an improved access to a larger market.

In the world of rapid change in technology and conditions in the market, a country may not be sure that its current comparative advantages will be secured in the future. So, a country may wish to secure markets for the widest variety of its goods and services against abrupt changes in the trade policy of its partners. International economic integration is an uphill job, but may be an attractive solution. Integration can be a risky enterprise for a small country in relation to protectionism in the short run. However, a defensive policy of protection may generate the economic decline of a small country in the long run. Few countries could accept this as their long-term goal. Integration may be a way out of this scenario. A willingness to cooperate with partner countries on the issue of the distribution of costs and benefits that accrue from the creation of a customs union and the settlement of disputes is of great importance for the smooth and beneficial operation, as well as for the survival of a customs union. International economic integration may be subject to various disputes. Most of them stem from the existence of NTBs. An effective dispute settlement mechanism is a necessary condition for the adhesion of the scheme.

NOTES

1 There are difficulties in explaining to a layman that half a loaf may be in certain cases worse than none!
2 Quotas are another instrument, however this instrument makes it pointless for producers to compete against each other. Quotas are more harmful than tariffs because their impact on rising prices to consumers is hidden. Hence, they can spread without check.
3 In general, integration in the EU has benefited third countries. The major exceptions are the countries that specialized in temperate agricultural goods covered by the CAP (Sapir, 1992, p. 1503). Hence, there was no need for retaliation!
4 This is part of the reason why highly protected countries, such as those in eastern Europe before the transition period had, in general, a poor export performance in western markets.
5 The problem with the subsidies is that all taxpayers contribute to them, not just those who are consumers, as is the case with tariffs.
6 Article VI of the GATT permits countries harmed to levy countervailing duties (unfair trading practice) in order to offset the impact of injurious foreign subsidies. Article XVI calls on member countries to observe self-restraints relative to export subsidies.
7 'Free trade' can not easily be fostered without reference to exchange rates. A depreciation in the value of the national currency in country A helps exporters, while local competitors in the importing country B may regard such a change as a 'subsidy' received by exporters in country A. US dollar sometimes fluctuates ± 30 per cent within one year relative to other major currencies. Fluctuations in exchange rates in the domestic currencies of the countries in the EU can jeopardize competition in the internal market. That is one of the reasons why the EU is pushing for the establishment of the monetary union.
8 As a general rule, antidumping and countervailing duties in the EU expire after five years.
9 'Strategic' does not have any military connotation here, but rather it refers to an industry with significant externalities (economies of scale or linkages with the rest of the economy).
10 The problem is that there may be costly errors in judgement, foreign retaliation may be provoked with the consequence in the undermining of the multilateral trading system.
11 This is another reinforcement of the second-best character of the theory of customs union.
12 Competition policy does not protect individual competitors, but rather the process of competition.
13 Hayek criticized the neo-classical model that is based on perfect competition in the following way: 'But I must be content with thus briefly indicating the absurdity of the usual procedure of starting the analysis with a situation in which all the facts are supposed to be known. This is a state of affairs which economic theory curiously calls "perfect competition". It leaves no room whatever for the activity called competition, which is presumed to have already done its task' (Hayek, 1978, p. 182).
14 Liberalization of imports has the strongest impact when exchange rates are stable. Volatility in the exchange rate market may enhance/loosen the effect of this policy instrument.

15 The response of the Luddites in the early nineteenth century to the introduction of looms and jennies was to destroy them.

16 Patent rights are there to protect somebody's codifiable innovation and knowledge, while trademarks protect the reputation of a firm. Other knowledge that comes from learning, trial and error is largely unprotected because it may not be put into 'blueprints'.

17 Timely, correct and cheap information is becoming a crucial input in the decision making process. A banker who is handling large funds over his PC terminal is a long way from the British general Sir Edward Pakenham who lost the battle of New Orleans and his life on 8 January 1815, fifteen days after the Treaty of Gent ended the war, but several days before the frigate arrived at his headquarters with the news about the end of the war (Lipsey, 1992a, p. 288).

18 The neo-classical doctrine relies on an elegant, but unrealistic, assumption that markets are perfect. Without such hypothesis, there is no case for the optimality in resource allocation.

19 Economies of scope are the outcome of the need for flexible (innovation driven) methods of production. This is because total production costs of manufacturing two separate goods may be higher than the costs of producing them together.

20 Rents are proceeds that are in surplus of what is necessary to cover costs of production and to yield an average return on investment. They are due to barriers to entry such as large sunk costs, economies of scale, externalities, advertising, regulatory policies, distribution and service networks, asymmetric information, as well as consumer loyalty to a certain brand.

21 Innovations do not only change the method of production of goods and services, but also our values and the way we live in an integral manner. For example, Hollywood films changed the way we lived and worked, how we saw the world, how the young courted (they were taken by the car away from the eyes of parents and chaperons) (Lipsey, 1993b, pp. 3–4).

22 'Schumpeterians' point to five long waves in modern history: (1) 1780–1840 steam power drove the industrial revolution; (2) 1840–1890 the introduction of railways; (3) 1890–1930 the introduction and production of electric power; (4) 1930–1980 cheap oil and cars; and (5) information technology.

23 While R&D and innovatory activities in the US is mainly led by the military and double-use industries where demand is limited, these activities are in other countries more consumer related, they are directed towards the development of goods and services for which demand exists everywhere. In addition, R&D is chiefly mission oriented towards big problems in countries such as the US, France and Britain. In countries such as Germany, Japan, Sweden or Switzerland, R&D is directed more towards the solution of practical problems.

24 Apart from the integration of separate markets, other supporting adjustment devices include deregulation and privatization.

25 The era of imaginative individuals as major sources of innovation belong to the nineteenth century and before. To fly to the moon involves the work of a large team of experts.

26 These irreversibilities include savings in factor (including energy) inputs per unit of output.

27 Economic growth may be propelled (among other elements) by the following three components (or by their combination): investment in capital and/or human resources, trade and technological change.

28 The time it takes to double national income per capita in the early stages of industrialization has fallen dramatically. It took Britain around sixty years to do that after 1780, some thirty-five years for Japan after 1885, Brazil eighteen years after 1961 and China ten years after 1977. The main reason is technological progress. Countries are able to purchase foreign technology to make their home

factors more productive. There is also another dimension to new technology. While it was an increase in the physical capacity to influence the environment and to produce goods that was brought by the industrial revolution in the nineteenth century, the current industrial revolution is more in the domain of a qualitative dimension.

29 'The great majority of innovations did *not* come from formal R&D (even in organisations like Du Pont...which had strong in-house R&D facilities). Most...came from production engineers, systems engineers, technicians, managers, maintenance personnel and of course production workers' (Freeman, 1994, p. 474).

30 If the claim that Beta is a technically superior system than the VHS system which won the market race, then the market choice did not represent the best economic outcome!

31 International agreements are usually ambiguous. This permits the diplomats to interpret them at home in their own favour. Conversely, constitutions and other domestic laws are (supposedly) clear. This is because domestic politicians want the voters to understand them in order to win their votes.

32 Strong advertising campaigns create awareness about 'differences' among, basically, very similar and easily substitutable goods (for instance, cars, printers, fax and xerox machines, audio and video cassettes, skis, soaps, toothpastes or TV sets). In addition, a large part of intra-industry trade is in parts and components.

33 Linder (1961, p. 102) noted that ships that brought European beer to Milwaukee took American beer back to Europe.

34 Verdoorn suggested that differences in the methods of manufacturing between the US and European firms was not in the size of firm/plant as in the length of the individual production run. The diversity of technical processes performed in the same type of plant was much smaller in the US than in Europe (Hague, 1960, p. 346). Compared with plants in the same industry, production runs in the US were several times larger than in Europe, even though the plants were owned by the same TNC (Pratten, 1971, pp. 195, 308–9; Pratten, 1988, pp. 69–70). On the other hand, even in the most efficient developed countries, manufacturing is to a large extent in plants of only moderate size. Differences in plant productivity are best explained by factors such as (1) inappropriate labour relations, in particular where many thousands of workers need to be employed together; (2) inadequate level of technical training; and (3) unsatisfactory structure of incentives (Prais, 1981, pp. 272 ff.). In support of one of these arguments, there is a finding that strikes grow exponentially with plant size (Geroski and Jacquemin, 1985, p. 174).

35 This refers to the nationality that belongs to the EU.

36 An exception to the general freedom of movement of goods is possible only in the case when such movement jeopardizes public morality, security and the health of humans, animals or plants (Article 36).

37 This programme is also known as the White Paper or the Cockfield Report.

38 Public procurement contracts that cross certain tresholds must be advertised in the *Official Journal* of the EU. For example, the threshold for public works is ECU 5 million, supply contracts in telecommunication is ECU 0.6 million and in the supply of water energy and transport is ECU 0.4 million. The supply of military goods is excluded from these rules. There are, of course, loopholes in the rules. For example, certain public works may be split in a number of smaller ones that are below the limit. Another way of avoiding EU scrutiny is to underestimate the value of the procured goods and services.

39 Regulation 418/85 includes a list of authorized and forbidden clauses in the agreement.

40 'Car prices in the European Union on 1 November 1996', European Commission, 14 February 1997. As for other consumer goods, the greatest convergence in

prices following the 1992 Programme was observed in highly traded goods, as well as in the ones that are more open to competition from non-EU producers. However, energy and construction are exceptions from such a trend. In general, a high degree of concentration in national markets is friendly with price disparity, while highly internationalized markets tend to ease price disparities (European Economy, 1996, pp. 134–139).

41 A special and still unresolved issue refers to takeovers by foreign firms. If the foreign buyer comes from a country with relatively cheap capital (low rate of interest) relative to the country of the target firm, such an acquirer has an advantage over other potential buyers that have access to financial markets that charge higher interest rates. If the authorities in the country of the target firm want to retain domestic ownership of such a business, they could restrict take-overs by foreign firms and/or give subsidies to the domestic acquirers. A much more effective policy to such direct interference in business would be to keep the domestic macroeconomic policy in order and, hence, have a domestic capital market competitive with the international one.

42 The exceptions are airlines and fibres. The two industries have already been highly concentrated for quite some time.

43 If to start a business require substantial sunk costs, then mere deregulation (the 1992 Programme) may not be enough. Further measures (such as subsidies) may be necessary to provide an investment impetus to firms.

44 The degree of concentration was much lower in the food and drink than in the chemical industry. It was higher at the national than at the EU level because of the barriers to trade (European Communities, 1991, p. 227).

45 Privatization in the former East Germany accounted for a part of the merger and acquisition activity in Germany.

46 This result was similar to the one reached in many studies on mergers in the US.

47 Another important tool for the control of dominance at the EU market and enhancing competition was the conclusion of the Uruguay Round in 1994. After ratification, the deal would liberalize further international trade, increase competition and, hence, modify/limit the non-competitive behaviour of EU industries concentrated in the internal market.

48 Smaller mergers are under the control of national authorities.

49 These thresholds also apply to firms that originate outside of the EU.

50 If competitive firms want to keep their lead, they need to follow developments not only in their own industry, but also in unrelated, but potentially competing ones. Examples of 'learning by watching' may be found in an almost overnight disappearance of the market for film cameras after the appearance of video cameras, redressing of the market for mechanical watches after the invention of digital ones, a shift from dot matrix to laser printers or fibre optics that evolved independently of the telecommunication technology.

51 The growing concentration of the semiconductor equipment and materials indus-tries by a few Japanese enterprises created a strategic threat to both commercial and defence interests. For example, because of the concerns of the socialist members of the Japanese Parliament in 1983, the MITI reportedly ordered Kyocera (a domestic manufacturer of high-technology ceramic products) not to take part in contracts to sell ceramic nose cones to the US Tomahawk missile programme (Graham and Krugman, 1991, p. 116). In another example, Nikon, one of only two Japanese suppliers of certain kinds of semiconductor-producing machinery, withheld its latest models from foreign customers for up to two years after making them available to Japanese clients (Tyson, 1992, p. 146). An 'expla-nation' was that the 'regular' customers needed to be served in a better way and prior to the others. The behaviour of IBM was not different. This firm has also refused to sell its components to other clients (Sharp and Pavitt, 1993, p. 144).

52 A refusal to supply goods or services was taken to be an infringement of Article 86. In the *United Brands* case (1976) the Commission found that United Brands, the major supplier of (Chiquita) bananas to most of the EU countries, abused its dominant position by refusing to supply green bananas to Olesen, a Danish ripener and distributor. Although Olesen had taken part in an advertising operation with one of United Brands' competitors, the Court found that the reaction of United Brands to competitive threat was excessive and, hence, abusive. The discontinuance to supply bananas was a significant intrusion into the independence of small and medium-sized firms. United Brands was fined ECU 1 million by the Commission. The Court reduced the fine to ECU 0.85 million.

53 This Article, however, neither outlaws nor discourages state ownership of enterprises.

54 EU Guidelines for state aid for small and medium-sized enterprises (1992) outline that these firms (fewer than 50 employees) may receive support of up to 15 per cent of investment cost. Enterprises with 50 to 250 employees may receive the same aid up to 7.5 per cent of their investment cost, while larger firms may get the same only in the assisted regions of the EU.

55 In the case of steel, shipbuilding or textiles, restructuring often means a reduction in production capacity.

56 A special type of public aid is in the form of public purchases. In Italy, for example, a law required that 30 per cent of contracts need to be awarded to firms based in the southern part of the country. The EU Court of Justice ruled in 1990 that such a law violated the public procurement directives. In other countries such as France or Germany there is no explicit buy-national law. None the less, publicly owned enterprises (railways, PTT) are 'expected' to prefer home-made goods and services to foreign ones.

57 The biggest state-aid case that came before the Commission was the $9.4 billion rescue package for Crédit Lyonnais, the French state-owned bank. It was approved in 1995. One can not avoid the impression that the approval did not have political motivations (*Financial Times*, 27 July 1995, p. 13).

58 The budget deficit in Germany was 2.9 per cent of GDP in 1992–4 period. The financing of state aid was equal to 88 per cent of that deficit.

59 When there are significant scale and learning economies, risk-loving firms have incentives to set current prices not on current costs, but rather on the costs they expect to achieve in the future once full economies of scale are reached.

60 If a country such as Germany sets higher standards than other EU countries, Germany could have carried on with the enforcement of those standards with trade restrictions. The purpose of Decision 3052/95 is to prevent such behaviour.

61 *Barter* terms of trade are measured by how many units of domestic good has to be exported to pay for one unit of imports. *Factoral* terms of trade are measured by how many hours of foreign labour can be paid by exporting the output of one hour of domestic labour.

62 Apart from tariff discrimination, other purposes of rules of origin include the determination of eligibility for quota and notification to the consumers that have preferences for goods of a certain origin.

63 Packaging and dilution with water do not change the essential features of a good, so they are not taken as important elements that change the origin of goods.

64 A supplementary tax 'replaced' the Poitiers customs clearance procedure in January 1983.

65 It was the US demand to exclude agriculture from the Agreement that created the GATT. Later on, that act had a backlash against the US in trade with the EU and Japan.

66 Between 1989 and 1991, the annual imports of Japanese cars into Italy more than doubled from 10,000 to 22,000 (*The Financial Times*, 5 August 1991).

67 Around a third of manufactured goods traded in the EU are covered by harmonized standards. The rest is covered by the national ones.

68 An example are cars produced by Nissan in Britain. France limited imports of Japanese cars to 3 per cent of the domestic market and claimed that the Nissan Bluebird cars produced in Britain were Japanese in origin. There was an earlier informal guideline for the local content of the Japanese cars produced in the EU. Those cars would have a preferential (domestic) treatment in the EU market if local EU content was at least 60 per cent. To get a national treatment (i.e. treated as goods produced domestically), France asked for an increase to 80 per cent of the EU origin in 1988. In order to qualify for the national treatment in the EU, the produced (assembled) cars need to have 80 per cent of local (EU) content.

3 Common Market

I INTRODUCTION

The entire analysis of customs unions applies to common markets too. Due to the free mobility of factors of production in a common market, the effects of a customs union are, however, substantially enriched. The effects on a more efficient allocation of resources (improvements in the locational advantages for business) are due to the free factor flow from low to high productivity businesses within the common market.

Apart from factor mobility, a condition for the integration of factor markets is the non-discrimination of factors originating in the partner countries. In this situation, factors respond to signals which include demand, higher productivity and returns within a common market. Integration of factor markets will be encountered as mobility of labour and mobility of capital in separate sections which follow.

II MOBILITY OF LABOUR

1 Introduction

A customs union involves product market integration. A common market adds to that development integration of factor markets. It is expected that the free flow of factors within the bloc will improve the allocation of resources over the one achieved in either a free trade area or a customs union. The neo-classical Hecksher–Ohlin trade theory concludes that a country with a rich supply of labour may either export labour-intensive goods or import capital and export labour, under the assumption that technology is the same in all countries. In either case the country is equally well off.

2 Equalization of factor prices

Let us assume a model which consists of two countries A and B, two final goods X and Y and two factors of production K and L, respectively. Suppose further that factor mobility is perfect within each country, but prohibited between countries. If there are no barriers to trade; and no distortions; and if technology is the same and freely accessible to both countries; and if production functions are homogeneous of the first degree; and if both goods are produced in both countries; and isoquants intersect only once (there is no factor intensity reversal), then free trade in goods will equalize relative prices in goods. This will equalize both relative factor prices and their returns between countries A and B, respectively. This stringent situation is illustrated in Figure 3.1.

In Figure 3.1 X_a represents the unit isocost line (the combination of factors which keeps output constant) for the good X in country A (production of which is relatively labour intensive), while X_b describes the same cost line for good X which is relatively capital intensive. Equilibrium is at point E where factor prices are equalized through trade at levels Or_e for capital and OW_e for labour. In this model trade is a substitute for factor mobility. An analogous condition holds in the common market.

The exclusion of balance-of-payments adjustments from comparative statistics implies that the adjustment process between the two distant points in time has worked well and that the balance is in equilibrium. Such a process in reality may, however, last even a generation. Thus a static model, which usually forgets the adjustment process, can be hardly justified. Capital accumulation, economies of scale and economic growth produce different results in the long run from the straightforward static model (Vosgerau, 1989, p. 219).

A free international trade in goods and factor movements are prevented by the existence of various barriers. In this framework, according to one view, commodity movements are still a substitute for factor movements. An increase in trade restrictions stimulates factor movements, while an increase in restrictions to international factor mobility enhances trade in goods (Mundell, 1957, p. 321).

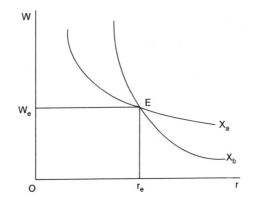

Figure 3.1 Equalization of factor prices

The assumption has been, so far, that technology was the same in all countries. This is, however, not always the case. The difference in technologies among countries enhances, rather than reduces, the opportunities for international capital mobility. Certain developing countries export raw materials in return for foreign investment which enables them to produce and later export manufactured goods (Purvis, 1972, p. 991). When technologies differ, factor mobility may increase the volume of trade, rather than reduce it. Factor mobility and commodity movements may act in this case as complements. Although theoretical explanations of the relation between trade and FDI still need to be well studied and explained, there certain evidence that FDI has increased trade in the EU (van Aarle, 1996, p. 137).[1]

Substitutability between trade in goods and mobility of factors (the Hecksher–Ohlin model) may be the exception, rather than the rule. If countries are quite different in relative factor endowments and with weak economies of scale, then individuals who draw their income from factors that are relatively scarce end up worse off as a result of trade. If countries are similar and trade is mostly motivated by economies of scale (intra-industry trade), then one might expect to find that even scarce factors gain (Krugman, 1990a, p. 80).

The basis for trade can be something other than a simple difference in factor endowments. Alternative bases for trade include returns to scale, imperfect competition, difference in market structure, difference in production and factor taxes, as well as differences in production technology. In this case free mobility of factors leaves countries relatively well endowed with the factor used 'intensively' in the production of export good (Markusen, 1983, p. 355). International mobility of factors and trade are taken to be complements, rather than substitutes in many occasions.[2] 'Globalization' of international business and integrated international operations of TNCs contribute to this kind of reasoning. This is most obvious in the EU where a high proportion of intra-group trade has been accompanied by an expansion of intra-group investment and the operation of TNCs.

If factor mobility leads to a reduction in the volume of trade in goods, then factor movements and trade in goods are substitutes. This is the case when there are differences in the prices of goods between countries. If labour moves from country A in which good X is dearer to country B in which this good is cheaper, this decreases the demand for and price of good X in country A and increases them in country B until the two prices are equalized. If relative differences in factor endowments are not the only basis for trade, international mobility of factors and trade may stimulate each other and become supplements (Markusen and Melvin, 1984).

The factor price equalization theorem anticipates that free trade will have as its consequence parity of wage levels among countries. This need not always be the case. Migration will be a necessary condition for the equalization of wages if the majority of labour in both high-wage countries and low-wage countries is employed in the production of non-tradable goods. In this case free trade is not a sufficient condition for the equalization of wages between the countries involved.

A study of relative differences in labour rewards in the EU found that there was a convergence in labour costs between the mid-1950s (that is before the EU was created) until the mid-1960s. From 1968 onwards the trend was reversed. The reasons for convergence may be found in free trade in goods and more liberal movements of capital and labour which came from the Mediterranean countries that were not members of the EU (Tovias, 1982). This approach was disputed as it did not provide an explanation for the converging trend in wages before the creation of the EU or the divergent trend after 1968. There is not even a single wage level within a country because of heterogeneous qualifications and employer demand in each sector. Due to imperfect mobility of labour, trade may be expected to lead to a convergence in prices of commodities and wages in industries that are involved in trade. A correlation should exist between the liberalization of internal trade and changes in the level of wages (Gremmen, 1985). In testing this idea a few errors were made, the most important being the expectation of an insignificant coefficient on the capital–labour ratio. Wage differences between the north and the south of Italy or the US reveal that this expectation is not correct. The results of the re-estimation found that the relation between the level of wages and trade intensity (the sum of countries' marginal propensities to import each others goods) is not as direct as Gremmen assumed. In addition, it was found that the capital–labour ratio remains an important determinant of factor prices even if international economic integration has advanced as far as it has in the EU. This is not to deny that increasing trade relations lead to decreasing wage differentials, but rather that trade intensity must be considered in conjunction with differences in the capital–labour ratio (van Mourik, 1987).

Free mobility of factors in a common market and an expectation of equalization of factor prices may be an attractive incentive for countries to close the gap in the levels of income and development within the integrated area. How this works in practice is not quite clear. The experience of the EU presented evidence that some corrective measures were necessary, such as social and regional funds.

Economies of scale make specialization more likely. Every technology requires different types of labour, so complete factor price equalization seems unlikely. Distortions such as tariffs, subsidies, taxes or costs of transport make equalization of factor prices real only in a strict model. In the real world there may appear only a tendency towards the equalization of factor prices.

Mobility of labour or labour responsiveness to demand has been a significant feature of economic life for a long period of time. Labour has not only moved among regions, but also among economic sectors. In the late 1950s, agriculture employed around 20 per cent of the labour force in most industrialized economies. In the 1990s, agriculture employed less than 5 per cent of the labour force in these countries.

The theoretical assumption that labour has a greater degree of mobility within a country than among countries may not always be substantiated. Inter-country mobility of labour between Ireland and other developed English-speaking countries has, perhaps, been much greater than internal Irish labour mobility. None the less, labour mobility should not always be taken in its 'technical' meaning of pure movements of persons from place A to place B. One has to bear in mind that these are the people who move with their skills, knowledge, experiences and organizational competences.

Outside of common markets, international labour migration is character-ized by a legal asymmetry. The Universal Declaration of Human Rights (1948), Article 13, denies the right to a country of origin to close its borders to *bona fide* emigrants. This country may not control the emigration flows according to its own interests. The country of destination, however, has an undisputed right to restrict the entry of immigrants, although this is not explicitly mentioned in the Declaration. In these circumstances migration flows are determined by demand. So, the will to move is a necessary condi-tion for labour migration, but it is not a sufficient one.

This section is structured as follows. We begin by looking at the costs and benefits of labour migration for countries of origin and countries of destina-tion, respectively. Next, we discuss labour mobility in the EU. The conclu-sion is that labour migration will be relatively high on the agenda over the coming decades because of unfavourable demographic trends in the EU and various push factors in the neighbouring regions.

3   Country of origin

If political instability and economic problems (push determinants) overcome the propensity to stay in the homeland (pull factors), then there are several reasons for the international migration of labour. The most significant include the possibility of finding a job which may be able to provide conditions for better living, as well as improved conditions for specialization and promotion. In these complex conditions migrants act as utility maxim-izing units subject to push and pull forces.

The migration of labour has its obstacles. They can be found both in receiving nations and in countries of origin. Socio-psychological obstacles to migration can include different languages,[3] recognition of qualifications, climate, religion, customs, diet and clothing. Such barriers to migration were high in the nineteenth century for intra-European mobility of labour. That was one of the reasons why Europe was a source of significant emigra-tion. In addition, socio-psychological obstacles may be part of the reason why Japan has almost closed borders for legal immigration. Economic obstacles include the lack of information about job openings, conditions of work, social security, legal systems, systems of dismissal (last in, first out) and the loss of seniority. During recession and unemployment periods there may be nationalistic, racial and religious tensions between the local population and immigrants. Trade unions may lobby against immigration, as well as for driving immigrants away.

Countries of origin have significant losses in manpower. Migrants are usually younger men who wish to take the risk of moving. These regions may have a tendency to become feminine and senilized. Potential producers leave while consumers remain behind. Countries of origin lose a part of their national wealth which was invested in the raising and education of their population. If the migrants are experienced and educated, then their positions may often be filled by less sophisticated staff. The result is lower productivity and lower national wealth.

The brain-drain argument is not convincing in all cases. Many of those who migrate can not always find adequate jobs in their home countries. The physician who leaves Burkina Faso is one thing. This country needs more medical services. A Mozambiquan astro-physicist is quite another. This country has few labs, telescopes and large computers, so it can not use the qualifications of this expert. It makes sense for this skilled person to go abroad and possibly send some money to his country of origin. However, if computer programmers emigrate from Mozambique, there is no point in this country importing computers, and without the import of new technology it will remain backward indefinitely! If the migrants return after a (long) period abroad, some of them may be old and/or ill, so they become consumers. This might all reduce the local tax base and increase the cost of social services to the remaining population.

Apart from these costs, countries of origin can obtain certain short-term gains from emigration. This movement of labour reduces the pressure which is caused by unemployment and reduces the payment of unemployment benefits (if they exist). Possible remittances of hard currency can reduce the balance-of-payments pressure, and if migrants return they can bring along hard currency savings and new skills which can help them to obtain or create better jobs. This can help the development efforts of the country.

If some countries do not have exportable goods they have to export labour services (if other countries want to accept that) in order to pay for imports. However, there is an asymmetry in the perception of labour mobility. When the rich north wants to send workers abroad, then that counts as trade in 'services'. When the poor south wants to do the same, it is regarded as 'immigration'!

The volume of possible remittances depends on the number of migrants, the length of their stay and on incentives. The shorter the stay of migrants abroad, the higher the probability that they will transfer or bring all their savings to their home countries. During short stays abroad, they intend to earn and save as much as possible. If they stay abroad for a longer time, then they may wish to enjoy a higher standard of living than during relatively short stays. They reduce the volume of funds which may potentially be remitted to their countries of origin. If the country of origin offers incentives for the transfer of these funds in the way of attractive rates of interest, rate of exchange, allowances for imports and investment, as well as if there is an overall stability, then there is a greater probability that funds will be attracted.

4   Country of destination

The supply of local labour and the level of economic activity determine the demand for foreign labour in the country of destination. A country may permit an inflow of foreign labour, but this country must bear in mind that these people come with all their virtues and vices. Foreign workers may face open and hidden clashes with the local population. The host country population may dislike foreigners because they take jobs from the domestic population,[4] they bring their customs, increase congestion, depress wages and because they send their savings abroad, to mention just a few reasons. In certain cases, such as the migration of retired persons from Scandinavia to Spain or from Canada to Florida, this should not be regarded as migration that is in response to wage differentials. These migrants do not work, they just spend and enjoy their life savings, and create permanent demand for certain services and jobs for the locals.[5]

The country of destination gains obvious benefits from immigration. The migrants are a very mobile segment of the labour force. Once they enter a country, they are not linked to any particular place. Mobility of local labour in the EU is quite low.[6] This is often due to the causes which include relatives and friends; spouses who have jobs that they do not want to leave; children who go to schools in which they are settled and because of homes which are still under mortgage.

The mobility of migrant labour within the country of destination has an impact on the national equalization of wages. Of course, every next wave of immigration depresses the wages offered to earlier immigrants. Foreign labour that is legally employed need not necessarily be cheaper than local labour as there is legislation requiring the payment of fair wages to all. However, foreign labour is more easily controlled by management.

In general, the country of destination may acquire labour which is cheaper and whose training has not been paid for by the domestic taxpayers. Migrants increase demand for housing, goods, they pay taxes (which may exceed what they receive in transfer payments and public services) and take jobs that are unattractive to the domestic workforce at the offered rates. These are jobs outdoors, in mines, foundries, construction, garbage collection, cleaning, hotels, restaurants and other monotonous work. The posts which are most threatened by migrants are the ones that are usually modestly paid. Migrants compete for these vacancies with the local youth and women who may have reduced opportunities for work. While offering lower wages for these jobs, countries of destination may partially reduce the price of inputs (labour) and partially increase competitiveness, at least in the short run. It is true that labour migration can lower real wages of competing labour in the country of immigration. However, that holds only in a static model. In a dynamic model that allows for growth, all income earners may become better off over an economic cycle.

Local labour may not have language barriers to move within the home country. Migrant workers may not know the language of the host country, so these people may not be able to take part in the social life. The only place where they may demonstrate themselves as creative beings is in production. These workers may sometimes work at a faster pace and better than the domestic ones. This may provoke clashes with the local workers as new production norms may be increased. Migrants may leave after a while, while the locals may be tied by those norms for a long time. Employers may sometimes prefer to conclude direct agreements with migrant workers than to employ domestic labour. It is not only that the migrant workers are working for lower wages than the domestic labour in the absence of legal protection, but also that foreigners may be dismissed with less consequences for the employer. Alternatively, the permits of foreign workers' might not be renewed.

5 European Union

It needs to be stated from the outset that the EU has no common policy regarding labour migration. Article 48 of the Treaty of Rome provides for the freedom of movement of workers within the EU. It also abolishes any discrimination among workers who are citizens of the member states.[7] In addition, Article 8a provides the citizens of the EU with an unrestricted right to move and reside within the territory of the EU. As for visas for non-EU nationals, Article 100c, authorized the Council to take decisions on that issue.

Following the Second World War, the migration of people in Europe had four distinct phases. First came the period from 1945 to the early 1960s. People moved because of the adjustment to the situation following the end of the war, as well as to the process of decolonization. For example, 12 million Germans were forced to leave central and eastern Europe. Most of them settled in Germany. Colonial powers such as Britain, Belgium, France and the Netherlands were affected by return migration from European colonies and the inflow of workers from former overseas territories. There were over a million French residents of Algeria who resettled in France during and after the Algerian war of independence. The second phase of the movement of people had an overlap with the preceding one. It lasted from 1955 to 1973. Labour shortages in certain countries led to openness for immigration. Labour from Italy, Spain, Portugal, Greece, Turkey, former Yugoslavia, Morocco and Tunisia was migrating northwards, mainly to Germany and France. Around 5 million people moved northwards during this period. Then came the third period of restrained migration from 1973 to 1988. Following the first oil price shock and the connected economic crises and social tensions, the recruitment of foreign labour was abruptly stopped. Policies that encouraged return migration were not working. The foreign population in the EU was, however, increasing as family members were joining workers who were already in the EU. In addition, this type of resident had higher fertility rates. The fourth phase started in 1988. It was linked with the dissolution of socialism, economic transition and ethnic wars. Hundreds of thousands of refugees and asylum seekers, as well as economic immigrants moved to the EU countries. Germany alone received 1.5 million new immigrants in 1992 (Zimmermann, 1995, pp. 46–47).

Conventional wisdom states that an abolition of barriers to international migration of labour would bring an increase in labour flow in relation to the previous situation. This hypothesis could be tested in the case of the EU. The total number of intra-EU migrants of the original six member countries was around half a million prior to 1960 which increased to a little over 800,000 in 1968. This volume of migrant workers remained almost constant until the early 1980s and since then it has decreased to 650,000 migrants. All other intra-EU migrations were national (from southern to northern Italy or from western regions of France into Paris), rather than inter-state. The inevitable conclusion is that the creation of the EU has not significantly changed intra-EU labour migrations. While intra-EU trade increased, the intra-EU migrations decreased. Trade and the migration of labour were substitutes! (Straubhaar, 1988).

The explanation for a greater migration of labour from third countries than within the EU can be found in part in the differences in production functions and barriers to trade among countries. The more similar the structure and the level of development between countries and the lower the barriers to trade, the greater will be the substitution effect between trade and labour migration. This also explains the migration of labour from Italy just after the creation of the EU, as well as the subsequent reduction in this flow.

The explanation for the decline in intra-EU labour mobility during the 1980s can be also found in significant improvements in the state of their local economies. Labour migration from Italy has slowed down since 1967. The same has happened in Greece since the early 1970s. Similar tendencies can be observed in the cases of Spain and Portugal since the mid-1980s. In addition, traditional countries of emigration such as Italy or Greece became targets for significant legal and illegal immigration. North Africans and Albanians were entering Italy in a clandestine way, while Greece was a target for similar migration by the Albanians. A certain number of Bulgarians, Serbs, Poles and Russians entered Greece legally, but stayed there after their permits expired.[8]

An interesting fact is Italy's transition over the past three decades from a net exporter to a net importer of non-European, mainly Mediterranean, illegal labour. Illegal immigrants work in and contribute to the growth of the informal economy. Costs of labour are both lower and more flexible in the black economy. This encourages firms to shift resources from the legal economy to the informal one. However, the technology available is less efficient in the underground economy. Hence, illegal immigration makes possible a transfer of capital (and labour) towards the informal economy. This may be favourable for the firms that avoid tax obligations, but it is damaging for the economy as a whole (Dell'Aringa and Neri, 1989, p. 134).

There is a special type of international mobility of labour which is often overlooked. Many TNCs mandate that their employees circulate and spend time in various affiliates in order to keep the corporation internationally and personally integrated. The staff often moves at regular intervals. Although this is recorded in statistics as international mobility of labour, it occurs within the same firm.

Exact data on the flow of migrants are deficient. Therefore, Table 3.1 presents no more than estimates of stock data of the population and migrants in the EU in 1993.[9] There were more than 5 million EU migrants and over 11 million non-EU immigrants in the EU in 1993. This volume of immigrants may prompt some to look at immigrants as the sixteenth nation of the EU. Migration of labour can be a significant feature even if countries are not formally integrated. More than two-thirds of migrants (a wider notion than migrant workers) in the EU up to the mid-1970s came from the non-member, mostly Mediterranean, countries. Despite all enlargements of the EU, more than two-thirds of all migrants in the EU still come from the

Table 3.1 Population and immigrants in the EU in 1993 (thousands)

Country	Total residents	Nationals	Total migrants	Migrants from EU	Migrants from non-EU
Austria	7,796	7,278	518	79	439
Belgium	10,068	9,159	909	542	367
Denmark	5,181	5,001	180	41	139
France	56,652	53,055	3,597	1,322	2,275
Finland	5,055	5,009	46	12	34
Germany	80,975	74,479	6,496	1,719	4,777
Greece	10,350	10,150	200	64	136
Ireland	3,563	3,473	90	—	—
Italy	56,960	56,037	923	160	763
Luxembourg	395	—	—	—	—
Netherlands	15,239	14,482	757	189	568
Portugal	9,865	9,743	122	33	89
Spain	39,048	38,655	393	181	212
Sweden	8,692	8,193	499	187	312
United Kingdom	57,222	55,202	2,020	770	1,250
EU	368,978	350,187	16,874	5,268	11,345

Source: Eurostat (1995)

non-member countries in 1993.[10] Apart from the non-EU migrants who have legal working permits one could estimate that there are around 10 per cent extra illegal immigrants.

The government is a significant employer in all EU countries. Therefore, many jobs may be closed to foreigners even if they are citizens of the EU partner countries. This potential obstacle to employment has been removed by the EU Court of Justice opinion that only those positions which are linked with national security may be reserved for domestic labour. It would be absurd to argue that a person loses skills, experience and knowledge after crossing a border. In order to facilitate labour mobility, in particular of highly educated labour, the EU sets qualitative (content of training) and quantitative (years of study, number of course hours) criteria which diplomas must meet in order to be awarded and mutually recognized.

Recessions now rarely affect only one country. During times of economic slow-down the unemployed among the EU labour force stayed in their country of origin. This was because the chances of finding employment abroad were smaller than at home. If there were some gaps between supply and demand in the labour market, labour migration from third countries was closing them, rather than internal EU flows. Reduced EU internal labour migration was due to a trend which was evening the income and productivity levels among the original six member countries, as well as the growth in the other EU countries that created domestic demand for labour. Hence, the expectation that the creation of a common market would significantly increase long-term intra-group migrations of labour was refuted in the case of the EU.

The free movement of people is one of the cornerstones of the single market in the EU. It is also one of the visible symbols for ordinary people that European integration actually works. Therefore, most EU countries signed an accord on the free circulation of people in the small Luxembourg village of Schengen in 1985 (the deal was revised in 1990). The nub of the Schengen Agreement was to shift passport controls from internal frontiers to external EU borders, to set a uniform visa policy, to increase cooperation among the national authorities that deal with the issues, as well as to coordinate asylum policies.[11] Once in, everyone can move freely in the Schengen countries. However, non-EU nationals can work only in the country that gave them the visa. The curiosity regarding the Schengen deal is that it was until the Treaty of Amsterdam (1997) a convention outside the EU Treaties.

After many delays the Agreement was put into effect in seven EU countries[12] in March 1995. The introduction of the deal in practice was coupled with many delays (for example, the creation of the Schengen Information System, a common database for wanted people and stolen goods). Once initiated, the system got into trouble. Faced with a wave of Islamic terrorist attacks, France effectively pulled out of the main commitment of the deal in June 1995. The country introduced land-border controls because of the fear of terrorism.[13] Those were the same reasons why Britain stayed out of the arrangement. No matter how genuine these fears of terrorism, drug smuggling and illegal immigration are, the truth is that, as a rule, terrorists and drug smugglers with their illicit cargoes are not caught on borders, but rather in the actual country after tip-offs. Another setback to the spirit of Schengen came when Spain threatened to suspend the key provisions of the Agreement when a Belgian court failed to authorize the deportation of two suspected Basque terrorists to Spain in 1996. Perhaps the largest chunk of illegal immigrants enter EU countries legally with short-term visas. Once those visas expire, they go 'underground'. Other EU and non-EU countries (Iceland and Norway) considered entering the Schengen Agreement. However, confidence in the Agreement was shaken.

6 Conclusion

Major labour movements took place from the Mediterranean countries into the EU during the 1960s and early 1970s. The exception was Italy which was in the EU since its establishment. Internal labour mobility in the EU has not played a significant role in European integration in spite of relatively significant differences in average wages (and productivity) among countries. However, a new type of human mobility emerges in the EU. It concerns students, professors and research staff supported by the EU.

The first generation of migrants is now ageing. The migration issue is no longer a question of labour movement, but rather one of integrating these people in the host countries. Almost a half of the migrant population was born in the host countries. This generation is confronted with different cultures and they are often in search of an identity. Their future depends on training and legal security regarding residence and employment rights in the receiving country. Certain EU countries such as Britain, France, Ireland and Italy allow dual citizenship. Others, such as Germany or Denmark, request that the people relinquish their old citizenship when becoming German or Danish. If a Turk gives up his citizenship, he/she has to forego the rural property rights in Turkey. This is one of the reasons why Turks in Germany are very cautious about becoming German.

An efficient EU immigration policy needs to be regulated by economic instruments. This may be based in future on two possible pillars (Straubhaar and Zimmermann, 1993, p. 233):

- Labour market needs to determine the volume of labour migration. There should be no legal restrictions for economically motivated migration. As soon as the migrant has a job, he or she should be allowed to enter the EU country. If the person is out of a job for a specified period (such as 6 or 12 months), the local authority may withdraw the residence permit from that person. Migrants may be invited to purchase citizenship and pay for it over a fixed period of time.

- The authorities need to set quotas for non-economically motivated (mass) migration such as refugees and asylum seekers.

The stagnating level of population in the EU combined with prosperous economic conditions in comparison with adjoining regions, create strong economic incentives for migration into the EU. Uncertainties regarding the transition process in central and eastern Europe create additional incentives for labour mobility towards the EU. The same holds for the south Mediterranean countries where Islamic fundamentalism, with its connected instabilities, are present.[14] These are important reasons for keeping migration relatively high on the policy agenda in the coming two decades. In addition, the EU will have to compete with North America for mobile professionals from the outside world.

III   MOBILITY OF CAPITAL

1   General considerations

Entrepreneurs view the creation of a common market, just like a customs union, as an economic signal that has a long-term nature as opposed to changes in prices which may embody only a temporary situation on the market. Entrepreneurs may form expectations with a higher degree of certainty. Hence, TNCs may enter such an expanding area, under certain conditions, and increase FDI by the creation of 'tariff factories'. The creation of tariff factories within an integrated area is a strategy that TNCs pursue not in order to take advantage of their efficiency or to employ a foreign resource (resource efficiency), but rather to benefit from (or avoid) the shield provided by the common external tariff and NTBs. This could be one of the reasons why Japanese TNCs were eager to establish their presence in the EU, prior to the full implementation of the 1992 Programme, and become EU residents in order to avoid threat of a possible 'Fortress Europe'. In addition to such an *investment creation effect*, new prospects for improved business without tariffs and quotas on trade within the region may prompt local firms to rearrange production facilities within the group. That may produce the *investment diversion effect*, that is, increased FDI in certain countries of the group and diminished FDI in others.

In principle, FDI asks for the freedom of establishment and, if possible, the national treatment in foreign markets. It is a distinct type of international capital flow as it has a strong risk-taking and, most often, industry-specific dimension. In addition, it is coupled with a transfer of technological know-how, as well as management and marketing skills.

Capital moves among countries in the form of portfolio and direct investment. Portfolio investment is most often just a short-term movement of claims which is speculative in nature. The main objectives include an increase in the value of assets and relative safety. This type of capital mobility may be induced by differences in interest rates. The recipient country may not use these funds for investment in fixed assets which may be repaid in the long run, so these movements of capital may be seen by the recipient country as hot, unstable and 'bad'. Volatility of portfolio investment complicates their analysis. The large number of portfolio investments, made in many cases by brokers, obscures who is doing what and why.

Foreign direct investment is often the result of decisions by TNCs. Therefore, FDI may be a relatively good proxy for the investment activities of TNCs (keeping in mind that TNCs may control operations abroad simply by giving licences).

There are three main types of trans-border business activities by TNCs. They involve investments that are: import substituting, resource based and rationalized (Dunning, 1988, p. 54). *Import substituting* investments seek new markets, but they replace trade. They are influenced by the relative size and growth of the foreign market in which the investment is made, the relative costs of supplying that market through imports or local production, as well as the relative advantage of engaging in direct local production or licensing.

Resource based investments are motivated by the availability and cost of both natural resources and labour in the target location. As the products of such investments are often exported abroad, the economic climate in foreign markets, transport costs and barriers to trade influence the attractiveness of such investment to TNCs.

Rationalized investments seek efficiency. They are, just like resource based investments, complementary to trade. Their attractiveness is found in cost considerations. They are influenced by the ease with which intermediate or final products (linked to economies of scale and specialization) can be traded on the international market. A case in question is the US loss of competitiveness as a site for labour intensive production and where the domestic enterprises from this area of manufacturing locate abroad.

On the one hand, there is a search by the efficiency-seeking enterprises, particularly some TNCs, for seamless and wide international markets regarding trade and investment. The *globalization* of economic activity is making national frontiers less divisive than was the case a few decades ago.[15] Such world-wide economic integration and integrated international production of goods and services whereby competitors are in each others' backyard are made possible by the expansion of information and telecommunication technologies.[16] That process is sometimes inverted, on the other hand, by the spread of *regionalism* (in the developing world) pushed by relatively inefficient firms and many governments that are driven by short-term election interests, even though the conditions for a relatively successful integration process, such as that in western Europe, may be largely absent. Regional integration (a second best solution) may resolve conflicts through positive cooperation but, if pushed to the limit, it may undermine multilateral (first best) trade and investment systems and fragment the world economy into conflicting regional blocs. Regionalism and globalization/multilateralism do not necessarily need to conflict. If the regional blocs adopt fairly liberal external trade and investment policies, and if they cooperate, the general outcome may be an overall welfare improvement.[17]

An enlarged market is an important gain for efficiency-seeking firms in a small country. In a situation without integration, foreign countries can simply threaten a small country that they will introduce protectionist measures against it. Such a warning can seriously undermine the quality of all economic decisions in the small country. Integration enhances and insures market access to the partner countries, as well as increasing the potential for the long-term competitiveness of a small country's economy. A common market eliminates or harmonizes national incentives to foreign TNCs to locate in the partner countries (which were previously subject to the countervailing duties). It also mitigates non-economic considerations, such as political pressures on third countries' investors to locate in a particular country.

All things being equal, foreign investors will locate in a country which offers the most favourable mix of cost of operation. None the less, FDI is made simpler by regionalization of the world economy and international economic integration. However, integration/regionalization is only a supporting tool for the tendencies that bring globalization of international business. Modern competitive firms are usually TNCs that globalize their business in the search for seamless and widest markets. Therefore, an increasing share of domestic output in developed countries is under the control of foreign TNCs. The same holds for an increasing share of foreign output of domestic TNCs. Strong FDI relations may exist even though the countries or groups of countries are not formally integrated. Look at the example of two-way FDI flows between the US and the EU.

A caveat for developing countries is that sometimes they use tariff proceeds for investment purposes. If that is the case, a customs union may dry up an important part of domestic investments by lowering tariff revenue. In a situation with many market imperfections, the opportunities for gains and losses are numerous. Hence, long-term gains in growth that originate in international economic integration may offset this loss of tariff revenue.

Targeting some key productive activities which have significant linkages with the rest of the economy may require some form of government intervention. Japan's decision to target steel and shipbuilding and toys in the 1950s and 1960s was highly profitable. This choice turned out to be questionable in the 1970s, so Japan turned to autos and machine tools. The Japanese have chosen electronics as their target in the 1980s and 1990s (Tyson, 1987, p. 70). This target may, in turn, become obsolete in the future. However, the selected sectors in the past have important spillover effects throughout the economy. Telecommunications affect the dissemination of information, computers have their impact on data processing, while transportation equipment affect the size of the market. These linkages make the

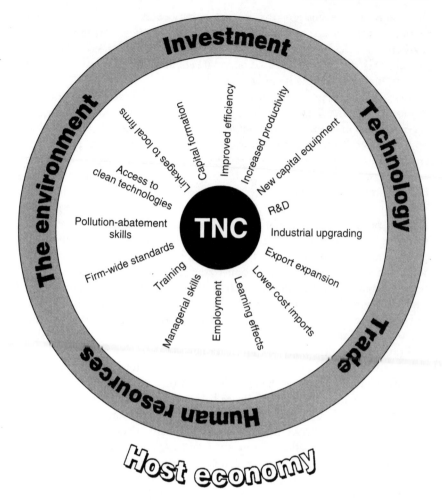

Figure 3.2 Transnational corporations and the growth process
Source: World Investment Report: Transnational Corporations as Engines of Growth. New York: United Nations, 1992.

private returns from these industries smaller than the social returns. The targeting of certain key industries, in a common market or other type of integration, which may have significant linkages with other sectors or partner countries may have important and long-term beneficial spillover effects on the member countries. Various linkages between the operation of TNCs and the growth process are presented in Figure 3.2.

When a firm wants to produce abroad it does not necessarily need to export capital. A firm may rent capital abroad instead of purchasing or building a production unit. Instead of using its own funds, a firm may borrow in its home, host country's or a third country's financial market. In the case of fixed exchange rates, countries may enter into a 'rate of interest war' in order to attract capital into their economies. Integrated capital markets with harmonized rates of interest and mobility of capital may prevent this outcome. While labour markets are regional, capital markets are national or, most likely, international.

Investment activity is one of the most sensitive indicators of a country's economic climate. What exactly it indicates, however, is not always clear. Increases in investment may indicate the emergence of new business opportunities, interest in the future, reactions to international competition and response to increasing cost pressures. In any case, sluggish investment activity, as during the 1970s, is an indication of rough economic times (Schatz and Wolter, 1987, p. 29).

Neither firms nor governments depend on savings in their home markets. Interest rates and demand for funds in one country are affected by money (short-term) and capital (long-term) markets in other countries due to the linkages among financial markets. Small countries are interest rate takers, so that even the national housing (non-traded good) market feels the impact from foreign markets by means of changes in interest rates. Free mobility of capital prevents the independent conduct of monetary policy. If a country lowers interest rates in relation to third countries, then capital will flow abroad. This also destabilizes the exchange rate if all else is equal. In addition, if a country increases interest rates in relation to foreign countries, if other things are constant, the capital will flow into this country. The supply of money increases, hence inflation is the consequence.

Financial markets may discriminate between big companies and countries on the one hand, and small companies and countries on the other. Large companies and countries provide greater security that the funds will be returned and interest paid. A large stock of assets provides this confidence. These markets may discriminate against risky investments such as sea bed research, new sources of energy and the like. By integration of capital markets, small countries may mitigate the effect of their relative disadvantage.

2 Transnational corporations

Any firm that owns or controls assets in more than one country may be called a TNC. It is a wider concept than FDI since it includes non-equity business participation in another country.[18] FDI is often the result of decisions by TNCs. Therefore, FDI may be a relatively good proxy for the investment activities of TNCs. A note of caution has to be added, however. TNCs may control trans-border business operations by non-equity involvement such as licensing (but must be assured that the goods or services provided conform with the original quality standards).

Large companies are in most cases TNCs. They do not have direct and complete responsibility to any government, but rather to their own ethos. Chauvinism is alien to the international firm, for their business decisions are not likely to be based on either ideological or nationalistic grounds (Rubin, 1970, p. 183). The most crucial determinants of FDI are the relative difference in returns and profit maximization in the long run, and market presence on the one hand, and availability of resources, expectations of growth in demand and political stability on the other. They may be more important than a country's participation in a regional economic bloc.

Other reasons for FDI instead of, or together with, exporting include taking advantage of the host country's financial incentives (subsidies, taxes), tariff protection, public purchases, market pre-emption, increase in market power, as well as empire-building ambitions. In addition, some goods or services must be adjusted in order to meet local needs (e.g. food) and this may be done in a cheaper way by locating at least a part of the production process near the place of consumption.

Most of the TNCs originate in countries with decentralized political systems such as the US, Britain and the Netherlands. These countries have the longest history in transnationalization of national economic activity. In these countries the TNCs and the state foster relations of complementarity. In centralized states the administration does not want to share power with any enterprise; however, this has changed in past decades.

If producers and government in a big country A make a credible threat to close its market to exporters from a small country B, then one of the options for country B is to establish 'fifth column' production in country A. This would save country B's market share in country A's market. If overheads are covered in country B's home market, then its firm in country A may sell on a marginal cost basis. Many European and Japanese TNCs have concentrated on breaking into the US market and become 'US nationals' in order to avoid unilateral US economic sanctions and changes in the US trade regime. Making profit has played a secondary role, at least in the short run. A similar observation can be made for a run of the non-EU TNCs to settle in the Union prior to the full implementation of the 1992 Programme.

Trade (export) and development of foreign markets may induce a TNC to embark upon FDI. There is, however, evidence to the contrary. On the one hand, FDI may forestall trade, if it is necessary for exploitation, production and export of raw materials. On the other hand, relative differences in the costs of labour between alternative locations do not play a prominent role for modern technologies. The share of the costs of labour is often minor in relation to capital. The success of Japanese firms in reducing their labour content is one of the factors contributing to the expansion of their direct investment into relatively high labour cost areas such as North America. Despite the advantage of cheaper labour in Italy, Greece and Portugal, relative to the central and northern EU countries, that advantage was met by labour outflow, rather than capital inflow in the 1960s.

Transnational corporations behave like other firms: they follow primarily the opportunities for making profit. Size and growth of the market (instead of mere differences in the cost of labour) seem to be the most prominent motivators for their trans-border business operations. That is why roughly 80 per cent of the activities of TNCs is in developed market economies measured by the stock of FDI. The developing countries and those in the transition region face very tough competition in attracting TNCs. Other motivators include the availability of resources (but this depends on the attitude of target countries towards TNCs), efficiency in production, diversification, available technology and exchange of threat (what Du Pont does in Europe, BASF will try to do in the US). A 'black and white' expectation regarding the location of activities due to capital mobility within a common market based on neo-classical theory does not exist. TNCs that use complex technologies do not worry about tariffs and quotas. They are concerned, rather, with domestic regulations such as environmental standards. A bit of government intervention may influence the location of TNCs with important implications for the future distribution of output and trade.

Foreign direct investment is for an enterprise in the function of long-term profit making opportunities abroad. Before embarking upon FDI, an enterprise compares alternative locations at home and at various places abroad. If investing abroad seems to be a more promising option, then the enterprise has to make sure that it possesses or can obtain certain income generating firm-specific advantages in production or transaction that could make it operate profitably in the foreign environment (Dunning, 1988, p. 42). Those advantages include exclusive or privileged access to specific assets and better organizing capabilities for both production and transactions.

Local firms have several advantages over foreign ones. First, they have a better knowledge of local consumer and supplier markets. Second, they do not have the costs of operating at a distance. Third, they often receive favours from the government. Fourth, they do not operate in a different, often hostile, language, tax, legal, exchange rate, social and political environment. Last but not least, TNCs may sometimes have some disadvantages in the eyes of certain local politicians in target countries. Basically: they are foreign and, often, relatively large.

A difficulty for TNCs may be that they have to attract key managers and technicians from the headquarters to a foreign subsidiary. This may require both higher wages for such personnel and higher allowances for their families. TNCs which extract and export natural resources are always at risk of becoming a target for nationalization. If a TNC wants to operate in such an environment, it must have or control a special and mobile advantage such as superior technology and management, a well known brand name and, especially important for services, access to markets and quality control than competitors in target countries. Due to these facts, it is no surprise that TNCs are more profitable and successful than local competitors in the same industry.

While firm-specific income generating and mobile advantages are a necessary condition for FDI, they are not a sufficient condition. If trade were free, firms could simply use their advantages by exporting instead of producing abroad. There exist various market imperfections that limit the size of the market for free trade and, hence, justify FDI. These include tariff and NTBs, differences in factor prices, sunk costs and aftersales service. Therefore, an enterprise with a specific and mobile income generating advantage considers a number of different possibilities and restraints at various foreign locations prior to settling abroad.

There are at least five basic theories that explain why firms engage in trans-border business activities and become TNCs.[19] First, the motivation to control foreign firms may not come from the need to employ assets in a prudent way in foreign markets, but rather to remove competition from other enterprises. Such a *market-power* approach by TNCs was advocated by Hymer (1976). The problem with this argument is that most of the TNCs (measured by their number) are small and medium sized. There were around 45,000 parent firms with over 280,000 foreign affiliates in 1995 (UNCTAD, 1997, p. xv). This shows that to become a TNC, a firm need not be a monopolist or an oligopolist at home and try to exercise that power abroad. If there is strong competition in the market for differentiated goods and services and an easy substitution is possible (perfumes, soaps, watches, clothing, vehicles, passenger air transport on certain lines, to mention just a few examples), then the market-power argument for the transnationaliza-tion of business is weakened.

Second, while the market-power model excludes potential rivals from competition, the *internalization* theory holds that an arm's-length relation among individual firms is in some cases less efficient (e.g. trade in techno-logy) than an intra-firm cooperative association. Profits may be maximized by means of an efficient and friendly intra-firm trade in intermediaries that eliminates sometimes excessive transaction costs (middlemen, exchange-rate risk, infringement of intellectual property rights, bargaining costs) when the business is conducted through the market. In these circumstances a hierarchical organization (an enterprise) may better reward parties in the longer term, as well as curb bargaining and incentives to cheat, than markets and external contractors. While Hymer conceives TNCs as vehicles for reaping monopoly profits and for the internalization of pecuniary external-ities, the internalization model looks at TNCs as a mode of business organ-ization that reduces transaction costs and internalizes non-pecuniary externalities. This model of FDI may be convincing in some cases, but it may not explain the structure and location of all FDI flows, since in addition to the internalization possibilities there ought to be ownership-specific and locational advantages for FDI.

Third, the *eclectic paradigm* (Dunning, 1988, pp. 42–45) explained the trans-border business activities of TNCs (production of goods and services) as a joint mix of three factors:

- First, in order to produce abroad and be successful, a TNC must have or control income-generating ownership-specific and mobile advantages (such as superior technology, brand name, access to wide markets, etc.) compared with the local firms (including other TNCs) in the potential host country.
- Second, there must be opportunities for the internalization of ownership-specific advantages. It should be in the interest of the enterprise to transfer these advantages abroad within its own organization, rather than sell the right to use these advantages to other firms located in the country of intended production.
- Third, locational (non-mobile) advantages refer to the gains of comparative or location-specific advantages of the target country. They refer both to the spatial distribution of resources and to those created by the government.[20]

If a firm possesses/controls ownership-specific advantages, then it may use licensing in order to penetrate foreign markets. If it has both ownership-specific and internalization advantages, such an enterprise may use exports as a means of entering foreign markets. It is only when an enterprise is able to take *simultaneous* advantage of ownership, internalization and locational advantages, that it will employ FDI as a means of operating in foreign markets. This model, however, does not apply to diversified and vertically integrated TNCs.

Fourth, the *product-cycle* model reasons that mature (and, perhaps, environmentally unsound) lines of production of goods (there is no explicit reference to services) are being passed on to the developing countries. That is the transnationalization of business. Such an argument can not pass the test of recent developments. There is a heavy concentration of FDI in developed countries, while the majority of developing countries are relatively neglected in FDI flows. In addition, countries start investing abroad at a much earlier stage of their development than before. The newly industrialized countries and many other developing countries are investing abroad. In many cases these investments are in the developed world. This may be prompted by the desire to be present in the developed countries' markets (closer to the customers), near the source of the major technological developments, as well as the strength of a host country's domestic currency.

Fifth, the *competitive international industry* model for the transnationalization of business refers to oligopolistic competition within the same industry and reactions to business moves by rivals. SMEs may, in their business, act independently. Large firms keep an eye on the actions of their rivals, i.e., they act strategically (pay attention to the likely reaction of their competitors to their own actions). What Exxon does in Europe, Shell will (try to) do in the US. Competition is not 'cut-throat', but rather 'stable' among several oligopolies.

Integrated countries may obtain benefits from the trans-border business activity of firms. These gains, specific to the operation of TNCs within the area, include not only tangible resources (transfer of capital on more favourable terms than could be obtained on capital markets, tax receipts, economies of scale, sourcing of inputs from local suppliers and employment) that it provides at lower cost than through the market, but also various intangible assets such as new technologies in production and management that make the existing resources more productive, positive externalities in production through linkages, international marketing networks that can overcome barriers for exports into foreign markets, new ideas, clustering of related firms, training of labour and competition. The pecuniary element of these spillovers is quite difficult to measure and could easily escape the attention of a non-economist. Monopolization, restrictive business practices, increased sourcing from the parent country with a negative impact on the balance of trade, transfer pricing, transfer of profits abroad[21] and polarization may be found on the other side of the benefits coin. All of them affect the allocation of resources that does not always have a favourable impact either on the integrated country or on the whole group.

Foreign ownership and control of domestic output facilities is often seen by the man in the street as a cost (if it is a cost at all) to the domestic economy that is brought by TNCs. A more seriously founded argument against the operation of TNCs is that they behave in the market in an anti competitive way through various business practices such as predatory pricing, monopolization or transfer pricing.

One of the host country's arguments against TNCs is their internal (transfer) pricing system.[22] TNCs internalize intermediate product and service[23] markets. Prices in trade among different sister enterprises are arrived at by non-market means.[24] For example, if transfer of technology is measured by international payments of royalties and fees, then around 80 per cent of payments are undertaken on an intra-firm basis (UNCTAD, 1994, pp. xxi–xxii). By doing so, TNCs may shift profits out of countries with relatively high taxes to those with the lowest corporate taxes (tax avoidance)[25] or they may oust competition by cross-subsidizing product lines. In order to shift profits, vertical TNCs may overprice imports of inputs and underprice exports. This pricing system may distort flows of trade. One way to control the operation of the TNCs in the host country could be to request that the internal pricing system between the parent and subsidiary should be treated as if they are two separate companies. The enforcement and control of this request may be seriously endangered if there are no substitutes for these internally traded goods and various (headquarters) services. Another solution may be to harmonize fiscal systems in countries where TNCs operate. None the less, a note of caution needs to be added. Transfer pricing perhaps is used much more than TNCs are willing to admit, but much less than is supposed by outsiders (Plasschaert, 1994, p. 13).

In any case, transfer pricing is not widespread in small TNCs, decentralized ones and those that operate in competitive markets.

Internalization of intermediate goods or services markets within TNCs is not always done with the primary goal of avoiding taxes on corporate profits. If a TNC wants to keep quality high in the supply of its goods and services, then local or out-of-the-firm suppliers may not necessarily be able to maintain these high standards requested by the TNC. Hence, the reason for keeping production (and pricing) internal to the TNC. None the less, fiddling with transfer pricing is more widespread in the developing countries than in the developed world. Their balance-of-payments position often drives developing countries to control flows of foreign exchange. Strict controls may induce TNCs to manipulate transfer pricing in order to protect and/or increase profits. The developing countries are not well equipped, first to detect, and, second, to control, manipulation of the internal prices of TNCs.

A potential case against TNCs is that they rely heavily on the R&D of their parent companies and/or head offices that can charge this in a way which might not be controlled by the host country. This can make both subsidiaries and host countries too dependent on foreign R&D and technology. Is this really the case? Some empirical research has shown that subsidiaries had more R&D in Canada than other domestic Canadian firms (Rugman, 1985, p. 486). European elevator companies keep their R&D for elevators for tall buildings in the US because this country has many tall buildings. While there is historical evidence that the major part of R&D takes place in the headquarters of TNCs, it is no longer the case on a large scale. In many instances foreign subsidiaries developed technologies that benefited the parent firm. For example, IBM's (US) breakthroughs in superconductor technology took place in Switzerland; Hoffmann–La Roche (Switzerland) developed important new pharmaceuticals in New Jersey (US); Toshiba made advances in audio technology in its British lab; and Matsushita has R&D facilities for air-conditioners in Malaysia. Affiliates of foreign TNCs in the US look a lot like the domestic firms. There are no particular signs of headquarters effects (Graham and Krugman, 1991, pp. 72–74, 117).[26]

A small country often does not have the available resources for basic research in relation to a big one. By imports of technology a small country may have access to the results of a much larger volume of R&D wherever carried out. It can be both complementary and supplementary to R&D already undertaken in the domestic economy. Relying on the domestic operation of foreign-owned TNCs is a superior choice for a risk-averse country than being dependent on foreign supplies of the same good produced elsewhere.

There is, however, a tendency to decentralize R&D within TNCs. One reason is the reduction in costs of research, while the other is the exploitation of host countries' incentives to R&D (subsidies, tax brakes, secure contracts). The basic research may remain in the headquarters while subsidiaries do applied development according to the local demand. It is often forgotten that many firms that create knowledge are not always either TNCs or big. The only condition for their creation is that they operate in a competitive environment which is often lacking in small countries.

The greatest power of TNCs stems from their high international mobility to enter and exit from an industry. TNCs have the possibility of acting as capital arbitrageurs. They may borrow in countries where the rate of interest is lowest and invest in countries where it expects the highest returns. TNCs may spread overheads and risk among their subsidiaries. These enterprises also extend control over international markets. If a subsidiary is producing final goods, then other parts of a TNC may increase export components to this subsidiary.

Many TNCs create sophisticated and complicated technologies. They avoid the transfer of this technology through the market in order to prevent competitors from copying it. The longer the technology gap with imitators, the longer the TNC can behave like a monopolist. Therefore, a TNC transfers technology usually only among its subsidiaries.

Relations between TNCs and host countries may sometimes be quite tense. Mining is an industry which requires a huge amount of investment before commercial exploitation. Various countries often compete and offer incentives for FDI. At this stage a TNC has the strongest bargaining position. When the TNCs are established in host countries they may react quite differently to changes in, for example, the host country's tax system or interest rates than domestic firms which may not be able to withdraw from the home market. Thus, TNCs may become a threat to the host country's national economic policies. To counter this danger, the common market member countries should coordinate and harmonize their policies regarding capital mobility and TNCs. A large amount of investment may, however, keep a TNC as a hostage of the host country. These sunk costs may represent a barrier to exit from the host country. It is now that the host country government can show the TNC who is boss. The host governments may renegotiate the deals with the TNCs. This kind of danger may induce the TNCs to borrow predominately on the host country financial market and transfer from elsewhere only the technical and managerial expertise. A possible closure of a subsidiary in the host country would cost some local jobs in both the subsidiary and supplying firms. The affected workers and their families may lobby in favour of the interests of TNCs. Those corporations may find allies among industries in the host country. As long as TNCs purchase from them, both subsidiaries and local firms may work together in lobbying the government for protection, subsidies, tax breaks and procurement agreements.

Mineral resources, including oil, are, as a rule, the property of the state in many developing countries. It is the government which negotiates terms of entry with TNCs. In manufacturing, the role of the government is somehow less pronounced. In this case, the government usually sets general terms of entry, performance and exit from an industry. While the developing countries, as a rule, regulate with greater scrutiny the conditions for entry of TNCs, industrialized countries control their exit and the possible consequences of loss of jobs.

In spite of the allegedly weaker environmental standards in the developing countries, a large-scale transfer of polluting business activities has not been transferred there. That is the consequence of the constant focus of TNCs on the developed countries and the adherence of TNCs to the application of environmental standards (often the same as their home country) that are superior to those prevailing in the host developing country.

The basis of the Organisation for Economic Cooperation and Development (OECD) Declaration on International Investment and Multinational Enterprises (1976) is the principle of national treatment of foreign companies. This principle means that, provided that national security is not jeopardized, TNCs have the same rights and obligations as domestic companies in similar situations. It does not equalize foreign suppliers on the importing country market with each other which the most favoured nation clause does, but rather, it refers to the treatment of foreign suppliers with domestic ones.

The greatest leverage on the TNCs may be exercised by resource-rich and prosperous countries such as Canada.[27] The experience of this country is one of the most interesting examples of control of TNCs. It is relevant, as a significant part of the economic integration between Canada and the US has a FDI dimension.

Both Canada and the US are signatories to the OECD Declaration. A few years before this Declaration was delivered, Canada established in 1973 the Foreign Investment Review Agency (FIRA) to survey inward FDI. This move was a reaction to a relatively large share of foreign ownership of Canadian industry. One may argue that much of the foreign ownership of the host country industry may be attributed to the level of the host country's tariffs, taxes, subsidies and other incentives. TNCs overcome tariff obstacles by setting up tariff factories in the host country. The intention of the FIRA was not to stop foreign investment in Canada, but rather to allow FDI only if it resulted in beneficial effects to Canada. The criterion upon which the FIRA evaluated both the takeovers of existing Canadian firms and the establishment of new businesses included expanded exports, use of Canadian resources, increase in investment, employment and productivity, as well as compatibility with the national industrial and other economic policies.

The rejection rate by the FIRA of 20 per cent was an important barrier for certain investors and was high compared to rates of some 1 per cent for other countries which used a similar screening process (Lipsey, 1985, p. 101). This made many firms withdraw their applications to avoid uncertain and costly application procedures while other firms which might be potential investors have not even applied. At the beginning of the 1980s the rejection rate by the FIRA was lowered. The Conservative government transformed the FIRA from a nationalistic authority aimed at increasing Canadian ownership in domestic industry into an organization for the attraction of FDI and in 1984 renamed it Investment Canada. The fear of too much foreign capital had given way to a fear of too little! (Lipsey and Smith, 1986, p. 53).

The local content condition may be criticized on the grounds that it distorts investors' input choices, stimulates sub-optimal input mixes and potentially increases prices. In a survey of 682 projects, it was found that in 83 per cent of the cases in which there was a requirement to accomplish the objectives of TRIMs such as local sourcing and exporting, the firms planned to do that anyway (UNCTC, 1991, p. 4). That is to say, TRIMS were redundant.

If the TNCs produce final goods in host countries and if they import raw materials and components from countries which are outside the common market instead of purchasing them from the local suppliers, then they may jeopardize the process of integration within a common market. This area may increase its external dependence, instead of reducing it. When the member countries of a common market compete amongst themselves for FDI in the absence of an agreed industrial policy, then one can not expect that the operation of the TNCs will result in an optimal allocation of resources within a common market or other types of international economic integration (Robson, 1983, p. 32). This has happened in the Caribbean region.

Transnational corporations treat their business in different countries as a single market operation. Therefore, their financial service is always central- ized as it may best meet the needs of the firm as a whole.[28] It represents the backbone of overall efficiency. This is most pronounced in the case where ownership-specific advantages of a TNC are generating high returns. Other operations such as employment, wage and labour relations are always decentralized within TNCs. Labour markets are local and often highly regulated, so decentralization of these issues is the optimal policy for TNCs. Multi-plant coordination of a growing part of business activities is one of the greatest advantages of TNCs. For example, Nike (an American 'producer' of sports goods) keeps its R&D in Oregon, but sub-contracts the actual manufacturing of those goods in some forty locations, principally in Asia. If wages increase in one country, Nike simply moves production into another.

It is popularly argued that TNCs invest most often in fast-growing manufacturing industries such as electronics and pharmaceutical industries. These industries thus 'fall into foreign hands'. Foreigners may thus hit the host country and interfere with sovereignty. An example was when the US introduced a ban on the export of technology for the gas pipeline from the then USSR to western Europe in the early 1980s. Many subsidiaries of US TNCs in western Europe were hit by this decision. It is much harder for a host country to hit the parent country of a TNC through a subsidiary.

As noted earlier, modern technologies complicate the employment impact of FDI. Modern technologies substitute capital for labour. A 'greenfield' entry on a new site adds to employment in the host country if it does not put out of business domestic competitors. A takeover of an existing firm does not necessarily increase employment and it may reduce it if this firm rationalizes the existing activity (Buckley and Artisien, 1987, p. 212). A subsidiary may start as an unit for marketing of the final good. If it develops further, it may become a product specialist which may increase employment (direct and indirect) of certain type of labour. However, one has to remember that employment is determined by demand for final goods and services.

Takeovers (mergers and acquisitions) provide ways for the 'external' growth of TNCs. They are attractive to TNCs which have wide international marketing networks and tempting to sellers who are interested in penetrating the widest possible market. This is even enhanced if the acquired (or merged) enterprise is not linked to any industrial group which helps to avoid conflicting interests. That is the reason why the Anglo-Saxon enterprises dominate cross-border mergers and acquisitions in Europe. TNCs may also grow 'internally' through subsidiaries. Mergers and acquisitions are virtually unknown in Japan.

A serious threat to the market structure of a host country may be introduced by a TNC. It may monopolize the whole domestic market and by predatory pricing prevent the entry to the industry of potential host country firms. It may introduce technologies which use relatively more of the resources in short supply (capital) and relatively less of the component which is abundant (labour) in the host country. TNCs may offer relatively higher wages to qualified domestic labour in order to attract it. This labour may flow from the host country's firms into TNCs. However, this may be due, in part, to the fact that the home firms do not value properly a resource which is in short supply. Vacancies in the domestic firms may be filled by less well trained labour which may have an adverse effect on the growth of production in the host country. Although technologies used by the TNCs in the host countries may not be the most up to date, they can be better than those which are currently in use in developing countries.

The policies of the TNCs may have an adverse impact on the allocation of resources in the host country under the condition that the existence and operation of the TNCs have a significant proportion of production, employment, purchases and sales in the host country. Developing countries may thus be more influenced in certain segments of industry by the operation of the TNCs than developed countries. This state of affairs asks for a coordinated approach towards TNCs by the regional groups in the developing world, as was the case with the controversial Decision 24 (1970) in the Andean Pact. It also required the establishment and enforcement of a common industrial policy. This can be supported by the regional development banks and/or by joint planning. Openness to and participation in an integrated network of international production of TNCs will contribute to the growth potential of the developing countries.

This analysis suggests that the TNCs do not pay much attention to the overall needs of the host countries. This is true. However, fulfilment of the social needs of the host country is not their duty. Nobody forces the host countries to accept TNCs. The fulfilment of these social demands is the role of the host country's government. In the situation with unemployed resources, inflation, foreign and budgetary debt, famine and underdevelopment, any coin of hard currency investment is precious. Any attempt of the host government to restrict the entry and operation of TNCs may dry up this thin trickle of capital inflow. Host countries sometimes behave (or used to) as if they wanted FDI, but did not want the foreign investor. Unfortunately, the developing countries are the ones that need these investments most. Economic adjustment in the developing world is facilitated in the presence of TNCs. These corporations have the know-how, ability to raise funds and the widespread marketing channels which help in export growth.

The estimates about the potential gains from the economic integration and operations of TNCs are generally based on the classical assumption that the set of traded goods is both complete and fixed. In such a case, the gains from trade and FDI appear to be quite small. Prices in the economy could be changed by government (tariff) intervention, so the quantity of produced and traded goods would change, but the list of the manufactured and traded goods would remain the same. Suppose now, that the list of goods is expandable. The neo-Schumpeterian economic model assumes that there are no limits for the introduction of new goods and services in an economy. Let us assume, in addition, that the introduction of a new commodity requires a large amount of fixed costs.[29] That is especially true in the case of the developing countries. Perfect competition and free trade exclude (major) fixed costs from consideration. Once the fixed costs are included in the picture, their presence is often used as a justification for the introduction of government intervention. When important fixed costs enter the model, a substantial amount of the good needs to be sold in order to make a profit. In such a case, a tariff on the good in question may reduce demand. If this reduction in (international) demand is important, then the commodity may never appear on the market. Losses from such a development or gains in the reverse case may not be easily estimated, at least, not for the time being. In any case, if the new goods are left out of consideration, then this kind of analysis can bring substantial underestimates of the welfare cost of trade restrictions (Romer, 1994). These new goods and services are brought to the developing countries by TNCs.

Despite a relative academic hostility, public sensitivity, polemics against foreigners which export home resources and some official consternation about the operation of TNCs, the situation has changed since the 1980s. All countries in the world welcome TNCs. There is a tendency towards a convergence in the national rules regulating FDI. Apart from some screening, these countries provide TNCs with various incentives which include the provision of infrastructure, subsidized loans, tax exemptions, export incentives, opportunities for complete ownership and exemptions from duties.

However, these countries have to bear in mind that they compete with other possible locations, hence there is a tendency towards a liberal and converging national system towards TNCs. The growing market in the EU and a wide market in the US are still the most preferred locations for TNCs. If other regions want to attract TNCs, then, ideally, they should have some 'unique selling point' that TNCs can not find in Europe or North America.

Apart from these drawbacks, a host country finds significant gains and invites the operation of the TNCs. These corporations may bring in technology which is superior to existing domestic technology. This promotes production capacity in the host country, jobs, tax proceeds, savings in unemployment benefits and may also create exports. TNCs enter into growth industries and provide technological expertise which would otherwise be missing. Some TNCs produce brand name drinks or cigarettes. These are goods whose consumption is burdened by excise duties. The governments may need or want these proceeds and become an ally of the TNCs. If there are some barriers to entry, such as huge initial capital investment in an industry, then TNCs may provide this advantage. When the host country's policy is to promote exports or substitute imports, then TNCs may fill part of this role. On the one hand, the major incentive for TNCs to locate their operations in a country or an integrated region is to offer them a growing market. International economic integration gives this opportunity. Other carrots include tax holidays, subsidies, tariff protection and secure public purchases. In the medium and longer term, the best policy is to influence the supply of educated local labour as an additional incentive to TNCs to select the country for the location of their operations. On the other hand, sticks include performance criteria, exports, employment, withholding taxes, as well as repatriation and re-investment rules.

Potential benefits from the involvement of TNCs may not be measured directly and in the short term. None the less, many of them can be listed. They include:

- access to wide international manufacturing and marketing networks;
- linkage of the economies of different countries;
- the introduction of new resources and capabilities in the national economy;
- an improvement in the quality of the existing resources and capabilities;
- increased capital formation and growth (creation of wealth);
- access to new technology, R&D, innovations, standards and know-how in production, management, marketing and pollution control;
- economies of scale and more efficient use of resources;
- improved efficiency in production and increased competitiveness;
- improved quality of output;
- product differentiation;
- externalities (including sourcing from the local firms);

- employment of local resources; and
- benefits of learning.

3 Intervention

If market imperfections permit rents (above average profits), then the governments of the integrated countries may wish to intervene. A larger market of an integrated area may be more able to absorb the cost of intervention owing to the spread of such costs than could be in the case of individual countries acting alone. For instance, a simplified (prisoner's dilemma) example is presented in Table 3.2. Suppose that there are just two firms capable of producing aircraft: British Aerospace in Britain and Aérospatiale in France. Assume also that due to sunk costs, R&D and economies of scale, only one firm can produce aircraft efficiently (profit-wise) within the EU and that public authorities prefer to purchase domestically made goods. The numbers in Table 3.2 then show the profit of the two firms. If there is no intervention by the government, the firm that moves first captures the market and makes a profit. If both produce: both lose; if neither produce: there is neither gain nor loss. The example is important since if only one country has the ability to produce aircraft, the government of the other may then try to persuade a foreign TNC to settle within its borders, thus putting the potential competitor from the partner country out of business. That is a strong case for a joint treatment of TNCs by the integration groups.

Now suppose that there is no domestic producer of aircraft in Britain and that the domestic government[30] decides that it may be sensible to have aircraft production located at home and to move first to strategically and irreversibly pre-empt any other player.[31] The reasons may include employment, export and prestige, but also, and more importantly, various externalities, including obtaining the leading edge in one of the high-technology industries and also national pride. The government decides to invite Boeing to come to Britain. As bait, it offers various subsidies and protection to capture the aircraft market in the integration arrangement with France.[32] The major reason for the subsidy is not simply to increase export sales, but rather to improve the terms of trade and secure rents for the home firm, a cluster of related domestic enterprises and, finally, for the country itself. Of course, such a policy may have a significant balance-of-payments effect in the medium and long term. Hence, the structure of markets and the operations of TNCs matter. Engineering comparative advantages of countries and

Table 3.2 Profit in the aircraft industry, without intervention

France \ Britain	Production	No production
Production	−3; −3	10; 0
No production	0; 10	0; 0

firms are becoming more important in modern footloose industries and are eroding, to an extent, inherited comparative advantages.[33] Basically, this is the way the new trade theory explains the success of Japan.[34]

What is important here is that the neo-classical model deals with the given and perfect resources and capabilities, while the new theory studies market imperfections and government intervention in a dynamic setup that suppresses market constraints and pushes economic frontiers outwards. It considers economies of scale, externalities, differentiated products, changing technology and FDI. These are all features of modern manufacturing. The new theory questions the proposition that free markets may successfully take advantage of the potential benefits in the new situation. Such an approach is different from the neo-classical one where TNCs were, by definition, excluded from consideration. The assumption in free markets is that there is no ground for trans-border business activities since the allocation of resources is perfect (first best solution). The new theory explains that countries can trade not only when their resource endowments and production capabilities are *different*, as in the neo-classical situation, but also when their resource endowment and production capabilities are *identical*. The case in question is the intra-industry trade (i.e. intra-EU trade in cars).

One thing, however, ought to be clear from the outset. The new theory does not replace the neo-classical one. The new theory only considers market imperfections that can be mitigated by intervention which may introduce an adjustment instrument into an already highly imperfect situation. Table 3.3 discloses the profits of two producers when the government of Britain subsidizes its (foreign owned/controlled) firm with monetary units that equal 5. If the firm in Britain decides to produce, it will always have the advantage over its potential French rival.

When market imperfections exist, the government of Britain can influence allocation of resources and specialization. None the less, to make accurate choices in the selection of national champions, the government ought to be competent and possess correct information, otherwise there may be costly commercial failures, such as the Franco-British Concorde project, or computers in France. Many governments in east Asia successfully intervened in the economy. But governments in many east European and developing countries were intervening much more, yet those countries did not have economic successes which are comparable those ones in east Asia. In any case, intervention is eased when the number of potentially competing firms is small and production output is standardized.

Table 3.3 Profit in the aircraft industry, with intervention

France \ Britain	Production	No production
Production	−3; 2	10; 0
No production	0; 15	0; 0

Moreover, governments need to keep in mind that general favours (subsidies) that are handed out to the domestic firms may trickle-out to foreign beneficiaries, located within the confines of the jurisdiction of the government that offers subsidies. A more effective policy may be to subsidize the development and upgrading of the domestic human capital as footloose capital is increasingly attracted, among other factors, by the local availability of skilled, highly trained and experienced labour.

In advanced countries such as the US, more than offered states offered and competed with substantial grants (and grant-equivalents) in order to attract the location of world-scale manufacturing projects. These grants are increasing. Michigan offered state and local incentives worth $120 million ($14,000 per job) to attract Mazda in 1984; Indiana offered $110 million ($51,000 per job) to Subaru–Isuzu in 1986; Kentucky offered $325 million ($108,000 per job) to Toyota in 1989 (UNCTC, 1991a, pp. 73–74). Alabama gave $252 million ($168,000 per job) to Mercedes–Benz in 1993, while North Carolina handed out $130 million ($108,000 per job) to BMW. In spite of strict rules of competition, countries in the EU are sometimes allowed to hand out 'incentives' to TNCs to settle within their confines. Britain gave $89 million ($29,675 per job) to Samsung in 1994, while France granted $111 million ($56,923 per job) to Mercedes–Benz and Swatch in 1995 (UNCTAD, 1995a, p. 18). These kind of subsidies are well beyond the financial capabilities of developing countries.

This simple model of strategic investment, industrial and trade policy is based on the expectation that the subsidized home production of a tradable good or service shifts monopoly profits (rents) to the home country and to the firms owned/controlled by it. These profits ought to be over and above the cost of the subsidy. If the domestic firms are affiliates of foreign TNCs, then the effect on the home country's welfare may be uncertain. No matter what the circumstances, the expectation that profit shifting may enhance the home country's welfare holds *only* when foreign countries do not retaliate against domestic subsidies. A cycle of retaliation and counter-retaliation would make everyone worse off. In addition, when there is a liberal treatment of FDI, bilateral trade deficits may point to misleading signals. For example, if Japan (or any other country) invests in China in order to take advantage of cheap labour and export output to the US, the bilateral deficit in trade between the US and Japan may shrink, but the deficit may increase because of extra exports from China to the US.

4 Transnational corporations and international economic integration

Many business activities entail high costs, uncertainties and face rapid changes in technology and demand, so the operation of such activities in relatively small markets may not be commercially viable from an efficiency point of view. As world-wide free trade may not be achieved in the short or medium term (if ever), as the first best neo-classical solution suggests, international economic integration may be an attractive second best policy option. Such integration, although to an extent an inward-looking strategy, widens/pools the markets of the participating countries. Larger and growing markets provide greater confidence than relatively smaller ones to both domestic and foreign investors.

Domestic markets in most countries are so small that even a high degree of protection of growth-propelling manufacturing industries and services aimed at supplying the local market may not be viable from the point of efficient employment of resources. By supplying a larger market provided by the integration arrangement, participating countries may increase production, capacity utilization, employment and investment; reduce vulnerability to external shocks; capture economies of scale; improve bargaining positions in international markets; and increase average standards of living. Those results are viewed in comparison to the situation in which all countries act alone under heavy domestic protection.

The production and distribution of goods and services in an integrated area does not take place exclusively by domestic firms, but also by TNCs and their affiliates. This point adds an extra element to the theoretical analysis that brings it closer to the real world, but it also introduces certain analytical drawbacks to the pure and simple theoretical models. In an early work, Mundell (1957) argued that within the HOS theoretical model, trade in goods and trade in factors may substitute each other. Markusen (1983) has shown that the flow of factors (operations of TNCs) are complementary to international trade, rather than substitutes, and that the proposition by Mundell may be only a special case. Moreover, FDI is due to market imperfections, since in a free trade situation the allocation of resources is perfect and there are no grounds for FDI whatsoever. None the less, TNCs provide for powerful enterprise-created links that may integrate national economies. However, a goal of countries should be to set realistic objectives in relation to integration: to see how TNCs fit into the picture; to structure their entry, operation and exit; as well as to negotiate deals. In addition, if the integrated countries master the production of goods and services to such an extent that it increases their international competitiveness, firms within the area may go abroad and themselves become TNCs. They may improve the employment of home resources and enter new markets beyond the confines of the market of the integrated area.

Suppose that a TNC as a monopolist exports a good to a group of integrated countries protected by a common binding quota. If, in addition, that TNC decides to locate within the integrated area, it may choose to produce there any quantity of the good it wishes. In such a case, the integration scheme (as a whole, but not necessarily every part of it) may gain significantly since there is an additional employment of the domestic factors, while domestic consumers also gain since the price of the good falls. In another case, when there are local firms competing with a TNC in the home market, the location of the TNC within the integrated area may benefit both consumers (price falls) and resource utilization since home firms ought to improve competitiveness if they want to remain in business. If such a process works well, then one may not justify restrictions on the operation of foreign TNCs in an integrated area (be it in the developed or developing world).

An arrangement that integrates countries may improve the terms of trade of the group with the rest of the world. If the price of a good or service that is imported to the group falls after integration, then such an arrangement increases the rents of the scheme to the detriment of those previously made by foreign firms. Suppose that country A and country B integrate. If a TNC outside the integration scheme that produces good X is located in country B prior to integration and continues to operate there after the regional arrangement is formed, then the price of good X may fall due to the possible competition in the integrated market or the increased efficiency that comes from economies of scale. If country A starts importing good X from country B, then there are benefits additional to trade creation for country A. The rents of the TNC dwindle, while the surplus of country A's consumers rises. That consequence of integration, from the standpoint of country A, is called the *foreign profit diversion effect*. When there is another TNC producing good Y in country A that starts to be exported to the partner country B after integration, then, from the perspective of country A, there is an opposite effect named *foreign profit creation effect* (Tironi, 1982, pp. 155–156).

The foreign profit creation/diversion effects are of vital importance to the integration schemes whose economic structures are dominated or influenced by TNCs. This may be the case in countries that are involved in the globalization of international business, as well as in many developing countries. If such countries integrate, then TNCs are mostly interested in favourable foreign profit creation effects. Suppose that there are two countries that contemplate integration and that each has in its market a different TNC that manufactures the same undifferentiated good. If the leverage of the two TNCs on decision making is significant in the two countries, then the TNCs may collude and undermine the integration efforts.

Governments usually respect the opinions of the business community, in particular if that business has a noted impact on the welfare of the country. Hence, in some cases, TNCs may even play one government against another and continue with an inefficient (from a resource allocation point of view), but profitable production for them.[35] That is one reason why the arrangements that integrate developing countries may include provisions that refer to TNCs. None the less, the policy stance of an integrated area towards TNCs depends on the basic objectives of the group. If the basic objective of the group is an increase in *employment*, then ownership of the firms does not matter at all. FDI is, after all, an investment. If the goal of the group is to *shift rents* towards the integrated countries, then it matters who is the owner of the manufacturing and service facilities.[36] In reality, however, governments are not indifferent to who owns 'national' assets.

Transnational corporations may introduce technologies which use relatively more resources in short supply (capital) and relatively less of the component which is abundant (labour) in the host country. TNCs may offer relatively higher wages to qualified domestic labour in order to attract it. This labour may flow from the host country's firms into TNCs. However, this may be due, in part, to the fact that the home firms do not value properly a resource that is in short supply. Vacancies in the domestic firms may be filled by less well trained labour which may have an adverse effect on the growth of production in the host country. Although technologies used by the TNCs in the host countries may not be the most up to date, they may be superior to those in use in developing countries (environmentally sound technologies are an obvious example).

If the integrated market of the (developing) countries is still small enough for the establishment of the cluster of related suppliers, then the major gainers may be TNCs that assemble goods and/or perform only limited (usually final) manufacturing operations. Such a tendency may be enhanced when the integrated countries have relaxed rules of origin for goods that qualify for liberal treatment in internal trade. Although the internal trade of the group increases, so does the extra-group import content of the traded goods. Broad regional deepening of production linkages does not take place. Estimates of the potential increase in trade ought to refer to the dual pattern of trade (imports of components from abroad and export of finalized goods within the group) and discount the gross increase in internal trade of the region. Instead of the expected relative reduction in the dependency on external markets, integration on such terms may have the completely opposite effect.

The governments of potential host countries may compete with each other with subsidies offered to TNCs in order to elicit their investment and location within the confines of their authority. In this game, TNCs may benefit since their bargaining power is enhanced. One outcome may be that TNCs locate in each country, supply the local protected market, engage in parallel production on a scale that is sub-optimal from a resource allocation point of view, while these countries lose interest in the integration process. Such a strategy requires a common competition policy, a joint industrialization programme and treatment of TNCs in a group of (developing) countries, otherwise the linkages with the suppliers from the local economy and integration partner country may be superficial. Integration may lead to a structure of production that is dominated by firms alien to the integrated group. A potentially positive absorption and spread of changes in the market (created by the involvement of TNCs) by the local enterprises does not take place.

Transnational corporations have an interest in promoting integration among developing countries with small markets, but only under the condition that these firms are not involved in the countries concerned prior to integration. In medium and large developing countries, the position of TNCs may be quite different, since TNCs do not seek integration among countries of this size. In fact, they may be a major obstacle for the forceful integration of developing countries. The primary concern of TNCs may not be efficiency in production, but rather the likely reactions of other TNCs, as well as the intention to avoid conflicts (UNCTAD, 1983, p. 12).

5 European Union

5.1 Issues

Coupled with the provisions on the monetary union, free capital mobility established by the EU means that the national monetary independence of the member countries was lost to a large degree. For example, if other things are equal, an increase in a member country's interest rate relative to those in the outside world, meant to cool the economy and curb inflation, would, in fact, expand the domestic quantity of money. Many TNCs would invest funds in that country in order to profit from higher rates of interest. In the reverse situation when a country lowers its rates of interest with the intention of stimulating economic activity by cheap loans, that would in fact contract the available funds as TNCs will move financial resources to countries with higher rates of interest (Panić, 1991, p. 212).

The establishment of the EU, as Mark 1 in the integration process, and its relative dynamism, has provoked the expansion of TNCs from the US to invest in this region during the 1960s and 1970s. The implementation of the 1992 Programme, as Mark 2 in the integration process, and the completion of the internal market was likely to increase investment of Japanese TNCs in the EU. However, the actual involvement also depended, in part, on the evolution of the tariffs and NTBs in the EU.

While Mark 1 in the integration process eliminated (among other things) tariffs on internal trade, the objective of Mark 2 was an elimination of NTBs on internal trade. That was supposed to increase efficiency of production (rationalized investments), reduce transaction costs, increase competition and demand and harmonize standards. That required certain adjustments of internal production in the EU. The rationale for the existence of 'tariff factories' was removed. Therefore, investment in the production that avoided internal EU barriers was significantly reduced or eliminated altogether. In any case, Mark 2 was expected to increase the operation, co-operative agreements, strategic alliances and investment of the TNCs that originate in the EU. An additional effect would be investment creation. In the longer term, they could look like those in the US that take full advantage of the economies of scale. The Europeans, on average, have more sophistic-ated tastes, and demand differentiated goods. Hence, large-scale production of homogenized goods as in the US has never been expected in the EU.

There was an initial fear by foreign TNCs that the EU would create a 'Fortress Europe' which would protect its home market with the 1992 Programme. Some of them rushed to establish themselves in the EU before the potential 'discrimination' took place. Target enterprises in the EU became overvalued to the extent that other locations, most notably in the US, seemed more attractive. In spite of that, the EU continued to be an interesting location for FDI, so foreign TNCs were also hoping to enter into strategic alliances with EU firms.

Horizontally integrated TNCs such as 3M responded to integration in the EU by specialization of production in their plants. 'Post it' notes are made in its British plant, while scotch tape is produced in its German unit. Previously, 3M produced a wide range of goods in each country in order to serve predominantly the local market. Vertically integrated TNCs such as Ford responded to the new opportunities by vertical specialization. Differentials and gear boxes are produced in France, while engines are made in Spain. In addition, there emerged a special kind of relation among the competing firms. A removal of NTBs on internal trade and liberalization of public procurement 'forced' inter-firm specialization in similar goods. For example, ICI (Britain) specialized in marine, decorative and industrial paints, while BASF (Germany) did the same in automobile paints (Dunning, 1994b, pp. 296–297).

5.2   Evolution

Unlike the Exxon–Florio amendment (1988) in the US that gave the president the right to block mergers, acquisitions or takeovers of domestic firms by foreign TNCs when such action is supposed to jeopardize national security, the EU does not have a common policy regarding FDI. Only Article 52 of the Treaty of Rome gives the right of establishment to businesses throughout the EU for the nationals of any member state. Japan is also without many formal barriers to inward FDI. None the less, the real obstacles to FDI in Japan are not found in the legal sphere. They exist as a cost of 'doing business in Japan' such as close and strong informal links among businesses, tight labour markets, language barriers and difficulties in obtaining the necessary data.

The impact of the creation of the EU on the attraction of FDI from the US was at the centre of the early studies of the relationship between integration (or, as it was than called, 'tariff discrimination' introduced by the EU and EFTA) and FDI. The expectation was that the allocation of FDI would be influenced by integration. In particular, that the establishment of the EU would lure TNCs to locate in this region. Scaperlanda (1967, p. 26) found, in the examination of the American FDI trend in Europe between 1951 and 1964, that the formation of the EU(6) has not attracted a large share of the American FDI. Since 1958, the value of FDI from the US in the EU(6) was $3.5 billion, while in non-EU Europe, it was $4 billion. Factors such as familiarity with the country in which the investment is to be located, differences in the application of technology and the financial liquidity to fund foreign investment, outweighed the influence of the creation of the EU(6) on the pattern of FDI. In addition, the American TNCs were more interested in the French market than that of the EU(6).

Instead of calculating the trend in FDI for the whole period 1951-64, merging both 'before' and 'after' the EU effects (as did Scaperlanda) and masking investment shifts, rather than revealing them, Wallis (1968) broke the period of analysis into two sub-periods. The share of the American FDI in the EU(6) moved along a continuous and increasing path in the period 1951-64 with a kink in 1958. Before 1958, the EU(6) share increased by 0.7 per cent a year, while after 1958, the average annual increase was 2.7 per cent.[37]

D'Arge (1969, 1971a, 1971b) tried to determine the impact of European integration on the American FDI in the EU and EFTA. The effect of the formation of a trading block on FDI may be along the following three lines:

• it may be a one-time (intercept) shift in trend;
• a gradual increase in trend (slope shift); or
• a combination of the other two.

The data showed that in the case of the EFTA, there was a positive intercept shift (a one-time effect), while in the period following the creation of the EU(6), there was a combination of shifts in both slope and intercept. Scaperlanda and Reiling (1971) suggested that European integration has not crucially influenced and changed the American FDI flows in this region. This was based on the similarity of trends in FDI between the EU(6) and EFTA after 1959, although there was a presumption that the EU would have a greater effect than the EFTA. None the less, one thing has to be kept in mind here. At that time, Britain was the country that received the largest share of American FDI. It was also a member of the EFTA [not the EU(6)]. Therefore, the early studies of the impact of integration on FDI do not show a clear picture regarding the relationship between the two variables. Clarification of the situation, however, came later on. Evidence was found that in the case of the American FDI in the EU(6), size and growth of market played an important role (Goldberg, 1972, p. 692; Scaperlanda and Balough, 1983, p. 389).

Econometric modelling of FDI is a formidable task. The results of various models depend greatly on the assumptions, so that the conclusions can only be tentative. None the less, there is general support for the hypothesis that tariff discrimination, regionalism and integration influence FDI. However, this can not be translated into a statement that an *x* per cent change in tariffs will induce a *y* per cent change in FDI. Therefore, strong policy recommendations on the basis of such models are reckless (Lunn, 1980, p. 99).

Recent studies report that the net effect of integration has been to increase both internal EU and non-EU investment in the Union. The elimination of import duties on internal EU trade encouraged non-EU investors to locate in the Union (Dunning and Robson, 1987, p. 113). An elimination of NTBs (1992 Programme) and a widening the internal market prompted both EU and third country TNCs to invest in the Union.[38]

The 1992 Programme prompted TNCs to rationalize their operations in the EU. The absence of any reference to TNCs from the official reports generated by the Single European Act such as Emerson *et al.* (1988) and the Cecchini Report (1988) comes as a surprising omission. The assumption in those reports seems to be that international specialization and trade is carried out by firms whose operational facilities are confined to a single country. Growth and predominance of TNCs in most areas of economic activity make this kind of analysis inappropriate (Panić, 1991, p. 204).

Britain has always been a relatively attractive location for TNCs, although its economic performance relative to other EU major economies has often been poor. What is the reason for this interest? Regional incentives are no more generous than in the rest of the EU.[39] English is often mentioned as one of the reasons for its appeal, although big TNCs were always able to afford to ease the language barrier. Location in Britain was supposed to serve as a springboard for the rest of the EU, but so too could be locations in other member countries. Where Britain, however, scores high is that it has labour with some degree of competence and it is relatively low paid (compared to other major countries in the EU), it has a good industrial infrastructure, as well as social and political stability.

Japanese TNCs were quite inclined to invest in Britain. However, they preferred to build new factories in rural areas, rather than to take over the existing plants. They also preferred takeovers to joint ventures. The advantages of the 'greenfield' entry was that previous managerial habits and labour relations were not inherited (Sharp and Shepherd, 1987, p. 60). In fact, where the Japanese TNCs had a clear comparative advantage they preferred greenfield starts, while where their comparative advantage was weaker, they were involved in alliances and joint ventures.

5.3   *Flow of foreign direct investment*

Table 3.4 summarized intra-EU(12) FDI flows during the period 1985–94. Panel A presents annual outflows of FDI in the individual member countries, while Panel B gives data on the FDI that were received from other EU partner countries. The discrepancy between the two panels comes for reasons that range from different definitions of FDI to the variety of collection systems, recording of short-term loans, borrowing on the local market, exchange rates, date of recording and accounting for authorized and actual investment.

The preferred locations for internal-EU(12) FDI were, according to Table 3.4, Britain, Germany, Benelux,[40] France, the Netherlands and Spain (Panel B).[41] Apart from Spain, these countries were at the same time major internal investors in the EU. Annual internal FDI flows in the EU were at relatively low levels in the mid-1980s. Those flows, however, quadrupled from ECU 11.3 billion in 1986 to ECU 44.9 billion in 1990. Since then, annual flows had ups and downs, but the important observation is that they have always been (well) above ECU 30 billion. For the 'core' countries of the EU the acceleration in the FDI trend (1986–90) coincided with the implementation of the 1992 Programme. Firms wanted to consolidate their competitive position prior to full implementation of the Programme. Internal flows of FDI in the EU, therefore, pointed to agglomeration tendencies.

Before Mark 2 in the integration process, the endogenous EU firms had, in general, primarily a national orientation, while foreign-owned TNCs (mainly American) had a pan-European business perspective. The removal of NTBs that came with the 1992 Programme aimed at addressing this disequilibrium in the European-business operations. It had an obvious and positive impact on internal FDI flows from 1989. The EU internal FDI flows became more important than outflows from the EU to third countries. Another interesting observation is that the southern countries such as Greece and Portugal (as well as Denmark) were largely left out of the EU internal flows of FDI.

The EU member countries were investing not only within the group, but also outside of it. Data on extra-EU(12) FDI flows are given in Table 3.5. Apart from 1990 and 1992, the EU was a net exporter of FDI. None the less, foreign investors have increased their interest in the EU. That was due to the 1992 Programme. Yamada and Yamada (1996) reported that the principal goal of Japanese investors in the EU was the avoidance of emerging protectionism in the EU. However, Thomsen and Nicolaides (1991, p. 103) argued that the 1992 Programme had not influenced the *quantity* of FDI in that period in the EU, but rather its *timing*.

If Table 3.4 is compared with Table 3.5, intra-EU FDI flows became more important for the EU than external ones from 1989. From that year EU investors started to invest more within the EU than outside of it. Earlier, regional integration was only one factor that influenced FDI flows from the EU countries within and out of the EU. Other factors, such as exchange rates, especially of the US dollar, might have played a more prominent role. While the liberalization of internal EU trade had a strong impact on trade integration, FDI flows show that until 1989 integration was stronger on the global plane than on the regional one.

The US and EFTA countries have always been both major targets for FDI from the EU and, at the same time, major sources of FDI coming into the EU. The US share of total foreign FDI in the EU was 34 per cent during the period 1985–94. The EFTA countries' portion was 30 per cent and that of Japan was 11 per cent during the same period.[42] The US was the preferred location for outward FDI from the EU. This country received 56 per cent of all EU outgoing FDI flows during the period 1985–94. The share of the EFTA was 10 per cent, while that of Japan was less than 1 per cent in the

Table 3.4 Intra-EU(12) flows of FDI, 1985–1994 (%)

	1985	1986	1987	1988	1989	1990	1991	1992	1993	1994	1985–94
A Outward flows											
Belgium/Luxembourg	6.5	4.0	11.8	8.9	5.9	7.4	12.2	16.2	12.6	12.4	10.4
Denmark	1.8	1.9	1.4	1.2	1.6	1.3	2.9	2.2	0.4	2.6	1.8
Germany	21.7	21.2	12.4	8.7	14.4	24.1	26.8	23.7	30.7	17.3	20.7
Greece	0.1	0.0	0.0	0.0	0.0	0.0	0.0	0.0	0.0	0.3	0.0
Spain	0.6	0.7	1.3	1.0	1.8	1.6	1.5	0.9	1.2	0.3	1.2
France	11.0	9.7	26.0	20.6	27.8	25.2	22.1	23.7	11.6	15.7	20.8
Ireland	0.6	0.6	0.5	1.1	1.3	1.6	1.7	1.1	1.2	4.0	1.6
Italy	3.8	6.1	5.3	4.8	2.8	5.0	4.6	10.6	5.6	5.3	5.5
Netherlands	9.5	29.1	11.7	27.7	16.6	21.1	19.0	9.6	7.6	25.1	17.8
Portugal	0.2	0.0	0.0	0.1	0.1	0.2	0.7	1.2	0.7	0.5	0.5
United Kingdom	42.6	26.1	27.7	25.2	25.6	11.8	8.6	10.6	28.3	17.2	19.3
EU 12	100.0	100.0	100.0	100.0	100.0	100.0	100.0	100.0	100.0	100.0	100.0
EU 12 Million ECUs	5,694	9,579	12,371	24,414	33,234	33,592	32,332	30,765	29,507	28,963	240,451
B Inward flows											
Belgium/Luxembourg	8.0	8.5	9.6	18.8	15.0	17.8	11.7	15.6	16.7	10.1	14.4
Denmark	0.1	0.6	1.4	0.7	1.4	0.3	0.7	1.3	0.5	1.7	0.8
Germany	9.9	5.2	3.6	6.8	13.7	16.8	19.8	16.7	10.3	23.1	14.8
Greece	1.8	1.2	0.8	0.4	0.7	0.5	0.9	0.8	0.7	1.0	0.8
Spain	9.6	10.3	12.4	9.4	9.5	10.8	14.2	10.9	11.3	13.8	11.4
France	19.9	12.7	10.9	21.9	11.1	9.5	9.6	14.7	10.5	17.8	12.9
Ireland	4.5	0.5	1.3	1.5	3.0	5.0	11.0	3.9	5.7	3.9	4.7
Italy	7.9	9.8	6.2	6.3	6.6	4.9	4.6	6.8	6.7	6.5	6.2
Netherlands	11.3	24.7	10.5	18.7	12.7	11.3	6.9	18.6	16.1	3.3	12.8
Portugal	3.0	1.0	1.5	1.6	2.1	2.0	2.6	2.6	1.5	2.7	2.1
United Kingdom	26.3	25.2	42.6	12.8	21.6	22.3	19.8	8.2	20.2	16.2	19.0
EU 12	100.0	100.0	100.0	100.0	100.0	100.0	100.0	100.0	100.0	100.0	100.0
EU 12 Million ECUs	6,204	11,319	12,316	20,219	35,736	44,998	37,477	45,982	34,057	30,764	279,072

Source: European Union Direct Investment Yearbook 1996 (Luxembourg: Eurostat, 1997)

Table 3.5 Extra-EU(12) flows of FDI, 1985–1994 (ECUs millions)

	1985	1986	1987	1988	1989	1990	1991	1992	1993	1994	1985–94
A Outward flows											
USA	10,061	17,772	23,885	22,120	24,053	7,155	9,232	6,455	13,357	5,453	139,544
Japan	34	104	-12	247	682	911	341	432	1,216	267	1,790
EFTA(7)	722	-163	1,789	2,593	1,992	3,226	2,471	2,676	4,054	6,317	25,678
Others	4,288	4,219	5,008	6,720	6,555	9,234	14,687	8,079	8,935	12,980	80,706
Extra EU(12)	15,105	21,932	30,670	31,680	33,282	20,527	26,732	17,642	25,130	25,017	247,717
%											
USA	66.6	81.0	77.9	69.8	72.3	34.9	34.5	36.6	53.2	21.8	56.3
Japan	0.2	0.5	0.0	0.8	2.0	4.4	1.3	2.4	-4.8	1.1	0.7
EFTA(7)	4.8	-0.7	5.8	8.2	6.0	15.7	9.2	15.2	16.1	25.3	10.4
Others	28.4	19.2	16.3	21.2	19.7	45.0	54.9	45.8	35.6	51.9	32.6
B Inward flows											
USA	1,788	2,660	2,337	2,551	9,846	9,178	5,411	12,011	10,477	7,963	64,222
Japan	719	465	1,572	2,584	4,354	5,406	1,682	1,825	1,577	1,336	21,520
EFTA(7)	1,838	3,258	3,833	8,509	8,351	11,284	6,883	3,912	3,506	4,933	56,307
Others	1,366	736	5,249	4,497	5,392	6,885	6,957	5,117	6,436	3,310	45,945
Extra EU(12)	5,711	7,119	12,991	18,141	27,943	32,753	20,933	22,865	21,996	17,542	187,994
%											
USA	31.3	37.4	18.0	14.1	35.2	28.0	25.8	52.5	47.6	45.4	34.2
Japan	12.6	6.5	12.1	14.2	15.6	16.5	8.0	8.0	7.2	7.6	11.4
EFTA(7)	32.2	45.8	29.5	46.9	29.9	34.5	32.9	17.1	15.9	28.1	30.0
Others	23.9	10.3	40.4	24.8	19.3	21.0	33.2	22.4	29.3	18.9	24.4

Source: European Union Direct Investment Yearbook 1996 (Luxembourg: Eurostat, 1997)

Table 3.6 Extra EU(12) and extra EU(15) FDI outflows and inflows (equity and other capital)

	Outflows to extra EU(12)								Outflows to extra EU(15)		
	1984	1985	1986	1987	1988	1989	1990	1991	1992	1993	1994
Belgium/Luxembourg	60	52	605	545	1,839	1,145	1,175	370	826	1,256	-2,336
Denmark	222	147	390	219	297	397	415	835	269	779	1,123
Germany	2,978	4,020	5,364	5,266	5,961	4,515	5,369	4,884	4,454	3,847	5,617
Greece	48	190	63	9	8	-1	3	-2	42	-7	-76
Spain	—	—	241	227	552	415	733	1,116	727	793	2,762
France	1,747	2,379	3,531	3,483	3,958	6,205	6,864	7,801	2,628	4,381	4,193
Ireland	100	108	40	86	598	835	22	997	343	2,664	-53
Italy	1,512	598	865	495	1,144	-242	1,031	4,362	1,911	1,442	1,101
Netherlands	1,011	2,373	1,029	3,607	2,612	5,182	4,497	3,179	—	2,978	3,035
Austria	—	—	—	—	—	—	—	—	67	6	76
Finland	—	14	97	4	149	143	235	77	299	177	472
Sweden	—	1,183	2,206	1,346	1,298	2,505	1,422	984	—	—	—
United Kingdom	9,627	5,105	9,799	16,728	14,710	14,819	392	3,130	504	4,704	4,381
Portugal	11	17	5	6	2	15	26	60	802	131	413
European Union[a]	17,407	15,105	21,932	30,670	31,680	33,282	20,527	26,732	17,828	24,157	21,530

	Inflows from extra EU(12)								Inflows from extra EU(15)		
	1984	1985	1986	1987	1988	1989	1990	1991	1992	1993	1994
Belgium/Luxembourg	64	507	151	693	1,282	1,868	1,355	1,774	1,995	2,935	2,830
Denmark	32	159	156	151	422	640	567	637	243	582	1,076
Germany	115	295	246	215	-383	1,670	2,187	440	513	2,012	2,186
Greece	-27	134	207	87	63	90	79	75	70	112	149
Spain	—	—	1,076	1,338	1,799	2,127	2,956	2,139	2,065	1,781	2,397
France	1,387	1,677	1,386	2,056	1,813	2,100	3,365	4,287	4,096	2,647	2,478
Ireland	-30	330	1	327	174	399	964	1,353	467	806	676
Italy	927	30	-456	1,745	3,063	291	3,020	1,288	940	673	416
Netherlands	139	507	938	664	947	2,704	3,013	2,807	—	272	232
Austria	—	—	—	—	—	—	—	—	317	227	376
Finland	—	10	85	12	25	44	180	-66	220	181	286
Sweden	—	188	683	249	622	927	603	552	—	—	—
United Kingdom	1,996	623	3,366	5,619	8,748	15,690	14,661	5,612	8,758	7,904	2,562
Portugal	135	122	47	97	211	365	586	520	504	1,024	1,760
European Union[a]	6,152	5,711	7,119	12,991	18,141	27,943	32,753	20,933	22,760	21,504	19,964

Note: [a] EU(12) until 1991 and EU(15) from then on.
Source: EUROSTAT (1997)

same period. An interesting feature is that the EU investors withdrew ECU 1.2 billion from Japan in 1993. Such large global inter-penetration of FDI reduces the chance that regional arrangements may turn into closed blocs. A 'hostage population' of TNCs may reduce the fear of retaliatory measures. Extensive FDI links between the US and the EU assisted in the relaxation of potential conflict between the two partners regarding market access. The same is not yet true with Japan. There is a hope that Japan will mature as a foreign investor in future and that potential conflict with that country will be defused. A drive towards a reciprocal treatment of FDI with Japan (or any other country) may not be highly productive. It is generally accepted that TNCs bring benefits that more than compensate for the possible costs. The EU is, after all, the major source of FDI, so the demand for a reciprocal treatment may be counterproductive. The principle of reciprocity in FDI often means the aligning of regulations upwards (reciprocal treatment in trade is often different as it levels down trade provisions).

Major EU investors in the third countries were Britain, Germany, France and the Netherlands during the period 1984–94 (Table 3.6). These countries were, at the same time, the major destination countries for the extra-EU FDI. In addition to these countries, external investors were also interested in the Benelux countries and Spain. The experience of Spain is valuable for other EU-rim countries. The country improved its infrastructure, it has an unimpeded access to the EU market and has a relatively abundant qualified and cheap (according to the EU standards) labour force. As such, it provided an attractive springboard for the external TNCs that are interested in operating on a pan-EU market. The noted enthusiasm of external investors in Spain points to a relative spread of external FDI in the EU.

EU countries started slowly to invest in the transition countries of central and eastern Europe. This is the only region in the world where international business has not yet expanded on a large scale (Africa apart). Therefore, some TNCs may wish to locate a part of their activities in that area instead of certain regions in the EU. Southern member countries of the EU may feel neglected because of outgoing FDI into the transition region, no matter how small these flows are. Such fears are, however, exaggerated. The southern region of the EU should not worry, at least not in the medium term. Most of the transition countries still have such distortions that it will take them quite some time to restructure. The alleged general 'exodus' of FDI and EU jobs is not well founded, although some EU industries may have certain adjustment pressures. If relatively low wages are the decisive factor for FDI in the transition countries, the EU would have already been flooded with cheap goods from those countries. Factors other than wages influence competitiveness of firms. They include productivity and capital stock. Therefore, southern EU member countries are still ahead of most of the transition countries in these matters. In addition, the Mediterranean region of the EU still has other advantages over the transition countries. Southern EU countries have direct access to the growing single EU market with more than

300 million consumers whose wealth is growing. They also have hard currencies, liberal treatment of TNCs and unrestricted capital mobility. These are features that most of the transition countries still lack.

Another advantage of the Mediterranean region of the EU is found in the economies of scale. This region of the EU is characterized by a lot of SMEs. Those firms have the chance to grow efficiently in the single market of the EU and take advantages of economies of scale. Large European firms have already taken most of the advantages which accrue from economies of scale. Hence, SMEs and countries in which they prevail have long-term potential for greater gains from the 1992 Programme.

The newly industrialized countries may also wish to invest in the EU in order to be present in a growing and affluent market, and also to have access to new technology. As for the TNCs from transition countries located in the EU, they can be expected to be active in trade-supporting services. Other than that, most of those TNCs are not expected to have either the technological or managerial or financial capacity to enter the EU on a large scale in another way in the near future.

6   Conclusion

A popular perception, based on shoddy economics, is that the export of goods is beneficial for the country and, therefore, it needs to be supported, while (certain) imports are perceived to be dangerous as they might jeopardize the national output and employment potential.[43] FDI is, however, treated in a different way. Outflows are being deterred as there is a fear that exporting capital means exporting exports and exporting jobs, while inflows are welcomed!

Capital mobility has its costs and benefits. If these effects are desirable, they should be stimulated, otherwise they should be taxed and/or controlled. Simultaneous inflows and outflows of FDI in integrated countries is possible and quite likely. This was confirmed in 1989 when intra-EU flows of FDI became more important than EU investment in third countries. FDI inflow may, however, be significant even without formal integration. Just look at trans-Atlantic FDI flows. TNCs primarily follow the opportunities for making profits in large and growing markets in the long term. Therefore, regional economic integration is *a*, rather than *the* cause of FDI.

The loss of the international competitive position of the EU in relation to the US, Japan and the newly industrialized countries (in several lines of production) in the 1970s and 1980s, has increased both interest in and the need for the strengthening of the competitiveness of TNCs from the EU. These TNCs are the key actors in improving the international competitiveness of the EU. Ambitious public research programmes in the EU, whose funds well exceed similar ones in the US and Japan, can help the EU first to catch up and later to improve its position *vis-à-vis* its major international competitors.

American FDI in the EU was market seeking in the 1950s and 1960s. The same was the case with Japanese FDI in the 1970s and 1980s. As EU consumers were not able to purchase what they wanted because of NTBs, Japanese TNCs invested in the EU in order to satisfy an existing and growing local demand. TNCs from both source countries have always been looking at the EU market as a single unit. Their advantages over the local EU enterprises included in certain cases not only a superior capability to innovate products and technologies, manage multi-plant production and supply, but also a willingness, experience and ability to serve consumers from close proximity, rather than through exports which was often the favourite method of operation of many national firms in the EU. There is, however, at least one difference between the Japanese and American FDI in the EU. Half of Japanese FDI was concentrated in banking and insurance in the early 1990s. At the same time, more than a half of American FDI was in the manufacturing industry. Therefore, Japanese FDI has relatively little impact, at present, on the EU manufacturing industry,[44] while the same is not true for the American TNCs (Buigues and Jacquemin, 1992, p. 22). This focus by Japanese investors may come as a surprise since Japan has the advantage in electronics and vehicles. A concentration of Japanese FDI in financial services (relying on human, rather than physical, capital) both in the EU and the US is, however, a partial reflection of Japanese balance-of-payments surpluses and the appreciation of the yen.[45]

In order to avoid the weakening of the competitive position of EU firms in global markets, the EU may follow two courses, although there may be a strong appeal to employ a mix of the two. First, the EU may increase protection of the domestic firms against foreign TNCs through measures such as rules of origin, local content requirements and other TRIMs. Second, the EU may open its domestic market and welcome foreign, in particular, Japanese TNCs to settle their operations in the EU. As widely argued, EU firms in a sizeable part of its manufacturing industry are less efficient than their counterparts in the US and Japan. Suppose that the EU adopts a liberal economic policy. If the EU firms adjust and withstand competition from foreign TNCs, they may, in relative terms, gain more from market liberalization than their foreign competitors.

The incomplete internal market in the EU was the major cause of a suboptimal production structure in the region. All economic agents, including TNCs, behave as welfare maximizing units in the long term, subject to the given conditions. These private agents should not be criticized for actions that may not conform to public objectives. The completion of the internal market in the EU which included a removal of NTBs assisted in a rationalization of production and enhanced the location-specific advantages of the EU. This will continue to increase both the size and growth of the EU market, which could, in turn, further increase investment expenditure in the region.

As one of the major players in the international capital mobility scene, the EU would like to see multilateral rules for FDI. These rules would include: the right of foreigners to invest and operate competitively in all sectors of the economy; only few exceptions to the general rule should be allowed; there should be no discrimination of foreign investors based on their origin; a 'stand still' commitment would prevent the introduction of new restrictions; and there should be a 'roll-back' principle to gradually eliminate national (or group) measures that run counter to the liberalization of FDI rules.

NOTES

1 The reader interested in the issue of the relation between trade and FDI is invited to consult UNCTAD (1996, pp. 71–125).

2 A high concentration of factors (designers in northern Italy, chemical engineers in Basle [Switzerland], financial experts in London and New York, or computer scientists in California or Boston) will create an additional comparative advantage which will, in turn, enhance trade.

3 Different languages are not an insurmountable problem for big TNCs. Philips, ABB and SKF use English as their corporate language, rather than Dutch, German or Swedish.

4 In a static world, free immigration of labour lowers (or prevents the increase of) the real wages of certain wage-earners in the receiving country.

5 There is a fine difference between immigration and immigrant policy. The former refers to the admission of foreigners into the receiving country. An immigrant policy deals with the treatment of resident foreigners. Neither of the two policies is well grasped in the EU countries.

6 It is estimated that labour is almost three times more mobile among the federal states in the US if compared with labour mobility within individual EU states. There are relatively good reasons for the American geographical rootlessness. The US is a very homogenized country indeed. If one pushes it to the limit, no matter where you go, the supply of goods and services is almost identical. Most American cities, towns and villages look similar. This may be one of the most important reasons why the majority of Americans move so easily and so often.

7 The rights of non-EU migrant workers depend on the bilateral agreement between their country of origin and the country of destination.

8 Unrestricted immigration in current conditions is out of the question. A highly restrictive immigration policy would tend to increase illegal immigration. One of the consequences of illegal immigration is insecurity and exploitation of the migrants, hence it has to be discouraged.

9 Migrants include migrant workers and members of their families that reside with them in the country of destination.

10 The difference from the data presented in Table 3.1 and the ones by Straubhaar (1988) come from the likely underestimation of the stock of migrants by Straubhaar, who relied only on the working permits issued by the country of destination.

11 The Dublin Convention (1990) of the 12 member countries provided for a joint procedure for asylum seekers. The Convention has reconfirmed the Schengen Agreement on this issue.

12 Benelux, France, Germany, Portugal and Spain. Austria, Denmark, Finland, Greece, Italy and Sweden signed the Schengen Agreement, but they have not

yet implemented it. Norway and Iceland will enjoy the benefits of enhanced cooperation with the Schengen group.

13 The French refused to implement the agreement and used the argument that terrorists might escape the vigilance of some of their co-signatories. In truth, France's hostility predated its latest experience of terrorism and owed more to the right-wing National Front's criticism of Schengen.

14 Important questions remain: Is the size of the Mediterranean sea sufficient to protect Europe from those troubles? Does the EU have to do more to prevent an uncontrolled mass immigration from the region? Does that include investment in the democratic institutions in these countries and investment in production in order to keep people employed there? Does it include more concessions in trade to these countries? Would that jeopardize the EU textile industry which relies in part on labour imported from the south Mediterranean counties?

15 Increased international mobility of factors, increased international intra-firm transactions, expanding international cooperative arrangements between firms, increasing importance of knowledge, as well as a reduction in transport and communication costs, support the process of 'globalization' and are constituent parts of it. In these circumstances, individual actions of national governments may not increase global welfare (pollution is an example). In those circumstances, certain supranational rules may be necessary in order to deliver more beneficial outcomes.

16 Trade is relatively more concentrated within regions than FDI. This suggests that trade plays a more prominent role in intra-regional integration arrangements, while FDI has a greater influence on global integration (UNCTAD, 1993, p. 7).

17 The pace of international trade liberalization since the 1960s, as well as the extension of the GATT into new areas such as services and agriculture might have been much slower in the absence of challenge posed by the progress in EU integration. The debate should not be between regionalism and multilateralism, but rather between liberalism and interventionism (Blackhurst and Henderson, 1993, p. 412).

18 As for the amount of FDI, the total world outward stock (the production potential) was an estimated $3.2 trillion in 1996, while the world-wide inflows of FDI in 1996 reached $350 billion. The distribution of the stock of FDI is asymmetrical. Around three-quarters of FDI stock is located in developed countries, while two-thirds of FDI stock is concentrated in 10 countries (UNCTAD, 1997). The sectoral distribution of FDI reveals that the industries that are absorbing the largest slices of FDI are those dominated by high technology and highly qualified personnel. The reasons for such a distribution may be found in the excessive transaction costs of arm's-length contacts through the market, so internalization of those links within a firm seems to be a better business choice.

19 In an early study, Weber (1909) offered two basic reasons why firms 'go to produce abroad'. The primary determinant is the achievement of lower labour and transport costs, while the secondary element is the benefit of large-scale production.

20 For example, governments may change over a certain period of time the availability, quality and cost of the domestic factors. The disposable tools for this policy include training of labour and education of management, R&D, science, transport and communication infrastructure and tax policies.

21 Transfer of profits out of the country takes place when TNCs do not find the country in question a promising location for the reinvestment of earnings. Such a transfer may send a warning signal to the government that something is wrong in the economy and that something needs to be done about it.

22 Intra-company pricing refers to transactions among related units of the same firm. Not every manipulation of transfer prices increases the overall profits of the

entire company, as these extra revenues stem from sales to outside customers (Plasschaert, 1994, p. 1).

23 Trade in services is expanding. Monitoring internal prices for services is a much more complex task than inspecting the same prices for goods by the employment of free market criteria.

24 Firms are reluctant to comment and release data on their internal prices. Hence, there is a black hole in this area of research.

25 Tax avoidance is a means that does not break any laws as this might be permitted according to the positive regulations. Tax evasion is different as it violates laws. In practice, the difference between the two practices is often ambiguous.

26 TNCs that come from the US and operate in the EU reported an annual R&D of almost $2,500 per employee in 1989. In contrast, Euro-affiliates of the Japanese TNCs reported R&D per employee of around $725 in the same year (Gittelman *et al.*, 1992, p. 18). The reasons for such behaviour of the Japanese TNCs include a relatively strong headquarters effect as the Japanese FDI in Europe is a fairly novel feature compared with the FDI from the US that has been present in the region on a larger scale since the 1950s. In addition, Japanese TNCs may be more involved in the EU in relatively mature manufacturing industries and services where R&D expenditure is not as high as in other activities.

27 Investment in natural resources has three distinct features. First, the location of non-renewable resources is not mutable; second, investments require huge amounts of capital which is linked with significant economies of scale; and three, processing of minerals is linked with a considerable consumption of energy.

28 For example, Pirelli (Italy) coordinates and guarantees its global financial duties from a Swiss affiliate which is in charge of finance for the whole corporation. The US affiliate of Siemens (Germany) transmitted daily financial data to headquarters, which is in charge of global financial management (UNCTAD, 1993, p. 124).

29 The introduction of a new good does not depend only on the fixed costs and expected benefits, but also on substitution and complementarity with the goods that already exist on the market.

30 The role of government as an organizing force in a market economy is increasingly being reexamined. Although there is an intention to reduce it's intervention, the fact is that countries in which the government has exerted a strong and positive influence have had the most impressive economic performance over the past two decades (Dunning, 1994a, p. 1).

31 According to an influential view, no matter what a government does in order to influence competitiveness and increase exports in the short run, would still cause the adjustment of the exchange rate and factor prices in the long run (Johnson and Krauss, 1973, p. 240). The new theory disputed such an approach and argued that in the presence of increasing returns to scale, externalities and the economies of learning, the policy of the government does matter. Such a policy may bring, if handled properly, irreversible advantages for the country in question.

32 In order to intervene/subsidize in an intelligent way, the government needs a lot of information that is quite costly to obtain. This concerns not only information about technology and demand, but also the reactions of other governments and TNCs. If fortunate, strategic policy is a magnificent policy. In practice, a subsidy in one country may provoke retaliation in another in the form of a subsidy or a countervailing duty. The retaliation and counter-retaliation chain makes everyone worse off. Integration may offer certain advantages to developing countries in a situation like that. It may inspire these countries to negotiate the distribution of strategic industries within the area or attract TNCs in order to maximize positive externalities and reduce unnecessary subsidies. The basic argument for intervention may be that without intervention in the area and owing to imperfections,

there may be *under-investment* in strategic industry. If, however, intervention is lousy, *over-investment* may be the consequence.

33 For example, trade within the EU is to a large extent of an intra-industry character. It is much more driven by economies of scale, than by the 'classic' comparative advantages of those countries.

34 If pushed to the limit, a national reaction to a monopoly in a foreign country is the creation of a national monopoly. That is fighting fire with fire (Curzon Price, 1993, p. 394)!

35 In the situation where TNCs do not dominate in the economy of a country or an integrated group of countries, then, of course, their impact may be marginal. The situation, however, in virtually all present-day regional groupings of developing countries is that TNCs play a dominant role (Robson, 1987, p. 209).

36 Educated management and a trained labour force (domestic human capital) is what matters for the country, rather than ownership of the business (Reich, 1990). Tyson (1991) disagreed with such view and argued that ownership still mattered. This view is, however, opposed to the traditional US stance that favours free trade and flow of capital.

37 'Fifteen years from now it is quite possible that the world's third largest industrial power, just after the United States and Russia, will not be Europe, but *American Industry in Europe*. Already, in the ninth year of the Common Market, this European market is basically American in organization' (Servan-Schreiber, 1969, p. 3).

38 The diversity of views expressed in the debate on the effect of European integration on FDI were surveyed by Yannopoulos (1990).

39 Government incentives influenced TNCs such as Ford to make new investments in the north west of the country and Wales. Honda, Nissan and Toyota benefited from public grants as they settled in regions with unemployment problems. However, those allowances were equally available in Britain to other firms from the EU or third countries, whether they were from car-production or other industries.

40 One has to be careful when interpreting the data for a country such as Luxembourg (or Switzerland). Such countries often act only as intermedies for the inflow and outflow of funds.

41 There was an increased flow of FDI in the EU-rim countries in 1991.

42 More than a half of all Japanese FDI is located in the US.

43 Through trade a country acquires useful things from abroad. Therefore imports is a gain, rather than a cost. To pay for imports, the country has to 'send' its useful goods and services abroad. In these terms exports is a cost, rather than a gain!

44 Toyota, however, plans to invest $1.5 billion and build a plant in Lens (France) in the near future. The capacity of the plant will be around 200,000 cars a year. Cars would be marketed from France all around Europe. From Nissan's British annual production of around 220,000 cars, only around 30 per cent are sold in Britain itself (*The Financial Times*, 18 March 1997, p. 2).

45 A distinct feature of Japanese FDI in manufacturing is that Japanese TNCs tend to invest in countries that have a certain advantage in the target manufacturing industry. For instance, Japanese FDI in machinery and precision instruments went to Germany, FDI in the production of cars went to Britain, while FDI in glass, stone and clay products went to Belgium (Yamawaki, 1991, p. 232).

4   Economic Union

None of the types of international economic integration may exist in its pure theoretical form. A customs union does not only deal with the elimination of tariffs and quotas and the introduction of the common external tariff, but also with industrial policy and specialization. It may also deal with NTBs and FDI from partner countries, as well as from outsiders. Free mobility of labour in a common market does not only require the elimination of discrimination of labour from partner countries, but also some degree of harmonization of social policy (social security, unemployment benefits, pension funds, vocational training). Without harmonization of these issues, distortions may be created which may induce labour to move in response to other signals than purely to its relative abundance/ scarcity and returns. The buffer against unacceptable costs which accrue from the free migration of labour and flow of capital can be found in regional policy. Therefore, common markets may have some elements of economic unions. In addition, an economic union need not be complete. The basic argument in favour of an economic union is found in its potential to increase the efficiency in the allocation of resources in relation to a common market.

The creation of an economic union can be defended by the same arguments which are used in favour of the creation, implementation and protection of a single economic policy in a country which has different regions. It can also be attacked by the same arguments that say that one policy for different regions does not make sense (as often heard in Canada). This chapter starts with a section on monetary policy because that is the field where the impact of international economic integration is quickest and most obvious. It is followed by a section on fiscal policy, which is necessary for the proper operation of an economic union. Industrial and regional (as well as social) policies are crucial for the survival of an economic union. While industrial policy is directed towards the creation of new wealth, regional (and social) policies are turned towards the distribution of already created wealth.

I MONETARY POLICY

1 Introduction

Monetary policy is a key element in the economic strategy of an economic and monetary union (EMU). As it is one of the most sensitive economic policies, the Treaties establishing the EU made special references to these issues. In fact, the Maastricht Treaty is almost entirely about the EMU. Integration of monetary policies in the EU is necessary not only for the stability of rates of exchange, prices, balance of payments and investment decisions, but also for the protection of the already achieved level of integration, as well as for the motivation for further integration in the future.

Relatively small countries may have an incentive to integrate into the monetary field in order to avoid the monetary domination of large countries. The joint money may overcome the disadvantage (vulnerability on external monetary shocks) of atomized currencies and it may become a rival to the moneys of larger countries in international currency markets. A common currency among the integrated countries may become an outward symbol, but it is not a necessary condition for a successful monetary union.

A monetary system between countries should be distinguished from a monetary union. Countries in a *monetary system* link their currencies together and act as a single unit in relation to third currencies. A *monetary union* among countries is an ambitious enterprise. It exists if there is either a single money (*de jure* EMU) or an irrevocable fixity among the rates of exchange of the participating countries together with a free mobility of goods and factors (*de facto* EMU). This prevents any alterations in the rates of exchange as indirect methods of non-tariff protection or as a subsidy to exports. It also means that the member countries should seek recourse to the capital markets in order to find funds to cover their budget deficit. Within an EMU, it should be as easy, for example, for a Frenchman to pay a German within Europe, as it is for a Welshman to pay an Englishman within the United Kingdom (Meade, 1973, p. 162).

A monetary union requires the following elements:

- convertibility (at least internal) of the participating countries' currencies;
- centralization of monetary policy;
- a single central bank or a system of central banks that control stabilization policies;
- unified performance on the international financial markets;
- capital market integration;
- identical rates of inflation;
- harmonization of fiscal systems;
- replacement of balance-of-payments disequilibria with regional imbalances;

- similar levels of economic development or a well-endowed fund for transfers of real resources to the less developed regions; and
- continuous consultation about and coordination of economic policies among the participating countries, as well as the adjustment of wages on the union level.

There may exist, also, a pseudo exchange rate union (Corden, 1972b). In this kind of union, member countries fix the exchange rates of their currencies and freely accept each others' monies. However, since there is no pooling of foreign reserves and no central monetary authority, such a union is not stable. Since there is no mechanism to coordinate national policies, an individual member country may choose to absorb real resources from the union partners by running with them a balance-of-payments deficit. In addition, such a country may change the effective exchange rates of other members by creating a deficit in the union's balance of payments with the rest of the world. A full EMU is not vulnerable to such instability. Foreign exchange rates are pooled and monetary policy is operated by a single monetary authority. In a pseudo exchange rate union, there is imperfect coordination of national monetary policies, but in a full EMU the problem is solved by policy centralization (Cobham, 1989, p. 204).

This chapter starts with the traditional single-criterion theory of monetary integration. A superior, that is, cost–benefit model, further develops consideration of monetary integration. Parallel currencies are presented before the analysis of the past and present monetary arrangements in the EU, in particular the Maastricht Treaty type of EMU that has nothing to do with the theoretical criteria for monetary integration.

2   Traditional model

2.1   *Exchange rate regimes*

Both flexible and fixed exchange rates have their virtues and vices. The benefits of a flexible exchange rate include their free floating according to demand and supply. This improves the allocation of resources and in liberal societies removes the need for government interference. There is no need whatsoever for foreign currency reserves, because balance-of-payments disequilibria are adjusted automatically. A country is free to pursue independently its national priorities regarding inflation, employment and interest rate targets. Any possible mistake in economic policy may be straightened out by continuous and smooth changes in rates of exchange.

There are, of course, several arguments against free floating. The most serious one is that this rate of exchange divides the economies of different countries. As such, it reduces the benefits of economies of scale. The floating rates of exchange stimulate speculation, uncertainty and instability. All the alleged criticisms about a smooth adjustment without the need for changes in reserves were disproved during the 1970s. Any change in the rate of exchange would have an impact on home prices. Its repercussions would be swifter in the countries which have a relatively greater degree of openness. There is, however, another problem with the floating rate of exchange. This is overshooting. Although some changes in economic policy are only announced and not yet implemented, the floating rates of exchange move and overshoot their long-run equilibrium.

The objections to fixed exchange rates are a mirror image of the virtues of the flexible rates. They include the following. Fixed exchange rates do not permit every country to pursue independently its own policy goals regarding employment and inflation. Countries have to subordinate their monetary policy to the requirements of the external balance. When the time comes for adjustment in the rate of exchange, it may be relatively large and disruptive in relation to the smooth, potentially frequent and small changes in the exchange rate in the case of the free float. The system of fixed rates of exchange requires reserves of foreign currencies for intervention in the currency market in order to defend the fixed parity. These funds may be derived from alternative productive uses.

The arguments in favour of fixed rates of exchange are those which justify the introduction of a single currency in a country. This system stimulates cooperation among countries as opposed to floating rates which encourage 'economic nationalism'. The most important feature of fixed rates of exchange is that they bring stability; prices are less inflationary; the allocation of resources is improved because decisions about investment are not delivered exclusively on the basis of short-term market signals; uncertainty is reduced and trade flows are stabilized. All this stimulates economic integration among countries. That is why the establishment of a free internal market in the EU in 1993 'needs' to be followed by a monetary union.

There is no general rule about which system of exchange rates is better. If a country has a balance-of-payments deficit, then it has to restore competitiveness. This can be done by a reduction in private and public consumption, so it requires cutting wages directly, or devaluation, which in turn cuts wages indirectly. But note, the choice of the exchange system here does *not* play a role at all. Reductions in real income are necessary under either exchange rate system.

It is a formidable task to offer a definite conclusion about the 'correct' system of exchange rates. The above choices contrast costs against benefits of a particular system. Once, when one comes to practice, the choice may often be between the costs of one system and the costs of another. In such a situation it comes as no surprise that economists can not be unanimous. Small countries may overcome, in an EMU, their disadvantage which stems from their relatively small economic size and thus those countries can create an area of economic stability. They may also reap the fruits of economic cooperation in an area where expectations may have a significant degree of accuracy.

Discussion about the exchange rate regimes (fixed, floating or managed), sheds light only on one side of a country's monetary policy in an international context. The other side deals with domestic monetary policy. Linkages between national money supply and rates of interest, as well as price levels must be also considered. Otherwise, the debate may be in vain.

Monetary integration means in its highest form that everybody within an EMU is free to use their own currency for any kind of payments to partners. The minimum definition of monetary integration is absence of restrictions, while the maximum definition requires the use of a single currency (Machlup, 1979, p. 23). Monetary integration may exist even without the integration of markets for goods and the integration of goods markets may exist without monetary integration. The former case is exemplified by countries in the West African Monetary Union which have a single currency, the CFA franc, and a similar monetary policy to France (their former colonial master), but there is little real integration of markets for goods, services and factors among them. The latter case may be found in the EFTA, where member countries have integrated their markets for manufactured goods, but there is no formal integration of the monetary policy among them.

2.2   Factor mobility

The traditional single criterion model of monetary integration started with the theory of optimum currency areas. This theory was a purely academic exercise during the 1960s. After a long while this theory was revived in the early 1990s. That was prompted by the intention to bolster the European Monetary System (EMS), as well as by the break-up of formerly federal states in central and eastern Europe, in particular the former USSR, which created problems of how to handle the new and separate currencies in most of the newly independent states which are 'small' and have their own currency for the first time in their history.

The theory of optimum currency areas was started by Mundell (1961). Economic adjustment can take place on international and national levels. On the international level, the basic issue of adjustment is whether the countries with trade deficits will accept inflation or deflation in their respective economies. On the national level, the pace of inflation in countries that have a single currency, but several regions, is regulated by the desire of the central authorities to permit unemployment in regions with a deficit. If the objective is the achievement of a greater degree of employment and stable prices in a world where there is more than one currency area, then this requires floating exchange rates based on regional instead of national currencies. As with Mundell, a region is the optimum currency area. Factor mobility is the criterion that determines a region. Within the currency areas factors are mobile, while between them, factors are immobile. Fluctuating rates of exchange are the adjustment mechanism between various currency areas, while factor mobility is the equilibrating mechanism within them.

Factor mobility as the criterion for an optimum currency area ought to be considered carefully. The difficulty with this model is that a region may be an economic unit, while the domain of a currency is an expression of national sovereignty which seldom coincides with a region.[1] In addition, factor mobility may change over time. Strong integration of goods and factor markets can tighten the budget constraint. Borrowing today implies higher taxes tomorrow. If factors (labour and capital) are free to move, that may give incentives to mobile factors to move to lower-tax jurisdictions which would erode the tax base in a high-tax country. Investors know that today's ability to borrow from a government is limited by its capability to tax tomorrow, and also its ability to tax tomorrow is restricted by factor mobility. Hence, investors will reduce or refuse their lending to governments threatening to exceed their borrowing capacity. The higher the integration of factor markets, the sooner this takes place (Eichengreen, 1993, p. 1335).

Mobility of capital is sensitive to the degree of economic activity and the outlook for economic prosperity. In the nineteenth century, labour and capital were flowing towards the Americas and Australia as the areas of promising development which needed those factors most. During the 'golden' 1960s, however, labour and capital were flowing towards the growing developed and relatively rich regions and countries.

Labour is not a homogeneous factor. Its full mobility may exist only in relatively small geographic areas or within a very specialized professional category. The experience of the EU(6) provides the best proof of this. The flow of labour in the EU in the 1960s and up to the mid-1970s came mostly from workers from the Mediterranean countries that were not members of the EU (with the exception of Italy). Those labour flows may not be taken as intra-EU labour mobility.

Regions within a single country grow at different rates. The same holds for countries in an EMU. These developments cause strain which is exacerbated if there are fewer opportunities for adjustment, such as factor mobility and fiscal compensations. However, it does not yet make a very sensible case for northern Italy (e.g. Padania) to have a separate currency, which creates a separate economy from the southern (Mafia ridden, subsidy consuming and Vatican dominated) part of the country. The cost of such monetary disintegration could be relatively high. However, quite a number of 'Padanians' have a very different opinion about the issue.

2.3 Openness

The second major approach focused attention on the degree of openness of a country (McKinnon, 1963). Commodities in a country may be distributed between tradables and non-tradables. The ratio between these goods determines the degree of its openness to trade. As a rule, the smaller the country, the greater the relative degree of its trade interaction with other countries. A high degree of openness embodies relatively high specialization of a country and it may be taken as the criterion for the optimum currency area.

When the tradable goods represent a significant part of home consumption (unless most of the consumer's goods are imported), then by a change in the rate of exchange, a country may hardly change real wages. Such a country (presumably small) is advised to enter into an EMU for it may not be an optimum currency area as a single unit (Corden, 1972). The greater a country's openness, the smaller the chances for the effective independent use of exchange rates as an instrument for economic stabilization.

Relatively small economies are advised to link their currencies with the currency of their major trading partner. This is the case when the former colonies link their currency to that of their former master (e.g. the CFA franc zone) or when some of the transition economies of central and eastern Europe link their currencies to the German mark. The second piece of advice to small economies which conduct a significant part of their trade among themselves is to link their currencies together. In the case of a single currency all financial dealings may be simpler. This is a part of the reason why the fifty federal states in the US may not be able to separately issue and operate their own currencies in an efficient way.[2] A similar observation may be applied to the sixteen federal states in Germany or the twenty-three Swiss cantons. Further evidence can be found in the serious problems in handling monetary affairs in most of the independent states that emerged from the former USSR.

If small open economies operate near full employment, then internal fiscal measures are advised for the adjustment of the balance of payments. Fixed exchange rates will be more productive in this case than flexible ones as they would have a less damaging effect on prices. A variation in the exchange rate will have a small response to the change in the level of imports because of high dependency on imports. Therefore, a variation in the rate of exchange should be much higher than in those countries which are relatively less open.

An alteration in the exchange rate will have a direct and significant impact on real income. Consumers and trade unions will request indexation of wages with a resulting change in prices and the exchange rate. If money illusion exists, the impression that changes in nominal (money) wages are identical to changes in real income, then a change in the exchange rate may be an effective means for adjusting balance of payments. However, money illusion is not a long-term phenomenon. It is no longer even a short-term event. An alteration in the exchange rate may not be effectively employed for the adjustment of balance of payments independently of other instruments. Flexible rates of exchange may be an efficient means for the adjustment of balance of payments of relatively large economies which are linked by small trade relations.

The assumptions in this model are that the equilibrium in the balance of payments is caused by microeconomic changes in demand and supply and, also, that prices in the outside world are stable. The argument about the relative stability of prices in the outside world cannot be substantiated for the period lasting around two decades since the early 1970s. When the prices in the outside world are fluctuating, that is directly conveyed to home prices through a fixed exchange rate. The openness of an economy may be the criterion for an optimum currency area if the outside world is more stable than the economic situation in a small open economy. Fixed exchange rates may force small open economies to pursue a more rigorous economic policy than under the fluctuating exchange rates regime which permits a policy of monetary 'indiscipline'. If money illusion does not exist, then the possibility of altering the exchange rate as an adjustment instrument becomes almost useless.

The Benelux countries and Denmark have participated in the EMS since its creation. Other small European countries (for example, Austria, Finland, Norway, Sweden and Switzerland) initially decided to stay out of the EMS and manage their exchange rates unilaterally, although these countries pay close attention to the developments in the EMS. The membership of most of those countries in the EU would make them strong insiders in the system. The argument of openness fails to explain why these countries still have national control over their exchange rate in spite of strong trade relations with the member countries of the EMS. In addition, it fails to explain why relatively large countries such as Germany and France opted for the EMS. However, the basic flaw of the optimum currency area theory is that it fails to distinguish between the case for fixed exchange rates and the situation when separate states join together in a common currency (McKinnon, 1994, p. 61).

2.4 Diversification

The third major contribution stated that countries whose production is diversified do not have to change their terms of trade with foreign countries as often as the less diversified countries (Kenen, 1969). An external shock in the form of a reduction in foreign demand for a country's major export item may have a relatively smaller impact on the diversified country's employment than on a specialized country's economy and employment. Finally, links between home and foreign demand, as well as export and investment, are weaker in the diversified country than in a specialized one. Large and frequent exchange rate changes are not necessary for a diversified country because of the overlap in the reduction and increase in demand for various export goods. This overlap may keep the proceeds from exports at a relatively stable level. In conclusion, Kenen suggested that fixed rates of exchange are suitable for diversified countries. Diversification is his criterion for the optimum currency area. It helps the stabilization of home investment and adjustment of the economy to external shocks. The US may be the closest example of such an economy. Countries with specialized economies and relatively low levels of diversification have a need to belong to currency areas with flexible rates of exchange. Such countries are more vulnerable to external shocks than are diversified economies. Examples may be found in Denmark, Iceland, New Zealand and most of the African countries.

While McKinnon deals with internal shocks to an economy, Kenen considers external ones. Kenen's argument may be weakened in the situation where the reduction in foreign demand occurs during a general fall in demand during recession. This reduces total demand, so a country's diversification does not help much in mitigating the fall in the demand for exports.

2.5   *Other strands*

Coordination of economic policies can be a criterion for a EMU (Werner, 1970). Economic policies which are not coordinated among countries may be a major reason for the disturbance in the equilibrium of the balance of payments. Coordination of economic, in particular, monetary policies, from a supranational centre requires political will on the part of the participating countries. A declaration towards such an objective was made in the Maastricht Treaty.

One criterion for monetary integration may be a similar level of inflation among the potential member countries (Fleming, 1971). Diverging ratios of employment to inflation among these countries will cause hardship. Countries with a balance-of-payments surplus would be driven to accept a higher level of inflation than when they are free to choose this ratio. Conversely, countries with deficits may be asked to tolerate a higher level of unemployment than they would be willing to accept if they were free to choose this level.

An optimum currency area may be defined as a region in which no part insists on creating money and having a monetary policy of its own (Machlup, 1979, p. 71). A monetary union which imposes minimum costs on the participating countries may be called an optimum currency area (Robson, 1983, p. 143). An optimum currency area may be alternatively defined as an area in which the net benefits of integration (e.g. increase in welfare in the form of greater stability in prices and smaller disturbances coming from abroad), outweigh the costs (restraint to individual uses of monetary and fiscal policies) (Grubel, 1984, p. 39). An optimum currency area aims at identifying a group of countries within which it is optimal to have fixed exchange rates while, at the same time, keeping certain flexibility in the exchange rate with the third countries (Thygesen, 1987, p. 163). Very small currency conversion costs and openness is likely to make the EU an optimal currency area, while high levels of government spending will make the EU less likely so (Canzoneri and Rogers, 1990, p. 422). An optimum currency area may also be defined as one that attains the macroeconomic objectives of internal balance (low unemployment and inflation) and external balance (a sustainable position in the balance of payments) (Tavlas, 1993a, p. 32).

The notion of an optimum currency area is theoretical, rather than practical. A region may be an economic unit which does not necessarily coincide with the domain of a currency. An optimum currency area may be able to sustain itself on its own. Its definition may ask for liberalization of all activities within it and its protection against the outside world. Despite their relevant arguments, these definitions can hardly be applied to countries in the real world, since the states are constituted in a sub-optimal way, so that full economic efficiency (regardless of the external world) can seldom, if ever, be achieved. A single criterion model has a narrower scope. Therefore, it is unable to present the costs and benefits of a EMU. The next task is to amend this shortcoming.

3 Costs and Benefits

3.1 Issues

A more practical and fruitful way to the analysis of an EMU is to study the optimum economic policy area, rather than the optimum currency area. A single state becomes increasingly ineffective as an independent policy-making unit in modern times of continuous changes in technology, relatively easy and cheap dissemination of information and frequent market changes. This is true for all countries in the world, but it is not true for all of them equally. Therefore, not all of them seek international solutions to their national problems. In a situation where economic problems assume global proportions there is only one optimum policy area: the world (Panić, 1988, pp. 317–330). The most pressing international economic problems can not be solved by countries acting in isolation. The solutions to these problems can be found in coordinated national economic management. A system of safeguards which would include assistance in the form of transfer of (real) resources to the countries which experience difficulties, is an essential feature for the survival of an efficient multilateral system of trade and payments.

The shortcomings of the traditional single-criterion and optimum-currency model of international monetary integration may be overcome by the 'new theory' of monetary integration that relies on the cost–benefit model. This model offers more satisfactory policy implications. The costs which may be brought by a country's participation in monetary integration may be traced to the losses of a country's right to alter independently its rate of exchange, its ratio between inflation and unemployment, its ability to handle regional development policy, as well as its seigniorage. Monetary integration brings a number of benefits. These include a dismissal of the exchange problems within the group of countries in the arrangement, an increase in influence in monetary affairs and an increase in monetary stability. The larger the integrated area, the larger the gains. Both the costs and benefits of monetary integration are analysed next.

3.2   Costs

First, the creation of a supranational body to conduct monetary policy (money supply, rate of interest and rate of exchange) in an EMU may be perceived as a significant loss of the participating countries' national *sovereignty*. This is the first cost, which may provoke adverse political, as well psychological consequences in countries that take part in the arrangement. The most sensitive issue may be the loss of the right to alter independently the rate of exchange. The loss occurs fully against the currencies of partner countries and partially against other countries. A right, often used selfishly, is gone. However, the gains here come from the pooling of the monetary policies of the member countries that can exercise a much greater leverage over their monetary policy in comparison to the situation prior to integration.

When policy makers want to adjust the balance of payments by means of alterations in a country's rate of exchange, then the most critical issue is the fall in real wages. Labour may accept a fall in real wages under the condition that the other alternative is (longer-term) unemployment. A reduction in the rate of exchange introduces an increase in the price for imported goods, as well as for some home-produced goods and services. The impact of the devaluation depends on the openness of a country. A reduction in real wages brings an advantage in the cost of labour and a relative decrease in the price of export goods in the short run. This classical scenario may be seriously questioned. Money illusion no longer has a significant impact on labour. Every increase in inflation and corresponding fall in real wages, under the assumption that there is no change in productivity, encourages labour and concerned trade unions to demand an increase in wages. The short-term cost advantage of devaluation is eroded by such increases.

Devaluation as an instrument of economic policy may not alone eliminate deficits in the balance of payments. The government may state that its policy objective is not to use devaluation in the fight against inflation. Such a policy goal may act as an important incentive to firms to resist higher costs because their goods would become uncompetitive on the foreign and, potentially, home market, if trade were free. A recession may be another, although less desirable, cure for inflation. Shrinking markets give firms incentives to keep prices low, while rising unemployment forces trade unions to resist increases in wages.

Exchange rates started to float in the early 1970s and did so for a decade. The experience has provided sufficient evidence that a country's autonomy in a situation of floating exchange rates is overstated. The reason is that a majority of countries are small and open. This leads to the conclusion that the sole use of the exchange rate as the adjustment mechanism of the balance of payments is of limited significance. Fiscal policy[3] and labour mobility are necessary supplements. The devaluation of a national currency is a sign of failure to manage the economy soundly and carefully according to international standards. The standards of international economic prudence show that it is the national bureaucracy which is the only loser from the deprivation of the right to devalue the national currency. Therefore, the loss in autonomy in the management of a country's rate of exchange as a policy instrument is of little real significance.

If, however, the rate of exchange of a group of countries such as the EU is fixed to an anchor currency such as the German mark, as was the case in the EMS till August 1993, the situation can change. If international capital markets are free, the loss of autonomy in the fixing of the exchange market does not matter as long as the economic cycles match each other. If the cycles differ, as has been the case in the EU, partner countries may be reluctant to follow the monetary policy of the anchor currency, since it may not match the necessary policy actions of the other participating countries.

Second, it was argued that floating rates of exchange permit unconstrained *choices between unemployment and inflation* in a country. On those grounds, countries may seem to be free to pursue their own stabilization policies. An EMU constrains the independent national choice of the rates of inflation, unemployment and interest rate. This national choice, as a second cost of monetary integration, is constrained by the choice of other partner countries. A loss of the right to deal independently may significantly jeopardize national preferences regarding the possible choices. The country with relatively low inflation and a balance-of-payments surplus may, in accordance with its economic and political strength, impose its own goals on other partner countries, because this country has much less pressure to adjust than the other countries. A common currency levels the competitiveness of the group in the monetary field. If a region's factor productivity is lower than the average in the group, then the regional/country authorities will have to 'tolerate' unemployment. Labour mobility (outflow) may be a solution to the problem. The higher the labour mobility, the more diversified the output pattern, and the more flexible prices and wages, the smoother the adjustment. Applied to the EU, only the relative diversification of the economic structure may pass the test for a smooth adjustment. Other macroeconomic criteria (labour mobility and flexible wages) do not fare well at all.

This consideration has been examined with geometric rigour by de Grauwe (1975a). It was proven that countries differ regarding the position of their Phillips curves, rates of productivity growth and the preferences of governments between unemployment and inflation. These are the differences that explain why, in the absence of an EMU, rates of inflation among countries will be equal only by accident. For a smooth operation of an EMU, the condition is not only balanced growth, but also equal unemployment rates, otherwise the EMU may not survive without inter-country compensatory transfer of resources. The mere integration of economic policy goals may not be effective without agreement on the means for achieving the agreed targets. If countries cope with a common problem and employ different tools, the outcome of harmonization of economic policy objectives only may do more harm than good.

The Phillips curve suggests that there is a measurable, inverse relation between unemployment and inflation. The government could reduce unemployment by means of demand stimulus such as an increase in budget deficit while the price for this policy is increased inflation. In Friedman's model, the rate of unemployment is independent of the rate of inflation. The followers of this school criticize Phillips curve theory for not seeing that continuous inflationary policy provokes changes in expectations about future inflation. They argue that there is only one rate of unemployment which is consistent with a constant rate of inflation. That is the natural rate of unemployment or the non-accelerating inflation rate of unemployment (NAIRU). No matter what a government does, the rate of unemployment may not fall below the national NAIRU. However, this rate is not fixed. It is determined by real factors which include minimum wage legislation, tax policy, dole money, labour mobility, the impetus for vocational training, payroll taxes,[4] as well as the choice between work and leisure. In another words, the NAIRU is determined by the structure of the labour market, rather than the amount of demand. Most of these factors are influenced by economic policy. Every attempt to lower the rate of unemployment below the NAIRU by means of monetary expansion will only accelerate inflation. Hence, the loss of this economic policy choice is also of limited significance.

The main way to reduce unemployment is to reduce the NAIRU. It can be done by reducing the social security benefits below the minimum wage for unskilled labour, shortening the time during which these benefits apply and by control over the demands of trade unions. Economic policy should be active in combating unemployment. The long-term unemployed have obsolete experience and training which makes them less attractive to potential employers. These unemployed compete less vigorously on the labour market and place less downward pressure on wages. The NAIRU increases with the expansion of the long-term unemployed. Economic policy should withdraw social benefits from those who refuse vocational training and/or jobs with the exception of anyone beyond the agreed age. The problem of the EU and its member countries is that they have not dealt with the long-term unemployed. These countries handed relatively generous benefits for long periods to the unemployed. Almost a half of the unemployed in the EU are out of work for over a year, while the same figure in the US is around 10 per cent.

The Canadian experience during 1950–62 with a fluctuating rate of exchange is illustrative. Canada intended to have monetary independence in relation to the US. Theoretical arguments (illusions) about greater national independence and freedom regarding employment policy in a flexible exchange rate situation seemed attractive. Canadian hopes were high. At the end of this period a mismanaged government intervention succeeded in destabilizing prices in Canada and growth stagnated. The decision to abandon flexible exchange rates showed that the benefits in the stability of employment and economic independence are smaller than the cost paid in economic instability and efficiency. Given the contemporary capital market integration among open economies, significant differences in real interest rates among different countries may not exist. Hence an open economy may not rely independently on this instrument of economic policy. In a situation where two or more currencies are close substitutes and where there exists free capital mobility, the central banks of these countries can not conduct independent monetary policies even under fluctuating exchange rates. Small open economies may be advised to link their monetary policies to those of their major partners in trade and investment.

Third, a serious problem in a monetary union may be traced in the *inflow of capital* into the prosperous regions. The regions losing this capital expect compensatory transfers from the prosperous ones. Those countries which feel that their destiny is to be losers from an EMU would not enter such an arrangement. The system of transfers may be a bribe to these regions/countries to participate. When there are budget deficits and expenditure cuts, the funds for transfers may not be found easily. None the less, the gainers may be quite happy to compensate the losers and protect the net gains from integration.

Fourth is the loss (if it is a loss) of *seigniorage* (also called the inflation tax) in an EMU. Instead of selling debt, a government may print money and, hence, raise revenue in order to cover its budget deficit. The government is taxing (inflation tax) the holders of cash held by the public and the commercial banks' low-interest bearing deposits/reserves held at the central bank.[5] In an EMU, inflating a national way out of economic crisis is not possible. Therefore, a country in need is supposed either to reduce its debt or to sell more reserves, or both.

To sum up, an EMU introduces significant losses in the constitutional autonomy of participating states, but real autonomy to conduct independent monetary policy for a small open country in the situation of convertibility, synchronized economic cycles and openness for trade and investment will remain almost intact.

3.3   Benefits

The benefits of monetary integration are numerous and intuitive in their nature. They are hardly quantifiable and are difficult to comprehend by the non-economist. The most important benefit of monetary integration is that it improves the integration of markets for goods, services and factors. Exchange rate risk for trade flows among the integrated countries is eliminated (false pricing that reflects distortions in the money exchange market is abolished), transaction[6] and hedging costs are reduced, so investors can make their decisions with a high degree of long-term confidence. Without a single currency, a German investor would look at an investment project in Britain as a riskier one than the same project in Germany. Intra-union direct investment is not controlled. That improves competition and allocation of resources. This brings an increase in influence in monetary affairs, as well as connections among major trading partners. Further, by coordinating monetary and fiscal policies, the participating countries are led to fewer distortions while combating macroeconomic disequilibria. This introduces a greater monetary stability. In a situation of stable prices, interest and exchange rates, trade flows are not volatile, as there is no exchange rate risk and uncertainty. This increases competition, economies of scale and mobility of factors that further improves the allocation of resources and increases economic growth. The central financial institution may be entitled to finance regional inequalities.

The pooling of national reserves of foreign currencies is also advantageous for the member countries of an EMU. By internalizing their foreign trade, these countries reduce their demand for foreign currency reserves. These reserves may not be necessary for trade within the group, but they may still be needed for trade with third countries. Anyway, there are certain economies in the use of reserves. Their level is reduced and overhead costs are spread on the participating countries. A single currency in the EU would save on the exchange reserves of the member states around $200 billion (*European Economy*, 1990, p. 178). That money can be easily spent on alternative and more productive uses.

The net effect of monetary integration may not be easily and directly quantified. Let us assume the reverse case. There were tremendous costs from the monetary disintegration of countries such as the former USSR or the former Yugoslavia. Just imagine the losses of the monetary disintegration of the US or Germany where each federal state independently handles its own currency! If there does not exist a control group of similar non-integrated countries, then there is no yardstick against which one may compare the relative performance of the countries which created an EMU. The cost which may be brought by monetary integration in the form of an increase in prices or unemployment are relatively easy identifiable, borne by the few and perhaps of a short-term nature. If that nature is not short term, then an indefinite intra-union system of transfer of resources is a necessary condition for the survival of the scheme. The benefits which accrue from monetary integration are long term in nature, they come in small amounts to everybody and they are hard to quantify with any precision. Moreover, these benefits create the potential for new capital formation (a permanent growth bonus) which will accelerate growth of output.

The 'new theory' of monetary integration suggests that there are somewhat fewer costs (loss of autonomy to handle domestic macroeconomic policies) and somewhat more benefits (gains in credibility in the combat against inflation) associated with monetary integration (Tavlas, 1993b, p. 682). The benefits of an EMU are larger the greater the intra-union factor mobility, the more diversified the economies, the higher the flexibility of wages, the greater the internal trade and the higher the synchronization of business cycles among the member countries. The EU can pass most of these tests, except for labour mobility and flexibility of wages.

4   Parallel currencies

There may be a question whether an irrevocable fixity of exchange rates is a sufficient condition for monetary integration or whether the introduction of a single currency is necessary in an EMU? Suppose that there are various currencies in an EMU which are tied by a fixed exchange rate. If there is an increase in the supply of any of these currencies, then convertibility may be maintained only by intervention, either in the form of the absorption of this currency by the monetary authorities or by a reduction in demand (restriction in transactions) for this currency. The first method represents monetary expansion, while the other is an act of disintegration.

A common currency may be an outward symbol, but is not a necessary condition for a successful EMU. Capital mobility and irrevocably fixed exchange rates of currencies in an EMU may create a single currency *de facto* in everything except, possibly, in name, while a single currency will create a monetary union *de jure*. A single currency will be ultimately necessary, because it makes the irrevocable fixity of exchange rates of the participating currencies completely credible. In addition, a single money will eliminate possible conversion charges, prices in the area will be fully transparent and there will be external benefits (such as introduction of a 'better' symmetry in the international monetary system). Countries will not have even the remote possibility of finding their way out of economic difficulties over devaluation and/or inflation. However, many international pledges towards fixed exchange rates have broken down! As soon as markets question the promise by the participants in the deal, this leads them to start speculating.

An evolutionary approach to the introduction of an EMU may be that a common currency exists side by side with currencies of the member countries. Once agents are used to dealing with the common currency, it may gradually replace the moneys of the participating countries. This is the case with parallel currencies. An important issue here is that the new, parallel currency, ought to be linked to the pace of economic activity, otherwise price stability can be in danger. In addition, it may bring an extra complication in the monetary affairs among the integrated countries. A gradual convergence among the currencies will make the participating currencies yield an identical return. They will become perfect substitutes. Monetary unification can take place.

Gradual monetary integration suffers from a serious flaw. It is a lack of credibility. During the transition phase, participating countries may find a way to step out temporarily from the arrangement. A system that permits some, even though remote, autonomy in the national monetary policy in a situation of free capital mobility is subject to speculative attacks (the most obvious example in the EU took place in July 1993). On the one hand, the longer the transition to a single currency, the greater the fragility of the system. On the other, a fast acceptance of a single money can provoke harsh regional disequilibria for which the countries may not be prepared (for example, a lack of well endowed regional funds). Policy makers need to balance the two sides before they decide. They also have to take into account the increase in unemployment in East Germany after reunification with the western part of the country in 1990. It resulted directly from an instant merger of the two economies on a very different level of development before they were ready for a full EMU. Should the same be repeated in the EU?

The above theoretical model about parallel currencies has two caveats. It ignores network effects and switching costs (Dowd and Greenaway, 1993a, p. 1180). For example, after the break-up of the former USSR (1992), the rouble was a currency which did not fit well into the new realities. Certain newly independent states continued to use roubles because of the network effects. They did so because most of their trading partners were using them. In addition, the switching costs from one currency to another are quite high. At the limit, it is better to use only one money because of the network effects, conversion charges and switching costs. If the benefits of a single currency outweigh these costs, welfare is maximized and it is justified, from the economic point of view, to switch to a single currency. In the case of the EU, the German mark would be the best option as the EU common currency. The mark has the biggest existing network, while the Bundesbank has greater credibility than any of the existing central banks in the EU (Dowd and Greenaway, 1993b, p. 243).

The currencies of member countries in an EMU are perfect substitutes. On the one hand, it would be meaningless to speak here about a parallel currency, since any parallel currency would be indistinguishable from national currencies in everything but name. The concept of a parallel currency becomes meaningful only in the intermediate stage of an EMU, when different currencies are not perfect substitutes because of transaction costs and/or exchange rate expectations. Reductions in exchange rate variability diminish the usefulness of a parallel (basket) currency as an instrument for risk diversification, unless transaction costs in the parallel (common) currency decline by more than the transaction costs in the component currencies. On the other hand, a parallel currency is unlikely to develop in a case where national currencies are only very imperfect substitutes, because of high conversion costs. Widespread use of a parallel currency alongside national currencies can therefore be expected only under a high degree of monetary integration (Gros, 1989, p. 224).

A common currency may replace national currencies after some period of adjustment. Stability in the monetary sphere may be a result. However, the new and single currency in the area would not solve the problem of the budget deficits of member countries that would be revealed, in part, as regional disequilibria.

Gresham's law says that in a situation of two currencies (in his example, gold and silver coins) circulating side by side in the economy, then 'the bad money will drive out the good', except where there is a fixed exchange rate between the two monies. This result has not materialized in some countries.[7]

5 The European Union ·

5.1 Background

Integration in the EU has advanced at a pace faster than envisaged in the Treaty of Rome. The customs union was fully established among the founding member countries in 1968, a year and a half ahead of schedule. This was one of the most significant initial achievements of the group.

After the initial success in the establishment of a customs union, the EU contemplated the establishment of an EMU. There were two schools of thought about how to implement this idea. They were the 'monetarists' and the 'economists'. The first school (Belgium, France and Luxembourg) argued that a promising EMU requires an irrevocable fixity of exchange rates of the participating countries from the outset. The member countries will, then, be driven to coordinate their economic policies in order to mitigate and, eventually, eliminate the discrepancies in their economies, necessary for a full EMU. They also argued in favour of a well endowed fund for the support of adjustments of the balance of payments. Complete freedom of capital movements should be permitted only after the establishment of a full EMU. The last request of this school was that supranationality should be on a relatively low level.

The school of 'economists' (Germany and the Netherlands) argued that fixed exchange rates for a group of countries that are on relatively different levels of development is a formidable task. They argued that the coordination of economic policies should be the primary task, because it would bring economic harmonization among the participating countries. They argued in favour of a free movement of capital from the outset and felt that fixed exchange rates may be introduced only after the fulfilment of the above conditions.

The Werner Report (1970) was offered as the blueprint for EMU in the EU. The Report required fixed exchange rates and free mobility of capital. Thus, it represented a compromise between the two schools. Super-optimism (EMU by 1980) was not rewarded because the Report over-estimated the will of the member states to abandon their monetary authority in favour of a supranational body, in particular in the light of the turmoil on the currency markets during the 1970s. This approach may have also failed because it wanted to fix rates of exchange without prior monetary reform among the member countries.

5.2   European Monetary System

The early 1970s were characterized by significant turbulence on the monetary scene. Currencies were fluctuating, so this state of affairs endangered the functioning of trade flows in the EU. The Council of Ministers requested the member governments not only to follow the ±2.25 per cent margins of fluctuation in relation to the dollar, but also to reduce the level of fluctuation among their respective currencies. This introduced the 'European snake' (common margins of fluctuation). If one plots the daily fluctuations of the currencies of the EU member states, then one would get a snake-like ribbon. The width of the snake depended on the fluctuation of the strongest and the weakest currencies, remaining always within the ±2.25 per cent fluctuation margins of the dollar tunnel. The creation of the 'snake' was mainly a European reaction to the hectic situation of the dollar on the international money market.

The main feature of the 'snake' was intervention. When the sum of the fluctuations in the 'snake' exceeded the margins, intervention was supposed to take place (the strongest currency should purchase the weakest one). The dollar tunnel disappeared in 1973, so the 'snake' found itself in the lake. The currencies in the 'snake' were entering and leaving the system quite often. This introduced uncertainty in trade relations in the EU. Apart from external pressures which the 'snake' was unable to resist, an internal shortcoming (different national monetary policies) also played a role. Something should have been done about that.

The member countries of the EU wanted not just to preserve the already achieved level of economic integration, but also to add to it. A further step was the creation of the EMS. The approach was completely different from the one which established the 'snake'. Instead of preparing various economic plans for political consideration, the EU member countries first delivered their political decision about the establishment of the system and, then, agreed about the technical/operational details of the system. The EMS was introduced in 1979.

The objectives of the EMS were:

- stabilization of exchange rates through closer monetary cooperation among the member countries;
- promotion of further integration of the group; and
- a contribution to the stabilization of international monetary relations.

The key role in the EMS is played by the European Currency Unit (ECU). The ECU is basically a 'cocktail' of fixed proportions of currencies of EU

Table 4.1 Composition of the ECU (%)

Currency	Weight in the 'basket'			
	1979–84	*1984–9*	*1989–94*	*1995*
1 German mark	33.0	32.0	30.1	32.7
2 French franc	19.8	19.0	19.0	20.8
3 Pound sterling	13.3	15.0	13.0	11.2
4 Dutch guilder	10.5	10.1	9.4	10.2
5 Belgian franc	9.3	8.2	7.6	8.4
6 Italian lira	9.5	10.2	10.15	7.2
7 Spanish peseta	—	—	5.3	4.2
8 Danish krone	3.1	2.7	2.45	2.7
9 Irish pound	1.1	1.2	1.1	1.1
10 Portuguese escudo	—	—	0.8	0.7
11 Greek drachma	—	1.3	0.8	0.5
12 Luxembourg franc	0.4	0.3	0.3	0.3
Total	100.0	100.0	100.0	100.0

Source: European Monetary Institute (1996)

member countries. The share of every currency in the ECU depends on the economic potential of the country (aggregate GDP), its share in intra-EU trade and the need for short-term monetary support. The composition of the ECU is presented in Table 4.1. Alterations in the composition of the ECU may occur every five years or when the share of each currency changes by at least 25 per cent in relation to the originally calculated value. In addition, the composition of the ECU can be changed when the currency of a new member country enters the 'basket'. The currency composition of the ECU was 'frozen' by Article 109g of Treaty of Rome (as revised by the Maastricht Treaty). This is why the currencies of Austria, Finland and Sweden are not included in the basket.

The exchange rate mechanism (ERM) of the EMS has been at the centre of controversy since its inception. Every currency in the EMS has its own central rate versus other partner currencies and the ECU. In relation to the partner currencies in the system individual currencies could fluctuate within a ±2.25 per cent band with the exception of the Spanish peseta and British pound which were permitted to float within a ±6 per cent limit. In 1990, eleven years after the creation of the EMS the special (±6 per cent floating band) treatment for the Italian lira ended. When a currency reaches its limit (upper or lower) of fluctuation in relation to another EMS partner currency, then intervention in the national currency of one of the two central banks is compulsory. Intervention within the margins of fluctuation may be either in the national currencies of the EMS members or in dollars.[8]

The fluctuation of each EMS currency against the ECU is slightly stricter. The Commission has individualized each currency's margin of fluctuation. It was strictest for the German mark ±1.51 per cent and widest for the Irish pound ±2.22 per cent (the currencies under the 'special treatment' had wider margins of fluctuation than the standard ones in relation to the ECU).

There was an implicit objective behind the relatively strict margins of fluctuation for currencies in the EMS. It was to drive member countries to accept similar economic policies and to converge. This convergence does not necessarily aim at averaging out the economic performance criteria. Although the EMS has not produced full convergence of the macro-economic indicators of the member countries, it seemed for quite some time that it was heading towards the desired outcome. The best signal was that most member countries remained in the EMS despite strains.

In order to prevent frequent interventions, the EMS has introduced an early-warning system in the form of a divergence indicator. The divergence threshold is ±75 per cent of a currency's fluctuation in relation to the ECU. The role of this indicator is ambiguous. As soon as the divergence threshold is reached, the countries in question are not formally required to do any-thing, even to consult. Therefore, this innovation has not so far played an important role in the EMS. None the less, consultation and cooperation of the monetary authorities of the EU member countries have compensated, at least in part, for this shortcoming.

The strongest arguments for the non-participating countries to join the ERM of the EMS seemed to be predominantly political. It was not integra-tion-prone for these countries to stay aloof from one of the most significant achievements of the EU. In addition, and more importantly, the creation of a genuine internal market for goods, services and factors will be incomplete without a single market for money.

The EMS funds for exchange market interventions are relatively well endowed. The very-short-term financing facility for compulsory interven-tions provides the participating central banks with an unlimited amount of partner currency loans. None the less, the Bundesbank does not accept in practice intervention without limits. The short-term monetary support dis-poses of 14 billion ECUs for the finance of temporary balance-of-payments deficits, while the medium-term support facility disposes of 11 billion ECUs (but the use of this mechanism is subject to certain conditions).

A country with the best performance in inflation, balance of payments, employment, growth and others has least pressure to adjust and, in relation to its size, it may call the tune in the shaping of other countries' economic variables. Hence, Germany was able to dominate within the EMS which operated asymmetrically in formulating the monetary policies of other member countries that had to bear the adjustment burden. Since inflation was reduced and other monetary variables generally aligned among most member countries, the EMS operated in a more symmetric way before the reunification of Germany in October 1990.[9]

The EMS can sometimes slow down the rate of economic adjustment of a member country. When countries borrow on the international financial markets, these markets do not consider exclusively the creditworthiness (reserves, deficits, experience in adjustments and outlooks) of the borrowing country. These markets also consider membership of the EMS and its possibilities for financial support. In this indirect way, financial markets take into account the reserves of other EMS countries. These markets believe that the partner countries will help the borrowing country in financial difficulties. This is a recognition of the relative success of the EMS. However, it may prevent a country accepting greater monetary discipline. A government may employ a a more ruthless method of eroding the real burden of debt and use inflation. In any case, a country which follows a policy of a relative monetary undiscipline will reduce domestic reserves and lose credit-worthiness in the long run. Foreign creditors may reasonably demand higher interest rates which usually deter investment and, hence, reduce the future economic potential of the country. An agreed limitation for national borrowing needs to be a part of an EMU.

Apart from funds for exchange market interventions, other EMS adjustment mechanisms include home price and income alterations, rates of interest, control of capital flows, as well as increased cooperation and exchange of information. Controls of internal trade flows are, of course, prohibited.

The rates of exchange in the EMS were semi-fixed. The EMS did not have as its goal the petrification of exchange rates among the member countries. The adjustments of the central rates may take place either every five years or according to needs. When all other mechanisms for intervention are used up, the country in question can ask for permission to change the central rate of its currency. The Council of Ministers decides about these changes (usually during the weekends, when the financial markets are closed). The effects of realignments (or in plain English, devaluations) may be eroded by inflation. So, the best and, surely, the hardest way for the stability of the system is that the deficit countries increase productivity above the EU average.

In spite of its relative rigidity, the EMS made the rates of exchange quasi-flexible. If a currency is in trouble which may not be solved by intervention, then the system permitted adjustments (revaluations and devaluations) of the central rate of exchange. This kind of adjustment has happened relatively often during the first years of the existence of the EMS.

A change of the central rate of a currency (devaluation) is still a permitted means for the restoration of competitiveness among EMS member countries. In a distant scenario without national currencies, even *de facto*, the restoration of national competitiveness could be achieved by an increase in productivity, reduction in wages or by labour migration to the advanced regions or all of these. The US is an example where wages are flexible and labour is highly mobile. At the same time a single currency has a smooth internal performance. The US interregional adjustments are eased by a system of implicit federal government transfers of real resources. The federal government spends much and taxes little in the backward or ill-performing states/regions, while it does the reverse in the advanced states/regions. A similar mechanism does not (yet) exist in the EU. The EU, with its vast internal market, does not yet have economic stabilizers on the American scale that are intended to ease the adjustment troubles of both countries and regions within them. There are, however, growing structural funds in the EU. The adjustment not only requires the transfer of real resources, but also measures to enhance mobility of factors from low to high productivity regions. On this account, the EU has so far failed.

All member countries of the EU have exchanged for ECUs 20 per cent of their gold reserves (the role of gold is partly reaffirmed)[10] and 20 per cent of their dollar reserves with the European Monetary Institute (until 1994, the European Fund for Monetary Cooperation). These assets are swapped on a revolving quarterly basis for ECUs. Hence the ECU is not a newly created reserve asset which is an addition to the existing stocks of reserves such as the special drawing rights. The creation of the ECU transforms a part of the existing reserve assets into another asset. The amount of ECUs issued changes every quarter in relation to the changes in member countries' volume of reserves, the price of gold and the dollar exchange rate. There were around 54 billion ECUs issued in 1996.

The ECU is used as: an accounting unit for intervention; a means of settlement among central banks; a part of international financial reserves; a basis for the calculation of the divergence indicator; a unit for the store of value (because of its relative stability) and a unit for financial transactions and statistics of the EU administration. There are, also, ECU-denominated bonds. Although the ECU is still a long way from day-to-day use by individuals, many banks open personal accounts in ECUs and offer an interest rate which is a weighted average of interest rates of the participant countries in the ECU. They also offer travellers' cheques denominated in ECUs. Interest rate differentials reflect mainly differences in the national rates of inflation. Once the exchange rates start to move with inflation differentials, the profitability of holding ECUs may diminish.

The ECU used by the monetary authorities is the official ECU, while businesses and the public use the private or commercial ECU. Nevertheless, the ECU market is not fragmented. All dealings are in a single ECU, as the definition of both is the same. A central bank may hold ECUs. If the national currency comes under pressure, the bank can sell ECUs and purchase the national currency. This may be a cheaper and less notable way of intervention than a direct borrowing of other currencies to buy domestic when the exchange rate is falling. The major reason for the relative spread in the use of private ECUs is the demand of business for simplifying transactions and, possibly, avoiding capital controls where they exist. The ECU is attractive because of its greater stability in relation to its components. Apart from the intra-firm trade, firms do not have great incentives to use the ECU when the rates of exchange are not stable (since they may wish to exploit the difference in prices). Non-European investors prefer to deal in a single currency rather than several different currencies. The market value of the

ECU is not directly influenced by the value of the dollar as it is not incorporated in the ECU basket as is the case with the special drawing rights. Therefore, dollar holders can buy ECUs and hedge against the dollar exchange risk.

Britain does not have capital controls, hence the volume of funds for intervention in order to protect a certain exchange rate should be quite large. Such interventions may endanger British monetary targets. Britain is a significant oil exporter, so the pound is a petro-currency. As such it is much more sensitive to actual and expected changes in the price of oil than any other EU currency. The reaction of the pound usually goes in the opposite direction from other EU currencies. As long as the exchange rate of the dollar (in which the price of oil is denominated) remains uncertain and as long as Britain remains a significant oil exporter, this potential over-reaction of the pound may remain. None the less, after a long period of absence, Britain decided to join the ERM of the EMS in 1990. Since the British goal was monetary stability and fight against inflation, the choice was astute. In addition, the EMS fully included one of the world's major currencies. During the first year of participation in the ERM, Britain reduced its rate of inflation to the German level (4 per cent). It took France a decade to achieve the same goal.

A shock came in September 1992. The demand for funds to cover the excessive costs of the reunification of Germany put pressure on its budget. In order to contain this inflationary pressure, Germany raised interest rates. At about the same time, the US wanted to revive demand by cutting interest rates. The dollar became cheaper, while the German mark became dearer. The divergency prompted speculation that hit the weaker currencies hard in the EMS. Currency market speculation forced Britain, followed by Italy, to suspend their membership in the ERM. The EMS was on the brink of a breakdown. A single EU currency would evade such a crisis. None the less, Britain had certain benefits from the 25 per cent depreciation in the value of the pound in the following months. For example, Philips moved the manufacturing of cathode tubes from the Netherlands to Britain. Likewise, Hoover relocated the production of vacuum cleaners from France to Britain, too.

Adjustments in the rates of exchange together with capital controls were used by some countries in the EMS, for example Italy and France, to control the domestic monetary system in an easier way than through other, relatively harsh means, such as recession. They were able to follow, to an extent and for some time, a different course in the national macroeconomic variables then their foreign partners. Capital, one of the major lubricants of the economy was 'forced' to remain at home. In addition, an outflow of capital pushes interest rates up. This slows down the economy, perhaps at a moment when it needs to grow. However, the problem is that capital controls retard structural adjustments that need to take place in any case. Although a short-term effect of controls may bring certain policy successes, the long-term costs of the structural transformation increase. This is why an interest rate policy may be now a preferred policy means.

Capital controls are effective ways to manage monetary affairs in a situation where money markets expect adjustments in the exchange rate.[11] Then, controls drive holders to keep (in the country) the currency that is about to be devalued. Controls may be permanent or temporary (as emergency measures to prevent speculative capital flows). In the absence of capital controls, devaluation of weak currencies can not be postponed; however, controls make the delay of devaluation possible. None the less, delays increase uncertainty about the rate of exchange in the future and, hence, jeopardize investment decisions. With capital controls, a relatively modest increase in the national rate of interest will achieve the desired monetary policy effect. Without capital controls, the only instrument that can be used with the same effect is a sudden and, usually, large increase in interest rates. The main defence of capital controls is not found in the fact that they are cost free, but rather that they are less costly than the movements of exchange rates and interest rates that would happen without these controls (Folkerts-Landau and Mathieson, 1989, p. 8).

The removal of the remaining capital controls in the EU in 1995 was one of the notable achievements of the 1992 Programme. It made residents of the EU sensitive to differences in interest rates. TNCs, including banks, as major beneficiaries of the dismantling of capital controls, are able to easily and swiftly change and diversify the currency composition and maturity of their financial portfolios. By doing that, TNCs and other money holders may jeopardize the objective of monetary policy of individual member countries in a situation with easy and cheap currency substitution. An increase in the national rate of interest in order to reduce the supply of money and 'cool' the economy will have the opposite effect. Increased interest rates will suddenly attract an inflow of foreign capital and increase the national supply of money. Such swift changes are not very likely in the flow of goods (and services.) Conversely, if the intention of the national government is to stimulate home economic activity by a reduction in interest rates, the effect of such a policy will be the opposite from the one intended. Capital will fly out of the country to locations where rates of interest are higher. Without capital controls investors speculate about which currency is to be devalued next. Enormous capital flows can destabilize exchange rates. With a daily trade of around 1 trillion dollars on foreign-exchange markets and with more than one currency in the market, it is possible to gamble. No national intervention can triumph over the speculators. This happened in the EU in the summers of 1992 and 1993. The grand dreams of an EMU in the relatively medium term were, in fact, pushed further into the future.

Without capital controls, large differences in the rate of interest among the EMS countries can not be sustained. In the new situation, the EU member countries have no other rational choice but to pool their national monetary policies and cooperate. Any increase in monetary instability among EU currencies will provoke the mobility of funds in the search for a greater security, thus making it impossible to maintain EMS parities without even greater harmonization of national monetary policies (Panić, 1991). The Bundesbank was calling the tune in the EMS. In that situation a pooling of monetary policies among the countries of the EU can increase the sovereignty of smaller countries because they would, in the new situation, have some say in the EU monetary policy making process. Although national central banks may become increasingly independent on their national governments, they need to enhance their reliance on other national central banks in the EU.

A reduction in the variance of economic indicators among countries may illustrate their economic convergence. The narrowing of the differences in the performance criteria among countries does not necessarily mean that their standards of living are becoming more equal. Membership of the EMS may be used by the national government as a convincing argument during the pursuance of a prudent national economic policy in the fight against the opposition. The EMS has introduced convergence in domestic monetary policies and inflation rates, but it has not been fully backed up by corresponding progress in the fiscal sector and external balance.

A mere convergence in the rate of inflation and other monetary variables may not be enough for the smooth operation of the single EU market. The EMS was not able to increase significantly the use of the ECU, the role of the European Fund for Monetary Cooperation was marginalized and the present form of the system was unable to bring spontaneous monetary integration. Those objectives might be achieved if there was a European central bank, a system of central banks or a common monetary authority. This did not happen before the implementation of the Maastricht Treaty because of a fear that the monetary issues would be passed on to a remote bureaucracy. Any government was afraid of losing monetary sovereignty: the right to cheat on its citizens, firms and other holders of its money without a promise to convert paper money into gold. Another fear was that they might not be able to pursue their own stabilization policy. Those anxieties were not well founded. In order to carry on with the national stabilization, balance of payments, regional, industrial and other policies, governments still have at their disposal taxes, certain subsidies, some procurement and budget deficits. The only (severe) restrictions to their sovereignty to choose stabilization policies are that they could not employ exchange-rate changes and have different rates of inflation from their partner countries.

It must be always kept in mind that in an EMU, the national governments still have a chance to tax and spend in the way they think is most appropriate. Budget deficits are still possible, but subject to only one condition: expenditure must be financed by borrowing (on commercial terms) instead of by printing domestic money. For example, borrowing and expenditure of the cantons in Switzerland and provinces in Canada are not subject to constraints. The *Länder* in Germany restrict borrowing only to the extent that it is necessary to finance investment, while the federal states in the US limit their outlays, applying a kind of balanced budget. Only in Australia does the federal government continuously supervise state debts.

The freedom to tax and spend in an EMU, however, is not absolute. As soon as a country's national finances jeopardize the stability of the union, such as excess imports that depress the value of a common currency, the union's authority may intervene. It may impose limits on the borrowing from the central bank and other sources, ceilings on the budget deficit, a request for non-interest-bearing deposits and impose fines. In a single-currency area, foreign debt has to be serviced by export earnings. The national debt, however, does not present an immediate real burden on the economy because it represents a transfer between present and future generations.

There may be a temptation for a country in a monetary system to run a budget deficit for quite some time according to current needs. Although governments are often safer borrowers in relation to private ones,[12] capital markets will increase interest rates to heavy borrowers when their creditworthiness is jeopardized. Big budget deficits keep long-term interest rates on a higher level than would otherwise be the case. This reduces the size and effectiveness of the cuts in short-term interest rates. The governments of the EU countries generally failed to do that during the 1980s, hence the lack of power in employing fiscal policy to prop up recovery in the 1990s. If a state in federations such as the US and Canada increases its borrowing, then the value of government bonds falls throughout the country. In this case, the federal government can step in to correct the distortion. However, such a well developed corrective mechanism does not yet exist in the EU.

6   European Monetary Union

During the discussions that led to the Maastricht Treaty, there were two extreme possibilities for the final shape of the EU Central Bank and a number of mixed ones. One extreme is the model of Germany's Bundesbank. It is independent from the government in the conduct of monetary policy and possibly, thereby, quite successful. The Bundesbank ensures stable prices, high employment, balanced foreign trade, as well as a constant and reasonable economic growth. The other extreme is the Bank of France. In this bank the government has a full stake, so France wanted to see a kind of 'accountability' of the EU Central Bank to the public bodies. As Germany was the engine of EU monetary stability until 1992–93, the Maastricht Treaty opted for its kind of central bank for the EU. The Bank is supposed to be very tough on inflation. However, that would cost the EU countries hundreds of thousands of existing and new jobs. Perhaps, but the primary source of the EU unemployment problem is *not* necessarily in a looser monetary or fiscal policy (although both of them were made inflexible by the Maastricht criteria for EMU), *but* rather in reforms of labour markets and the welfare system. Politicians might have realized somehow belatedly that the only 'soft' option for economic adjustment needs to come from flexibility in labour markets.

The main argument in favour of a common central bank is that it reduces uncertainties and conflicts about and among national monetary policies. It does so by providing a forum in which national views can be represented and resolved, as well as by reducing the discretion that national monetary authorities have in the implementation of (divergent) policies. In the absence of a central bank, national conflicts are resolved by market forces with adverse externalities for efforts to promote greater stability of exchange rates (Folkerts–Landau and Mathieson, 1989, p. 15). However, a question still remains: do the appointed central bankers possess a superior knowledge about the country's long-term needs than the governments that represent the elected opinion of the public?

Many EU member countries preferred to see a 'German-influenced' EU Bank, rather than the continuation of the prevailing system that is 'German-controlled'. In the system with binding rules and procedures, the smaller EU countries may be represented on the Bank's board where they could, at least to an extent, shape policy. Therefore, their sovereignty may be *increased* in comparison to the previous situation. Independent central banks, such as the judiciary, are constitutional institutions since they are not accountable to the elected government or parliament. Their autonomy comes from a general consensus about long-term economic objectives and from the fact that their instruments may be badly abused by the political majority of the day (Vaubel, 1990, p. 941).

The Delors Report (1989) gave an impetus to the creation of the EMU. It envisaged the EMU in three stages. Its wise approach was not to state any specific date apart from mid-1990 for the beginning of the first stage. During the first stage, the member countries would strengthen the coordination of their economic and monetary policies. The removal of the remaining capital controls would require this in any case. All countries would enter the ERM of the EMS. Stage two would be marked by the creation of the European Central Bank (a system of central banks or a monetary authority). The major macroeconomic indicators would be set for all member countries including the size and financing of the budget deficit. In addition, the margins of fluctuation in the ERM would be narrowed. The first two stages would not be fully stable, as there would be the potential for speculative attacks. In the last stage of the creation of the EMU, a common central bank would be the only authority responsible for the conduct of monetary policy through-out the EU. Exchange rates among the national currencies would be perman-ently fixed without any fluctuations. A single currency would emerge. It may be a necessary condition for a genuine single market where a national competitiveness would not be influenced by alterations in exchange rates. This was the blueprint for the finalization of the Maastricht Treaty.

The British proposed in 1990 an alternative plan that would introduce a 'hard ECU' as the thirteenth currency at that time, in stage two, as a parallel currency. It would be an additional anti-inflationary control on governments that intend to ease national monetary policy. It would be issued by the Central Bank in exchange for deposits of national currencies. The 'hard ECU' would be managed in such a way that each national central bank would compensate the Union's Central Bank for any loses caused by devaluation of its currency and that any inflating national central bank would buy back its national currency with, for example, dollars or yen. Wide acceptability of the 'hard ECUs' would prevent national central banks from inflating. The problem with this plan is that the British saw it as an end in itself, not as a vehicle towards a single currency of the EU. This plan received little support during negotiations over EMU.

After the currency disturbances of September 1992 when Britain and Italy left the ERM, a new and bigger shock took place at the end of July 1993 when there was the actual demise of the ERM of the EMS. Germany's need to obtain funds to finance the reintegration of its eastern region increased interest rates. The country placed its national interest ahead of the concerns of the EU by refusing to cut interest rates.[13] This produced a currency crisis. To ease the strain, a way out was found in an increase in the margins for the fluctuations of the currencies participating in the ERM. They were widened from ±2.25 per cent to ±15 per cent from the central parity. The 'dirty float' began. The EMS revealed its fragility. However, a step back from the EMU path was a preferable action than total suspension of the EMS. The widening of opportunities to fluctuate within the ERM increased the room for differences in the national economic policies. Even though this was a possibility, it was not exercised. The countries endeavoured to keep the exchange rate of their currencies within the 'old' margins of fluctuation. None the less, the mere existence of the permitted wider margins for fluctuations introduced an element of uncertainty.

A condition for the establishment of the EMU is that 'normal' (without a definition) fluctuation margins for currencies need to be observed for at least two years. However, what is 'normal' in the situation when the ERM remains only in name? The wide increase in fluctuation margins made a mockery of the Maastricht Treaty's intentions to introduce a single currency in the relatively near future. One needs to remember, however, that exchange rate movements of 15 per cent are quite common outside the EU.

The Maastricht Treaty is in essence mostly about the EMU. This is voiced both in the Preamble and Articles B and G, respectively. That was an expected step after the establishment of a free internal market in 1993. For a free flow of goods and services, as well as for an efficient allocation of resources, a necessary condition is a degree of stability in exchange rates and a removal of conversion costs.

According to the Maastricht Treaty, EMU is to be achieved in three stages. During the first, there was a reinforcement of coordination of economic and monetary policies of the member countries. The second stage started in January 1994 with the establishment of the European Monetary Institute (EMI) in Frankfurt. This took place in an unsettled exchange rate environment. The EMI is to coordinate the EU members' monetary policies and prepare the conditions for the final stage. The central banks of the member states need to become independent before the end of the second stage when the EMI would be transformed into an independent European Central Bank (ECB). There would be, in fact, the European System of Central Banks. It would be composed of the ECB and the central banks of the member states.

There is a chance that Frankfurt may take the major part of trade in the EU single currency if the pound stays out of this project. Having an EMU whose major financial markets are off-shore would be, on the surface, an unusual arrangement. London has, however, already become the market where trading in the German mark, Europe's most important currency, takes place. Hence, its position on the financial markets should not be seriously threatened.

According to the letter of the Treaty, the Council of Ministers was supposed to decide by a qualified majority, not later than 31 December 1996, whether a majority (at least eight) of the EU countries fulfil the following five necessary criteria for the third stage of the EMU (Article 109j and Protocol on the Convergence Criteria).

- a high degree of price stability (inflation within the margin of 1.5 per cent of the three best-performing EU countries);
- sound public financial position (budget deficit of less than 3 per cent of the GDP);[14]
- a national debt of less than 60 per cent of GDP;[15]
- the observance of the 'normal' fluctuation margins (no devaluation within the EU exchange rate mechanism for at least two preceding years); and
- the durability of convergence of economic policies that needs to be reflected in the long-term interest rate levels (interest rate has to be within the 2 per cent margin of the three best-performing EU countries).

The final decision about the eligibility of the countries is expected to be taken in May 1998.[16]

If a country fails one (or, perhaps, two conditions), but if it makes good progress on these issues, it may be let into the EMU. If the Council is not able to decide about the beginning of the third stage, the Maastricht Treaty stipulates that it would begin on 1 January 1999 for the countries which fulfil the necessary conditions for the EMU. These countries would irrevocably fix their exchange rates and the ECU would subsequently replace the national currencies under the name of the euro. This will unleash the full potential of the genuine single market in the EU. The ECB would follow its primary commitment of price stability and, consequently, set interest rates and conduct foreign-exchange operations. In addition, the ECB would support economic growth and employment. The ECB would report regularly to the EU finance ministers (meetings of the ECOFIN which would issue broad economic-policy guidelines) and to the European Parliament. In any case, the implementation of the five criteria for the third stage of the EMU, if implemented strictly, would have a deflationary effect on the economy of the EU.

In the rush to meet the Maastricht criteria for the third stage of the EMU, governments introduced additional (temporary) taxes, took on austerity measures and, consequently, restrained flexibility of fiscal policy. The consequences were numerous industrial actions, as well as high taxation, an obstacle to employment.

In any case, as officially declared, the planned schedule for the introduction of the euro is expected to observe the following timetable:

- *February 1996*: start of the banknote competition
- *December 1996*: winning design selected
- *Mid-1998*: start of printing
- *January 1999*: scheduled start of EMU (stage three); one-for-one conversion of the ECU for the euro; irrevocable fixation of the rate of exchange of the currencies in the EMU
- *Mid-2001*: currency delivered to EMU central banks
- *January 2002*: notes and coins enter circulation *alongside* national currencies which will no longer be legal tender six months after the introduction of the euro
- *July 2002*: the euro is the only legal tender in the EMU countries

The objective of the Stability Pact, reached in December 1996 in Dublin, is keeping any EMU on track. Germany wanted to have automatic fines for any EMU country that has a budget deficit of over 3 per cent. However, France argued that sanctions for excessive borrowing of member states must be a political matter. The final agreement was that the Council of Ministers (excluding the country being hit) can penalize the country with a fine of up to 0.5 per cent of its GDP. The countries are excepted from fines if their economies shrink by over 2 per cent.

The Maastricht convergence criteria are arbitrary. Economic theory suggests other conditions for monetary integration such as flexibility in labour markets, labour mobility and fiscal transfers. The Maastricht criteria could be met once the countries are *in* the EMU; however, *before* such Union takes place it may be extremely hard to do so. 'The Maastricht treaty has it back to front.... On balance the Maastricht convergence criteria are *obstacles* to a monetary union in Europe' (de Grauwe, 1994, pp. 159–161). The question is whether the difficult road towards the EMS as structured by the Maastricht Treaty is becoming impossible?[17]

It is certain that very few countries will meet in full the Maastricht convergence criteria for the EMU. If the EMU takes place only among the select group of countries, excluded countries will face divergence, rather than convergence in certain macroeconomic variables, because of the fact that they have been left out of the arrangement. Exchange rates between the full EMU countries and those that are outside would remain volatile.[18] This would have an adverse impact on trade flows in the single market of the EU. Therefore, one may wish to put less emphasis on convergence criteria and more on strengthening the future monetary institutions of the EU. First, if the Board of Directors of the ECB fails to maintain price stability, there should be a procedure for their removal. Second, if a country (such as Belgium or Italy) fails to satisfy budgetary standards, it would be denied voting power on the Board of Directors of the ECB (de Grauwe, 1996). When first spelled out in 1995, these ideas had economic grounds, but they seemed initially to be politically naive. However, the Stability Pact 'made a note of them'.

A way out may be found either in changing the criteria or in altering the timetable. If the criteria are changed, the arrangement may not be acceptable to Germany. Hence, the answer is self-evident. The problem with changing the timetable is that once the timetable and the deadlines are altered, for instance postponed for a few years, this may terminate the whole project.[19] A delay may be justified by the need to deregulate economies, in particular product and labour markets, as well as welfare systems. That requires a certain period of time. After all, the 'process of creating an ever closer union' (Preamble to the Maastricht Treaty) is not necessarily only linked to the EMS (at least as structured so far)! The abandonment of the 1999 deadline does not mean departure from the idea of an EMU.

The reunification of Germany was the major instigator of the Maastricht Treaty, as well as the reason for the Treaty's disappointing implementation. The EMS became too rigid to adjust to disequilibrating blows such as the reunification of Germany and the consequent budget deficits. The high German interest rates (because of the decision to pay for the reunification[20] by borrowing, rather than by raising taxes) and the need of the economies in recession to get cheap loans, produced the upheaval that speculators desired. If EMU is founded on foreign policy considerations, it comes as no surprise that German voters are highly sceptical about it. The exchange rate crisis was a good reminder to the policy makers that markets can not be avoided. Capital markets will always test the resolve of governments to defend the narrow bands of the exchange rate. As long as economies are in recession, governments will not enter such a contest. The wreckage of the ERM of the EMS is one of the symbols of the evident 'weakness' of the governments and power of markets.

As so much political capital has been invested in the EMU, one may guess that it may take place as planned, but it will be based on a flexible interpretation of the Maastricht criteria. Hence, it may not be very stable. Policymakers need to think about a contingency plan for what to do three years following the start of the EMU if it falls apart.

7 Conclusion

Monetary integration is a field where genuine economic integration among countries is tested. The EU countries wanted to supplement the customs union and the frontier-free internal market with an EMU[21] that would secure trade flows. The politicians succeeded in achieving a more modest goal. The EMS was a voluntary and complicated system of semi-fixed exchange rates which was supported by certain cooperation by central banks. The success in the attainment of the original objectives of the EMS were obvious. The EMS introduced a certain degree of monetary stability up to 1992 by a reduction in inflation differentials and by a lowering in the volatility of the exchange rates.

Less developed regions/countries in the EMU and those with deficits in balance of payments would be deprived from employing devaluation as a means of adjustment. These countries/regions would have to do better than the others in the EU in reducing costs and increasing productivity. Hence the need for regional, industrial and social policies and aid at the EU level. Otherwise, the less developed and deficit countries/regions may threaten to use protectionism and jeopardize the whole EMU programme. Once countries are seriously committed to integration and place the long-term interests of the EU above the short-term national ones, it is harder to stop than to go ahead with it. One of the major problems regarding this view is that Germany, the hegemonic country in the EMS, did not do that in 1993!

The rationale for common EU economic policies exists in the case where the Union is better placed to do certain things than the member countries (subsidiarity). One can hardly think of a better example of this than in the case of monetary and trade/competition policies. An EMU would further promote and strengthen integration in the EU, but, as structured so far, it is not the only approach to an 'ever closer union'. Economic efficiency would be increased because of improved allocation of savings and investment due to the elimination of exchange-rate risk and reduction in the cost of capital. However, a mere EMU would not be the end of the story. Fiscal harmonization and budgetary coordination would be the next step, as they would contribute to the full effectiveness of the stabilization policy.

Although the EU does not have either high mobility of labour or flexibility in wages which may provoke high adjustment costs, an EMU is welcome not only because of the internal market, but also because of the external issues. There are serious doubts about the future stability and value of the dollar because of the rising US foreign debt (over 1 trillion dollars in 1997). A strong alternative currency as the euro (if it is strong) is welcome. Portfolio switching into the euro may keep its value high. If this happens, there will be considerable fluctuations in the exchange rate between the dollar and the euro

8 West African Monetary Union

The West African Monetary Union (WAMU) consists of seven West African states. They are Benin, Burkina Faso, Ivory Coast, Mali, Niger, Senegal and Togo. Membership of the WAMU varied over time. Mauritania participated in the WAMU from its inception in 1962, but withdrew in 1972; Togo joined in 1963; while Mali withdrew from the WAMU, but rejoined in1984. The WAMU has provided these countries for almost three decades with a freely circulating common currency, the CFA (Communauté Financière Africaine) franc. This currency was linked by a fixed rate of exchange to the French franc without any changes from 1948 till 1994 at the rate of 1 French franc = 50 CFA francs. The CFA franc is issued by a common central bank which pools the member countries' reserves. France is very involved in this system because of guarantees of an unlimited convertibility of CFA francs into French francs at the fixed exchange rate. Such free and unlimited convertibility contributed to the capital drain and added to other causes which culminated in a devaluation of 50 per cent in January 1994.

The role of WAMU was passive in the first decade of its existence. The WAMU's central bank was charged with the maintenance of liquidity (money supply/GNP) and not with responsibilities for maintaining monetary and price stability and balance-of-payments equilibrium (Robson, 1983, p. 150). Its monetary policy was centralized in the Paris headquarters although the WAMU kept agencies in each member country. The WAMU's monetary policy was not coordinated with the fiscal policies of the member countries. At the beginning of the 1960s these countries were heavily dependent on France for all external economic affairs. The WAMU countries became linked to the EU by the Yaoundé and, subsequently, the Lomé conventions which provide trade preferences and aid from the EU. They, also, joined the IMF and the World Bank. The WAMU countries thereby increased the number of external economic partners. Anyway, France has preserved dominant position in the region. The WAMU countries intended to reduce the strong French influence and increase their autonomy in the monetary sphere. This brought certain reforms in 1974.

Reform was founded on the grounds that a monetary union among the member countries was necessary for faster economic development, but that the monetary arrangements should be organized differently than before. The most important changes occurred regarding the rediscount facilities. Instead of a 10 per cent annual increase in the money supply as before, the reform allowed a 45 per cent annual increase in the money supply in each country (this amount would be rediscounted by the WAMU central bank). This has increased the power of the National Credit Committees. Foreign reserves of the member countries may be diversified, but at least 65 per cent of them should be in French francs.[22] The WAMU countries align their exchange rate policy with France while, in return, France guarantees free convertibility of CFA francs. The site of the central bank was transferred from Paris to Dakar. Prior to the reform, decisions of the central bank were made by the two-thirds majority where France had half of the bank's Board membership. After the reform the decisions were made by simple majority. France is represented on the Board by two directors, like every other country.

It is difficult to create a counterfactual world in which one may evaluate the degree of success of any monetary union. However, there is one important benefit of being linked in a monetary union. Some of the poorest countries in a volatile area have low monetary credibility. Being involved in a monetary union prevents governments printing money without control in order to finance deficit. The relative performance of the CFA franc zone countries can be compared to other developing countries. The performance of the CFA franc countries was relatively poorer than that of all other developing countries in the period 1960–73, while their economic performance in relation to this group of countries was significantly improved during the 1974–82 period. A more suitable 'control group' of developing countries can be taken for comparison. This group can be found among other sub-Saharan countries. These countries are much more similar to the CFA franc countries in climate, endowment of factors and so on. The WAMU countries grew significantly faster than the group of other sub-Saharan countries (Devarajan and de Melo, 1987, p. 491). This result may support the view that participation in a monetary union and its 'discipline' was much more helpful for the economic adjustment of countries during the period of floating and sharp increases in prices than the free and uncoordinated float of other sub-Saharan countries. Although there was the possibility of changing parity of the CFA franc, the WAMU has kept a fixed parity with the French franc. Such exceptional stability has been a major factor in the creation and maintenance of confidence in the CFA franc (Guillaumont and Guillaumont, 1989, p. 144). Therefore, claims that the WAMU does not operate for the benefit of its member countries may not be well founded. The best proof is that the membership of the WAMU has first stabilized and then increased in number.

The future of the WAMU may be uncertain. Other African countries have devalued their currencies, so the share of WAMU countries in the continent's exports may be in danger. The smuggling of goods from weak currency countries into the WAMU, the relative strength of the French franc and a fall in the prices of primary commodities, except oil, require another devaluation and possibly a loosening of the link with the French franc. Although the devaluation of 1994 brought one-time positive benefits regarding the regional balance of trade,[23] regional competitiveness is not a monetary phenomenon. The roots of the problem are in the structure of the economy and political organization of the countries in the region which can not be permanently solved by devaluations. The reforms of these areas do not take place at a satisfactory pace.

II FISCAL POLICY AND THE BUDGET

1 Introduction

It is a common assumption in the standard theory of customs unions that by the elimination of tariffs and quotas trade within an integrated area becomes free (but for the existence of the common external tariff). It is also assumed that foreign trade is fostered by relative differences in national production functions and resource endowments. This is just an illusion. It is not only the tariff and quota systems that distort the free flow of trade, but also fiscal impediments such as subsidies and taxes create distortions. The focus of the White Paper (1985) and the 1992 Programme was mostly on the elimination of frontier controls. After the creation of a genuine internal market in 1993 and steps towards the EMU attention needs to be directed towards tax harmonization in the EU. Should taxes be unified throughout the EU, or should they be set independently by each country and markets allowed to equilibrate trade flows and, supposedly, introduce approximation in taxes, or should national preferences deriving from a variety of geographical or social reasons be reflected in tax diversity among the EU countries?

This chapter deals with the structure and harmonization of taxes, as well as the budgetary questions in the EU. It starts with fiscal policy issues. Sections 3 and 4, respectively, present a discussion of direct and indirect taxes. A brief analysis of the EU budget is contained in section 5. The conclusion is that there is considerable room for improvement in the field of fiscal and budgetary integration.

2 Fiscal policy

The fiscal policy of a country deals with the influence of the demand, size, revenues and expenditure of the public sector. It influences both the provision and consumption of a range of goods and services. In addition, it affects the allocation of resources (efficiency), economic stabilization (reduction in the fluctuation of macroeconomic variables around desired, planned or possible levels) and equity in the distribution of national wealth. Fiscal policy can also reflect strategic behaviour of national governments. By offering preferential tax treatment to TNCs, governments may change/ improve their competitiveness in relation to other countries. Applied to an EMU, fiscal federalism (a supranational fiscal authority) needs to take care of a certain transfer of resources from prosperous countries/sectors to needy ones, as well as to promote mobility of resources.

Harmonization of the fiscal system among countries has two meanings. First, the lower form of fiscal harmonization may be equated with coopera- tion among countries. These countries exchange information and/or enter into loose agreements about the ways and types of taxation. Second, in its higher meaning, fiscal harmonization means the standardization of mutual tax systems regarding methods, types and rates of taxes and tax exemptions (Prest, 1983, p. 61).

A prudent fiscal policy should ensure that the government at all its levels (local, regional and central) should spend only on those activities where it can use resources in a better way than the private sector. Taxes should be high enough to cover that cost, but levied in a way that distorts the economy as little as possible (although there are some valid social cases for distortion, which include conservation of energy and control of pollution). The budget should be roughly in balance during the economic cycle. The problem that must be avoided is to resist the burdening of too narrow a tax base, otherwise tax rates will be high and distorting. As for the collection of taxes, they ought to be other than taxes on trade and company profits. These two types of taxes are the most distorting. Unfortunately, they are the most common taxes in the developing world. Taxes on trade (both export and import) prevent specialization, while loophole-ridden taxes on company profits distort investment decisions. Sales taxes (e.g. value added tax) may be the most attractive alternative.

The integration of fiscal policies in an EMU refers to the role of public finance and the part played by the budget. The theory of fiscal integration deals with the issue of optimal fiscal domains in an EMU (Robson, 1987, p. 89). It studies the rationale, structure and impact of fiscal (tax and budgetary systems) of the integrated countries. Integration of fiscal policies implies not only a harmonization of national systems of taxes and subsidies, but also issues such as public expenditure, transfers (redistribution) within and between countries, regions, economic sectors and individuals; combat of cyclical disturbances; stabilization policy; and tax evasion. The highest type of fiscal integration among countries represents a unified system of taxes and subsidies, as well as the existence of a single budget that is empowered to cope with all economic issues of common concern. This has, however, only been achieved in centralized federal states.

Fiscal neutrality among the integrated countries refers to a situation in which a supplier or a consumer of a good or service is indifferent about being taxed in any of the integrated countries. This is an important prere- quisite for the efficient allocation of resources and for the operation of an EMU.[24] The fiscal authorities should be quite cautious while assessing taxes and spending tax receipts. If they tax a significant part of profit or income, then they may destroy incentives for business, savings and investment. They may stimulate factors to flow to locations where they can maximize net returns. This can, however, be a powerful tool for the direction of certain business activities towards specific locations (tax heavens). Such a policy may find a certain social justification (e.g. equity), although it may be questionable from an efficiency standpoint.

The member countries of an EMU may basically finance a common budget according to the principles of benefit and ability to pay. First, the principle of benefit is based on the rule of clear balances or *juste retour* (a fair return). Those that get the favours from the budget expenditure ought to contribute to these public funds in proportion to the benefits they receive. Second, economic benefits of integration do not accrue to the participating countries only through the transfers of (common) public funds. The most important gains come from a secure freedom for intra-group trade, mobility of factors, specialization, acceleration in economic activity and the like. Such a neo-classical expectation may not require 'corrective measures' since all countries and regions benefit from integration. However, in the case of imperfect markets and economies of scale, this expectation may not materialize. In the new situation, the principle of the ability to pay features highly. Individual contributions and receipts from the common budget do not have to be equal. Net contributions reflect a country's ability to pay. A nominal net contributory position of a country can well be more than compensated by various spillovers that stem from the membership of an EMU. Therefore, the *juste retour* principle may get a new dimension: it is a discreet, but continuous, flow of resources from the rich and thriving to the less-well-off member countries and those in (temporary) need.

Fiscal policy has a direct (blunt) effect on income of factors, as well as consumption of goods and services. This is in contrast to monetary policy that does the same, but in an indirect (fine tuning) way through financial markets. By a simple change in transfers and rates of taxes and subsidies, the fiscal authority may directly affect expenditure and consumption. However, the problem with fiscal policy is that it is usually passing through a long parliamentary procedure and its changes may be taking place once (or only a few times) a year. Monetary policy may do the same job as fiscal policy, but in a discreet manner and, potentially, much faster. By changing interest or exchange rates, a government may react swiftly to the emerging crises and opportunities. Such a quick reaction is not always possible with fiscal policy. Hence the need for the coordination of fiscal and monetary policies in an EMU. If they work one against the other, neither would be effective and the result may be damaging. Stabilization and investment policies for a small country may be more effective in an EMU, than in a situation where these policies are pursued in an independent, uncoordinated and often conflicting way with countries that are major economic partners. If intra-union trade is high in proportion to total external trade of the unionized countries, then the stability in the group exchange rates is a necessary condition for the protection of these flows.

The issue that needs to be addressed next is the classification of taxes. According to their base, taxes may be levied on income (direct taxes) and consumption (indirect taxes). Direct taxes charge incomes of firms and individuals (factor returns), as well as property ownership. These taxes are effective at the end of the production process. They have an impact on the mobility of factors. A change in these taxes has a direct impact on tax-payers' purchasing power. Indirect taxes are applied to consumption. They affect movements of goods and services. An alteration of these taxes changes the prices of goods and services.

3   Direct taxes

3.1   Corporate taxes

The international aspect of corporate taxation refers to the taxation of TNCs. Differences in corporate taxes among countries in which a free capital mobility is permitted may endanger the efficient allocation of resources if capital owners tend to maximize their net profits in the short run. Other things being equal, capital would flow to countries with a relatively low level of corporate taxes (although this is only one of the variables that influence investment decisions). TNCs decide about their trans-border business activities not only according to the production-efficiency criteria, but also according to others that include differences in tax rates, subsidies, market growth, trade regime, competition, stability and so on.

Corporate taxes may be collected according to several *methods*. These are the classical, integrated and dual or imputation systems. A classical, or a separate, system represents one extreme. According to it, a firm is taken as a separate entity, distinct from its shareholders. Corporations are taxed irrespective of whether profits are distributed or not. At the same time, shareholders' income is taxed notwithstanding the fact that the corporation has already paid taxes on its profit.

An integrated system represents another extreme which is relevant for theoretical considerations. Here, a corporation is viewed just as a collection of shareholders. Corporate tax is eliminated while shareholders pay tax on their portion of corporate profits. Hence, personal income tax and corporate tax are integrated in full. It is, however, very hard to implement this system because of the practical problems of allocating corporate income to possibly thousands of shareholders.

The dual (two rate, split rate) system falls between the two extreme systems. A corporation pays tax at a lower rate if profits are distributed than in the case when they are not.

Imputation is another intermediate system for taxing corporations. In contrast to the dual system, however, relief is provided here at the shareholder level. Corporations pay taxes just as in the classical system, while shareholders receive credit, usually in the year they receive dividends, for the tax already paid by the corporation.

Computation of corporate profits has provoked many controversies. The authorities of several states in the US[25] apply the unitary or formulary apportionment method for the taxation of TNCs. This arbitrary and controversial method was inspired, in part, by the problem of transfer pricing. A TNC derives its income not only in the place of its residence, but also from operations of its subsidiaries. The rationale for the unitary method is that profits of the TNC accrue from its global operations, so that a TNC needs to be taken as a single unit. The tax authorities, in particular in California, reach beyond the borders of their own jurisdiction. Because of an increasing diversity and volume of international transactions and the globalization of business activities, it is hard to assess exactly the individual affiliate's contribution to the overall profit of a TNC (UNCTAD, 1993, p. 209). If instead of the employment of the still prevailing (and perhaps superior) cost-plus or resale-minus method, the unitary system is applied, then the tax authorities relate sales, assets and/or payroll expenditure of the affiliate under their jurisdiction to the TNC's world-wide sales, assets and/or payroll outlays. The business community adamantly and rightly disputes such a mechanical view that averages the global operations of a TNC across the board. Profit uniformity at all stages of production and at all international locations does not prevail.

In a 'globalized' international economy there may be continuous multi-jurisdictional conflicts regarding taxation of TNCs. The national tax authorities take a semi-arbitrary unitary method and assess the share of global profits of the TNC that should be taxed within the confines of their jurisdiction. This approach contrasts sharply with the traditional separate accounting rules (arm's-length method) for tax assessment among distinct fiscal authorities because it is not (necessarily) arbitrary. Although the unitary method has elicited support from certain intellectuals, the business community is adamantly opposed to this method of taxation. This opposition comes not only from the increased administrative costs for the TNCs, but it also runs contrary to the US constitutional provision that the federal government (not the ones in the constituting states) is in charge of foreign commerce.

If the unitary principle is applied only in one or a few (but not all) locations where a TNC operates, the following two cases are possible. First, if the operation of the affiliate is more profitable than the average overall profitability of the TNC, then the local authority that applies the unitary method of corporate taxation would collect less tax proceeds than it could by the application of the cost-plus method. Second, if business operations of the affiliate are less profitable than the average-universal profitability of the TNC, then the local tax office will collect more tax proceeds than under the alternative collection method. The second case directly harms the profitability of the affiliate, reduces the corporate funds for the potential investment and, hence, the long-term interests of the host country. In 1994, after 17 years of legal battle, the US Supreme Court decided in favour of California regarding the unitary method of taxation (Barclays Bank lost the case). The Court held that unitary taxation did not violate the foreign commerce clause. The implications of the decision are not fully clear. If profitability of a TNC is higher in California than elsewhere in the world, this company may benefit from unitary tax assessment. California, however, allows taxpayers to choose between unitary tax assessment and the 'water's edge' method (taxation of income within the confines of the US), a system close to the universally accepted arm's-length method.

The main distortion that is brought by unitary taxation is that it is different from the standard arm's-length taxation principle. In addition, states using the unitary method adopt a formula favourable to themselves. Many states use different formulae (more distortions) and the outcome is the creation of a potentially higher aggregate taxable income than the aggregate economic income.

The main objective of corporate taxation is not to increase the price of goods and services, but rather to capture a part of the firm's profit. Frequent changes in the corporation-tax systems should be avoided. They increase uncertainty and the administrative burden on firms. Unless they are favourable for business, these variations distort the decision-making process about investment and may have a long-term negative effect on capital that will withdraw or reduce investment in these destinations.

A firm may pass on the tax burden to consumers in the form of higher prices for its goods and services or to its employees, by reduced wages, or a combination of the two. By passing on the tax burden, it may reduce, in part or in full, the impact of the tax on its profit. The possibility for the passing on of the tax burden depends on the idiosyncrasies of the goods/services and the labour market. If a firm is free to set its prices, then it depends on competition if this passing on is possible. If prices are regulated, then the way of passing on the tax burden is different. Suppose that the prices do not rise. A firm may reduce the quality of its output in order to save profits. In the reverse case when prices do not fall, it may improve the quality of its output and after-sales service in order to increase its competitiveness and save or increase its market share.

The importance of the distribution of the tax burden between individuals and firms may be analysed in the following example. Suppose that P_d stands for the price paid by consumers. If one imposes a tax of t dollars per unit of output on the suppliers, then the price P_s which they receive is:

$$P_s = P_d - t \qquad (4.1)$$

The condition for equilibrium is:

$$P_s(q) = P_d(q) - t \qquad (4.2)$$

Assume that one imposes the same tax of t dollars per unit of purchased good on the buyers. The price paid by consumers is:

$$P_d = P_s + t \qquad (4.3)$$

The condition for equilibrium in this case is:

$$P_d(q) = P_s(q) + t \qquad (4.4)$$

Note that the two conditions for equilibrium 4.2 and 4.4 are the same. Thus the quantity, P_s and P_d in equilibrium are independent of whether the tax is levied on demanders (individuals) or suppliers (firms). The volume of government revenue does not change. What changes is the composition of revenue, which may provoke hot political debate. This is obviously not understood by many tax authorities.

There is a school of integrationists who argue that income has to be taxed as a whole in spite of differences in its source. It says that all taxes are ultimately borne by the people. This view opposes the school of absolutists who argue that firms are separate legal entities that need to be taxed in their own capacity (under the assumption that they do not pass on the tax burden either to their employees or consumers). Another reason for the separate treatment of corporations is that they use government services without fully paying for them. This has an impact on the reduction of costs of operation. Tax authorities can use their policy to regulate investment of firms and to control their monopoly position. On these grounds, tax instruments can influence the behaviour of the business sector.

If private capital flows are a significant feature of economic relations among countries, some of those countries may find an incentive to negotiate tax treaties in order to avoid double taxation and, possibly, achieve tax neutrality. Tax neutrality between investment in home country A and foreign country B is achieved when firms are indifferent (other things being equal) between investing, producing and selling in either country. In this case, the foreign country's tax equals the corporate tax plus the withholding tax (tax on the transfer of profits). If under a condition of free capital mobility country A's firm finds country B's taxes equal to country A's, then there is tax neutrality between these two countries.[26] If not, investment will flow to the country that has relatively lower taxes.

Cooperation among the tax authorities in partner countries is necessary for the smooth operation of the economies of the integrated countries. This demand is amplified if the desired goals are a free mobility of capital, free competition, efficient allocation of resources, 'fairness' in the distribution of revenues among the member countries and the elimination of administrative difficulties. This is of special importance in a situation of fixed exchange rates and free capital mobility. Measures to reduce the risks of tax evasion can take the form of a generalized withholding tax to all EMU residents and/ or a commitment of banks to disclose information about interest received by the union residents. Therefore, the need to create conduit companies, as intermediary subsidiaries that take advantage of tax treaties in order to reduce withholding taxes, can be eliminated. As tax harmonization deals with difficult and deeply rooted national customs, the EU has put the harmonization issue aside. The Single Market Programme from 1993 and the moves towards the EMU are supposed to perform the sophisticated, behind-the-scenes market-led pressure on countries to approximate taxes, since the high-tax countries, other things being equal, would lose competitiveness of their goods and services, and also be less attractive locations for FDI.

3.2   Corporate taxes in the European Union

The basic Treaties of the EU are short on the tax provisions. There are just a few provisions in the Treaty of Rome that refer to the general issue of taxation. Article 95 stipulates that imported products from the partner countries may not be taxed more highly than comparable domestic goods. This has introduced the principle of destination for value added tax (VAT), as well as non-discrimination in the EU internal commerce. Article 96 introduced tax neutrality. It states that any repayment of tax on the goods exported to the EU partner countries may not exceed the taxes actually paid on the good in question. Article 99 requires harmonization of indirect taxes, while Article 100 indirectly demands approximation of laws that affect the establishment or operation of the common market. Article 100a excludes fiscal matters from the majority voting procedure. The unanimity principle has prevented fast progress in the approximation of fiscal matters in the EU.

Table 4.2 illustrates, in a simplified way, differences in corporate tax systems in the EU countries. It does not take into account any of the surtaxes, surcharges, local taxes, credits, exemptions, special treatment of SMEs and the like, that apply in nearly all EU countries. The differences in systems and rates of corporate taxes point at the distortions of the tax neutrality for investment in the EU. Therefore, the Commission thought about proposing a single corporate-tax rate for the EU, but stepped back from the idea. A special committee proposed a minimum tax rate (30 per cent) and a maximum rate (40 per cent) that may be introduced in the EU countries. The proposed rates may be meaningful only if the tax base is also harmonized.[27] The problem has been identified, but the solution is not always easy to find. A TNC is ready to pay relatively higher corporate

Table 4.2   Systems and rates of corporate taxes in EU countries in 1997

Country	System	Rate (%)
1 Austria	Classical	34
2 Belgium	Classical	40
3 Denmark	Classical	34
4 Finland	Imputation	28
5 France	Imputation	37
6 Germany	Dual and imputation	30 (distributed) 45 (retained)
7 Greece	Corporate tax, no tax on shareholder	35 (40 for foreign companies)
8 Ireland	Imputation	36
9 Italy	Imputation	37
10 Luxembourg	Classical	32
11 The Netherlands	Classical	35–36
12 Portugal	Imputation	36
13 Spain	Imputation	35
14 Sweden	Classical	28
15 United Kingdom	Imputation	31

Source: International Bureau of Fiscal Documentation (1997)

taxes in country A if it supplies the business sector with educated labour, infrastructure, lower social contributions, even trade protection, relative to country B where the corporate tax rate is lower.

Harmonizing or equalizing corporate tax rates in the EU aims at introducing an identical distortion across the EU. However, the corporate tax distorts another important variable for firms. That is, the form of financing. A corporate tax punishes enterprises that raise their capital through equity, rather than debt. This is because interest payments can be deducted from taxable profits, while the return on equity can not. Probably the best solution may be to eliminate utterly corporate taxes. Taxes on corporate profit could be collected from shareholders' income and/or on corporate cash flow before the interest is paid (not as now, after the deductions for the interest payments). That would be in line with a tendency to stay away from taxes that hurt capital formation.

Differences in corporate taxation distort the operation of the EU internal market. The Ruding Committee (1992) reaffirmed this observation, but recommended that the existing system of corporate taxation is retained. That is to say, that the state in which profits of a TNC originate should continue to tax them in full (i.e. both distributed and retained profits should be taxed). If the profits are transferred to the parent country, this state should exempt them from taxation or allow a tax credit for the taxes already paid in the country where they were made. This reflects difficulties in harmonization of taxes on the international level. It seems that tax reform *within* countries needs to precede tax reform *between* them.[28]

Juridical double taxation arises when a single economic income is taxed twice. If a firm (TNC) operates in two countries, its profit may be taxed by the two national tax authorities. It is often forgotten that what matters for TNCs is not the fact that profits are taxed twice, but rather the level of total taxation. If the profit of country A's TNC earned in country B has been taxed by country B, then country A may exempt this TNC from taxes on that part of its income earned in country B. Another method for solving this problem is that country A provides credit to its TNCs on taxes paid in country B. In this case the tax burden on country A's corporation operating in country B is the same as the one made from purely home operations in country A, provided that country B's taxes are lower or equal to those in country A.

The solution to the double taxation problem may also be found elsewhere. One of the possible solutions is the unitary method (with all its controversies) of collection of corporate taxes. A second one is the profit split method. Income of the distinct affiliates of a TNC is split in relation to the functions they perform and the associated risk. The difference between the profit split and the unitary method is that the former applies a functional analysis that is unique to each transaction, while the latter averages out all transactions. A third potential solution is the mutual agreement procedure where the national tax authorities discuss and try to correct tax discrepancies. In fact, they try to find a smooth way for the application of an existing method. The EU *Convention on the Elimination of Double Taxation in Connection with the Adjustment of Profits of Associated Enterprises* (1990) provided for binding arbitration related to the adjustment of profits of associated enterprises. A fourth answer may be found in advance-pricing agreements. This is, again, the application of an existing method. A TNC may acquire an advance agreement from the tax authority on the system for the allocation of its profit. This method represents a departure from the usual tax procedure (tax audits may take place even a few years after a transaction has taken place) since it refers to the unknown future evolution (UNCTAD, 1993, pp. 207–210).

3.3   *Personal income tax*

Differences in personal income taxes between countries and different regions within them may have effects on the mobility of labour. Actual labour mobility depends on a number of factors that include the chance of finding employment, improved standard of living, social obstacles, social security benefits and immigration rules. Differences in personal income taxes may be neither the most decisive nor the only incentive for labour to move. This difference is of significant influence only for the movement of the upper-middle class and the rich.

It is a generally accepted principle that taxes are applied in those countries in which income originated. In addition, most countries tax the global income of their residents, but with foreign tax relief. A person originating in country A who works for part of the year in country B and the rest of the year in country A would pay income tax on pay earned in country B and ask for tax credit while paying income tax in country A for the rest of the taxable income. This person's tax payment would be the same as if the whole income had been earned in country A, unless country B's income tax is higher than that in country A.

A tax ratio relates tax revenues to the GNP of a country. This ratio has been increasing over time. There are at least three reasons for such evolution. First, the welfare state has increased social care transfers. These are financed mostly by social security levies. Second, economic development and an increase in opportunities have had their impact on the growth of taxable incomes. Taxpayers were climbing into higher brackets, so these proceeds increased. Third, inflation has increased nominal tax revenues and devalued their real value.

Personal income tax is taken to be one of the most genuine rights of a state. There is little chance of this tax being harmonized in an EMU. The EU is fully aware of this issue, so it has few ambitions in the sphere of personal income taxation. On the one hand, a free mobility of labour in the EU may provide a behind-the-scenes pressure for a harmonization of national personal income taxes. On the other hand, that pressure may not be that great because of the still considerable social obstacles[29] to moving from one country to another.

A notable exception has often been the taxation of income of frontier and migrant workers. Tax agreements generally avoid double taxation, both in the country of destination (where the income was made) and the country of origin (where the income maker resides). Troublesome issues remain regarding deductions, allowances and applicable rates. Granting an allowance to a non-resident worker may involve a concession. This would be the case when the same allowance is offered by the country of residence. Generally, full taxation in the country of residence with a credit for tax paid in the source country is the solution (Cnossen, 1986, p. 558).

4 Indirect taxes

Indirect taxes are levied on the consumption of goods and services. They influence the retail price, and hence affect patterns of trade and consumption. Sales and turnover taxes, excise duties and tariffs are the basic indirect taxes. In contrast with direct taxes, indirect taxes are seldom progressive. The principles for the levying of these taxes will be considered before the analysis of indirect taxes.

4.1 Principles of destination and origin

Tax authorities are aware of the possible impact that indirect taxes have on trade in goods and services. Therefore, they introduced a safety device in the form of the destination and origin principle for taxation. That is of a great importance to those countries that integrate. According to the principle of destination taxes on goods are applied in the country of their consumption. That is the norm accepted in the GATT. According to the principle of origin taxes apply in the country of their production.

The destination principle states that consumption of all goods in one destination should be subject to the same tax irrespective of its origin. This principle removes tax distortions on competition between goods on the consuming country's market. The goods compete on equal tax conditions. This principle does not interfere with the location of production. It is widely accepted in international trade relations. The problem is that this principle may give the illusion that it stimulates exports and acts as a quasi-tariff on imports. This issue will be discussed shortly.

The origin or production principle asserts that all goods produced in one country should be taxed in that country, despite the possibility that these goods may be exported or consumed at home. If the production tax on good X in country A is lower than the same tax on the same good in country B, then if exported at zero transport and other costs, good X produced in country A will have a tax advantage in country B's market over country B's home-made good X. This introduces a distortion that interferes with the location of production between the countries. For allocational neutrality, a harmonized rate of tax, between countries, is a necessary condition.

Even within a customs union or a common market, there may exist fiscal frontiers if the member countries accept the principle of destination. The fiscal authorities of each country should know until where and when they are entitled to tax consumption of goods or services. The origin principle may have an advantage, for it does not require fiscal frontiers. This conserves scarce resources.

Taxes levied according to the destination and origin principles differ regarding their revenue impact. These two principles determine to which government the proceeds accrue. A full economic optimization can not be achieved if there are different tax rates levied on various goods. Suppose that country A levies a VAT at the rate of 25 per cent on cars only, while the partner country B applies a uniform tax at the rate of 10 per cent on all goods. Suppose that both countries apply the destination principle for tax collection. In this case, the production in either country would be maximized because it would not be affected by the tax. Consumption would, however, be distorted. The relative consumer prices would be distorted because cars are dearer relative to clothes in country A, than they are in country B. Consequently, country A's consumers buy fewer cars and more clothes than they would do otherwise. The opposite tendency prevails in country B. In this case, trade between the two countries would not be optimal. Conversely, suppose that the two countries collect taxes according to the origin principle. In this case trade would be optimized for the relative consumer prices would be the same in either country. So, although trade is optimized, tax would still distort the maximization of production. That is because producer prices, net of tax, would be reduced in a disproportionate way. Country A producers would be stimulated to produce clothes, rather than cars, while the opposite tendency would prevail in country B. Once indirect tax is not levied at a uniform rate on all goods, the choice is between the destination principle that maximizes production, but does not optimize trade and the origin principle that optimizes trade, but does not maximize production (Robson, 1987, pp. 122-123).

The principle of destination offers a chance for tax evasion that is unavailable (if the records are not faked) with the origin principle. If taxes differ, then a consumer may be tempted to purchase a good in the state in which the relative tax burden is lower and consume it in the country where the tax burden is relatively higher. Consumers may easily purchase goods in one country and send or bring them to another one, or order these goods from abroad. This tax evasion depends on the differences in taxation, cost of transport and cooperation of buyers and sellers which do not inform the tax authorities if they know that the objective of certain purchases is tax evasion. The revenue effect of a standard tax at a rate of 40 per cent in a country where tax evasion is widespread (e.g. the 'olive-oil belt' countries of the EU) may be much smaller than the revenue impact of the same tax at a rate of 10 per cent in the country where tax evasion is not a common practice.

The tax system in the US relies on corporate and personal income taxes applied at the origin principle. The west European tax authorities rely upon consumption taxes with the application of the destination principle. If the Europeans export goods to the US, they may have an advantage embodied in the difference in the tax systems. The US may contemplate the introduction of a border tax adjustment. This step may involve an addition to or reduction in the taxes already paid in Europe. The objective would be to keep competition in the US market on the same tax footing.

While the origin principle does not involve visible border tax adjustment, the destination principle includes it to the full extent of the tax. The long-run effect of either principle is, however, the same. In general equilibrium, any short-run advantage by one country will be eliminated in the long run by changes in the rate of exchange and domestic prices (Johnson and Krauss, 1973, p. 241). The US is a net importer of manufactured goods from Europe and Japan. It is advantageous, however, for the US to have these two exporting countries administer taxes on a destination, rather than origin basis (Hamilton and Whalley, 1986, p. 377). This is correct in the short run. In the long run general equilibrium, the operation of exchange rates and factor prices (Johnson-Krauss law) would, presumably, eliminate any short-run (dis)advantage to these countries.[30]

4.2 Sales and turnover taxes

Sales and turnover taxes are payments to the government that are applied to all taxable goods and services except those subject to excise duties. Turnover tax is applied during the process of production, while if the tax is applied during sales to the final consumer it is called a sales tax. There are two *methods* for the collection of the sales tax. One is the cumulative multi-stage cascade method, while the other method is called VAT. Apart from these two multi-phase methods for the collection of the sales tax, there is a one-stage method. This method is applied only once, either at the stage of production or at the wholesale or retail sales phase. The following analysis will deal with the multi-phase methods.

4.3   Cumulative multi-stage cascade method

According to the cumulative multi-stage cascade method for the collection of sales tax, the tax is applied every time goods and services are transferred against payment. The tax base includes the aggregate value of goods that includes previously paid taxes on raw materials and inputs. The levying and collection of this tax is relatively simple, the tax burden may appear to be distributed over a larger number of taxpayers and the rate of sales tax applied by this method is relatively lower than the rate applied by the VAT method.

Firms may be stimulated by this method of collection of sales tax to integrate vertically in order to pay tax only at the last stage of the production process. This may have a favourable impact on the expansion of the business activities of firms (diversification). It may, however, cause a misallocation of resources. This artificial vertical integration may erode the advantages of specialization and the efficiency of numerous SMEs if the vertically integrated firm ceases to use their output or if it absorbs them.

4.4   Value added tax

This method of collection of sales tax is applied every time a good or service is sold, but it applies only on the value that is added in the respective phase of production. That is the difference between the price paid for inputs and the price received for output. The application of VAT starts at the beginning of the production process and ends up in the retail sale to the final consumer. The VAT avoids double or multiple taxation of the previous stages of production. Every taxpayer has to prove to the tax authorities, by an invoice, that the tax has been paid in the previous stages of production. Hence, there is a kind of a self-regulating mechanism.

At the early stages of economic development, countries have relatively simple tax systems which apply only to a few goods and services. As countries develop, they tend to introduce a tax system that is more sophisticated, with a wider and more neutral tax base and coverage, and that is more efficient. Taxes on international trade (exports and imports) ought to be replaced by sales taxes that are collected by the VAT method. A relatively low rate of tax applied according to this method can raise a lot of proceeds. It does not distort the economy, because it is neutral to the production mix of home and imported factors. In addition, it does not discriminate between production for home and foreign markets. The VAT is neutral regarding the vertical integration of firms, so specialized SMEs may remain in business. If sales tax is collected according to the VAT method, then it would be harder to evade it in comparison to the situation where tax is collected only at the retail stage.

The VAT, on the principle of destination is accepted in the EU as the method for the collection of sales tax. The method is harmonized, but there is a wide range of differences in the rates of this tax among the EU countries. If the objective is to have a single rate of this tax, then there exists considerable room for improvement in the future. The elimination of fiscal frontiers in the EU in 1993 placed certain market pressures on tax authorities to 'align' the national VAT rates and prices, otherwise firms would lose business, in particular, in the frontier regions.

The White Paper (1985) proposed the setting up of the EU Clearing House System. Its role would be to ensure that the VAT collected in the exporting member country and deduced in the importing member country was reimbursed to the latter. The crucial feature in this system would play across EU-book-keeping and computerization. This system would, in principle, create a situation for taxable persons within the EU identical to the one that prevails in the member countries. In spite of the potential benefits of such a tax system, it was criticized on the grounds that it would be bureaucratic and costly.

In practice, however, the existence of widely diverging rates of tax and tax exemptions may expose the system to the risk of fraud and evasion. The EU was aware that some fraud and evasion already exists, but the scale of such distortions after the removal of fiscal frontiers without harmonization would, potentially, increase. Therefore, a minimum standard VAT rate of 15 per cent on most goods became a legal obligation in the EU from October 1992. It is relatively understandable for Britain (as well as Ireland and Greece) to protest against alignment since cross-border shopping is not a common feature in those countries as they have no common land frontier with the rest of the EU. However, for Austria, the Benelux countries, France and Germany, it is easy to accept such cross-border shopping arguments as it is common in those countries.

A move towards the origin principle (collection of tax during production) would require a system for redistribution of revenues (refunds) from the country where the goods were produced and taxed to the one where they are consumed. The effect of such a system would be as if the tax had been levied on consumption. Although there were concerns in some member countries because of the need to find alternative employment for thousands of customs officers, the fiscal frontiers among the EU countries were removed in 1993. That was the most visible benefit of the implementation of the 1992 Programme.[31] Consumers are now free to purchase goods in any EU country and bring them home with very few restrictions, provided that the imported goods are only for their personal consumption. There are, of course, exceptions; but, only two. The purchase of new cars is taxed in the country of registration, while mail-order purchases are taxed in the country of destination.

In any case the tax system of the EU was only transitional, until 1997 when the entire tax system was supposed to have been reassessed and made permanent. The final tax system will be moved towards the origin principle, but the deadline has been postponed. According to the interim system (introduced in 1993) companies pay the VAT in the country of consumption. This system replaced time-consuming tax controls and payments at the EU internal borders with a demanding centralized reporting system carried out by the companies themselves. The final system will allow firms to pay the VAT in the country of origin, as if all EU member countries were a single country. The burden of redistribution of VAT revenue will then fall on the member states. This would be advantagous to businesses as they would not have to differentiate between domestic and intra-EU sales. None the less, there will be two problems. First, a clearing-house system will have to redistribute revenue around the EU as countries that export a lot will benefit from the system, while those that import a lot will lose. Second, the origin-based tax system will enhance the need for a higher harmonization of VAT rates. In the meantime, the current transitory system seems to be operating quite well. This will, of course, be taken into account during the reassessment of the tax system.

Table 4.3 illustrates differences in VAT rates in the EU countries. The underlined rates are the standard ones, as well as the lower rates for food, clothing and other essential items. Portugal has lower rates in its autonomous regions. Ireland and Britain use the zero rate for food, books and children's clothing. The other countries generally apply an exception with credit (which comes down to the same thing as a zero rate) to exports and supplies assimilated to exports, such as supplies to embassies, to ships leaving the country and the like. In Ireland and Britain these supplies are also covered by the zero rate.

A broad-based VAT can be criticized on the grounds that it is regressive. The reason for the regressive impact of the VAT in the EU can be found in the structure of national demand. Consumption to which VAT applies, usually embraces a relatively higher proportion of the GNP in the less advanced member countries than in the richer ones. Other components of demand, such as investment, that is presumably higher in the advanced countries, is not burdened by the VAT. The low-income segment of the population can be helped by transfer payments. This can make VAT directly progressive. Zero rating, exemptions and multiple rates do not always directly assist the low-income group of the population intended to be helped.

The EU conducted a wide-ranging survey in the second half of the 1980s. About 20,000 businessmen from 12 member countries of the EU were asked

Table 4.3   VAT rates in EU countries in 1997

Country	VAT rate (%)
1 Austria	10, <u>20</u>
2 Belgium	1, <u>6</u>, 12, <u>21</u>
3 Denmark	<u>25</u>
4 Finland	6, <u>12</u>, <u>17</u>, <u>22</u>
5 France	2.1, <u>5.5</u>, <u>20.6</u>
6 Germany	7, <u>15</u>
7 Greece	4, <u>8</u>, <u>18</u>
8 Ireland	<u>0</u>, 3.3, 12.5, <u>21</u>
9 Italy	4, <u>10</u>, 16, <u>19</u>
10 Luxembourg	<u>3</u>, 6, <u>12</u>, <u>15</u>
11 Netherlands	<u>6</u>, <u>17.5</u>
12 Portugal	<u>5</u>, 12, <u>17</u>
13 Spain	<u>4</u>, <u>7</u>, <u>16</u>
14 Sweden	6, 12, <u>25</u>
15 United Kingdom	<u>0</u>, <u>17.5</u>

Source: International Bureau of Fiscal Documentation (1997)

to rank the worst barriers to free trade. The most damaging of all were overt obstacles. Different national technical standards, administrative and customs formalities were at the top of the list. Differences in rates of VAT and excise duties were at the bottom of the list of eight barriers (Emerson *et al.*, 1988, pp. 44–46).

4.5   Excise duties

Excise duties are a type of indirect tax that are levied for the purpose of raising public revenue. They are applied in almost every country to tobacco, spirits and liquid fuels. Excise duties are also applied in some countries to coffee, tea, cocoa, salt, bananas, light bulbs and playing cards. These duties are levied only once. It is usually at the stage of production or import. Another property of excise duties is that they are generally high in relation to other taxes.

While the VAT is proportional to the value of output, an excise duty may be based either on the *ad valorem* principle (retail or wholesale price) or it may be a specific tax. Within the EU, tobacco products are subject to both. There is a specific tax per cigarette and an *ad valorem* tax based on the retail price of the cigarettes concerned (Kay, 1990, p. 34).

Table 4.4 presents the rates of excise duties in the EU member countries and the minimum EU rates. There is a wide variety in the rates of excise duties among the member countries. This difference is due to the various choices of fiscal and health authorities. If the difference in excise duties among countries exceeds the costs of the reallocation of resources or transport, it will have a distorting effect on the allocation of resources or pattern of trade. The difference in the excise duty on 1,000 litres of petrol of ECU

Table 4.4   Excise duty rates in EU countries in 1992

Country	Pure alcohol (ECU per hl)	Wine (ECU per hl)	Beer ECU per hl)	Cigarettes		Petrol ECU per 1,000 l)
				ECU per 1,000	ad valorem (%)	
1 Austria	739	0	1	17	41	406
2 Belgium	1,607	37	1	9	50	479
3 Denmark	3,698	87	3	80	21	467
4 Finland	5,016	284	11	12	50	532
5 France	1,381	3	1	5	55	585
6 Germany	1,327	0	1	43	25	562
7 Greece	550	0	1	3	54	406
8 Ireland	2,757	272	9	72	17	378
9 Italy	593	0	1	3	53	527
10 Luxembourg	1,037	0	1	3	54	408
11 Netherlands	1,540	50	2	38	21	566
12 Portugal	715	0	1	7	56	479
13 Spain	552	0	1	3	50	394
14 Sweden	5,132	284	10	81	0	498
15 United Kingdom	2,634	180	5	74	20	462
EU min.	550	0	1	–	–	337

Source: Commission of the EU (1995)

191 between France and Spain is significant when one bears in mind that it costs just a few ECUs to transport this amount of fuel by pipeline.

The VAT is calculated on the price of a good that includes the excise duty. Any change in the excise duties will produce differences in the VAT revenue. Hence the need for harmonization of excise duties too. One solution to maintain national fiscal frontiers within the EU could be done in a similar way to that by which the US retains different liquor duties among its states. Liquor and cigarettes should bear the national tax authority stamp. Only the nationally stamped goods could be purchased legally within a state. Import for personal consumption would be unlimited, while bulk intra-EU commercial transport and trade in these goods without the proper tax clearance would be forbidden. The rates proposed by the Commission should be viewed only as a yardstick for approximation as it would be most difficult and highly uncertain to try to unify excise duties throughout the EU member countries (waiting for Godot).

The goods that are subject to excise duties are normally stored in bonded warehouses that are controlled by the public authorities. Once the goods are taken out for consumption, the excise duty is levied. If the goods are exported, the excise duty is not charged upon the presentation of a proof of export. The importing country of these goods controls the import at the frontier where it establishes liability for excise duties of these goods. This ensures that excise duty is charged in the country where the goods are consumed. After the removal of tax and other frontiers, the wide divergence in excise duties would distort trade, because of a real danger of fraud and evasion. The White Paper proposed as a solution a linkage system for bonded warehouses for products subject to excise duties and the approximation of these charges in the EU.

The benefits that accrue from the elimination of fiscal frontiers in an EMU include the following. The investment decisions of the firms are improved as the tax system increases the degree of certainty in relation to the situation when every country manages its own taxes. A removal of tax posts at the frontiers saves resources and, more importantly, increases the opportunities for competition. Of course, some facilities for random anti-terrorist, health, veterinary and illegal immigration checks may be necessary. Finally, harmonization of the tax system would enhance the equalization of prices and lower the distortions due to different systems and rates of taxation.

5 Budget of the European Union

5.1 Introduction

Together with the law and its enforcement, the budget, its revenue and expenditure, is one of the most essential instruments that an economic and/or political organization may employ to fulfil its role. The budget should cover not only administrative costs, but also dispose of funds for intervention in the economy. Otherwise, the role of such an organization will be limited to mere consultation and, perhaps, research of certain issues. Most international organizations cover only their administrative expenses. A rare exception is the EU, which returns and redistributes around 95 per cent of its receipts. The budgets of the member countries reduce their expenditure for their own interventions in the fields where the EU has competence and where it intervenes.

The theory of fiscal federalism looks at a central fiscal authority and considers its relations with the lower administrative levels. In a general case, this consideration is complicated by the existence of different currencies that take part in the venture and that are not irrevocably linked through the fixed exchange rate. If an EMU is to conduct an effective stabilization policy it should be endowed with the power to tax and borrow. This implies that its budget may be not only in balance, but more importantly, in temporary deficit or surplus over an economic cycle. An EMU may not necessarily directly tax firms and individuals, as it may tax member governments. In order to maximize welfare, the EMU needs to decide about the preferred distribution of functions among distinct governments (principles of subsidiarity, cooperation or competition). It should also act upon that decision and allocate public goods and services that ought to be provided commonly, and others, that are to be supplied at a national or local level.

A common approach to the macroeconomic management of an EMU is subject to a number of pitfalls. The first one is the issue of a common stance on major macroeconomic variables. Even if the member countries agree on the major objectives (rate of exchange, inflation, rate of interest, balance-of-payments position, unemployment and the like) they also have to agree on the economic policy instruments and their timing. Even though the countries concur about the major macroeconomic goals, they may use different, and often conflicting, means to achieve the stated objectives. Instead of improving the economic situation such an economic policy may well worsen it. Therefore, it is not only the main economic goals that the member countries should agree upon, but also they should concur regarding the methods that should be employed to achieve them. This means that a common fiscal and common monetary policy require each other in harmony in an EMU.

Integration of fiscal policy in the absence of integration of monetary policy and vice versa in an EMU may be a futile effort. Of course, the agreed economic policy would not need to have an equal effect on all member countries. Similarly, as in a single country, public economic policy does not have identical effects on all regions or industries. One solution to this problem may be found in the creation of built-in stabilizers, such as the transfer of resources among the member states or among regions within a country. In spite of the above disputes among economists, there is a certain agreement that economic stabilization can be influenced in the short run by the joint action of fiscal and monetary policies. It may control expenditure, employment and output around their 'natural' levels and avoid excess demand that creates inflation. If economic ties among countries are highly interlaced, then the optimal solutions to economic issues may be found in a joint action of the countries concerned, rather than in an atomized and uncoordinated way.

5.2   European Union

The EU is on its way towards an EMU. None the less, the absolute and relative size of its budget is rather small in relation to its share of the joint GNP of the member states, as well as the potential impact on the economic life of the EU. As such, it differs from the national budgets since it neither plays a significant role in economic stabilization, nor allocation of resources (apart from agriculture). In addition, its stabilization role is further jeopardized by the request that it must be in annual balance without any provision to take on loans to finance the possible deficits (Article 199 of the Treaty of Rome).

The budget of the EU is subject to the principle of annuality. That is to say, financial operations need to be executed within the given budget year. This eases the control of the work of the EU executive branch. The financial year is equal to the calendar year. The Union, however, has sometimes to engage in multiannual financial operations. These operations are continuously expanding. Therefore, those dual requirements are reflected in the entry of two distinct appropriations. First, the commitment appropriations refer to the total cost in the current financial year of the obligations that are to be carried out over a period of more than one financial year. Second, the payment appropriations cover expenditure (to the limit entered in the current annual budget) that result from the commitments undertaken in the current financial year and/or preceding financial years.

The Treaty of Rome (Article 203) sets two types of EU budgetary outlays. They are compulsory and non-compulsory expenditures. The distinction between the two kinds of expenditure is basically political, so it is often a source of conflict between the Parliament and the Council of Ministers. A vague definition of the two kinds of expenditures was drafted in 1982 by a joint Declaration of the Commission, Council of Ministers and Parliament. It stated that compulsory expenditure from the budget is obligatory for the EU in order to make it meet its obligations. It refers both to the internal and external tasks that stem from the Treaties and other Acts. All other expenditure is non-compulsory. The Council has the last word on compulsory expenditure, while the Parliament decides on the non-compulsory outlays. The Parliament may increase the amount of non-compulsory expenditure by amending the draft budget. The maximum rate of increase in relation to the preceding fiscal year depends on the trend of the increase in the GNP in the EU, average variation in the budgets of the member states, trends in the cost of living, as well as on the approval by the Council. Before the drafting of a new budget, the presidents of the three institutions have a 'trialogue' meeting to determine the grouping of the new budget chapters and the ones for which the legal basis might have changed.

5.3 Expenditure

The budgetary crises of the 1980s prompted the EU institutions to reconsider budgetary procedure and discipline. The budget was sometimes balanced by accounting tricks dubbed 'creative accounting'. Certain payments were deferred till the following year, when it was expected that the financial conditions would improve. As a part of the reform, the Commission, the Council and the European Parliament concluded the binding Interinstitutional Agreement in 1988. A reference point for the budgetary expenditure was the financial perspective from 1988 to 1992. The new Interinstitutional Agreement covers the period 1993 to 1999.

The financial perspective marks the maximum amount of payment appropriations for the various chapters of EU expenditure. It is not, however, a multiannual budget, as the usual annual budgetary procedure is still a key element for the decision about the exact volume of budgetary expenditure (but up to the ceiling provided by the financial perspective). The three institutions agree to respect the annual expenditure ceiling for each expenditure item. The ceilings, however, need to be sufficiently large in order to allow for the flexibility necessary for the budgetary management. The ceiling may be revised in either direction, but that depends only on unforeseen events (such as German reunification, the violent disintegration of the former Yugoslavia or aid to Rwanda) that took place after the Inter-institutional Agreement was signed.

The reform of the budget of 1988 had three additional aspects. First, the total own resources of the EU budget were not linked to the VAT contribution. Instead, resources needed to cover the budgetary expenditure had a ceiling in appropriations for payments. That overall ceiling was fixed for each year from 1988 to 1992 as a percentage of the Union's GNP (e.g. 1.15 per cent in 1989 and 1.2 per cent in 1992). The new ceilings would gradually increase from 1.20 per cent to 1.27 per cent in the period which ends in 1999. Second, the budgetary discipline, as a shared responsibility of the Commission, the Council and the Parliament, was increased. Its major objective was to check farm expenditure. The means to achieving that is a guideline that may not increase by more than 74 per cent of the annual rate of growth of the GNP of the EU. Third was the coordination and increase in effectiveness of the three Structural Funds (European Agricultural Guarantee and Guidance Fund, European Regional Development Fund and European Social Fund). The objectives included the adjustment of regions whose development was below the EU average, structural conversion in the regions hit by industrial decline, the fight against long-term unemployment, the occupational integration of young people, the adjustment of the farm structure and development of rural areas.

The European Council (Edinburgh, 1992) reaffirmed the basic goals of the EU budgetary policy. Following the doubling of the Structural Fund appropriations from 1988 to 1992, the EU was able to continue its regional and social development efforts. The expenditure in future would mainly affect those EU *regions* in which average GNP per capita is less than 75 per cent of the EU average. The expenditure from the Cohesion Fund in those *countries* where the per capita GNP is less than 90 per cent of the EU average (Greece, Ireland, Portugal and Spain) is to help those countries comply with the EU legislation. This needs to be done by financing transport infrastructure or environmental projects. In addition, expenditure on internal policies is supposed to increase in future. The main priority will be the financing of the trans-European transport, telecommunications and energy networks. Emphasis will be given to the cross-frontier links between the national networks. As for external action, the EU will pay attention to emergency aid (primarily to the countries in the vicinity: transition countries and the Mediterranean region, basically to prevent undesired migratory inflows of people), as well as loan guarantees.

EU expenditure has expanded and diversified remarkably since its inception. Table 4.5 presents budgetary expenditure in 1996. The guarantee expenditure of the CAP disposes of half of the entire budget. Hence, in

Table 4.5 The 1996 budget expenditure (ECUs millions)

Chapter	Payments	
	Amount	%
1 Common Agricultural Policy (guarantee expenditure)	41,320.0	49.4
2 Structural funds	26,005.6	31.1
of which:		
– Agriculture Guidance	3,859.4	4.6
– ERDF	10,663.1	12.8
– ESF	6,031.6	7.2
– Cohesion Fund	1,919.3	2.3
– Fisheries	314.0	0.4
3 Research	3,096.6	3.7
4 External action	4,718.2	5.6
5 Administration	4,128.6	4.9
6 Repayments and other	2,611.4	3.1
General budget	*81,888,4*	*98.0*
European Development Fund	1,434.0	1.7
European Coal and Steel Community	247.0	0.3
Grand total	83,569.4	100.0

Source: *The Community Budget: The Facts and Figures* (Brussels: EC, 1996)

relative terms, not much remains for many other EU economic policies. Structural funds of the EU include the European Regional Development Fund (ERDF), European Social Fund (ESF), the Guidance Section of the Agricultural Fund and, from 1993, the Cohesion Fund. Outlays on transport and fisheries are also included in this chapter. The share of Structural funds is 31 per cent of the budget. A notable feature of the components of this chapter is that their shares are continuously rising in the general budget over time. The (ab)use of structural funds may become a serious stumbling block in the future, just as agricultural expenditure has continued to be for decades.

Administrative operations cost the EU only 5 per cent of its budget, while the rest of the budget is redistributed mostly to the member countries. This distinguishes the EU from other international organizations, since elsewhere, the budget is used mainly for the administrative expenditure.

5.4 Revenue

The EU budget was financed by the national contributions of member states until 1970. After that, the EU got its 'own' resources, including customs duties, agricultural levies and a budget-balancing resource of up to 1 per cent of the VAT base (the base was increased to 1.4 per cent in 1985). Own resources of the EU budget represent a one-time tax revenue allocated to the EU. They accrue automatically to the EU without any need for additional decisions by national governments. A reform of finances in 1988 changed and expanded own financial resources of the EU. These resources are: customs duties; agricultural, sugar and isoglucose levies; VAT resources; the fourth resource; and miscellaneous revenue.

Table 4.6 presents the EU budget revenue in 1996. Customs duties and agricultural levies are the 'natural' proceeds of a customs union. First, customs duties that are applied on imports of goods from non-member countries represent 15 per cent of revenue. Their relative impact is diminishing over time as tariffs are being continuously reduced through the GATT rounds of tariff negotiations. This trend may be partly compensated by an increase in the volume of trade with external countries, but recession can reduce the level of economic activity and, consequently, reduce imports.

Second, agricultural levies (2 per cent of the budget revenue) are variable charges applied on imports of farm goods included in the CAP, and that are imported from third countries. They are a changeable source of revenue for they depend on the volume of imports that relies in part on weather conditions and partly on the trade concessions that the EU offers to foreign partners. Another element in this fluctuation is that world market prices for agricultural goods frequently change. The EU is becoming increasingly self-sufficient in a number of agricultural products of the temperate zone, hence there is a reduction in demand for imports. Sugar and isoglucose levies are charges on producers that are supposed to make them share the financial burden of market support for production and storage.

Third, the VAT contribution includes 49 per cent of the revenue. It is calculated for each member country by the application of a uniform rate of 1.4 per cent to the national VAT base. This base may not exceed 55 per cent of the national GNP.

Fourth is a relatively new source known as the 'fourth resource'. It is closely related to a country's ability to pay. This revenue item provided 33 per cent of the EU budget. Together with the VAT resources, it is the only dynamic component of the budgetary revenue as it is derived from the application of a rate to the GNP of each member country. It is an additional source as it is calculated during the budgetary procedure in order to top up the difference between the budgetary expenditure and (insufficient) revenue that accrues from other sources.

The fifth revenue item is negligible relative to the total budget. It covers miscellaneous revenue such as deductions from the salaries of the EU civil servants, fines and possible surpluses from preceding years.

5.5 Problems

The preceding considerations revealed that both EU budget expenditure and revenue were related neither to the EU need to influence economic life (save for agriculture) as national governments can do nor, until, recently to the relative economic wealth of the member countries. Instead of singling out

Table 4.6 The financing of the 1996 budget (ECUs millions)

Country	Agricultural levies	%	Customs duties	%	VAT	%	Fourth resource	%	Total	%
Belgium	117.8	2.8	855.8	27.5	1,235.3	41.4	848.0	27.3	3,106.9	100.0
Denmark	45.2	2.9	219.6	14.0	770.8	49.3	528.8	33.8	1,564.4	100.0
Germany	472.7	1.9	3,591.0	14.7	12,863.5	52.7	7,493.6	30.7	24,420.8	100.0
Greece	26.5	2.2	135.0	11.3	664.3	55.5	370.7	31.0	1,196.5	100.0
Spain	105.4	2.0	546.1	10.5	2,812.2	54.2	1,724.6	33.2	5,188.3	100.0
France	364.9	2.5	1,203.0	8.4	7,971.1	55.6	4,799.3	33.5	14,338.3	100.0
Ireland	11.0	1.4	229.5	29.9	347.5	45.3	179.6	23.3	767.6	100.0
Italy	194.5	2.0	953.6	9.7	5,098.2	51.7	3,622.4	36.7	9,868.8	100.0
Luxembourg	0.1	0.0	15.1	8.3	110.7	60.5	57.2	31.2	183.1	100.0
Netherlands	149.0	3.2	1,325.8	28.0	2,038.8	43.1	1,215.4	25.7	4,729.0	100.0
Austria	44.4	1.9	361.9	15.4	1,214.8	51.7	727.7	31.0	2,348.8	100.0
Portugal	95.9	7.9	134.6	11.1	647.3	53.4	334.5	27.6	1,212.3	100.0
Finland	23.9	1.9	235.0	19.0	589.8	47.6	390.4	31.5	1,239.1	100.0
Sweden	62.9	2.7	580.9	24.8	998.2	42.7	698.4	29.8	2,340.4	100.0
United Kingdom	249.2	2.8	2,466.0	28.0	2379.8	27.0	3,721.0	42.2	8,816.1	100.0
Other									568.1	
Total	1,963.4	2.4	12,852.9	15.7	39,792.3	48.9	26,711.8	32.6	81,888.4	100.0

Source: The Community Budget: The Facts and Figures (Brussels: EC, 1996).

economic areas that need to be influenced at the EU level, and then creating the necessary funds, the EU still continues to pick up policies that can fit into these limited funds. It should not be forgotten, however, that it is neither the absolute nor the relative size of the budget that matters. What matters is the size of funds that are necessary to change certain behaviour in the desired direction. In some cases this amount can be rather minuscule, such as the development of SMEs where a simple freedom of establishment, tax incentives and loan guarantees can do the job. In others, such as agriculture, infrastructure or adjustment out of obsolete industries, the amounts required to change behaviour in the desired way can be quite large.

When the member countries of the EU agree to pursue a common policy, one can also expect that the means for the carrying out of that policy may also be transferred upwards towards the EU institutions. The problem is that the member countries take the EU as the appropriate plane for the conduct of common policies in certain cases, but they are quite unyielding (mainly Britain) when new funds have to be collected. Reforms of the EU budget are resisted by the regions and countries that benefit from the present structure (mainly the agricultural regions in the north and the less developed ones in the south). An increased expenditure on economic activities (other than agriculture), without extra funds, can jeopardize the current distribution of costs and benefits. Without the ability to increase or substantially reorganize spending, the EU should endeavour to coordinate its own expenditure with that of the member countries. The application of common rules on the size and trend in public expenditure are expected to lead to the final stage of the EMU. They need to be followed as fiscal 'indiscipline' by one or several member countries may affect the fiscal policy of the EU as a whole.

The EU budget absorbs only around 1 per cent of the combined GNP of its member countries. Compared with the national budgets (agriculture apart) it plays only a limited role in the redistribution of income and allocation of resources. Its role in economic stabilization has never existed. The influential MacDougall Report (1977) noted that in federal states such as the US and Germany, federal spending was in the neighbourhood of 20-25 per cent of GNP. Such an increase in the EU spending can not be reasonably expected in the near future. In the pre-federal stage of the EU, a budget that absorbs 5-7 per cent of the combined GNP (without transfers for defence) could have an impact on economic stabilization and an evening of regional disparities. Such a budget might be able to influence social (unemployment, education, health, retirement), regional and external aid policies. Resources might be found either in the transfer of funds from the national budgets and/or in an increase in the 'fourth' budgetary resource. The problem is that the member countries are still reluctant to increase the budgetary powers of the EU. If the EU gets more resources for its budget, the total public expenditure in the EU, compared with similar uncoordinated outlays of member states, may be reduced because of the economies of scale. A budget with increased resources may represent a built-in stabilizer for macroeconomic management. In addition, transfers among regions may enhance economic convergence and strengthen the cohesion of the EU.

In contrast to a variety of revenue sources employed to fill the national budgets, the EU budget is financed from a narrow range of taxes. On the expenditure side, there is a high concentration of resources in one area: farming. This contrasts with the much diversified public expenditure in member countries. However, the possibility of changing such a pattern of EU revenue still remains in the hands of member countries and is left to their willingness to enhance the powers of the EU. The EU should avoid a situation in the future in which member countries have a single monetary policy and, at the same time, largely decentralized and uncoordinated fiscal policies.

Apart from all the stated problems, the EU has a strong indirect means for controlling a significant part of public expenditure in all member countries. That is EU competition policy. State aids absorb a sizeable chunk of the national budgets. To control these outlays it does not require extra expenditure from the EU budget.[32] One may expect that in the near future an extensive reform of the EU budget will, unfortunately, not happen. An event like this would be coupled with considerable political sensitivity. Instead, what may take place is the reform, or rather restructuring (in relative terms), within the framework of the existing budget. Increased contributions to the EU budget according to the level of national wealth or the principle of the ability to pay should further be encouraged.

6 Conclusion

A country or a group of countries that frequently change fiscal systems end up on the track away from liberalization, may be regarded as potentially risky locations for investment. This may provoke a reduction in the inflow and an increase in the outflow of capital to the relatively more stable and growing destinations. Complete unification of fiscal systems, however, may not be a prerequisite for the smooth functioning of an EMU. The US is the best example in support of this argument. The federal states in the US have differences in their respective tax systems. This system has functioned relatively satisfactorily without any tax posts between the states for a number of decades. However, one must note that the differences in the tax systems among the federal states in the US are not that great. There exists a significant degree of harmonization among tax systems in federal units.

A genuine internal market in the EU requires a degree of harmonization of indirect taxes among its member countries. Otherwise, member governments will have to accept substantial diversions in revenues. It is widely believed that a difference in sales tax of up to 5 per cent can introduce distortions that may be acceptable among the integrated countries and that will not bring unbearable budgetary problems. However, the problem arises when the national budgets have different trends regarding their deficits. Alterations in the national tax systems in such situations can bring serious political difficulties.

As for the possibility for a significant degree of harmonization (or, in an extreme case, unification) of fiscal systems in the EMU, there are certain reasons for pessimism. A tax policy is one of the most fundamental national sovereign rights. Recall Britain's vehement opposition to the inclusion of fiscal matters in the majority-voting issues in the Single European Act. The achievement of national goals within a fiscal policy do not necessarily coincide at all times with those of other partners. Although an EMU may agree on the basic objectives, their achievement may be left to the member countries which may sometimes wish to use different and potentially conflicting instruments. None the less, the sophisticated market led approach (bottom-up) to integration in tax matters that came from the Single European Act (a removal of fiscal frontiers) might compel national tax authorities to align their tax rates and systems. Otherwise, other things being equal, businesses may move to and settle in the countries where tax treatment is most favourable. This bottom-up approach by the EU is a significant shift from the earlier policy proposals that argued in favour of full tax harmonization (top-down).

The public is sensitive to changes in tax systems. Full fiscal harmonization in the EMU may require an increase in taxes in some countries (e.g. Germany) while it may require their decrease in others (e.g. Denmark and Ireland). In the low-tax countries there is an opposition to tax increases, while in the high-tax countries, there is a fear of revenue losses. Therefore, a partial fiscal harmonization (only agreed taxes) might be a good first step. One of the flaws of the Single Market Programme of the EU is that very little has been done in the area of taxation. Harmonization of fiscal systems of the countries that are in the EMU requires caution, gradualism and, more than anything else, the political will which economic theory cannot predict.

The Maastricht Treaty has enhanced the role of the EU institutions. New EU-wide policies and responsibilities require EU to play a much more prominent part than before the Maastricht Treaty. This involves an increase in common resources, as well as the coordination of fiscal, monetary, social and regional policies. The EU ought to have the right to tax and spend in its own right, at least up to the agreed limit. How to persuade the national governments to abandon a part of their fiscal sovereignty in favour of the EU in order to reap the rewards of fiscal integration is a question to be dealt with in politics and diplomacy.

III   INDUSTRIAL POLICY IN MANUFACTURING AND SERVICES

1   Introduction

Explicit industrial policy as a part of overall economic policy has not been at the centre of research interest in industrialized countries up to the mid-1970s. This is due to underlying economic developments. During the 1960s and early 1970s these countries experienced relatively fast economic growth with low rates of inflation and unemployment. Prices of raw materials were stable and relatively low, while labour flowed without major disturbances from agriculture to the manufacturing and services sectors. Excess demand for labour was met by a steady inflow of labour from abroad. This period was also characterized by sporadic government intervention to influence the pattern of national manufacturing and services production. Relatively free markets were operating smoothly without significant disruption. During this period, the GATT was active in the lowering of tariffs.

The 'golden' 1960s were followed by a period whose first characteristic was a sharp increase in the price of oil in 1973. This triggered rises in inflation, unemployment and a deceleration in the rate of growth throughout the world. International competition increased sharply because suppliers were fighting on shrinking markets. It seemed that the free market system was not capable of coping satisfactorily with this situation. There appeared an awareness about a need for alternative strategies (i.e. those based on intervention in manufacturing, services and trade) to cope with the new situation. Industrial policy could be seen as a supply-side response to market imperfections. Discussion was less about the formation of capital and more about its allocation. It was also more about the adjustment policy than about an industrial policy (a term not liked by either the politicians or the neo-classical economists). None the less, the gloves were off for the debate about industrial policy in the developed market economies.

This section is structured as follows. The explanation of the rationale (market failure) for an industrial policy is followed by a consideration of the meaning of this policy. Various issues related to industrial policy are considered in a separate part, just as is the case with the problem of picking winners or losers in industry. Industrial policy in the manufacturing sector, including the technology policy, of the EU is presented before the analysis of industrial policy in the services sector. At the end of the section, there is a certain doubt about the possibility of implementing a sound industrial policy, both in a single democratic country or in economic unions because of various interests and coordination problems.

2 Background

The classical economic model based on free trade and perfect competition predicted that *laissez-faire* is universally beneficial and costless. The new theory of strategic[33] trade and industrial policy demonstrated cases where intervention (including an industrial policy) can play a useful role in mitigating the shortcomings of market imperfections. In general, economic adjustment (reallocation of resources) is prompted by an increase in GNP, as well as changes in demand, technology, prices, foreign competition, marketing and organization of markets which all contribute to a potential loss in current competitiveness. This adjustment is neither smooth nor easy nor costless, hence the need for an industrial policy. Instead of relying on the inherited and nature-based advantages, industrial policy may help in the conscious shaping of a country's comparative advantage through the supply of trained labour and educated management of a specific profile (e.g. engineers vs. priests); tax, infrastructure, public purchase and R&D policies. One thing, however, has to be clear from the outset. Both intervention (action) and *laissez-faire* (non-intervention) have an impact on the structure of industry. The challenge for a government is to profit from the balance between the best features of the two approaches. That is, however, not at all easy.

Countries in the EU and the US have responded to the circumstances prevailing during the 1970s primarily by protectionism. These and other industrialized countries realized that the solution to lagging productivity, recession and deteriorating export performance could be found in policies that affect the development of national industry. None the less, inadequate economic performance is not a sufficient condition for the justification of industrial policy. The question is not whether the economy is operating (un)satisfactorily, but rather whether an industrial policy might have achieved a better result than a free market system (Adams, 1983, p. 405). Any policy has to be tested according to its gains and losses in a dynamic context.

Once free markets lose credibility as efficient conductors of an economy, interventions (in various economic policies) seem inevitable. Now, the question is how can the government intervene in the most efficient and least harmful way? The choice might be between the risk of leaving the economy to the imperfect entrepreneurs or, possibly, the even greater danger of having it run by imperfect governments (Curzon Price, 1981, p. 20). However, there is no *a priori* reason why an economy run by imperfect governments is possibly at even greater risk than an economy run by imperfect businessmen and vice versa. Both of them are second best operators.

Risk-taking (entrepreneurship) has always been a significant engine of economic growth. The benefits of risk-taking are not without peril, of course. The greatest part of the cost of adjustment to the changed situation is borne by those who are powerless. Therefore, governments quite often followed a defensive policy whose objective was to ensure employment in the short run and evade social tensions, at least during their term in office. The socialization of risk in the form of various economic policies may introduce a safer life, but may also prevent both the free operation of individual entrepreneurial activity and an even greater increase in the economic pie. This process may be seen as a reconciliation of the public's desire to see a happy marriage between progress and stability (Blais, 1986, p. 41). Interestingly, the British experience has shown that rescuing declining industries (such as coal) to protect jobs was not a safe method of re-election.

Tax-payers and consumers have increased their awareness of the costs of such an exercise. However, the influence of trade unions in declining industries can still mobilize a strong lobby in many countries. Those who have full confidence in the operation of a free market system say that the market will take care of itself. Why bother to change those things which will happen on their own? This school of thought fails to consider a number of serious market imperfections.

The most influential reasons for intervention may be found in the loss of a competitive position, the management of expansion of new and the decline of old industries, the handling of industries subject to scale effects and externalities, as well as attracting footloose industries (Lipsey, 1987a, p. 117). Fostering strategic industries[34] which have strong forward and backward linkages with the rest of the economy can be very attractive policy goal. These industries supply external or non-priced gains to the whole economy. Growing industries such as semiconductors and electronics have a much more profound spillover effect on the economy than the furniture or clothing industry.

Another classification of the reasons for an industrial policy groups them in three broad categories. There are respectable, false and non-economic arguments in favour of intervention (Curzon Price, 1990, pp. 159–167):

- Respectable arguments include *market failures* because, in practice, a perfect competition model does not always lead to a stable equilibrium. However, the problem is that a market failure such as wage rigidity or monopolies can be traced to a previous intervention by the government. *Domestic distortions* may be used as another pretext for intervention. A uniform VAT system may be neutral regarding the consumption of goods or services. If one wants to reduce the VAT rate on food, a share of resources may shift to that industry at the time when telecommunications or data processing may employ them in a more effective way. *Infant industries* offer an appealing reason for intervention, but the problem is that there are many old 'infants' that may never become self-sustaining. Is Airbus one of them? One can build an intellectually respectable case for industrial policy on *positive externalities* and spillover effects (Krugman, 1993, pp. 160–161).[35] These include benefits from the setting of common technical standards for production and/or operation of goods, e.g. telecommunications. However, there may be costly mistakes in targeting, such as computers in France, Concorde (Britain and France), or petrochemicals and aluminium in Japan prior to the first oil shock. The process may become too politicized and subject to strong lobbying as in the case of *public goods* that everyone wants and consumes, although these goods could be produced at a commercial loss.
- The first false argument in favour of intervention is the issue of *employment*. If employment subsidies extend the life of jobs in declining

businesses, these funds are taken from growing industries that might need them to expand their operations and that could improve job opportunities both in quality and quantity in the future. The proponents of the *balance-of-payments* argument for intervention often forget that resources that move into protected industries could relinquish those industries in which export opportunities may be more favourable. Hence a drop in imports may provoke a fall in exports.

- Non-economic arguments can be quite strong. It is often hard to dispute the issue of *national security*. This is a political process that eludes the prediction abilities of the economist. The problem is that it may be pushed to the limit where most industries can be labelled as essential for national defence. In general, a possible nuclear war and 'smart bombs' reduce the weight of the national security argument for intervention. Long-term supply contracts from allies and stockpiling may be considered prior to intervention. *Social arguments* for intervention that distributes, rather than creates wealth, such as regional development or the protection of the environment may have certain non-economic weight during the discussion about intervention.

The relative shares of the manufacturing industry and agriculture in GDP and employment have been continuously declining in the industrialized countries over the past decades. GDP and employment in these countries on average consists mostly of services (60 per cent), while the rest is distributed between manufacturing (35 per cent) and agriculture (5 per cent). Hence, the process of deindustrialization leads countries to a post- industrial society. These countries could be better called service rather than industrialized economies, because manufacturing industry is a statistically 'shrinking' sector in relation to services.[36] One has to be very cautious with such generalizations. Many services (around a half) are directly linked with the manufacturing of goods such as transport, financial, telecommunication and other business services that cover everything from cleaning offices to business consultancy and advertising.[37] These services are not directly aimed at individuals for their personal consumption. If they are added directly to the relative share of manufacturing and agriculture, these sectors may significantly increase their relative share in the national economy. In fact, they are most intimately linked with each other. In regions with poor services, manufacturing industry performs below its potential. Hence, the relation between manufacturing and services is not one way. New manufacturing technologies require new, better and/or more services, while services (such as R&D) may create new manufacturing technologies that may, in turn, create demand for services etc. Profound changes in the structure of manufacturing and services have blurred the distinction between the two economic sectors.

A relative increase in the demand for services and growth in this sector was made possible by an increase in the productivity of the manufacturing sector. This has made more resources available for the services sector of the economy. An increase in productivity has lowered the price of manufactured goods, hence there appeared an increase in disposable funds for the consumption of services. This makes industrial policy interesting for consideration.[38] The importance of manufacturing was considered by the MIT Commission on Industrial Policy. The Commission found for the US that (Dertouzos *et al.*, 1990, pp. 39–42):

- Imports of goods and services were ten times as large as exports of services in 1987. It is necessary to manufacture and export goods in order to pay for imports. The more the resources are relocated to services the lower the chances to equilibrate the foreign balance.
- Moving resources from the manufacturing industry into services will cause a shift from a sector with a relatively high productivity growth to one where it is lower.
- Almost all R&D is done by the manufacturing sector.
- National defence depends on the purchase of a lot of manufacturing goods. If the country starts to depend on foreign suppliers, national security may be placed in jeopardy.

3 What is the meaning of an industrial policy?

The literature on modern industrial policy started its development in the early 1980s. There appeared various definitions of industrial policy. Before surveying them, one should keep in mind the difference between competition and industrial policy. The former is directed towards the freeing of market forces, while the latter seeks to channel them (Geroski, 1987, p. 57). In addition, industrial policy may sometimes have strong anti-competitive effects, such as the need for the concentration of business because of economies of scale.

Some definitions of industrial policy are specific and selective. Industrial policy can be defined as coordinated targeting. It is the selection of parts of the economy such as firms, projects or industries for special treatment (targeting), which is coupled with a coordinated government plan to influence industrial structure in defined ways (coordination) (Brander, 1987, p. 4). Industrial policy implies policies that relate to specific industries, such as the correction of restrictive business practices (Pinder, 1982, p. 44). Industrial policies can be those government policies that are intended to have a direct effect on a particular industry or firm (McFetridge, 1985, p. 1). Industrial policy is aimed at particular industries (and firms as their components) in order to reach ends that are perceived by the government to be beneficial for the country as a whole (Chang, 1994, p. 60). This definition does not, however, distinguish between the short- and long-term time perspective. Different policies need to be employed to achieve efficiency if the time perspective changes.

Other definitions of industrial policy are broad, often overloaded, and include many areas of public policy. For example, industrial policy includes all government actions that affect industry such as domestic and foreign investment, innovation, external trade, regional and labour policies, environmental features and all other aspects (Donges, 1980, p. 189). Industrial policy can be any government measure or set of measures used to promote or prevent structural change (Curzon Price, 1981, p. 17). Industrial policy may mean all measures that improve the economy's supply potential: anything that will improve growth, productivity and competitiveness (Adams and Klein, 1983, p. 3). Another look at industrial policy can take it to mean a government policy action that is aimed at or motivated by problems within specific sectors. These 'problems' are presumably in both declining and expanding (manufacturing or service) industries. The solutions to these problems need not necessarily be sector-specific although that is a possibility (Tyson and Zysman, 1987a, p. 19). Initiation and coordination of government activities in order to influence and improve the productivity and competitiveness of particular industries or the whole economy is industrial policy (Johnson, 1984, p. 8). Industrial policy can be defined as the set of selective measures adopted by the state to alter industrial organization (Blais, 1986, p. 4). Another definition states that its focus has been on the ideal relation between governments and markets. Industrial policy need not be equated with national planning. It is, rather, a formula for making the economy adaptable and dynamic (Reich, 1982, pp. 75, 79). The term industrial policy describes that group of policies whose explicit objective is to influence the operation of industry (Sharp and Shepherd, 1987, p. 107). An industrial policy implies intervention by a government which seeks to promote particular industries in some way. This may be either to stimulate production and growth of an industry's size or to promote export sales (Whalley, 1987, p. 84). This definition does not, however, include government influence on the decline of and exit from an industry. Industrial policy may be equated with intervention employed to cope with market failures or a price system and that affects the allocation of resources (Komiya, 1988, p. 4). All acts and policies of a government that relate to industry, constitute industrial policy (Bayliss and El-Agraa, 1990, p. 137). Industrial policy is defined by the World Bank 'as government efforts to alter industrial structure to promote productivity-based growth' (World Bank, 1993, p. 304). Does this mean that aid to ailing industries falls out of the scope of industrial policy? Industrial policy includes all actions that are taken to advance industrial development beyond what is allowed by the free market system (Lall, 1994, p. 651). Industrial policy may also mean a set of public interventions through taxes, subsidies and regulations on domestic products or factors of production that attempt to modify the allocation of domestic resources that is the consequence of the free operation of market forces (Gual, 1995, p. 9). To formulate a definition of industrial policy may be hard. One US Supreme Court Justice tried to find a definition of pornography and said: 'You know it when you see it, but you can't define it, so it may be with industrial policy' (Audretsch, 1989, p. 10).

A critical definition of industrial policy states that it is the label used to describe a wide-ranging, ill-assorted collection of micro-based supply-side initiatives that are designed to improve market performance in a variety of mutually inconsistent ways. Intervention is typically demanded in cases with market failures and where major changes need to be effected quickly (Geroski, 1989, p. 21).

Industrial policy may mean different things for various countries at different times. Developing countries look at industrial policy as a means of economic development. They may favour certain industries over others. Once these countries become developed, industrial policy may be directed towards fostering free competition. In the ex-centrally planned economies, industrial policy meant planning and imposing production and investment targets in each sector and industry within it.

Industrialized countries have had implicit industrial policies for a long period. They were embodied in trade, competition, tax, R&D, standardization, education, public procurement and other policies that have derived effects on the industrial structure. This is due to the interdependence of economic policies within the economic system. Therefore, some countries have joint ministries of industry and international trade. This is the case, for instance, with the British Department of Trade and Industry (DTI) and the Japanese Ministry of International Trade and Industry (MITI), although there are differences in the powers and role in the economy between the two ministries.

In most developed countries the whole period after the Second World War was characterized by reductions in tariffs, as well as measures to prevent the demise of declining industries. Governments' industrial policies may be a simple continuation of the old protectionism by more sophisticated means (Pinder *et al.*, 1979, p. 9). Governments' tax and transfer policies have had their impact on demand, which affected manufacturing production. By direct production and supply of public goods, as well as through public procurement, governments influenced, at least in part, the industrial structure of their economies. Other government policies, such as foreign policy, have nothing directly to do with the increase in the economic pie of the country. However, they can influence industrial structure and employment. This is the case when some governments ban the export of high-technology goods abroad.

Various economic policies have their impact on industrial policy. It is not only trade policy, but also social, regional, energy, transport and others. Hence, most definitions of industrial policy include, at least implicitly, the need for a stable economic environment and coordination of various economic policies. Only then may specific targeting of industrial policy have its full contribution to economic growth and improvement in productivity and competitiveness with the final objective being an increase in the standard of living. On such grounds, broad definitions of industrial policy may embrace all of these facets. Hence, industrial policy is an economic policy that shapes a country's comparative advantage. Its objective is to influence the change in national economic structure (reallocation in resources) in order to enhance the creation and growth of national wealth, rather than to distribute it.

Three (non-mutually exclusive) broad types of industrial policy include macroeconomic, sectoral and microeconomic orientation. The macroeconomic orientation is least interventionist because it leaves the operation of industries and firms to market forces. This policy orientation simply improves the general economic climate for business. Sector-specific orientation becomes relevant when market failures affect certain industries. It tries to amend the particular market shortcoming. Microeconomic orientation of industrial policy may direct a government to act directly towards specific firms or industrial groups (Jacquemin, 1984, pp. 4–5).

There are another three broad types of industrial policy. They are market oriented, interventionist or mixed. The first type (market oriented) fosters competition and free markets. The second (interventionist) policy may be conducted as in the centrally planned economies. In practice, industrial policy is most often a mixture of the former two. Most of the countries may be classified as 'massaged-market economies'.[39] The only thing which most often differs between countries is not whether they intervene or not, but rather the degree and form of intervention in industry.

Industrial policy may be adjustment-prone and adjustment-averse. Adjustment-prone industrial policy stimulates adjustment of various industries to enter into new production, remain competitive or ease the exit from selected lines of production. Adjustment-averse industrial policy is the policy of protection which impedes changes in an economy by preserving the status quo.

4   Industrial policy issues

The standard comparative-advantage and factor-proportions theories of international trade may be satisfactory for the explanation of trade in primary goods. They are, however, less so for the explanation of trade in industrial goods. Manufacturing can be seen as a collection of industries with no factor abundance base. On those grounds it is difficult to explain why France exports perfumes while Japan exports copiers, cameras and VCRs, or why the Swiss export chocolate, chemicals and watches.

A country's comparative advantage is not only given by resource endowment, but is shaped over time by the actions of both business and government. Government economic policies may affect comparative advantage over time by influencing the quantity and quality of labour, capital, incentives and technology. The comparative advantage in manufacturing industries is not an unchangeable condition of nature, but often the outcome of economic policies which affect incentives to save, invest, innovate, diffuse technology and acquire human capital.

Until the 1970s market imperfections were at the margin of orthodox economic analysis, but these imperfections are at the heart of the analysis of the new theory of trade and industrial policy. A country's size; regional disequilibria; skill, mobility and unionization of labour; R&D; sunk costs; economies of scale; competition and bankruptcy laws are just a few imperfections. To ignore them is to miss the point that their effects can be mitigated by economic policy (Tyson, 1987, pp. 67–71). In the field of industry, a government disposes of a number of instruments. These include trade policy (tariffs and NTBs) that may reduce competition and anti-trust policy that increases it; preferential tax treatment; non-commercial loans and loan guarantees as a support to the risk capital; exports, insurance and other subsidies; public procurement; support to education and vocational re-training; assistance to workers to improve their professional and geographical mobility; and the provision of public or publicly financed R&D.

Free competition within an economic union brings costs of adjustment to which the governments, voters and citizens are not indifferent. It is often forgotten that increased competition brings benefits of economic restructuring. Costs of adjustment are often highly concentrated on the (vociferous) few and are usually temporary, while the benefits are dispersed over a long period of time and throughout the society, but in relatively small instalments to everyone. In the real, second best and imperfect world, there may be enough scope for both market mechanism and select intervention (economic policy).

The role of governments as organizers of national economies is coming under increasing inquiry. Governments can play at least four roles in the economic activity. They are:

- initiation,
- supervision,
- ownership of assets, and
- arbitration.

In spite of a general agreement about the need to reduce the extent of public intervention in the allocation of resources in a national economy, it is a fact that the countries that had the most impressive economic achievements during the past two decades were those whose governments exerted a strong and positive influence over all facets of commercial affairs (Dunning, 1994a, p. 1).

A general reduction in tariffs and NTBs, as well as economic integration, may increase a country's market. However, free markets are myopic about producing the necessary structural adjustments from the vantage point of the long-term needs of the society. This adjustment (the transfer of resources from the lagging to the growing industries) may not necessarily be a swift, cheap and smooth process. In addition, it is a risky operation as the future of the expanding industries is not very certain in the long run. If shrewd (a big if), adjustment policies (intervention) may facilitate these shifts by providing incentives and support to the private businesses to adjust to the new situation, and intervention may then have a certain justification.

One can make predictions about the model of economic adjustment based on the characteristics of a country's financial system. First, if this system relies on capital markets that allocate resources by competitively established prices, the adjustment process is company-led. The allocation decisions are the responsibility of firms, as in the case of the US. Second, in a credit-based financial system where the government is administering prices, the adjustment process is state-led (such as the past experiences of Japan and France). Lastly, in a credit-based system where price formation is dominated by banks, the adjustment process can be considered as negotiated. An example could be found in Germany (Zysman, 1983, p. 18).

The key question in the debate on industrial policy (the relationship of states and market) still remains: can imperfect governments make this shift any better than imperfect markets? Generally not, but this does not mean that market solutions are always superior to the other ones. Just as the dangers of market failure are often exaggerated, so are the competencies of governments. None the less, there are certain cases where a government's intervention (policy) may fare better than a free market solution. Here are cases in which intervention may be justified.

First, the time horizon that private markets take account of is relatively short. They may not foresee countries' long-term needs in changing circumstances, capabilities and opportunities with a high degree of accuracy. Japanese manufacturing is financed to a large extent by bank credits while the US industry uses this source of finance to a much lower extent. This means that the manager of a Japanese firm who asks for a loan can inform the home bank manager that he is looking for longer-term capital as he expects that profits will come in the ship which is due to arrive in the forthcoming few years. The manager of an American firm in the similar situation must be sure that he can see the smoke of the ship in the distance. Hence, the US industrial production is much more affected by the short-term interests of shareholders than the Japanese. The major goal of Japanese and German bank and enterprise managers is to ensure a firm's long-term competitive position in the market and favour risky investments such as the commercialization of new technologies. In contrast, the US system favours readily measurable physical (mergers and acquisitions) over intangible assets such as education or R&D. A government policy may change this short-term foresight towards longer-term economic considerations.

Second, in a different case, risk-averse governments may organize stockpiling in order to cushion the effect of a possible crisis. Private markets may not have the inclination and/or funds to do the same in the long run. A government may estimate the cost of this kind of risk in terms of GDP that would be sacrificed in the case of an unexpected reduction in the availability of certain inputs.

Third, governments may wish to keep some facilities for the home production as a bargaining chip with foreign suppliers while negotiating prices
in long-term supply contracts. This should deter foreign monopolies from
charging monopoly prices.

Fourth, market forces are quite efficient in allocating resources among
producers and allocating goods and services among consumers in simple and
static settings. Much of the power of markets in these circumstances emerges
from the fact that prices convey all the necessary information to participants
in the market. This enables them to act independently, without explicit
coordination, and still reach a collectively efficient solution. It is possible
that markets can, at least in principle, solve simple and static problems in a
remarkably efficient way, but it is not entirely surprising to find out that the
free market game is less successful in more demanding circumstances with
market imperfections. Adjustment problems appear because of the unsatisfactory operation of the market/price game viewed from the long-term
vantage point. It is the objective, or endeavour, of forward-looking intervention to put the economy on the path towards the desired long-term
equilibrium.

Fifth, basic research provides significant positive externalities (spillovers)
throughout the economy. These social gains in most cases are difficult for
private markets to grasp because the private risks and costs may be very high
in the light of uncertain benefits and their appropriation. In addition, without intervention, such as patents and other intellectual property rights, free
markets can not guarantee sufficient pecuniary returns to the private innovator. The fruits of successful basic research fuel technological progress in
the country. This research is funded in full or in part by the government in
direct (subsidy) or indirect (tax relief) ways in most countries. Governments
and private businesses share the risk.

Sixth, industrial policy may ease economic adjustment in a more efficient
and equitable way than free market forces. This policy may provide support
for R&D, education and training, support for geographical and professional
mobility of labour, investment subsidies, protection and other support for
the improvement of infrastructure during the early fragile times of a new
industry. Free market forces fail to do so. As for the adjustment and exit
from ailing industries, government policy may offer unemployment benefits
and vocational training. Industrial policy can, to an extent, both anticipate
and shape these changes. It can be involved either directly in picking the
winners/losers or indirectly by creating the business environment in which
firms can make choices in a potentially successful and desirable way.

Seventh, agriculture is a sector in which every government intervenes.
Due to the impact of weather conditions, free market forces can not achieve
the reliability of supply and stability of incomes of the farm population
relative to the labour force in the manufacturing sector. In addition, governments seek to secure the domestic supply of farm goods in circumstances of
war, as well protecting the landscape and environment.

The eighth reason for the introduction of an industrial policy is that this policy may be able to respond, with various internal and external (retaliatory) measures, to the economic policies of foreigners. Left alone, the market forces may take advantage of foreign policies in the short run, but if the long-term strategy of foreigners is to undermine the importing country's home production by means of predatory pricing in order to create an international monopoly, then the long-term effect may be detrimental for the importing country's welfare. An industrial policy may be a suitable response because it can change the possible free market outcome.

Tariffs (trade policy) have historically been the most important instrument of industrial policy. Due to a number of rounds of multilateral reduction in tariffs under the GATT, the use of this instrument has been restricted and reduced, but there have appeared other methods of intervention. Some of these personify protectionist pressures against adjustment, while others are adjustment oriented. They include: subsidies for exports, production, R&D and investment; NTBs; tax, exchange rate and credit policy; public purchases; price and exchange controls; regulation of the market (such as licensing); technical standards; direct production by the state; provision of infrastructure; competition and concentration policy.

The most benign intervention is the kind that does not harm other businesses and sectors. The most effective instruments of such an industrial policy include macroeconomic stability, education and the provision of infrastructure. Low inflation, a stable exchange rate and slightly positive real rates of interest may be the best tools of such an industrial policy. Savings will increase and entrepreneurs will have the chance to observe and shape their future with a relatively high degree of accuracy. Well educated management and well trained labour (investment in human capital) provide the economy with the most valuable assets capable of solving problems. Moreover, in many cases private businesses are not interested in investment in infrastructure (sewage systems, certain roads or bridges, etc.), so the government needs to step in.

Many of these instruments may be applied to a single target simultaneously, and may sometimes be in conflict. If the objective is to increase efficiency, then competition and concentration may be conflicting. It was accepted that many industries may not operate efficiently without a certain degree of concentration dictated by minimum efficient economies of scale. So, this has to be accepted. Small countries usually do not have very restrictive anti-monopoly laws, because efficient production for their home (unprotected) market and possibly foreign ones often allows the existence of only one efficient production unit. Countries such as France foster a policy of concentration and efficiency, while others such as the US, due to the huge home market, have strong anti-monopoly legislation which favours free competition. Inward-looking industries that are in the ailing phase of their lifecycle traditionally lobby in every country for protection, while the emerging industries, which are oriented to the widest international market, support free trade.

It was a strong belief in Europe during the 1960s that big American-style companies were the key factor for the economic growth of a country. These enterprises may, among other things, spend substantial funds on R&D and increase their international competitiveness. Hence, mergers and acquisitions were encouraged. That policy left Europe with a number of slumbering industrial giants, ill equipped to face the challenges of the 1970s and 1980s (Geroski and Jacquemin, 1985, p. 175). However, experience has shown that those countries that spend most on R&D do not necessarily have the highest rates of growth. It was also realized that SMEs,[40] largely forgotten or marginal in the traditional economic analysis, are the important factors for economic revival and employment. Subsequently the policy which strongly encouraged mergers and acquisitions was abandoned. It is now recognized that the jobs created by SMEs are greater in number than those created by large companies per unit of investment. This may be one of the outcomes of the business policy of (large) firms that want to avoid conflicts with organized labour. Product differentiation demands production on a smaller scale and decentralization of business. This is radically different from the prevailing theoretical expectations during the 1960s.

An expansion of SMEs started after the first oil shock (1973). However, jobs created by SMEs often have the disadvantage of being relatively less secure than those in big firms. Being small, these firms need to be flexible if they want to withstand competition. Flexible SMEs often use hit-and-run tactics in their business, linked with low sunk costs, as they can react faster to new business opportunities than more rigid large firms. However, SMEs often do not have capabilities to behave 'strategically' and exert as strong lobbying power as big businesses can. None the less, SMEs are necessary for the balanced growth of an economy, as they provide certain links among various sub-sectors. In general, neither large businesses nor SMEs can be efficient in isolation. They both need each other. Big businesses may use specialized SMEs as subcontractors and buffers against fluctuations in demand.

While industrial policy deals with select industries, the policy on SMEs refers to a group of firms of a specific size. It is supposed to rectify market imperfections that work against relatively smaller firms (uncertain future; high risk; low value of assets, although their quality may not necessarily be 'low'). This policy also exploits the positive aspects of relative smallness, such as organizational flexibility, fast and smooth flow of information, product differentiation and custom-made goods and services.

Subsidies may be a distorting instrument of industrial policy. They may diminish incentives for the advance of profitable firms if they are always taxed in order to provide the government with revenue for subsidies to inefficient enterprises. A subsidy that stimulates the introduction of new capital may distort a firm's choice of technologies. This is relevant for firms that use capital and labour in different proportions. If a firm has to pay the full cost of capital it might choose another technology. A one-time subsidy to investment may help a firm buy time and adjust to an unexpected change in demand or technology. If the value of subsidies and other favours is smaller than the additional value added in the given industry, then subsidization may be justified (but this calculation can be quite difficult). If subsidies are provided on a permanent basis for the protection of employment to an industry or firm, its management does not need to perform its role as efficiently as would be the case in those enterprises or industries where market criteria dominate. A permanently subsidized industry or firm is a very likely candidate for nationalization.

A common view of the world holds that firms play Cournot–Nash games against all other players (each firm decides on a course of action, e.g. output, on the assumption that the behaviour of the other firms remains constant), while the governments play a Stackleberg game (the agent knows the reaction functions of all others) against firms and Cournot–Nash against other governments (Brander and Spencer, 1985, p. 84). Unfortunately these are all games that can produce relatively unstable solutions and fluctuations in prices. Collusion among the players may lead to a relatively stable (Chamberlin) solution.

The promotion of the adjustment of some industries does not always go smoothly. Some ailing industries are well established, relatively large employers of labour and possess a strong political lobby. This is often the case with the steel industry. Some steel firms are, however, quite successful in their adjustment. This is the case with the US Steel Company which closed thirteen steel making units and diversified out of steel. This company invested funds in a shopping centre in Pittsburgh, Pennsylvania, and a chemical business in Texas. Steel making accounted for only 11 per cent of US Steel's operating income (Trebilcock, 1986, p. 141). Other steel companies prefer a quiet life. They neither innovate nor compete, but they are able to mobilize powerful political forces and government policy instruments (e.g. tariffs, quotas, subsidies) in order to resist adjustment (contraction in output and labour redundancies). Response to shocks such as an increase in labour costs was met by a number of US firms by sticking to the same technology, but investing abroad where labour costs were lower. The response of Japanese firms to the same shock was to change technology and increase productivity. In addition, certain Japanese TNCs, operating in the US, increased the US content of their goods over and above the domestic content of their US counterparts in the same industry. A number of US firms wanted to compete on the home market with the Japanese TNCs not necessarily on the basis of productivity, but rather on the grounds of low labour costs. Therefore, many US firms started to source heavily from abroad (developing countries) or to transfer their labour-intensive operations there. Japanese TNCs operating in the US increased productivity, so by the mid-1980s, for example, colour TVs sold in the US by the domestically owned firms had less local content than those made by the Japanese competitors. Honda and Nissan each had a local content of over 60 per cent in their cars produced in the US in 1987. That was expected to increase to 75 per cent over the following ten years (Graham and Krugman, 1991, pp. 78–79).

The newly industrialized countries have substantially increased their competitiveness in traditional industries such as steel and shipbuilding. Their output position is irreversible in the medium and, perhaps, long term. These industries can not be recovered in the developed market economies on the grounds of reductions in wages. Such a policy would involve a waste of resources, as trade unions would resist cuts in wages to meet the level of wages prevailing in the newly industrialized countries which have productivity at a level comparable to that in developed market economies.

Sufficient subsidies would always keep output (in ailing industries) at a level which would not survive in free market conditions. Emerging industries, where investment risk is quite high, have to offer the prospects of relatively higher rewards than elsewhere in the economy in order to attract factors. Gains in productivity in these new businesses may be able to cushion increases in pecuniary rewards to investors without increases in prices. However, faced with the possibility of higher wages in one industry, trade unions may press for increases in wages elsewhere in the economy. Without increases in productivity, the result may be an increase in prices throughout the economy. None the less, the emerging industries where productivity is higher than elsewhere in the economy may be a lap ahead of other businesses in this race.

The policy of shoring up a 'dying' industry for an excessively long period is like moving forwards, but looking backwards. The policy of compensation to redundant labour may be preferable to shoring up ailing firms. Compensation to redundant labour needs to be provided by the public authorities because the whole society benefits from the process of industrial change and adjustment. Shareholders of dying firms should not be compensated for the depreciated value of their shares. They should channel their funds into the growing businesses that need fresh capital for expansion, not to those that are declining and that do not need it (Curzon Price, 1981, pp. 27–29).

In contrast with declining industries, emerging ones require venture capital: they may be quite small, numerous, unstable and with uncertain future. When they are in trouble their voice may not be heard as loudly as that of declining industries. Investment in the emerging firms is risky because many of them collapse before they reach maturity.[41] However, these firms are the greatest propelling agents of a modern economy. Although many of them disappear from the market, many of them stay and new ones are created. The high birth-rate of new firms is the best indication of the vitality of the system which creates incentives, so that many new enterprises may be started and the risk accepted. Alfred Marshall drew the analogy between the forest (industry, sector or the whole economy) and the trees (individual firms). The trees may grow and decay for individual reasons (such as the prodigal character of the owner's wife), but what is important for the economy is that the forest grows.

When economic adjustment is spread over a number of years, it may appear that it is easier and less costly per unit of time. Some 'breathing space' for structural change (slowing down the attrition or keeping the ailing industries alive) may be obtained, but this argument is not always valid. First, the damage to the rest of the economy is greater the longer a depressed industry is allowed to last and, second, it is not obvious that prolonged adjustment is really any easier to bear than quick surgery. Even direct costs may turn out, in practice, to be higher (Curzon Price, 1981, p. 120).

All protectionist measures offered to an industry ought to be conditional, otherwise the problems of the industry can be exacerbated. If the protected industry is a declining one, then its adjustment may be postponed or reversed by production or employment subsidies. This increases costs to society in the long run because the desired change (transfer of resources from low-profit to high-profit industries) does not take place. The adjustment policy needs to be of limited duration. It should involve both public funds and private capital, as well as make the cost of action as transparent as possible. In addition, the recipients of assistance should be expected to develop comparative advantages prior to the termination of that help. Market processes should be encouraged and managerial practices improved.

There was a controversial argument that protectionism did not cost the US economy any more than the trade deficit did. The real harm done by protectionism (reduction in the efficiency of production because of a fragmentation of markets, as well as prevention of specialization and economies of scale) is more modest than was usually assumed in the case of the US. The major industrial nations suffer more, in economic terms, from the relatively unattractive problems for economic analysis such as 'avoidable traffic congestion and unnecessary waste in defence contracting than they do from protectionism. To take the most extreme example, the cost to taxpayers of the savings and loan bailout alone will be at least five times as large as the annual cost to US consumers of all US import restrictions' (Krugman, 1990b, p. 36). The reasons why *protectionism* features relatively highly on the public agenda can be found in politics and symbolism. Politically, free trade offsets economic nationalism, while symbolically, free trade is a cornerstone of liberal democracies. In addition, people from protected businesses such as agriculture and declining manufacturing industries tend to vote in large numbers, unlike the rest of the population.

Direct subsidies for R&D or indirect subsidies in the form of public procurement are powerful instruments for the support of industries that introduce new goods and services. The volume of demand and its structure provides the most important incentive for production. This is also crucial for the strategic industries, whose activities provide external and unpriced gains through linkages and externalities to the rest of the economy (examples include the machine tool industry, computers, telecommunications and data-processing).[42] If start-up costs create a barrier to entry into a strategic industry, the government may step in and help out. If the governments of other countries are subsidizing their strategic industries, the case for intervention by the domestic government can look very persuasive. In the early unstable phase of the introduction of a new good or service, a secure government demand provides a powerful impetus for the firm to develop the product and open new markets. If this production does not become self-sustaining within a specified period of time, then it may never become profitable and resources that may be allocated for protection may be used elsewhere in the future with a greater efficiency in improving competitiveness. The costs of subsidies need to be considered before intervention. A subsidy to one firm is a tax on others. If there is the chance of big returns in the future, such a tax might be worth bearing, but the gains are impossible to judge in advance. Once a government starts handing out subsidies, demands for more go on expanding without end. At that point political power, rather than 'economic sense' determines who gets what. The long isolation of an industry from market forces may remove incentives for the swift reaction to signals that comes from competition in international markets.

Protection may be given to an industry on the condition that the schedule of protection/intervention will be revised downward over time. If protection is not temporary and selective, it may create serious adjustment problems and increase costs in the future. The strategy of selection and the transitory nature of protection may provide a limited adjustment period to an industry by mitigating the full impact of international competition. This programme does not ensure the existence of inefficient industries and firms, but rather their adjustment and exit from the declining businesses. The self-liquidation of protection is perhaps the only means for maintaining the incentives to adjust. If the adjustment programmes offer funds to firms, then there must be an obligation that these funds are spent on specified activities. Adjustment programmes should be overseen by technical advisory boards that represent a wide community (Tyson and Zysman, 1987b, p. 425).

Public intervention in many countries has, primarily, but not exclusively, been directed towards the problem industries. These were usually coal, steel, textile, footwear and agriculture. However, there appeared a growing interest in intervening in the emerging industries. Intervention there is in the form of providing or subsidizing innovation, R&D in firms, special tax treatment of new technologies (tax holidays and subsidies), training of labour, education of management, government procurement, provision of infrastructure, as well as more general instruments such as planning, policy guidelines and exchange of information.

The level of industrial policy can be general and specific. The choice is between discrimination and non-discrimination. The degree of intervention should be as high as possible. This means it needs to be general, i.e. available to every industry and enterprise. Once the policy is installed, the market is the best tool for the fine tuning of the economy, creation and exploiting unforeseen opportunities, as well as the selection of the firms or industries that should take advantage of the policy instruments. Market forces prevent players from the inefficient employment of resources. The policy should be tailored to suit local needs (industry or firm) in cases where there are no externalities. In addition, it ought to be used only as a last resort because the government does not have infallible knowledge and may well make the wrong choice, as was the case with the French and British Concorde project.

5 Picking the winner/loser

The new theory of trade and strategic industrial policy found, in contrast to the neo-classical theory, certain manufacturing and service industries that are relatively more important to an economy than others. These are the industries with economies of scale, wide forward and backward linkages and unpriced spillover effects (externalities) on the rest of the economy. Privileges to these industries *may* create a new irreversible competitive advantage for a country.[43] It needs to be clear from the outset that the findings of the new theory are not prescriptions for economic policy, but rather an agenda for further research (Krugman, 1993, p. 164). If industrial policy is selective, then it is coupled with a policy of picking the winner (creating a national champion) or picking (bailing out) the loser. This has always been difficult, risky and demanded considerable and costly information. If this were not so, than you would probably not read this book, but rather look at the stock market report, invest and increase the value of your assets by several zeros daily. If the choice of tomorrow's winner is wrong and requires permanent subsidies, such an industry/firm may become the day after tomorrow's loser. If one intervenes, it is important to have reasonable aims and to use policy tools preferably in an indirect way and be ready to pull back whenever there are undesirable events in order to prevent even greater damage.

Picking the winner can usually be found in those countries whose domestic market is small and unable to support the competition of several firms operating at the optimum level of efficiency. National free market policies can be fostered in large countries such as the US, which can leave market forces to select the best suppliers. Smaller countries usually have to rely on selective policies which are potentially riskier. They have to make the best use of the limited amount of available resources. These resources have to be concentrated on select industries (specialization). Such an industrial and trade policy may be termed 'cautious activism', which should not be taken to mean protectionism.

While France relied on a relatively centralized model of the economy, Germany fostered a decentralized model. However, both countries have achieved a relatively comparable level of economic success (de Ghellinck, 1988, p. 140). While picking the winner, the government chooses between supporting emerging industries and propping up ailing ones (protection of the existing structure which is adjustment-averse). The balance between the two depends upon both the power of the industries involved and the intentions of the government.

The policy of singling out certain industries or firms for special treatment sets the problems of all the others aside. The 'neglected' businesses may be at a relative disadvantage because they cannot count on direct support by the state if they happen to be in need. In addition, they are taxed in one way or another in order to provide funds for the public support of the 'privileged' businesses. This drains funds for investment in the promising enterprises. The neglect of emerging and expanding industries may reduce the inclination of entrepreneurs for risk-taking and jeopardize the growth of the economy in the future. If a government can not formulate the basic structural objectives of national economic policy, then it should leave that to the politically strongest segment of business.[44] Policy will be formulated in a hurry in response to the political pressures of the moment, with the likely outcome of protecting troubled industries. Independence, resistance to business pressures and clear economic objectives of the government remove extemporizations in economic policies. Otherwise, the industrial policy of the country would be an instrument for supporting obsolete industries and a brake on expanding ones (Tyson and Zysman, 1987a, p. 22). The history of trade and industrial policy (just look at the GATT rounds of negotiations) reveals how hard it is to combat the entrenched interests of producers.

Output grows fastest in emerging industries. These industries may not necessarily create a significant volume of direct employment, but due to linkages and other externalities, they have a strong potential for the creation of indirect jobs. There has, however, been a notable technological improvement in declining industries such as textiles and steel. So, the distinction between the two kinds of industries is, in general, mostly for analytical purposes. A smart option for the risk-averse developing country may be to choose first the establishment of a good 'declining' industry, rather than an uncertain expanding one. Of course, the potential consequence of this choice may be a decline in the standard of living relative to countries that have gone for a different development model and are successful (?!) in its implementation.

Targeting is linked to three basic issues. These are: which industries or firms should receive support, what kind of support should be provided and, finally, for how long? The industries that are singled out for 'special treatment' are usually those that are significant employers and those that have important externalities. In addition, if the private markets do not favour risky investments such as the development of alternative sources of energy, then the government may also single out such investments for special treatment.

If domestic regulations regarding safety standards are stricter and more costly then abroad, than, other things being equal, this may place home firms at a relative disadvantage in competition with foreigners. Such a case may be used as an argument for demanding some public 'support'. Political reasons such as national defence and pride may influence decisions about the support of certain industries. Assistance should cease as soon as the beneficiary becomes profitable; or once it becomes obvious that this will never happen; or after the expiration of the specified period of assistance.

Japan is an example of a country that has reaped the fruits of conscious targeting of certain industries. This country has always been one step ahead of its competitors with regard to new technologies[45] in the targeted industries. During the 1960s the targets were steel and shipbuilding because of their significant externalities. Another target was the production of toys. During the 1970s the targets were machine tools and cars. The target for the 1980s was electronics (copiers, computers, audio and video equipment). For the 1990s it is semiconductors. This may be taken as an example of the shaping of comparative advantage in a dynamic context. Japanese 'targeting' was first and foremost an information-collecting, interpretation and transmission process which helped the individual firms to make investment decisions. In addition, it guided the government in allocating, basically, indirect support to businesses. Japan emphasized intervention in technological *areas* that created a large bilateral trade surplus with the US, rather than intervention in *firms*.[46]

Japanese targeting has not been successful in all cases, however, for a variety of reasons. For example, this country targeted the production of aluminium and petrochemicals before the first oil shock, after which such a choice was not justified. The MITI was against the development of cars during the 1960s since the US and Europe were ahead of Japan in these industries. In spite of official opposition to the expansion of the car manufacturing industry, Japanese corporations were against the MITI and pushed ahead with the manufacturing of cars. Their policy was right and yielded positive results.

Elsewhere in the developed market economies, the policy of targeting has not always been that smooth. After the Second World War, industrial policy relied partly on the unorganized labour that was flowing from agriculture and abroad into the manufacturing industry. This situation has changed. Trade unions organize labour that can influence (i.e. postpone) economic adjustment, even though it may be to the long-term detriment of the economy.

France is a country whose concern was in the creation of large and efficient firms that could compete in international markets. This country was not very concerned with home competition. France's Interministerial Committee for Development of Strategic Industries targeted the key industries, defined the strategy and picked a firm as a national champion to implement that programme. The implementation method was a contract between the government and the firm. The government did not, however, have perfect foresight. Mistaken judgements happened in very costly projects such as computers and Concorde. Although the Concorde project was a success in the high-technology industry, it was a commercial failure (the project started in 1962 when fuel was cheap).

The French strategy for computers was to try to build large mainframes in order to compete directly with IBM, rather than to begin with small computers or peripheral equipment. This was too ambitious for the relatively undeveloped French firms to cope with, so the effort failed. The mistake might have been avoided if the government industrial policy-makers had consulted more with private experts. Private firms also make mistakes, but they are less likely to ignore market forces (in particular when they use loans) than government officials. This was the main reason why the Japanese targeting was more successful than French. The early French mistakes, however, were not in vain. During the Airbus[47] project, the government learned to select the segment of the market for which demand would be high. It also tied customers by early purchasing of aircraft parts in exchange for orders (Carliner, 1988, p. 164).

Direct targeting of certain industries or firms has not been a striking feature of US industrial policy. This system was established in such a way as to foster individual freedom, not to discriminate among firms or industries. The only exceptions are agriculture and sporadic bailouts of firms such as Lockheed (1971) or Chrysler (1979). Government consumption on all levels, however, creates a big overall demand pull to the economy due to a huge general expenditure and the budget deficit. As a part of public expenditure is defence-related, selective public procurement or subsidized insurance indirectly influences the development and expansion of high technologies. Hence, the argument that the US government does not intervene in the economy does not hold water at all. In special situations (e.g. during the Second World War), the US had an explicit industrial policy.[48] In addition, the US has become the major producer of food in the world as a consequence of calculated economic and other policies that included various (including credit) subsidies.

Human capital and human resource management are the key factors in increasing a country's comparative advantage in a situation of rapidly changing technology and market conditions. Basic choices such as the education of priests or engineers, singers or mathematicians, lawyers or designers influence a country's competitiveness. Macroeconomic policy may just support, in an important way, the creation of comparative advantage, but it is human capital (properly organized, valued and continuously educated) that presents the major lever in the enhancement of a country's competitive advantage.

One has to keep in mind that there is a big redistribution of income: from those less skilled or fortunate, towards those with high skills. This takes place within each country, but also on the international scale.[49] 'Old' rules where real wages go hand in hand with an increase in productivity do not apply any more. High productivity no longer warrants high wages. With high international mobility of goods and capital there is always somebody elsewhere willing to do the same job for less money (Krugman, 1996b).

During the nineteenth and early twentieth century, bright pupils were steered towards the classics in Oxford and Cambridge in Britain, while technical subjects were reserved for the less gifted. The situation was the reverse in France, Germany and Japan. After the Second World War, British industry begun to recruit widely from the universities. A career in industry, even if a third choice after the Foreign Office and the BBC, became socially acceptable for the sons (and increasingly the daughters) of the Establishment (Sharp and Shepherd, 1987, pp. 83–84).

Some may argue that government planners and other public officials in Japan, France and Germany may be more competent and sophisticated than managers in the private firms in these countries. The best and most ambitious students aspire to government service. In North America, society has a different attitude. Many people look on government jobs as inferior to those in the private sector because, among other things, they are less well paid. It is not surprising to find that Japan, France and Germany have an industrial policy, while the US and Canada do not, at least no overt industrial policies. Nevertheless, shoddy economic policies in these two countries might be easily amended if civil servants were given a freer hand by the system (Brander, 1987, p. 40).

6   European Union

6.1   Rationale

The grounds for the introduction of an industrial policy in the EU can be identified in at least seven related areas:

- If uncoordinated, national policies may introduce a wasteful duplication either of scarce resources for R&D or investment in productive assets of suboptimal capacity. If minimum efficient economies of scale demand access to a market that is wider than the national one then there is a case for a common EU approach to the issue. Some competition in the diversity of R&D, ideas and production is necessary because it can be a source of creativity. None the less, the authorities need to strike a harmonious balance between competition and coordination, in order to profit from both of them. Hence, a certain coordination of industrial policies at the EU level contributes to the efficiency of the policy.
- A common or a coordinated industrial policy in a large and expanding EU market may wield a deeper (positive or negative) impact on the economy than any isolated national policy can, no matter how big the national market of a member country.
- With a free mobility of factors in the EU, any disequilibria in a national economy may first provoke an immediate and a large outflow or inflow of capital and, afterwards, other factors if the disequilibria are not

corrected. If a government wants to cool down the economy and increase the rate of interest, the result may be the opposite from the desired one. High rates of interest will provoke a large inflow of foreign hot capital and the economy may become 'overheated'. Therefore, the deeper the integration in the EU, the less effective become the national macro-economic policies that are pursued in isolation. A common or coordinated EU policy in such circumstances is a more effective choice than the sum of national ones.

- Although EU firms are rivals on the EU internal market, they are allies in competition against firms from third countries both on the world and internal EU market. If national economic policies used to tackle the same problem are different and have undesirable and unwanted spillover effects on the EU partner countries, then there are grounds for the introduction of subsidiarity, i.e. a common industrial policy of the EU.
- Another argument may be found in the 'unfair' trade and industrial practices of foreign rivals. An EU industrial policy may be a counter-measure.
- No matter how disputed in theory, the concern about employment always carries weight in daily politics.
- Last, but not least, there is a case for externalities which create market failure (the difference between private and social benefits). When there are undesired spillover effects across the frontiers of a single country from, for example, large investments in certain businesses that pollute, then the appropriate response to such events can be found in a common EU policy.

In spite of the arguments in favour of an EU industrial policy, one should not get the impression that it has to be a substitute for national policies. On the contrary, they should be complements. In fact, the EU policy needs to refer only to those areas where it has the potential to fare better than national policies can. In general, policies at EU level need to be as general as possible, while those on the local plane need to be custom-made. There has to be coordination between the EU and national/local policies in order to avoid the implementation of conflicting instruments even when there is an agreement about the major goals to be attained.

One of the principal things that the Treaty of Rome sought to achieve was to increase the competitiveness of domestic firms relative to the US at the time of the creation of the EU. The intention was to take advantage of the economies of scale which were provided by an enlarged EU market. It was primarily the expansion of domestic demand that stimulated the development of both the US and, later, Japan. Competitiveness was created in these two countries on the basis of the secure, even protected, large domestic market. A large domestic market in any EU member state was lacking in comparison both to the US and Japan. The creation of the EU was conceived to amend this 'disadvantage'.

In the small European countries industrial policy was often defensive (e.g. subsidies to protect employment), rather than aggressive (e.g. risky entry into new industries). Relatively weak anti-merger laws created the potential for the establishment of large European corporations in the 1960s which could, it was thought at that time, successfully compete with their US and Japanese rivals. However, the problem was not merely in the size of firms in the EU. Fragmented by NTBs, the internal market of the EU had as a consequence economic rigidity, and shielded many national firms both from the EU-internal competition and the necessary adjustment. The outcome was that in certain industries and relative to the US and Japan, the EU came close to being a 'manufacturing museum'.

Protectionism has been the instrument of the EU industrial policy in spite of the costs and postponement of adjustment. Resistance to abandoning obsolete technologies and industries permitted others, most notably Japan, to gain the competitive edge and penetrate the EU market with many high-technology goods. EU manufacturing has valuable attributes in these industries where the growth of demand is slow. Competitive advantage is relatively smaller in the expanding industries. Without domestic restructuring and with the exception of German, Dutch and certain firms from a few other countries, foreign TNCs that are located in the EU and that operate in the expanding industries may be among the major beneficiaries of any gains from Programme 1992. If the instruments of protection and cartelization (e.g. in the coal and steel industry) are not coupled with other tools of industrial policy (e.g. contraction of obsolete industries or assistance for a limited time for the introduction of new technologies), then such a policy will be ineffective from the resource viewpoint. It may be pursued by those who choose to do so and can afford to be wasteful.

6.2   Evolution

The first attempt to introduce a 'real' industrial policy by the EU dates back to 1970. The Commission's *Memorandum on Industrial Policy* (the Colonna Report) was a project to shape the structure of EU industry and set priorities for a common action. As there was no strong legal basis for the introduction of a common industrial policy in the Treaty of Rome, the Report restricted itself only to ambitious general statements and five recommendations. First, the Report foresaw the creation of a single EU market (such as the US) based on the abolition of internal barriers to trade. Second, it required the harmonization of legal and fiscal rules that would ease the establishment of enterprises throughout the EU. It envisaged the creation of a European Company Statute. Third, although the EU had existed for more than a decade, firms were very slow to merge businesses across national boundaries. As TNCs were perceived to be important vehicles for improvements in competitiveness and technology relative to foreign rivals, there was a need for the support (intervention) of intra-EU mergers and acquisitions.[50]

Fourth, changing demand conditions cause the need for economic adjustment. This adaptation could be made smooth if there was an encouragement of geographical and occupational mobility of labour and upgraded business management. The last recommendation was an extension of the EU solidarity regarding foreign competition, R&D and finance. Consideration of the Report ran into difficulty as there were two opposing views. On the one hand, Germany did not want any interference into industrial policy either on the national or the EU level. On the other hand, France was in favour of coordination of national economic policies. Other countries sided with one or other of these views.

The following step in the shaping of EU industrial policy was a *Memorandum on the Technological and Industrial Policy Programme* (the Spinelli Report) of 1973. Basically, it was a scaled-down version of the Colonna Report. The new Report argued in favour of the exchange of information, the coordination of national R&D policies, joint R&D projects and the elimination of national technical barriers. The broad strategy did not succeed in full because of different economic philosophies among the member countries. After the oil crisis the member countries pursued nationalistic industrial policies and were not very interested in a joint approach to the issue. In fact, they passed on to the EU the adjustment of the problem industries (steel, shipbuilding, textile and in some cases even cars) via trade, social and regional policies, while keeping the management of expanding industries in national hands. During this period there was only a certain coordination of technical standards and joint actions in R&D.

A profound step towards the elimination of NTBs on internal trade, competition and, hence, industrial policy came with the introduction of the programme *Completing the Internal Market* (the Cockfield Report) of 1985. This supply-side oriented 'technical' Programme had 282 industry-specific legislative proposals for the elimination of NTBs, as well as a timetable for their implementation by the end of 1992. The adoption of the Cockfield White Paper (1985) and the Single European Act (1987) provided the EU with the means to implement the 1992 Programme. The objective was the achievement of a genuine single internal market through the adoption and implementation of 282 measures (directives). This was the outcome of the political determination of the member states to eliminate NTBs on internal trade and change their 'atomized' industrial policies. The EU tried to employ its resources in a more efficient way by a reduction of physical, technical and fiscal barriers to internal trade (elimination of X-inefficiencies). The classic integration method (elimination of tariffs and quotas) in the EU exhausted its static effects at the end of 1960s. A new approach, the ousting of NTBs, favoured full factor mobility. It was implemented in order to create a genuine frontier-free internal market in the EU. The stress was on a change in the rules, rather than on additional funds. The creation of a homogeneous internal market, such as that in the US which benefits from enormous economies of scale, was not expected. The

Europeans have, on average, far more refined and deeply rooted tastes, hence they benefit from variety. They demand and are often ready to pay for superior quality and diversity. All that the 1992 Programme was about was an improvement in competition and market access to diverse national, regional and local markets, as well as the introduction of flexible modes of production.

The abolition of customs duties and quotas in the EU benefited only those industries that serve *private* consumers. There is also another market, that for goods and services consumed by *governments*. Industries that employ new technologies fail to serve the entire EU market for these goods and services and benefit from economies of scale due to the existence of NTBs. These national industries compete for public funds and orders. That is why EU firms tended to cooperate more with partners in the US or Japan, than among themselves. By a joint venture with a Japanese firm, an EU enterprise made up for its technological gap without forgoing the protectionist shield and/or privileges in the form of public procurement, major export contracts, tax reliefs and R&D accorded by the state (Defraigne, 1984, p. 369). The outcome of such a policy was a non-existence of EU standards for high-technology goods, as well as the existence of relatively large and protected national corporations, which were not very interested in intra-EU industrial cooperation. These firms were unable to respond swiftly to changes in the international market. An obvious example of this sluggishness was the relatively slow adjustment to the oil shocks.

EU company law was to help carry out the objectives of the Treaty of Rome regarding the harmonious development of economic activities in the Union. Therefore, the Commission proposed the European Company Statute in 1989. The arguments in favour of the Statute include the elimination of the difficulties that come from the current national tax systems for those firms that operate in several EU countries. Business in the entire EU market would be made simpler if the firms were incorporated under a single code of law. The absence of this Statute is estimated to cost business ECU 30 billion a year.[51] On the other side is the case against the Statute. Increased interference by the EU may jeopardize national sovereignty.

The Commission was not without further ideas on industrial policy. A communication on *Industrial Policy in an Open and Competitive Environment* (the Bangemann Communication) of 1990 had, basically, the following three proposals. First, industrial policy needed to be adjustment-friendly. This has to take place within the framework of a liberal trade policy. Second, the EU industrial policy has to be in accord with other common policies. They need to reinforce each other. Third, difficulties within industries or regions need to be settled by the employment of horizontal measures. The means for the achievement of these ideas should include an improvement in the operation of both the internal market and the international market, as well as the creation of an investment-friendly environment for risk-taking in the EU.

The 1993 Delors' White Paper, *Growth, Competitiveness, Employment,* aimed at the preparation of the EU for the twenty-first century. The major goal was a reduction in unemployment. This was to be done, among other means, by an ambitious wave of investment from various sources into the following areas: ECU 400 billion over 15 years into transport and energy in trans-European networks; ECU 150 billion until the year 2000 into tele-communications; and ECU 280 billion over 12 years into environment-related projects. The Council of Ministers did not support the project and budgetary austerity measures cast it aside.

The impact of the opening up of the internal EU market as a consequence of the 1992 Programme is most obvious in highly regulated (and hence fragmented) industries such as pharmaceuticals. A major regulatory change in the EU took place with the initiation of the European Agency for the Evaluation of Medicinal Products in 1995. The opening up of the EU market would alter the business practices of firms in the industry in the following seven ways (Chaudhry *et al.*, 1994):

- *Market authorization*: National regulatory authorities that control the introduction of new products at different rates wield influence not only on trade, but also on the health and life of patients. To change that, the European Agency for the Evaluation of Medicinal Products became the single decision-making body of in the EU in 1995. Pharmaceutical firms can, however, use a two-tier system. They can choose either a centralized procedure leading to a single authorization for the entire EU (this procedure is mandatory for products derived from biotechnology) or a decentralized method based on mutual recognition of national marketing authorizations. The apparent choice of firms should be to select the country with the least amount of regulatory delay and, then, apply the principle of mutual recognition to a product.
- *Dependence on domestic market*: More than 60 per cent of sales of pharmaceutical firms located in France, Germany, Greece, Italy, Portugal or Spain were to the domestic market. This was the consequence of preferential government procurement from local firms, inistence on local R&D and local-content requirements. Following the opening up of the EU market, the business of those firms selling primarily on the national market will be in jeopardy.
- *Parallel trade*: The EU Court of Justice ruled in favour of parallel impor-ters (*Centrafarm* v. *Sterling Drug*, 1974), i.e. purchasing of drugs in a low-price market, repacking and diverting them to other markets. The principle is that ethical drugs are permitted to move freely from one country to another if the importing country provides a marketing authorization. If there are price differentials for the same drug between EU countries, this type of trade will continue to exist.
- *Regulated prices*: Price differences for drugs among EU countries exist because of various factors that include price-control schemes, different

costs of production, variations in exchange rates, differences in re-
imbursement systems, transfer pricing, patent status, package sizes, rebates
and taxes. Sometimes the difference in price for the same drug between the
country in which it is the cheapest and that where it is the most expensive is
ten times! The opening up of the EU market will tend to bring a slow
convergence in prices for drugs. The progress will be relatively slow as
many of the distortions mentioned will continue in the future too.

- *Expenditure for R&D*: Competition will stimulate innovation. R&D for
  new drugs directed at the regional and global market will increase. R&D
  in the pharmaceuticals industry has always been mission oriented, regardless of integration.
- *Rationalization of operation*: Producing a drug involves the manufacture
  of the active substance and, subsequently, the conversion of this ingredi-
  ent into dosage forms. The first part has been centralized in the EU, while
  the second has been decentralized. Many plants were not benefiting from
  economies of scale as they were operating between one-third and one-half
  of their capacity. Plant closures, as a consequence of market opening in
  the EU, will bring benefits in the form of economies of scale.
- *Mergers and acquisitions*: The integration of various firms in the pharmaceutical industry is expected to consolidate the industry. Examples
  include the purchase of Syntex by Hoffmann–La Roche and a mergers
  between Smith Kline and Beecham, Bristol–Myers and Squibb or Ciba–
  Geigy and Sandoz into Novartis.

When a large corporation from a declining industry closes down in an old
industrial city, the first reaction by the state is often to offer subsidies to
large new corporations to settle there. If an industrial rhinoceros is caught or
attracted, it is usually loyal in this area only as long as the carrot lasts. If the
firms are uncertain that the incentives will last up to the end of the invest-
ment/production programme, they will not enter into this business. Risk-
averse enterprises may in this situation request larger incentives and/or
single out projects with relatively high rates of return. Locally created jobs
can be found in the development of SMEs. Of course, SMEs may not create
enough jobs in the short run to make up for the loss of posts in an area
where a large corporation closed down. However, SMEs were a source of
more than a half of net created jobs in countries such as the US in the past
decade or two. SMEs can flourish in the EU even more than was the case until
now. Some 17 million SMEs employed around 70 million people in the EU in
1994.[52] Their output can be efficient on the grounds of economies of scale and
specialization because they can serve one segment of the entire EU, rather
than a local or national market (if demand for their output exists there).

A policy of support to SMEs is different from one that fosters the development of a few national champions that are easy to control. Until the
1980s, even the EU regarded SMEs as unstable and marginal firms. It is
true that the life of many SMEs is much shorter than the life of big firms;

many of SMEs disappear from the market before they reach maturity, but many new ones are created. That should not be a worrying sign at all. It shows that the economic system is healthy and that it allows many new business opportunities to be tried out. Since the mid-1980s, the EU approach towards SMEs has changed. Many industrial policy programmes started to support this type of enterprises. SMEs are of vital importance when the market is in the process of opening (1992 Programme). Euro-Info Centres act as 'marriage' agencies for SMEs and support the establishment of business networks among these firms. This evolutionary and cumulative process needs to be sustained by an educational system that supplies businesses with labour that is and will be in demand. None the less, the EU must be much more explicit in its industrial policy towards SMEs in the future than was the case in the past.

Spain has traditionally been a relatively closed economy, hence it was interesting to explore the impact of the 1992 Programme on the Spanish SMEs. Although the economy was protected, exporting was widespread among Spain's SMEs even before this country joined the EU in 1986. Jarillo and Martínez (1991) surveyed a sample of SMEs three years after Spanish entry to the EU which was when the 1992 Programme was in full swing. They found that:

- almost all SMEs started exporting even when the Spanish economy was still relatively isolated from the rest of the world;
- the costs of production were declining as a competitive advantage, while design, style and superior technology had an increasing importance;
- two-thirds of the SMEs were exporting to the EU even before 1986; and
- some SMEs saw the 1992 Programme as a threat (the group of firms for which international activities were secondary to their main business in Spain), while none saw it as a new opportunity as access to the EU market had been almost free since the mid-1970s.

Hence, the 1992 Programme was perceived by the Spanish SMEs as a negative or as a non-event! In spite of that conclusion, there is a large gap in our knowledge of the relationship between economic integration and the behaviour of SMEs.

The opening up of the EU market prompted by the 1992 Programme brought several advantages to SMEs. They include the rationalization of distribution networks; cheaper and fewer inspections of conformity standards; diversification of suppliers; more efficient stock controls; and savings in time and cost of transport. None the less, there are certain flaws. Many SMEs do not fully understand the operation of the EU market. For example, many SMEs are familiar with the concept, but relatively few of them know the conditions under which they can use 'CE' marking which shows that the good was produced in the EU and that it meets EU standards. The EU policy regarding SMEs will have to refer to these and similar issues.

6.3   Technology policy

Determining factors of industrial structures of the developed market economies since the 1960s have included changes in technologies, foreign competition, environmental issues, changing employment patterns, as well as an ageing population. With this in mind, the EU Commission was initially more concerned with the industries in crisis. None the less, from the 1980s it started to be involved with industries of the future. These are the ones that have strategic importance for competitiveness. Therefore, the EU created various technology-push programmes in the mid-1980s. In the creation of those programmes, the Commission has always had to balance the interests of Directorates General for competition that argues in favour of *laissez-faire*, and electronics and telecommunications that argues in favour of an industrial policy (intervention). These programmes have (indirectly) created a technology policy of the EU.

With the exception of Euroatom, R&D occurred before that in the domain of national governments. A part of the inspiration for such an approach came from the Japanese experience in the public support offered to industries by the MITI in the form of an exchange of information, cooperation and a partial funding of R&D projects. The legal basis for the EU action in the R&D was given in the Single European Act (Title VI). Although there were certain earlier actions, the member governments decided for the first time to pass on significant funds for R&D from national to EU programmes. According to the Single European Act, the EU will strengthen its scientific and technological bases and encourage competitiveness at international level (Article 130f). The Commission and the member states are supposed to coordinate policies and programmes carried out at the national level (Article 130h). The EU needs to adopt a multiannual framework programme for its R&D projects (Article 130i). In the implementation of its long-term R&D programme the EU may cooperate with third countries or international organizations (Article 130m). The goal is to have closer links between research institutes and entrepreneurs throughout the EU in order to alter the old perception that science (i.e. R&D) in Europe is culture, while in the US it is business.

In a situation in which strong national elements still dominate, the EU should endeavour to coordinate national policies, promote cooperation in R&D and production, and support the flexibility of the industrial structure. Coordination of national policies should be in the decaying industries in a way that avoids an integration-unfriendly beggar-thy-neighbour policy. In the light of the irreversible changes started by the 1992 Programme, activities in the expanding industries should introduce common EU standards that provide room for the large-scale production and improvement in competitiveness. The objective is to avoid the creation of incompatible standards as happened with the PAL and SECAM television systems. The EU has opted for the MAC standard in the emerging high-definition television system. Although it will be applied throughout the EU for the next generation of television, it may be different from the Japanese and US (perhaps superior) standards. Making the EU market different from the foreign ones will reduce the benefits of economies of scale, but it will at the same time provide a temporary shield to the EU producers from external competition which may be the 'real' objective of devising different standards. If the EU, Japan and the US accept three different standards for a high-definition television system, and if experience is a good guide, it seems likely that the Japanese could excel in the production of TV sets that satisfy all three standards.

EU dependency on third-country suppliers of high-technology goods has several sources. On the supply side, there is a gap between investment in R&D in the EU countries on the one hand and US[53] and Japan on the other; a relatively insufficient allocation of human resources in R&D in Europe; and delays in the passing on of the results of R&D into production and marketing. On the demand side, there are still various national 'attitudes' (e.g. buy domestic) that limit potential demand for high-technology products in EU countries; lower receptiveness of European firms to new products compared with their US or Japanese rivals; a lack of stronger links between producers and consumers in Europe; and inadequate training in new technologies (Jacquemin and Sapir, 1991, pp. 44–45).[54] Various EU technology programmes are supposed to redress such a situation.

Philips and Thomson led the lobby of European companies that were pushing national governments for the completion of the EU internal market as the principal cure for countering the Japanese ability to be always a few steps ahead in the business game. The Round Table of European Industrialists was successful in eliciting support from governments for the 1992 Programme. When the US announced the 'Star Wars' project in 1983, EU industrialists started to worry. First the Japanese took over a large part of the market for consumer electronics, then the Americans were on the way to dominate that for advanced industrial goods. Following that, the Round Table (rent-seekers), created in 1983, was pushing for the creation of a transnational industrial policy in the form of EU support for high-technology research projects. In spite of budgetary restrictions, the big EU industrialists were successful again (Curzon Price, 1993, pp. 399–400).

The EU policy in R&D is carried out in the form of four-year Framework Programmes that started in 1984. The purpose of these medium-term instruments is to integrate and coordinate all assistance/aid that is given to R&D in the EU.[55] These programmes lay down objectives, priorities and the budget for EU-sponsored R&D. By distributing funds on selected research actions, the EU sets guidelines for specific R&D programmes. Based on the findings of the FAST (Forecasting and Assessment in Science and Technology) programme,[56] the EU started a score of publicly supported programmes for industrial cooperation among the EU firms in the R&D stage. Most of the programmes would be beyond the financial capability of the participating countries if they were supposed to finance them and accept the risk on their own. These programmes include the following 'winners':

- A dozen renowned enterprises in information technology from Britain, France, Germany, Italy and the Netherlands wanted to pool resources, share the risk and extract certain subsidies.[57] Their pressure group (the Round Table) was lobbying both national governments and the Commission to adopt the European Programme for Research in Information Technology (ESPRIT) and try to 'correct market failures' in R&D. The Commission was receptive to the idea and together with the Round Table won the approval from the national governments. The EU adopted the Programme, i.e. picked a winner, in 1984. Within ESPRIT the EU finances half of the cost of the project that is in line with the EU terms of reference and that is proposed by two or more firms from different EU countries. The other half of the funds has to come from the participating firms and national sources. The project has to refer only to pre-competitive R&D. The Commission has been refusing to subsidize joint production. The reason is that it wants to avoid all criticisms by the US about subsidies.[58]
- Research and Development in Advanced Communication for Europe (RACE) is a spillover programme from the ESPRIT. It aims at advancing the telecommunication network in Europe in the future by the means that include standardization and coordination of national telecom services.
- Basic Research in Industrial Technologies in Europe (BRITE) aspires to revitalize traditional industries in the EU. It is to be done through the introduction of new technologies in these industries. It is unclear what is so 'strategic' about these industries. Perhaps the concern here is more about employment, than anything else. Public money is spent on projects that financial markets find unbecoming.
- The Biotechnology Action Programme (BAP) is small relative to its 'strategic' potential in the future.
- European Collaborative Linkage of Agriculture and Industry through Research (ECLAIR) is like the BAP: relatively small, but with great potential for finding solutions regarding food in the future. It contributes to the establishment and reinforcement of inter-sectoral links between agriculture and manufacturing.

EUREKA (European Research Cooperation Agency) was a programme started by 17 countries (from the EU and the EFTA) on the French initiative in 1985. It was in response to the Strategic Defence Initiative ('Star Wars') of the US. Its objective is the development and *production* of high-technology goods. It is not confined only to pre-competitive R&D as the other programmes are. Other countries (such as Turkey) may be included in some of its programmes. EUREKA is, however, *not* an institution of the EU. It has a small secretariat in Brussels and has gained popularity in the business community.

The Fourth Framework Programme (1994–98) disposes of ECU 13.2 billion. The five 'winners' are cars, trains, aeronautics, vaccinations and educational software. These EU-wide programmes ought to be supported by a number of national plans that spread and reinforce links among the parties involved in R&D and the implementation of the results of those efforts. A lot of public money has been poured in to R&D over the past decade in the EU, but the results have been very slow in coming. Of course, the effects of fundamental R&D can not be predicted with a high degree of accuracy. As public funds are limited and as the results of R&D are more important than the origin of the work, companies from foreign countries may take part in the R&D projects of the EU on a case-by-case basis, but without any financial help from the Commission. Production in the world is becoming more and more globalized. Therefore, 'forcing' cooperation in R&D only within the EU may squander a part of the taxpayers' money. What global production in the world requires is an open (global) industrial and trade-policy system.

Inter-firm strategic alliances in the development of technology in the EU increased sharply during 1980s. In addition, there was a relatively vigorous involvement by the Commission in projects on the cost-sharing basis. Over 70 per cent of the private (largely non-subsidized) strategic-technology alliances were related to the joint R&D of new core technologies in informatics, new materials and biotechnology. A major field of cooperation was in information technologies as over 40 per cent of all strategic-technology alliances were in this field (Hagedoorn and Schakenraad, 1993, p. 373). A comparison between the established 'private' cooperation in R&D and the one that was sponsored by the EU found that they resemble each other for leading enterprises. In fact, the 'subsidized R&D networks are added to already existing or emerging private networks and merely reproduce the basic structure of European large firm co-operation' (Hagedoorn and Schakenraad, 1993, p. 387). If so, one fails to understand why leading and large firms in the EU need subsidies! If the 'official' network largely reproduces the already existing 'private' one, then it may be redundant. Financial resources may be used elsewhere (for instance, programmes that are not in the field of informatics such as biotechnology or education or infrastructure). Whether such replication of R&D networks is the outcome of the lobbying muscle of powerful firms or whether it is necessary to accelerate R&D in the private sector because of significant externalities, needs to be answered in the future.[59] Perhaps such a waste of scarce public money will be checked in the future by the WTO rules on subsidization.

The experience of Japan is also instructive. During the 1960s the MITI targeted the production of steel and shipbuilding as the 'winners'. Intervention (support) was relatively heavy. At that time the Japanese corporations had an identical business choice and were investing in these industries. Such private investments would have happened even without government intervention. At about the same time, Japanese firms also wanted to start developing car and electronics industries. The two industries were not on the priority list of the MITI. None the less, private businesses went it alone in their investments and were successful without public support (if one leaves aside the relatively closed domestic market).

A changed and improved new industrial strategy of the EU and its member states needs to take into account first and foremost the crucial role played by the development of human capital for the long-term competitiveness of the economy. In addition, there may be a certain need for selective intervention in the form of subsidies, promotion of cooperation and information exchange during the pre-commercial phase of R&D projects that may give (oligopolistic) advantages to EU producers relative to foreign rivals. If deemed appropriate, selective intervention in new technologies needs to be aimed at those expanding industries where the EU businesses already have or could create internal resources. This means that EU efforts and funds should not be focused only on the replication of industries where the US and Japan are strongest (cooperation with them may be a better choice), but primarily where there are grounds for the development of genuine EU technologies and comparative advantages.[60] One of them could be found in biotechnology. Not only now, but also in the coming decades there will be an increased overlap between mechanical, electronic, chemical, medical and biotechnology industries. The EU has a reasonable chance of becoming a leader in this field. However, there are many perils in this area. Although there are important scientific achievements in genetic engineering (e.g. cloning of animals [sheep] in Britain in 1996–97) there are serious ethical, moral, social and religious questions related to such issues. In addition, there may come serious negative side-effects from biotechnology as was the case with 'mad cow disease'[61] in Britain in 1996.

6.4   The way forward

The competitiveness of a country's goods and services in modern times is more created than inherited. The leader in certain lines of production can not be sure that this position will endure in the long run. Therefore, one can find scope for industrial cooperation in the EU. It could be established both in the pre-commercial and during the commercialization stages of R&D. In this way inefficient duplication or multiplication of R&D would be eliminated and resources saved and directed elsewhere. However, the creation of knowledge is not enough to keep a country on a competitive edge. That knowledge needs to be applied in practice. Here the US fares much better than the EU. The US system and culture offers wide opportunities to start and re-start promising businesses. If someone with sound profit-making ideas fails (for whatever reasons) in Boston, there are further chances in Seattle or San Francisco. The Americans look at certain business failures as if they are scars on the Prussian officer's face. In Europe, the situation is different. If your business start-up fails, you can forget one for a while, unless you cross the Atlantic!

As the 1992 Programme eliminated most NTBs on internal EU trade, its largest impact was and will continue to be felt in sensitive businesses.[62] These are the ones that were shielded by relatively high NTBs and which had the effect of large price distortions. These include the production of goods that are publicly procured either in the high-technology business (e.g. office machines, telecommunications and medico-surgical equipment) or in traditional manufacturing such as electrical and railway equipment, pharmaceuticals, wine and boilermaking. Business that were protected with relatively modest NTBs will also continue to be affected by market liberalization. These include motor vehicles, aerospace equipment, basic chemicals, machine tools for metals, as well as textile and sewing machines.

There was a fear by the outsiders that the 1992 Programme could lead to the creation of 'Fortress Europe' as a mixture of intra-EU liberalization and an increase in the existing level of external protection. However, the EU neither had such a plan, nor would it serve its long-term interests. If a 'fortress' was mentioned, it was only as a potential bargaining chip with major trading partners. It was expected that the 1992 Programme would lead, among other things, to increased competition and efficiency which would reduce prices in the EU. Therefore, even without a change in the existing level of nominal protection, the real level may rise. An extra increase would not be either necessary or desirable. On the contrary, increased efficiency may prompt the EU to reduce the current level of protection as happened in the Uruguay Round deal. None the less, the 1992 Programme has influenced the timing of external FDI in the EU. Many foreign TNCs entered the EU in order to become an 'internal' resident of the EU prior to full implementation of the 1992 Programme. They wanted to pre-empt any potential moves towards the creation of a fortress after 1993.

Potential changes in the rules of origin and local content may, however, discriminate against 'internal' goods with a relatively high external import content. This may be reinforced by a discriminatory application of testing procedures and standards. A fortress mentality may be introduced in the EU through the social(ist) over-regulation of labour issues. If this is done in future, it could provoke protectionist winds that would make the security of current jobs more important than the long-term efficiency and adjustment of the economy.

The impetus to the economic life once offered by a customs union as Mark 1 in the process of integration in the EU was exhausted at the end of 1960s. Something greater and fresher was needed. The genuine EU internal market with an unimpeded flow of goods, services and factors from 1993 ended Mark 2 in the integration process. It provided the EU with the new propelling force. The member countries decided to reintroduce the principle of majority voting (save for fiscal, national border controls, working conditions and environmental issues) in order to ease the procedure for the implementation of the Programme.

The EU member countries realized that the costs of 'non-Europe' were too high to be ignored. An EU without frontiers, of course for the domestic residents, as envisaged in the White Paper could increase GNP in the EU up to 7 per cent and employment by 5 million new jobs, if accompanied by matching national policies (Emerson *et al.* 1988, p. 165). The 'sacrifices' for those real gains were more freedom for business and less regulation. The opponents of the 1992 Programme have not been able to create a more attractive and feasible economic strategy and ultimately gave these efforts up. Only the inefficient ones and the others that fail to compete and adjust would lose out in the new situation. As there was no chain of bankruptcies throughout the EU, this is an indication that business has absorbed the 1992 Programme without any serious and negative shocks. However, the Programme was merely the first step. One has to keep in mind that the 1992 Programme is merely a medium-term strategy. The Maastricht Treaty rearranged the decision-making process in the EU and set the 'agenda' for the EMU. If (a very big if) that is realized according to the plan and timetable, there is no way of knowing what will come after that. This is a highly political question because it is linked to the transfer of other responsibilities to the EU level.

Tables 4.7, 4.8 and 4.9, respectively, show annual percentage changes in GDP, manufacturing output and capital formation in the EU countries

Table 4.7   Real GDP in the EU countries, US and Japan, 1987–1996 (annual % change)

Country	1987	1988	1989	1990	1991	1992	1993	1994	1995	1996
1 Austria[a]	1.7	4.1	3.8	4.6	2.8	2.0	0.4	3.0	1.8	0.7
2 Belgium	2.2	4.9	3.6	3.8	2.2	1.8	−1.6	2.2	1.9	1.2
3 Denmark	0.3	1.2	0.6	2.0	1.3	0.8	1.5	4.4	2.8	2.0
4 Finland[a]	4.0	5.4	5.4	0.3	−7.1	−3.6	−1.2	4.4	4.2	2.8
5 France	2.3	4.5	4.1	2.2	0.8	1.3	−1.5	2.9	2.2	1.2
6 Germany	1.4	3.7	3.4	5.1	5.0	2.2	−1.2	2.9	1.9	1.3
7 Greece	−0.7	4.1	3.5	−0.2	3.2	0.8	−0.5	1.0	2.0	2.5
8 Ireland	4.6	4.5	6.4	7.1	2.9	5.0	4.0	6.5	10.3	6.5
9 Italy	3.1	4.1	2.9	2.2	1.2	0.7	−1.2	2.2	3.0	0.8
10 Luxembourg	2.9	5.6	6.8	3.2	3.1	1.9	0.0	3.3	3.2	2.6
11 Netherlands	0.9	2.6	4.7	3.9	2.3	2.0	0.8	3.4	2.1	2.5
12 Portugal	5.3	3.9	5.2	4.1	2.1	1.1	−1.2	0.9	2.6	2.3
13 Spain	5.6	5.2	4.8	3.7	2.2	0.7	−1.2	2.1	2.8	2.3
14 Sweden[a]	2.8	2.3	2.4	0.7	−1.1	−1.4	−2.2	2.6	3.0	0.8
15 United Kingdom	4.8	4.4	2.1	0.5	−2.0	−0.5	2.3	3.9	2.6	2.3
United States	3.1	3.9	2.5	0.8	−1.0	2.7	2.2	3.5	2.0	2.3
Japan	4.1	6.2	4.7	4.8	4.3	1.1	−0.2	0.5	0.9	3.5

Source: National statistics and UN ECE
Note: [a] Joined the EU in 1995

Table 4.8 Industrial production in the EU countries, US and Japan, 1987–1995 (annual % change)

Country	1987	1988	1989	1990	1991	1992	1993	1994	1995
1 Austria[a]	1.0	4.4	5.9	7.4	−1.8	−1.1	−2.0	4.0	5.4
2 Belgium	2.2	6.5	3.4	3.8	−2.0	−0.5	−5.2	1.8	4.2
3 Denmark	—	—	—	—	—	—	—	—	—
4 Finland[a]	4.2	5.8	2.4	0.4	−9.8	2.5	5.1	11.5	7.5
5 France	1.9	4.7	4.1	1.9	0.2	−1.1	−3.7	3.8	1.5
6 Germany	0.4	3.6	5.0	5.1	2.9	−1.9	−6.3	1.3	2.1
7 Greece	−1.5	5.1	1.9	−2.4	−1.4	−1.2	−2.1	0.9	2.3
8 Ireland	9.1	10.6	11.6	4.6	3.2	9.3	5.6	11.0	18.8
9 Italy	2.6	6.9	3.9	−0.7	−0.9	−1.3	−2.2	6.8	5.5
10 Luxembourg	—	—	—	—	−0.1	−0.8	−2.5	5.9	1.4
11 Netherlands	1.0	0.1	5.1	2.3	3.9	0.2	−1.1	3.0	2.3
12 Portugal	4.4	3.7	6.8	8.9	0.1	−3.4	−2.6	−0.2	4.6
13 Spain	4.7	3.0	4.5	0.1	−0.9	2.9	4.7	7.0	4.7
14 Sweden[a]	2.6	1.3	3.6	2.7	5.6	3.5	0.2	10.5	10.6
15 United Kingdom	3.2	3.6	0.4	0.5	3.9	0.2	2.1	5.0	2.5
United States	5.0	5.5	2.5	1.0	1.7	3.3	3.5	5.9	3.2
Japan	—	11.0	4.8	4.2	1.8	5.7	4.2	1.2	3.3

Source: National statistics and UN ECE
Note: [a] Joined the EU in 1995

Table 4.9 Real gross fixed capital formation in the EU countries, US and Japan, 1987–1996 (annual % change)

Country	1987	1988	1989	1990	1991	1992	1993	1994	1995	1996
1 Austria[a]	3.1	6.0	6.1	5.8	6.3	1.7	−1.6	6.7	2.3	0.7
2 Belgium	5.6	15.2	14.5	8.3	−1.5	0.2	−6.7	3.0	3.0	3.1
3 Denmark	−3.8	−6.6	1.0	−0.9	−5.7	−7.2	−2.3	3.0	10.2	5.2
4 Finland[a]	5.4	10.5	14.1	−4.9	−20.3	−16.9	−19.2	−0.3	7.7	9.2
5 France	4.8	9.6	7.0	2.9	0.0	−3.1	−5.8	1.6	2.8	0.7
6 Germany	2.1	4.6	6.5	8.7	5.8	3.5	−5.6	4.3	1.5	−2.0
7 Greece	−5.1	8.9	10.0	4.8	−4.5	0.5	−2.7	0.6	5.8	9.5
8 Ireland	−2.3	3.3	15.8	9.5	−8.2	−1.9	−0.5	8.7	10.1	9.0
9 Italy	5.0	6.9	4.3	3.3	0.6	−1.7	−13.1	0.2	5.9	1.7
10 Luxembourg	14.5	14.2	9.7	2.5	9.8	−2.1	3.9	2.4	3.5	3.7
11 Netherlands	1.1	4.5	4.9	3.6	0.2	0.6	−3.1	1.6	6.7	3.3
12 Portugal	15.1	15.0	5.6	6.0	2.4	5.4	−4.8	3.9	5.4	5.0
13 Spain	14.0	14.0	13.8	6.9	1.3	−4.1	−10.6	1.8	8.2	4.3
14 Sweden[a]	7.6	5.8	11.8	−0.5	−8.9	−10.8	−17.2	−0.2	10.6	9.4
15 United Kingdom	9.6	14.2	7.2	−3.1	−9.5	−1.5	0.6	2.9	−0.2	4.4
United States	−0.5	4.2	0.1	−2.8	−8.0	5.7	5.1	7.9	5.2	5.3
Japan	9.6	11.9	9.3	8.8	3.7	−1.1	−1.8	−2.3	0.8	4.2

Source: National statistics and UN ECE.
Note: [a] Joined the EU in 1995

during the period 1987–96. Memorandum items in the tables are indicators for the US and Japan. Although the performance of individual countries differ, there is general harmony in the economic cycles in the EU countries. The most obvious example was in 1993 when most of the EU countries were in recession. That was the first year when the 'genuine internal market' in the EU started to operate! In addition, industrial production and investments in the EU stated to suffer even from 1991. It would be, however, cynical to associate those negative macroeconomic trends with the potential failure of the 1992 Programme. Integration is after all no more than a *supporting* instrument to general national macroeconomic policies. Once they are in order, integration can contribute to their reinforcement.

The year 1992 came and passed, but the economies of the EU have not yet exhibited a big expansion in economic activity in spite of the large-scale expectations about the beneficial effects from the implementation of Programme 1992. Has something gone wrong? Perhaps not. Economic integration, including the single-market programme, is an ongoing process. It is not a programme with clear deadlines after which one may measure the overall effects with only a small margin of error. Research on the effects of the 1992 Programme suffers from an identification problem. It is a common shortcoming of all studies that deal with the effects of international economic integration. It is hard to know which changes in the economy and the reaction of enterprises are due to the 1992 Programme and which would have happened anyway (for example, because of imports of improved foreign technology or 'globalization' of business and competition)! It may take another decade or so until all the effects of Programme 1992 are fully absorbed by the economies of the EU. Perhaps, again a 'perhaps', the biggest effect on the economies of the EU already took place at the end of 1980s. Part of the support for this thesis can be found in business concentration deals peaking in 1990. It needs to be kept in mind that the 1992 Programme is *a*, rather than *the* reason for change.

In spite of 'grand' expectations at the start of the 1992 Programme by Emerson *et al.* (1988) regarding employment and growth, the outrun in practice was much more modest, although not negligible. The 1992 Programme created between 300,000 and 900,000 jobs, while an extra increase of EU income was 1.1–1.5 per cent over the period 1987–93 (European Commission, 1997).

EU direct intervention in the manufacturing industry was primarily aimed at declining industries such as steel, shipbuilding and textiles during the 1970s and early 1980s. After 1985, the major emphasis of the policy changed. The EU became much more involved in the expanding high-technology industries through its R&D policy. This should not be taken to mean that the EU is no longer concerned with obsolete 'industries', or that it was not interested in the support and development of advanced industries in the past. On the contrary. EU involvement with both types of manufacturing industries existed in the past, and it continues in the present. What changed, was only the order of priorities. None the less, high on the agenda for the future are five priorities:

- promotion of investment into intangible assets,
- advancement of industrial cooperation,
- paying special attention to services, energy, biotechnology and information technology,
- strengthening of competition, and
- modernization of public intervention.

7 Services

7.1 Issues

While actual physical existence determines goods, such a direct relation does not exist for services. A service may be given to various receivers. It can be to a person for a haircut, education, entertainment or transport; a legal entity such as a firm or government for banking or construction; an object such as an aeroplane for guidance, repairs or airport services; or goods for transport or storage. Certain services can be provided to a variety of receivers. For example, banking, insurance, transport, telecommunication, leasing, data processing and legal advice could be offered to individuals, businesses and governments.

In general, the services sector in the developed market economies contributes by more than a half both to the GNP and to employment. The share of services has been continuously increasing. These deindustrialization tendencies have been shifting emphasis towards the services sector as one of the key solutions to the problem of unemployment and growth. Employment in the manufacturing sector in the EU declined from 33 million to 30 million between 1980 and 1990. At the same time employment in the services sector increased from 44 to 54 million. Newly created jobs in the services sector more than compensated for job losses in manufacturing. Production of almost all services takes place in every country. The same is, however, not true for the manufacturing of cars, lorries, aircraft or steel. Hence, the alleged importance of the creation of new jobs in the services sector.

Notwithstanding its importance and impact on the economy, the services sector has been neglected in economic analysis for a long time. Classical economists such as Adam Smith and Karl Marx neglected services as the residual sector of the economy on the grounds that it does not have durable properties and no facility for physical accumulation. The production and consumption of services is simultaneous and it requires a degree of mobility of factors. Therefore, the classical economists turned their attention towards physical goods.

On the 'technical' side, services differ from other business activities in at least the following five ways (Buigues and Sapir, 1993, p. xi):

- The production and consumption of services happen at the same time and at the same place. Therefore, they are regarded as non-tradable as they can not be stored. Because of a relatively low level of internationalization, the right of establishment (FDI) is essential for the provision of services abroad. Although services account for around a half of the GDP of the EU, their share is around 20 per cent in total trade. This epitomizes the non-tradable nature of many services. On the other hand, services account for around a half of all FDI in the EU. Internationalization of services is lowest in distribution, road transport and construction; average in telecommunications, financial and business services; and relatively high in air transport and hotel chains.

- The quality of services can not be easily verified in advance of consumption. Non-price competition such as reputation often plays a key role during the decision-making process by consumers. This is important in longer-term relations such as in financial services. Experience plays a part even in one-time relationships in certain cases and places.[63]

- Governments in all countries intervene in services more than in other economic activities, because of market failures. These include imperfect competition in a number of services, asymmetric information between providers and consumers (the sellers potentially know more about a service, such as an insurance policy, than the buyers) and externalities.[64] Public intervention influences entry, operation, competition and exit from the sector. Regulation is high and competition low in financial services, air transport and telecommunications. Therefore, only a few big companies exist in those industries. Reputation plays a big role in finance, economies of scope in air transport, while in telecommunications there are relatively large sunk costs and economies of scale (most countries have a single public firm providing the service). Competition tends to be higher and regulation easier in road transport, business services, construction and hotels.

- Debates about the (im)possibility of the government to intervene (in)efficiently to correct the above market failures, as well as changes in technology contributed to an ebb in deregulation in the sector first in the US at the end of 1970s, then in Britain during the early 1980s, which subsequently spread to the rest of Europe.

- Services are characterized by a relatively slow growth of labour productivity. Their rate of productivity growth during the period 1970–90 was half of what it was in the manufacturing sector. There are at least two explanations for such development. First, competition in services is obstructed by a high degree of regulation and, second, the substitution of capital for labour is more limited in services than in manufacturing. Technological innovations, however, increased labour productivity in telecommunications and air transport during that period.

Differences between services and other economic activities are not confined only to the 'technical' side. There is also a social dimension. First, half of the employees in services were women in 1990. This is in sharp contrast with the manufacturing sector where women have only one in five jobs. Second, there are many more part-time employees in the services sector than in manufacturing. Third, and linked with the former issue, is an expansion of temporary work contracts in services. Fourth, there is a relatively high level of non-employees. Fifth, labour unions are not spread in the services sector. The exceptions are transport and telecommunication services. Sixth, SMEs are dominant types of business organization in most service industries.

There are other reasons that make the analysis of services tricky. One is a lack of any profound theory. A wide definition states that a service is a change in the condition of a person, or a good belonging to some economic unit, which is brought about as a result of the activity of some other economic unit (Hill, 1977, p. 317). Without a proper definition, the measuring unit is lacking. Trade statistics, however, list thousands of items for the goods on the one hand, but record only a handful of services on the other. Although many services are not tradable, progress in information and telecom technology make many services eligible for international trade. Nevertheless, trade in many services is not recorded. The service part of a good, such as repair, may be incorporated in the total price of traded goods. Apart from transport, financial and telecommunication services, in principle, an entry into and exit from a service industry is relatively cheap and easy. However, there are regulatory barriers to such (dis)orderly operation in the service businesses. TNCs release little data on their internal trade in services, while other establishments in the sector reluctantly make public this information, as this can endanger their competitive position. In addition, information can be easily, swiftly and cheaply distributed, which jeopardizes property rights. Such a lack of hard statistical information makes trade in services difficult to study.

It is easier to sell goods than services in foreign markets. While barriers to trade in goods can be eliminated at the border, problems for the suppliers of services usually start once they pass the frontier control. Provision of services often requires the right of establishment and national treatment of enterprises. Providers of a service need to be present in person in order to be able to provide many services to their receivers.

Experts may enter and settle in foreign countries, but their qualifications and licences may not be recognized by the host authorities. Public authorities regulate the supply of services to a much higher degree than they do the production of goods. They often regulate public shareholding, quality and quantity of supply, rates and conditions of operation. Fiscal incentives are often more easily given to firms in the manufacturing industry than to those in the services sector. Because of the wide coverage of regulation of industries in the services sector, an easing or a removal of control of the establishment in services can have a much greater impact on trade and investment in the sector than would be the case in the trade and production of goods.

Small and open countries that are net importers of goods may not chose to rely solely on their domestic manufacturing industry, which need not operate on an efficient scale. These countries may choose to develop service industries which can create the proceeds to pay for imports of goods. In general, the Netherlands developed trade, Austria tourism, Norway and Greece shipping, while Switzerland and Luxembourg are highly specialized in financial services.

The issues linked to trade in services have often been neglected in the past. The rules relating to these problems were not negotiated. Trade in services, however, exceeded $1,000 billion in 1993 (almost a third of world trade in goods) so it comes as no surprise that services were included in the Uruguay Round Accord and the WTO.

The services sector of an economy changes its structure over time. The traditional services (such as transport, legal, banking and insurance) are enriched by the new and fast growing ones (such as telecommunications, information, data processing, engineering and management consultancy). Services and the jobs which they create may be broadly classified into two groups: (1) those that require high skills and pay (such as business, financial, engineering, consulting and legal advice), and (2) those that are geared to consumer and welfare needs. The suppliers of services in this second group receive poor training, have a high turnover and low pay (such as jobs in shops, hotels and restaurants). Economic development in its post-industrial phase should be aimed at the creation of jobs in the former group, rather than the latter (Tyson, 1987, p. 79).

7.2   European Union

Articles 52 to 68 of the Treaty of Rome grant the right of establishment to EU residents, freedom to supply services throughout the region and freedom of movement for capital. Article 90 states that public enterprises and those with special or exclusive rights to provide services of general economic interest 'shall be subject to...the rules on competition, in so far as the application of such rules does not obstruct the performance, in law or in fact, of the particular tasks assigned to them'. Compared with trade in goods, these rights have not yet materialized in practice on a large scale. The major reason was the various national restrictions (NTBs). In fact, around half of the 282 measures that came from the 1992 Programme related to services such as finance, transport and telecommunications. It was in the financial services (banking and insurance) that the 1992 Programme advanced most swiftly. On the one hand, this was due to the impressive changes in technology (data processing and telecommunications services), while on the other, to international efforts to liberalize trade in services under the auspices of the Uruguay Round.

There is a question whether the changes prompted by the 1992 Programme have the same effects on services as they have on manufacturing? The question is, in fact, whether there will be an impact by the Programme on the geographical location of services in the EU as happened with manufacturing. For certain services that are tradable because of data-processing and telecommunications possibilities, such as accounting, there will be some centralization and reallocation of business. For most others, significant changes are not expected in the short and medium term. Skilled accountants are able to move around the EU and offer their services, but the Greek islands (tourism) will remain where they are!

The financial services deal with promises to pay. In a world of developed telecom services, these promises can move instantaneously all around the globe. Customs posts do not matter in this business. None the less, restrictive rights of establishment may limit the freedom to supply these services. Traditionally, monetary power was jealously protected and saved for domestic authorities. This has changed in past decades. International mobility of capital can hardly be stopped, therefore countries try to make the best use of it. Financial services not only generate employment and earnings themselves but also, and more importantly, the efficient allocation of resources and the competitiveness of the manufacturing sector depends on wide choice, efficient and low costs of financial services.

The still evolving legislative framework for the single EU market in services is based on the following four principal elements:

- *Freedom of establishment.* Enterprises from other EU countries may not be discriminated and need to receive the national treatment in the country of operation. This is important in services sector because of the necessity for direct contact between the providers and consumers of services. There needs to be a single licence for the provision of services throughout the EU. This means that a firm that is entitled to provide services in one EU country has the same right in another EU country. The country that issues such a licence is primarily responsible for the control of the licensed firm on behalf of the rest of the EU.
- *Liberalization of cross-border trade in services.* This element increases the possibility of cross-border provision of services without the actual physical establishment of the business in the host country. A gradual inclusion of cabotage (internal transport service within a country) in air and road transport are the key changes of the programme.
- *Harmonization of the national rules.* This eases the trans-border establishment of business and the provision of services. This is relevant for telecommunications (technical standards) and financial (solvency) services.
- *Common rules of competition.*

According to the First Banking Directive (1977), EU-resident banks are free to open branches throughout the Union, but this was subject to the host-country authorization. Foreign banks could not compete successfully with local banks, as the costs of establishment differ widely among countries. In addition, foreign banks may be excluded from certain services (securities) which are reserved for the local residents. The Second Banking Directive (1989) brought a major breakthrough in the EU banking industry as it introduced the single banking licence. From 1993, member countries of the EU accepted the home-country control principle, as well as a mutual recognition of each others' licensing rules for the banks. Full harmonization of the banking laws in the EU countries is, however, neither easy nor necessary. Banking laws among the states in the US differ, but this has never been a big handicap to the economic performance of the country. As financial services became globalized, the challenge to the EU and its member countries is to adjust to this change and remain competitive, became mature or lose out to other competitors. If third-country banks wish to benefit from the single market in the EU, a draft of the Second Banking Directive has asked for reciprocal treatment from them. Subsequently, it became evident that it would be an unrealistic provision in relation to US banks. These banks are not allowed to enter certain financial operations (such as securities) across the boundaries of federal states. It would be unreasonable to give EU banks operating in the US a more favourable treatment than domestic US banks and/or that the US would change the domestic rules because of a different regulation in the EU. In the end, the reciprocity provision will not apply to subsidiaries of US banks that were established in the EU prior to 1 January 1993.

The insurance business is very special and complex indeed. There are few homogeneous products and there is usually a long-term relation between the parties. If a consumer purchases a bottle of Scotch whisky, he still has the pleasure to consume this drink even if the producer goes out of business. The same is not true for an insurance policy. Control of the insurance business is exercised by regulating entry into this business. Insurers in the EU are granted the general right to establish, but they are often permitted to solicit business only through the local agencies. This is particularly true for compulsory insurance.[65] The rationale for such restrictions can be found in the protection of consumers' interests because of the asymmetric information between the seller and the buyer (the seller may know much more about the policy than the buyer),[66] but it can be employed for the protection of local businesses too. Where a sound case for the protection of local consumers ends, and where a barrier to trade in the insurance business and protection of the local industry begins is hard to identify. Buyers of an insurance policy may appreciate the benefits of relatively tougher regulation, but may not wish to accept the higher costs involved.[67]

Progress in the EU was faster in the non-life than in the life insurance business. The directive (1988) on the freedom to supply non-life insurance distinguished between two kinds of risks. First, the home-country regulation covers mass risks (commercial risks) and large risks (transport, marine, aviation). Second, the national regulation that applies to personal insurance depends on where the policy-holder resides. Progress in integrating the insurance business in the EU has not advanced as much as in the field of banking. EU insurance companies were allowed to compete only under the host country rules, which significantly reduces the chance of real competition. In fact, the insurance industry is least affected by the 'globalization' of business. Highly protected national insurance markets would require a lot of harmonization before real competition takes place in this field and before a 'single EU insurance passport' is introduced in this business. The process may take longer than in banking because distortions in the insurance business were much more complex, and because the reasoning from the *Cassis de Dijon* case has not yet been applied to insurance services.

As part of the implementation of the internal-market programme, personal insurance policies started to be sold and advertised freely in the EU in 1994. But the insurers and the consumers were not rejoicing in full. One reason is that the national tax treatment will still favour the local companies. These firms have a wide network of tied agents that may not be easily and swiftly replicated by foreign competitors. Another includes national restraints on the sale of certain types of policies. For example, Italy banned the sale of kidnap insurance because of the concern that it would encourage abductions.

Uncoordinated national laws can no longer provide the basis for the future developments of financial services in the EU. This is increasingly important in the light of rising globalization and a loss of an EU-specific dimension in business, especially in banking. If the EU wants to preserve or, even, increase the existing amount of business and employment that goes with it, the crucial thing is that it fosters the development of an open and efficient market for financial services. Consumers will get a wider choice, better quality and cheaper financial services which is essential for the competitiveness of the manufacturing industry and the whole economy.

The *Debauve* case (1980) dealt with advertising. It showed how complicated may be cases in the services sector. Belgium prohibited advertising on TV. None the less, cable TV programmes that originated in other countries without such restrictions and which were marketed in Belgium contained advertising messages. The issue was whether the government of Belgium had the right to ban advertising on channels received in the country, but which originate in other countries. The EU Court concluded that in the absence of the EU action, each member state would regulate and even prohibit advertising on the TV on its territory on the grounds of general interest. The question here is what was the 'general interest' in this case? A typical argument for regulation would be the protection of consumers (viewers). An increase in the choice of channels would not be against the interests of the viewers notwithstanding the fact that foreign programmes contain advertising spots or not. Therefore, the argument that an improvement in the welfare of those in Belgium wished to watch foreign channels was increased by the ban, can not hold water (Hindley, 1991, p. 279). If Belgian viewers watch foreign programmes (with or without advertising), they will watch fewer domestic channels. Hence, support for the public financing for domestic TV will decrease. An additional reason for the Belgian policy was the protection of the advertising revenue of the local newspapers.

Both large scale and flexible modes of production require efficient and reliable transport services. The sophistication in demand by the consumers and a reduction in the own-account transportation have redressed demand for this service. A just-in-time delivery system (frequent, punctual and reliable shipments) was the outcome of sophisticated logistics which reduced storage costs. All that would be reinforced and advanced by competitive transport services. The majority of firms in the haulage industry are small or medium-sized. Around 95 per cent of the companies have less than six vehicles. This reflects the fact that road haulage markets are mainly local (Carlén, 1994, p. 89). Two-thirds of all goods transported by road in the EU are within a distance of 50 km, a further 20 per cent within distances of between 50 and 150 km, leaving only 14 per cent for distances of over 150 km (Commission, 1992, p. 11). While in most of the EU countries road transport is geared towards the domestic service (most obvious in Greece, Spain and Portugal), the Netherlands and Belgium direct around a half of their respective road transport services to other countries because of their ports of Rotterdam and Antwerp.

The operation of commercial transport vehicles and the supply of transport services was highly restricted throughout the EU. Free competition did not exist. This can be understood because all countries apply qualitative controls (safety standards), but also used quantitative controls. Cabotage was generally prohibited, while bilateral permits negotiated between member states regulated haulage between them.

The EU was relatively successful in introducing special transport permits valid for a limited time throughout the EU. However, the number of these permits was relatively small in relation to demand. The shortage of international haulage licences which were acceptable for business throughout the EU has created a black market for them. The price of an annual permit for a lorry to carry goods around the EU can be as high as a fifth of a lorry's operating costs. International road transport in the EU was fully liberalized from 1993. Liberal rules for the EU road haulage including cabotage, will significantly increase the efficiency of transport and reduce the costs of this service to the manufacturing sector, trade and distribution.[68] There is a quota of around 30,000 authorizations (valid for two months) for cabotage in the EU. It will be progressively increased until 1998, after which EU hauliers will be free to pick up or deliver their cargo anywhere in the EU without any restrictions. The Single Administrative Document for carrying goods among the member countries of the EU is a significant step in the direction of improving the transport service.

The EU skies were open to all EU-domiciled air-transport companies in 1997. These companies are allowed to operate domestic air service in the EU country of their choice. In addition, they can offer air-transport services between EU countries. However, anyone who expects tectonic changes in this market will be disappointed. Few companies are likely to start a domestic air service in other countries. Barriers to 'real' competition in this industry involve various national bilateral deals holding sway over long flights to non-European destinations. Alitalia can not operate flights between Paris and New York because the Franco-American deal does not allow for such a possibility. These bilateral deals are the result of arrangements between governments, not airlines. Hence the solution needs to be found in administration. None the less, there are slow moves towards reshaping the EU air travel market.

One of the fastest growing industries in the services sector is telecommunication. This is due to the profound technological changes since the 1960s which include communication via satellite, microwaves and digital technology. New goods and services, such as fax machines, electronic mail and mobile phones also appeared. ECU 450 billion are invested in the EU information industry. The natural monopoly argument for the provision of long-distance services has vanished, although it may still be valid for the local phone service because of the economies of scale and sunk costs. Local phone companies, however, have an access to several competing long-distance networks. The EU policy in the telecommunication field was slow and late to appear. During the mid-1980s, the EU was concentrating its efforts on R&D and common standardization. Subsequently, the intention of having an open network was translated into a directive in 1990. In addition, public contracts that exceed ECU 0.6 million in the industry must be transparent and officially published. Directive 96/19/EC introduced full competition in the telecommunication market in 1998, although Greece, Portugal and Spain may get a five-year implementation period. This means that EU consumers should have the right to have a phone connected, access to new services, have services of a specified quality and benefit from new methods of solving problems between the consumer and the provider of the service.

Business services have high rates of growth too. They include accountancy, auditing, legal, R&D, information, data processing, computing and various engineering and management consultancy services. Different technical standards, licensing of professionals and government procurement of services represent barriers to the free supply of services throughout the EU. A liberal treatment of these services may reduce their costs and increase the efficiency of business. In a world with continuous changes in technology, markets, laws and the like, as long as consultants manage to stay at least one step ahead of their clients, their services will survive.

7.3   *The way forward*

The policy of the EU towards services should be founded on three major freedoms. They are the freedom to establish business, the freedom to offer services and the freedom to transfer capital. Deregulation in the services sector will increase competition which will reduce costs for consumers, increase opportunities and improve the competitive position of the entire economy. Apart from deregulation, the promotion of the development of the EU-wide service industries needs to be encouraged. Initial steps towards this objective include recognition of qualifications, single banking and insurance licences, removal of restrictions on transport and the opening up of government procurement over a certain (small) threshold to all EU suppliers.

Although the general interests of a member country do not always conform with the overall interest of the EU, the EU Court has often been reluctant to question national stances. This has limited the effectiveness of Articles 59–66, as well as Article 90 of the Treaty of Rome. While the *Cassis de Dijon* case was applied to internal trade in goods, the application of the same principle to services is waiting for 'better times'. The 'soft' stance of the EU regarding restrictive agreements and abuse of dominant position in services can not easily be explained only by the properties of services; one also needs to add the influence of entrenched businesses, lobbies and the public protection of specific interests. None the less, the attitude is slowly changing in favour of the view that regulation which limits competition prevents, rather than stimulates, efficiency in services such as telecommunication, transport and finance.

As the provision of most services has a local character (many of them are non-tradable), there will be no big change in their location as the local incumbents have established and operating retail networks and their own reputation (accounting may be an exception). Because of this aspect of services, national regulation will remain dominant in many industries within the services sector in the future. The structure of ownership, however, may change as local firms enter into the network of large TNCs in the industry. However, one should not exaggerate the potential expansion of TNCs in the services sector as most mergers and acquisitions in the sector have a strong national dimension. An international, i.e. EU dimension in the services sector is growing in the insurance industry. Allianz, the biggest insurer in the EU made 48 per cent of its premium income outside Germany in 1990, compared with only 18 per cent in 1985 (Sapir, 1993, p. 37).

The impact of the 1992 Programme on services may not be immediately obvious. It will take a long time to materialize in the future. The 1992 Programme may bring certain benefits to the consumers of services. However, large-scale benefits may be missing because of important barriers that include the reputation of the already established service firms, past experience, excess capacity and cultural differences. It may be wrong to expect that the genuine internal market will cause an equalization of prices of services throughout the EU. Prices will only tend to converge because of increased competition. None the less, certain price differentials will still persist because of differences in productivity, taxation and needs of the local markets.

8 Conclusion

Consideration of the various problems which appear during the creation and implementation of an industrial policy in the manufacturing and services sectors of a country has given an insight into the magnitude of the problems in this field which face schemes to integrate countries. There is at least one forceful argument that favours the introduction of an industrial policy. The neo-conservative school argues that a free market system is the best existing method for solving economic problems. However, that can not be accepted without reservations. Neither the economic performance of the US prior to the New Deal, nor the contemporary economic performance in the most successful industrialized countries such as Germany, Japan or Sweden, supports this view. Strategic government intervention and comprehensive social welfare programmes, rather than free markets have been the engines of economic success throughout the advanced industrial world (Tyson and Zysman, 1987b, p. 426). In fact, free markets were no more than 'fine tuning' policy choices of the government.

If a country's policy is flexible towards the manufacturing industry in response to market signals (as in Japan) or if it shapes the market (as in France), it has a greater possibility of adapting than countries which have largely prevented change (such as Britain). Industrial policy that ignores market signals and that supports declining industries introduces confusion over future developments and increases the cost of inevitable change. These costs may be much higher in the future than they were in the past because of social rigidities and rapid changes in technology. The success of an industrial policy may be tested by its effectiveness in shifting resources from ailing industries, not how effective it is in preventing this adjustment.

The policy of picking the winner (a strategic industry with important externalities) *ex ante* may propel the economy of a country in the future. This may have a favourable outcome for the country or the EU if the choice is correct, if this policy is coordinated with the suppliers of inputs and if it is limited to a defined period of time in which the national champion is expected to become self-reliant. The other interventionist approach of the rescue (*ex post*) may just postpone the attrition of the assisted industry and increase the overall costs of change to the society. The shifts out of obsolete industries into modern ones seems easy in theory, but can be quite difficult, costly and slow in practice. This is, of course, a matter of political choice. The inability to do something is different from an unwillingness to do it. The EU opted for the creation of an environment that favours change. None the less, its direct industrial policy is in many respects a set of R&D policies (coupled with public procurement). Other dimensions of industrial policy can be implemented within the domain of competition and trade policies. There is a hope that the 'social dimension' in the future of the EU will remain only a set of non-obligatory standards that will not mislead the EU into the complacency that would kill the urge for continuous change for the better.

The shaping of an industrial policy in every country requires detailed data about the available factors, competition, externalities, policies of the major trading partners, as well as about the tax, legal and political environment. Even then, industrial policy prescriptions should be taken with great caution. At the time when Britain was industrializing it was the textile industry which was the leader in technology. The required capital for the start-up of a firm was much smaller than for a steel mill which was leading the manufacturing industry when Germany started to industrialize. The problems of development had to be solved by government incentives (intervention) and bank loans. Modern industries not only require capital investment (in many cases this entails reliance on banks) but also, and more importantly, they involve investment in highly qualified personnel. Education policy is always shaped to a large extent by the government.

There are certain reasons for pessimism about the possibility of the creation and implementation of an effective industrial policy in a decentralized country or a group that integrates countries. There are many agents and issues which should be taken into account during the decision-making process. Various agents have their special impact on industrial policy. They include ministries of trade, finance, social affairs, education, regional development, defence and foreign affairs. Most of these departments exist at the federal, regional and local levels. There are also labour unions, banks and industrial associations. They all have diverse and often conflicting goals. The complexity of coordination, communication and harmonization of all those players increases exponentially with their number. In spite of all those organizational difficulties, rewards are challenging.[69] However, numerous agents may, of course, be a source of creativity, but in practice they often turn out to be a source of disagreement over the distribution of instruments of industrial policy. The interaction of all those players has an amalgamating effect on the national industrial policy. To reconcile all these diverse demands is a great political challenge.

Luckily, the evidence in the cases of Japan and Germany may serve as an example to other countries in the shaping of national industrial policies. The crucial property of a promising industrial policy is that if it can not be organized on the central level, then it ought to coordinate measures taken at lower levels. Without a consensus about the basic objectives of industrial policy among the major players and their commitment to these goals, the success of this policy will not come about. Exchange of views, mutual understanding, trust, support and then, an agreement about the goals and means of industrial policy between governments at all levels, business community and labour is an essential element of its effectiveness.

While the EU creates conditions for competition, its member countries implement their own national industrial policies. The divergence in the industrial policy philosophies among the member countries and a lack of funds prevented the EU from playing a more influential role. The variety of the national uncoordinated policies introduced confusion and uncertainty regarding the future actions of the EU. Until the member countries take advantage of a vast internal market, they may lose the competitive edge in many industries to Japan, US and newly industrialized countries in future. If it attempts to be durable and successful an EU industrial policy will require the agreement of the member states about their objectives and policy means. A new philosophy by the Commission regarding industrial policy in the EU is based on the idea that this policy needs primarily to offer a stable macro-economic environment. It is hoped that enterprises can be left alone within such ambience to do their best to remain competitive.

The 'golden' rules for a respectable industrial policy include the following:

- The policy should not harm other parts of the economy.
- The policy needs to be continuous and stable.
- The policy instruments should reinforce each other.
- Inflation needs to be low, rates of interest positive and exchange rates stable. In such an environment incentives exist for savings and investment.
- Public borrowing needs to be small in order to give better opportunities to the private sector for obtaining investment funds.
- If necessary, intervention needs to be general and offer support to industries, rather than individual firms within them.
- There always needs to be an element of choice among various courses of action, as well as the flexibility to respond to crises and opportunities.
- If certain support (such as subsidies, tariffs or quotas) is offered, it should have a timetable, be transparent and be of limited duration after which it has to be withdrawn.
- There needs to be a reference to investment in human capital. Well trained labour and an educated management are the most valuable assets that an economy can have. The policy needs to support the acquisition of new skills and promote the flexibility needed for adapting to constant changes in the economy and technology.[70]
- Measures to ease the adjustment frictions are often a necessary element in an industrial policy. Emphasis needs to be on expanding, rather than declining industries.
- The policy should not neglect the creation of SMEs that establish valuable links throughout the economy, not only among the large firms, but also between producers and consumers.

- There needs to be a consensus among the major players (employers, employees and the government) in the economy about the global economic goals and means for their achievement. These players should also be committed to the achievement of the agreed goals. This implies that the long-term vision of the goals needs to be realistic.
- Public support to R&D and innovation should increase the exchange of information among the interested parties.
- As private capital is generally uninterested in investment in infrastructure, the government needs to step into this field.

Although industrial policy is wider than trade or competition policy, the frontier between them is obscure. Whether an industrial policy increases the national GDP in relation to what will happen without it can be debated for a long time without a solution to satisfy everyone. A promising industrial policy should neither shield the expanding industries from competition for an excessively long period of time, nor prevent the attrition of declining industries forever. It ought to facilitate the movements of factors from obsolete to modern industries. It has to be well coordinated on all levels of government with other economic policies that affect the manufacturing and services sectors. Without successful communication, harmonization and coordination, intervention in industry will be similar to the work of a brain-damaged octopus. This holds both for single countries and integration schemes. None the less, traditional behaviour is sometimes hard to change in reality, even though the need for change is recognized. The EU has chosen a path which creates the conditions for change according to market criteria of efficiency. It is up to the economic agents to take advantages of these opportunities.

IV   REGIONAL POLICY

1   Introduction

The prevailing attitude towards regional policy was one of non-intervention until the economic crisis in the 1930s. As the allocation of resources is perfect in a situation of free trade,[71] intervention in the form of regional policy is not necessary. Such a 'classic' premise has not, however, passed the test of time. The reasons for the alteration of the classic idea included not only transport costs, but also other market imperfections such as economies of scale or externalities. In those circumstances, an industrial policy is generally directed towards an increase in national or regional production potential and capabilities through a (supposedly) efficient allocation of resources from the national standpoint.[72] The objective of a regional policy is, however, to influence the distribution of the created wealth and to contribute to the easing and eventual solution to the 'regional problem'. In spite of intervention in regional affairs, there appeared a recent move towards the abandoning or, at least, easing and changing intervention in regional matters.

There is still a controversy regarding the issue of what constitutes the 'regional problem'. If taken together, there are several elements that may provide an insight into the issue. First, there is the case when different regions grow at uneven rates for a longer period of time, so the policy action aspires to reduce that problem. Second, intervention may also aim at an equalization of consumption or GDP per capita among different regions. Third, the government may be interested in the relatively equal access of the population throughout the country/union to an adequate level of public goods and services. Another interest of the public authorities might include a spatially stable distribution of economic activities and population in order to avoid negative externalities. Governments intervene in regional matters at least because of the following three reasons:

- *equity* (this social motive is based on public pressure on the government to try to achieve a 'proper' balance and an 'orderly' distribution of national wealth among different regions);
- *efficiency* (the desire to employ, sustain and increase national economic potentials and capabilities); and
- *strategic behaviour* (public authorities want to shape the comparative advantages of the country).

Intervention in the form of a regional policy is not a simple task as there are constant changes in technology, competition and demography.

This section is structured as follows. Part 2 spells out basic theoretical ideas regarding regional policy, in particular, in an integrated area. That is followed by a consideration of objectives and instruments of a regional policy in part 3. Various aspects of regional policy in the EU are the subject matter of part 4. The conclusion is that the EU has to pay attention to regional matters in particular because of the fact that in an EMU, balance-of-payments disequilibria are replaced by regional disparities.

2 Theory

The neo-classical or convergence school of thought argues that the 'regional problem' is not a problem at all. A free movement of goods, services and factors would, under certain assumptions, equalize factor earnings and living standards in all regions. In spite of this, even *laissez-faire* governments may be seriously tempted to intervene in the economy as the adjustment process may work so slowly that it is not politically acceptable. Another school emphasized growing disparities, rather than equalization among regions. Imperfect markets with economies of scale, constrained mobility of factors or externalities may increase the attractiveness of already advanced areas and widen regional gaps, rather than reduce them.

Determinants of industrial location include considerations about access to raw materials, energy and labour; access to markets; competition; government (dis)incentives and the cost of transport. An advance in transport and communication technologies has made transport costs rarely the most important determinant for the location of business. While considering feasible locations for business, a firm may prefer a least-cost location and ignore the demand side of the function. In the reverse case, a firm may emphasize demand and neglect everything else. In practice, a firm considers both of these issues simultaneously.

Urbanization is one of the important features of a modern society. One of the reasons for this development is a declining share of labour relative to capital in agriculture. Another incentive for urbanization comes from the fact that many manufacturing and service operations depend on access to public services, in particular in the countries that are known for intervention. That is why lobbyists cluster in cities such as Brussels or Washington, DC. Footloose industries are less reliant on natural inputs. In some cases they may place more emphasis on the proximity to final markets which further adds to the urbanization trend.

Industrial development was shaped in the past by a host of economic and historic factors. Many of them were quite accidental. One of the most attractive locations for setting up business was in the past on crossroads or at the mouth of a river. During the colonial period, colonial powers obtained natural resources from their provinces. In many cases they prevented the development of manufacturing in colonies as they wanted to secure those outer markets for the exports of domestic manufactured goods. Local competition was ousted. If certain development of manufacturing activities did take place it was usually in port cities and was limited to primary processing.

Once the development of a business activity starts in an area and if the system is flexible, then it attracts other activities to the region. The location of a firm was influenced in the past both by the endowment of immobile local resources and by flows of mobile factors. A modern firm is highly mobile in its search for profitable opportunities, not only within its region or country, but also internationally. For a footloose firm, the advantages of one location in relation to others are much more people-dependent than subject to resource endowments. Up until the 1960s it seemed to be more efficient to move people to jobs by migration. The footloose element of many modern industries supports production in relatively small and flexible units. Hence, there is an arbitrary and uncertain element in the location of firms from such as industry. Locations that are close to consumers save in transport costs of final output, while other locations may save in the cost of production. In some cases, costs of inputs, economies of scale and forwarding outlays may favour peripheral locations, while in others a preference may be for those that are close to consumers.

A relatively modest start for an industry or a firm could have irreversible effects for a specific location or a region. For example, there are interesting stories of why certain firms/industries are located where they are:

- There was a recession in Seattle (Washington) after the First World War. The economy of the region was based on fishing, production of timber and ship/boat building. At about the same time demand for aircraft (made of wood) started to emerge. There were unemployed boat-builders and other inputs. Workers had the talents to make wooden boats, so they could easily make a fully covered boat (i.e. the body of an aeroplane), they knew how to fix a propeller, and that is how it all started with Boeing.
- The US film industry started in California because that state has excellent light. Although modern filming and lighting technology no longer depends on natural light, the clustering of the film industry in California continued.
- Nestlé was established in Vevey (Switzerland). There was a brook that could be used to turn a mill-wheel (with a hammer). It was used for the cracking of cocoa nuts and producting cocoa powder and, hence, chocolate. There has been no production in Vevey for a long time, but Nestlé kept its headquarters there.
- Marble is still carved in Carrara (Italy) where craftsmen have chipped away for centuries, even though much of the stone is now imported.
- Most of the supply of the ski boots comes from clusters of firms in Veneto[73] (Italy), the region with the esteemed history of producing 'good' shoes.
- Although BMW has a respectable history of producing motorcycles, when it came to the making of moto-cross engines, the Germans turned to the Italians based in and around the Veneto and Emiglia Romana.
- Stalin admired classical ballet. Hence, the central plan allocated the 'necessary' resources for the education and training of ballet dancers and their teachers. The Russians still excel in the education and supply of highest quality dancers of classical ballet.
- Fine beer is produced only in relatively few 'regions'. They include countries with a very long tradition and technology such as Germany, the Czech Republic, the Netherlands, Belgium and Denmark, basically because of high quality hops and water, as well as know-how.

As products mature, the production cycle can render some previously unattractive locations for business worthy of consideration. Following invention, innovation is the process by which these inventions are put into commercial use, while technology transfer is the process by which new products are transformed into 'old' goods elsewhere. An increasing number of new goods in the north usually creates demand all around the world. Hence, relative prices of northern goods rise in relation to the prices of southern commodities. It is profitable to invest in the north, so capital moves there from the south. Similarly, technology transfer shifts at least a part of demand towards goods produced in the south. This catch-up by the south, makes a certain amount of capital move there, so the relative income of southern workers increases. This process may 'hurt' the technical leader. Therefore, northern countries have an interest in innovating continuously, not just to grow, in order to maintain their real incomes (Krugman, 1990a).

There is, however, a drive that may help out the lagging regions in an integrated area. Suppose that the initial elimination of barriers to the movement of goods, services and factors in a common market spurs an inflow of factors to already industrialized areas where they benefit from economies of scale and externalities. If all barriers to internal trade and factor movements are eliminated or become insignificant, firms may benefit from economies of scale and externalities in other (less advanced or peripheral) regions where the variable costs of production are potentially lower than in the centre of the manufacturing or service activity (Krugman and Venables, 1990, p. 74). In this case, the less developed region or a country that takes part in a common market is likely to benefit on two accounts. First its industries get firms that benefit from economies of scale and, second, their former industrial structure that was typified by a lack of open competition is altered. Therefore in theory, economic integration may, but not necessarily will, bring greater benefits to the regions/countries that lag in their development behind the centre of economic activity. However, if production linkages (forward and backward) are strong and internal to an industry such as in chemicals or financial services, and imperfect competition prevails, economic integration will trigger agglomeration tendencies. If those linkages are not limited to a relatively narrow industry group, but are strong *across* industries and sectors, integration will produce agglomeration tendencies in select spots. If labour is not mobile, the whole process will tend to open up new and widen existing regional wage differentials (Venables, 1995). Although this may produce deindustrialization tendencies in the peripheral regions, this does not mean that integration is not desirable. Education and regional policies increase the attractiveness of Spain as a location for various manufacturing industries. This was discovered not only by the external, but also by the EU investors.

Others may, however, argue that the outcome may be the reverse of the one just described, and that an active regional policy is necessary, in particular, in a EMU. An outflow of migrants will discourage an entry of new businesses into the region which will further weaken the economic position of the area in question. None the less, such a vicious circle has not taken place in the EU. What seems likely to be the case in the EU is that the regional disparities were slowly narrowing until the early 1970s; that was followed by a decade-long period of widening of regional gaps after which the regional gap among the member countries more or less stabilized.[74]

The national rate of growth of capital stock (without FDI and foreign loans) depends on home savings and investment. Suppose that one region/country initially accumulates more capital than the other. In the following period both regions grow, but the one with more capital grows faster than the one with less capital. As manufacturing capital grows, the relative prices of manufacturing goods fall. After a certain period of time, there is a point where the lagging region's industry can not compete internationally and it begins to shrink. Once this process starts, the new theory of trade and strategic industrial policy suggests, there is no check. Economies of scale may drive prices down in the capital-abundant region and the lagging region's manufacturing industry disappears. In this model, relatively small beginnings can have large and irreversible final consequences for the manufacturing structure of a country, its competitiveness and trade (Krugman, 1990a, pp. 99–100). A lesson for the EU is that the 1992 Programme provided opportunities to concentrate firms in select hot spots,[75] as well as for rationalization of business operations. In the US, for example, there is a high concentration of aero-industries around Seattle, electronics in the Silicon Valley or Boston's Route 128 (because of the existence of the best universities in the vicinity), cars around Detroit or insurance in Hartford, Connecticut. In Europe, the production of knives is clustered in Solingen, watches in the Swiss Jura, financial services in London, certain pharmaceuticals in Basle, fashion garments and motorcycles in northern Italy ('Padania'), but the European car industry has never created a cluster similar to Detroit. However, once the concentration of business becomes too high, there are negative externalities such as pollution, congestion and an increase in the price of land. This may have an impact on the spread and decentralization of businesses and their shift to other regions as firms may wish to leave the 'threatened' regions.

One of the consequences of the 1992 Programme was that clusters of firms are becoming more visible.[76] A relatively high geographic concentration of related firms in comparatively small areas eases the exchange of information. Frankfurt, London and Paris are places that create jobs faster than the rest of the national economy. However, there is a problem. Regions outside a large metropolitan area seem to remain poor. Success, like many other things, seems to cluster too.

There are many causes of regional disequilibria. They include market rigidities such as relatively low mobility of factors; geographical factors; differences in the availability of resources; education of management and training of labour; regional economic structure (in some regions declining industries, in others growing ones); institutional factors such as the centralization of public institutions (Paris is an obvious example); and national wage setting in spite of differences in productivity (Vanhove and Klaassen, 1987, pp. 2–7). Regional disparities appear in numerous forms. They include not only differences in income levels per capita, rates of growth or rates of unemployment, economies of scale, externalities, output and consumption structures, productivity, but also age structure, population density and the pattern of migration.

Regional policy was neglected in the EU before its first enlargement in 1973. That was followed by a period of interest in an active regional policy. However, enthusiasm for that policy waned in the 1990s. But can regional policy work at all? That was the question asked by de la Fuente and Vives (1995). Governments introduced regional policies in order to promote growth in poor regions. The policy was based on the assumption of market failures. The instruments of the policy included investment aid, direct investment by the state, wage subsidies, tax allowances, licensing and the provision of infrastructure and services. Since the 1990s, the emphasis of the policy moved away from the attraction of extra-regional investment and general subsidies, towards the development of endogenous regional growth and human resources. The situation regarding regional policy in the EU has been ambivalent. On the one hand, cohesion is becoming a *leitmotif* of European integration, hence the involvement in this issue. On the other hand, market liberalization and an active regional policy (intervention) do not go hand in hand! As an automatic market-led adjustment mechanism operates too slowly to be politically acceptable, the EU funds for regional development and social issues emphasize supply-side intervention because they provide assistance to infrastructure and training. Public intervention in regional issues is still a highly controversial issue. Is there a self-equilibrating process among the regions in the long term or not? Is intervention (regional policy) necessary or not?

Regional policy is basically aimed at influencing economic adjustment in the four (theoretical) types of regions.

- The regions with a relatively high share of agriculture in production and employment. These are usually underdeveloped rural areas with relatively low levels of income, high levels of unemployment and poorly developed infrastructure.
- This policy tries to have an adjustment impact in regions whose former prosperity was founded on industries that are now in decline, such as coal, steel, shipbuilding or textiles. These are the regions that failed to keep pace with changes in technology and were unable to withstand external competition (in some cases because of excessive protection). In the case of recession, labour in these regions is the first to be made redundant.
- The regions with a high concentration of manufacturing have congestion and pollution problems. In these areas, of course, there exist benefits from the joint use of goods and services available in these areas. Regional policy may, however, try to reduce the existing congestion and pollution and/or prevent their further increase.
- Regional policy helps the solution of adjustment problems in frontier regions which are far from the strongest areas (poles of growth) of a country's or union's economic activity.

The above discussion has shown that there is a great deal of uncertainty regarding the impact of international economic integration on regional matters. One thing, however, needs to be mentioned here. Having a 'peripheral' location is not an irreversible economic disadvantage. Its impact can be mitigated and, even, reversed as has been successfully shown by countries such as Australia or Japan. What matters most for economic competitiveness is the efficient development and employment of the most precious economic factor: human capital!

Jobs can be located in regions where there are people with suitable qualifications, training and experience. Therefore, regions with unskilled labour can not be expected to attract a significant proportion of industries that use modern technologies employing trained labour and educated management. Location of business near large and/or growing markets saves in transport costs. If returns to scale were constant, as the neo-classical theory assumes, this could have equalizing tendencies for factor-owners' rewards in different regions. With economies of scale, these tendencies may increase, rather than decrease, regional disequilibria.

Convergence in the level of development among different regions is not a self-operating process. It works easier during an economic recovery than during recessions. Lagging regions/countries have usually a higher proportion of both 'sensitive industries' and public enterprises than prosperous ones. Therefore, they may be hit harder by a recession and budgetary restrictions than other regions.

The regional problem was usually tackled around the 1960s with supply-side subsidies for the provision of infrastructure and the reallocation of various (public) manufacturing and service industries. Foreign competition, in particular from the newly industrialized countries, placed in jeopardy a number of industries that failed to adjust. As there had been little luck with earlier approaches to the regional problem,[77] coupled with austerity programmes in public finances, there was a major change in regional policies during the 1980s. Outright subsidies were reduced or slashed and the policy was supplemented by a system intended to make the lagging regions more self-reliant and that supports indigenous development. This included the development of human resources, the attraction of private investors (in particular foreign ones) and the provision of technical services.

Recent research suggests a great deal of apprehension regarding the introduction of a regional policy. The long-term rate of regional convergence is quite comparable across countries in spite of highly different efforts to promote regional equality (Barro and Sala-i-Martin, 1991; Sala-i-Martin, 1994).

3 Objectives and instruments

A region may be more easily discerned than defined. The definition of a region depends on the problem which one encounters. A region is both a geographical phenomenon with its distinctions from others; it also has political, governmental and administrative features; and it is an ethnic and social concept with its human and cultural characteristics. A region is also an economic concept with its endowment factors, their combinations and mobility. Therefore, a region can be defined in theory as a geographic area that consists of adjoining particles with similar unit incomes and more interdependence of incomes than between regions (Bird, 1972, p. 272). A region of a country or an economic union may be thought of as an open economy.

Regional policy is intervention by the state in order to influence the 'orderly' distribution of economic activity and to reduce social and economic differences among regions. It was usually a reactive (*ex post*) policy which primarily tried to reduce the existing regional disparities, rather than a policy that primarily prevented the creation of new regional disequilibria.

Trade liberalization and/or economic integration can provoke economic adjustment (reallocation of resources). Enhanced competition may force certain regions to embark upon a painful, but potentially rewarding, transfer of resources from unprofitable into profitable economic activities. These regions often blame integration or trade liberalization for adjustment 'pains'. However, this objection may not always be justified. The most basic reason for the painful adjustment process is due to the earlier protection. The policy of long and excessive sheltering of the domestic economy reduced the pace of reaction of local enterprises on international structural pressures and, hence, increased the cost of adjustment in the future. The adjustment costs may be there, but the benefits *may* more than compensate for the effort!

Relatively low wages may attract investment into the region, however, there may be at the same time certain agglomeration and concentration tendencies in other regions. If there is a nationwide setting of wages, this may act as a structural barrier that works against the lagging regions. As there is no flexibility in the level of wages among various regions in spite of differences in productivity, the less developed areas do not have the capacity to respond to this situation. One cannot know in advance where the balance will tilt. Certain developed regions may become more developed, while some less developed regions/countries may become poorer (if nothing is done to alleviate the situation), but certain less developed regions may move to the group of advanced ones.

The objectives of a regional policy are various, but their common denominator is that they aim at the utilization of regions' unemployed or underemployed resources and potentials, attracting the missing factors, as well as increasing output and incomes. In the congested or polluted areas, this policy restricts the expansion of firms and stimulates exit from the region. In the developing countries, the primary concern is economic development. This is most often coupled with regional imbalances, but their solution is not as high on the agenda as increases in economic potentials. In areas of economic integration, the problem of regional (in)equalities is of great concern. Countries are reluctant to lag for a long time in development behind their partners. This is of great concern in monetary unions (the goal of the EU) where there are no balance-of-payments disequilibria, but rather regional disparities. Depressed regions/countries will no longer resort to devaluation as there is a single currency, while advanced regions/countries will not always be willing to finance regional disequilibria without proof that there is structural adjustment taking place in the regions assisted.

The first justification for a regional policy (intervention that is supposed to assist in the process of economic adjustment), as contrasted with the free-market adjustment, can be found in the structural deficiencies of regions. These include: market rigidities, conditions of access to the market and the structure of output. When there exist such imperfections, a free market system is 'unable' to achieve satisfactory equilibrium from the social stand-point in the short and medium term, so there may be a need for intervention in order to increase output.

Regional imports consists of goods and services. In France, for example, most of the country's regions purchase financial, insurance, legal and other services from Paris. All this cannot be quantified with ease. A reduction in a region's exports, for instance, may be obvious from the outset. Regional solutions to these disequilibria are inhibited by rules of competition and by the existence of a single currency. Hence, the second 'justification' for regional intervention in an economic union.

The third reason for intervention may be found in the employment of factors. The neo-classical theory of international trade usually assumes free and full international mobility of factors that ensures full employment. However, even Adam Smith noted that a man is the most difficult 'com-modity' to transport. During recession, the employment situation is difficult everywhere, therefore the potential advantages of some regions that are abundant in labour are removed. Reduced mobility of labour prevents the equalization of discrepancies in economic unions. Hence, growth in one region may create conditions for even higher growth in the same region and increase inequalities among regions (polarization effect). This may, however, act as a 'locomotive' for development in other regions as there may be increased markets for food, economies of scale and innovation in other regions (spread effect). In order to adopt the idea that there are benefits from the spread effect, one must assume that there is a complementarity between the regions in question.

In a situation closer to reality and which includes economies of scale, large sunk costs, externalities and other market failures, adjustment does not happen according to such a relatively smooth neo-classical expectation. The regional absorption capacity of new technologies requires continuous learning, adaptation, development of human capital and established indus-trial culture. Therefore, the introduction of new technologies may be quite risky. That is why certain technologies diffuse quite slowly among the regions. The reallocation of resources induced by the spread effect works at a (much) slower pace than may be politically acceptable, hence the need for intervention.

The fourth rationale could be found in the 'need' for compensation. Two opposing forces created by economic integration affect regional development. The first one, specialization, leads to a convergence in regional incomes. Backward regions tend to specialize in labour intensive production according to their comparative advantage. This can have as a consequence a faster increase in wages in those regions than in the rich ones. The second force includes economies of scale and externalities. It can lead to a divergence in regional incomes. As integration extends the size of the market, firms take advantage of economies of scale and externalities. The EU 1992 Programme provided certain incentives for the concentration of businesses. This may benefit some regions more than others, in fact there is the possibility that certain (small and backward) regions may actually be hurt by integration if there are no instruments for compensation. Hence, another justification for a regional policy.

Subsidies may be one of the tools of a regional policy. However, a distribution of subsidies is always subject to political pressures. The final disbursement of subsidies often reflects more the balance of political powers than the comparative (dis)advantage of a region. At the end of the process, regional policies executed in such a way may do more harm than good, or at best, they may have a dubious effect. None the less, public policies in the backward regions, such as support to education, infrastructure, select public goods and help for the creation of SMEs in the form of loan guarantees for the start-up of a business, have the potential to assist regional development.

The fifth reason for intervention may be found in the improved allocation of resources. Free markets usually direct capital towards already developed regions in the short and medium term. Private investors tend to increase the speed of the safe return of the funds they invested and to save as much as possible on investment in infrastructure. It may be understandable why they direct their funds towards the already advanced regions. These tendencies of agglomeration (adjoint locations of linked productions),[78] where the developed tend to be more developed while the underdeveloped remain at best where they are, have significant private benefits on the one hand, as well as social costs and benefits on the other. A society may reap the benefits of large-scale efficient production. However, if private entrepreneurs are not impeded in their decision-making by a government policy, the location of their business may introduce significant social costs such as pollution, congestion and traffic jams in some regions and unemployment and increased social assistance in others.

The sixth reason for intervention may be found in the improvement in stabilization (macroeconomic) policy. Regional differences in rates of unemployment may reduce the opportunities to control inflation and manipulate a stabilization policy. The reduction of inflation in some regions may increase unemployment in others. This may not always be the desired outcome. Diversified regions with a variety in employment opportunities will be able to adjust in a less painful way than the specialized regions with entrenched market rigidities.

The seventh justification for an introduction of regional policy is that it may reduce public expenditure in the assisted region in the long run. Public support to firms to locate in certain regions may propel economic activity in these regions. Unemployment may drop, so welfare payments may be reduced and tax receipts may be increased and spent on something else in the long run. In addition, 'employment' in public administration used to provide a shelter to the unemployed. Such artificial employment may be reduced or even eliminated once the private sector (with higher wages) starts thriving in the assisted region.

The eighth rationale points out that regional policy is targeted at regions with some disadvantage (underdevelopment, unemployment, obsolete output structure or pollution). The benefits of a regional policy are not confined only to the assisted area. Part of the benefit is enjoyed by other regions through externalities. The benefit area of a regional policy is larger than the assisted area itself. That is why the Germans or the Swedes have a certain interest in helping out the Irish or Portuguese. Integration may be enhanced, unwanted migration of labour may be prevented, factors may be employed in a superior way and there may be important non-economic gains.

Finally, apart from the above arguments for regional policy that mostly deal with 'economic' efficiency, there are political grounds which are at least as important as the economic ones. Solidarity, tolerance and perception of a common future are the core of any social community. The mitigation of economic disparities among the constituent regions may be the necessary reason for the unity of a state or an economic union. That is relevant as the costs and benefits of international economic integration tend to be unequally spread among the participating countries in a situation of market imperfections. Arguments of equality require the solution and/or mitigation of intolerable or growing differences in the distribution of wealth among the population which lives in different regions. The national political system does not always take fully into account the needs of backward regions. For example, the national system of setting wages may on the one hand significantly reduce the wage-cost advantages of many regions, while on the other hand welfare expenditure can contribute to a greater regional equilibrium. Complete equalization in the standards of living in different regions is neither possible nor desirable because it may relax incentives for change and improvement. What is needed in regional matters is a continuous adjustment of regional development within commonly agreed guidelines, as well as the protection of the standard of living accepted as desirable by the group.

Regional intervention may be quite costly. In addition, there may be an inefficient replication of certain efforts on various levels of government. Therefore, one may use the subsidiarity argument in favour of a EU regional policy. The EU is best placed to coordinate various regional actions, improve their efficiency and to collect and transfer resources from the prosperous to the backward regions of the EU.

The goals of regional policy such as balanced growth, equal shares of social and cultural progress of the society, solidarity, regional distinctiveness and stability, are vague and may not be accurately measured. Specific objectives such as job creation, reduction in unemployment, housing and development of infrastructure introduce fewer problems in quantification. In the implementation of a regional policy care has to be given during the selection of policy tools in order to ensure that the policy does not evolve into protection of the present economic structure, as that prevents structural adjustment and the efficient division of labour.

Instruments of regional policy are often directed towards entrepreneurs and factor owners. They can be employed either directly (e.g. support of the existing or shifting towards the new business activities) or indirectly (e.g. improvement in infrastructure). Their joint effects may increase employment, investment and output in the assisted regions, at least in the short term.

The dilemma of the state may be to stimulate regional development through private investment, on the one hand, and/or to invest directly in production and infrastructure for which there is no interest in the private sector. The available policy tools include those that provide incentives and disincentives to firms to move into or out of specific regions. Major instruments include: regional allocation of capital, investment, infrastructure, output, social security and wage subsidies; vocational training; public procurement and provision of goods, services and infrastructure; reductions in interest rates; tax concessions; decentralization of government offices, education and health services; reductions in energy and public transportation costs; free locations; licences for the location of business; and trade protection.

If offered, cash grants may be preferred regional policy instruments to reduced tax liabilities. Grants apply directly to all firms while reduced tax liabilities help only those that are profitable. Trade restrictions are not the wisest instruments of a regional policy. The costs fall on the whole economic union, while they bring benefits to one or only a few regions.

Disincentives for regional expansion in congested areas are a relatively novel feature. In Britain, for example, they appeared in the form of industrial development certificates that should be obtained prior to expansion or location in the non-assisted regions. However, after the second oil shock, as unemployment increased, those certificates were abandoned as an instrument of regional policy. In France, for instance, there were certain constraints on the expansion of manufacturing and service industries in the Paris region. They included a special tax on office floor construction and authorizations for large-scale investments.

The policy of moving workers to jobs regards the regional problem exclusively as one of unemployment. It neglects the fact that other problems in a region may be worsened further by this 'forced' mobility of labour. The productive sector of the population moves out of the region while the consuming sector remains in it. The local tax base may not be able to provide funds in order to cover the costs of local health care, schools and other social services. The overall situation may be worsened by the multiplier effect. In advanced regions that receive the migrants, there may also be new disequilibria created. The additional population increases congestion and rents for a certain type of housing, which may reduce the quality of life there.

Unemployment rates may be one of the most telling indicators of regional variations. If labour mobility is relatively low, then the movement of jobs to workers may diminish regional disparities in unemployment. Against this action is the fact that it may increase costs as alternative locations may not be optimal for the efficient conduct of business. However, as more industries become footloose, these costs to firms may diminish. Improvements in infrastructure, including the training of labour and the education of management together with the spread of timely information, help the location of footloose industries which are at the beginning of their product cycle in the assisted regions.

4 European Union

4.1 Introduction

International economic integration may, in certain cases, aggravate the situation of already backward and peripheral regions in comparison to previous circumstances. This is recognized in part by the existence of national regional policies. None the less, having a peripheral location does not mean that a country has destined to have a poor economic performance. The accumulation and efficient employment of human (and physical) capital is the most important factor for a country's economic performance. Although countries such as New Zealand, Australia, even Japan or South Korea, have relatively unfavourable geographical locations regarding major transport routes, the irreversibility of their 'peripheral' position was mitigated and more than compensated for by the accumulation and efficient employment of the national human and physical capital. The location of Spain at the fringe of the EU was alleviated by the expansion of infrastructure and further development of human and physical capital. It is expected that Greece and Portugal, as well as prospective newcomers from the transition region, will do the same in the future.

The regional policy of an economic union can be justified at least on the grounds of harmonization of national regional policies and the (re)distribution of wealth within the group. Policy coordination at the central level is defended on the grounds that it prevents clashes of different national regional policies with common objectives. The policy needs to ensure, at the very least, that the existing regional problems are not made worse by economic integration, otherwise the less developed regions/countries will have no incentives to participate in the project.

4.2   Evolution

The evolution of the regional policy of the EU can be divided into three broad phases. Regional issues did not feature highly on the agenda among the original six member countries. At that time, only Italy gave weight to the regional problem because of its southern part. That is why there was hardly any regional policy in the EU till 1973. Following the entry of Britain, Denmark and Ireland in the same year, the situation changed in the enlarged EU. The second phase in the development of the regional policy started following the first enlargement of the EU. Britain was particularly interested in having regional issues included in the EU. Hence, there was the creation of the first tools for the implementation of the policy in the form of the European Regional Development Fund (ERDF). The entry of Greece (1981), and later Spain and Portugal in 1986, amplified the desire and need for a EU regional policy. This policy mainly gives benefits to the EU-rim countries (Britain, Greece, Ireland, Italy, Portugal and Spain), just as the CAP favours the 'northern' countries.[79] The third phase started with the reform of policy and the ERDF in 1988. The concept of an EMU gave fresh impetus for further development of the regional policy.

Following the first enlargement of the EU, the new regional conditions of the EU were officially analysed for the first time in the *Report on the Regional Problems of the Enlarged Community* (the Thomson Report) of 1973. The Report identified two types of regions in the EU that have problems. First, those are the farming regions that are located in the periphery of the EU. The Italian Mezzogiorno or Ireland fit into this group. In both regions there is a relatively high long-term structural unemployment and dependence on farming. Second, the problem regions are also the ones that have a high proportion of regional output and employment in the declining industries. These problem regions have a slow rate of shifting resources out of those industries and a relatively high level of long-term structural unemployment. Certain regions in Britain fit into this group. A renegotiation of the British entry and the concerns by Italy and Ireland led to the creation of the ERDF in 1975 under Article 235 of the Treaty of Rome. However, the ERDF would provide resources for regional development that are only *additional* to the sources that are available for regional development from the national funds.

4.3   Regional discrepancies

Differences in economic development among regions exist in every country, but at the EU level they seem much larger. Less-developed regions in one country may have different characteristics from less-developed regions in others, including large variations in income. In addition, congestion in southern Italy is greater than that in the south-west of France. Table 4.10 presents GDP per capita in the EU countries at market prices during the period

Table 4.10   GDP per capita in ECUs, 1990–1994

Country	1990	1991	1992	1993	1994
Luxembourg	21,770	23,100	24,860	26,860	28,520
Denmark	19,970	20,310	21,080	22,160	23,660
Germany	18,690	17,400	18,890	20,100	21,150
Austria	16,140	17,100	18,190	19,450	20,670
France	16,690	17,140	17,950	18,630	19,460
Belgium	15,200	15,970	17,000	17,850	18,870
Sweden	21,130	22,460	22,080	18,130	18,850
Netherlands	14,940	15,570	16,300	17,270	18,070
Finland	21,290	19,570	16,290	14,160	16,230
United Kingdom	13,450	14,240	14,000	13,930	14,780
Italy	14,950	16,130	16,284	14,490	14,750
Ireland	10,070	10,410	11,110	11,330	12,440
Spain	9,950	10,950	11,390	10,430	10,380
Greece	6,340	6,880	7,160	7,410	7,630
Portugal	5,350	6,350	7,450	7,324	7,430
EU (15)	14,890	15,400	15,970	15,940	16,650
Japan	18,690	21,860	22,680	28,720	30,950
United States	17,430	18,280	18,150	20,970	21,720

Source: EUROSTAT (1995)

1990–94 ordered according to the relative hight in 1994. The comparison of the relative difference in GDP per capita among regions and countries at current exchange rates may well overestimate the real difference between the advanced and backward regions or countries. The difference between Luxembourg as the richest country according to this measure, and Portugal as the least developed, was 3.8 : 1 in 1994.

A useful device for overcoming part of the problem associated with the inter-country comparison of GDP at market prices can be found in the use of current purchasing-power standard (PPS). This statistical indicator is based on the relative prices of a basket of representative and comparable goods. The PPS represents more adequately the real level of the local purchasing power and it often gives significantly different results from the ones given in current ECUs, in particular during times when there are serious changes in the rates of exchange. As the PPS is not affected (in the short term) by fluctuations in the exchange market, it is more appropriate to use this indicator for countries such as Greece, Italy, Portugal and Spain, than the current ECU values. Significant differences between data given in current ECUs and those in the PPS are assigned to the differences in price levels in the member countries. If the level of prices in an individual member country is higher than the EU average, then the GDP per capita is higher in current ECUs than according the PPS. The reverse is true for the countries that have the GDP per capita in current ECUs below the EU average. In these countries, the PPS gives a higher value than the GDP in current prices.[80]

Table 4.11 provides data on the differences in GDP per capita in the EU at purchasing-power standard during the period 1990–94. This kind of presentation changes, to an extent, the picture of the relative wealth of countries in comparison with Table 4.10. The difference in average real income according to this indicator was between the richest, Luxembourg, and the poorest, Greece, 2.6:1 in 1994. These contrasts are also an indication of differences in the level of economic development, while disparities in unemployment rates may be one of the indications of a relatively poor capacity to adjust to various economic shocks. It also has consequences for the regional problem as the local output is below its potential.

The two tables reveal an interesting feature. That is the relative decline of Britain, the world economic leader in the 19th century. While according to the GDP per capita in current prices Italy closely approached Britain during the period of observation, according to the purchasing-power standard, Italy was on a higher level of development than Britain throughout 1990s. If one adds the impact of global warming, Britain will soon join the 'olive-oil zone' of the EU that is bothered with regional problems.[81]

Data for 1992 in the PPS[82] reveal that the most developed regions of the EU, those with per capita GDP of 150 per cent or more of the EU average (100), were Hamburg (196 per cent), Darmstadt (174 per cent), Brussels (174 per cent), Paris (169 per cent), Vienna (166 per cent), Oberbayern (157 per cent), Luxembourg (156 per cent) and Bremen (155 per cent). On the other hand, the most backward regions were the ones that had GDP per capita 50 per cent or less than the EU average (100). They were the five new German

Table 4.11   GDP per capita, purchasing power standard in ECUs, 1990–1994

Country	1990	1991	1992	1993	1994
Luxembourg	21,620	23,250	24,580	25,420	26,140
Denmark	15,300	16,480	16,650	17,740	18,810
Belgium	15,190	16,210	17,300	17,950	18,540
Austria	16,650	17,380	17,100	17,720	18,480
France	16,200	17,270	17,710	17,420	18,120
Germany	17,050	16,070	17,080	17,150	17,890
Netherlands	14,820	15,510	16,060	16,310	16,900
Italy	14,900	15,920	16,470	16,120	16,770
United Kingdom	14,610	14,790	15,500	15,800	16,660
Sweden	17,010	16,880	15,700	15,590	16,140
Finland	16,200	15,540	13,760	14,400	15,210
Ireland	10,400	11,290	12,250	12,830	13,970
Spain	10,940	11,990	12,160	12,330	12,790
Portugal	8,680	9,710	10,410	10,940	11,220
Greece	8,430	9,040	9,610	10,000	10,160
EU (15)	14,730	15,220	15,760	15,840	16,520
Japan	16,270	17,760	18,720	18,900	19,278
United States	20,550	21,180	22,440	22,750	23,890

Source: EUROSTAT (1995)

Länder (38–44 per cent, each); the Greek regions of Voreio Aigaio (45 per cent) and Iperios (47 per cent); the French overseas departments of Guadeloupe (37 per cent) and Réunion (45 per cent); and the Portuguese regions of Alentejo (41 per cent), Açores (41 per cent), Madeira (44 per cent) and Centro (48 per cent). There are regional differences within countries too.[83] These discrepancies may be capable of dividing the EU. The objective of the EU is to mitigate the existing and prevent the creation of new regional imbalances.

In spite of the relative backwardness measured by the differences in GDP per capita relative to the average in the EU, the most thriving parts of the EU can be found in the sizeable regions of both Spain and Portugal.

4.4 Action

Local regional policies that are carried out by the member states and their regional authorities, on the one hand, can have an advantage over the EU regional policy because the local authorities may be better informed about local needs and problems. On the other hand, the EU is better placed to coordinate regional, as well as other national policies. In addition, the EU may contribute own resources, introduce common priorities and standards, as well as take into account regional interests when it reaches certain policy decisions. The EU has to make sure through the employment of the rules of competition that the member governments do not distort competition by a 'subsidy war'. Normally, the EU puts a ceiling on the permitted subsidy per establishment and/or a job created in various regions.

The ERDF was established in 1975. Its expenditure was allocated to the member states in fixed quotas. Those national quotas were set according to the following four criteria:

- the national average GDP per capita had to be below the EU average;
- the assisted region had to have an above-average dependence to farming or a declining industry;
- there had to be structural unemployment in and/or emigration from the region; and
- the EU policies such as free trade had to be having a detrimental impact on the region.

If put in simple terms, the governments of the member states had to submit regional projects to the EU to meet the allocated financial quota and to commit certain funds themselves to these projects, and the EU funds were obtained. The EU did not have any leverage on the selection process. It was simply reacting to national initiatives. There was also a minuscule non-quota section of the ERDF which absorbed only 5 per cent of the resources. The EU was able to use these funds freely. Such a situation was criticized and the ERDF was reformed in 1985.

The reformed ERDF divided its funds among the EU member states by indicative ranges instead of fixed quotas as was the earlier case. Those indicative ranges only guarantee that the government will receive the minimum range over the period of three years if it submitted a sufficient number of quality projects. The projects submitted will be evaluated according to criteria that are consistent with the EU priorities and objectives. The intention of the EU is to receive a greater number of applications in order to increase competition among various proposals. The ERDF support may be up to 55 per cent of public expenditure on regional projects, it is allowed to co-finance programmes and it may prop up the development of indigenous potential in regions. The ERDF also attempts to mobilize local resources because it is increasingly difficult to attract private investment from wealthy to poor regions. Additional attention is devoted to the coordination of both member countries' regional policies and EU policies that have an impact on regions (CAP, trade, environment, for example).

A further modification of EU regional policy came after putting into effect the Single European Act (1987) and the entry of Spain and Portugal which intensified the regional problem. The Act introduced a new Title into the Treaty of Rome on Economic and Social Cohesion. Article 130a requests the promotion of a harmonious development in the EU and 'reducing disparities between the level of development of the various regions'. Article 130b requires the coordination of economic policies among the member countries and authorizes the EU to support those actions and objectives set in the Article 130b through Structural Funds. Apart from these grant-awarding funds, the EU has loan-awarding institutions (European Investment Bank and European Coal and Steel Community) that are also involved in regional projects.

Special regional problems emerged in the EU in 1986 after the entry of Spain and Portugal. Therefore, during the preparations for enlargement, the EU introduced the Integrated Mediterranean Programme in 1985. The goal of this coordinated Programme was to help the Mediterranean regions of the EU (Greece and the southern regions of Italy and France with a combined population of around 50 million) to adjust to competition from the two new member countries. The Programme disposed of ECU 4.1 billion in grants and ECU 2.5 billion in loans over a period of seven years. It integrated all available sources of finance on the levels of the EU, national, regional and local authorities. In addition, it coordinated other policies of the EU. The Programme was not aimed only at adjustment of agricultural production (olive oil, wine, fruit, vegetables), but also at the adjustment of existing and the creation of new SMEs. Alternative employment for jobs lost in agriculture was to be found in services (tourism) and SMEs. Apart from the border regions of Finland, the entry of three developed countries (Austria, Finland and Sweden) in 1995 has not introduced new regional distortions in the EU.

The adjustment of the regional policy and the ERDF that took place in 1988 had one basic objective. It was to improve the coordination of various structural funds in order to support the 1992 Programme. The 1988 reform introduced the following six basic *principles*:

- member countries are to submit plans according to priority objectives;
- there needs to be a partnership between the administration on the local, regional and national level;
- the EU measures play only an additional role;
- there needs to be compatibility with other EU policies such as competition and environment;
- different EU policies need to be coordinated; and
- resources need to be concentrated on the least-developed regions.

At the same time, five priority *objectives* of the regional policy included:

- promotion of the development of the backward regions (Objective 1);
- economic adjustment and conversion of the production structure in the regions that were affected by a large-scale industrial decline (Objective 2);
- a fight against structural unemployment (Objective 3);
- the promotion of youth employment (Objective 4);
- structural adjustment in agriculture, in particular, in the regions affected by the reform of the CAP and fisheries (Objective 5a); and
- promotion of development in rural areas (Objective 5b).

Another decision in the reform package was to more than double the resources of Structural Funds from ECU 6.3 billion in 1987 to ECU 14.1 billion in 1993.[84] None the less, these funds had to be only an additional regional expenditure to that undertaken by the national governments. The objective was to make the structural policy a tool with a real impact, to move from an *ad hoc* project to multiannual programme financing, to improve the predictability of the policy (as the funds were planned for a period of five years) and increased partnership with the authorities that are involved in the regional policy at all levels of the government. In practice, all these tasks turned out to be quite bureaucratic; the methodology for the designation of regions that had to receive assistance permitted a high degree of political influence, so the coverage of the assisted areas was wider than originally planned, and support was less concentrated (Bachtler and Mitchie, 1993, pp. 722–723).

The provisions that regulate the operation of the Structural Funds were revised in 1993. The main thrust of the 1988 reform was, none the less, preserved. Alterations included only a simplification of the decision-making procedure and its greater transparency; the planning period over which the Structural Funds operate was extended to six years (1993–99); the resources for the period 1994–99 would total ECU 144.5 billion; and there was the inclusion of a few new regions that are eligible for the assistance.

As always when there is a disbursement of funds, the Commission has to be careful. It has to find a balance between its intention to have effective policies that do not introduce distortions that may be damaging for the EU in the long term, on the one hand, and subsidy-seeking regions and firms on the other. To be eligible for the EU assistance, the disadvantaged region has to have per capita GDP of 75 per cent or less of the EU average. In reality, the application of this official ceiling was quite 'flexible' as aid was given also to the regions that had average income of 80 per cent of the EU average.

The regional policy of the EU is simply a supranational addition to, instead of being a partial replacement of various national regional policies. Its first shortcoming is that the ERDF is modest in relation to regional needs. It should not be forgotten, however, that the regional policy of the EU is a relatively novel feature. It is improving over time. The share of Structural Funds was almost a third of the entire expenditure from the EU Budget in 1994. The effort to reduce disparities between rich and poor countries in the EU is great in circumstances of relatively slow growth and cuts in expenditure. Another brake on the development of regional policy are the national governments, as they prevent, in some cases, greater involvement of the EU in their own regional affairs. A greater degree of coordination of national economic policies may avoid prodigalities of scarce EU funds and may result in help to the rich in the relatively less developed regions to the detriment of the poor in the developed ones.

There could appear a tendency of redirection of structural spending from rural to urban areas. Regional problems are starting to concentrate in the urban areas of the backward regions. The beneficiaries of the economic integration in the EU are urban areas in the central regions. This process also created disadvantages in urban areas, but in *other* regions of the EU. This is because the EU is a heavily urbanized group of countries.

The impact of the 1992 Programme on regional disequilibria in the EU is ambiguous. There is an identification problem. First and foremost, one needs to answer difficult questions: what are the short- and long-term effects of the 1992 Programme on the regions and, then, what is the impact of the changes on the regional disequilibria that would have happened on their own? If the longer-term effects of Programme 1992 include the liberalization of EU trade, then output may continue to be concentrated in the already advanced regions in order to benefit from positive externalities (this implies a fall in output and wages in the less advanced regions). However, internal trade liberalization may reallocate some of the EU production activities towards the periphery in order to take advantage of lower wages and other production costs there. As the outcome is uncertain in a situation with market imperfections, the effects of Programme 1992 on the regions will be debated for quite some time.

Traditional forms of the national regional policy started to decline from the early 1990s in most of the EU member countries. Denmark, for example, abolished all regional development grants and loans in 1991. The Dutch have restricted their regional assistance to a relatively small part of the country in the north. Owing to budgetary constraints, France had to scale down its regional aid. Germany has severely curtailed regional policy in the western part of the country, while placing priorities in the new eastern *Länder*. Even the less developed countries such as Greece or Ireland had to be careful with their regional expenditure because of the restrictions that originate in recession. The new spirit of national regional policies in the EU countries includes (Bachtler and Michie, 1993, pp. 721–722):

- reduction of the importance of regional policy in the northern countries;
- transfer of responsibilities to regional and local levels;
- automatic aid becomes replaced by discretionary assistance; and
- increased involvement of the Commission in regional matters, in particular through the rules on competition.

Contemporary regional policy also includes the local development of producer services. This is a feature that started to be slowly incorporated into this policy only in the latter half of the 1980s. None the less, the creation of jobs in new manufacturing businesses, their extension in existing ones or relocation of businesses still account for the major part of regional intervention. The Commission may authorize investment aid of up to 75 per cent net grant equivalent in the least developed regions. The same limit is 30 per cent in other areas where aid is allowed. The upper limit for aid in the least-favoured areas is intended to increase the competitiveness of these regions in attracting private investment. In practice, the country that has such regions within its confines may face severe budgetary problems and lack the necessary funds to finance projects in these areas. Hence, the impact of this concession is significantly eroded. In any case, a relatively high proportion of the allowed aid of up to 75 per cent may seriously question the degree of commercial risk borne by the private firm (Yuill *et al.*, 1994, p. 100).

As time passes, one observes an expanding sway being exercised by the Commission in regional matters in the EU. This is done mainly through the competition rules. National governments also conduct regional policies, however, they are increasingly becoming selective and make sure that the policy provides value for money. In addition, outright general assistance to the regions is being replaced by transparent grants for capital investment.[85]

There is concern among member countries that the Commission relies heavily on quantitative indicators in the designation of areas for assistance and that it does not take into consideration to a sufficient degree the specific circumstances of each area. For example, unemployment data in rural areas may hide the 'real' regional problem as there may be strong emigration tendencies from those areas. Unemployment rates that are below the national average do not reflect a buoyant local economy, but rather a lack of local job opportunities. The quantitative approach by the Commission may be justified on the grounds that it must be impartial. The Commission can be questioned in its work by the European Parliament or by the Court of Justice so it must have a certain justification for its action. Although quantitative criteria play an important role in the first phase of the consideration of the problem by the Commission, the second phase of analysis provides for a greater flexibility and consideration of other, more qualitative elements (Yuill *et al.*, 1994, pp. 98–100).

4.5   Mezzogiorno

Some forty years of regional policies in Italy have failed to deliver any sizeable and continual catching-up by the Mezzogiorno[86] with the rest of the Italian economy. One of the policy tools that was used to support industrialization in the region were law provisions that requested public corporations to direct the majority of their investments towards the south. These firms were regarded in the receiving area more as providers of jobs (hence, as supporters of the local demand) than as contributors to the growth of the national economy. As such, a relatively low efficiency of investment in the Mezzogiorno comes as no surprise at all. Because of these 'results' there was growing pressure for a reconsideration of the public policy towards the south, as well as open opposition to the policy from the northern regions of the country.

During the first half of the 1950s GDP per capita in the south of Italy was around 55 per cent of the north and centre of the country. The same ratio was 57 per cent in the second half of the 1980s. In spite of this, the Mezzogiorno can not be described as a 'poor' region, in particular, in terms of consumption. The artificially high levels of consumption are supported by large transfers of resources from outside the region. Therefore, the Mezzogiorno may be described as a structurally dependent economy (*European Economy*, 1993, pp. 21–22).

The development of infrastructure should not be undertaken without a close coordination with other policy measures. For example, poor transport links may 'protect' local industries in the backward regions as was the case in southern Italy. Once the Autostrada del Sole was built, it led to a chain of bankruptcies in the local food, textiles and clothing businesses.

The source of the regional problem of the Mezzogiorno lies not necessarily in a lack of funds or infrastructure, but rather in the non-material sphere. One of the major obstacles can be found in the absence of an 'entrepreneurial culture'. In addition, a survey of TNCs that already operate in or consider investment in the Mezzogiorno revealed that the major obstacles to foreign investors in the region include the existence of criminal organizations and political factors. A lack of infrastructure featured highly only for those TNCs that have not yet established their branches there. Factors that contributed to the attractiveness of the Mezzogiorno included the availability of relatively low-cost labour (both quantity and quality), the availability of land, as well as various public incentives to settle business operations there.[87]

Dissatisfaction with previous regional policies carried out since the 1950s, pressure from the northern regions and involvement of the Commission in regional and competition affairs, contributed to the introduction of Law 488 in December 1992. This Law effectively abolished special intervention (*intervento straordinario*) for the Mezzogiorno and extended the coverage of the policy (grant-based support) also to the centre-north of Italy. This means that regional policy in Italy is no longer tantamount to a policy directed at the southern part of the country. The abolition of this special treatment for the Mezzogiorno may be considered as one of the most significant developments in regional policies during the past four decades.

5 Conclusion

If a country or an economic union has differences in the levels of development and/or living standards among constituent regions that do not have at least a tendency towards equalization, such a country/economic union may not be regarded as having a well-integrated economy. Therefore, all countries and economic unions have a certain commitment to reduce regional disequilibria for various economic and, more importantly, non-economic reasons. The intentions of the EU regional policy are to diminish the existing and prevent new regional disparities. If a regional policy is to be effective, then the authorities at all levels of the government have to coordinate their activities in order to influence decisions about the allocation of resources. In spite of these coercive powers, regional policies of countries had relatively limited achievements. It should come as no surprise that the achievements of the regional policy of the EU which often relies more on persuasion and on certain funds than on coercion, are scant indeed.

Regional policy has been based on a number of compromises, hence the purity of principles suffered. Previous attempts to shape regional policy relied mainly on the alleviation of transport and communication costs through the expansion of infrastructure, as well as the mitigation of agglomeration disequilibria. More recently, attention shifted towards a greater self-reliance for those regions that are lagging in development, as well as the enhancement of enterprise competitiveness in these regions.

Demand, technology and supplies of factors often change. Regions that fail to adjust continuously to the new challenges remain depressed. One of the broad objectives of regional policy is to help the redistribution of economic activity among different regions. Its impact cannot be measured easily as it is not a simple task to construct a counterfactual world that would specify what would have happened without this policy. The difference between the actual and counterfactual situation may be attributed to regional policy.

Raw materials are traded without major restrictions, while it is the manufacturing industry and services that are protected. On these grounds, the resource exporting regions (countries) may be supporters of free trade in a country or an economic union, because they would be able to obtain manufactured goods at more favourable terms of trade.

The question, however, arises as to whether regional policy increases or decreases market imperfections. In the second best world, all answers are possible, but not always desirable. If the costs of such policy are less than the benefits which it brings, then the policy is justified. The rationale for a regional policy, which basically redistributes income (equity), must be found in solidarity among regions that constitute countries and/or the EU, as well as the fact that the benefit area is larger than the assisted region.

There are at least three major arguments in favour of the regional policy in the EU. First, in the absence of policy instruments such as tariffs, NTBs, devaluation or rates of interest, regions that are not able to adjust as fast as the rest of the EU, face increases in unemployment and decreases in living standards. In this situation, there is some case for the demand for short-term fiscal transfers at the EU level to ease the adjustment process. The possibility of such transfers in unforeseen cases ought to be permanent in an EMU. Otherwise, when in need, the regions that are in trouble may not be sure that other partner countries will provide resources on a case-by-case basis. EMU may not be able to operate efficiently without an effective regional policy. Structural funds are expected to involve around 35 per cent of the EU budget in 1999. Second, coordination of national regional policies at the EU level can avoid self-defeating divergent regional programmes that were taken in isolation. Third, footloose industries, economies of scale and externalities do not guarantee that integration will bring an equitable dispersion of economic activities. Some direction for economic adjustment and allocation of resources in the form of regional policy may be necessary. Expanding Structural Funds are employed in the EU in order to preserve unity with diversity in the group.

It is hard to locate the point where regional competition distorts competition beyond the interest of the EU. Hence uncertainty over regional policy will continue in the future. There are many arbitrary elements in the policy, as well as special cases. EU regional policy has revealed its limitations. It is still an unconsolidated policy with deficient policy instruments. If this is so in the case of integration of the fifteen current member countries that are on the road to establishing an EMU, the situation will be worse if certain central European transition countries join the EU in the future. A solution to the regional development problem, as well as to achieving a certain balance among various regions is an urgent, difficult, but highly rewarding challenge for the EU, in particular, in the light of moves towards an EMU. Instability in the regional policy at national and EU levels seems likely to continue. It is plausible that a trend towards decentralization in the creation and execution of regional policy will continue in the future. There is, however, a danger in the expansion of regional incentives that compete with each other. In contrast to the decentralization and trimming down in the national regional policies, EU regional policy has continued to widen its coverage and scope.

NOTES

1 Separate countries may, *de facto*, share a common currency. For example, Estonia's Law on Security for Estonian Kroon (1992), Clause 2, directly links the exchange rate of the kroon to the German mark. The Estonian Central Bank is forbidden to devalue the kroon. However, devaluation can take place, but only if the law is changed. The usual parliamentary procedure is necessary for that action. There have been no cases so far in history, where authorization for the devaluation of a national currency has been loudly trumpeted by a parliament.

2 Some Californians may argue, perhaps rightly, that this is not so in the case of their own state.

3 The impact of fiscal policy for the fast fine tuning of the economy should not be exaggerated. A country's fiscal policy is almost as a rule an annual event. It passes through a long parliamentary procedure. Therefore, it is the monetary policy that is continuously at hand to equilibrate the economy. Fiscal policy is not a replacement, but rather a less-flexible supplement.

4 If payroll taxes are high, firms are less willing to hire new or even keep existing staff.

5 If a government can not or does not want to tax businesses and individuals, it may print money and tax everybody through inflation. Keynes wrote about such an inflation tax that 'a government can live for a long time ... by printing money. The method is condemned, but its efficacy, up to a point, must be admitted. ... so long as the public use the money at all, the government can continue to raise resources by inflation' (Keynes, 1923, p. 23).

6 Businesses in the EU yearly convert several trillion ECU at an annual cost for the conversion charges of over ECU 15 billion or about 0.4 per cent of the EU's GDP (*European Economy*, 1990, p. 63). This is the only cost of the monetary non-union that may be relatively easy to quantify.

7 In the early 1980s firms in the former Yugoslavia were permitted to sell their home-made durable goods to domestic private buyers for hard currency. These buyers received price rebates and priority in delivery. Due to shortages and accelerating inflation, domestic private hard-currency holders increased their purchases in order to hedge against inflation. The growth of this type of home trade relative to the 'normal' trade in the (sinking) domestic currency has been increasing. The discrimination of home firms against the domestic currency has been spreading. Firms were happy because they received hard currency without the effort required to export, while consumers were happy because they were able to get what they wanted. Subsequently, the domestic sales for hard currency were banned because they reduced the effectiveness of the domestic monetary policy. This is an example of where a weak domestic currency (prior to state intervention) was crowded out from domestic trade by a relatively strong foreign currency (the German mark). Hard currency was not, however, driven out of Yugoslav private savings. Around 80 per cent of these savings were in foreign hard currency in Yugoslav banks. This was the way to protect savings from rising home inflation and negative interest rates on savings in the home currency. A new restatement of Gresham's law had in that case the reverse meaning: good money drove out the bad.

8 Greece and Portugal did not participate in the ERM as those countries were at a lower level of development relative to the core EU countries, so they wanted time for a gradual adjustment. This made the EMS incomplete even in its first phase. A few other countries were out of the ERM, but they joined this part of the EMS later.

9 Belgium and Luxembourg have shared a monetary union since 1921. It has worked relatively well. One reason for such an operation is that one partner

dominates the relationship. This monetary union has not brought either a political union or a centralist state. An interesting issue is, however, what happens if tensions arise between partners of a similar weight?

10 The US is trying to persuade central banks to keep reserves in US dollars as those reserves bring interest. However, the US dollar may easily fluctuate ± 30 per cents a year relative to other major currencies. Many central bankers think that the reserves need to be kept in assets that are subject to much greater discipline than the US dollar is.

11 An alternative policy instrument could be (interest-free, one-for-one) deposit requirements.

12 An appraisal of the relative safety of a borrower introduces many problems. The value of assets in the private sector is determined by the net present value of the stream of profit that those assets earn. As for the public assets, there are many that do not yield a financial return (military camps, for example). Their value can be assessed in an indirect way through replacement costs.

13 Solidarity in the EU is still quite fragile when major national interests are in question. The Bretton Woods currency system collapsed because of similar reasons. Countries refused to forgo control over the domestic money supply for the sake of external equilibrium.

14 The budget-deficit condition provoked most criticism. A country with a heavy public debt has good reason to have episodes with inflation: it is to reduce the real burden of its debt. Paul de Grauwe argued that France had been more successful than Germany in keeping the domestic budget deficit low over the past 25 years. Yet the franc was weak, while the mark was strong. Low budget deficit is not sufficient in ensuring a strong currency. Other factors such as monetary policy are necessary. During the same period France had higher inflation than Germany. Tough monetary policy, rather than strict adherence to the 3 per cent budget deficit criterion will make the euro strong (*Financial Times*, 11 July 1997).

15 While annual budget deficits may happen depending on the business cycle, the overall national debt may need to be controlled in a different way than is proposed in the Maastricht Treaty. Instead of putting a cap on the public debts (and on the budget deficit) which are, indeed, on various levels among the EU countries, a more effective way may be to install instruments that discourage trends of growing debts and deficits, and that encourage their continuous reduction.

16 The question (perhaps, theoretical) is: what if the Council of Ministers decides that none of the countries satisfies the criteria for the single currency?

17 In 1912 the blueprint for *Titanic* looked perfect. It was said to be unsinkable. In EMU's case, even the blueprint is full of holes (*The Economist*, 27 July 1996, p. 14).

18 Once the euro replaces the national currencies, the internal EU trade would be transacted in the euro. Hence, 'international' trade will be smaller. Policy-makers in the EU *may* pay less attention to exchange rates than they usually do. If the policy goal is internal stability, rather than stability in the exchange rate, cooperation between the major international players may be weak and the result may be instability in the currency market.

19 How will financial markets react if the project is postponed? How will they react to an EMU in which certain important countries are not taking part? If the project is posponed once, why should it not be postponed once more?

20 The net annual fiscal transfers from the western part of Germany to the eastern part of the country were around DM 150 billion throughout the 1990s. They will be necessary for around a decade. The danger is that such 'gifts' may ruin local incentives for entrepreneurship and self-relying adjustment and create a structurally dependent economy as is the case with the Italian Mezzogiorno.

21 The emu is a large flightless bird.
22 From 1939 to 1973, the French treasury was in charge of all foreign exchange reserves.
23 To safeguard these gains, policy-makers must follow tight fiscal and wage controls.
24 Allocation of resources is production efficient if all producers face the same tax for the same good or service. It is consumption efficient if all consumers face the same tax for the consumption of the same good or service.
25 Alaska, Arizona, California, Colorado, Connecticut, District of Columbia, Illinois, Indiana, Iowa, Kansas, Massachusetts, New Hampshire, New Jersey, New York, Ohio, Rhode Island and West Virginia. Because of controversies regarding the unitary system of computation of corporate profits, certain states are considering abandoning this system.
26 This assumes that country A grants either an exception or a full foreign-tax credit.
27 There is also a problem of inflation. Depreciation may be calculated according historic costs, but how should capital gains be taxed to reflect inflation? Luckily, the governments of most of the EU countries continue to be tough on inflation.
28 Cnossen (1995) provided a survey of options for the reform of corporate taxes in the EU.
29 For example, language, seniority, xenophobia, social and family ties.
30 The new theory of trade and strategic industrial policy disputes the Johnson–Krauss argument. In a real situation with imperfect markets (increasing returns to scale, externalities and the economies of learning), once the production of, for example, aircraft or fast trains starts at a very restricted number of locations in the world, it perpetuates itself. There is no room in the world even for five producers of the wide-body passenger aircraft. In this case, the exchange-rate argument (Johnson–Krauss) is of little help for the small and medium-sized countries.
31 Apart from making life and travel easier for the EU residents, the business community saves too. They are spared from the preparation of some 60 million customs and tax documents a year. The abolition of border checks saves around ECU 8 billion a year to the EU member states (*Business International*, 15 July 1991, p. 237). In 1988, the EU introduced the Single Administrative Document to replace some 30 documents that were required in order to allow goods to move within the EU. This Document was not required for internal trade after 1993, but is used for goods that cross an EU external frontier.
32 Fraud against the EU budget is on a rise. It was ECU 1.3 billion in 1996 (*Financial Times*, 7 May 1997 p. 2).
33 'Strategic' is not taken here to have any military sense, but rather, its meaning refers to businesses that have important forward and backward links with other industries, as well as strong and positive externalities (spillovers) on the rest of the economy.
34 Technologies that are 'critical' for a large country's competitiveness and/or defence include those that deal with new materials, energy sources and environment; biotechnology and pharmacy; manufacturing including the production of tools; information gathering, communications, data processing and computers; transportation and aeronautics, including navigation. Because of large sunk costs and economies of scale, small and medium-sized countries do not have the means and the need (if they have the chance to acquire through trade some of these goods, services or technologies) to develop all or most of these technologies and operate them in a commercially viable pattern. What these countries may do instead is select a 'critical' mass of vital technologies or some part of them (e.g. components, basic chemicals etc.) and try to excel in these market niches as is the case with Switzerland, Austria, Benelux or the Scandinavian countries.

35 There is a growing awareness that *most* external economies apply at a regional or metropolitan level, rather than at an international one. Therefore, the fears that external economies will be dissipated abroad is mostly wrong (Krugman, 1993, pp. 161, 167).

36 It needs to be noted that a part of the manufacturing jobs from developed countries have gone to the developing world.

37 Over 90 per of R&D expenditures in the US is accounted for by the manufacturing sector (Bhagwati, 1989, p. 449).

38 Akio Morita, the chairman of Sony Corporation, argued that 'an economy can be only as strong as its manufacturing base. An economy that does not manufacture well cannot continue to invest adequately in itself. An economy whose only growth is in the service sector is built on sand. Certainly, the service sector is an important and growing economic force. But it cannot thrive on its own, serving hamburgers to itself and shifting money from one side to another. An advanced service economy can thrive only on the strength of an advanced manufacturing economy underlying it ... The notion of a postindustrial economy that is based principally on services is a dubious one' (Morita, 1992, p. 79).

39 The term 'massaged-market economies' was first used by Lipsey (1993b, p. 12).

40 A common definition of an SME used the number of employees as the determining factor. Small enterprises are taken to be those with up to 25 employees, while medium-sized ones have up to 250 workers.

41 Entrepreneurs (sometimes seen as 'maniacs with a vision') often have genuine ideas, but many of them do not have the necessary knowledge about how to run a business.

42 New technologies are less and less sector or industry specific. The same holds for modern firms. Many of them may not be easily put in the group of enterprises that belongs to only one industry or sector.

43 A few examples are given in the section on regional policy.

44 Groups that lobby in Brussels include 400 trade associations, around 300 large firms, 150 non-profit pressure groups, 120 regional and local governments and 180 specialist law firms (*The Economist*, 15 April 1995, p. 26). A very high concentration of lobby services in Washington, DC, made, in some cases, a collection of certain (private) interests stronger than those of the government.

45 A lack of natural resources made Japan invest in the development of human and technological capital.

46 In spite of the success in certain high-technology industries, average living standards in Japan are below those of the US. Part of the explanation may be found in the relatively high proportion of Japanese national resources that are devoted to stagnant industries relative to the US.

47 Airbus was established in 1970. It is a publicly sponsored consortium of British (British Aerospace, 20 per cent), French (Aérospatiale, 37.9 per cent), German (Deutsche Airbus, 37.9 per cent) and Spanish (CASA, 4.2 per cent) enterprises. It was established without the involvement of the EU and under the French law as a Groupement d'Intérêt Economique. As such, it makes no profits or losses in its own right. This means that the accounts of the group are available only to the four shareholders. Unlike Boeing's profitability, which is open to the public, Airbus's accounts are concealed from the public and the profit disguised in the accounts of its shareholders. It is, therefore, hard to assess the commercial success of the best known consortium in Europe. Why then does Boeing not pressure the US administration to do something about this? As around a half of the value built into Airbuses has a US origin, the producers of these components have a strong lobbying power in Washington, DC, and could counter that of Boeing.

Airbus received in subsidies for new models of aircraft in the period 1970–94 between $10 and $20 billion, depending on whether the source of the data is

Europe or America (*The Economist*, 8 July 1995, p. 14). If these subsidies have been granted for such a long time and in such a large volume, one wonders if the man-made comparative advantage has really been successful!

Airbus is expected to become a limited company in 1999. Only a fully integrated company can know what its costs are and introduce policies that will drive costs down in order to keep the company competitive. Such a corporate strategy is enhanced because of Boeing's takeover of McDonnell-Douglas which in 1997 sells 7 out of 10 commercial aircraft, with more than 100 seats.

48 The policy goal was to acquire the production of war materials. There was little concern about antitrust laws, international competitiveness or competing national objectives (Badaracco and Yoffie, 1983, p. 99). Governments have always affected industrial development through trade policy, public procurement, taxes and subsidies, as well as provision of public goods.

49 One has, however, to remember extreme cases which are not very numerous, but exist everywhere. The most highly paid people are not always highly educated. Many pop singers or sportspeople have a poor education. However, one cluster of educated people that is being paid most are lawyers (in the countries where law means something) and managers.

50 The absence of EU corporate law presented a serious problem. Big national corporations that tried to merge on the EU level such as Fiat-Citroën, Agfa-Gevaert, Dunlop-Pirelli or Fokker-VFW, gave those projects up. A notable exception is Airbus Industrie (set up in 1970). The pan-EU TNCs that survived to 'adolescence' were those (Philips, Shell, Unilever) that existed long before the establishment of the EU.

51 *Single Market News*, February 1996, p. 13.

52 *European Voice*, 4 January 1996, p. 22.

53 In the period 1987–93, the total public funds for R&D in the US were ECU 168 billion, while in Europe, 'only' ECU 66 billion were allocated for that purpose (Jacquemin, 1996a, p. 176). Europe invests 2 per cent of GNP in R&D, while the same investment in the US is 3 per cent. Japan invests even more in R&D (Micossi, 1996, p. 160).

54 In the US small high-technology firms sell as much as a half of their output to the federal government and benefit from R&D support. In contrast, public procurement in Europe is effected through a small number of large national suppliers. This suggests that fostering of a free entry and mobility within flexible industries may be a superior policy choice than supporting a few giants that react to changes with some delay (Geroski and Jacquemin, 1985, p. 177).

55 The First Framework Programme (1984–87) disposed of a budget of ECU 3.7 billion, the Second Framework Programme (1987–91) had a budget of ECU 6.5 billion, while the Third Framework Programme (1991–94) was allocated ECU 8.8 billion.

56 FAST is a shared-cost programme involving a number of research and forecasting centres in the EU. It is an instrument for studying future developments, as well as the impact and social uses of science and technology.

57 One wonders why renowned and leading-edge companies need support and cartelization at all?

58 Indeed, the Commission tried to argue that it does not operate a large-scale industrial policy, but rather a series of R&D programmes (Curzon Price, 1990, p. 178).

59 Decisions that are taken at EU level are easy targets for special lobbies as they are too far from the public to monitor. The co-decision procedure between the Council and the Parliament introduced by the Maastricht Treaty tried to ameliorate this shortcoming. This is a step forward compared with the past, but there is

still a danger that the EU technology policy may become a sophisticated way of new protectionism.

60 The EU invested in industries in which is a high risk of failure and where Japan and the US are the strongest. A relative failure of electronics in the EU is due, in part, to the fact that the domestic firms were sheltered from foreign competition. On the other hand, where competition was global, for example in commercial aircraft, Airbus had certain successes.

61 A 'layperson' would say: 'Cows were created as herbivorous animals. Don't make them eat meat products!'

62 They include businesses in both manufacturing and services sectors. The impact on services is discussed below.

63 Do you remember your first (or for that matter even your second or third) cab drive from the airport in a south European country as a foreigner? If not, you certainly will!

64 Positive externalities take place in services, such as telecommunications, where the value for one user increases with the total number of all users. A negative externality may be found, for example, in financial services, where the failure of one bank may cause trouble to a number of others (Sapir, 1993, p. 27).

65 The number of car accidents per motor car or per inhabitant may be higher in one country relative to another. Hence, due to higher risk, certain differences in insurance premiums among countries will remain in spite of increased competition.

66 'As patriotism is the last refuge of scoundrels (according to Dr Johnson), the welfare of widows, orphans, and the incompetent is the last refuge of supporters of regulation. Individuals free to make their own decisions will indeed make mistakes. Even if potential buyers are clearly informed of the regulatory regime, some will not understand its significance. Even if large amounts of information are available on that significance, some will not bother to obtain it... Protection of the foolish against error provides a rationale for almost infinite extension' (Hindley, 1991, pp. 272–273).

67 Everyone may appreciate the benefits of a car such as a BMW or a Mercedes. It is quite another thing, however, whether consumers are willing to pay or have the means to pay for such a motor car. A small Fiat may be the ultimate limit for many of them.

68 The US offered a convincing example of deregulation of the inter-state transport services in 1980.

69 Without the highest degree of coordination one would not be able to fly to the moon and return safely to the Earth.

70 Education may be a subsidised input for which the business sector has not paid the full price. None the less, countervailing duties can not be introduced by foreign partners as education often takes a long time and can not be easily and directly valued as is the case with other subsidies, such as those for exports.

71 The tacit assumption has always been that there are no transport costs.

72 A strategic industrial (and trade) policy is based on a number of assumptions that include non-retaliation by foreign partners and (perfect) information and forecasts.

73 Moon boots were also invented there.

74 The economic history of integrated states such as the US points to the fact that integration is associated with regional convergence which predominates over economic divergence in the long run. This process is rather slow, around 2 per cent a year, but it is sustained over a long period of time (Barro and Sala-i-Martin, 1991, p. 154).

75 See discussion of mergers and acquisitions in the chapter on customs union (Chapter 2).

76 Positive feedback economics may find parallels in non-linear physics. For example, ferromagnetic materials consist of mutually reinforcing elements. Small perturbations at critical times influence which outcome is selected, and the chosen outcome may have higher energy (that is, be less favourable) than other possible end states (Arthur, 1990, p. 99).

77 This should not be taken to mean that regional policy is ineffective in general terms. Given the means and the structure of the problem in the case of the EU, however, the policy has not yielded significant positive results.

78 The non-linear probability theory can predict the behaviour of systems subject to increasing returns. Suppose that balls of a different colour are added to a table. The probability that the next ball will have a specific colour depends on the current proportion of colours. Increasing returns occur when a red ball is more likely to be added when there is already a high proportion of red balls (Arthur, 1990, p. 98).

79 Federal countries such as the US, Canada, Australia or Switzerland have different regional policies from that of the EU.

80 The difference between the GDP per capita and according to the PPS is particularly striking in the case of the memorandum country of Japan.

81 Britain changed its regional policy in 1980. The most important features of this alteration included the following three elements. First, the regional disequilibria started to be seen as a problem of a *region*, rather than a *national* issue. Therefore it needs to be resolved by indigenous development, rather than by a transfer of resources and business activity from elsewhere. Second, direct subsidies for employment were replaced by a system of regional aid programmes that are based on employment creation through improved competitiveness. Third, the policy became increasingly reliant on employment cost-effectiveness (Wren, 1990, p. 62).

82 Eurostat (1995), 'Statistics in focus: regions', no. 1.

83 In Finland, for instance, the southern regions of Åland and Uusimaa (including Helsinki) are the most prosperous. GDP per capita there is 120 per cent of the EU average (100). The rest of the country has an income that is 90 per cent of the EU average.

84 The European Coal and Steel Community has exerted its own influence on regions that are involved in coal, iron and steel industries. Loans were given for the retraining and redeployment of workers, as well as for a modernization of the industry. The European Investment Bank has been giving loans for projects in the less developed regions of the EU.

85 Regional support started to include producer services and incentives for the introduction of innovations such as licences or patents.

86 The Mezzogiorno is the area south of Lazio.

87 *Business Europe*, 31 May 1991, p. 3.

5 Integration Schemes

I INTRODUCTION

The founders of GATT recognized the importance of economic integration between countries. That process can have identical economic rationale as integration within a single country that has different regions. Hence, regional economic integration, according to the WTO (1995) does not pose an inherent threat to global integration. None the less, the GATT (Article XXIV) constrains the level of the common external tariff and other trade measures in customs unions. On the whole, these trade measures should not be higher or more restrictive than those of the member countries prior to the integration agreement. Between 1947 and 1995 a total of ninety-eight integration agreements had been notified to the GATT. Membership of those integration groups can be seen in Annex I. However, only six agreements were 'cleared' by the working party through the consensus principle. For others, including the 'clearance' of the Treaty of Rome that established the EEC in 1957 the result was inconclusive. One of the reasons why there was no definite agreement in the working party were the ambiguous effects of integration on nonmembers. Therefore, this inconclusive nature of the Treaty of Rome in this respect set the pattern that dominated nearly all future reviews of integration agreements notified under Article XXIV.

Intra-group trade has a rising long-term trend, at least in Europe and North America. That development, however, was not associated with a significant alteration in the relevance of extra-group trade in relation to total output in the two regions. In spite of various concerns, the WTO (1995) did not find conclusive evidence about the emergence of a 'fortress' mentality in integration arrangements. The conclusion was that regional integration was complementary to the multilateral trading system. Regional economic integration had an overall favourable impact on the pace of global economic integration. However, various NTBs pose an obstacle to deeper integration in the future.

The objective of this chapter is to provide no more than a brief reminder on international economic integration arrangements in the developed and developing countries, as well as the integration efforts of the countries in central and eastern Europe. The most striking absence is the lack of a section on the EU. The reason for omitting the EU is that this group is so rich in developments, problems and achievements that it is difficult for it to be properly represented in a relatively brief section. Therefore, the interested reader is invited to consult economic texts on the issue.[1] Unfortunately, the international integration schemes were successful only in the developed world. Elsewhere, they either collapsed or, at best, lingered on feebly. Rare exceptions can be found in south-east Asia or certain promising emerging groups in Latin America. Certain schemes were referred to for the 'historical record' only. This does not mean that there is no potential for a certain degree of economic integration throughout the (developing) world. In fact, many integration schemes in that region are going through a phase of innovation. However, the new development that will feature high in the future is north–south integration as started among the US, Canada and Mexico, around South Africa, the customs union between the EU and Turkey,[2] as well as the EU and select countries in central and eastern Europe.

The chapter is structured such that section II refers to the integration schemes in the developed world and the countries of central and eastern Europe. This is followed by a description of schemes among the developing countries in section III.[3] Reference is made to the relevant integration groups in Latin America, Africa and south-east Asia.

II DEVELOPED COUNTRIES

1 Introduction

A consideration of the EFTA, economic integration in north America and that between Australia and New Zealand open a brief discussion about integration schemes among the developed countries. It is followed by speculation about the possible reaction of east Asian countries to the new wave of regionalism in the world. The presentation of previous integration efforts among the formerly centrally planned economies are outlined mainly for historical and educational purposes, in order not to repeat past mistakes. The possibilities for economic integration among the countries of central and eastern Europe[4] and their potential entry into the EU follow. At the end of the section, there is an explanation why small, rich and highly specialized countries such as Norway and Switzerland have chosen to stay out of the EU.

2 European Free Trade Association

A look at the EFTA and its experience is relevant as free trade areas have been mushrooming all over the world. The relatively small, developed, specialized and open EFTA countries did not have a genuine objective of economic integration of the group (created in 1960), but rather the establishment of good commercial relations with the EU. The EFTA countries have always traded significantly more with the EU than within the group. That is one of the reasons why there were no serious disputes in internal trade and why economic adjustment to integration in the group was smooth. High specialization and geographical distance between the EFTA countries explain this distribution of trade. Following the departure of Britain in 1973, the EFTA consisted only of small countries. If compared with the EU, major omissions from the coverage of internal free trade are agriculture, services and free movement of labour and capital. The success or failure of any free trade area depends to a large extent on how it deals with technical matters such as NTBs and rules of competition that include restrictive business practices, technical standards, subsidies, dumping, public procurement, rules of origin and dispute settlements. The process of cooperation in the EFTA went so smoothly and at such a microeconomic level, that the entire history of the group seemed to be uneventful (Curzon Price, 1987; 1997). The only exceptions were departures of Britain, Denmark, Ireland, Austria, Sweden and Finland to join the EU.

3   North American Free Trade Agreement

Canada had five theoretical options regarding its trade future in the mid-1980s. First was a continuation with the status quo of gradual moves towards free trade liberalization through the slow process of multilateral negotiations under the auspices of the GATT. The problem with that approach was that tariffs were declining while the proliferating NTBs were beyond the scope of the GATT until the mid–1990s. Hence, this option was considered to be too risky for Canada. Second was an active inward-looking trade and industrial policy. The chances for the success of such policy were judged to be small, while the risks of foreign (mainly US) retaliation were expected to be high. Third, was the option of fostering ties with Europe and the developing countries. The experience from this approach was not encouraging. Canada had tried to promote trade with Europe in the early 1970s when that region had an annual share of 20 per cent in the Canadian exports, but in spite of the 'encouragement' of relations, exports to that region fell to 8 per cent in 1984. The fourth choice was an aggressive policy of multilateralism. Canada should push for negotiations in the GATT and preserve its commercial interest as it would negotiate with the US in a group of countries, rather than alone. Lipsey and Smith (1986) were not convinced that for Canada, multilateral negotiations with the US, were preferable to bilateral ones, and they thought that any gains would be too small for Canada and would come too late. The fifth option for Canada was bilateral trade liberalization and formal integration[5] with the US. This option, in the form of a free trade area, was the only one that provided a real chance for major improvement in the Canadian economy. Such a deal would secure access for Canadian firms to a market of over 250 million consumers, it would support economies of scale and a reduction of prices per unit of output. In addition, this would increase the competitiveness of Canadian goods in the third markets and, ultimately, it was assessed that the general effect of the deal would be an increase in Canadian living standards of between 4 and 7 per cent (Lipsey and Smith, 1986).

Once the free trade agreement between the US and Canada was signed and implemented, there were moves to include Mexico in the North American Free Trade Agreement (NAFTA). If the US were to enter into a bilateral free trade deal with Mexico and, then, to conclude similar arrangements with other (Latin American) countries, then that would create a hub-and-spoke model of integration (which was undesirable for Canada and other involved countries). The US, as the regional hub, would have a separate agreement with each spoke country. As such, the US would have advantages of negotiating individually with each partner country, as well as being the only country with tariff-free access to the markets of all participants, with locational advantages for FDI. If low-wage Mexico were included in the NAFTA, the fear was that it would divert trade.[6] However, what matters in international competition is not how much local labour is paid in terms of purchasing power, but rather how much unit costs of production compare internationally at the ongoing exchange rates. If the level of wages were the determining factors of international trade, then the markets of the US and Canada would be flooded with Mexican goods. Other factors, such as capital stock (its quantity and quality) and productivity play more prominent roles. An integration arrangement between the two developed countries (the US and Canada) and one developing country (Mexico) would make the trade and industrial policies of the three countries more outward-looking and less focused on uncompetitive import-competing industries (Lipsey, 1990). Mexico, however, joined OECD in 1994.

The striking feature of the NAFTA (1994) is that it is an arrangement that includes countries with significant differences in per capita incomes. That is why Mexico was given a 'transition period' of seven years for the elimination of tariffs, which was a bit longer than was the case with Canada and the US. During that period, *maquiladoras* in Mexico are expected to disappear under the NAFTA. Mexico and Canada were in favour of relatively liberal rules of origin because of the positive impact of such rules on the Japanese FDI in the two countries and the potential exports of goods to the US. Initially, the required local content of goods for liberal treatment in the NAFTA was 50 per cent, but that would increase to and stay at 62.5 per cent from the year 2002. There are still problems within the group regarding issues such as the environment, subsidies and agriculture. One has to keep in mind that NAFTA is not a group such as the EU with a free mobility of labour and transfers of various funds which brings different effects from integration from those of a simple free trade area. If one bears in mind that the entire economy of Mexico is equal to that of Massachusetts, it becomes clear that 'economics' (large market, economies of scale, jobs and growth) has not played a primary role in this integration group. The US is very concerned about stability at its southern border. Hence, the NAFTA needs to be seen as a tool that is supposed to help a friendly Mexican government succeed in its reform and development process (Krugman, 1996a, p. 165).[7] None the less, an open regional approach by the NAFTA regarding new members such as Chile or a few other Latin American states may be the way to dissolve criticism that the NAFTA is undermining the multilateral trading system.

4   Pacific countries and 'new regionalism'

Concerns about 'Fortress North America' prompted by the protectionist interests in the US could provoke reactions in the countries of the Pacific region (English and Smith, 1993). In spite of the integration of countries at a significantly different level of per capita income and concerns about adjustments in the labour market in the US and Canada, negotiations on the NAFTA followed a relatively speedy timetable. The free trade deal will eliminate tariffs on internal trade among the three member countries. None the less, restrictive rules of origin are the major means of protection. They are most restrictive for vehicles, textiles and apparel. A trans-Pacific extension of free trade would, perhaps, have taken place if the result of the Uruguay Round had been slim. As that was not the case, reactive regionalism in the Pacific is not feasible. Some Latin American and Caribbean countries may achieve accession to NAFTA, but even that may take a considerable period of time.

The 'new regionalism' has its impact on east Asian countries. Economic integration in Europe is deepening and widening, it is expanding in north America and there is a new interest in integration in south America. What is the place and future of east Asia in the new wave of international economic integration? If the multilateral trading process does not operate in a satisfactory way for the countries of east Asia, should they create a regional trading bloc of their own? The countries in the region would increase their bargaining power *vis-à-vis* other economic groups. Most of the countries in the region followed similar economic strategies and created competitive, rather than complementary, economic structures (but they have a different type and degree of protection). Hence, they have a strong orientation towards extra-regional markets. Joint bargaining would be beneficial for the group. However, an east Asian trading bloc may not materialize in reality. There are several reasons for this. These include a possible tough reaction from north America which could end up in a 'trade war'. If east Asian countries threaten to form a trading bloc in order to influence the trade policy of north America, then such threat has to be credible. Who is going to lead east Asian countries 'against' north America? Is it Japan, China, South Korea or some other country? Weak political leadership and national resistance to a surrender of trade and industrial policy to a common institution prevent the creation of a regional economic bloc. An Asia–Pacific group would suffer from a similar problem of effectiveness. Therefore, east Asian countries need to continue to support a multilateral trading system. In addition, the emerging Asia Pacific Economic Cooperation (APEC), created in 1989, should be used as a forum for discussing issues related to the liberalization of global trade (a kind of Asian OECD) (Young, 1993).[8] Although there is a 'grand plan' to have a free trade area in the Pacific region by the year 2020, real action by the group is occurring at a snail's pace. Would it be simple to make those deals at the WTO?

5 Australia and New Zealand

Integration arrangements between Australia and New Zealand have escaped attention by many in Europe and North America. These two high-income countries with a specialization in primary commodities have had a free trade agreement since 1966. It was replaced by an agreement on Closer Economic Relations in 1983. Free trade in goods within the group was achieved in 1990, five years ahead of the deadline specified in the Agreement. Apart from a select list of services (e.g. shipping, aviation and telecommunications), there has been an internal free trade in this sector from 1989. In spite of these successes, internal trade in goods and services is still not entirely 'free' as there are no common taxes/subsidies, nor common external tariff[9] and differences in domestic policies such as technical standards and business law still persist. Market forces will drive the economies of Australia and New Zealand towards deeper integration, hence the two countries may proceed in the future towards a kind of a single market (Lloyd, 1991).

6 Central and eastern Europe

Economic integration in the region of central and eastern Europe continued for the major part of the second half of the 20th century within the Council for Mutual Economic Assistance (CMEA). Majority voting in that group was prohibited. This may be why the CMEA did not have any real powers (endless bilateral negotiations made progress in integration slow). This was also why the Soviets were not able to control fully all member countries. Although market competition did not play a significant role, a certain type of competition between different plans was still present in the group. 'Socialist prices' in the CMEA trade were supposed to embody 'equality' in economic relations in contrast to cyclical 'capitalist prices' that personified inequality in economic relations. None the less, the just 'socialist prices' were always calculated on the basis of world market (capitalist) prices. In a system where the major concern was with quantity, rather than quality and value in the market, prices did not respond either to costs or to the relation between demand and supply. Therefore, it was hard to understand why CMEA countries spent so much time bargaining over prices or why there was a world market price formula. Bilateral balancing of trade was reducing the extent of external trade and, hence, kept trade at a lower level than in the countries at a similar stage of development with a market-based economic system. Such a trading system was integration unfriendly for the CMEA. Different reforms attempted changes within the socialist system, but that did not lead anywhere. An overhaul of the entire system was necessary. As it was unable to resist the challenge of economic transition towards a market-type economy, the CMEA vanished in 1991. For details about the operation of the CMEA consult Annex II.

Although the CMEA collaped, there was a certain external and internal interest in fostering economic links among the central European transition countries. The Visegrád[10] countries, however, declared joining the EU as their primary individual objective. Challenges regarding possible 'eastern enlargement' of the EU are presented in Annex III. The key problems relating to economic integration in this central European group include the actual interest of the partner countries in integration within this group[11] and the real enthusiasm of the EU to accept them. Hence, the Visegrád group may be seen by the participating countries as a waiting room (vehicle) for entry into the EU (end). In addition, integration may be seen as a means of gaining regional co-operation 'maturity' for joining the EU. The EU may also use the Visegrád group as a safety belt from potential turbulence in other eastern European countries. The Central European Free Trade Agreement (CEFTA) took effect in 1993. It was expected that the regional free trade area in manufactured goods would be gradually established in 1998 (originally 2001). The impact of the CEFTA on the participating countries can be, at best, only marginal. Member countries trade mostly with the EU, while the level of internal CEFTA trade is relatively small (less than 10 per cent of their external trade). This should come as no surprise since modernization of the CEFTA economies, and a process of economic transition towards a market economy and growth is hardly possible without trade with the developed market economies. Perhaps, internal CEFTA trade would increase if the countries of the group were within the EU, a case that took place in trade between Spain and Portugal following their entry of the EU. The possibility of expanding the group to include other transition countries, the option preferred by the EU, may be resisted by the original CEFTA countries, as this may endanger or delay the accession of the 'original four' to the EU. An expansion of the CEFTA group may be seen by the original 'four countries' as an alternative, rather than as instrumental for integration with the EU (Richter and Tóth, 1994). The CEFTA, however, enlarged. It involves 90 million consumers as Slovenia joined in 1996, while Romania did the same in 1997.

7   Norway and Switzerland

It was argued in theory that relatively small countries have an inclination towards international economic integration. What were the reasons, then, for relatively small, highly developed and specialized countries such as Norway and Switzerland to choose repeatedly not to join the EU? In theory, an economic rationale for economic integration with the EU exist in both of those countries. In fact, the two countries have been 'integrated' with the EU since 1973 through a free trade arrangement for manufactured goods. This allowed the two countries to have their own farm policies.[12] It also permitted Norway to have its own fisheries and natural resources policy, while Switzerland was saved from an unrestricted inflow of foreign (EU) labour. The major reasons for resisting full and formal integration with the EU are mostly political. A fear of the loss of sovereignty to external forces (no matter how little it remained in the economic sphere) looms large in both countries. Diverse institutions, social cleavages and experiences with foreign rulers, still present significant obstacles in Norway and Switzerland to their formally joining the EU. Unless there are new overriding political incentives such as security considerations and/or an increased voice in EU affairs, the voters in the two countries will still prefer to preserve the status quo (Gstöhl, 1996). The cost of such a policy is a certain loss of R&D, FDI and banking business.

III DEVELOPING COUNTRIES

1 Introduction

The 'traditional' schemes that integrate developing countries, structured along the lines of the neo-classical theory of integration, have not lived up to the great expectations of their founders and most, in fact, failed and collapsed. Most of them can be arbitrarily placed in two broad groups. One is based on the liberalization of trade, while the rationale of the other is specialization in production (Mytelka, 1994, pp. 24–25). The former scheme was motivated by pure trade and based on the neo-classical theoretical model. The attention of countries was directed mainly towards the common external trade protection of the integrated countries and to a reduction and elimination of barriers to the intra-group trade. It is, then, left to the *market forces* to determine the allocation of resources in the region. Attempts to establish a regional agency that organizes and/or harmonizes industrial policy was largely left out of the arrangement. The organizational structure of these schemes was relatively unsophisticated.[13]

The second simplified theoretical model of integration among the developing countries focused, in practice, on the specialization in production. The stated goals were to increase the relatively slim level of development in manufacturing industry, to reap economies of scale, to enhance complementarity in manufacturing, to establish linkages in production and to introduce a certain degree of regional planning. Owing to the relatively backward technologies in production and management, as well as to a lack of investment funds, TNCs could be an attractive (initial) choice for bridging that gap. The involvement of TNCs as a means for the mitigation of market imperfections in those groups was addressed, and sought to reach a coordinated approach towards TNCs. To put it in simple terms, *intervention* was the background *leitmotif* in the integration of these countries and the allocation of resources. In fact, rather than directing integration energies towards the establishment of production and other business linkages among countries, these groups expended much of their potential on distributing the benefits that might accrue from integration. The groups that suit the model of integration that has as its objective the specialization in production require a more complex institutional structure than trade models.[14]

Economic integration among the developing countries was in the past, to a large extent, a waste of time and resources.[15] The following text explains how and why that took place and how an emerging scheme in the south of Latin America attempts to reverse the past experience (although it has yet to reinforce its achievements and prove itself in the future).

2   Latin America

2.1   *The Latin American Free Trade Area and the Andean Pact*

Economic integration of countries in Latin America has the longest history among the developing countries. The countries involved include, with a few exceptions,[16] the entire region. None the less, the integration effort (compared to the achievements of the EU) has passed through very hard times. On the one hand, within the Latin American Free Trade Area (LAFTA), sub-regional groups, such as the Andean Pact were formed in 1969 while integration of the southern countries (MERCOSUR) is a relatively novel feature. On the other hand, the LAFTA was replaced by the Latin American Integration Association (LAIA) in 1980 with no significant effect on any change/improvement in the economic performance of the participating countries. The real basic objective of the LAIA was to provide a security buffer against the global recession and, in particular, the one that was taking place in Latin America.

The major instrument of integration was a free trade area. Trade was at the forefront of the arrangement, while other objectives, most notably growth and development, played second fiddle. The Preamble to the Treaty of Montevideo (1960) was long on intentions (it mentioned even the creation of a common market), but short on substance. The signatory countries have not pledged much more than to negotiate liberalization of trade in the future. This referred to tariffs, but not to NTBs. The heavily protected private sector in Latin American countries was not keen on integration. It wanted to protect the well entrenched domestic position and did not want to 'rock the boat' with integration and expose itself to an uncertain and risky adjustment. Hence one of the reasons for the failure of the LAFTA.

A kind of new energy to the scheme came in 1970s. The member countries concluded industrial complementary agreements. Basically, these were arrangements that offered certain tariff concession only to those countries that participated in them. The major users and beneficiaries of these agreements, and hence integration, were TNCs since they were the major players in the negotiations and design of the agreements. In addition, there were commercial agreements among firms from participating countries. The role of the governments was merely to ratify, or not, any deals concluded by private businesses.

Since it is basically a free trade area, the LAFTA cannot be criticized on the grounds that it has failed to develop, harmonize and implement industrial, regional, social or other economic policies. Perhaps, an alternative integration arrangement, with the potential for a greater success and fortified with an (effective) enforcement mechanism, ought to include these features. The instrument that dealt with manufacturing, the industrial complementary agreements, were used by foreign TNCs that wanted to penetrate the markets of the participating countries.

The LAFTA Treaty includes a very interesting feature. This is, the *super-MFN provision*, which provides that any bilateral arrangement reached by any LAFTA country is to be extended to *all* other LAFTA/LAIA member countries. If that is the case, then whatever Mexico achieved in negotiations with the US and Canada about NAFTA, should be automatically extended, under the LAFTA/LAIA, to other Central and Latin American countries. The LAFTA/LAIA provisions are, however, not backed by any strong enforcement tool (Whalley, 1992, pp. 130–131).

Although economic integration in Latin America has featured high on the agenda in various discussions since the beginning of the 1960s, at least three real elements have worked against integration. First, the national economic strategies of a number of countries were inward-looking. The most obvious example is Brazil, the country with, indeed, a very large domestic market. As such, it might not be, in theory, as interested in integration as the relatively smaller countries. Second, the economic relations of the countries in the region have been complex. These include not only relations among countries of different size and economic potential within the region, but also relations between the Latin American countries and the developed market economies. Third, as a market with substantial potential for growth, TNCs from the US, on the one hand, and from Europe and Japan, on the other, have been competing in the region. In any case, regional integration, in particular in trade, among the Latin American countries has, in general, been below expectations.

Attention devoted primarily to trade in the LAFTA was not sufficiently appealing to involve large countries in deeper integration. This was, however, not always the case with the relatively small countries. As a reaction to the 'impotent' LAFTA, a sub-regional group, the *Andean Pact*, was formed in 1969.[17] The major significance of the Pact may be found in its different approach to integration, as well as the anxiety of the small countries that they might be economically ousted by the large partner countries. The crux of the new arrangement was in industrial development through joint programming. The member countries have, however, been reluctant to extend the concessions to other countries in the LAFTA region. This has, of course, slowed down integration efforts in the LAFTA and has also fragmented it (Finch, 1988, pp. 252–253).

The joint programming in the manufacturing industry was supposed to be growth-oriented and to pay special attention to the equitable distribution of gains from integration. This was a reaction to the dissatisfaction of the smaller member countries with the uneven distribution of benefits within the LAFTA. The developing countries that integrated became experienced enough to give a more prominent role to the issues of coordinated development in their integration schemes.

Treatment of FDI in the Andean Pact received a high priority. FDI was regulated by several decisions that were usually quite restrictive. Such a policy reflected the introverted, even autarkic, strategy of the group. This was the major reason why Chile left the Pact in 1976. Eliminating the fortress mentality, as well as liberalizing trade and FDI did not, for Chile, go hand in hand with Pact membership. The unilateral liberalizing action by Chile had a positive economic impact on the country. Nogués and Quintanilla (1992, p. 20) argued that unilateral, rather than regional or multilateral, reforms were the most efficient strategies for improving the economic prospect of Latin America. In order to increase the inflow of FDI, the initial restrictive demands of the Pact were gradually eased over time.

The Sectoral Programme of Industrial Development aspired to rationalize the industrial structure of the member countries by the plan. The Programme ought to assure both the optimal utilization of resources and even development among the countries. What really happened, however, was quite different from these noble objectives. For example, metal working and vehicle producing facilities were allocated to those countries that already housed similar facilities. For industries that were new to the region, the allocations were easier in theory, but little has happened in practice. So the existing structure of production was petrified.

The standstill, almost collapse, of the Andean Pact, was amplified by the evasion of the equal distribution of benefits, since relatively smaller countries had little real say in the decision-making process; a politicization of integration issues; and inconsistent national economic policies (El-Agraa and Hojman, 1988, pp. 264–265). That comes as no surprise since the governments in many countries in the region have changed very often. The Andean countries have been trading very little among themselves. The share of their internal trade was only 5 per cent of their external trade. An extra element came from the inhospitable nature of the terrain which provided formidable barriers for the creation of an integrated system of transport. In addition, some member countries, such as Colombia and Venezuela, were aspiring to follow a policy of closer ties with Mexico, in order to be involved, in one way or another, with the NAFTA.

One of the most widely cited attempts to introduce a common policy towards TNCs in the groups that integrate developing countries was Decision 24 (1970) of the Andean Pact. That was the first effort by an integration scheme of developing countries to reach and implement an organized and collaborative approach towards TNCs. It ought to be mentioned at the outset that the goal of Decision 24 was not to obstruct inflow of FDI into the region. On the contrary, member countries wanted to encourage such an inflow, but in a 'structured' way that would benefit members of the Pact and increase economic efficiency there. In addition, they wanted to increase the bargaining power of home firms in relation to foreign TNCs in order to promote an 'equitable' distribution of gains from FDI.

The thrust of a complicated and controversial Decision 24 was the regulation of FDI and transfer of technology. It permitted the establishment of national screening and registering bureau; outlawed new FDI in utilities and services; prohibited an annual reinvestment of corporate profit of more than 5 per cent without approval; allowed the annual transfer of profit of up to 14 per cent; and compelled TNCs to disclose all data that relate to the transferred technology, including those on the pricing of inputs. In addition, the expectation from the divestment stipulation (the most polemic feature) imposed on TNCs, was a gradual reduction in foreign ownership of local assets, national capital accumulation and a basis for the development of local technology (Mytelka, 1979, p. 190).

Foreign investors loudly criticized Decision 24 as an unfriendly measure, but in practice, they took a more pragmatic and longer-term approach. In spite of stringent conditions for FDI, the flows to the region have not decreased. Far more important instrument for attracting FDI to the region were size and growth of the local market, as well as national policies and the macroeconomic situation, rather than the potentially stringent Decision 24 and economic integration.

In order to enhance the inflow of FDI in the region the group replaced Decision 24 and introduced a more liberal Decision 220 in 1987. This move introduced a set of common rules for FDI, but gave independence to the member states in implementing the policy. Decision 220 was replaced in 1991 by Decision 291. This represents the biggest turning point in the group since its inception. Decision 291 reversed the alleged dislike of the old approach towards FDI and removed obstacles to the free flow of FDI. It symbolizes a total departure of the group from the doubtful import substitution economic strategy of the Pact in favour of a de-regulated and export-oriented model of development, as well as being a major transformation since the inception of the group.[18] The Andean Pact opened its doors completely to TNCs. The most important feature of Decision 291 was related to the national treatment of TNCs. The intention of the group was to remove obstacles to FDI and promote a free inflow of capital to the region. The Pact, however, started to 'crumble' in 1997. Peru left the group and started to approach both MERCOSUR and APEC. Obviously, bigger blocs are more attractive.

2.2   The Southern Common Market

Trade conflicts with the US and EU (farm goods) inspired Brazil and Argentina to revitalize their mutual economic relations. This was the background to the decision of Argentina and Brazil to sign 17 partial agreements in 1986 and expedite integration on a bilateral basis. These partial agreements included ones that permit duty-free trade in capital goods and cars. This segmented arrangement, rather than one that liberalizes trade across the board, may prove to be quite clumsy since a tit for tat negotiation tactic may prevent a free adjustment of the whole economy to a deeper integration.

So-called 'integration' of Argentina and Brazil lured Paraguay and Uruguay to join them in 1991 and create Mercado Común del Sur (MERCOSUR)[19] by the Treaty of Asuncion. The ambitious goal of this second-generation integration group in Latin America was to create the Southern Common Market with over 200 million consumers. The first 'positive' step towards the implementation of the plan was an across-the-board cut in tariff rates on the internal trade in 1991. A change of approach to integration in Argentina and Brazil was indeed noteworthy. A set of tailor-made fractional arrangements was replaced by generally liberalized and integrated trade. An Inter-governmental Common Market Council (that meets twice a year) and a relatively small permanent secretariat in Montevideo are in contrast with the excessive baroque-type structures of previous integration schemes in the region. Although that may be seen as an advantage relative to the past integration efforts, the flaw is that even small technical problems may end up consuming the energies of ministers and presidents and may generate a lot of hot air in tit for tat bargaining at the highest level.

The group intends to move from a free trade area, through a customs union and on to a common market.[20] According to the plan, a common external tariff was introduced in 1995, but its complete operation will start at the beginning of 2001. The local content requirement for preferential treatment in trade is 60 per cent. There are no commitments to a free factor mobility, hence a common regional market remains only a desire for the future. Economic and monetary union was not stated as a goal, although there was a recognized need to co-ordinate macroeconomic policies.

The first integration-related signs were encouraging. Average internal trade in MERCOSUR as a share of total external trade grew from 9 per cent in 1990 to 18 per cent in 1994. None the less, there is still important unused potential for an increase in the regional economic links. One of the hindrances is, however, a deficient transport infrastructure (roads, bridges, different railway gauges). These infrastructural shortcomings are a consequence of the past mistrust among the countries in the region. However, the situation started being rectified in the early 1990s. Other obstacles to integration still demonstrate the deeply rooted legacy of the past protectionism. Yet another stumbling bloc is the confusingly diverse economic policies of the member countries. For example, while Argentina was pegging its currency to the dollar, Brazil was slowly devaluing. In addition, Brazil, as a big country, has relatively little inclination towards regional integration and introduces unilateral trade barriers at its own will.[21] In 1995, it increased tariffs on imported cars to 70 per cent. As Argentina was not initially excluded from those tariffs, this brought MERCOSUR close to breaking point. Unless such incidents are avoided in the future, the relatively fast pace of regional integration may be slowed down.

MERCOSUR might be on the way to breaking with the inward-oriented tradition of the first generation Latin American integration arrangements such as the LAFTA. Thus, in future MERCOSUR could be an attractive grouping for other countries in Latin America. Chile signed a free trade deal with the group in 1996, while there are also opportunities for the development of relations with the Andean Pact countries. Hence, the regional arrangement is wide open. In addition, TNCs such as General Motors, Toyota, Volkswagen and Mercedes–Benz all announced plans in 1996 for new investment in southern Brazil.

It is relatively early to predict whether southern integration is irreversible given the regional history of many integration schemes that did not take off. None the less, there are two positive developments. One is the pledge to a liberal trade regime, while the other is the rule of democratic[22] governments that see MERCOSUR as a long-term project of regional integration among the participating countries. This has provided an incentive to intra-regional and external TNCs[23] to invest in the region. If integration-prone approaches continue to develop in the region, then the potential Western Hemisphere Free Trade Area may be a deal between the NAFTA (led by the US) and MERCOSUR (led by Brazil). But would it be a completely new institution or would it be an extension of the NAFTA? Interest in the deal would be reinforced if the countries such as Brazil grow at relatively high rates without major interruptions. Regional integration can provide a supporting tool for growth, but it will never be a substitute for sound national macroeconomic policies.

2.3 The Central American Common Market

The Central American Common Market (CACM), established in 1960, had a misleading name from the outset. The group was similar to a customs union as factor mobility was not allowed. In spite of a relatively long time integrating, the 'real' effect of the CACM group has been quite small.

The member countries intended to industrialize by means of integration. The instrument employed was the creation of a customs union. The market was enlarged, but it was still too small to permit more than a single (monopolistic) firm that operated efficiently in most manufacturing industries.

Industrialization should be accomplished by an import substitution strategy. Since backward linkages were weak, consumer goods that were produced in the group had a substantial import content.

Industrialists have not been a strong pressure group in the region in comparison to the land-owners. Therefore, investors have considered returns between the manufacturing industry and agriculture, rather than between different manufacturing industries. If profits were made and if returns justified such a decision, then investment was usually made outside the manufacturing sector. In spite of the initial increase in regional trade, supported by a relatively stable macroeconomic situation, the major cause of CACM failure can be found in the lack of an established structure within which industrialization of the group can arise (Bulmer-Thomas, 1988, pp. 302–303). In addition, the macroeconomic situation worsened at the end of the 1970s and the introduction of exchange controls led to further disintegration of the group since the goods traded with the CACM partners were not high priority.

A stagnation of the CACM started after the war between El Salvador and Honduras in 1969 and the subsequent exit of Honduras from the scheme. After that, rapid decline of the group followed throughout the 1980s when member countries were faced with oil shocks, budget deficits, unemployment and inflation; they acted unilaterally and restricted even the intra-group trade. The actual role of the CACM moved from economic integration to an arena for soliciting peace.

The small markets of CACM member countries were not attractive to TNCs prior to the establishment of the scheme. After its creation, interest by the TNCs increased. Out of 155 foreign manufacturing subsidiaries at the end of 1960s, only 10 had settled more than one plant in the CACM (UNCTAD, 1983, p. 14). Although such a concentration of sellers might point to the existence of economies of scale and a potential benefit to the integrated countries, in practice, the situation was different. TNCs were sourcing components from outside of the area and they were uninterested in exporting output to third countries. If the member countries had chosen an outward oriented economic strategy, the outcome would have been, perhaps, different. Although there are still various impediments to integration in the region, that range from military to economic issues, the CACM is still there. The new surge of interest in integration may trigger its revival.

2.4   The Enterprise for the Americas and Western Hemisphere Free Trade Area

The Enterprise for the Americas Initiative announced by the US in 1990 aspired to support market reforms throughout Latin America. The means for backing these reforms included an increase in trade and FDI, relieving foreign debt, as well as environmental control and improvement. The bilateral framework agreements, quite loose in origin, between the US and almost all Latin American countries, set the agenda for consultations.[24] There is a stated willingness by the US to enter into free trade arrangements with Latin American countries on bilateral bases, although the Latin American group would prefer a multilateral deal. However, a country that is to be considered eligible for free trade has to satisfy 'indicators of readiness' which include a stable market and macroeconomic system, outward orientation and a pledge to the multilateral trading system. These framework agreements were, as their name suggests, merely a prelude to what may take place in the (distant) future. Latin American countries are quite interested in achieving secure economic links with the US since intra-Latin American trade and FDI are less important for these countries than similar ties with the US.

The Enterprise for the Americas Initiative may have a profound and, even, undermining effect on integration among the Latin American countries. As is well known, many of those countries are much more interested in wide and secure trade access and FDI relations with the US than among themselves. Internal trade within integration groups of the developing countries does not offer even a medium-term alternative to their economic relations with one of the hub partners in the developed world. Mexico is an example of this.

The Enterprise for the Americas Initiative may be a step towards the Western Hemisphere Free Trade Area (from Alaska to Tierra del Fuego).[25] Although it is not its stated goal, the Initiative may evolve in the textbook example of the hub and spoke model of international economic integration with dominance by the US. Increased trade with the US may further undermine the relatively low level of trade within the region and increase the dependence on the hub country. With the uncertain future of (democratic) governments in the region and proliferating economic sanctions on an *ad hoc* basis without any universally applicable criteria for their introduction and lifting (everyone is somewhere a sinner), considerable economic reliance on a big hub partner may be the reason for concern. 'Indicators of readiness' for preferential treatment are a powerful mechanism for discrimination. In addition, countries that enter into a preferential deal with the US may present an obstacle to further liberalization in the region since their initial preferences may be eroded by the expansion of the preferential scheme.

Lipsey (1992, p. 17) presented arguments why Canada and all Latin American countries should resist the hub and spoke model of integration in the western hemisphere:

- As the hub country, the US is the only one with free entry to the markets of all participating countries. On the reverse side of the coin, all other spoke countries have free access only to the US market. The clear beneficiary of such an arrangement is the US.
- Locating a plant in any of the spoke countries offers free access only to the local market and the US. Investment in the US provides a free access

to all countries in the arrangement. TNCs will definitely keep that option in mind. The US would be the only beneficiary of such FDI diversion.

- The US is in a better bargaining position than its other partners. Smaller partners may have to forgo many of their spheres of interest and may not wish to 'rock the boat' with their common cause in certain matters simply in order not to jeopardize negotiations and free access to the US market.

The leaders of thirty-four western hemisphere countries agreed in Miami in 1994 to negotiate a Free Trade Deal of the Americas by 2005 and implement it by 2015. Many things have changed since that time. For example, there is not yet any date when the countries (or their groups) should start 'hard talking' and Brazil is primarily interested in consolidating MERCOSUR. Hence, the western hemisphere free trade deal will have to wait for quite a while.

3   Africa

3.1   East African Community

Paradoxically, economic integration in the East African Community (EAC) (1967–77) among Kenya, Tanzania and Uganda can be observed not as a way towards regional integration, but rather as a step towards disintegration of the countries in the region. These countries were 'integrated' before they achieved independence. However, the colonial era arrangement could not be expected to continue without alteration as there was an issue about the distribution of benefits of integration. Tanzania and Uganda felt that regional integration favoured Kenya. In theory, a regional transfer tax was supposed to provide certain protection to industries in the less developed countries in the group. In practice, it encouraged replication of industries in the EAC countries. The East African Development Bank was supposed to complement the financing of projects that would make the economies of the countries complementary. The countries, however, did not go far regarding their industrial planning. Regional problems were exacerbated by ideological differences as Kenya was 'capitalist' and welcomed foreign investors while Tanzania was 'socialist' and resisted it. Economic integration in the group was perceived as a zero, even a negative-sum game. In those circumstances, the EAC faded away as there was no interest by the participants in keeping it alive (Hazlewood, 1988).

3.2   Customs and Economic Union of Central Africa

The major novelty brought by the Customs and Economic Union of Central Africa (Union Douanière et Economique de l'Afrique Centrale – UDEAC) in trade relations of its members by was the single tax (*taxe unique*). Goods manufactured in UDEAC and sold in more than one of its member states were subject to a single tax that was always lower than the customs duty. The single tax was supposed to provide incentives for industrialization in the region. UDEAC countries started to compete with each other in order to attract foreign investors with incentives that included duty-free imports of capital goods and other inputs. TNCs entered the region and dominated manufacturing industries in UDEAC countries. They segmented local markets, linked them to inputs with the markets of developed countries and created an oligopolistic, even monopolistic, local market structure. A replication of manufacturing in small batches in the countries of the group increased the costs of production, but TNCs were able to pass these high costs of production on to consumers in the form of higher prices. A lack of any coherent industrial planning, distribution of benefits and an absence of an effective regional financial institution may be the primary culprits for the weak progress of integration in UDEAC (Mytelka, 1984).

3.3 Economic Community of West African States

Nigeria was the country that led the creation of the Economic Community of West African States (ECOWAS) in 1975 as a means for the reduction of French influence in the region. In addition, Nigeria, a noted exporter of oil, intended to use the group as a way of increasing its economic and political authority in the region. The ambitious goal was to create a common market in the region. The sixteen countries in the group are a mix of diverse, mainly, but not exclusively, anglophone and francophone countries. As the production structure of the countries in the region is generally characterized by a monoculture, it comes as no surprise that internal trade in ECOWAS was unimportant for participating countries (around 3 per cent of total exports during the 1970s and double that in the subsequent decades). The Fund for Co-operation, Compensation and Development, although conceived as a means for the promotion of a fair and equitable distribution of benefits of integration had very limited effect on the group because of the financing problem. Real progress in economic development in a situation of severe poverty may not depend much, or primarily, in the short and medium term on the integration arrangement, but rather on the discovery and exploitation of natural resources and an ample inflow of foreign aid and investment. Useful industrial, regional and social policies may be necessary for the alleviation of the rough times linked to the distribution of the costs and benefits of integration. The existence of smaller integration groups within ECOWAS such as the Mano River Union, the Economic Community of West Africa[26] (a French tool to check the influence of Nigeria in the region from 1973) and the Senegambian Confederation made decision making difficult. The member countries were not always convinced that the ECOWAS offered a better arrangement than the smaller and more cosy integration groups. A policy of trade liberalization in the absence of supporting regional and industrial policies in ECOWAS was mainly responsible for keeping the group only at the blueprint stage (Robson, 1983). A revision of the Treaty (1993) of the group brought no visible change in the life of the ECOWAS.

3.4   South African Customs Union

The Southern African Customs Union (SACU) was created in 1910 between South Africa and its neighbours (Botswana, Lesotho, Swaziland and Namibia). It was underpinned by a monetary arrangement in which the South African rand was the dominant currency. This arrangement between a 'developed' (according to many criteria applied for African countries) and several developing countries had as one of its consequences trade diversion. In particular, South Africa was not the cheapest source of supply for many items imported by its partners in the deal. There is a system for the redistribution of customs revenue that is supposed to favour the less developed countries and compensate them for the costs of polarization and loss of fiscal discretion. In spite of the problems of trade diversion and a polarization of economic activity towards South Africa, even during the apartheid days, the SACU members maintained an interest to keep and strengthen the scheme. New political realities in the post-apartheid South Africa could breathe new life into economic integration in the group. However, a definite opinion about the success of the group in past decades cannot be given as the hub country, South Africa, was subject to economic sanctions and isolation.

The Southern African Economic Community[27] was occupied in the past with 'cooperation' in transport and communication. Intra-regional trade has always been around 5 per cent of total external trade. The intentions of the group to be involved in deeper regional 'integration' will require an alignment of trade and other economic policies with other schemes that operate in the region. It is possible that various sub-regional groups of countries may proceed with integration at different speeds. If the economy of South Africa exhibits strong growth, it may have a similar 'locomotive' role on the economies of neighbouring countries to that of the US on Mexico.

3.5   The Preferential Trade Area

The Preferential Trade Area (PTA) for Eastern and Southern African States, established in 1984, had the objective of promoting cooperation in the areas of trade, manufacturing, agriculture, monetary affairs and transport and communication services. Tariffs on a select number of goods that were traded internally were reduced by up to 70 per cent. A preferential treatment of trade in goods is granted only to those produced in facilities that were majority owned by the residents of the PTA countries. A clearing house handled a sizeable proportion of settlements in regional trade.

The PTA failed to deliver obvious benefits to the member countries, hence it was replaced by a much more ambitious Common Market for Eastern and

Southern Africa (COMESA) in 1994. An additional goal of the new arrangement is the creation of a monetary union. There are few grounds to expect that it will fare better than ECOWAS (Robson 1997 p. 350).

3.6 Arab countries

Integration among the Arab countries in North Africa and the Middle East is characterized by the frequent establishment and the even more habitual breakdown of the integration schemes. This might be surprising since all these countries share a common language and religion.[28] Of course, the distribution of natural wealth is very uneven among the countries, but there is a number of fusing elements among the countries that may, potentially, make the integration process smooth. None the less, numerous attempts to integrate these countries got nowhere, principally because of stark political differences. This is very discouraging for investments that look at the wider markets that integration provides. TNCs have been active in the region almost exclusively in the exploitation of one natural resource, hydrocarbons.

3.7 African experience

In spite of many attempts to integrate on a regional scale, overlapping membership in various groups as well as investing of scare resources into those enterprises (building of institutions, customs systems, industrial projects, etc.) the economies of most African countries remained detached from each other. As a matter of comparison, in 1989 the GNP of all sub-Saharan African countries was roughly equal to that of Belgium. Suppose now that the economy of Belgium was splintered into around forty independent and isolated countries with different languages, administration, currency, taxation, army and an inefficient transport and communications system! Their economic growth remained low, while the majority of countries saw little structural change until 1990s. The major reasons for the poor results of integration arrangements in the region include a disparity in the level of economic development of the countries, import-substitution policies and constant problems with the distribution of gains from integration. If this is taken together, it comes as no surprise that intra-regional trade has always been very small (just a few per cent of their total trade) and even declining. Economic integration in the region may be fruitful in the future if the countries abandon their past economic policies and introduce transparent, balanced and market-oriented policies. Other types of integration policies have already been tried out in the region with results that were at best disappointing. Perhaps, a look to the north, as Mexico did, may offer better results, even though such an approach may be criticized on the grounds that it may reintroduce the old colonial links. Project-based cooperation among African states, as well as stronger economic relations with the 'northern' countries (based on a free access of 'sensitive' products to northern markets) may be beneficial for both regions.

4   South-east Asia

It is hard to imagine an integration scheme that unites such diverse countries as the Association of South East Asian Nations (ASEAN). The member countries contrast not only regarding their size and level of development, but are also heterogeneous due to a host of social issues such as language, history, religion and culture. The approach of ASEAN to integration was in stark contrast to most of the schemes that integrate developing countries. Instead of grand programmes for trade liberalization, joint production and a vast institutional structure, the ASEAN approached integration differently. The institutional structure was light and there were no formal and detailed blueprints for integration. The Bangkok Declaration (1967) merely calls, in a general way, for the participating countries to cooperate in areas of regional interest. There was no supranational institutional setup and the activities all followed the principle of unanimity in decision making.

Such a low profile, and even a slow approach to regional integration, might have worked in support of the ASEAN. The diversity among the countries was so immense that, probably, not many other approaches could have survived. The main instruments of cooperation were preferential trade, industrial projects and industrial complementarity.

In spite of the preferences for intra-group trade, the member countries trade mostly with developed countries. None the less, internal trade in the ASEAN countries is by far the largest in comparison to all other integration groups among the developing countries (around 20 per cent of external trade). This relative level of internal trade may be quite misleading since a notable part of it is directed through Singapore which is not the final destination of goods. In fact, an important share of internal trade is redirected to external markets, in particular, to the US. A further increase in internal trade was expected to be brought by the decisions reached in the Manila Summit (1987). Coverage of the preferential trade arrangements was expanded to include more commodity items, preferences granted were widened and the exclusion lists of 'sensitive items' were limited to 10 per cent of traded goods. Although such a move could enhance links within the region, the ASEAN countries approved in 1992 (Singapore Summit) an agreement to create an ASEAN Free Trade Area within the coming fifteen years.[29]

The goals of the ASEAN Free Trade Area (agreed, but not yet implemented, a quarter of a century after the establishment of the ASEAN), include a reduction in the level of tariffs on the manufactured goods to a level not higher than 20 per cent in five to eight years, and to a level of up to 5 per cent before the year 2008. Such a (long) timetable is in place because of the accommodation of the demands of the less-developed ASEAN countries (such as Indonesia and the Philippines), as well as national differences on the policy stances regarding different economic sectors and industries within them. Primary farm goods and services are beyond the scope of the free trade regime. A further issue that may frustrate a deeper free trade area is NTBs originating in differences in national taxes, standards and political connections in doing business.[30]

The new free trade area arrangement refers only to manufactured goods (services and agriculture are omitted, just like in the EFTA). Although everything moves very slowly in the ASEAN, the free trade area technique of integration within the region may have a realistic chance of success. With few exceptions, the member countries of the ASEAN are among the swiftest growing economies in the world. It makes sense to settle a single production unit with significant economies of scale for standardized goods in a market of almost 500 million consumers (following the entry of Vietnam in 1995 and Burma and Laos in 1997) with fast growing incomes, than to locate seven separate sub-optimal units that serve local markets. This may here a profound influence on the inflow of FDI into the region. However, the problem with the enlargement of the ASEAN is that some of the poorest countries in the world joined the group. That may divert the energies of the ASEAN away from trade liberalization.

As a more integrated group, the ASEAN countries may have greater leverage in international talks on trade, bearing in mind the potential splintering of the world market into trade blocs. In addition to the perils of protectionism in the US and EU, another element that encourages efforts towards tighter integration in the ASEAN is the enduring and rapid growth of Asia.

The ASEAN government-to-government *industrial projects* had as their objective the installation of large-scale capital-intensive ventures. They were perceived to be flexible ventures and, therefore, only the interested ASEAN parties took part in them. The urea projects for Indonesia and Malaysia, the diesel engine project for Singapore, the soda-ash project for Thailand and the superphosphate project for the Philippines were in the first package deal to be considered in 1976. To help these projects get off the ground, the government of Japan promised $1 billion in soft loans. However, the package of projects soon got into various kinds of trouble. Owing to a host of political and economic reasons, one being monopoly rights, only those projects in Indonesia and Malaysia were initiated and that was made possible by Japanese assistance (Wong, 1988, p. 323).

The purpose of the ASEAN industrial projects was to introduce new, grand and state-led industrial projects, while the goal of *industrial complementation schemes* was for link the existing manufacturing industries (promote complementarity) without government intervention and serve as a substitute for industrial projects. Since the industrial projects were largely unsuccessful, cooperation energy shifted towards the industrial complementarity. None the less, the approval process was so cumbersome that it rendered it unattractive to investors. The Manila Summit (1987) made the approval process simpler, increased the margin of tariff preference to 90 per cent for approved products and proposed an increase in the foreign equity participation to 60 per cent. Since the changes were subsequently accepted, there was certain initial interest in the usage of those facilities.

The concept of *joint ventures* in the group, even though they were among flexible private firms, was attractive in theory. What happened in practice was different. The member countries followed similar industrial strategies and they competed with their goods more than they complemented each other. As such, an across-the-board tariff reduction within the group could jeopardize national industrialization strategies in spite of a plethora of NTBs that are still in effect. Since in the ASEAN national strategies took priority over regional ones, the common interest of the group always assumed secondary status, hence the record of joint manufacturing efforts in the ASEAN was quite poor. In fact, in the case of ASEAN, regional economic integration played an insignificant part in the economic success of the countries in the region. What mattered first and foremost for that success was the soundness of the national macroeconomic situation, as well as national economic policies.

None of the integration projects mentioned provided a leap forward to a deeper integration. The ASEAN group can be seen more as a conflict resolution mechanism than a genuine international economic integration group. The regional market is still largely a sum of separate markets of the member countries. The group has, nevertheless, established a dialogue with major trading partners. The member countries have had, with a few exceptions, an open mind and open policy towards FDI. Economic strategy was almost always open towards the rest of the world and the involvement of foreign TNCs was most pronounced in the electronics industries in the region. Strong engines of manufacturing growth to the countries in the region came from the involvement of TNCs, initially because of relatively low labour costs. TNCs brought with them not only the necessary manufacturing and management technologies, but also employment and wide international marketing networks. The indigenous business community was receptive to the establishment of sourcing, subcontracting and other links with TNCs, which had positive externalities for the host country. This was particularly important since the output of the TNCs was basically (in the initial stage) for export, mainly, but not exclusively, to the US. Relatively competition-prone ASEAN industrialists were very receptive towards the positive externalities that came from the involvement of TNCs in their national economies. In fact, the learning, absorption, extension and upgrading process of the business in the new circumstances made them certain that they were capable of competing successfully on the national, regional and international market without protective national/regional economic policies.

In spite of all the integration efforts, national trade policies remained largely independent from each other in the group. In fact, only Brunei and Singapore were free-trade nations in the group. Hence, what was the major valued-added of the group to its member countries? Well, ASEAN (an economic integration enigma) provided a communication channel for member countries in discussions about economic and political relations with major trading partners. In addition, an outward-oriented model of cooperation instead of inward-oriented industrial policies gave ASEAN an international reputation in the past. One of the major lessons that ASEAN can offer to other schemes is that economic 'integration' is no more than a supporting tool to a sound *national* economic policy (Langhammer, 1991).

5 Conclusion

Integration groups among the developing countries were not propelled by a high and/or fast growing internal trade or FDI. Intra-group trade played a minor role in these schemes. This is even truer for intra-regional FDI. The main instrument of integration in many integration schemes among the developing countries, as structured in the past, was trade liberalization. It was very hard to move integration efforts beyond the opening stage. The opening up of the regional market, although on a limited scale, was an instrument that prompted a certain involvement of TNCs in the groups. The only exception is the Andean Pact where the core of the arrangement was the structuring of this involvement of TNCs in the region, even although the success of the policy has not materialized. Only in the ASEAN were countries able to take a common and FDI friendly joint stance towards foreign TNCs from the outset. TNCs have been contributing to the local fixed capital formation and technology in production and management, as well as in wide international marketing networks that were export friendly and that supported the general ASEAN trade openness. None the less, the soundness of the national economic policy and macroeconomic stability has always played an important role in attracting of FDI, rather than a country's participation in the regional integration scheme. Therefore, an exploration of the ways for north–south integration, as took place in the NAFTA, provides a promising research area in the future.

NOTES

1 A. El-Agraa (ed.)(1994), *The Economics of the European Community*, New York: Harvester Wheatsheaf; C. Dent (1997), *The European Economy*, London: Routledge; T. Hitiris (1994), *European Community Economics*, New York: Harvester Wheatsheaf; M. Jovanović (1997), *European Economic Integration: Limits and Prospects*, London: Routledge; W. Molle (1994), *The Economics of European Integration*, Aldershot: Dartmouth; D. Swann (1995), *The Economics of the Common Market*, Harmondsworth: Penguin Books; D. Swann (1996), *European Economic Integration: The Common Market, European Union and Beyond*, Cheltenham: Edward Elgar; and L. Tsoukalis (1993), *The New European Economy*, Oxford: Oxford University Press.

2 Interestingly enough the major beneficiary of the customs union between the EU and Turkey is most likely to be the EU! Most of the Turkish exports to the EU were liberalized even before the customs union deal, which simply formalized trade relations. On the other hand, Turkey had to open its market to the imports from the EU.

3 For select readings on each of the referred group, the interested reader is invited to consult El-Agraa (1977) and Jovanović (1998d).

4 Countries of central and eastern Europe are often referred to as 'transition countries'. Transition as a term is a finite process. However, after a decade of 'transition towards a market-type economy' the end of this process in not yet in sight. It seems that 'economic transition' has turned into a policy of long-term economic development.

5 80 per cent of trade was free of tariffs and additional 15 per cent were subject to tariffs of 5 per cent or less.

6 Interestingly enough, this issue did not feature high on the agenda when Greece, Spain and Portugal were entering the EU, but may be of relevance once the potential eastern enlargement takes place in the future.

7 Only 117,000 Americans have applied for the benefits offered to workers displaced by the NAFTA. If compared with 1.5 million who lose their jobs each year from factory closures, slack demand and corporate restructuring (*The Economist*, 5 July 1997 p. 17), the cost of adjustment for the US, does not seen too high.

8 A free trade area between the US and Japan can not be envisaged for a long time, as it would be linked with many controversial issues such as rice, textiles, steel, computers and biotechnology. Barriers such as national business relations, industrial structures, relations with the government and distribution systems are so different that a mere free trade arrangement would not be sufficient to overcome them.

9 'Averaging' of tariffs could present problems as they are lower in New Zealand than in Australia.

10 The town in Hungary where the leaders of the Czech Republic, Hungary, Poland and Slovakia met in 1991 and agreed to start negotiations on the establishment of a free trade area.

11 The Czech and Slovaks split in 1993. One may ask where their real interest is to get together again?

12 On average, they were more expensive and trade distorting than the Common Agricultural Policy of the EU.

13 Schemes that may fit into this group include the Latin American Free Trade Area, the Latin American Integration Association, the Southern Common Market, the Economic Community of West African States and the Preferential Trade Area for Eastern and Southern African States.

14 Schemes that could fit into this group include the Andean Pact, the Central American Common Market, the East African Community and some aspects of the Association of South East Asian Nations.

15 'If a certain level of integration cannot be made to work, the reaction of policy-makers has typically been to embark on something more elaborate, more advanced and more demanding in terms of administrative requirements and political commitment' (Robson, 1997, p. 348).

16 Guyana, Suriname, French Guyana and Cuba.

17 The Andean Pact was established among Bolivia, Colombia, Chile, Ecuador, Peru and Venezuela. It was regarded for some time to be the model for economic integration among the developing countries.

18 The merits of import-substitution strategies of growth have been debated for a long time. Neo-liberals dispute its value. Others measure the success of such a strategy by rates of growth. Although Brazil followed an import-substitution

strategy, its average annual rate of growth during the 1950s and 1960s was around 7 per cent.

19 MERCOSUL is the abbreviation in Portuguese.

20 A cynic would exclaim: 'Oh, again, one more Latin American grand plan that is going to hibernate!'

21 For Brazil the MERCOSUR increases the 'local' market by a quarter, while for Argentina, the increase of the market is four-fold.

22 However, trans-border links among national political parties still have to be developed.

23 This was most obvious in the car-making and food businesses.

24 Abolishment of tariff and NTBs, protection of FDI and intellectual property rights, as well as settlement of disputes.

25 The exception is Cuba unless there is a change to democracy.

26 *Communauté Economique de l'Afrique de l'Ouest* (CEAO).

27 Angola, Botswana, Lesotho, Malawi, Mozambique, Namibia, Swaziland, South Africa, Tanzania, Zambia and Zimbabwe.

28 A similar structure is also in Latin America where it has proceeded at a slow pace in the past.

29 A more 'compact' integration agreement in the form of a customs union might not be very realistic in the near future because of enormous differences in the level of income (per capita) and approaches to economic policy.

30 The preferential trading agreement covers 15,000 items in the ASEAN. Countries are granted the right to exclude 'sensitive' items from such a preferential trade. Contrary to expectations the preferential regime has not had a strong impact on internal trade. Intra-ASEAN trade takes 20 per cent of trade of the member countries. Out of that volume of trade less than 1 per cent is affected by preferential treatment. Many regional preferences were without real substance. For example, the Philippines grants preferential access to snowploughs (Business Asia, 2 September 1991, p. 304).

6 Measurement of the Effects of International Economic Integration

I INTRODUCTION

It is no strange thing in economics to find out that the development of the theory on a particular topic and the development of empirical research have pursued rather different courses. It is difficult to imagine a better example of this divergence than the study of the effects of international economic integration (Mayes, 1988, p. 42). Various studies have attempted to measure the effects of international economic integration. Some of them intended to show the advance in integration as the interlace of economic ties among countries. Others wanted to measure the increase in welfare. Yet another group of studies strove to measure the distribution of the costs and benefits of integration. However, the theory of international economic integration encountered in this book is so complex that it cannot be represented mathematically with a great precision.

II MODELS

Econometric models which attempt to measure the effects of international economic integration can be divided into those which are *ex ante* and *ex post*. The former models are often founded on a simple extrapolation of trends. These models can not be based on reliable data, but rather on estimations. The problem represents the fact that one has no reliable data on future developments. It is assumed that the future flow of foreign trade is a function of income, production, relative prices, change in the level of trade barriers, substitutability among import sources, as well as between imports and domestic production.

The *ex post* models attempt to measure a hypothetical situation (the counterfactual world or anti-monde) which may represent what could have happened with trade in a situation without integration. The difference between the actual and expected imports of each of the participating countries represents trade creation, while the same difference in imports from outside countries shows trade diversion. These differences may be attributed to autonomous changes in prices, changes in income and competition, reductions in barriers to trade and to errors.

The models may single out a reduction or removal of trade barriers trade as the most important reason for the change in the pattern of trade. This may not be the most reliable way for the assessment of effects of integration. Trade may have been diverted from third countries because of FDI which have substituted imports, not only because of changes in tariff structure. Instead of comparing the actual behaviour with what would have happened without integration and attributing all the difference to integration, one should better compare what a model predicts with integration to what it predicts without integration (Mayes, 1988, p. 45). By doing that, the possible biases may be reduced. None the less, one can neither be fully certain about what would have happened without integration, nor about the influence of integration on the economic policies of member countries.

Most of the quantitative studies measure trade creation, trade diversion and output effects mainly in the context of the EU. An early influential study found that trade among the member countries of the EU was 50 per cent higher in 1969 than would be the case without integration (Williamson and Bottrill, 1973, p. 139). Another study found that there was a 25 per cent increase in both exports and imports in EFTA in the 1959–65 period (EFTA, 1969, p. 10).

There exists a fair degree of agreement among various studies that trade creation outweighs trade diversion. The disagreement exists regarding the magnitude of this difference. The net effect of trade flows is usually positive (trade creating), but is relatively small. This is obvious from surveys by Mayes (1978)[1] and El-Agraa (1989). In spite of their relative magnitude (smallness) the perceived static gains always lend support to a number of economists' and certain politicians' arguments in favour of integration (and the other way around).

The reason for the relative smallness in the measured gains from regional agreements is that some countries that take part in integration may trade a relatively small part of their goods and services within the group. That is most obvious in the schemes that integrate developing countries (see Table 2.8). Alternative explanations should also be found. Mere trade creation/diversion effects do not properly represent changes in welfare. The total effect of regional economic integration is a blend of various effects of integration in the long run. Countries might not embark upon international economic integration because of clear balances in trade with partners, but rather to reap the dynamic benefits of integration such as an enhancement in opportunities for specialization, economies of scale and increased welfare. Hence, the net trade creation/diversion effect is only a minor part of the answer to why countries integrate.[2]

While traditional general equilibrium models reported small welfare gains from integration, that is, less than 1 per cent of GNP in the EU (Lipsey, 1960, p. 511),[3] this is not the case with modern analysis which considers imperfect competition and economies of scale. Brada and Méndez (1988) estimated two dynamic effects of integration: levels of investment and growth in productivity in six integration schemes. Faster productivity effects were found only in two, while increased investment levels were discovered in five groups. The modest dynamic gains discovered reflected the cumulative effects of around two decades of integration. Therefore, according to the authors, these dynamic gains could not explain the rapid growth of west European countries during the 1960s, nor be a strong justification for external countries to join the existing groups, nor be used as arguments for the creation of new ones.

A complex general equilibrium model that considered economies of scale and imperfect competition was offered by Harris (1984a) and applied to Canada. Although it had limitations that included only one fixed factor (labour) and one internationally mobile factor (capital), Harris considered situations both with and without product differentiation. The findings were that trade liberazation provoked intra-industry adjustment and a reallocation of resources and that trade liberalization gave incentives to the expansion of economies of scale as a response to access to larger markets and competitive pressure from abroad.

Various studies of the potential effects of the Canada–US free trade agreement (1988), estimated a relatively modest long-run increase in the Canadian real income, between 1 and 3 per cent (Government of Canada, 1988, pp. 30–32). The only exception was the study by Harris and Cox (1985) which estimated an increase of 9 per cent. However, that study was prepared in 1984 and was based on outdated estimates of tariff rates, economies of scale and NTBs. The explanation for the relatively modest trade-creating effects of economic integration in Europe and North America could be found in the already high trade among partners prior to integration. The estimated modest gains from integration had two impacts on public debate about the issue. Internal dimension is that if the gains were so meager, why should one bother to integrate? The external dimension is that when the effects of integration are so small, then there is little need for retaliation by third countries. However, a major benefit of the deal for Canada was security of access to the US market.

The 1985 'White Paper' set out the 1992 Programme in the EU. The Union acted first, and only afterwards attempted to assess the potential impact of its action. Cecchini (1988) analysed the effects of completing the EU internal market elimination of both NTBs and fragmented national markets by the end of 1992. It was also published as the *Cost of Non-Europe* (Emerson et al., 1988). This project estimated the impact of the removal of all trade barriers on internal trade, freedom to provide services, economies of scale, the effect of competition on corporate behaviour and procurement on the EU. As such, it became a valuable benchmark for subsequent research. The major results of the Emerson's project were as follows:

- The estimated partial-equilibrium economic gains were between ECU 175 and 255 billion in 1988 prices. Most of those gains would come in the form of savings from the elimination of custom formalities and technical barriers to trade, liberalization of public procurement, economies of scale, freedom to provide services, reduction in X-inefficiency, as well as a downward convergence in prices.
- The above would increase EU GNP by 5 per cent of the 1988 level. If economic policies were coordinated, then the increase in GNP might be in the range between 2.5 and 6.5 per cent in the medium term.
- The extra non-inflationary economic growth would create up to 5 million new jobs in the medium term.

The above figures, according to the study, were unlikely to be overestimates because the methodology excluded the effects of important dynamic gains such as technological innovation, learning economies of scale and the emergence of 'truly European companies'. Such gains, which might occur under certain conditions (accommodating economic policy), even though they have a one-time character, were hard to resist.

The results of the above study may well be underestimated as they excluded certain types of continuing and likely dynamic benefits. These indirect effects are difficult to measure. They include technological innovation which depends on the existence of competition; the impact of the growth of GNP on long-term savings, investment and rate of growth; the dynamic effects of economies of scale, learning by doing and know-how will be most obvious in the fast-growing high-technology industries where market segmentation seriously limited the scope for these benefits and jeopardized performance in the future; and the big EU market would induce EU enterprises to change their business behaviour in that they would foster the emergence of truly EU companies and business strategies which are better suited to secure a superior place in competition both within and out of the EU.

The macroeconomic effects of integration depend on several variables. They include the following:

- changes in the volume and structure of trade in goods and services between the partners,
- changes in the balance of trade,
- created and lost jobs in the integrated countries,
- changes in wage rates,
- alterations in the real rates of exchange,
- changes in prices,
- accumulation effects (human and physical capital),
- creation of new goods and services,
- FDI,
- retaliation by the 'injured' countries/regions, and
- changes in GNP.

A number of equations, many assumptions about unknown parameters (elasticities and cross-elasticities of demand and supply, substitution rate between capital and labour, or expenditure functions), require high-powered econometric models and make results shaky. Very often only the authors of the models (and a few others) understand the exercise (Hufbauer and Schott, 1992, p. 51).

The greatest benefits of the 1992 Programme in the EU are not expected from one-off effects, as studies by Cecchini/Emerson suggest. They will come from continuous dynamic influences. Baldwin (1989) argued that Cecchini/Emerson (C/E in Figure 6.1) significantly underestimated the dynamic effects of the 1992 Programme, for they concentrated on the impact of the single market on the level of output. The one-time efficiency gains from the 1992 Programme will be multiplied into a substantial 'medium-term growth bonus' (B in Figure 6.1). A rise in savings and investment, due to the initial 2.5 to 6.5 per cent growth in the GNP, will increase EU capital stock. The medium-term growth bonus might evolve into the long-term one, adding permanently between 0.2 and 0.9 per cent to the EU long-term growth rate. The static part of it would be spread over five to seven years following completion of the internal market at the end of 1992. It may take about ten years for the realization of a half of the medium-term 'growth bonus'. Baldwin concluded that the most important impact of the 1992 Programme may be on growth of the EU, not on its effect on resource allocation. If this analysis is correct, then the gains of the 1992 Programme may be between 13 and 33 per cent of the EU GNP. This type of analysis, along the lines by Romer (1986), could be discouraging for all critics that argued that the Cecchini/Emerson results were high.

Contrary to the view of Baldwin, Peck (1989) thought that the estimates by the Commission of the European Communities of the potential gains of the 1992 Programme were overestimates. His own assessment of the gains of

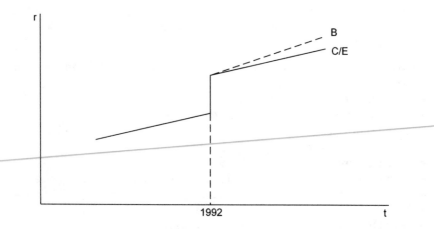

Figure 6.1 Growth effects of the 1992 Programme

the 1992 Programme was that it may increase GDP of the EU by 2 per cent. Hence, the computation of the Commission overestimated the potential gains by a factor of 2 or 3 (Peck, 1989, p. 289). In addition, he referred to the argument that it was difficult to increase significantly the growth-rate of an economy.

Smith and Venables (1988) also studied the effects of the 1992 Programme on economic welfare. Increased competition and a fuller exploitation of economies of scale due to the change in the size of firms were expected to raise welfare in the EU. The partial equilibrium model calibrated to 10 separate industries included imperfect competition, economies of scale and differentiated products. The results of both Cournot and Bertand behaviour were presented, although the authors regarded Cournot competition as a more satisfactory model. Simulations were carried out both in the cases where there was a fixed number of firms and where entry in and exit from an industry was possible. The results showed that the gains from integration could be quite significant for certain industries as they exceeded 4 per cent of base consumption.

A general equilibrium model for the estimation of the impact of the 1992 Programme was developed by Gasiorek, Smith and Venables (1992). Their starting point was that the partial equilibrium models were potentially mis-leading as they did not capture the impact of a change in one industry on others in imperfectly competitive markets. Another limitation of the partial equilibrium model was that they assumed horizontal input-supply curves. In the general equilibrium model, they considered 8 countries and 5 factors (8×5 model) and cases when markets are both segmented and integrated. If one neglected restrictive assumptions of the model that gave a crude approx-imation of the real world and an imperfect set of data, the results supported the view that intra-EU liberalization of trade had pro-competitive effects that could make a substantial contribution to welfare. Most of the welfare gains were attributable to the competition effect and economies of scale, although this was partly offset by a loss in the variety, trade diversion and deterioration in terms of trade with the third countries as certain benefits of lower costs of the EU goods were passed on to foreign consumers.

A Communication from the EU Commission based on replies from 13,000 enterprises offered an *ex post* assessment of the impact of the 1992 Programme (European Commission, 1997). It was found that:

- there was solid evidence of the positive effects of the Single Market Programme;
- growing competition between firms in both manufacturing and services;
- an accelerated pace of industrial restructuring;
- a wider range of products and services available to the public sector, industrial and and domestic consumers at lower prices, particularly in newly liberalized services such as transport, financial services, telecom-munications and broadcasting;

- faster and cheaper cross-frontier deliveries resulting from the absence of cross-border controls on goods;
- greater inter-state mobility of workers, as well as students and retired people;
- between 300,000 and 900,000 more new jobs were created than would be the case without the 1992 Programme;
- there was an extra increase in EU income of 1.1–1.5 per cent over the period 1987–93;
- inflation rates are 1.0–1.5 per cent lower than would be the case in the absence of 1992 Programme;
- there was an increase in economic convergence and cohesion between different EU regions.

The model estimated that the GDP for the EU (12) in 1994 was in the range of 1.1–1.5 per cent above the level that would have prevailed in the absence of 1992 Programme. That was the gain in the range of ECU 60–80 billion, an increase as if an income the size of Portugal's economy (ECU 75 billion in 1994) had been added to the EU. The gains came from the increase in competition/efficiency and the rise in total factor productivity (each accounting about a half of the total effect) (*European Economy*, 1996 pp. 166–167). The elimination of trade barriers reduced the segmentation of the national market, increased competition and decreased costs (and prices).

The above quantitative findings were disappointing compared with the earlier official estimations and expectations when the 1992 Programme was launched. The new data by the Commission are more in line with the expectations by Peck (1989) than in accord with any other *ex ante* estimation.[4]

There are several arguments that may be put forward to explain these results. They include the following:

- Although the 1992 Programme was 'formally' implemented and the Single Market introduced in 1993, the process of actually 'digesting' all the changes still needs additional time. In spite of the big wave of (defensive) mergers and acquisitions around the year 1990, the exploitation of new opportunities for output and business on an enlarged market (free of NTBs) will require more time. This is relevant both for the manufacturing sector end, even more important, for services.
- The reunification of Germany has affected the performance of the EU.

III CONCLUSION

Econometrics has advanced a great deal since the 1960s, but it is still unable to solve some important methodological issues. The problem is bolstered by the complexity of the modern economy. Has it grown in such a way and is it changing so fast that it has become unmeasurable? It is, however, recognized that it is better to measure in some way, even with all the limitations of modelling, than not to measure at all. The problems which appear concern the choice of assumptions: the base year and length of time series before and after integration. The structure of foreign trade changes throughout time, new goods and services appear, old ones disappear while tastes change. The quality of goods and services changes over time and technology becomes more productive. Capacity utilization within broadly defined sectors escapes scrutiny. All these issues jeopardize generalizations about the long-term structure and pattern of trade. Business cycles make comparisons of prices among countries questionable. A part of trade flows (traditional trade or unique commodities) is independent of international economic integration. Hence, inter-temporal estimates are very complex indeed.

While trade creation indicates new imports of goods from partner countries and a reduction of the same quantity of domestic production, trade diversion indicates a reduction of imports from (and production in) third countries, as well as new imports and production in partner countries. Therefore, a comprehensive measurement of the effects of integration does not require only analysis of trade data, but also data on production (El-Agraa, 1989, p. 346).

Changes other than international economic integration need be considered too. These refer to a reduction of tariffs and NTBs to trade under the auspices of the GATT/WTO. These modifications are not a direct consequence of the creation of either the EU or the EFTA although regional integration deals contributed to the negotiations about the reductions in tariffs and NTBs. Other alterations include the introduction of convertibility in the late 1950s and an increase in US investment in western Europe. Hence, formal integration is not the only reason for an increase in economic and investment activity.

Assumptions about unchangeable market shares for the purpose of the extrapolation of trends means that technology, competition, costs, tastes, elasticities and economic policy are fixed. The availability and comparability of data may be also criticized. Actual production and trade does not mean that all potentials are fully utilized. Unfortunately, there exists no model which accurately measures unused potential.

Customs duties are made public, but their implementation is often formidable. Only a part of the reduction in tariffs is passed on to the consumers in the form of lower prices. The prices of imported goods are often set (by means of various taxes and price discrimination policies of firms[5]) with reference to competing home goods if they exist. Technology and inputs for the standardized products are available to all producers, but the final goods are often produced at different prices. The answer to this question may be found in X-inefficiency.

Adjustment to integration is not instantaneous. Integration and growth-induced forces are interlaced. Integration-induced effects may dominate the more sudden the integration. Growth-induced effects may dominate over a longer time. The more gradual the integration and the longer the period of observation, the more the effects will be mixed up (Lipsey, 1976, p. 38). Part of the answer to this problem may be found in models inspired by the work of Romer (1986).

The analysis has revealed that there are serious drawbacks in the econometric modelling and interpretation of the results of international economic integration. All models should be viewed with a certain degree of suspicion as they rely on a number of restrictive assumptions and a complexity of the effects. One wonders if slightly different assumptions might have not produced a completely different econometric result. The final outcome of all estimations is always a blend of various effects. The whole analysis, therefore, suffers from an identification problem, that is, how to distinguish between the effects of integration from the various other influences. This has so far been unfortunate for econometrics, not for the effects of international economic integration.

Baldwin (1993) treated the problems of measurement of dynamic effects of international economic integration. Certain politicians and many economists believe that economic integration is an engine of growth. The available estimates of the effects of integration do not fully justify these expectations. While the static effects of economic integration were believed to produce more output from a given set of inputs, the dynamic effects were assumed to affect the accumulation of factors. The measurement of both effects is tricky, in particular in the case of the dynamic effects as it takes decades to accumulate factors and to reach a new steady-state equilibrium. In addition, integration does not affect all industries and all participating countries in an identical way. Problems are also amplified by our lack of a full understanding of what governs investment in human and physical capital in the short and medium term. The same holds for savings. The variable impact of integration on different industries and countries is the principal drawback of the quantitative estimates. In general, economic integration is expected to have the strongest impact on the competitive behaviour and productivity in traded goods and industries characterized by the economies of scale. These are activities that employ a lot of human and physical capital, hence economic integration has the potential to increase the return on capital.

There is, sometimes, conflicting evidence regarding the effects of integration, in particular, regarding the 1992 Programme. For example, Neven (1990) concluded that the 1992 Programme was relatively unimportant to the northern EU member countries since they have already used most of the potential for large-scale production. Alternatively, Smith and Venables (1988) and Cecchini/Emerson believed that the potential for economies of scale were significant throughout the EU. This puzzle reveals that there does not yet exist a full understanding of the determinants of trade and production patterns in the EU and that the analyses of integration will remain speculative (Norman, 1990, p. 52).

A meaningful comparison of the gap in price for a good in different parts of an integrated area ought to reflect not only the transport costs, as was traditionally the case, but also the consumption pattern in different countries. The problems of measurement become immense because income, tastes, traditions and climate may be very different even within the confines of a single country. The greater the diversity of the integrated countries the harder the test.

A pragmatic way to encounter the effects of international economic integration may be to follow the structure of home consumption (proportions of home made goods, commodities imported from partner countries and goods from third countries). Another way may be to compare the relative prices of equal goods and services on the markets of the integrated countries. In a well integrated area such as the US with no differences in tastes, income and climate, these prices may differ only for costs of transport.

The magnitude of the effects of international economic integration will be debated for a long time. It is widely accepted that integration increases potentials for economic gains. The actual and perceived distribution of costs and benefits of these effects matters a lot. However, when one participant gains from integration it does not mean that others lose. It is essential that every participant gains more in the long term than is able to gain when acting alone.

In spite of significant improvements in techniques for measuring the effects of international economic integration the studies presented reveal an important puzzle. That is our lack of full understanding of the determinants, operation and effect of integration on trade, production, investment and consumption. Until this is solved, the nature of the analysis of integration will remain speculative. Attempts to solve these problems, in particular the dynamic ones, will be on the research agenda for the future.

NOTES

1 If one removed barriers to trade such as tariffs, quotas and biased public procurement, one might reasonably expect an increase in trade (trade creation). If such domestic barriers were removed from commerce with foreign country A, but not with country B, as is the case in customs unions, imports from country A may increase at the expense of the imports from country B (trade diversion). Mayes considered three types of quantitative models. First were residual (*ex post*) models. They compared various hypothetical situations (often referred to as the anti-monde of what would have happened had the integration not taken place) to the actual situation. Second were simple analytic (*ex ante*) models that tried to predict the course of developments in the near future. Third were the dynamic models. The process of integration takes place over time and is not limited to the simple static effects of trade creation and diversion. However, analytical tools were, at the time, modest for such a complicated econometric exercise.

2 A non-market-based economic system and integration in the former CMEA created controversies. Dietz (1986) attempted to estimate effects of trade in the CMEA. One view was that in this group the Soviet Union, at that time, used political clout in order to obtain economic advantages in trade relations with east European countries. Another one was that the Soviet Union was heavily

subsidizing these countries through the CMEA pricing system. These gains/loses included the difference in the world market price (most notably for energy) and the internal CMEA price for the same good. The finding was that the Soviet Union gave subsidies to its CMEA partners, but these were much smaller than the ones estimated in earlier studies.

3 Balassa (1967) employed an *ex post* model for the comparison of income elasticities of import demand in intra-area and extra-area trade, for periods that preceded and followed integration in the EU. There was evidence of trade creation and no indication of trade diversion.

4 The interested reader is invited to consult Sapir (1996) for another assessment of the effects of the 1992 Programme.

5 Different pricing of the same model of a car in various member countries of the EU is a prime example of such a policy.

7 Conclusion

Free trade and an unimpeded movement of factors is the first best policy in a world which does not have any distortions, but this is only a hypothetical scenario. The real situation is full of market imperfections that may be corrected and/or exploited by the employment of an economic policy (intervention). The rationale for international economic integration can be found in the case where market imperfections exist. When one distortion (e.g. a universal tariff of a country) is replaced by another (e.g. the common external tariff of a customs union) the net effect may be obscure. Theory about regional economic integration (an introverted economic strategy, to a degree) is the analysis of second best situations. It is, therefore, not surprising that general theoretical principles may not be found. What matters, however, is not solely the predictions of theory, but rather what happens in real life.

The gains that international economic integration provides can be summarized as follows:

- Integration extends, improves and secures the markets for a country's goods and services against abrupt changes in the trade policy of partners in the future. Hence, integration can be seen as an 'insurance policy' against sudden and unilateral economic actions by partners in the deal.
- Improvement in the efficiency of the use of resources due to increased competition, specialization and returns to scale. This increases average standards of living.
- Integration results in more efficient manufacturing and service sectors.
- Creation of new technologies, goods and services.
- Integration reduces the cost of a national import-substitution policy.
- International action limits, to an extent, the possibility for unnecessary public intervention in the economy because it extends the scope of economic policy across several countries.
- Wider and secure markets increase investment opportunities for both domestic firms and TNCs. Expectations may be established with an increased degree of security.
- Trade creation and trade diversion.

- International coordination of economic policies.
- Creation of the potential for monetary stability.
- Relatively larger markets have a potentially greater capacity for coping with various distortions than smaller markets, because larger markets may more easily offset the impact of both favourable and unfavourable effects. Vulnerability to external shocks can be reduced.
- Integration arrangements also exist because trade barriers can be adapted according to the preferences of the countries involved.
- Integration partners have a greater degree of mutual understanding and trust, that is often lacking on the global scale. A relatively small number of participants may create cosy relations, make monitoring of the deal easier and friendly while positive cooperation within the group may potentially help the exchange favours, reach agreement and (perhaps) settle disputes in a faster and more efficient way than is the case in multilateral institutions.
- Improvement in bargaining positions with external partners.
- Terms of trade effects and gains to exporters provide benefits from preferential trading agreements that are not available from unilateral trade liberalization policies.
- Stimulation of economic growth.

Given the above motives for regional integration, it is not necessary to resort exclusively to non-economic reasons for economic integration. However, there are still many unanswered and emerging questions regarding international economic integration. Annex IV provides a brief list of research topics for the future.

A customs union or any regional trading bloc may be seen as a compromise between two groups of protagonists promoting seemingly irreconcilable principles of economic policy: free-traders and protectionists. Having made the compromise in a regional group, the former are happy about the abolition of barriers on intra-bloc trade, while the latter are glad about the continuation of barriers against extra-bloc imports. Does it make any sense to ask who has made the greater concession in reaching the compromise? The question makes sense indeed, and the answer depends on the height of the trade barriers abolished and that of the barriers retained (Machlup, 1979, p. 102).

It is hard to forecast with a high degree of accuracy when and how the effects of integration will turn out. In the short term, just after the lifting of barriers to trade, production, GNP and commerce may increase while some prices may fall. In addition, some increase in unemployment may occur in the short run because of intensified competition and the unfinished adjustment process. In the medium and long term, structural adjustment takes place and economies of scale occur, retraining and mobility of labour reduces unemployment because new jobs are being created. Market rigidities are being eased as agents change their behaviour due to increased opportunities for business and competition. It is in this context that the dynamic effects of integration are materialized.[1]

When there exist economies of scale, changes in technology, sunk costs, imperfect competition and/or FDI, it is select intervention in the form of economic policy (for example, investment/production subsidies; development of human resources through education; protection for a limited period of time) which may successfully correct those market imperfections. The theory of strategic trade and industrial policy which takes into account market imperfections, supplements the smooth and straightforward conclusions of the neo-classical theory. Under certain assumptions, free trade may be an attractive economic policy. In more realistic conditions, however, judicious intervention (of which integration/regionalization is a part) may fare even better. This is only a possibility, not a definite outcome as the 'lone-wolf' development strategies of Sweden (until it joined the EU in 1995), Switzerland, Taiwan, South Korea, Singapore or Hong Kong have shown. However, the economic performance of these countries may be the exception, rather than a general rule. None the less, in 'normal' circumstances countries grow richer together, not at each others' expense. Hence the need for cooperation (if not integration) on a larger international scale.

A relatively big and integrated market is not a guarantee in itself that international economic integration will bring both satisfactory and desired economic outcomes. This evidence can be found in the cases of Russia and India, as well as China (perhaps until the 1990s). Contrasting evidence can be traced in the impressive experience in individualistic development of the small countries mentioned. A country's prosperity does not depend on its size and natural resources, since more important are human resources, as well as the political and regulatory framework. None the less, relatively larger markets may have the potential for a greater capacity in coping with the various distortions than smaller markets, because they may more easily offset the impact of both favourable and unfavourable effects. This presents the case in favour of integration. Although all countries are not under the same kind of pressure to adjust, joint action by countries may offer attractive economies of scale in economic policy relative to the situation where each country acts alone.

Large and developed countries depend to a lesser degree on external relations than do small countries. In theory, these countries may have a diversified economic structure which allows for an autarchic economic policy, while such a policy for small countries in a situation with economies of scale and other externalities does not have an economic rationale. Without a secure and free access to a market wider than the national one, a relatively limited domestic market and demand in small countries often prevents the employment of the most efficient technology, even if trade barriers are prohibitive. If some production takes place, the consequences include short production runs, high prices and lower standard of living. The efficient operation of many modern technologies requires secure access to the widest market, which does not exist in small, and sometimes, medium-sized countries. That is why large economies such as the US, Germany, France or Brazil get involved in economic integration. The elimination of tariffs, NTBs, restrictions on factor mobility, as well as the international coordination of economic policies and integration can be solutions to this problem of country size. The goal is to increase, improve and secure access to markets by the participating countries.

In a situation of imperfect competition, a score of various economic outcomes can happen. This is different from the case of perfect competition where a narrow range of outcomes is clear. The objective of this book is not to give *carte blanche* to intervention, it is much more modest than that. This book argues that in a situation with market imperfections, 'smart' intervention (integration is a part of it), under certain conditions, may have a more favourable welfare outcome than the 'free' play of market forces. This does not supplant the neo-classical economic model, but rather enriches it with another possibility that needs to be considered during the policy-making process. Any theoretically respectable case for intervention may often find support for the wrong reasons. Intervention is capable of provoking a chain of retaliations and counter-retaliations which may impoverish everybody.

Regional economic integration is not an enterprise without risks of adjustment. On those grounds some countries may accept protectionism as an attractive alternative to integration. National protectionism may offer in the short run some advantages over a relatively outward oriented economic policy that includes integration. Such a choice is defensive in its nature. International markets and technology continuously increase their speed of change. To petrify the status quo by endless protection is the surest way to economic disaster in the long run, when every country will face the need to adjust. If economic policy provides a friendly environment with continuous adjustment, then the costs of relatively smooth shifts may be smaller than the big-bang adjustment which may occur after a long period of protection, as was exemplified by the long, difficult and uncertain transition process towards a market-type economy in the countries of central and eastern Europe.

Free competition within the group is not likely to destroy all business in some of the participating countries. Two instruments will prevent such a disastrous scenario. First is the adjustment period to new circumstances that will gradually enable firms to reallocate resources. A country with serious adjustment problems may seek free access to the markets of partner countries some time before it offers the same concession to these partners. The exchange rate is the second safety valve which will prevent such a catastrophe. The experience of the EU, EFTA and NAFTA showed that economic adjustment to integration took place smoothly. Trade, production, economic growth and employment had an increasing trend in the long term. If structural problems did occur, then they were due to increases in prices for oil, competition from the newly industrializing countries or, most often, a poor national macroeconomic policy, not integration.

International economic integration limits, to an extent, the possibility for unnecessary public intervention in the economy because it extends the scope of economic policy to at least two countries. The result is increased competition which may create more efficient industry and services sectors. An additional benefit of integration is that it reduces the cost of a national import-substitution policy. Integration is, however, not a cure for all economic ills. It is only a supporting tool to the national economic policy. Integration creates opportunities for increased competition on an enlarged market, but it also depends on an astute macroeconomic policy and similar policies in education (investment in human capital that is supposed to solve problems), R&D and investment in capital goods, as well as the interest of firms to take advantages of the newly created environment.

One of the difficulties of international economic integration is that its gains accrue in the long run to everybody, but in relatively small instalments. The costs of integration may be more easily identified. They affect certain visible and vociferous segments of business and labour, but their effects may have only a relatively short-term impact on the national economy. The coordination of economic policies which may be brought by regional integration has the potential to exercise its full beneficial effects only in the long run. These joint economic policies should not be abandoned even if they do not bring the desired results in the short run. Enhanced competition and economies of scale exert a downward pressure on costs and prices. This enables an increase in non-inflationary growth. None the less, it is unclear how this would happen in practice. It may occur through increased output with unchanged inflation or less price inflation or, and most likely, a mixture of both. One real problem is that the gains of international economic integration may not be easily comprehended by non-economists.

External countries may experience unfavourable effects from integration. Trade diversion is an example. But if integrated countries grow at a faster rate than in the case without integration, their income may increase and, by such acceleration, the integrated countries may expand their trade with outside countries. Although the EU was in recession in 1992, EU imports from third countries continued to grow in spite of fears of a 'Fortress Europe'.

The theory of international economic integration has been basically Eurocentric as Europe was the area where regional integration has had its most significant impact since the 1950s. Its application to the case of developing countries may be enhanced by cost–benefit analysis. The classical theory of customs unions found that a customs union among the developing countries would be trade diverting in most cases. This is due to the fact that the developing countries are for many goods and services higher-cost suppliers than industrialized and newly industrialized countries. The existing structure of production and trade does not provide a rationale for economic integration among many developing countries. It is, however, the potential for change in this structure which could provide the rationale for integration among the developing countries. Integration and adequate intervention (economic policy) may offer attractive gains. None the less, previous integration arrangements among developing countries have had at best very limited results. In certain cases, they were a waste of time and resources. The potential for the future may be found in north–south integration as was the case with Mexico which integrated with the US and Canada. Integration between partners at different levels of development may take place in the future in the EU once a select group of central European countries satisfies conditions for entry and is accepted to join the EU. A certain kind of economic 'cooperation' in the Pacific region may take place in the coming decades and some 'stronger economic links' across the Mediterranean may be discussed in a (distant) future.

Countries throughout the world have revived their interest in regional economic integration since the early 1990s. Regional free trade arrangements are expanding all around the world. However, past attempts at integration have been achieved with very different degrees of success in relation to the stated objectives, expectations and potential. One of the possible explanations for the slowness in economic integration may be traced to the non-acceptance of supranationality. Small countries, in particular, have to learn that it is much less a matter of actual economic sovereignty and integration, and much more a choice between one or another form of interdependence.

In spite of various economic arguments in favour of integration, there are still a number of controversies as the real and full dynamic gains and costs of integration are still not known. If regional integration is now here to stay for a long time, what are the disposable means to make these trading blocs complementary with the multilateral trading system? The situation at the end of the 1990s is much different from that in the 1960s when south–south integration deals were operated in an inward-looking environment. Many of the integration schemes among the developing countries were mistakes that are not worth repeating. The potential for the expansion of intra-regional trade was simply not there. In that situation, a promising avenue is to explore possibilities for north–south integration in the future (de Melo and Panagariya, 1992). A potentially encouraging example for the future along the north–south integration lines to Latin American (and other) developing countries is set by the NAFTA.[2] However, there are also certain potentials for the regional integration among the developing countries in the MERCOSUR, but this group still has to prove itself in the future.

An inevitable question is whether integration/regionalism is a good or a bad thing? The answer to this depends on a further question: for whom? For the multilateral trading system it may be bad. For individual countries it may not be the case in the short term. Many countries did not have much confidence in the multilateral trading system. In general, regional integration arrangements were neither in themselves liberal nor 'illiberal'. Their impact on trade depended on the provisions of the scheme, the way in which they evolved and the potential collision with the trade policies of third countries. The pace of post-1960s trade liberalization trends and the entry of the GATT/WTO into new fields such as agriculture and services might be slower in the absence of the challenge posed by the evolution of the EU. Hence, regional integration in Europe has been 'friendly' to multilateral trade liberalization (Blackhurst and Henderson, 1993).

The costs of regional integration arrangements such as the NAFTA and the EU's 1992 Programme on world welfare may exceed the benefits; however, this is only a possibility, not a certainty.[3] The erosion of the multilateral process was a consequence of the declining role of the US and growing importance of new players (such as Japan) in the world economy; change in the structure of production (the move towards knowledge-intensive goods and services and operations of TNCs); and the changing character of protectionism ('voluntary' export restraint deals, harassment by countervailing measures, etc.). An answer to these challenges was found in regionalism. For example, the 1992 Programme of the EU was an agreement to coordinate policies that have historically been regarded as domestic. The case against free trade agreements is their possibility of harming efforts to deal with problems of the multilateral system. Key players, such as the EU and partners in the NAFTA, diverted certain political energies away from working on the problems of the GATT. If these energies were directed towards the GATT, perhaps, the Uruguay Round of negotiations could have had better results than the regional solutions! Could the GATT really have done much better in the absence of moves towards regional free trade areas? This did not seem to be too likely. In fact, the multilateral trading situation would not be much better without the recent 'great' free trade agreements, and could easily have been worse (Krugman, 1995)![4]

In spite of observations that regional integration was supporting multilateral trade liberalization, rather that preventing it, there is a warning note. Integration reduced incentives to take into account global welfare. Hence, it may still be puzzling if the member countries of the EU would have been on a higher or lower level of protection without the EU or not? The decision-making process in Brussels makes the EU prone to yielding to various lobbies such as farmers and producers of iron, steel and cars. The common policy of the EU was often set in such a way to reflect that of the most protectionist member country. Hence, the existence of the EU on the international trading system has not been entirely benign.

Dr Samuel Johnson's (1709–84) remark 'Like a dog walking on his hind legs. It is not well done, but you are surprised to find it done at all' aptly describes integration arrangements among countries. International economic integration increases the potential for significant world-wide improvements in economic welfare. However, countries have to organize themselves both individually and collectively to reap these benefits. National economic policies concerning investment, industrial change, R&D, mobility of people and knowledge, investment in human capital (education) that develops and extends skills, experience and organizational competencies of the most important factor is crucial for the efficiency side of the economy; and regional and social matters, on the equity side of it, are absolutely crucial for the success, evolution, cohesion and survival of integration schemes.[5]

The main conclusion is that international economic integration is a desirable economic strategy for small and medium-sized countries in a world with continuous changes in technology and market situation. Integration can increase and secure foreign markets for a variety of a country's goods and services in the future and, hence, mitigate the inevitable costs of adjustment to change. The opponents of integration for small countries would have to answer the question: how much is it worth to lose the market and other potentials for expanded business for the 'gain' to retain the sovereign right to carry on with (a bad) home economic policy which is insulated from international influences?

International economic integration is not an economic policy choice which would frighten small and medium-sized countries. The only thing which these countries will lose while integrating is the illusion that international economic integration is a bad policy choice.

NOTES

1 There was (and perhaps still is) a confusion that external trade policy including integration affects the aggregate level of employment. Trade policy alters the structure of employment within different economic sectors and the overall standard of living, i.e. the kind of jobs available, rather then whether they are available or not.

   A relatively high and stubborn unemployment rate in the EU is mainly due to rigid national labour markets, not to European integration. Primary measures to cope with the problem are at *national*, not EU level. Perhaps, without integration, unemployment would be even higher.

2 An earlier example of integration of partners at a different level of economic development was the entry of Greece, Portugal and Spain into the EU. A customs union between the EU and Turkey is another example. Future examples could include eastern enlargement of the EU.

3 The distorting effects of the EU's Common Agricultural Policy on international trade must always be kept in mind.

4 Renato Ruggiero, Director-General of the WTO, wrote in the comment to the *International Herald Tribune* (28 November 1996) that 'regional agreements have been a generally positive force for liberalization'.

5 The equity side of economic life is provoked by the polarization effect due to market imperfections and it is requested by the desire of the 'losers' to share the benefits of integration.

Annex I
GATT: Regional Integration
Agreements

Regional integration agreements notified to GATT since its inception are listed in chronological order according to the date of signature. (Agreements have at times been concluded by countries in the same geographic region, and in other cases, have involved countries in different regions, but the term 'regional integration' covers both.) For each entry, seven columns of information are provided: (i) name of the agreement; (ii) participating countries; (iii) the form in which the agreement was presented (for example, free trade area, customs union or preferential trade arrangement); (iv) the document reference for the text of the agreement; (v) the date of signature; (vi) the date of entry into force; and (vii) the GATT action taken and section B corresponding document references. Section A of the table concerns agreements notified under Article XXIV, and section B concerns agreements covered by or notified under the 1979 Enabling Clause.

I TRADE AGREEMENTS NOTIFIED UNDER ARTICLE XXIV

In accordance with the Decision of the Council of 25 October 1972 (19S/13), contracting parties that sign an agreement falling within the terms of Article XXIV are to inscribe the item on the agenda of the first meeting of the Council following its signature. Members of the agreement provide the text of the agreement to contracting parties in order to permit them to review the agreement. The third column of the table describes the manner in which the agreement was presented by its members in the GATT (for example, free-trade area, customs union). This information reflects GATT provisions and may consequently not convey other aspects of the agreement (for example, liberalization of services, commitments regarding labour standards or competition policies). The final column reports the last GATT action taken. A working party is generally established which submits a report and recommendations, if any, to the Council. The entry does not contain reference to the biennial reporting requirement established for regional agreements under the Decision of 26 November 1971 (L/3641). Contracting parties claiming to have completed the implementation of free trade areas or customs unions (for example, the European Community, the European Free Trade Area, the Australia–New Zealand Closer Economic Relations Agreement) have not submitted reports, and the calendar for such reports has not been revived since 1987.

	Name	Participating countries	Presented as	Text	Signature	Entry into force	GATT action taken and document references
1.	South Africa-Southern Rhodesia Customs Union Agreement[1]	South Africa and Zimbabwe (Southern Rhodesia)	Interim agreement for the formation of a customs union	CP.3/96.	6 Dec. 1948	1 Apr. 1949	Working Party Report adopted on 18 May 1949 (II/176). Declaration of 18 May 1949 (II/29). Decision of 17 Nov. 1954 (3S/47).
2.	El Salvador-Nicaragua Free Trade Area	El Salvador and Nicaragua	Free trade area	CP/104/Add.1	9 Mar. 1951	21 Aug. 1951	Decision of 25 Oct. 1951 (II/30).
3.	European Economic Community (EEC) and European Atomic Energy Community[2]	Belgium, France, Germany, Italy, Luxembourg and Netherlands	Customs union and common market for nuclear products	L/626	25 Mar. 1957	1 Jan. 1958	Committee Report adopted on 29 Nov. 1957 (6S/70). Report of the Intersessional Committee and Thirteenth Session (7S/69).
4.	Participation of Nicaragua in the Central American Free Trade Area[3]	Costa Rica, El Salvador, Guatemala, Honduras and Nicaragua	Free trade area	L/891	10 June 1958	2 June 1959	Decision of 13 Nov. 1956 (5S/29).
5.	Equatorial Customs Union and Cameroon	Cameroon,[4] Central African Republic, Chad, Congo and Gabon	Customs union	L/2061	23 June 1959	1 July 1962	Working Party Report adopted on 2 Mar. 1964 (12S/73).
6.	European Free Trade Association (EFTA)[5]	Austria, Denmark, Norway, Portugal, Sweden, Switzerland[6] and United Kingdom	Free trade area	L/1167	4 Jan. 1960	3 May 1960	Working Party Report adopted on 4 June 1960 (9S/70). Conclusions adopted on 18 Nov. 1960 (9S/20).
7.	Latin American Free Trade Association (LAFTA)[7]	Argentina, Brazil, Chile, Peru and Uruguay	Interim agreement leading to the formation of a free trade area	L/1157	18 Feb. 1960	2 June 1961	Working Party Report adopted on 18 Nov. 1960 (9S/87). Conclusions adopted on 18 Nov. 1960 (9S/21).

	Name	Participating countries	Presented as	Text	Signature	Entry into force	GATT action taken and document references
8.	Participation of Nicaragua in the General Treaty for Central American Economic Integration[8]	Costa Rica, El Salvador, Guatemala, Honduras and Nicaragua	Interim agreement leading to the formation of a free trade area and equalization of customs duties and charges	L/1425 and Add.1	13 Dec. 1960	June 1961	Working Party Report adopted on 23 Nov. 1961 (10S/98). Decision of 23 Nov. 1961 (10S/48).
9.	Borneo Free Trade Area[9]	Sarawak and North Borneo	Free trade area	L/1630	1961[10]	1 Jan. 1962	Oral statement by the Chairman of the CONTRACTING PARTIES (SR.19/12).
10.	EFTA-Finland Association Agreement (FINEFTA)[11]	EFTA member states (Austria, Denmark, Norway, Portugal, Sweden, Switzerland and United Kingdom) and Finland	Interim agreement for the formation of a free trade area	L/1451	27 Mar. 1961	26 June 1961	Working Party Report adopted on 23 Nov. 1961 (10S/101). Conclusions adopted on 23 Nov. 1961 (10S/24).
11.	Ghana-Upper Volta Trade Agreement	Ghana and Burkina Faso (Upper Volta)	Free trade area	L/1766	28 June 1961	9 May 1962	Working Party established. Oral statement by the Chairman of the CONTRACTING PARTIES referring the agreement to the Working Party established to examine the African Common Market (SR.20/4).
12.	EEC-Greece Association Agreement[12]	EEC member states (Belgium, France, Germany, Italy, Luxembourg and Netherlands) and Greece	Interim agreement for the formation of a customs union	L/1601	9 July 1961	1 Nov. 1962	Working Party Report adopted on 15 Nov. 1962 (11S/149). Conclusions adopted on 15 Nov. 1962 (11S/56).

No.	Name	Type	Document	Date	Date	Working Party
13.	African Common Market	Algeria, United Arab Republic, Ghana, Guinea, Mali and Morocco	Customs union	L/1835	1 Apr. 1962	1 July 1963	Working Party established (SR.20/4).
14.	EEC-Association with African and Malagasy States (Yaoundé I)[13]	EEC member states (Belgium, France, Germany, Italy, Luxembourg and Netherlands), and Burundi, Cameroon, Central African Republic, Chad, Congo, Côte d'Ivoire, Benin (Dahomey), Burkina Faso (Upper Volta), Gabon, Madagascar (Malagasy Republic), Mali, Mauritania, Niger, Rwanda, Senegal, Somalia and Togo	Interim agreements for the formation of bilateral free trade areas between the EEC and each member state	L/2160/Add.1	20 July 1963	1 Jan. 1964	Working Party Report on Yaoundé I and EEC-PTOM I adopted on 4 Apr. 1966 (14S/100). Conclusions adopted on 4 Apr. 1966 (14S/22).
15.	EEC-Turkey Association Agreement[14]	EEC member states (Belgium, France, Germany, Italy, Luxembourg and Netherlands) and Turkey	Interim agreement for the formation of a customs union	L/2155/Add.1	12 Sept. 1963	1 Dec. 1964	Working Party Report adopted on 25 Mar. 1965 (13S/59).
16.	EEC-Association with certain non-European countries and territories maintaining special relations with France and the Netherlands (EEC-PTOM I)[15]	EEC member states (Belgium, France, Germany, Italy, Luxembourg and Netherlands), and Comoros Archipelago, French Polynesia, French Somali Coast, Southern and Antarctic Territories, Mayotte, New Caledonia and Dependencies, St. Pierre and Miquelon, Suriname, Wallis and Fortuna Islands and Netherlands Antilles	Free trade area	L/2342	25 Feb. 1964	1 June 1964	Working Party Report on Yaoundé I and EEC-PTOM I adopted on 4 Apr. 1966 (14S/100). Conclusions adopted on 4 Apr. 1966 (14S/22).
17.	Arab Common Market	Egypt, Iraq, Jordan and Syria	Interim agreement for the formation of a free trade area leading to a customs union	L/2366 and Corr.2	13 Aug. 1964	1 Jan. 1965	Working Party Report adopted on 6 Apr. 1966 (14S/94). Conclusions adopted on 6 Apr. 1966 (14S/20).

	Name	Participating countries	Presented as	Text	Signature	Entry into force	GATT action taken and document references
18.	Australia–New Zealand Free-Trade Agreement[16]	Australia and New Zealand	Interim agreement for the formation of a free trade area	L/2485/ Add.1	31 Aug. 1965	1 Jan. 1966	Working Party Report adopted on 5 Apr. 1966 (14S/115). Conclusions adopted on 5 Apr. 1966 (14S/22).
19.	Ireland–United Kingdom Free Trade Area Agreement[17]	Ireland and United Kingdom	Free trade area	L/2552/ Add.1	14 Dec. 1965	1 July 1966	Working-Party Report adopted 5 Apr. 1966 (14S/122). Conclusions adopted on 5 Apr. 1966 (14S/23).
20.	Caribbean Free-Trade Agreement (CARIFTA)[18]	Antigua, Barbados, Guyana and Trinidad and Tobago	Free trade area	L/3074	15 Dec. 1965	1 May 1968	Working Party Report adopted on 9 Nov. 1971 (18S/129).
21.	EEC-Tunisia Association Agreement[19]	EEC member States (Belgium, France, Germany, Italy, Luxembourg and Netherlands) and Tunisia	Interim agreement for the formation of a free trade area	L/3226/ Add.1 and Corr.1	28 Mar. 1969	1 Sept. 1969	Working Party Report adopted on 29 Sept. 1970 (18S/149).
22.	EEC-Morocco Association Agreement[20]	EEC member States (Belgium, France, Germany, Italy, Luxembourg and Netherlands) and Morocco	Interim agreement for the formation of a free trade area	L/3227/ Add.1 and Corr.1	31 Mar. 1969	1 Sept. 1969	Working Party Report adopted on 29 Sept. 1970 (18S/149).
23.	EEC-Association with African and Malagasy States (Yaoundé II)[21]	Member States of Yaoundé I and Mauritius[22]	Bilateral free trade areas between the EEC and each member state	L/3283	29 July 1969	1 Jan. 1971	Working Party Report adopted on 2 Dec. 1970 (18S/133).
24.	EEC-Association Agreement with the East African States (Arusha II Agreement)[23]	EEC member States (Belgium, France, Germany, Italy, Luxembourg and Netherlands) and Tanzania, Uganda and Kenya[24]	Free trade area	L/3369	24 Sept. 1969	1 Jan. 1971	Working Party Report adopted on 25 Oct. 1972 (19S/97).

	Agreement	Parties	Type of agreement	Document	Date(s)	Entry into force	Working Party Report
25.	EFTA and FINEFTA-Accession of Iceland	EFTA member States (Austria, Denmark, Norway, Portugal, Sweden, Switzerland and United Kingdom) and Finland and Iceland	Interim agreement for the formation of a free trade area	L/3328	4 Dec. 1969	1 Mar. 1970	Working Party Report adopted on 29 Sept. 1970 (18S/174).
26.	EEC-Israel Agreement[25]	EEC member States (Belgium, France, Germany, Italy, Luxembourg and Netherlands) and Israel	Interim agreement for the formation of a free trade area	L/3428 and Corr. 1	29 June 1970	1 Oct. 1970	Working Party Report adopted on 6 Oct. 1971 (18S/158).
27.	EEC-Spain Agreement[26]	EEC member States (Belgium, France, Germany, Italy, Luxembourg and Netherlands) and Spain	Interim agreement for the formation of a free trade area	L/3427 and Corr. 1	29 June 1970	1 Oct. 1970	Working Party Report adopted on 6 Oct. 1971 (18S/166).
28.	EEC-Association with certain non-European countries and territories (EEC-PTOM II)[27]	Member States of EEC-PTOM I	Free trade area	L/3467	29 Sept. 1970	1 Jan. 1971	Working Party Report adopted on 9 Nov. 1971 (18S/143).
29.	EEC-Turkey Additional Protocol to the Association Agreement and Interim Agreement[28]	EEC member States (Belgium, France, Germany, Italy, Luxembourg and Netherlands) and Turkey	Additional Protocol and Interim Agreement specifying transitional stage of formation of customs union	L/3554 L/3554/Add. 1, 2	23 Nov. 1970 27 July 1971	1 Jan. 1973 1 Sept. 1971	Working Party Report adopted on 25 Oct. 1972 (19S/102).
30.	EEC-Malta Association Agreement[29]	EEC member States (Belgium, France, Germany, Italy, Luxembourg and Netherlands) and Malta	Interim agreement for the formation of a customs union	L/3512	5 Dec. 1970	1 Apr. 1971	Working Party Report adopted on 29 May 1972 (19S/90).
31.	EEC-Accession of Denmark, Ireland and United Kingdom[30]	EEC member States (Belgium, France, Germany, Italy, Luxembourg and Netherlands) and Denmark, Ireland and United Kingdom	Customs union	L/3677	22 Jan. 1972	1 Jan. 1973	Working Party established. Oral statement of the Chairman (C/M/107).

Name	Participating countries	Presented as	Text	Signature	Entry into force	GATT action taken and document references
32. EEC-Austria Agreement[31]	EEC member States (Belgium, Denmark, France, Germany, Ireland, Italy, Luxembourg, Netherlands and United Kingdom) and Austria	Free trade area; coverage of ECSC products	L/3755/ Add.1 L/ 3783/Add.1	22 July 1972 (EEC-Austria) 22 July 1972 (ECSC-Austria)	1 Oct. 1972 (EEC-Austria) 1 Jan. 1974 (ECSC-Austria)	Working Party Report adopted on 19 Oct. 1973 (20S/145).
33. EEC-Switzerland and Liechtenstein Agreement	EEC member States (Belgium, Denmark, France, Germany, Ireland, Italy, Luxembourg, Netherlands and United Kingdom) and Switzerland and Liechtenstein	Free trade area; coverage of ECSC products	L/3758/Add. 1	22 July 1972 (EEC-Switzerland and Liechtenstein) 22 July 1972 (ECSC-Switzerland and Liechtenstein)	1 Jan. 1973 (EEC-Switzerland and Liechtenstein) 1 Jan. 1974 (ECSC-Switzerland and Liechtenstein)	Working Party Report adopted on 19 Oct. 1973 (20S/196).
34. EEC-Portugal Free Trade Agreement[32]	EEC member States (Belgium, Denmark, France, Germany, Ireland, Italy, Luxembourg, Netherlands and United Kingdom) and Portugal	Interim agreement for the formation of a free trade area	L/3781/Add. 1 and Corr. 1	22 July 1972	1 Jan. 1973 (EEC-Portugal) 1 Jan. 1974 (ECSC-Portugal)	Working Party Report adopted on 19 Oct. 1973 (20S/171).
35. EEC-Sweden Agreement[33]	EEC member States (Belgium, Denmark, France, Germany, Ireland, Italy, Luxembourg, Netherlands and United Kingdom) and Sweden	Free trade area; coverage of ECSC products	L/3782/Add. 1	22 July 1972 (EEC-Sweden) 22 July 1972 (ECSC-Sweden)	1 Jan. 1973 (EEC-Sweden) 1 Jan. 1974 (ECSC-Sweden)	Working Party Report adopted on 19 Oct. 1973 (20S/183).

No.	Agreement	Parties	Coverage	Document	Signature	Entry into force	Working Party Report
36.	EEC-Iceland Agreement	EEC member States (Belgium, Denmark, France, Germany, Italy, Luxembourg, Netherlands and United Kingdom) and Iceland	Free trade area; coverage of ECSC products	L/3780/Add. 1	22 July 1972 (EEC-Iceland) 22 July 1972 (ECSC-Iceland)	1 Apr. 1973 (EEC-Iceland) 1 Jan. 1974 (ECSC-Iceland)	Working Party Report adopted on 19 Oct. 1973 (20S/158).
37.	EEC-Lebanon Agreement[34]	EEC member States (Belgium, Denmark, France, Germany, Italy, Luxembourg, Netherlands and United Kingdom) and Lebanon	Interim agreement for the formation of a free trade area; Protocol to the agreement relating to new members of the EEC (Denmark, Ireland and United Kingdom)	L/4002	18 Dec. 1972 6 Nov. 1973	1 Jan. 1975	Working Party Report adopted on 3 Feb. 1975 (22S/43).
38.	EEC-Egypt Agreement[35]	EEC member States (Belgium, Denmark, France, Germany, Italy, Luxembourg, Netherlands and United Kingdom) and Egypt	Interim agreement for the formation of a free trade area; Protocol to the agreement relating to new members of EEC (Denmark, Ireland and United Kingdom)	L/3938/Add. 1	18 Dec. 1972 19 Dec. 1972	1 Nov. 1973	Working Party Report adopted on 19 July 1974 (21S/102).
39.	EEC-Cyprus Association Agreement[36]	EEC member States (Belgium, Denmark, France, Germany, Italy, Luxembourg, Netherlands and United Kingdom) and Cyprus	Interim agreement for the formation of a customs union	L/3870	19 Dec. 1972	1 June 1973	Working Party Report adopted on 21 June 1974 (21S/94).
40.	EEC-Norway Agreement	EEC member States (Belgium, Denmark, France, Germany, Italy, Luxembourg, Netherlands and United Kingdom) and Norway	Free trade area; coverage of ECSC products	L/3872 and Add. 1	14 May 1973 (EEC-Norway) 14 May 1973 (ECSC-Norway)	1 July 1973 (EEC-Norway) 1 Jan. 1975 (ECSC-Norway)	Working Party Report adopted on 28 Mar. 1974 (21S/83).

	Name	Participating countries	Presented as	Text	Signature	Entry into force	GATT action taken and document references
41.	EEC-Turkey Agreement	EEC member States (Belgium, Denmark, France, Germany, Ireland, Italy, Luxembourg, Netherlands and United Kingdom) and Turkey	Free trade area; coverage of ECSC products. Extension of association agreement to ECSC products and to new members of the EEC	L/3980	30 June 1973 (ECSC-Turkey) 30 June 1973 (EEC-Turkey)	1 Mar. 1986 (ECSC-Turkey) 1 Mar. 1986 (EEC-Turkey)	Working Party Report adopted on 21 Oct. 1974 (21S/108).
42.	Caribbean Community and Common Market (CARICOM)[37]	Barbados, Guyana, Jamaica and Trinidad and Tobago[38]	Interim agreement for the formation of a customs union	L/4083	4 July 1973	1 Aug. 1973	Working Party Report adopted on 2 Mar. 1977 (24S/68).
43.	EEC-Finland Agreement[39]	EEC member States (Belgium, Denmark, France, Germany, Ireland, Italy, Luxembourg, Netherlands and United Kingdom) and Finland	Free trade area; coverage of ECSC products	L/3973 and Corr. 1	5 Oct. 1973 (EEC-Finalnd) 5 Oct. 1973 (ECSC-Finland)	1 Jan. 1974 (EEC-Finland) 1 Jan. 1975 (ECSC-Finland)	Working Party Report adopted on 21 Oct. 1974 (21S/76).
44.	Bulgaria-Finland Agreement	Bulgaria and Finland	Free trade area	L/4137/Add. 1	26 Apr. 1974	1 Jan. 1975	Working Party established. Oral interim Report of the Chairman of the Working Party (C/M/117).
45.	Finland-Hungary Agreement on the Reciprocal Removal of Obstacles to Trade[40]	Finland and Hungary	Interim agreement for the formation of a free trade area	L/4136/Add. 1	2 May 1974	1 Jan. 1975	Working Party Report adopted on 31 Oct. 1975 (22S/47). Second Report adopted on 23 May 1977 (24S/107).

No.	Agreement	Parties	Description	Document			Working Party Report
46.	Czechoslovakia-Finland Agreement[41]	Czechoslovakia and Finland	Interim agreement for the formation of a free trade area	L/4138/Add. 1	19 Sept. 1974	1 Jan. 1975	Working Party Report adopted on 14 June 1976 (23S/67). Second Report adopted on 6 Nov. 1979 (26S/327).
47.	ACP-EEC Lomé Convention (First Lomé Convention)[42]	EEC member States (Belgium, Denmark, France, Germany, Ireland, Italy, Luxembourg, Netherlands and United Kingdom) and Bahamas, Barbados, Botswana, Burundi, Burkina Faso (Upper Volta), Cameroon, Central African Republic, Chad, Congo, Cote d'Ivoire, Benin (Dahomey), Ethiopia, Fiji, Gabon, Gambia, Ghana, Grenada, Guinea, Guinea Bissau, Equatorial Guinea, Guyana, Jamaica, Kenya, Lesotho, Liberia, Malawi, Madagascar (Malagasy Republic), Mali, Mauritius, Mauritania, Niger, Nigeria, Rwanda, Senegal, Sierra Leone, Somalia, Sudan, Swaziland, Tanzania, Togo, Tonga, Trinidad and Tobago, Uganda, Western Samoa, Zaire and Zambia[43]	Preferential, non-reciprocal access to the EEC market (Part IV claim)	L/4193, L/4198	28 Feb. 1975	1 Apr. 1976	Working Party Report adopted on 15 July 1976 (23S/46).
48.	Finland-German Democratic Republic Agreement[44]	Finland and German Democratic Republic	Interim agreement for the formation of a free trade area	L/4211	4 Mar. 1975	1 July 1975	Working Party Interim Report adopted on 2 Mar. 1977 (24S/106).[45]
49.	EEC-Greece Extension of Association Agreement[46]	EEC member States (Belgium, Denmark, France, Germany, Ireland, Italy, Luxembourg, Netherlands and United Kingdom) and Greece	Extension of the association agreement to new members of the EEC (Denmark, Ireland and United Kingdom)	L/4206	28 Apr. 1975	1 July 1975	Working Party Report adopted on 14 June 1976 (23S/64).

	Name	Participating countries	Presented as	Text	Signature	Entry into force	GATT action taken and document references
50.	EEC-Israel Agreement[47]	EEC member States (Belgium, Denmark, France, Germany, Ireland, Italy, Luxembourg, Netherlands and United Kingdom) and Israel	Agreement on the implementation of free trade area treatment; coverage of ECSC products	L/4194/ Add. 1	11 May 1975 (EEC-Israel) 11 May 1975 (ECSC-Israel)	1 July 1975 (EEC-Israel) 1 May 1978 (ECSC-Israel)	Working Party Report adopted on 15 July 1976 (23S/55).
51.	EEC-Tunisia Agreement[48]	EEC member States (Belgium, Denmark, France, Germany, Ireland, Italy, Luxembourg, Netherlands and United Kingdom) and Tunisia	Preferential non-reciprocal access to the EEC market (Part IV claim); coverage of ECSC products	L/4379	25 Apr. 1976 (EEC-Tunisia) 25 Apr. 1976 (ECSC-Tunisia)	1 July 1976 (EEC-Tunisia) 1 Nov. 1978 (ECSC-Tunisia)	Working Party Report adopted on 11 Nov. 1977 (24S/97).
52.	EEC-Algeria Interim Agreement[49]	EEC member States (Belgium, Denmark, France, Germany, Ireland, Italy, Luxembourg, Netherlands and United Kingdom) and Algeria	Preferential non-reciprocal access to the EEC market (Part IV claim); coverage of ECSC products	L/4380	26 Apr. 1976 (EEC-Algeria) 26 Apr. 1976 (ECSC-Algeria)	1 July 1976 (EEC-Algeria) 1 Nov. 1979 (ECSC-Algeria)	Working Party Report adopted 11 Nov. 1977 (24S/80).
53.	EEC-Morocco Co-operation Agreement[50]	EEC member States (Belgium, Denmark, France, Germany, Ireland, Italy, Luxembourg, Netherlands and United Kingdom) and Morocco	Preferential non-reciprocal access to the EEC market (Part IV claim); coverage of ECSC products	L/4381	27 Apr. 1976 (EEC-Morocco) 27 Apr. 1976 (ECSC-Morocco)	1 July 1976 (EEC-Morocco) 1 Nov. 1978 (ECSC-Morocco)	Working Party Report adopted on 11 Nov. 1977 (24S/88).
54.	EEC-Portugal Interim Agreement[51]	EEC member States (Belgium, Denmark, France, Germany, Ireland, Italy, Luxembourg, Netherlands and United Kingdom) and Portugal	Extension of free trade agreement	L/4419	20 Sept. 1976	1 Nov. 1976	Working Party Report adopted on 26 July 1977 (24S/73).
55.	Finland-Poland Agreement[52]	Finland and Poland	Interim agreement for the formation of a free trade area	L/4652	29 Sept. 1976	1 Apr. 1978	Working Party Report adopted on 26 Mar. 1980 (27S/136).

No.	Agreement	Parties	Type	Document	Signed	Entry into force	Working Party Report
56.	Australia-Papua New Guinea Trade and Commercial Relations Agreement (PATCRA)[53]	Australia and Papua New Guinea	Preferential non-reciprocal access to the Australian market	L/4451/Add.1	6 Nov. 1976	1 Feb. 1977	Working Party Report adopted on 11 Nov. 1977 (24S/63).
57.	EEC-Jordan Interim Agreement[54]	EEC member States (Belgium, Denmark, France, Germany, Ireland, Italy, Luxembourg, Netherlands and United Kingdom) and Jordan	Preferential non-reciprocal access to the EEC market (Part IV claim)	L/4523	18 Jan. 1977	1 July 1977	Working Party Report adopted on 17 May 1978 (25S/133).
58.	EEC-Syria Interim Agreement	EEC member States (Belgium, Denmark, France, Germany, Ireland, Italy, Luxembourg, Netherlands and United Kingdom) and Syria	Preferential non-reciprocal access to the EEC market (Part IV claim)	L/4522	18 Jan. 1977	1 July 1977	Working Party Report adopted on 17 May 1978 (25S/123).
59.	EEC-Egypt Interim Agreement[55]	EEC member States (Belgium, Denmark, France, Germany, Ireland, Italy, Luxembourg, Netherlands and United Kingdom) and Egypt	Preferential non-reciprocal access to the EEC market (Part IV claim)	L/4521	18 Jan. 1977	1 July 1977	Working Party Report adopted on 17 May 1978 (25S/114).
60.	EEC-Lebanon Interim Agreement[56]	EEC member States (Belgium, Denmark, France, Germany, Ireland, Italy, Luxembourg, Netherlands and United Kingdom) and Lebanon	Preferential non-reciprocal access to the EEC market (Part IV claim)	L/4524	3 May 1977	1 July 1977	Working Party Report adopted on 17 May 1978 (25S/142).
61.	EEC-Accession of Greece	EEC member States (Belgium, Denmark, France, Germany, Ireland, Italy, Luxembourg, Netherlands and United Kingdom) and Greece	Customs union	L/4845	28 May 1979	1 Jan. 1981	Working Party Report adopted on 9 Mar. 1983 (30S/168).
62.	EFTA-Spain Agreement[57]	EFTA member States (Austria, Iceland, Norway, Portugal, Sweden and Switzerland) and Spain	Interim agreement for the formation of a free trade area	L/4867	26 June 1979	1 May 1980	Working Party Report adopted on 10 Nov. 1980 (27S/127).

	Name	Participating countries	Presented as	Text	Signature	Entry into force	GATT action taken and document references
63.	ACP-EEC Second Lomé Convention[58]	Member States of the First Lomé Convention[59]	Preferential non-reciprocal access to the EEC market (Part IV claim)	L/5098	31 Oct. 1979	1 Jan. 1981	Working Party Report adopted on 31 Mar. 1982 (29S/119).
64.	EEC-Yugoslavia Agreement	EEC member States (Belgium, Denmark, France, Germany, Ireland, Italy, Luxembourg, Netherlands and United Kingdom) and Yugoslavia	Preferential non-reciprocal access to the EEC market (Part IV claim)	L/5007 and Add.1	6 May 1980	1 July 1980	Working Party Report adopted on 6 Oct. 1981 (28S/115).
65.	Australia-New Zealand Closer Economic Relations Trade Agreement (ANZCERT)[60]	Australia and New Zealand	Free trade area	L/5475	28 Mar. 1983	1 Jan. 1983	Working Party Report adopted on 2 Oct. 1984 (31S/170).
66.	ACP-EEC Third Lomé Convention[61]	Member States of the Second Lomé Convention and Mozambique[62]	Preferential non-reciprocal access to the EEC market (Part IV claim)	L/6109 and Add.1	8 Dec. 1984	1 Mar. 1986	Working Party Report adopted on 22 Sept. 1988 (35S/321).
67.	Israel-United States Free Trade Agreement	Israel and United States	Interim agreement for the formation of a free trade area	L/5862	22 Apr. 1985	1 Sept. 1985	Working Party Report adopted on 14 May 1987 (34S/58).
68.	EEC-Accession of Portugal and Spain[63]	EEC member States (Belgium, Denmark, France, Germany, Greece, Ireland, Italy, Luxembourg, Netherlands and United Kingdom) and Spain and Portugal	Customs union	L/5936 and Addenda	12 June 1985	1 Jan. 1986	Working Party Report adopted on 19–20 Oct. 1988 (35S/293).
69.	Canada-United States Free Trade Agreement[64]	Canada and United States	Interim agreement for the formation of a free trade area	L/6464 and Add.1	2 Jan. 1988	1 Jan. 1989	Working Party Report adopted on 12 Nov. 1991 (38S/47).

No.	Agreement	Parties	Description	Document	Date	Date	Remarks
70.	ACP-EEC Fourth Lomé Convention[65]	Member States of the Third Lomé Convention, plus Dominican Republic, Haiti and St. Christopher and Nevis	Preferential, non-reciprocal access to the EEC market (Part IV claim)	L/7153/Add.1	15 Dec. 1989	1 Mar. 1990	Working Party Report adopted on 4 October 1994 (L/7502).
71.	EFTA-Turkey Free Trade Agreement	EFTA member States (Austria, Finland, Iceland, Liechtenstein, Norway, Sweden and Switzerland) and Turkey	Interim agreement for the formation of a free trade area	L/6989/Add.1	10 Dec. 1991	30 Apr. 1992	Working Party Report adopted on 17 Dec. 1993 (L/7336).
72.	EC-Poland Interim Agreement	EC member States (Belgium, Denmark, France, Germany, Greece, Ireland, Italy, Luxembourg, Netherlands, Portugal, Spain and United Kingdom) and Poland	Interim agreement for the formation of a free trade area; coverage of ECSC products	L/6992/Add.1	16 Dec. 1991	1 Mar. 1992	Working Party on agreements between the EC and the Visegrad countries established on 30 Apr. 1992.
73.	EC-Czech and Slovak Federal Republic Interim Agreement	EC member States (Belgium, Denmark, France, Germany, Greece, Ireland, Italy, Luxembourg, Netherlands, Portugal, Spain and United Kingdom) and Czech and Slovak Federal Republic	Interim agreement for the formation of a free trade area; coverage of ECSC products	L/6992/Add.1	16 Dec. 1991	1 Mar. 1992	Working Party on agreements between the EC and the Visegrad countries established on 30 Apr. 1992.
74.	EC-Hungary Interim Agreement	EC member States (Belgium, Denmark, France, Germany, Greece, Ireland, Italy, Luxembourg, Netherlands, Portugal, Spain and United Kingdom) and Hungary	Interim agreement for the formation of a free trade area; coverage of ECSC products	L/6992/Add.1	16 Dec. 1991	1 Mar. 1992	Working Party on agreements between the EC and the Visegrad countries established on 30 Apr. 1992.
75.	Estonia-Finland Protocol Regarding Temporary Arrangements on Trade and Economic Co-operation	Estonia and Finland	Free trade area	L/7130/Add.1	13 Feb. 1992	1 May 1993	Working Party Report on agreements between Finland and the Baltic countries adopted on 17 Dec. 1993 (L/7339).

	Name	Participating countries	Presented as	Text	Signature	Entry into force	GATT action taken and document references
76.	Lithuania-Sweden Free Trade Agreement	Lithuania and Sweden	Free trade area	L/7036	17 Mar. 1992	15 Aug. 1992	Working Party Report on agreements between Sweden and the Baltic countries adopted on 17 Dec. 1993 (L/7338).
77.	Czech and Slovak Federal Republic-EFTA Free Trade Agreement	EFTA member States (Austria, Finland, Iceland, Liechtenstein, Norway, Sweden and Switzerland) and Czech and Slovak Federal Republic	Interim agreement for the formation of a free trade area	L/7041/ Add.1	20 Mar. 1992	1 July 1992	Working Party Report adopted on 8 Dec. 1994 (L/7570).
78.	Estonia-Sweden Free Trade Agreement	Estonia and Sweden	Free trade area	L/7036	31 Mar. 1992	1 July 1992	Working Party Report on agreements between Sweden and the Baltic countries adopted on 17 Dec. 1993 (L/7338).
79.	Latvia-Sweden Free Trade Agreement	Latvia and Sweden	Free trade area	L/7036	31 Mar. 1992	1 July 1992	Working Party Report on agreements between Sweden and the Baltic countries adopted on 17 Dec. 1993 (L/7338).
80.	Finland-Lithuania Protocol Regarding Temporary Arrangements on Trade and Economic Co-operation	Finland and Lithuania	Free trade area	L/7130/ Add.1	5 June 1992	1 May 1993	Working Party Report on agreements between Finland and the Baltic countries adopted on 17 Dec. 1993 (L/7339).
81.	Latvia-Norway Free-Trade Agreement	Latvia and Norway	Free trade area	L/7104/ Add.1	15 June 1992	Provisionally applied from 1 July 1992	Working Party Report on agreements between Norway and the Baltic countries adopted on 17 Dec. 1993 (L/7337).
82.	Estonia-Norway Free-Trade Agreement	Estonia and Norway	Free trade area	L/7104/ Add. 1	15 June 1992	Provisionally applied from 1 July 1992	Working Party Report on agreements between Norway and the Baltic countries adopted on 17 Dec. 1993 (L/7337).

No.	Agreement	Parties	Type	Document	Date	Application	Working Party
83.	Lithuania-Norway Free-Trade Agreement	Lithuania and Norway	Free trade area	L/7104/Add.1	15 June 1992	Provisionally applied from 1 July 1992	Working Party Report on agreements between Norway and the Baltic countries adopted on 17 Dec. 1993 (L/7337).
84.	EFTA-Israel Free Trade Agreement	EFTA member States (Austria, Finland, Iceland, Liechtenstein, Norway, Sweden and Switzerland) and Israel	Interim agreement for the formation of a free trade area	L/7129 and Add.1	17 Sept. 1992	1 Jan. 1993	Working Party established on 9–10 Feb. 1993.
85.	Czech Republic-Slovak Republic Customs Union Agreement[66]	Czech Republic and Slovak Republic	Customs union	L/7212	28 Oct. 1992	1 Jan. 1993	Working Party Report adopted on 4 Oct. 1994 (L/7501).
86.	Lithuania-Switzerland Free-Trade Agreement	Lithuania and Switzerland	Free trade area	L/7223/Add.1	24 Nov. 1992	Provisionally applied from 1 Apr. 1993	Working Party established on agreements between Switzerland and the Baltic States on 16–17 June 1993.
87.	Finland-Latvia Protocol Regarding Temporary Arrangements on Trade and Economic Co-operation	Finland and Latvia	Free trade area	L/7130/Add.1	26 Nov. 1992	1 July 1993	Working Party Report on agreements between Finland and the Baltic States adopted on 17 Dec. 1993 (L/7339).
88.	EFTA-Romania Free Trade Agreement	EFTA member States (Austria, Finland, Iceland, Liechtenstein, Norway, Sweden and Switzerland) and Romania	Interim agreement for the formation of a free trade area	L/7215/Add.1	10 Dec. 1992	1 May 1993[67]	Working Party established on 16–17 June 1993.
89.	EFTA-Poland Free Trade Agreement	EFTA member States (Austria, Finland, Iceland, Liechtenstein, Norway, Sweden and Switzerland) and Poland	Interim agreement for the formation of a free trade area	L/7372/Add.1	10 Dec. 1992	15 Nov. 1993	Working Party established on 25–26 Jan. 1994.

	Name	Participating countries	Presented as	Text	Signature	Entry into force	GATT action taken and document references
90.	North American Free Trade Agreement (NAFTA)[68]	Canada, Mexico and United States	Free trade area	L/7176/ Add.1	17 Dec. 1992	1 Jan. 1994	Working Party established on 23 Mar. 1994.
91.	Estonia-Switzerland Free-Trade Agreement	Estonia and Switzerland	Free trade area	L/7223/ Add.1	21 Dec. 1992	Provisionally applied from 1 Apr. 1993	Working Party established on agreements between Switzerland and the Baltic States on 16–17 June 1993.
92.	Central European Free Trade Agreement (CEFTA)	Czech Republic, Hungary, Poland and Slovak Republic	Interim agreement for the formation of a free trade area	L/7495/ Add.1	21 Dec. 1992	Provisionally applied from 1 Mar. 1993	Working Party established on 20 July 1994.
93.	Latvia-Switzerland Free-Trade Agreement	Latvia and Switzerland	Free trade area	L/7223/ Add.1	22 Dec. 1992	Provisionally applied from 1 Apr. 1993	Working Party established on agreements between Switzerland and the Baltic States on 16–17 June 1992.
94.	EFTA-Hungary Free Trade Agreement	EFTA member States (Austria, Finland, Iceland, Liechtenstein, Norway, Sweden and Switzerland) and Hungary	Interim agreement for the formation of a free trade area	L/7360/ Add.1	29 Mar. 1993	1 Oct. 1993[69]	Working Party established on 25–26 Jan. 1994.
95.	EFTA-Bulgaria Free Trade Agreement	EFTA member States (Austria, Finland, Iceland, Liechtenstein, Norway, Sweden and Switzerland) and Bulgaria	Interim agreement for the formation of a free trade area	L/7257 and Add.1	29 May 1993	1 July 1993[70]	Working Party established on 27 Oct. 1993.
96.	Czech Republic-Slovenia Free Trade Agreement	Czech Republic and Slovenia	Free trade area	L/7447/ Add.1	4 Dec. 1993	Provisionally applied since 1 Jan. 1994	Working Party on agreements between Slovenia and the Czech Rep. and Slovak Rep. established on 21 June 1994.
97.	Slovak Republic-Slovenia Free Trade Agreement	Slovak Republic and Slovenia	Free trade area	L/7448/ Add.1	22 Dec. 1993	Provisionally applied since 1 Jan. 1994	Working Party on agreements between Slovenia and the Czech Rep. and Slovak Rep. established on 21 June 1994.

Name	Participating countries	Presented as	Text of agreement	Signature	Entry into force	GATT action taken and document references
EC-Accession of Austria, Finland and Sweden	EC member States (Belgium, Denmark, France, Germany, Greece, Ireland, Italy, Luxembourg, Netherlands, Portugal, Spain and United Kingdom) and Austria, Finland and Sweden	Customs union	L/7614/Add.1		1 July 1994	1 Jan. 1995

II. AGREEMENTS COVERED OR NOTIFIED UNDER THE 1979 ENABLING CLAUSE

Since 1979, developing countries having concluded agreements have notified them under the Enabling Clause (Decision of 28 November 1979 on 'Differential and More Favourable Treatment, Reciprocity and Fuller Participation of Developing Countries'). For agreements notified under the Enabling Clause, the item is inscribed on the agenda of the Committee on Trade and Development (CTD). Subsequent actions of the CTD may include 'noting' the agreement, requesting additional information, establishing a working party and adopting its reports, reviewing reports made by members on developments under the agreement. The table also includes agreements reached between developing countries which provide for the exchange of preferences on a selected group of products ('preferential trade arrangement') for which a waiver was granted by the CONTRACTING PARTIES prior to the entry into force of the Enabling Clause, under which they were subsequently covered.

Name	Participating countries	Presented as	Text of agreement	Signature	Entry into force	GATT action taken and document references
1. Trade Expansion and Co-operation Agreement	Egypt (United Arab Republic), India and Yugoslavia	Preferential trade arrangement	L/2980/Add.1	23 Dec. 1967	1 Apr. 1968	Working Party Report adopted on 14 Nov. 1968 (16S/83). Decision of 14 Nov. 1968 (16S/17) granting a waiver from Article I:1, extended through the Decisions of 20 Feb. 1970 (17S/21), of 22 Mar. 1973 (20S/23), of 13 Nov. 1973 (20S/23), and of 14 Mar. 1978 (25S/8).

	Name	Participating countries	Presented as	Text	Signature	Entry into force	GATT action taken and document references
2.	First Agreement on Trade Negotiations Among Developing Member Countries of the Economic and Social Commission for Asia and the Pacific (Bangkok Agreement)	Bangladesh, India, Lao People's Democratic Republic, Philippines, Republic of Korea, Sri Lanka and Thailand	Preferential trade arrangement	L/4418	31 July 1975	17 June 1976	Working Party Report adopted on 14 Mar. 1978 (25S/109). Decision of 14 Mar. 1978 waiving the obligations of the parties under Article I (25S/6). Report to the CTD in 1982 (L/5243) and review (COM.TD/112). Report to the CTD in 1990 (L/6718) and review (L/6744).
3.	Agreement on ASEAN Preferential Trading Arrangement[71]	Indonesia, Malaysia, Philippines, Singapore and Thailand[72]	Preferential trade arrangement	L/4581	24 Feb. 1977	1 Jan. 1978	Working Party Report adopted 29 Jan. 1979 (26S/321). Decision of 29 Jan. 1979 waiving the obligations of the parties under Article 1 (26S/224). Report (L/5455) and review by the CTD (COM.TD/114). Report (L/6569) and review by the CTD (L/6605).
4.	Latin American Integration Association (LAIA)[73]	Argentina, Bolivia, Brazil, Chile, Colombia, Ecuador, Mexico, Paraguay, Peru, Uruguay and Venezuela	Preferential trade arrangement	L/5342	12 Aug. 1980	18 Mar. 1981	Reports to the Committee on Trade and Development (COM.TD/W/416 and Add.1, L/6158 and Add.1, L/6531, L/6946, L/6985 and Add.1).
5.	South Pacific Regional Trade and Economic Agreement (SPARTECA)	Australia and New Zealand, and Cook Islands, Fiji, Kiribati, Niue, Papua New Guinea, Solomon Islands, Tonga, Tuvalu and Western Samoa[74]	Preferential non-reciprocal access to the markets of Australia and New Zealand	L/5100	15 July 1980	1 Jan. 1981	Decision of Council requiring the submission of reports by Australia and New Zealand in accordance with the procedure for the examination of biennial reports on regional agreements, agreed on 26 Nov. 1971 (C/M/148). Reports to the Committee on Trade and Development (L/5488).

No.	Name	Members	Type	Document	Date	Date	Committee
6.	Unified Economic Agreement among the States of the Gulf Co-operation Council	Bahrain, Kuwait, Oman, Qatar, Saudi Arabia and United Arab Emirates	Preferential trade arrangement	L/5676	8 June 1981	1 Mar. 1983	Noted by the Committee on Trade and Development (L/5735).
7.	Andean Group[75]	Bolivia, Colombia, Ecuador, Peru and Venezuela	Customs union	L/6737	12 May 1987	25 May 1988	Reports to the Committee on Trade and Development (L/6737, L/7089, L/6841, L/7088).).
8.	Southern Common Market (MERCOSUR)	Argentina, Brazil, Paraguay and Uruguay	Interim agreement for the formation of a customs union	L/7370 and Add. 1	26 Mar. 1991	9 Nov. 1991	Working Party established on 28 May 1993 under the Committee on Trade and Development.
9.	Additional Protocol on Preferential Tariffs among members of the Organisation for Economic Co-operation	Islamic Rep. of Iran, Pakistan and Turkey[76]	Preferential trade arrangement	L/7047	23 May 1991	Not available	
10.	Common Effective Preferential Tariff Scheme for the ASEAN Free Trade Area[77]	Brunei Darussalam, Indonesia, Malaysia, Philippines, Singapore and Thailand	Interim agreement for the formation of a free trade area	L/7111 and Add. 1	28 Jan. 1991	28 Jan. 1991	Reports to the Committee on Trade and Development (L/7111/Add. 1, L/7309/Rev.1, L/7491, L/7546 and Add.1).
11.	Trade Agreement between Thailand and Lao People's Democratic Republic	Lao People's Democratic Republic and Thailand	Preferential trade arrangement	L/6947	20 June 1991	20 June 1991	

Source: World Trade Organization (1995). *Regionalism and the World Trading System* (Geneva: World Trade Organization)

Notes

1. Agreement terminated on 1 July 1955 and immediately superseded by a preferential trade agreement notified to GATT (Working Party Report adopted on 3 Dec. 1955 (14S/72)), and the subject of a waiver from Article 1.1 under the Decision of 3 Dec. 1955 (14S/17).

2. In 1952 the members of the European Coal and Steel Community (ECSC) obtained a waiver from Article 1.1 under the Decision of 10 Nov. 1952 (1S/17) which expired in 1958. Denmark, Ireland and the United Kingdom acceded to the EC on 1 Jan. 1973, Greece acceded on 1 Jan. 1981, Portugal and Spain acceded on 1 Jan. 1986, and Austria, Finland and Sweden acceded on 1 Jan. 1995.

3. Nicaragua was the only member of the Multilateral Central American Free Trade and Economic Integration Treaty which was a GATT contracting party at the time of its formation. See entry for the participation of Nicaragua in the General Treaty for Central American Integration.

4. Cameroon joined the customs union on 23 June 1961. The common external tariff was implemented on 1 July 1962.

5. Denmark and the United Kingdom withdrew from EFTA on 1 Jan. 1973 upon accession to the EC, and Portugal withdrew on 1 Jan. 1986 upon accession to the EC. Iceland acceded to EFTA on 1 Mar. 1970, Finland acceded on 1 Jan. 1986, and Liechtenstein acceded on 1 Sept. 1991. Austria, Finland and Sweden withdrew from EFTA on 1 Jan. 1995 upon accession to the EC.

6. The GATT Protocol of Accession of Switzerland provides that the customs territory of Switzerland is deemed to include the territory of the Principality of Liechtenstein as long as the customs union treaty with Switzerland is in force.

7. The 1980 Montevideo Treaty establishing the LAIA superseded the 1960 Montevideo Treaty establishing the LAFTA.

8. The 1961 Treaty reduced the period for the establishment of a free-trade area among members of the Central American Free Trade Area from ten to five years and provided for the equalization of import duties within five years.

9. At the time of the formation of the free-trade area, Borneo and Sarawak were dependent territories of the United Kingdom. On 30 Oct. 1963, the government of Malaysia assumed the responsibility for the conduct of the external affairs of the former states of the Federation of Malay, including the states of Borneo and Sarawak (L/2077).

10. The date of signature is not available to the GATT Secretariat.

11. On 1 Jan. 1986, Finland acceded to EFTA. Finland withdrew from EFTA on 1 Jan. 1995 upon accession to the EC.

12. The Association agreement was extended in 1973 to cover the accession of Denmark, Ireland and the United Kingdom to the EC. Greece acceded to the EC on 1 Jan. 1981.

13. Superseded by the 1971 Yaoundé II, which was superseded by the 1976 First Lomé Convention and its Second, Third and Fourth successor agreements.

14. The Association agreement was supplemented by an Additional Protocol (with effect from 1 Jan. 1973) establishing conditions, arrangements and a timetable for a transitional stage to the customs union. The Association agreement was extended in 1973 to ECSC products and to new members of the EEC (with effect from 1 Mar. 1986). The tariff preferences on citrus products were the subject of a dispute settlement proceeding 'European Community – Tariff treatment on imports of citrus products from certain countries in the Mediterranean region' in 1985. The Panel's report remains unadopted.

15. Superseded by the 1971 EEC-PTOM II.

16. Superseded by the 1983 Australia-New Zealand Closer Economic Relations Trade Agreement (ANCERT).

17. Ireland and the United Kingdom acceded to the EC on 1 Jan. 1973.

18. Superseded by the 1973 CARICOM.

19. Superseded by the 1976 Co-operation Agreement.

20. Superseded by the 1976 Co-operation Agreement.

21. Superseded by the 1976 First Lomé Convention and its Second, Third and Fourth successor agreements.

22. An Association Agreement between Mauritius and the Yaoundé Convention was signed on 12 May 1972 and entered into force on 1 June 1973.

23. Superseded by the 1976 First Lomé Convention and its Second, Third and Fourth successor agreements.

24. Kenya, Tanzania and Uganda concluded the Treaty for East African Co-operation in 1967.

25. Superseded by the 1975 Agreement on the implementation of free-trade area treatment and extended to cover ECSC products.

26. Spain acceded to the EC on 1 Jan. 1986. The tariff preferences on citrus products were the subject of a dispute settlement proceeding 'European Community – Tariff treatment on imports of citrus products from certain countries in the Mediterranean region' in 1985. The Panel's report remains unadopted.

27. Superseded the 1964 EEC-PTOM I.

28. Supplemented the 1964 Association Agreement. The Association agreement was extended in 1973 to ECSC products and the new members of the EEC (with effect from 1 Mar. 1986).

29. The tariff preferences on citrus products were the subject of a dispute settlement proceeding 'European Community – Tariff treatment on imports of citrus products from certain countries in the Mediterranean region' in 1985. The Panel's report remains unadopted.

30. Denmark and the United Kingdom withdrew from EFTA upon their accession to the EC. Ireland and the United Kingdom had concluded a free-trade agreement in 1966. The notification also concerned the proposed accession of EFTA member Norway, which did not subsequently ratify the treaty with the EC.

31. Austria acceded to the EC on 1 Jan. 1995.

32. Portugal acceded to the EC on 1 Jan. 1986.

33. Sweden acceded to the EC on 1 Jan. 1995.

34. Other agreements covering trade matters between the EEC and Lebanon include the 1965 Agreement on Trade and Technical Cooperation, and the 1973 Protocol relating to the Agreement. The Agreements notified to the GATT in 1973 include one Agreement between the original six members of the EEC and Lebanon signed in 1972, and a Protocol extending the Agreement to Denmark, Ireland and the United Kingdom, signed in 1973.

35. Superseded by the 1977 Agreement.

36. The tariff preferences on citrus products were the subject of a dispute settlement proceeding 'European Community – Tariff treatment on imports of citrus products from certain countries in the Mediterranean region' in 1985. The Panel's report remains unadopted.

37. Superseded the 1968 CARIFTA.

38. Bahamas, Belize, Dominica, Grenada, Montserrat, St. Lucia and St. Vincent acceded to the Treaty establishing the CARICOM in May 1974; Antigua and Barbuda and St. Kitts and Nevis acceded in July 1974.

39. Finland acceded to the EC on 1 Jan. 1995.

40. See also the 1993 EFTA-Hungary Free Trade Agreement. The 1975 Agreement shall remain in force until the substance of its mutual benefits has been fully overtaken by the later Agreement.

41. See also the 1991 EFTA-Czech and Slovak Federal Republic Free Trade Agreement. The 1975 Agreement shall remain in force until the substance of its mutual benefits has been fully overtaken by the later Agreement. Following the dissolution of the former Czech and Slovak Federal Republic as of 1 Jan. 1993, agreements were signed by the two successor states with EFTA that provide for the continuing application of the 1991 Agreement (L/7220).

42. The membership of the Agreement includes that of the 1971 Yaoundé and Arusha Agreements.

43. Accessions to the First Lomé Convention include Cape Verde on 28 Mar. 1977, Comoros on 13 Sept. 1976, Djibouti on 2 Feb. 1978, Dominica on 26 Feb. 1979, Kiribati on 30 Oct. 1979, Papua New Guinea and Sao Tome and Principe on 28 Mar. 1977, St. Lucia on 28 June 1979, St. Vincent and the Grenadines on 27 Feb. 1980, Seychelles on 27 Aug. 1976, Solomon Islands on 27 Sept. 1978, Surinam on 16 July 1976, and Tuvalu on 17 Jan. 1979.

44. The Agreement is no longer in force following the unification of Germany in 1989.

45. The Working Party had planned to reconvene in 18 months time after the adoption of the Interim Report to continue its examination of the Agreement.

46. Supplemented the 1962 Agreement. Greece acceded to the EC on 1 Jan. 1981.

47. Superseded the 1973 Agreement. The tariff preferences on citrus products were the subject of a dispute settlement proceeding 'European Community – Tariff treatment on imports of citrus products from certain countries in the Mediterranean region' in 1985. The Panel's report remains unadopted.

48. Superseded the 1969 Agreement. The tariff preferences on citrus products were the subject of a dispute settlement proceeding 'European Community – Tariff treatment on imports of citrus products from certain countries in the Mediterranean region' in 1985. The Panel's report remains unadopted.

49. The tariff preferences on citrus products were the subject of a dispute settlement proceeding 'European Community – Tariff treatment on imports of citrus products from certain countries in the Mediterranean region' in 1985. The Panel's report remains unadopted.

50. Superseded the 1969 Agreement. An Interim Agreement allowed for the trade provisions to be implemented with effect from 1 July 1976. The tariff preferences on citrus products were the subject of a dispute settlement proceeding 'European Community – Tariff treatment on imports of citrus products from certain countries in the Mediterranean region' in 1985. The Panel's report remains unadopted.

51. Supplemented the 1973 Agreement. Portugal acceded to the EC on 1 Jan. 1986.

52. See also the 1993 EFTA-Poland Free Trade Agreement. The 1978 Agreement shall remain in force until the substance of the mutual benefits under the earlier Agreement has been fully overtaken by the later Agreement.

53. Australia obtained a waiver from Article 1.1 for preferences granted to products imported from Papua New Guinea under the Decision of 24 Oct. 1953 (2S/18). PATCRA covers trade and commercial relations between Australia and Papua New Guinea, while Papua New Guinea obtains trade concessions from New Zealand under SPARTECA (see under Enabling Clause in the chapter on Article 1).

54. The tariff preferences on citrus products were the subject of a dispute settlement proceeding 'European Community – Tariff treatment on imports of citrus products from certain countries in the Mediterranean region' in 1985. The Panel's report remains unadopted.

55. The tariff preferences on citrus products were the subject of a dispute settlement proceeding 'European Community – Tariff treatment on imports of citrus products from certain countries in the Mediterranean region' in 1985. The Panel's report remains unadopted.

56. The tariff preferences on citrus products were the subject of a dispute settlement proceeding 'European Community – Tariff treatment on imports of citrus products from certain countries in the Mediterranean region' in 1985. The Panel's report remains unadopted.

57. Spain acceded to the EC on 1 Jan. 1986.

58. Superseded the First Lomé Convention. Successor agreements are the Third and Fourth Lomé Conventions.

59. Greece acceded to the EEC on 1 Jan. 1981. Antigua and Barbuda acceded to the Second Lomé Convention on 30 July 1982, Belize on 5 Mar. 1982, Vanuatu on 18 Mar. 1981 and Zimbabwe on 1 Mar. 1982.

60. Superseded the 1966 Australia-New Zealand Free Trade Agreement.

61. Superseded the Second Lomé Convention. Successor agreement is the Fourth Lomé Convention.

62. Portugal and Spain acceded to the EEC on 1 Jan. 1986.

63. Superseded previous Agreements between the EEC and Portugal and Spain.

64. The provisions of this agreement have been partially superseded by 1994 NAFTA.

65. Superseded the Third Lomé Convention. Preferential treatment on bananas imported from ACP countries was the subject of two dispute settlement proceedings. 'EEC-Member states' import regimes for bananas' in February 1993 and 'EEC-Import regime for bananas' in June 1993. Both Panel reports remained unadopted. The GATT Contracting Parties members of the Fourth Lomé Convention were granted a waiver on 9 Dec. 1994 from the provisions of paragraph 1 of Article I of the General Agreement, until 29 Feb. 2000, to the extent necessary to permit the European Communities to provide preferential treatment for products originating in ACP States as required by the relevant provisions of the Fourth Lomé Convention (L/7604).

66. Established following the dissolution of the Czech and Slovak Federal Republic on 1 Jan. 1993.

67. Entered into force for Sweden and Romania on 1 May 1993. The Agreement is being provisionally applied by Switzerland and Liechtenstein pending ratification. The Agreement will enter into force for other EFTA member states when ratification is completed.

68. Between Canada and the United States, members of the Canada-United States Free Trade Agreement, the NAFTA prevails to the extent of inconsistency, except as otherwise provided for in NAFTA.

69. Entered into force for Austria, Hungary, and Sweden on 1 Oct. 1993. The Agreement and arrangements are also being provisionally applied since 1 Oct. 1993 by Switzerland and Liechtenstein pending their ratification. The Agreement and arrangements will enter into force for Finland and Iceland when the ratification process is completed.

70. Entered into force for Sweden on 1 July 1993. The Agreement and arrangements are being provisionally applied since 1 July 1993 by Norway, Switzerland and Liechtenstein, pending their ratification. The Agreement and arrangements will enter into force for Finland and Iceland when the ratification process is completed.

71. Supplemented by 1991 agreement on the Common Effective Preferential Tariff Scheme for the ASEAN Free Trade Area.

72. Brunei Darussalam joined ASEAN in 1984.

73. The 1980 Montevideo Treaty establishing the LAIA superseded the 1960 Montevideo Treaty establishing the LAFTA. In the LAIA framework, liberalization is carried out on a sectoral basis through two mechanisms: Regional Scope Agreements, covering all members of LAIA, which give preferential treatment on a regional basis, and Partial Scope Agreements, concluded by sub-groups of LAIA, which offer preferential treatment to the signatories only. It is through a Partial Scope Agreement that the current economic integration initiatives are taking place. Partial Scope Agreements which have been notified under the Enabling Clause include L/5689, L/6158 and Add.1, COM.TD/W/469, L/6531, L/6946, as well as the MERCOSUR.
74. In 1982, New Zealand notified the extension of the agreement to Nauru and Vanuatu.
75. The 1987 Cartagena Agreement superseded the 1969 Cartagena Agreement which established the Andean Group, concluded in the context of the 1960 Treaty of Montevideo establishing the LAFTA. In 1988, the Cartagena Agreement became independent as regards aspects relating to the 1960 Montevideo Treaty which had expired. The Andean Group was originally composed of Bolivia, Chile, Colombia, Ecuador and Peru. Chile withdrew from the Treaty in Oct. 1976 and Venezuela acceded to the Agreement in 1973.
76. Subsequent participants include Azerbajan, Kyrgzstan, Tajikstan, Turkmenistan and Uzbekistan.
77. Supplemented the 1978 Agreement on ASEAN Preferential Trading Arrangements.

Annex II
Council for Mutual Economic Assistance

I INTRODUCTION

The Council for Mutual Economic Assistance (CMEA) or Comecon existed for four decades. Regretably it did not live up to its potential or to the expectations of its members. This situation was due to the following two reasons. First, the former USSR was territorially the largest country in the world. As such it had a vast domestic market which permitted diversification in production so that international trade was (presumably) not a key factor in its economic prosperity. Second, such a situation in the CMEA was also due to central planning which worked out detailed tasks regarding production, investments, prices and trade. Foreign trade flows were not due to differences in absolute and comparative costs among countries, but, rather, they were only an extension of the plan. Many of the impediments to trade which are studied in the theory of international economic integration (tariffs, quotas, taxes) did not appear in the CMEA system.

A Communiqué announced the establishment of the CMEA in 1949. The Statute of this group was, however, delivered a decade after the Communiqué. The main objectives of this institution were the continuous increase in the welfare of the people in all CMEA member countries, as well as the gradual equalization of the level of economic development among the member countries. Other goals (development and improvement of economic cooperation, development of socialist economic integration and acceleration of economic and technical progress) seem more like means towards achieving the main objective. The principles upon which the CMEA was founded were the sovereign equality of all member countries, voluntary membership, socialist internationalism, mutual benefit and fraternal assistance.

II BASIC FEATURES

Majority voting within the CMEA was prohibited. This was the real reason why the CMEA did not have any real power, as well as why the former USSR had not succeeded in completely controlling all CMEA member countries.[1] The group's institutional set-up was complicated. There were very many CMEA bodies. The CMEA intended to compensate for the lack of real power by means of a formidable institutional structure. Decision-making in this bureaucratic labyrinth was very slow because every country could block any proposals by dissenting.

It was after the promulgation of the CMEA Statute that 'The Basic Principles of International Socialist Division of Labour' were accepted in 1962. 'The Basic Principles' set down guidelines for future cooperation among the CMEA countries. During the 1950s there were great disequilibria in the economies of the CMEA countries. On the one hand, there were shortages of consumer goods, while on the other, there was a glut of producer goods. This situation brought open dissatisfaction in Hungary in 1956 which was 'pacified' by the Soviet intervention. Little attention had been paid to specialization until that time. On the basis of the 'Basic Principles', the socialist division of labour was implemented through the coordination of economic plans and specialization in production on the basis of the employment of disposable factors in each country. As a relatively less developed country in the CMEA, Romania did not want to accept this kind of specialization, for under this pattern, the development of industry in Romania would be impeded.

Romanian opposition to the introduction of supranational planning within the CMEA was supported by Hungary and Czechoslovakia. The latter two countries were implementing reforms directed towards a socialist system in which the market played an important role. A relative dilution of the CMEA was prevented by the intervention of the Warsaw Pact in Cze-choslovakia in 1968. After that event the former USSR had to find a way to close ranks within the CMEA.

'The Comprehensive Programme of Socialist Economic Integration' was presented and accepted in 1971. The 'Comprehensive Programme' was basically a list of proposals which refer to a number of issues in economics and science, and which dealt with a long period of time (15–20 years). The pivotal clause within the 'Comprehensive Programme' is joint planning and joint investment projects in the priority sectors (raw materials and energy, machine industry, food, consumer goods industries and transport). If a CMEA country was not interested in decision making with respect to an issue, then the decision or recommendation would not refer to the country in question. This principle of 'interested party' was implemented in the CMEA structure as protection against the introduction of suprana-tionality.

Competition takes place among firms in market economies. In centrally planned economies competition existed among different plans which were offered to the central decision-making body. The adjustment of national plans meant at an earlier stage only an exchange of information for bilateral trade negotiations. This was changed so that the procedure began three years before the end of the five-year period covered by the plan. This gave time to the planners to change and supplement their investment plans. The adjustment of plans among the CMEA countries was done on the basis of mutual prognoses, consultations, planning of the interested countries in certain fields, exchange of experience and planning principles. The intention was to consciously link bilateral and multilateral measures for the development of cooperation in economics, science and technology.

Planning, as a process in which the future of a certain field is consciously shaped, has a theoretical advantage because mistakes and costs which can cause 'blind market forces' are deliberately avoided. The politicization of integration, however, reduced the advantages of planning, and with regard to the speed of integration, it was much slower than in the market model. Endless bilateral negotiations made the integration progress very slow. This could easily be a sign that countries did not desire it enthusiastically (on such terms).

During the negotiation process about common projects, negotiators from the member countries appraised costs and benefits of the project in question, compared projects with alternatives, estimated concessions given to and received from partners and, finally, compared possible projects with national priorities in development. This was a complicated, time-consuming and difficult task (Robson, 1987, p. 218).

There have been around twenty common projects; most of them in energy and raw materials. Common investments were made in the country which was endowed with a substantial amount of mineral resources. This attitude by the CMEA had as its consequence the fact that most common projects were located in the former USSR. The most important projects were found in a common infrastructure in energy which was the greatest source of pride in the CMEA, for they represented genuine integration. The Druzhba oil pipeline was 5,500 km long and linked oil wells in the former USSR with consumers in the former German Democratic Republic, Poland, Hungary and the former Czechoslovakia. The Soyuz gas pipeline was 2,750 km long and supplied European countries with Soviet natural gas. The Mir was a huge electric grid that linked the CMEA countries from Mongolia to eastern Europe. Other important common projects included the production of cellulose and asbestos in the former USSR, the production of cobalt and nickel in Cuba and cotton spinning in Poland.

The greatest part of the above mentioned projects were directed towards the production and transport of primary products from the former USSR. This was how the European CMEA member countries compensated the former USSR for the supply of resources which could be easily sold on the international market for hard currency. Investments of the European member countries in the former USSR were done in the form of the export of goods, labour and know-how. European member countries of the CMEA protested at the low interest rates which they received, payments in kind and high costs of projects. However, the security of supplies from the former USSR in the future compensated for these worries.

III FACTOR MOBILITY

Mobility of capital within the CMEA framework was of little importance. If the funds moved, then it was due to the interest of the countries to which the funds belonged. From the point of view of normative economics, the funds should move from those countries which have a surplus of capital (in which profit and interest rates are relatively lower) to those countries which have a shortage of capital (in which profit and interest rates are relatively higher) and in which there exists confidence that the invested funds will be recovered. Capital mobility within and out of the CMEA, however, had a political dimension. The CMEA countries, just like governments in the west, 'exported' capital everywhere they wanted to win friends and exert political influence.

The International Investment Bank (IIB) was established in 1970 in order to finance the common investments necessitated by the 'socialist division of labour'. The IIB gave medium and long-term loans which were in most cases of benefit to all CMEA member countries. The capital of the Bank was 1 billion transferable roubles. The IIB was also entitled to take funds from the international capital market. In the beginning Romania did not want to participate in the IIB, because decisions were made in this Bank according to majority vote (each country had one vote), but subsequently joined. This decision-making process was in contrast to the operation of all other CMEA bodies. None the less, there was a lack of interest in the active operation of the IIB. This can be explained by the need of the relatively advanced countries of the CMEA for investments in their own economy. In this situation the relatively advanced countries did not want to help, to any great extent, the development of relatively less advanced CMEA countries. In addition, the rate of interest on the one hand, and profitability, supply and demand of funds on the other, were not connected.

According to CMEA opinion, labour movements were inherent to capitalism. These flows were of very little significance in the CMEA, although there existed differences among member countries in the relative level of wages due partly to the relative abundance or shortage of labour. Labour flows between the relatively backward countries of the CMEA towards the relatively advanced ones (from Bulgaria to the former USSR, from Poland to the former German Democratic Republic) were observed. In 1989–90 (the fall of the Berlin Wall) there was a massive flow of population out of the CMEA, in particular from the former German Democratic Republic to the FR Germany before reunification in 1989.

The exchange of scientific and technical information between the CMEA member countries was formally very developed. It was based on the critique of capitalism in which private owners control scientific achievements and prevent a wide application of new ideas in order to make super-normal profit. There was, however, a problem in financing research in the CMEA. Relatively advanced countries did not have much incentive to share the fruits of their achievements with other users because of high costs and uncertainty of research which they bore alone. Recipients of the scientific information had neither the interest nor the funds to take part in research when they could get the results of such research free from others. Therefore, the CMEA countries tried to compensate for their relative backwardness in technology by purchasing western equipment and licences.

IV   PRICES IN TRADE

Eastern European theorists maintained throughout the 'socialist period' that capitalism was in crisis and that it had a destabilizing cyclical effect and caused speculative movements of prices. On these grounds, the CMEA endeavoured to find its own socialist prices (which embodied 'equality' in economic relations) in contrast to capitalist prices (which personify inequality). In the centrally planned system of economic autarky a concern with quantity rather than value was dominant.

Fluctuations in prices could endanger the planned nature of the CMEA economies. The economic results of this system were measured in metres, litres and tonnes, not in money, which was only an accounting unit. Prices in this system responded neither to costs of production nor to the relation of supply and demand. They also did not reflect the relative abundance or shortage of goods and services. They were set arbitrarily and were used for accounting purposes only. Hence, they did not play any role in the allocation of resources. The gap between prices and the cost of production was caused by relatively low prices for producers goods, low rates of interest and as taxes which burden consumer goods. The system of prices in the CMEA member countries gave neither a satisfactory nor a rational denominator for the production of goods and services. It was much more suited to a large closed economy than to a small developed and specialized country which pursues a policy of openness in trade and investment.

Domestic rationality in production can be tested by comparison with prices on the world market. It is not a simple self-comparison, but rather a comparison with the most efficient world producers. Trade and comparison with the most advanced world economies could give a positive impetus to economic development in the region. The CMEA member countries negotiated about volume and structure of trade, as well as bargained about prices (terms of trade). Every country's administration decided own prices, so that prices among the states could not be compared. In their internal trade, the CMEA countries intended to 'clear' the world market (capitalist) prices of cyclical and speculative movements and used the five-year weighted averages. Following the sharp increase in the world market price for oil, the prices for intra-CMEA trade, on the basis of a Soviet request, were delivered every year from 1976 (instead of every five years). The bases were world market prices from the preceding five years.

This system of prices did not cause problems for standardized goods (raw materials); however, problems arose regarding manufactured goods. One could ask the question: should a Bulgarian computer be worth as much as a Japanese one? Such a system of 'just and equivalent socialist prices' in trade within the CMEA was very slow to bring the beneficial effects which come from the world market. At the same time, it isolated the CMEA from the abrupt and disadvantageous effects which came in the form of sharp increases in prices which distort planning. It could also bring odd situations. Prices for oil in the CMEA were rising between 1982 and 1986 while they were decreasing on the world market!

The CMEA member countries used current world market prices in trade with third countries while in their internal trade, they used prices which were reached after bilateral negotiations on the basis of historic world prices as explained above. These bilateral negotiations were quite tough as it was no easy task to get the world market price for each particular good. Commodity exchanges deal with only a limited number of goods. In addition, the bulk of world trade is covered by long-term contracts which do not necessarily have a close relation to current world market prices. Prices played no role in the allocation of resources in the centrally planned system. Therefore, it is hard to understand why the CMEA countries spent so much time bargaining over prices or why there was a world market price formula.

The CMEA price system enabled the former USSR in the 1955–59 period to charge 15 per cent higher prices during exports to the CMEA partner countries, while on the import side the former USSR paid to the same partners 15 per cent lower prices for the same or similar import goods than to the western countries (Mendershausen, 1959; 1960). On these grounds the former USSR could take advantage of the CMEA member countries by means of its monopolistic position. Such a result can be questioned on several grounds. Econometric problems arise regarding the comparison of data, price, quantity and quality of goods. In addition, the former USSR had to accept higher prices from the western partners in order to attract them for trade. At the same time the former USSR had to offer relatively lower prices in exports in order to penetrate the western markets and earn the necessary hard currency to pay for imports.

If the terms of trade were favourable to the former USSR until the 1960s, after that period the situation altered. The former USSR exported mainly primary goods and energy to its CMEA partners while the partners exported industrial goods in exchange. Relative prices of manufactured goods rose in relation to prices for primary goods, so that the terms of trade were working against the former USSR within the CMEA. This tendency was manifested in 1975 when the Soviets insisted on a change in the pricing system. These potential losses from trade, or subsidies to the CMEA partners, took place when the former USSR exported energy and raw materials below the world market price and when it imported manufactured goods at prices higher than those which prevailed on the world market for goods of similar quality. The former USSR may have consciously directed such subsidies to the CMEA partner countries in order to prevent or stimulate policy changes in these countries. One of the crucial factors which induced Britain and France to decolonize was the need by their colonies to be subsidized. However, it appears that the Soviets in the past compensated for possible losses in trade within the CMEA by using their political influence.

Various studies found the existence of Soviet subsidies to the CMEA partners. Where they disagreed was in the magnitude of these subsidies. The accumulated Soviet subsidies over the period 1973–84 due to divergent price developments on the CMEA and world markets amounted to 18.8 billion transferable roubles (Dietz, 1986) which is three times less than in another estimate even for 1980 (Marrese and Vanous, 1983). Yet another study reported Soviet aid in all forms to eastern Europe of around 134 billion dollars between 1971 and 1980 (Bunce, 1985). The major source of these subsidies was the price (and its change) of energy.

The leaders in the former USSR did not want its population to be aware that the CMEA partners were being subsidized. Socialist cooperation was supposed to be founded on 'equality'. Therefore, it was unnecessary to compensate partners for their friendship. In addition, Soviet citizens would not be happy to learn that their country subsidized other partner countries with higher living standards! At the same time, east European political leaders did not want their population to know that national sovereignty was being 'sold' in return for the Soviet subsidies to help the running of their economies (Marrese, 1986, p. 311).

Prices were relatively stable in the CMEA countries and direct inflation did not exist. None the less, producer prices differed from consumer prices due to bonuses, subsidies and taxes. These 'additives' can create quite a significant gap between the two kinds of prices, although the planners attempted to keep consumer prices fixed. Inflation of a kind, however, existed. It appeared in the form of shortages, cutting of the supplies of electricity, restrictions on foreign travel, long queues in front of shops, low quality of goods and the like. The solution to the price problem in the CMEA countries was to be found in domestic reforms which would introduce the market system of production according to market needs. By doing this, one would avoid the absurd situation in which the Soviet sewing machine producers received bonuses for fulfilling their plan, although there were piles of sewing machines in the shops which nobody wanted to buy!

V TRADE

Trade, FDI and specialization (division of labour) represent the core of international economic integration. Because of the non-market formation of prices within the CMEA, the trade data which were released by the CMEA were most usually useless for international comparisons, as well as calculations of trade creation and trade diversion. Of course, this did not hold for data which referred to litres, metres or tonnes.

The CMEA could not be taken as a customs union. Indirectly, customs protection was replaced by a complicated system of direct control of foreign trade quotas which were set by the plan. State ownership of the means of production, state foreign trade monopoly and a high degree of self-sufficiency removed the need for the existence of customs duties.

Customs duties might have some justification when they protect an infant industry for a limited period of time; reduce consumption of imported goods in order to curtail and redirect home consumption; and when the proceeds are needed for the budget in the short term. Since the state could get funds from enterprises without obstacles and directly protect/promote firms and industries, there was no need for customs duties in the centrally planned system. Since the 1970s the CMEA countries started introducing tariffs. The main reason for this move was the creation of the base for negotiation and concessions in trade from the west.

Intra-CMEA trade has been characterized by bilateralism (the most protectionist economic system), during the entire life of this organization. Bilateralism is a kind of exchange control. It is usually introduced when countries face severe payment problems for which the more subtle kinds of intervention are not sufficient to achieve the desired policy objectives (van Brabant, 1980, p. 128). If the bilaterally negotiated price for a good is too high for a country, then this country tries to produce the good at home. If this option is expensive, then the country purchases it from the western countries. Either action is integration averse. The goal of bilateral balancing was economic independence. In the case of deficit, the currencies of the CMEA countries were not accepted internationally, they have little reserves, while the opportunities to arrange *ex post* loans were limited. These countries did not want to become too dependent on unplanned capital imports which might jeopardize their major policy objective, independence (van Brabant, 1980, p. 114). Therefore, the level of trade of the CMEA countries was lower than was the case for market economies at a comparable level of development.

Bilateral balancing in trade among the CMEA member countries used to be routine occurrence. Since the mid–1970s and the energy crisis, this has not been the case in trade between the former USSR and all other CMEA member countries. The former USSR became a creditor of these countries. These disequilibria in trade enabled the former USSR to 'favour' (large 'credits') some countries or 'punish' (small 'credits') others.

A specific CMEA trade took place in hard and soft goods. Hard goods in the CMEA were either deficient goods (food) or those that could be sold easily for hard currency (raw materials). These goods became an accepted means of payment because of their scarcity. Countries which were abundant in raw materials (the former USSR and to an extent Poland and Romania) were under pressure from the other CMEA countries. Countries which had 'soft' (manufactured) goods tried to swap them for as many 'hard' goods as possible. Sellers of 'hard' goods requested in return better quality 'soft' ones. As a rule, however, hard goods were traded for hard goods and soft goods were traded for soft goods. Note that money did not fit into this barter! Holders of money were not even sure that their national currency was fully convertible into the home goods they wanted.

VI   REFORMS

A permanent increase in welfare (consumption by kind and volume) of the citizens of the CMEA member countries was the rationale for the existence of the CMEA. With an increase in the economic development, consumers (public and private) request improvements in the quality and increase in choice of goods and services. This required an improvement in the operation of the economy. The rate of growth has continuously fallen in the CMEA countries since 1960s. One reason is found in the relatively low starting base of the CMEA countries in the post-war period, with the exception of Czechoslovakia and the former German Democratic Republic. The other reason was the exhaustion of the effects of extensive economic development. This development model relied on increases in employment, investment and the plentiful use of raw materials. Such a model had its full justification in the CMEA at the time, but its achievements were limited to one-time positive effects. Such a development model offered little opportunities for development in the long-term.

An increase in the rate of growth, prevention of its fall or, at least, maintaining this rate at the current level, together with the introduction of intensive economic development (based on increases in productivity and efficiency in production, that is, better use of inputs per unit of output) were the reasons for reform of the centrally planned system in the CMEA countries. In order to turn unfavourable domestic economic flows, the CMEA countries looked westwards for loans and modern technology. In a situation of forced full employment, additional loans increased the quantity of money, so that the existing economic disproportions become more pronounced.

The central plan is not capable of satisfactorily harmonizing infrastructure, production and the trade of each good and service out of the millions that circulate within every economy. Nor has it been able to take account of changing consumer preferences, world market prices, new technology, new mineral discovery and weather conditions. The consequences of central planning systems included shortages of goods, services and spare parts, poor quality of output, delays in delivery, separation of producers from consumers and lack of interest in their interrelationship, lack of direct competition which stimulates innovation, as well as protection from the impact of the world market. These shortcomings can be removed to a large extent by a kind of self-regulating market system. Of course, the immediate and, possibly, short-term reaction would be a change in prices, inflation, economic cycles and unemployment.

The interlacing of trade ties between integrated partners is a measure of the degree of integration. Bilateralism in trade and inconvertibility of currencies in the CMEA expressed a disconnection among the CMEA partners, which within four decades, have developed neither competition nor large-scale cooperation. The CMEA has not lived up to its potential in a great many areas. Hence, the controversial thesis by Sobell (1984) that the CMEA was a highly integrated scheme can not be accepted.

Production for the foreign market is harder than for the domestic market. A firm's production in the CMEA was not subordinated to consumer demand, but rather to the central plan. Firms produced not in order make profit, but rather to fulfil the plan targets. Their existence was not imperilled by import competition. When the plan was fulfilled, the firm received bonuses. These favours were much more easily obtained through negotiations with the central planning administration about the production targets, than through efforts in exports.

Attitudes towards reforms differed among the countries. This was not only due to the shape of the economy, but also to the country's objectives and the ability of their leaders to carry them out. Hungary tried to soften the rigid central planning system in 1968. However, the hangover from the old way of conducting the economy was such that even after the reform, the state still controlled over 80 per cent of the GNP. The dominant role of the state sector and control of the economy prevented the operation of market forces and may be a major factor for the economic crisis. The Hungarian model of reform was interesting to study, but not to follow.

Poland tried to reform its economy during the 1970s by a heavy investment programme. It took loans from the west. The technical capacity of the economy was transformed, but the economic system remained the same. This led to investments in a number of projects that turned out to be unprofitable. Protectionism and a lack of competition, owing to the system of central planning, was to blame for the wrong choices. A profound economic crisis in Poland in the late 1980s was due to an increase in the rates of interest and an inability of projects to service foreign hard currency debt. The result was high inflation.

The leaders of the CMEA countries considered ways for improving the operation of the CMEA on a number of occasions during 1980s. They identified priority industries for cooperation and development. These industries included food, energy, transport, consumer goods and science and technology. The problem was that these industries had priority in the preceding two decades too. The centrally planned economic system was unable to solve these issues and presented a hindrance to the economic development and prosperity of the CMEA member countries.

Perestroika in the former USSR was a step towards a greater openness of the economy and the society in the mid–1980s. But the citizens began to be nervous about its achievements. What they saw were longer queues, soaring inflation, a decline in real income and a rationing of meat and dairy products. They felt that they were worse off than before and disregarded doubtful statistics which sometimes offered a different statistical conclusion.

Market-type reforms which started in eastern Europe and the former USSR in the late 1980s, aimed at discovering the sources of competitive advantage which are found in developed market economies. They should start with innovative small private firms. In many developed countries, the average size of firm is becoming smaller, not bigger. SMEs create the necessary web among different parts of the economy. The lack of SMEs came from the basic weakness of the centrally planned system. In the situation where shortages prevail and without the confidence that the planned and agreed quantities of inputs will be delivered in time, the only way to obtain, in a reliable way, the necessary inputs was to make them oneself (and to stockpile). Firms did not have the choice between make and buy. Such a situation increased prices per unit of output, reduced competitiveness and weakened links among firms.

The enterprises in eastern Europe and the former USSR had very soft budget constraints. The were taking loans without any fear of going bust. If the projects were profitable, enterprises and management would receive bonuses and medals. If they were unprofitable, the government was always there to bail them out. Proprietors of firms in a market economy, the shareholders, are not only interested in the income generating capacity of their assets, but also, and equally important, in the market value of their assets. A mistaken judgement about investment will be instantaneously reflected in the market value of the shares. This was missing in the CMEA countries. Since workers in the centrally planned economies did not have shares in their firms, they were afraid of investment in new technology that would make them redundant. Hence, driven by their short-term income maximizing goals, they requested from the management and the state increases in wages, rather than investment in new technology to respond to a change in demand. Even if they did have shares, there was no reliable stock market to trade them on.

VII CONCLUSION

Various piecemeal reforms within the framework of the central planning system in the Eastern Europe and the former USSR had very limited success. Central planning is quite tough and it successfully resisted profound reforms. This became obvious at the end of 1989 when an overhaul of the whole economic system and its replacement by a kind of a market-type economic one came about.

The CMEA decided in 1990 to abolish coordination of national plans and multilateral cooperation. These were the most important functions of the whole organization. Since 1991 all CMEA trade was conducted at world prices in convertible currencies. Not much, then, was left of the CMEA, hence the group vanished in the same year.

NOTES

1 The Luxembourg Agreement effectually prohibited majority voting in the EU, but the Single European Act re-introduced this way of voting for certain issues in the EU.

Annex III
The Eastern Enlargement of the European Union

I INTRODUCTION

The EU is at an important turning point. A new EU is in the process of forming, but it is not known yet what kind of shape it will take. There is a chance to alter the EU beyond recognition, hence the stakes are quite high.

Occasional inter-governmental conferences (IGCs) provide political guidelines for the future course of the EU. They have always presented one of the major opportunities for reshaping the EU. The seventh IGC that started in Turin in March 1996 and ended up in June 1997 where the Treaty of Amsterdam was expected to provide an answer about the future shape of the EU. One of the major items on the agenda was the institutional, political and economic preparation of the EU for the decades to come when the EU may even double its number of member countries from the current fifteen states. Six months following the completion of the seventh IGC, negotiations about enlargement of the EU may start. Cyprus is the first country in line.[1] Other countries that may follow include a select group of advanced central European transition countries.[2]

Previous Conferences (one has to recall that the term IGC is of relatively recent origin) that introduced changes in the process of European integration were the following seven:

- European integration, as we now know it, started with the Schuman/Monnet Plan (1950) and culminated with the Treaty of Paris.
- The second started in 1955 and led to the Treaty of Rome.
- The third was initiated in 1970 in order to revise Article 203 of the Treaty of Rome on the financing of the EU.
- The fourth began in 1985 and led to the Single European Act.
- The fifth and sixth started in 1990. One considered the extension of the Single European Market into an EMU. The other focused on internal and external political issues. Together, they produced the Maastricht Treaty.
- The seventh IGC was requested by Article N(2) of the Maastricht Treaty. It started as specified in 1996 and ended up in June 1997. Major agenda items included institutional reform, eastern enlargement and security

issues. The Treaty of Amsterdam has not, however, provided answers to any of the crucial issues. Hence, hard solutions are postponed until an unspecified date in the future.

Economic transition towards a market-based system and a decentralized decision-making process are again making the transition countries able to take advantage of being fully included in the market based international trading system. However, the success of integration of the transition economies into the international trading system depends on at least two factors. The first is the transformation of their economic system towards a market-based one,[3] while the other hinges on the openness of the western markets for goods and services from transition countries.

II RELATIONS BETWEEN THE EUROPEAN UNION AND TRANSITION COUNTRIES

Formal links between the EU and the countries in central and eastern Europe have not existed for a very long time. This was one of the impediments to trade liberalization between the two economic groups. The two opposing economic blocs and systems discriminated against each other in their trade relations. There was little that the east was able to offer to the west in return for the most-favoured nation (MFN) status in trade. This continued until the end of the cold war in 1989. The transition process introduced a significant change in these relations. From piecemeal assistance and trade concessions, certain transition countries won Association Agreements with the EU in the new situation. It all started with the EU granting the Generalized System of Preferences (GSP), over Trade and Cooperation Agreements, to the Association Agreements.

One of the significant features of the transition process is the change in the direction of trade. After the collapse of the CMEA, transition countries redirected their trade westwards, in a relatively short period of time, in particular towards the EU. Although a change in the pattern of trade took place, a portion of goods released from CMEA trade, cannot easily find market outlets in the EU. Those goods cannot always satisfy the quality, quantity, design and other standards that prevail in the EU. In addition, and very important, goods that might be potentially important as exports items for the transition countries are often regarded as 'sensitive' in the EU.

Initially, transition countries were at the very bottom of the EU pyramid of privileges. Only Romania and the former Yugoslavia benefited from the GSP. Other transition economies were facing all the trade obstacles for exports to the EU. Hence the former Soviet policy of keeping friendly countries in the camp not only through political and military means, but also through economic ties was lavishly assisted by the trade policy of the EU. In order to curtail the technological capabilities of the former socialist countries, the west established the Coordinating Committee on Multilateral

Export Controls (COCOM). Its objective was during and after the cold war the prevention of the transfer of high technology to the then socialist countries which may enhance their fire-power.[4] As this was not necessary after the collapse of socialism, the COCOM was replaced by the Wassenaar Agreement[5] which includes Russia. The Secretariat of the new organization started work in Vienna in 1996.[6]

It was as late as in 1989, but as early as the start of the transition process, that trade relations between the two regions started to 'normalize'. The G–7 and the EU took the first step to assist transition countries in their reform towards a market-type system, as well as to regulate relations. This was a unilateral decision to grant GSP and to curtail certain quantitative restrictions on trade with transition countries. Subsequently, most of the transition economies were removed from the list of state-trading countries.

The second step in the formalization and normalization of economic relations between the two groups was the conclusion of Trade and Cooperation Agreements with the transition countries that did not have them.[7] The trade provisions of these Agreements allow for reciprocal MFN treatment and trade concessions, they remove specified quantitative restrictions and seek further liberalization of mutual trade. This type of agreement was concluded between the EU and the former USSR in 1990. After the disintegration of that country, most of the newly independent states accepted the obligations coming from that Agreement in 1992.

In order to coordinate western aid to Hungary and Poland in their transition process to a market-based economic system, political pluralism and democracy, the EU started the PHARE[8] Programme in 1989. Assistance from this programme was extended later to most of the transition countries in central and eastern Europe. The goal of the PHARE Programme is an improvement in the access to markets, promotion of investment, transfer of know-how, adjustment in the farm sector, food aid, environmental protection and vocational training. Its focus is the development of and support to the private sector in the transition countries. The Programme has additional multiplier effects. It provides incentives to other donors and instigates private interest and investment through various studies. The most recent trend is to direct the PHARE assistance into the projects linked with infrastructure and the strengthening of democratic institutions and public administrations, as well as preparation for the full entry of the EU.

Following this assistance, the latest step in the formalization of relations is the liberalization of economic relations brought Association Agreements (Europe Agreements) between the EU and select transition countries. Short of full membership, the new arrangement with the EFTA and the deal with 70 African, Caribbean and Pacific (ACP) countries, these Agreements[9] are supposed to be the most favourable arrangements that the EU can offer to foreign countries. These Agreements mention in the Preamble the possibility of full membership for transition countries in the EU in the future, but for certain countries this may be a very distant future.

Different agreements offered to transition economies reflect the degree of the reform process achieved in the these countries, as well as their capabilities to compete. Although the need to aid transition countries through trade concessions is recognized and some actions are taken to create a free trade area between the EU and select transition countries, there are NTBs that seriously hinder exports from transition economies to the EU. This is most obvious in goods in which transition countries have a comparative advantage such as steel, textile, clothing, bulk chemicals and farm products.

Europe Agreements between the select group of transition countries take account of their efforts and achievements in the transition process. These countries had the fastest ever 'graduation' on the EU pyramid of trade privileges (Figure AIII.1). They started with GSP, over trade and cooperation agreements to reach association agreements that offer the possibility of full membership in the EU in the future. These countries are the most serious candidates for the entry of the EU. The goal of these agreements is the establishment of a free trade area in the manufactured goods between the partners within a period of ten years maximum from the entry into force of the deals. They also provide for improved access for certain farm goods. All this is expected to reinforce the reform process in the transition countries and increase stability in the relations between the partners. None the less, annual trade by the EU with the entire transition region is approximately the same as EU trade with Switzerland alone!

Other major provisions of the Association Agreements refer to the political dialogue among partners (this does not cost anything to the EU budget), as well as safeguard measures. During the times of recession and when jobs are at stake, there is an increased pressure on the authorities to introduce safeguard measures against foreign suppliers. The Agreements stipulate that if the EU producers are seriously injured or if there are dangerous developments within an EU industry that jeopardize the economic activity of the EU, there is a possibility that the EU will undertake (unspecified) safeguard measures. So, uncertainty prevails!

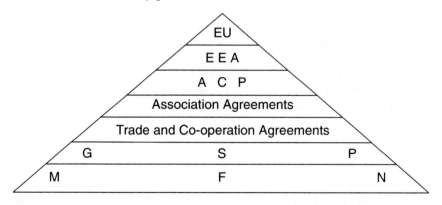

Figure AIII.1 Pyramid of privileges in trade with the European Union.

Rules of origin provide a potential benefit for associated countries. It is not only the goods that originate in either of the associated countries or in the EU that are entitled to preferential treatment, but also the Agreements allow for the cumulation of origin among the associated countries. Although this may sound like a concession, on the cost side of the coin, this interferes with the input mix in production. Instead of procuring inputs that may have superior features (price, quality, design), firms may be 'pushed' by the origin rules to select inputs that qualify for preferential treatment in exports.

There are strong arguments in support of a kind of re-establishment (re-integration is not a favoured term in central and eastern Europe) of broken economic ties among the transition countries. The Central European Free Trade Association, the Visegrád Group,[10] was created by the Czech Republic, Hungary, Poland and Slovakia in 1993, Slovenia joined in 1996, while Romania joined in 1997 (the group has 90 million people). The EU supported this type of integration; however the countries in the Visegrád scheme intend to join the EU, not to foster large-scale integration within the group. Otherwise that may keep them away from the EU. The intra-Visegrád group trade is relatively small, but it may increase once the member countries enter the EU as was the case with Spain and Portugal.

Regarding concessions in trade, the EU may think about a larger-scale cumulation of origin for the goods coming from transition economies in the future. A proposal by the Commission for the future does not go as far as to include the cumulation of origin of the goods from all transition economies for preferential treatment. Rather, it intends to offer something less ambitious. That is, a cumulation of origin for all goods that originate in the associated transition countries and the remaining EFTA countries.

Most of the anti-dumping actions against transition economies deal with sensitive goods. These products (agriculture, textile, steel and bulk chemicals) are the production lines in which transition countries have relative advantages in production and trade. Most of exports from transition economies are concentrated in these goods, although they present only a small share of the EU imports and consumption. For example, even in the sensitive iron and steel trade, the EU imports from transition countries was less than 3 per cent of the EU apparent consumption (UN/ECE, 1994, p. 154). Because of such a stance on dumping in the EU, uncertainty in trade relations with the transition region continues! That is unfriendly both regarding domestic and foreign investment. Investment is not undertaken if firms fear that their exports-related output will be subject to protectionist measures by the EU. None the less, apart from farm trade, various barriers to trade will disappear (e.g. on textiles) during 1997.

Association Agreements may have a negative impact on the transition countries, even though that is not their goal. These agreements are opening up the markets of partner countries (although there are NTBs on trade in 'sensitive goods'). The Czech prime minister, Klaus, criticized his country's

Europe Agreement as one of the causes of a sharp increase in deficit in trade with the EU. That deficit was 8.6 per cent of the Czech GDP in 1996 (*The Financial Times*, 18 July 1997).

One should not, however, downgrade the impact of Association Agreements on the transition countries. These Agreements introduce an element of stability into otherwise potentially volatile trade relations. An important thing is that the EU accepted certain bold and liberalization prone steps even in trade in sensitive goods. The Agreements offer some vision for economic relations for the future. This view is supported by a general belief that concessions in trade may be the most effective way in which the west can help transition countries in their difficult, but in the longer term rewarding, transition process.

The transition process does not progress in all countries at the same pace. Apart from the Baltic states, most of the countries that emerged from the former Soviet Union are those that lag behind the central-European transition economies. The term transition is by definition a finite process. However, after almost a decade of 'transition', it is hard to say when the transition countries would become market economies in the EU sense! The process of transition might have turned into a process of economic development. Therefore, the EU intends to conclude Partnership and Cooperation Agreements with most of the former Soviet countries. This type of accord will offer more than the usual trade and cooperation agreement, but it falls short of the benefits offered by Association Agreements. A bargaining problem is that Russia wants to be treated as if it were a member country of the WTO. The EU can not accept that prior to the establishment of a market-type economy in Russia. This is important since rules on costs and prices, on goods and services still do not follow market principles. What may emerge is a safeguard and/or an evolutionary clause that Russia may get a free trade agreement in industrial goods with the EU, if it enters into and adheres to the rules of the WTO. In the meantime, the EU has offered the countries of the Commonwealth of Independent States the TACIS[11] Programme which is similar to that (PHARE) given to the central European transition countries.[12] In any case, Russia intends, in a few years time, to submit an application for full membership of the EU.

III ENTRY INTO THE EUROPEAN UNION

1 Costs and benefits

Transition economies share political, security and economic motives for joining the EU. Politically, the transition countries still have young and relatively fragile democratic systems. This fragility comes from unfulfilled grand hopes that the change for the better towards a market-type democratic system can take place in a relatively short period of time and at a relatively small cost regarding economic and job security issues. Although the immediate threat of armed conflict is not very likely, there is still a certain apprehension regarding the division of 'spheres of influence' between the west (EU and, principally, Germany) and Russia. The central, east European and Baltic states obtained their freedom from the 'eastern bloc' and have concerns about preserving their independence. In addition, they have certain anxieties about 'losing' that independence to the west. An entry into the North Atlantic Treaty Organization (NATO) would require significant readjustment of military hardware and its alignment to the standards of the group. In the situation of an undercapitalized economy (which may have different investment priorities), this could be done through a new set of loans from the west. This is a sophisticated financial way to 'tie' these countries into NATO.[13] As for the economic issues, there are gains and costs for the transition countries from entry of the EU.

The major benefit for the transition countries would be secure access to the huge EU market. This is particularly relevant for goods that are 'sensitive' for the EU (farm products, textiles, steel, chemicals) as the transition countries have a comparative advantage in the production of those goods. For transition countries entry would mean a kind of an 'insurance policy' that the EU trade regime will remain open for their exports. The second gain for the transition countries would be an opportunity for the migration of labour into the rest of the EU following the specified adjustment period, even though this may have a two-edged effect. If the educated and the experienced leave transition economies, productivity in the transition region will suffer and funds for the education of experts will be lost. None the less, a relatively tight labour market in the rest of the EU could prevent such a scenario. In addition, experience has shown that labour migration (wars apart) takes place chiefly if labour cannot find employment in its country of origin. A third benefit from entry includes access to the structural and other funds of the EU. All this would give an impetus to the strengthening of the market system in the economies that are still passing through the transition process (van Brabant, 1996).

All these gains are not without risks. In some cases, the costs are quite serious. Transition countries still have fragile economies that would be exposed to fierce competition on the EU market. These adjustment troubles are well known even for the relatively advanced centrally planned economy of East Germany after the *Anschluss* of 1989. Gross annual transfers from the western part of the reunified Germany to the eastern one were around DM 200 billion (Table AIII.1). Such massive aid will be necessary at least until the year 2005 in order to let the former East Germany adjust to the new situation and catch up with the rest of the country and the EU. However, there is a question whether such massive aid is necessary in the medium and long term. Aid may kill local incentives to adjust and create a structurally dependent economy out of the former East Germany as was the case with the Italian Mezzogiorno. If the relatively advanced eastern part of Germany needs such massive transfers, one fears to think about the potential transfers

Table AIII.1   Intra-German transfers (from the West to the East), 1992–1996
(DM billions)

Transfer	1992	1993	1994	1995	1996
Gross	156	194	215	212	198
Net	122	154	172	148	144

Source: *Frankfurter Allgemeine Zeitung*, 2 October 1996

to the other transition countries that desire to enter the EU. Are they, perhaps, aspiring to do and get too much too soon? The Maastricht criteria for the EMU press for budgetary cuts throughout the EU. One does not know where the funds would come from to accommodate this eastern enlargement. The Cannes summit (1995) allocated 'only' ECU 6.7 billion to the PHARE Programme for the period 1995–99!

Transition is a lengthy and costly process. The question even for the other advanced transition countries that aspire to join the EU is who will finance such a 'wholesale' transition and adjustment cost to the membership. Second, the acceptance and implementation of the continuously evolving *acquis communautaire* is costly not only for the new members, but also for those countries that are already in the EU. Being less developed, the transition countries have both a lower financial capacity and a higher need to incorporate the EU rules. *Acquis communautaire* consists of around 11,000 pieces of EU legislation. Many things are highly regulated in the EU. They include not only health, environment and consumer protection, but also safety at work and social standards. Many of these issues do not directly increase productivity. In a situation with out-of-date capital stock, there is a dilemma in the transition countries that are on the way towards the EU. Should they invest scarce capital first into upgrading output potential or do something else?[14] Third, although there are certain positive developments regarding monetary aggregates in the transition countries, the criteria for the EMU may create barriers to entry.

The EU is also interested in enlargement for various political, security, ecological and economic reasons. However, if one asks the question what can 'eastern countries' specifically contribute to the EU?, the answer is rather subdued. Is the 'eastern' market with cheap labour and a certain possibility for investment an opportunity or a threat? One has to remember that European integration started in the early 1950s, not for economic reasons, but rather for the preservation of peace. That political goal was to be achieved through economic means by making war between Germany and France impossible. The southern enlargement of the EU, although costly in financial terms had the objective of stabilizing democracy in Greece, Spain and Portugal, following a period of dictatorship. Identical arguments can be used regarding the potential eastern enlargement of the EU. Stability and predictability at the eastern border is in the interests of the EU. Ecological and economic factors also exist. Modernization of the economies of the transition countries may create and retain certain high technology jobs in manufacturing and services in the EU. None the less, all that is linked to at least two types of economic cost. First is the need to finance the adjustment of the new countries to the new situation in the EU. With the Maastricht criteria for the EMU, there are serious austerity measures. One has noted the cost of adjustment of the former East Germany which has the advantage of already being formally absorbed into the reintegrated Germany. The question is where the funds would come from? The second cost would come from the loss of jobs and business in the 'sensitive' industries and agriculture of the EU because of the penetration of goods from the east. Those industries may exert a strong lobbying pressure on policy makers.

2   Criteria for entry

'Any European state may apply to become a Member of the Union' (Article O of the Maastricht Treaty).[15] This is the only Maastricht Treaty-based (sufficient) condition for a country to be considered for a full membership of the EU. In addition to this explicit (Treaty-based condition), there are several necessary and tacit, economic and political requirements for entry. These were defined in the Copenhagen summit in 1993. The potential candidate country must fulfil three conditions. It must have a market economy, a democratic political system and accept *acquis communautaire*.

First, the potential applicant country must have a market economy. Apart from the Czech Republic and Slovakia, not a single transition country had a fully functioning market economy even before they became centrally planned countries (van Brabant, 1996). Entry, in particular, an early entry, into the EU may cause serious external upheaval for any transition country. Their economies are not yet fully adjusted to the market-type economic system and their manufacturing and services sectors are still fragile.[16] Early entry into the EU without full macroeconomic stabilization and modernization of the output structure may be disastrous for the transition countries. They will not be able to withstand the strict rules for competition with EU producers in most industries. (The example of the former East Germany after reunification is quite instructive.) This would shatter any chance for further development of their fledgeling social and political democracies. Transition fatigue is obvious in all transition countries. This is exemplified in the return of the 'recycled' communists to office. Therefore, entry into the EU in the distant future needs to be thoroughly thought out and should be coupled with serious preparation. The EU needs to assist transition countries in order to invest in its own peaceful and prosperous neighbourhood in the future. The question is not any more whether transition countries need to be incorporated into the EU. Rather, it is how costly is it going to be to existing EU members and when and how long will it take?

The second condition is that the prospective country should have a stable democratic political system. This means a multi-party parliament, rule of law and respect for human and minority rights. This also includes good neighbourly relations and no territorial disputes. With regard to the last, not a single transition country passes the test. Neither do certain EU countries fare well here. Just consider Northern Ireland. However, the advantage is that they are already in the EU, a group which has no desire to get into any more trouble. There are some signs that the prospect of EU membership may ease tensions, as happened with Hungary and Romania in 1996.

The third condition is related to *acquis communautaire*. The prospective member country must accept and implement this set of rules. The only possibility for negotiation is the length of the adjustment period (otherwise there would be a two-speed EU) and the funds that will help to implement the *acquis communautaire*.

The fourth, tacit, requirement is that entry should not jeopardize the EU's financial resources. In addition, widening of the EU should not jeopardize any deepening of the integration process. If there are no changes in EU policies and if the original four Visegrád countries enter the EU, various estimates state that the annual transfers from the EU to the original four countries will cost the EU around ECU 50 billion a year.[17] That is roughly half of the entire EU budget for fifteen countries!

Transition economies need to 'catch up' in economic development with the EU (Table AIII.2). It is in the interest of the EU to help them achieve this goal. However, this will not be swift at all. For example, if a transition country such as Poland starts at 60 per cent of the Portuguese level and if

Table AIII.2 GDP per capita in 1994 and annual growth rates in select candidate countries, 1992–1997

Country	GDP per capita in USD 1994 (PPP)[a]	Annual growth rate (%)					
		1992	1993	1994	1995	1996	1997[b]
Cyprus	10,260	—	1.8	5.8	4.8	2.4	3.5
Czech Republic	7,910	−6.4	−0.9	2.6	5.2	4.4	4.0
Slovenia	7,020	−5.4	1.3	5.3	4.8	3.5	4.0
Hungary	6,310	−3.0	−0.8	2.9	1.5	0.5	2.0
Slovakia	6,660	−7.0	−4.1	4.8	7.4	6.9	6.0
Poland	5,380	2.6	3.8	5.2	7.0	6.0	5.0
Estonia	4,510	−14.1	−8.6	−2.7	2.5	3.5	4.0
Latvia	5,170	−34.9	−14.9	0.6	−1.6	2.5	3.5
Bulgaria	4,230	−7.3	−1.5	1.8	2.5	−10.0	3.0
Lithuania	3,240	−39.3	−30.4	1.0	2.5	4.0	5.0
Romania	2,920	−8.8	1.5	3.9	6.9	4.1	−2.0
Malta	7,460	—	4.5	5.0	9.0	4.0	4.0

Source: UN/ECE, IMF and World Bank (1997)
Notes: [a] The average GDP in the EU was USD 18,170 in 1994. [b] estimate

the continuous annual rate of growth of GDP in that transition country is 4 per cent, while that in Portugal is 2 per cent, it will take Poland more than twenty years to catch up with Portugal (CEPR, 1992, p. 65; Baldwin, 1995, pp. 477–478). One has to remember that most transition economies have shown positive rates of growth from 1994 only. There are still certain questions about the sustainability of these rates in the future.[18]

The southern EU countries are concerned with the possible entry of some of the east European countries, even in the distant future, since the new-comers may be democratic, but they are still 'poor' countries. Hence, they will compete with the 'Club Med' of the EU for regional and other aid. France and Spain would like to see a 'balanced' approach between the potential eastern enlargement of the EU and the policy of 'openness' towards south Mediterranean countries. The prospect of a rejuvenated old division of 'spheres of influence' has a corrosive effect on the unity of the EU, as proclaimed by the Maastricht Treaty.

The entry of the east European transition countries need not worry the EU Mediterranean nations, at least for another fifteen years or so. The most developed of the 'new democracies' lag a good deal behind the 'poorest', Portugal, in economic terms. Southern EU countries need not fear in the medium term the entry of select transition countries to the EU, and the potential 'exodus' of jobs eastwards because of lower wages there. If relatively low wages were the determining factor for location of production, then the EU would be flooded with cheap goods from these countries. Other factors, apart from wages, such as productivity, the capital stock and stability, play a more decisive role in many instances than relative wages. The Mediterranean EU countries are well ahead of the transition countries in those matters.

In order to assist the prospective transition countries in preparing for entry, the Essen summit of 1994 outlined the 'pre-accession strategy' of the EU. The key element is assistance to the select group of transition countries in making themselves ready for integration into the EU internal market. The prospective central European member countries committed themselves, among other things, to approximate their legislation to that of the EU. The gap in political, economic and social organization and development between the EU and potential new members has to narrow. Otherwise, new members will not assume the full set of obligations or enjoy all the benefits of being in the EU. Europe Agreements, structured dialogue and the PHARE Programme are the major tools of the 'pre-accession strategy'. In addition, the Cannes summit (1995) endorsed the White Paper, a reference document that can guide prospective member countries through the labyrinth of the EU legislation in order to make the assimilation task simpler.

As part of the 'pre-accession strategy', the EU sent a 200–page questionnaire to potential member countries to assess their eligibility for membership. The answers present an important input into the preparations of opinions about eligibility for entry by the Commission. Apart from deciding

the eligibility of each country, the Commission is in charge of the preparation of three other documents. The first deals with the impact of the
enlargement on the EU, the second considers the financial framework,
while the third, a composite document, is to offer a general assessment. In
addition, to ease potential entry, the EU in January 1996 opened the Technical Assistance Information Exchange Office (TAIEX). This is a one-stop
shop for information and technical/legal advice on EU legislation, enforcement and infrastructure.

All these necessary conditions for entry into the EU reveal that the Union
has very high discretionary powers and flexibility to select would-be members. With this in mind, the chances of even the most advanced transition
countries seem bleak for quite some time in the future, unless and until the
entry rules change and the economic situation in the transition countries
improves. The EU has neither intentions nor funds to include countries that
have an economic structure that would tilt towards agriculture or primary
commodities. Such an attitude by the EU may be hypocritical from a political vantage point since the west used almost half a century to encourage
these countries to join the free market and democratic world! The moral is:
calm down, please, Czechs, Slovenians, Hungarians, Poles and Estonians;
and others. An 'optimistic' scenario is that if 'all goes well', meaning smooth
negotiations of perhaps around a decade and an adjustment process of
another decade, it will take the most advanced transition countries some
twenty years to become full members of the EU.

The field where a coordination and, even, a certain unification of action
between the EU and the 'prospective' member countries is most likely in
future is politics.[19] It costs the EU nothing, while the transition countries
may feel that something is going on between them and the EU. None the
less, the most that central Europeans should hope for in the long term is a
kind of arrangement similar to the one that was implemented between the
EU and most of the EFTA countries (European Economic Area) in 1994.
That is, full membership minus the CAP, minus labour mobility, and minus
structural funds.

IV CONCLUSION

The EU is in a particular (temporary) crisis. On the political front, it has
been unable to solve the neighbouring Yugoslav black hole. This proves that
the EU still plays a relatively minor role in the resolution of grave international crises (although others did not fare much better).[20] In the economic
field it is incapable of creating new jobs and reducing unemployment. As for
the EMU, the EU is still quite far away from that goal as followed by the
letter of the Maastricht Treaty.

Various agreements between the EU and transition countries offer preferential treatment and introduce a certain 'order' into economic relations. It
is a very positive step in relation to the pre-transition era, although it should

not be an end in itself. Further unilateral steps need to be taken by the EU if the transition process hopes to continue. However, when jobs are at risk, in particular during recession and in pre-election times, short-term considerations by the EU may overshadow the longer-term gains.

A plethora of agreements by the EU with transition countries offers an improved access to the EU market. These technical agreements are a paradise for lawyers and consultants. This variety of arrangements can complicate life. What may happen in the future is that the EU will replace the glut of agreements with one single one, at least for certain groups of advanced transition countries. These economies may slowly be on the way towards the European Economic Area. None the less, there is a lot of anxiety about relations between the EU and the transition economies, as there are still risks and uncertainties in the transition region. This is why the transition economies now have a partnership with the EU instead of membership.

A new IGC that will start at least a year before the next enlargement will confront the most comprehensive political reform of the EU since its creation. It will have to deal with a number of political minefields on the way to preserving unity with diversity in the EU. The IGC may, perhaps, aim at relatively less to make the EU better. A consideration of the issue of timing and terms of enlargement is highly speculative.[21] A hypothetical early expectation for full membership of the most advanced transition economies is the year 2015! None the less, entry depends on political will (and the funds) of the EU countries. If that exists, then entry can be made faster and easier. However, the funds and the political will existed even when Spain and Portugal were negotiating entry with the EU, but their entry took several years more than expected. Hence, all official statements about (very) early entry to the EU, by even around the year 2002, need to be taken with a pinch of salt.

The EU as we know it, is over, however what will come out of the IGC is as yet unknown. Perhaps it will not be known until the very last second of negotiations, as has usually been the case in similar occasions. As a rule, when France and Germany and, perhaps one other larger EU country reach an agreement during the final moments of negotiation, they draw others into the deal.[22] Only once the exact terms for the entry are known, one will be able to make an analysis about the potential (high) costs of any eastern enlargement of the EU.

Eastern enlargement of the EU will be quite costly: both for the EU and for the select group of central European countries. Is it necessary to do so much so fast on both sides? It is true that the central European transition countries have 'no other option' but to join the EU. It is also true that they survived a 'big-boom' adjustment following the transition process. However, the 'big-boom' was a one-off affair. Integration in the EU is a constantly evolving process. Unless the transition countries are well prepared, they may face similar problems that Germany encountered with the absorption of the eastern part of the country. The forthcoming eastern enlargement of the EU will be the best prepared enlargement to date. A cynic would say that this why enlargement will not take place (at least for quite some time).[23] None the less, enlargement of the EU is a highly charged political process that can not be predicted with any accuracy.

Although Germany (together with Britain) would like to see an expanded EU, pushing for this enlargement along with a tighter EMU may end up achieving neither! Even the majority of the German population may be not convinced that the EMU as planned is acceptable. In addition, the Maastricht-type EMU is based on criteria that are unknown in monetary integration theory.

European integration has always been based on a political decision about securing peace and liberty in Europe. This is the purpose of the EU, although many have forgotten about it! European integration is aimed at mitigating the impact of old rivalries and their replacement by mutual economic advantages and social prosperity. Eastern enlargement is, for the EU, neither about extra efficiency or growth. It is neither about the creation of new jobs.[24] Its basic objective is to give a certain support to friendly countries and governments and a chance to succeed in their reform process. Therefore, eastern enlargement of the EU has to be given a chance, but at more of a jog than a sprint. *Festina lente*! (Hurry, slowly!)

NOTES

1　Malta is no longer enthusiastic about the EU.
2　Turkey applied for membership of the EU in 1987. In spite of the likely Greek veto and the negative opinion by the commission in 1989, too many in the EU consider Turkey not to qualify on economic, political (e.g. the treatment of Kurds), religious and cultural grounds. However, Greece may act as a handy scapegoat for a much wider European resistance towards the accession of Turkey. For example, a prominent christian Democrat in the European Parliament, Wilfried Martens, said 'The EU is in the process of building a civilization in which Turkey has no place'. In addition, top Dutch politicians have audibly doubted if Turkey should be let in the EU 'because there are too many of them and they are too poor – and they are Muslims' (*The Economist*, 15 March 1997, p. 31).
3　The transition process has three features: liberalization, stabilization and modernization. It is much longer and costlier that foreseen at the end of 1980s. All these changes happened in undercapitalized economies.
4　The goods whose trade was followed by the COCOM were divided into three lists: nuclear-related exports, conventional weaponry and dual-use (civil or military) goods and technologies.
5　Wassenaar is a suburb of the Hague.
6　The purpose of the new organization is to control and prevent trade in technology for atomic, chemical and bacteriological weapons, in particular, to areas of tensions and countries (such as Iraq, Iran, North Korea and Libya) that may abuse them.
7　Trade and Cooperation Agreements entered into force for Hungary in 1988, Poland 1989, former Czechoslovakia 1990, while for Bulgaria and Romania it was 1991.
8　Poland, Hungary: Assistance for Economic Restructuring.

9 Europe Agreements were signed with Hungary, Poland and the former Czecho-slovakia in 1991. Bulgaria and Romania concluded Association Agreements in 1993, the Baltic states did the same in 1995 and Slovenia in 1996.

10 The major problems of the Visegrád group include the following. First, this integration arrangement means different things to different countries. The Czechs see it as a purely free-trade-area-to-be by the year 2000. Others would like it to be a bit more than that. Second, internal trade is relatively small. More than a half of the total trade of the member countries is with the EU.

11 Technical Assistance for the Commonwealth of Independent States.

12 The difference between the two Programmes is that most TACIS assistance is still linked to technical advices, while PHARE assistance is moving from that stage into infrastructure.

13 There are several questions for the politicians. Is, perhaps, a democratic Russia, a far more important element for the peace and stability of Europe, than the expansion of NATO? Is the anxiety of Russia about the eastern enlargement of NATO justified? Isn't it true that the 'West' started wars with Russia three times during the past two centuries (not the other way around)? Is eastern enlargement of NATO a long-term preparation for the fourth military attack?

14 It is true that not all the measures are to be accepted and implemented by the newcomers before entry.

15 Article 237 of the Treaty of Rome regulates the same issue in the identical way. None the less, the unresolved question is what are the European states? Are those the ones that are members of the UN Economic Commission for Europe (include among others Canada and Uzbekistan)? Does religion matter?

16 The EU may even think about excluding agriculture from possible entry talks with the transition economies, although that is the sector where these countries may have comparative advantages. Alternatively, if the farm sector is included in negotiations, it may receive a longer transition period, just as was the case in the deals with Spain and Portugal.

17 A short survey of select studies is given by Baldwin (1995).

18 Davenport (1995, p. 20) reported the results of several studies that attempt to estimate the necessary annual investment requirement of the central European countries in order to double GDP per capita over ten years. The estimates are between USD 103 and 344 billion! One just wonders where that money will come from.

19 Examples include the involvement of certain transition countries in the war against Iraq (1991) or cooperation in peacekeeping operations in the former Yugoslavia.

20 The fragile Dayton Peace Accord (1995) reflected the fact that the warring parties were temporarily tired of war.

21 Once the Treaty is revised, it may need to go through the national parliaments for ratification, even through referendums. Memories about the difficulties of ratific-ation of the Maastricht Treaty are still quite fresh.

22 Remember that revisions of the Treaty have to be legally unanimous.

23 Remember that the initial opinion of the Commission about the accession of Greece was negative.

24 If all ten applicant countries enter the EU, that would increase the EU's popula-tion by around 30 per cent, but its GDP by only 4 per cent (*The Economist*, 31 May 1997).

Annex IV
Research Topics for the Future

The objective of this Annex is to provide a select list of future research topics in the field of international economic integration. This topics include the following:

- A research issue needs to be a theoretical consideration of economic integration between countries on different levels of development: integration between the EU and transition economies. (For example. Is integration, such as a free trade area between, the US, Canada and Mexico, without a special treatment for the weaker country a good thing? What are the chances of integration between South Africa and its neighbours? What are the potential and chances of economic integration in the Pacific region?)
- In spite of significant improvements in techniques for measuring the effects of international economic integration, there is still a considerable dilemma. That is, our lack of a full understanding of the determinants, operation and effect of integration on trade, production, investment and consumption. Until this is solved, the nature of the analysis of integration will remain speculative (just take a sample look at the index of this book under 'uncertainty'). Attempts to solve these problems, in particular the dynamic ones, need to be on the research agenda in the future.
- Relations between regionalism and multilateral solutions to the trade and investment problems offer another challenging research topic. Is there a way to prevent the creation and evolution of regional blocs that inhibit global liberalization?
- The relation between economic integration and NTBs has received relatively little research attention so far. The same is the case with the theory of customs union and imperfect competition.
- Another global item for research is the impact of integration on various industries. Integration has had the strongest impact on higher value-added industries with significant economies of scale. This, however, has to be studied in greater detail, in particular, its relevance for developing countries.

- In the case of integration among developing countries, should one think first about a free mobility of labour and capital in their integration attempts and, only then, about the movement of goods and services?
- One should not forget the development of the theory of public choice. What do the voters want regarding economic integration and are ready, able and willing to pay for in terms of taxes, prices and security of employment?[1] Does that public choice change over time? How do you adjust integration arrangements to accommodate these changes?
- What are the ways of overcoming difficulties in integrating diverse financial market structures (e.g. instruments of supervision and regulation) when countries decide to form a monetary union? In the absence of some degree of harmonization, is it possible to create incentives for regulatory arbitrage in which financial institutions migrate to the relatively more lax regulatory jurisdiction within the group?[2]
- Another topic may be inspired by the old literature on trade creation and trade diversion. One may examine whether monetary unions create or divert trade in financial services. For instance, if Britain were not a part of the monetary union of the EU, would British banks lose much business to German or French banks? What would be the effects on the Swiss and US banking businesses?
- The US has a huge and mouting foreign debt. Hence, there will be an erosion in the confidence in the stability of the dollar. What would be the effect of a massive switch in international reserves from unstable dollars into stable euros?
- Monetary integration between the EU and transition countries is a promising research area. The same holds for capital market integration and international monetary stability. In addition, the Maastricht Treaty introduced tough fiscal criteria for monetary union. Hence, the tax burden increased, job creation was prevented in the EU by another restriction as the flexibility of fiscal policy was narrowed. Alternative ways for reaching the same goals with less damaging consequences will be an interesting research topic.
- There are also unresolved issues regarding fiscal federalism in integration groups with members at different level of development.
- The future of the inflow of foreign labour in the EU is highly uncertain. On the one hand, an ageing population in the EU will demand extra expenditure by the state. On the other hand, an inflow of foreign labour to rectify certain demographic trends in the EU, may ease the pressure from labour shortages in the EU. But an inflow from where? An 'orderly' inflow from the countries in transition or a 'disorderly' inflow from the Islamic and unstable countries which pass through a demographic 'explosion' such as the south Mediterranean countries and Turkey? Some background research on how to cope with such developments is still lacking.
- There is a large shady area in our knowledge regarding the necessity of an industrial and technology policy (intervention) for an increase in compe-

titiveness of an integrated group. Is simple economic integration and liberalization in an enlarged market sufficient for an increase in competitiveness? What are the corporate strategies regarding economic integration? How will they change over time? Is business consolidation (mergers and acquisitions) a necessary consequence of an enlarging and integrating market? Is it going to be reversed in the future? What is the impact of integration on concentration ratios? What is the *ex post* impact of the 1992 Programme on consumers (i.e. have prices fallen or not increased; by how much)?

- Answers to many issues relating to economic integration, imperfect competition and NTBs are still pending. The same holds for economic integration, on the one hand, and linkages between competition, industrial and trade policies, on the other.
- Integration issues related to FDI such as competition, competitiveness, the attraction of TNCs, sectoral distribution, new technology and trade, offer research topics that will not be easily exhausted.
- What is the relation between international economic integration and SMEs?
- What is the impact of economic integration and the opening up of an internal market (1992 Programme) on the penetration of external suppliers? What is the impact of a lack of fiscal harmonization on competition (in the EU, for instance)?
- Is there a need for the harmonization of regulation in an integrating group of countries, or can/should one leave competition within national regulations about, for example, labour or environment issues?
- There is still a puzzle regarding the question of the location of firms and economic integration.
- As regional policies had very limited results in the past, one wonders if it is necessary to have such a policy at the level of an integration scheme? If not, how to reconcile economic and monetary union among countries that are on different level of economic development? Can one leave the solution of the 'regional problem' exclusively to market forces? How to cope with the regional problem of the EU once the transition countries start entering the EU?
- As for the services sector, the question is whether a liberal regulatory framework within a group of countries is sufficient to cause the integration of this sector? If not, what else is necessary? Why?
- High and ever increasing environmental standards will continue to introduce NTBs to trade. How to cope with that problem? Is it a mutual recognition of national standards in the EU or should the highest standards be imposed throughout the group? If the highest standards are to be imposed in the EU, then certain countries may face financial difficulties in implementing them. Who should/is willing to pay for that? The national taxpayers, the taxpayers of the standard-imposing country and/or the EU?

- Last, but not least, there is the question of regional integration and the multilateral rules for trade and investment. Almost all countries in the world are and will be involved in a certain type of integration arrangement. International economic integration is now here to stay. The issue is the strengthening of the complementarity between regional economic integration and the WTO, and the prevention of regional groups turning into blocs that inhibit global liberalization. Researchers and practitioners will have to find the ways and make sure that integration and the multilateral process continue to reinforce each other in the decades to come.

In any event, there are so many dilemmas regarding international economic integration that anyone embarking upon studying these issues should not worry that the circle is closed and that their research efforts will be in vain.

NOTES

1 Recall the changing mood of public support for the Maastricht Treaty, and anxiety regarding monetary integration in the EU.
2 Germany has an aversion to allowing short-term debt instruments unlike the British reliance on them for the conduct of monetary policy and liquidity management of its banks.

Bibliography

Adams, G. (1983). 'Criteria for US Industrial Policy Strategies', in *Industrial Policies for Growth and Competitiveness* (eds G. Adams and L. Klein). Lexington, MA: Lexington Books, pp. 393–418.

Adams, G. and A. Bolino (1983). 'Meaning of industrial policy', in *Industrial Policies for Growth and Competitiveness* (eds G. Adams and L. Klein). Lexington, MA: Lexington Books, pp. 13–20.

Adams, G. and L. Klein (1983). 'Economic evolution of industrial policies for growth and competitiveness: overview', in *Industrial Policies for Growth and Competitiveness* (eds G. Adams and L. Klein). Lexington, MA: Lexington Books, pp. 3–11.

Allen, P. (1983). 'Policies to correct cyclical imbalance within a monetary union', *Journal of Common Market Studies*, pp. 313–327.

Allen, P. and P. Kenen (1980). *Asset Markets, Exchange Rates and Economic Integration*. Cambridge: Cambridge University Press.

Andréoso-O'Callaghan, B. and C. Noonan (1996). 'European intra-industry trade: emerging industrial specialization in central and eastern europe', *Journal of World Trade*, pp. 139–168.

Ardy, B. (1988). 'The national incidence of the EC budget', *Journal of Common Market Studies*, pp. 401–429.

Armington, P. (1969). 'A theory of demand for products distinguished by place of production', *IMF Staff Papers*, pp. 159–178.

Armstrong, H. (1985). 'The reform of European Community regional policy', *Journal of Common Market Studies*, pp. 319–343.

Arthur, B. (1990). 'Positive feedbacks in the economy', *Scientific American* (February), pp. 92–9.

Ashcroft, B. (1980). *The Evaluation of Regional Policy in Europe: A Survey and Critique*. Glasgow: University of Strathclyde.

Audretsch, D. (1989). *The Market and the State*. New York: New York University Press.

Audretsch, D. (1993). 'Industrial policy and international competitiveness', in *Industrial Policy in the European Community* (ed. P. Nicolaides). Dordrecht: Martinus Nijhoff, pp. 67–105.

Bachtler, J. and R. Michie (1993). 'The restructuring of regional policy in the European Community', *Regional Studies*, pp. 719–725.

Bachtler, J. and R. Michie (1995). 'A new era in EU regional policy evaluation? The apprisal of the structural funds', *Regional Studies*, pp. 745–751.

Badaracco, J. and D. Yoffie (1983). 'Industrial policy: it can't happen here', *Harvard Business Review* (November–December), pp. 97–105.

Balassa, B. (1967). 'Trade creation and trade diversion in the European Common Market', *Economic Journal*, pp. 1–17.

Balassa, B. (1973). *The Theory of Economic Integration*. London: George Allen & Unwin.

Balassa, B. (1986a). 'Intra-industry specialisation', *European Economic Review*, pp. 27–42.

Balassa, B. (1986b). 'The determinants of intra-industry specialization in the United States trade', *Oxford Economic Papers*, pp. 220–233.

Balassa, B., and L. Bauwens (1988). 'The determinants of intra-European trade in manufactured goods', *European Economic Review*, pp. 1421–1437.

Balasubramanyam, V. and D. Greenaway (1992). 'Economic integration and foreign direct investment: Japanese investment in the EC', *Journal of Common Market Studies*, pp. 175–193.

Baldwin, R. (1989). 'The growth effects of 1992', *Economic Policy*, pp. 248–270.

Baldwin, R. (1993). 'On the measurement of dynamic effects of integration', *Empirica*, pp. 129–145.

Baldwin, R. (1995a). 'The eastern enlargement of the European Union', *European Economic Review*, pp. 474–481.

Baldwin, R. (1995b). 'A domino theory of regionalism', in *Expanding Membership of the European Union* (eds R. Baldwin, Pertti Haaparanta and Jaakko Kiander). Cambridge: Cambridge University Press, pp. 25–48.

Baldwin, R. P. Haaparanta and J. Kiander (eds) (1995). *Expanding Membership of the European Union*. Cambridge: Cambridge University Press.

Baldwin, R. and A. Venables (1995). 'Regional economic integration', in *Handbook of International Economics* (eds G. Grossman and K. Rogoff). Amsterdam: Elsevier, pp. 1597–1646.

Barro, R. and X. Sala-i-Martin (1991). 'Convergence across states and regions', *Brookings Papers on Economic Activity*, pp. 107–182.

Bayliss, B. (1985). 'Competition and industrial policy', in *The Economics of the European Community* (ed. A. El-Agraa). Oxford: Philip Allan, pp. 209–227.

Bayliss, B. and A. El-Agraa (1990). 'Competition and industrial policies with emphasis on competition policy', in *Economies of the European Community* (ed. A. El-Agraa). New York: St Martin's Press, pp. 137–155.

Beije, P., J. Groenewegen, K. van Paridon and J. Paelinck (eds) (1985). *A Competitive Future for Europe?* Rotterdam: Erasmus University.

Berglas, E. (1979). 'Preferential trading theory: the n commodity case', *Journal of Political Economy*, pp. 315–331.

Bhagwati, J. (1971). 'Trade diverting customs unions and welfare improvement: a clarification', *Economic Journal*, pp. 580–587.

Bhagwati, J. (1973). 'A reply to Professor Kirman', *Economic Journal*, pp. 895–897.

Bhagwati, J. (1989). 'United States trade policy at the crossroads', *World Economy*, pp. 439–480.

Bhagwati, J. and A. Panagariya (1996). 'The theory of preferential trade agreements: historical evolution and current trends', *American Economic Review*, pp. 82–87.

Bhatia, R. (1985). *The West African Monetary Union*. Washington: IMF.

Bird, R. (1972). 'The need for regional policy in a common market', in *International Economic Integration* (ed. P. Robson). Harmondsworth: Penguin Books, pp. 257–277.

Bird, R. (1975). 'International aspects of integration', *National Tax Journal*, pp. 302–314.

Bird, R. and D. Brean (1985). 'Canada/US tax relations: issues and perspectives', in *Canada/United States Trade and Investment Issues* (eds D. Fretz, R. Stern and J. Whalley). Toronto: Ontario Economic Council, pp. 391–425.

Blackhurst, R, and D. Henderson (1993). 'Regional integration arrangements, world integration and GATT', in *Regional Integration and the Global Trading System* (eds K. Anderson and R. Blackhurst). New York: Harvester Wheatsheaf, pp. 408–435.

Blais, A. (1986). 'Industrial policy in advanced capitalist democracies', in *Industrial Policy* (ed. A. Blais). Toronto: University of Toronto Press, pp. 1–53.

Bos, M. and H. Nelson (1988). 'Indirect taxation and the completion of the internal market of the EC', *Journal of Common Market Studies*, pp. 27–44.

Bowles, P. and B. MacLean (1996). 'Regional trading blocs: will east Asia be next?', *Cambridge Journal of Economics*, pp. 393–412.

Brada, J. and J. Méndez (1985). 'Economic integration among developed, developing and centrally planned economies: a comparative analysis', *Review of Economics and Statistics*, pp. 549–556.

Brada, J. and J. Méndez (1988). 'An estimate of the dynamic effects of economic integration', *Review of Economics and Statistics*, pp. 163–168.

Brander, J. (1987). 'Shaping comparative advantage: trade policy, industrial policy, and economic performance', in *Shaping Comparative Advantage* (eds R.G. Lipsey and W. Dobson). Toronto: C.D. Howe Institute, pp. 1–55.

Brander, J. and B. Spencer (1985). 'Export subsidies and international market share rivalry', *Journal of International Economics*, pp. 83–100.

Buckley, P. and P. Artisien (1987). 'Policy issues of intra-EC direct investment', *Journal of Common Market Studies*, pp. 207–230.

Buigues, P. and A. Jacquemin (1992). 'Foreign direct investment and exports in the Common Market', paper presented at the Japanese Direct Investment in a Unifying Europe, conference held in INSEAD, Fontainebleau, 26–27 June 1992, mimeo.

Buigues, P., A. Jacquemin and A. Sapir (eds) (1995). *European Policies on Competition, Trade and Industry*. Aldershot: Edward Elgar.

Buigues, P. and A. Sapir (1993). 'Market services and European integration: issues and challenges', *European Economy Social Europe*, no. 3, pp. ix–xx.

Bulmer-Thomas, V. (1988). 'The Central American Common Market', in *International Economic Integration* (ed. A. El-Agraa). Houndmills: Macmillan, pp. 284–313.

Bunce, V. (1985). 'The empire strides back: the evolution of the eastern bloc from a Soviet asset to a Soviet liability', *International Organization*, pp. 1–46.

Camagni, R. (1992). 'Development scenarios and policy guidelines for the lagging regions in the 1990s', *Regional Studies*, pp. 361–374.

Campa, J. and T. Sorenson (1996). 'Are trade blocs conducive to free trade?', *Scandinavian Journal of Economics*, pp. 263–273.

Cantwell, J. (1987). 'The reorganization of European industries after integration: selected evidence on the role of multinational enterprise activities', *Journal of Common Market Studies*, pp. 127–151.

Canzoneri, M. and C. Rogers (1990). 'Is the European Community an optimal currency area? Optimal taxation versus the cost of multiple currencies', *American Economic Review*, pp. 419–433.

Carlén, B. (1994). 'Road transport', *EFTA Occasional Paper*, no. 49, pp. 81–111.

Carliner, G. (1988). 'Industrial policies for emerging industries', in *Strategic Trade Policy and the New International Economics* (ed. P. Krugman). Cambridge, MA: The MIT Press, pp. 147–168.

Caves, R. (1985). *Multinational Enterprise and Economic Analysis*. Cambridge: Cambridge University Press.

Caves, R. and R. Jones (1985). *World Trade and Payments*. Boston: Little, Brown and Company.

Cecchini, P. (1988). *The European Challenge 1992*. Aldershot: Wildwood House.

CEPR (1992). *Is Bigger Better? The Economics of EC Enlargement*. London: Centre for Economic Policy Research.

Chang, H. (1994). *The Political Economy of Industrial Policy*. London: Macmillan.

Chaudhry, P., P. Dacin and P. Peter (1994). 'The pharmaceutical industry and European Community integration', *European Management Journal*, pp. 442–453.

Choi, J. and E. Yu (1984). 'Customs unions under increasing returns to scale', *Economica*, pp. 195–203.

Cnossen, S. (1986). 'Tax harmonization in the European Community', *Bulletin for International Fiscal Documentation*, pp. 545–563.

Cnossen, S. (1995). 'Reforming and coordinating company taxes in the European Union', paper presented at the conference Changing Role of the Public Sector: Transition in the 1990s, Lisbon, 21–24 August 1995.

Cnossen, S. (1996). 'Company taxes in the European Union: criteria and options for reform', *Fiscal studies*, pp. 67-97.

Cobham, D. (1989). 'Strategies for monetary integration revisited', *Journal of Common Market Studies*, pp. 203–218.

Cobham, D. and P. Robson (1994). 'Monetary integration in Africa: a deliberately European perspective', *World Development*, pp. 285–299.

Coffey, P. (ed.) (1988). *Main Economic Policy Areas of the EEC towards 1992.* Dordrecht: Kluwer.

Collier, P. (1979). 'The welfare effects of customs unions: an anatomy', *Economic Journal*, pp. 84–95.

Collins, C. (1985). 'Social policy', in *The Economics of the European Economic Community* (ed. A. El-Agraa). Oxford: Philip Allan, pp. 262–287.

Commission of the EC (1990). 'One market, one money', *European Economy*, October.

Commission of the EC (1992). *The Future Development of the Common Transport Policy.* Brussels: European Commission.

Conklin, D. and T. Courchene (eds)(1985). *Canadian Trade at a Crossroads: Optionsfor New International Agreements.* Toronto: Ontario Economic Council.

Cooper, C. and B. Massel (1965a). 'A new look at customs union theory', *Economic Journal*, pp. 742–747.

Cooper, C. and B. Massel (1965b). 'Toward a general theory of customs unions for developing countries', *Journal of Political Economy*, pp. 461–476.

Corado, C. and J. de Melo (1986). 'An ex-ante model for estimating the impact on trade flows of a country's Joining a Customs Union', *Journal of Development Economics*, pp. 153–166.

Corden, W. (1972a). 'Economies of scale and customs union theory', *Journal of Political Economy*, pp. 465–475.

Corden, W. (1972b). *Monetary Integration.* Princeton: Essays in International Finance, Princeton University.

Corden, W. (1976). 'Customs union theory and the nonuniformity of tariffs', *Journal of International Economics*, pp. 99–106.

Corden, W. (1979). 'Intra-Industry trade and factors proportion theory', in *On the Economics of Intra-industry Trade* (ed. H. Giersch). Tubingen: J.C.B. Mohr, pp. 3–12.

Corden, W. (1984). 'The normative theory of international trade', in *Handbook of International Economics* (eds R. Jones and P. Kenen). Amsterdam: North Holland, pp. 63–130.

Corden, W. (1990). 'Strategic trade policy. How new? How sensible', Working Paper 396, Washington: World Bank.

Courchene, T. (1987). *Social Policy in the 1990s, Agenda for Reform.* Toronto: C.D. Howe Institute.

Croxford, G., M. Wise and B. Chalkley, (1987). 'The reform of the European Development Fund', *Journal of Common Market Studies*, pp. 25–38.

Curzon, V. (1974). *The Essentials of Economic Integration.* London: Macmillan.

Curzon Price, V. (1981). *Industrial Policies in the European Community.* London: Macmillan.

Curzon Price, V. (1987). *Free Trade Areas, the European Experience*. Toronto: C.D. Howe Institute.

Curzon Price, V. (1988a). 'The European Free Trade Association', in *International Economic Integration* (ed. A. El-Agraa). London: Macmillan, pp. 96–127.

Curzon Price, V. (1988b). *1992: Europe's Last Chance? From Common Market to Single Market*. London: Institute of Economic Affairs.

Curzon Price, V. (1990). 'Competition and industrial policies with emphasis on industrial policy', in *Economics of the European Community* (ed. A. El-Agraa). New York: St Martin's Press, pp. 156–186.

Curzon Price, V. (1991). 'The threat of "Fortress Europe" from the development of social and industrial policies at a European level', *Aussenwirtschaft*, pp. 119–138.

Curzon Price, V. (1993). 'EEC's strategic trade-cum-industrial policy: a public choice analysis', in *National Constitutions and International Economic Law* (eds M. Hilf and E. Petersmann). Deventer: Kluwer, pp. 391–405.

Curzon Price, V. (1996). 'Residual obstacles to trade in the Single European Market', *Euryopa*, Institut européen de l'Universite de Genève.

Curzon Price, V. (1997). 'The European Free Trade Association' in *Economic Integration Worldwide* (ed. A. El-Agraa). London: Macmillan, pp. 175–202.

d'Arge, R. (1969). 'Note on customs unions and direct foreign investment', *Economic Journal*, pp. 324–333.

d'Arge, R. (1971a). 'Customs unions and direct foreign investment', *Economic Journal*, pp. 352–355.

d'Arge, R. (1971b). 'A reply', *Economic Journal*, pp. 357–359.

Davenport, M. (1995). 'Fostering integration of countries in transition in central and eastern Europe in the world economy and the implications for the developing countries', UNCTAD, ITD/7, 31 October 1995.

de Bandt, J. (1985). 'French industrial policies', in *A Competitive Future for Europe?* (eds P. Beije, J Groenewegen, K. van Paridon and J. Paelinck). Rotterdam: Erasmus University, pp. 65–79.

Defraigne, P. (1984). 'Towards concerted industrial policies in the EC', in *European Industry: Public Policy and Corporate Strategy* (ed. A. Jacquemin). Oxford: Clarendon Press, pp. 368–377.

de Ghellinck, E. (1988). 'European industrial policy against the background of the Single European Act', in *Main Economic Policy Areas of the EEC – Towards 1992* (ed. P. Coffey). Dordrecht: Kluwer, pp. 133–156.

de Grauwe, P. (1975a). 'Conditions for monetary integration – a geometric interpretation', *Weltwirtschaftliches Archiv*, pp. 634–646.

de Grauwe, P. (1975b). 'The interaction of monetary policies in a group of European countries', *Journal of International Economics*, pp. 207–228.

de Grauwe, P. (1987). 'International trade and economic growth in the European Monetary System', *European Economic Review*, pp. 389–398.

de Grauwe, P. (1989). 'Economic policy and political democracy', *European Affairs*, no. 1, pp. 66–72.

de Grauwe, P. (1994). 'Towards EMU without the EMS', *Economic Policy*, pp. 149–185.

de Grauwe, P. (1996). 'The economics of convergence: towards monetary union in Europe', *Weltwirtschaftliches Archiv*, pp. 1–27.

de la Fuente, A. and X. Vives (1995). 'Infrastructure and education as instruments of regional policy in the European Community', *Economic Policy*, pp. 13–51.

Dell'Aringa, C., and F. Neri (1989). 'Illegal immigrants and the informal economy in Italy', in *European Factor Mobility* (eds I. Gordon and A. Thirlwall). New York: St Martin's Press, pp. 133–147.

Delors, J. (1989). *Report on Economic and Monetary Union in the European Community*. Brussels: EC.

de Melo, J., and A. Panagariya (1992). *The New Regionalism in Trade Policy.* Washington: The World Bank.

Dennis, G. (1981). 'United Kingdom's monetary independence and membership of the European Monetary System', in *European Monetary System and International Monetary Reform* (eds J. Abraham and M. Vanden Abeele). Bruxelles: Editions de l'Université de Bruxelles, pp. 139–155.

Dent, C. (1997). *The European Economy: The Global Context.* London: Routledge.

Dertouzos, M., R. Lester and R. Solow (1990). *Made in America.* New York: HarperPerennial.

Devarajan, S. and J. de Melo (1987). 'Evaluating participation in African monetary unions: a statistical analysis of the CFA zones', *World Development*, pp. 483–496.

Dietz, R. (1986). 'Soviet foregone gains in trade with the CMEA six: a reapprisal', *Comparative Economic Studies*, pp. 69–94.

Donges, J. (1980). 'Industrial policies in West Germany's not so market-oriented economy', *The World Economy*, pp. 185–204.

Dore, R. (1986). *Structural Adjustment in Japan, 1970–82.* Geneva: ILO.

Dosi, G. (1988). 'Sources, procedures and microeconomic effects of innovation', *Journal of Economic Literature*, pp. 1120–1171.

Dosi, G., K. Pavitt and L. Soete (1990). *The Economics of Technical Change and International Trade.* New York: Harvester Wheatsheaf.

Dowd, K. and D. Greenaway (1993a). 'Currency competition, network externalities and switching costs: towards an alternative view of optimum currency areas', *Economic Journal*, pp. 1180–1189.

Dowd, K. and D. Greenaway (1993b). 'A single currency for Europe?', *Greek Economic Review*, pp. 227–244.

Drabek, Z. and D. Greenaway (1984). 'Economic integration and intra-indusrtry trade: the EEC and CMEA compared', *Kyklos*, pp. 444–469.

Drysdale, P. and R. Garnaut (1993). 'The Pacific: an application of a general theory of economic integration', in *Pacific Dynamism and International Economic System* (eds F. Bergsten and M. Noland). Washington: Institute for International Economics, pp. 183–223.

Dunning, J. (1969). 'Foreign capital and economic growth in Europe', in *Economic Integration in Europe* (ed. G. Denton). London: Weidenfeld & Nicolson, pp. 246–285.

Dunning, J. (1988). *Explaining International Production.* London: Unwin Hyman.

Dunning, J. (1994a). 'Globalization: the challenge for national economic regimes', *Discussion Paper*, no 186, Department of Economics, University of Reading.

Dunning, J. (1994b). 'MNE activity: comparing the NAFTA and the European Community', in *Multinationals in North America* (ed. L. Eden). Calgary: University of Calgary Press, pp. 277–308.

Dunning, J. and P. Robson (1987). 'Multinational corporate integration and regional economic integration', *Journal of Common Market Studies*, pp. 103–124.

EFTA (1969). 'The effects of EFTA on the economies of member states', *EFTA Bulletin* (January).

Eichengreen, B. (1993). 'European monetary unification', *Journal of Economic Literature*, pp. 1321–1357.

El-Agraa, A. (1985a). 'General introduction', in *The Economics of the European Community* (ed. A. El-Agraa). Oxford: Philip Allan, pp. 1–8.

El-Agraa, A. (1985b). 'European monetary integration', in *The Economics of the European Community* (ed. A. El-Agraa). Oxford: Philip Allan, pp. 93–111.

El-Agraa, A. (1989). *The Theory and Measurement of International Economic Integration.* New York: St Martin's Press.

El-Agraa, A. (ed.) (1988). *International Economic Integration.* Houndmills: Macmillan.

El-Agraa, A. (ed.) (1994). *The Economics of the European Community*. New York. Harvester Wheatsheaf.

El-Agraa, A. (ed.) (1997). *Economic Integration Worldwide*. London: Macmillan.

El-Agraa, A. and D. Hojman (1988). 'The Andean Pact', in *International Economic Integration* (ed. A. El-Agraa). Houndmills: Macmillan, pp. 257–266.

Emerson, M., M. Aujean, M. Catinat, P. Goybet and A. Jacquemin (1988). 'The economics of 1992', *European Economy*, March.

English, E. and M. Smith (1993). 'NAFTA and pacific partnership: advancing multi-lateralism?' in *Pacific Dynamism and the International Economic System* (eds F. Bergsten and M. Noland). Washington: Institute for International Economics, pp. 159–182.

Ethier, W. and L. Svensson (1986). 'The theorems of international trade with factor mobility', *Journal of International Economics*, pp. 21–42.

European Commission (1997). *The Impact and Effectiveness of the Single Market*. Luxembourg: EU.

European Communities (1991). *XXth Report on Competition Policy*. Brussels: European Communities.

European Economy (1990). *One Market? One Money* No 44.

European Economy (1993). *The Economic and Financial Situation in Italy*, No 1.

European Economy (1994). *Competition and Integration; Community Merger Control Policy*, No 57.

European Economy (1996). *Economic Evaluation of the Internal Market*, No. 4.

Finch, M. (1988). 'The Latin American Free Trade Association', in *International Economic Integration* (ed. A. El-Agraa). Houndmills: Macmillan, pp. 237–256.

Flam, H. and E. Helpman (1987). 'Industrial policy under monopolistic competition', *Journal of International Economics*, pp. 79–102.

Fleming, M. (1971). 'On exchange rate unification', *Economic Journal*, pp. 467–486.

Folkerts-Landau, D. and D. Mathieson (1989). *The European Monetary System in the Context of the Integration of European Financial Markets*. Washington: IMF.

Franko, L. (1977). 'European multinational enterprises in the integration process', in *The Multinational Enterprise in a Hostile World* (eds G. Curzon and V. Curzon). London: Macmillan, pp. 58–67.

Freeman, C. (1994). 'The economics of technical change', *Cambridge Journal of Economics*, pp. 463–514.

Fretz, D., R. Stern and J. Whalley (eds) (1985). *Canada/United States Trade and Investment Issues*. Toronto: Ontario Economic Council.

Gasiorek, M., A. Smith and A. Venables (1992). '1992: trade and welfare – a general equilibrium model', in *Trade Flows and Trade Policy after 1992* (ed. A. Winters). Cambridge: Cambridge University Press, pp. 35–62.

Georgakopoulos, T., C. Paraskevopoulos and J. Smithin (1994). *Economic Integration between Unequal Partners*. Aldershot: Edward Elgar.

Geroski, P. (1987). 'Brander's "Shaping comparative advantage": some comments', in *Shaping Comparative Advantage* (eds R. G. Lipsey and W. Dobson). Toronto: C.D. Howe Institute, pp. 57–64.

Geroski, P. (1988). 'Competition and innovation', in Commission of the European Communities, *Studies on the Economics of Integration*. Brussels: European Community, pp. 339–388.

Geroski, P. (1989). 'European industrial policy and industrial policy in Europe', *Oxford Review of Economic Policy*, pp. 20–36.

Geroski, P. and A. Jacquemin (1985). 'Industrial change, barriers to mobility, and European industrial policy', *Economic Policy*, pp. 170–218.

Gittelman, M., E. Graham and H. Fukukawa (1992). 'Affiliates of Japanese firms in the European Community: performance and structure', paper presented at the

Japanese Direct Investment in a Unifying Europe, conference held in INSEAD, Fontainebleau, 26–27 June 1992, mimeo.

Gleiser, H., A. Jacquemin and J. Petit (1980). 'Exports in an imperfect competition framework: an analysis of 1,446 exporters', *Quarterly Journal of Economics*, pp. 507–524.

Goldberg, M. (1972). 'The determinants of U.S. direct investment in the E.E.C.: comment', *American Economic Review*, pp. 692–699.

Government of Canada (1988). *The Canada–U.S. Free Trade Agreement: An Economic Assessment*. Ottawa: Department of Finance.

Gowland, D. and S. James (eds) (1991). *European Policy after 1992*. Aldershot: Dartmouth.

Graham, E. and P. Krugman (1991). *Foreign Direct Investment in the United States*. Washington: Institute for International Economics.

Gray, P., T. Pugel and I. Walter (1986). *International trade, Employment and Structural Adjustment: The United States*. Geneva: ILO.

Greenaway, D. (1987). 'Intra-industry trade, intra-firm trade and European integration', *Journal of Common Market Studies*, pp. 153–172.

Greenaway, D. and C. Milner (1987). 'Intra-industry trade: current perspectives and unresolved issues', *Weltwirschaftliches Archiv*, pp. 39–57.

Greenaway, D. and P. Tharakan (eds) (1986). *Imperfect Competition and International Trade*. Brighton: Wheatsheaf Books.

Gremmen, H. (1985). 'Testing the factor price equalization theorem in the EC: an alternative approach', *Journal of Common Market Studies*, pp. 277–286.

Gros, D. (1989). 'Paradigms for the monetary union of Europe', *Journal of Common Market Studies*, pp. 219–230.

Grubel, H. (1967). 'Intra-industry specialization and the pattern of trade', *Canadian Journal of Economics and Political Science*, pp. 374–388.

Grubel, H. (1970). 'The theory of optimum currency areas', *Canadian Journal of Economics*, pp. 318–324.

Grubel, H. (1984). *The International Monetary System*. Harmondsworth: Penguin Books.

Gstöhl, S. (1996). 'Switzerland, Norway and the European Union: the odd ones out', *Euryopa*, Institut européen de l'Universite de Genève.

Gual, J. (1995). 'The three common policies: an economic analysis', in *European Policies on Competition, Trade and Industry* (eds P. Buigues, A. Jacquemin and A. Sapir). Aldershot: Edward Elgar, pp. 3–48.

Guillaumont, P. and S. (1989). 'The implications of European monetary union for African countries', *Journal of Common Market Studies*, pp. 139–153.

Haberler, G. (1964). 'Integration and growth of the world economy in historical perspective', *American Economic Review*, pp. 1–22.

Hagedoorn, J. and J. Schakenraad (1993). 'A comparison of private and subsidized R&D partnerships in the European information technology industry', *Journal of Common Market Studies*, pp. 373–390.

Hague, D. (1960). 'Report on the proceedings: summary record of the debate', in *Economic Consequences of the Size of Nations* (ed. E. Robinson). London: Macmillan, pp. 333–438.

Hall, G. (ed.) (1986). *European Industrial Policy*. London: Croom Helm.

Hamilton, B. and J. Whalley (1986). 'Border tax adjustment and US trade', *Journal of International Economics*, pp. 377–383.

Harris, R. (1984a). *Trade, Industrial Policy and Canadian Manufacturing*. Toronto: Ontario Economic Council.

Harris, R. (1984b). 'Applied general equilibrium analysis of small open economies with scale economies and imperfect competition', *American Economic Review*, pp. 1016–1032.

Harris, R. and D. Cox (1985). 'Summary of a project on the general equilibrium evaluation of Canadian trade policy', in *Canada–US Free Trade* (ed. J. Whalley). Toronto: University of Toronto Press, pp. 157–177.

Haverman, J. (1996). 'Some welfare effects of sequential customs union formation', *Canadian Journal of Economics*, pp. 941–958.

Hayek, F. (1978). *New Studies in Philosophy, Politics, Economics and the History of Ideas*. London: Routledge.

Hazlewood, A. (1988). 'The East African Community', in *International Economic Integration* (ed. A. El-Agraa). Houndmills: Macmillan, pp. 166–189.

Helleiner, G. (1996). 'Why small countries worry: neglected issues in current analyses of the benefits and costs for small countries of integrating with large ones', *World Economy*, pp. 759–763.

Helpman, E. (1984). 'Increasing returns, imperfect markets and trade theory', in *Handbook of International Economics* (eds R. Jones and P. Kenen). Amsterdam: North Holland, pp. 325–366.

Helpman, E. and P. Krugman (1986). *Market Structure and Foreign Trade*. Cambridge, MA: The MIT Press.

Herin, J. (1986). 'Rules of origin and differences between tariff levels in EFTA and in the EC', Occasional Paper No 16, EFTA, Geneva.

Hiemenz, U. (1994). *Regional Integration in Europe and Its Effects on Developing Countries*. Tübingen: J.C.B. Mohr.

Hill, T. (1977). 'On goods and services', *Review of Income and Wealth*, pp. 315–338.

Hindley, B. (1991). 'Creating an integrated market for financial services', in *European Economic Integration* (eds G. Faulhaber and G. Tamburini). Boston: Kluwer, pp. 263–288.

Hitiris, T. (1994). *European Community Economics*. New York: Harvester Wheatsheaf.

Holmes, P. (1991). 'Non-tariff barriers', in *The Economics of the Single European Act* (eds G. McKenzie and A. Venables). Houndmills: Macmillan, pp. 27–50.

Holmes, P. and A. Smith (1995). 'Automobile industry', in *European Policies on Competition, Trade and Industry* (eds P. Buigues, A. Jacquemin and A. Sapir). Aldershot: Edward Elgar, pp. 125–159.

Holzman, F. (1976). *International Trade under Communism*. New York: Basic Books.

Hufbauer, G., and J. Schott (1992). *North American Free Trade*. Washington: Institute for International Economics.

Hymer, S., (1976). *The International Operations of National Firms: A Study of Direct Foreign Investment*. Boston: MIT Press.

Ishiyama, Y. (1975). 'The theory of optimum currency areas: a survey', *IMF Staff Papers*, pp. 344–378.

Jacquemin, A. (1979). 'European industrial policies and competition', in *Economic Policies of the Common Market* (ed. P. Coffey). London: Macmillan, pp. 22–51.

Jacquemin, A. (1983). 'Industrial policies and the community', in *Main Economic Policy Areas of the EEC* (ed. P. Coffey). The Hague: Martinus Nijhoff, pp. 27–58.

Jacquemin, A. (ed.) (1984). *European Industry: Public Policy and Corporate Strategy*. Oxford: Clarendon Press.

Jacquemin, A. (1990a). 'Mergers and European policy', in *Merger and Competition Policy in the European Community* (ed. P. Admiraal). Oxford: Basil Blackwell, pp. 1–38.

Jacquemin, A. (1990b). 'Horizontal concentration and European merger policy', *European Economic Review*, pp. 539–550.

Jacquemin, A. (1996a). 'Les enjeux de la compétitivité européenne et la politique industrielle communautaire en matière d'innovation', *Revue du Marché commun et de l'Union européenne*, March, pp. 175–181.

Jacquemin, A. (1996b). 'Towards an internationalisation of competition policy', *World Economy*, pp. 781–789.

Jacquemin, A. (1996c). 'Theories of industrial organization and competition policy: what are the links?', Discussion Paper No 9607, Université Catholique de Louvain, Département des Sciences Economiques.

Jacquemin, A. and A. Sapir (1988). 'International trade and integration in the European Community', *European Economic Review*, pp. 1439–1449.

Jacquemin, A. and A. Sapir (eds) (1989). *The European Internal Market*. Oxford: Oxford University Press.

Jacquemin, A. and A. Sapir (1991). 'The internal and external opening-up of the Single Community Market: efficiency gains, adjustment costs and new Community instruments', *International Spectator*, pp. 29–48.

Jacquemin, A. and A. Sapir (1996). 'Is European hard core credible? A statistical analysis', *Kyklos*, pp. 105–117.

Jacquemin, A. and D. Wright (1993). 'Corporate strategies and European challenges post-1992', *Journal of Common Market Studies*, pp. 525–537.

Jarillo, J. and J. Martnez (1991). 'The international expansion of Spanish firms: towards an integrative framework for international strategy', in *Corporate and Industry Strategies for Europe* (eds L. Mattsson and B. Stymne). Amsterdam: Elsevier, pp. 283–302.

Johnson, C. (1984). 'The idea of industrial policy', in *The Industrial Policy Debate* (ed. C. Johnson). San Francisco: Institute for Contemporary Studies.

Johnson, H. (1962). *Money, Trade and Economic Growth*. London: George Allen & Unwin.

Johnson, H. (1973). 'An economic theory of protectionism, tariff bargaining and the formation of customs unions', in *The Economics of Integration* (ed. M. Krauss). London: George Allen & Unwin, pp. 64–103.

Johnson, H. (1974). 'Trade-diverting customs unions: a comment', *Economic Journal*, pp. 618–621.

Johnson, H. and M. Krauss (1973). 'Border taxes, border tax adjustment, comparative advantage and the balance of payments', in *Economics of Integration* (ed. M. Krauss). London: George Allen & Unwin, pp. 239–253.

Jones, A. (1985). 'The theory of economic integration', in *The Economics of the European Community* (ed. A. El-Agraa). Oxford: Philip Allan, pp. 71–92.

Jones, R. and J. Neary (1984). 'The positive theory of international trade', in *Handbook of International Economics* (eds R. Jones and P. Kenen). Amsterdam: North Holland, pp. 1–62.

Jovanović, M. (1989). 'Industrial policy and international trade (shaping comparative advantage)', *Economic Analysis*, pp. 55–77.

Jovanović, M. (1995). 'Economic integration among developing countries and foreign direct investment', *Economia Internazionale*, pp. 209–243.

Jovanović, M. (1997a). *European Economic Integration: Limits and Prospects*. London: Routledge.

Jovanović, M. (1997b). 'Probing leviathan: the eastern enlargement of the European Union', *European Review*, pp. 353–70.

Jovanović, M. (ed.) (1998a). *International Economic Integration: Critical Perspectives on the World Economy – Theory and Measurement* (Volume I). London: Routledge.

Jovanović, M. (ed.) (1998b). *International Economic Integration: Critical Perspectives on the World Economy – Monetary, Fiscal and Factor Mobility Issues* (Volume II). London: Routledge.

Jovanović, M. (ed.) (1998c). *International Economic Integration: Critical Perspectives on the World Economy – General Issues* (Volume III). London: Routledge.

Jovanović M. (ed.) (1998d). *International Economic Integration: Critical Perspectives on the World Economy – Integration Schemes* (Volume IV). London: Routledge.

Kahnert, F., P. Richards, E. Stoutjesdijk and P. Thomopoulos (1969). *Economic Integration among Developing Countries*. Paris: OECD.

Kaldor, N. (1971). 'The dynamic effects of the common market', in *Destiny or Delusion: Britain and the Common Market* (ed. D. Evans). London: Victor Gollancz, pp. 59–83.

Kay, J. (1990). 'Tax policy: a survey', *Economic Journal*, pp. 18–75.

Keen, M. and S. Smith (1996). 'The future of value added tax in the European union', *Economic Policy*, pp. 375–420.

Kemp, M. and H. Wan (1976). 'An elementary proposal concerning the formation of customs unions', *Journal of International Economics*, pp. 95–97.

Kenen, P. (1969). 'The theory of optimun currency areas: an eclectic view', in *Monetary Problems of the International Economy* (eds R. Mundell and A. Swoboda). Chicago: University of Chicago Press, pp. 41–60.

Keynes, J. (1923). *A Tract on Monetary Reform*. London: Royal Economic Society.

Kindleberger, C. and D. Audretsch (eds) (1984). *The Multinational Corporation in the 1980s*. Cambridge, MA: The MIT Press.

Kirman, A. (1973). 'Trade diverting customs unions and welfare improvement: a comment', *Economic Journal*, pp. 890–893.

Kojima, K. (1996). *Trade, Investment and Pacific Economic Integration*. Tokyo: Bunshindo.

Komiya, R. (1988). 'Introduction', in *Industrial Policy of Japan* (eds R. Komiya, M. Okuno and K. Suzumura). Tokyo: Academic Press, pp. 1–22.

Krauss, M. (1972). 'Recent developments in customs unions theory: an interpretative survey', *Journal of Economic Literature*, pp. 413–436.

Krauss, M. (ed.) (1973). *The Economics of Integration*. London: George Allen & Unwin.

Krauss, M. and R. Bird (1973). 'The value added tax: critique of a review', in *Economics of Integration* (ed. M. Krauss). London: George Allen & Unwin, pp. 254–264.

Kreinin, M. (1964). 'On the dynamic effects of a customs union', *Journal of Political Economy*, pp. 193–195.

Kreinin, M. (1969). 'Trade creation and trade diversion by the EEC and EFTA', *Economia Internazionale*, pp. 273–280.

Krugman, P. (1981). 'Intraindustry specialization and the gains from trade', *Journal of Political Economy*, pp. 959–973.

Krugman, P. (ed.) (1988). *Strategic Trade Policy and the New International Economics*. Cambridge, MA: The MIT Press.

Krugman, P. (1990a). *Rethinking International Trade*. Cambridge, MA: The MIT Press.

Krugman, P. (1990b). 'Protectionism: try it, you'll like it', *International Economy*, June–July, pp. 35–39.

Krugman, P. (1991). 'Is bilateralism bad?', in *International Trade and Trade Policy* (eds E. Helpman and A. Razin). Cambridge, MA: The MIT Press, pp. 9–23.

Krugman, P. (1993). 'The current case for industrial policy', in *Protectionism and World Welfare* (ed. D. Salvatore). Cambridge: Cambridge University Press, pp. 160–179.

Krugman, P. (1995). 'The move toward free trade zones', in *International Economics and International Trade Policy* (ed. P. King). New York: McGraw-Hill, pp. 162–182.

Krugman, P. (1996a). *Pop Internationalism*. Cambridge, MA: The MIT Press.

Krugman, P. (1996b). 'The Adam Smith address: what difference does globalization make', *Business Economics*, pp. 7–10.

Krugman, P. and A. Venables (1990). 'Integration and the competitiveness of peripheral industry', in *Unity with Diversity in the European Economy: the Commu-*

nity's Southern Frontier (eds C. Bliss and J. Braga de Macedo). Cambridge: Cambridge University Press, pp. 56–75.

Krugman, P. and A. Venables (1996). 'Integration, specialization and adjustment', *European Economic Review*, pp. 959–967.

Kumar, M. (1985). International trade and industrial concentration', *Oxford Economic Papers*, pp. 125–133.

Lall, S. (1994). 'The east Asian miracle: does the bell toll for industrial strategy?', *World Development*, pp. 645–654.

Lancaster, K. (1980). 'Intra-industry trade under perfect monopolistic competition', *Journal of International Economics*, pp. 151–175.

Langhammer, R. (1991). 'ASEAN economic co-operation: a stock taking from a political economy point of view', *ASEAN Economic Bulletin*, pp. 137–150.

Langhammer, R. and U. Hiemenz (1990). *Regional Integration among Developing Countries*. Tübingen: J.C.B. Mohr.

Leamer, E. (1984). *Sources of International Comparative Advantage*. Cambridge, MA: The MIT Press.

Levin, R., A. Klevorick, R. Nelson and S. Winter (1987). 'Appropriating the returns from industrial research and development', *Brookings Papers on Economic Activity*, pp. 783–820.

Linder, S. (1961). *An Essay on Trade and Transformation*. Uppsala: Almquist & Wiksells.

Lipsey, R. G. (1957). 'The theory of customs unions: trade diversion and welfare', *Economica*, pp. 40–46.

Lipsey, R. G. (1960). 'The theory of customs unions: a general survey', *Economic Journal*, pp. 496–513.

Lipsey, R. G. (1970). *The Theory of Customs Unions: A General Equilibrium Analysis*. London: Weidenfeld & Nicolson.

Lipsey, R. G. (1976). 'Comments', in *Economic Integration Worldwide, Regional, Sectoral* (ed. F. Machlup). London: Macmillan, pp. 37–40.

Lipsey, R. G. (1984). 'Can the market economy survive?' in *Probing Leviathan: An Investigation of Government in the Economy* (ed. G. Lermer). Vancouver: The Frazer Institute, pp. 3–37.

Lipsey, R. G. (1985). 'Canada and the United States: The Economic Dimension', in *Canada and the United States: Enduring Friendship, Persistent Stress* (eds C. Doran and J. Stigler). New York: Prentice Hall, pp. 69–108.

Lipsey, R. G. (1987a). 'Report on the workshop', in *Shaping Comparative Advantage* (eds R. G. Lipsey and W. Dobson). Toronto: C.D. Howe Institute, pp. 109–153.

Lipsey, R. G. (1987b). 'models matter when discussing competitivness: a technical note', in *Shaping Comparative Advantage* (eds R. G. Lipsey and W. Dobson). Toronto: C.D. Howe Institute, pp. 155–166.

Lipsey, R. G. (1988). 'Sovereignty: culturally, economically and socially', in *Free Trade – The Real Story* (ed. J. Crispo). Toronto: Gage, pp. 148–160.

Lipsey, R. G. (1990). 'Canada at the US–Mexico free trade dance: Wallflower or partner'. *Commentary 20*. Toronto: C. D. Howe Institute.

Lipsey, R. G. (1992). 'Getting there: the path to a WHFTA and its structure', Simon Fraser University, Vancouver, mimeo.

Lipsey, R. G. (1992a). 'Global change and economic policy', in *The Culture and the Power of Knowledge* (eds N. Stehr and R. Ericson). New York: De Gruyter, pp. 279–299.

Lipsey, R. G. (1993a). 'The changing technoeconomic paradigm and some implications for economic policy', Canadian Institute for Advanced Research, Vancouver, mimeo.

Lipsey, R. G. (1993b). 'Globalisation, technological change and economic growth', Annual Sir Charles Carter Lecture, mimeo.

Lipsey, R. G. (1994). 'Markets, technological change and economic growth', *Pakistan Development Review*, vol. 33, no. 4, pp. 327–352.

Lipsey, R. G. and W. Dobson (eds) (1987). *Shaping Comparative Advantage*. Toronto: C. D. Howe Institute.

Lipsey, R. G. and K. Lancaster (1956–57). 'The general theory of the second best', *Review of Economic Studies*, pp. 11–32.

Lipsey, R. G. and M. Smith (1986). *Taking the initiative: Canada's Trade Options in a Turbulent World*. Toronto: C. D. Howe Institute.

Lipsey, R. G. and M. Smith (1989). 'The Canada-US free trade agreement: special case or wave of the future?', in *Free Trade Areas and U.S. Trade Policy* (ed. J. Schott). Washington: Institute for International Economics, pp. 317–335.

Lipsey, R. G. and R. York, (1988). *Evaluating the Free Trade Deal: A Guided Tour through the Canada-US Agreement*. Toronto: C.D. Howe Institute.

Lloyd, P. (1982). '3 × 3 theory of customs unions', *Journal of International Economics*, pp. 41–63.

Lloyd, P. (1991). 'The future of CER – a single market for Australia and New Zealand', *CEDA*, Monograph, no. 96.

Lundgren, N. (1969). 'Customs unions of industrialized west European countries', in *Economic Integration in Europe* (ed. G. Denton). London: Weidenfeld & Nicolson, pp. 25–54.

Lunn, J. (1980). 'Determinants of US direct investment in the EEC', *European Economic Review*, pp. 93–101.

Lunn, J. (1983). 'Determinants of US direct investment in the EEC', *European Economic Review*, pp. 391–393.

MacDougall, G. (1977). *Report of the Study Group on the Role of Public Finance in European Integration*. Brussels: EC.

Machlup, F. (ed.) (1976). *Economic Integration Worldwide, Regional, Sectoral*. London: Macmillan.

Machlup, F. (1979). *A History of Thought on Economic Integration*. London: Macmillan.

Maksimova, M. (1976). 'Comments on paper types of economic tntegration by B. Balassa', in *Economic Integration Worldwide, Regional, Sectoral* (ed. F. Machlup). London: Macmillan, pp. 32–36.

Marer, P. and J. Montias (1988). 'The Council for Mutual Economic Assistance', in *International Economic Integration* (ed. A. El-Agraa). London: Macmillan, pp. 128–165.

Markusen, J. (1983). 'Factor movements and commodity trade as complements', *Journal of International Economics*, pp. 341–356.

Markusen, J. and J. Melvin, (1984). *The Theory of International Trade and Its Canadian Applications*. Toronto: Butterworths.

Marrese, M. (1986). 'CMEA: effective but cumbersome political economy', *International Organization*, pp. 287–327.

Marrese, M. and J. Vanous (1983). *Soviet Subsidization of Trade with Eastern Europe: A Soviet Perspective*. Berkeley: Institute of International Studies, University of California.

Mayes, D. (1978). 'The effects of economic integration on trade', *Journal of Common Market Studies*, pp. 1–23.

Mayes, D. (1985). 'Factor mobility', in *The Economics of the European Community* (ed. A. El-Agraa). Oxford: Philip Allan, pp. 124–150.

Mayes, G. (1987). 'European industrial policy', in *European Integration and industry* (eds M. Macmillen, D. Mayes and P. van Veen). Tilburg: Tilburg University Press, pp. 247–265.

Mayes, D. (1988). 'The problems of quantitative estimation of integration effects', in *International Economic Integration* (ed. A. El-Agraa). London: Macmillan, pp. 42–58.

McFetridge, D. (1985). 'The economics of industrial policy', in *Canadian Industrial Policy in Action* (ed. D. McFetridge). Toronto: University of Toronto Press, pp. 1–49.

McFetridge, D. (ed.) (1986). *Economics of Industrial Policy and Strategy*. Toronto: University of Toronto Press.

McKinnon, R. (1963). 'Optimum currency area', *American Economic Review*, pp. 717–725.

McKinnon, R. (1994). 'A common monetary standard or a common currency for Europe? The fiscal constraints', *Rivista di Politica Economica*, pp. 59–79.

McKay, D. and W. Grant (1983). 'Industrial policies in OECD countries: an overview', *Journal of Public Policy*, pp. 1–12.

Meade, J. (1968). *The Pure Theory of Customs Unions*. Amsterdam: North Holland.

Meade, J. (1973). 'The balance of payments problems of a European free-trade area', in *The Economics of Integration* (ed. M. Krauss). London: George Allen and Unwin, pp. 155–176.

Melvin, J. (1985). 'The regional impact of tariffs', in *Canada-United States Free Trade* (ed. J. Whalley). Toronto: University of Toronto Press, pp. 313–324.

Melvin, M. (1985). 'Currency substitution and western European monetary unification', *Economica*, pp. 79–91.

Mendershausen, H. (1959). 'Terms of trade between the Soviet Union and smaller communist countries 1955–57', *Review of Economics and Statistics*, pp. 106–118.

Mendershausen, H. (1960). 'Terms of Soviet-satellite trade: a broadened analysis', *Review of Economics and Statistics*, pp. 152–163.

Mendes, A. Marques (1986). 'The contribution of the European Community to economic growth', *Journal of Common Market Studies*, pp. 260–277.

Mendes, A. Marques (1987). *Economic Integration and Growth in Europe*. London: Croom Helm.

Mennis, B. and K. Sauvant (1976). *Emerging Forms of Transnational Community*. Lexington: Lexington Books.

Merrit, G. (1988). 'Social policy rethink', *European Affairs*, no. 1, pp. 88–94.

Michaely, M. (1976). 'The assumptions of Jacob Viner's theory of customs unions', *Journal of International Economics*, pp. 75–93.

Michaely, M. (1977). *Theory of Commercial Policy*. Oxford: Philip Allan.

Micossi, S. (1996). 'Nouvelles orientations de la politique industrielle dans l'Union européene', *Revue du Marché commun et de l'Union européenne*, pp. 158–164.

Mishan, E. (1976). 'The welfare gains of a trade diverting customs union reinterpreted', *Economic Journal*, pp. 669–672.

Molle, W. (1988). 'Regional policy', in *Main Economic Policy Areas of the EEC towards 1992* (ed. P. Coffey). Dordrecht: Kluwer, pp. 67–97.

Molle, W. (1991). *The Economics of European Integration*. Aldershot: Dartmouth.

Molle, W. and A. van Mourik (1988). 'International movements of labour under conditions of economic integration: the case of western Europe', *Journal of Common Market Studies*, pp. 317–342.

Morita, A. (1992). 'Partnering for competitiveness: the role of Japanese business', *Harvard Business Review* (May-June), pp. 76–83.

Mundell, R. (1957). 'International trade and factor mobility', *America Economic Review*, pp. 321–335.

Mundell, R. (1961). 'A theory of optimum currency areas', *American Economic Review*, pp. 657–665.

Mwase, N. (1994). 'The southern African customs union in a post-apartheid southern Africa', *Journal of World Trade*, pp. 119–130.

Mytelka, L. (1979). *Regional Development in a Global Economy*. New Haven: Yale University Press.

Mytelka, L. (1984). 'Competition, conflict and decline in the Union Douanière et Economique de l'Afrique Centrale (UDEAC)', in *African Regional Organizations* (ed. D. Mazzeo). Cambridge: Cambridge University Press, pp. 131–149.

Mytelka, L. (1994). 'Regional co-operation and the new logic of international competition', in *South–South Co-operation in a Global Perspective* (ed. L. Mytelka). Paris: OECD, pp. 21–54.

Mytelka, L. and M. Delapierre (1987). 'The alliance strategies of European firms in the information technology industry and the role of ESPRIT', *Journal of Common Market Studies*, pp. 231–253.

Nayyar, D. (1988). 'The political economy of international trade in services', *Cambridge Journal of Economics*, pp. 279–298.

Neven, D. (1990). 'EEC integration towards 1992: some distributional aspects', *Economic Policy*, pp. 14–46.

Nevin, E. (1985). 'Regional policy', in *The Economics of the European Community* (ed. A. El-Agraa). Oxford: Philip Allan, pp. 338–361.

Nogués, J. and R. Quintanilla (1992). 'Latin America's integration and the multilateral trading system', paper presented at the World Bank Conference on New Dimensions in Regional Integration, Washington, 2–3 April 1992.

Norman, V. (1990). 'Discussion of D. Neven's paper', *Economic Policy*, pp. 49–52.

Norman, V. (1995). 'The theory of market integration – a retrospective view', in *35 Years of Free Trade in Europe, Messages for the Future* (ed. E. Ems). Geneva: EFTA, pp. 19–36.

Owen, N. (1976). 'Scale economies in the EEC', *European Economic Review*, pp. 143–163.

Palmeter, D. (1993). 'Rules of origin in customs unions and free trade areas', in *Regional Integration and the Global Trading System* (eds K. Anderson and R. Blackhurst). New York: Harvester Wheatsheaf, pp. 326–343.

Panić, M. (1988). *National Management of the International Economy*. London: Macmillan.

Panić, M. (1991). 'The impact of multinationals on national economic policies', in *Multinationals and Europe 1992* (eds B. Burgenmeier and J. Mucchelli). London: Routledge, pp. 204–222.

Panić, M. and C. Schioppa (1989). 'Europe's long-term capital flows since 1971', in *European Factor Mobility* (eds I. Gordon and A. Thirlwall). New York: St Martin's Press, pp. 166–194.

Peck, M. (1989). 'Industrial organization and the gains from Europe 1992', *Brookings Papers on Economic Activity*, pp. 277–299.

Pelkmans, J. (1980). 'Economic theories of integration revisited', *Journal of Common Market Studies*, pp. 333–353.

Pelkmans, J. (1984). *Market Integration in the European Community*. The Hague: Martinus Nijhoff.

Pelkmans, J. and A. Winters (1988). *Europe's Domestic Market*. London: Routledge.

Petith, H. (1977). 'European integration and the terms of trade', *Economic Journal*, pp. 262–272.

Pinder, J. (1969). 'Problems of European integration', in *Economic Integration in Europe* (ed. G. Denton). London: Weidenfeld and Nicolson, pp. 143–170.

Pinder, J. (1982). 'Causes and kinds of industrial policy', in *National Strategies and the World Economy* (ed. J. Pinder). London: Croom Helm, pp. 41–52.

Pinder, J., T. Hosomi and W. Diebold (1979). *Industrial Policy and International Economy*. New York: The Trilateral Commission.

Plasschaert, S. (1994). 'Introduction: transfer pricing and taxation', in *Transnational Corporations: Transfer Pricing and Taxation* (ed. S. Plasschaert). London: Routledge, pp. 1–21.

Pomfret, R. (1986a). 'The trade-diverting bias of preferential trading arrangements', *Journal of Common Market Studies*, pp. 109–117.

Pomfret, R. (1986b). 'The theory of preferential trading arrangements', *Weltwirtschaftliches Archiv*, pp. 439–465.

Prais, S. (1981). *Productivity and Industrial Structure*. Cambridge: Cambridge University Press.

Pratten, C. (1971). *Economies of Scale and Manufacturing Industry*. Cambridge: Cambridge University Press.

Pratten, C. (1988). 'A survey of the economies of scale', in *Studies on the Economics of Integration, Research on the Costs of Non-Europe, vol. 2*, Brussels: European Communities, pp. 11–165.

President's Commission on Industrial Competitiveness (1985). *Global Competition: The New Reality* (Volumes 1 and 2). Washington: U.S. Government Printing Office.

Prest, A. (1979). 'Fiscal policy', in *Economic Policies of the Common Market* (ed. P. Coffey). London: Macmillan, pp. 69–97.

Prest, A. (1983). 'Fiscal policy', in *Main Economic Policy Areas of the EEC* (ed. P. Coffey). The Hague: Martinus Nijhoff, pp. 58–90.

Purvis. D. (1972). 'Technology, trade and factor mobility', *Economic Journal*, pp. 991–999.

Reich, R. (1982). 'Why the U.S. needs an industrial policy', *Harvard Business Review*, January–February, pp. 74–81.

Reich, R. (1990). 'Who is us', *Harvard Business Review*, pp. 53–64.

Reich, S. (1989). 'Roads to follow: regulating direct foreign investment', *International Organization*, pp. 543–584.

Renshaw, G. (1986). *Adjustment and Economic Performance in industrialised Countries: A Synthesis*. Geneva: ILO.

Richter, S. and L. Tóth (1994). 'Perspectives for economic cooperation among the Visegrád Group countries', *WIIW*, no. 156, November 1994.

Riezman, R. (1979). 'A 3 × 3 model of customs unions', *Journal of International Economics*, pp. 341–354.

Robson, P. (1968). *Economic Integration in Africa*. London: George Allen & Unwin.

Robson, P. (ed.) (1972). *International Economic Integration*. Harmondsworth: Penguin Books.

Robson, P. (1980). *The Economics of International Integration*. London: George Allen & Unwin.

Robson, P. (1983). *Integration, Development and Equity*. London: George Allen & Unwin.

Robson, P. (1987). *The Economics of International Integration*. London: George Allen and Unwin.

Robson, P. (1997). 'Integration in Sub-Saharan Africa', in *Economic Integration Worldwide* (ed. A. El-Agraa). London: Macmillan, pp. 348–367.

Romer, P. (1986). 'Increasing returns and long-run growth', *Journal of Political Economy*, pp. 1002–1037.

Romer, P. (1994). 'New goods, old theory and the welfare costs of trade restrictions', *Journal of Development Economics*, pp. 5–38.

Rubin, S. (1970). 'The international firm and the national jurisdiction', in *The International Corporation* (ed. C. Kindleberger). Cambridge, MA: The MIT Press, pp. 179–204.

Ruding Committee (1992). *Conclusions and Recommendations of the Committee of Independent Experts on Company Taxation*. Luxembourg: European Communities.

Rugman, A. (1985). 'The behaviour of US subsidiaries in Canada: implications for trade and investment', in *Canada/United States Trade and Investments Issues* (eds D. Fretz, R. Stern and J. Whalley). Toronto: Ontario Economic Council, pp. 460–473.

Sala-i-Martin, X. (1994). Regional cohesion: evidence and theories of regional growth and convergence', CEPR Discussion Paper, no. 1075.

Sapir, A. (1992). 'Regional integration in Europe', *Economic Journal*, pp. 1491–1506.

Sapir, A. (1993). 'Structural dimension', *European Economy Social Europe*, no. 3, pp. 23–39.

Sapir, A. (1996). 'The effects of Europe's internal market program on production and trade: a first assessment', *Weltwirschaftliches Archiv*, pp. 456–475.

Sapir, A., P. Buigues and A. Jacquemin (1993). 'European competition policy in manufacturing and services: a two-speed approach?', *Oxford Review of Economic Policy*, pp. 113–131.

Scaperlanda, A. (1967). 'The EEC and US foreign investment: some empirical evidence', *Economic Journal*, pp. 22–26.

Scaperlanda, A. and E. Reiling (1971). 'A comment on a note on customs unions and direct foreign investment', *Economic Journal*, pp. 355–357.

Scaperlanda, A. and R. Balough (1983). 'Determinants of US direct investment in Europe', *European Economic Journal*, pp. 381–390.

Schatz, K. and F. Wolter (1987). *Structural Adjustment in the Federal Republic of Germany*. Geneva: ILO.

Schmalensee, R. (1988). 'Industrial economics: an overview', *Economic Journal*, pp. 643–681.

Schmitt, N. (1990). 'New international trade theories and Europe 1992: some results relevant for EFTA countries', *Journal of Common Market Studies*, pp. 53–73.

Schott, J. (ed.) (1989). *Free Trade Areas and U.S. Trade Policy*. Washington: Institute for International Economics.

Schott, J. and M. Smith (1988). 'Services and investment', in *The Canada–US Free Trade Agreement* (eds J. Schott and M. Smith). Washington: Institute for International Economics, pp. 137–158.

Scitowsky, T. (1967). *Economic Theory and Western European Integration*. London: George Allen and Unwin.

Scott, A. (1986). 'Britain and the EMS: an appraisal of the Report of the Treasury and Civil Service Committee', *Journal of Common Market Studies*, pp. 187–201.

Sellekaerts, W. (1973). 'How meaningful are empirical studies on trade creation and diversion?', *Weltwirschaftliches Archiv*, pp. 519–553.

Servan-Schreiber, J. (1969). *The American Challenge*. New York: Atheneum.

Sharp, M. and K. Pavitt (1993). 'Technology policy in the 1990s: old trends and new realities', *Journal of Common Market Studies*, pp. 129–151.

Sharp, M. and G. Shepherd (1987). *Managing Change in British Industry*. Geneva: ILO.

Shoup, C. (1972). 'Taxation aspects of international economic integration', in *International Economic Integration* (ed. P. Robson). Harmondsworth: Penguin Books, pp. 197–218.

Sidjanski, D. (1997). 'Networks of European pressure groups', *Euryopa*, Institut européen de l'Université de Genève.

Sleuwaegen, L. (1987) 'Multinationals, the European Community and Belgium', *Journal of Common Market Studies*, pp. 255–272.

Smith, A. and A. Venables (1988). 'Completing the internal market in the European Community', *European Economic Review*, pp. 1501–1525.

Snape, R. (1990). 'Principles in trade in services', in *The Uruguay Round: Services in the World Economy* (eds P. Messerlin and K. Sauvant). New York: United Nations Centre on Transnational Corporations, pp. 5–11.

Sobell, V. (1984). *The Red Market – Industrial Co-operation and Specialisation in Comecan*. Aldershot: Gower.

Spinelli, A. (1973). *Action Programme in the Field of Technological and Industrial Policy*. Brussels: EC.

Straubhaar, T. (1988). 'International labour migration within a common market: some aspects of EC experience', *Journal of Common Market Studies*, pp. 45–62.

Straubhaar, T. and K. Zimmermann (1993). 'Towards a European migration policy', *Population Research and Policy Review*, pp. 225–241.

Swann, D. (1978). *The Economics of the Common Market*. Harmondsworth: Penguin Books.

Swann, D. (1996). *European Economic Integration: The Common Market, European Union and beyond*. Cheltenham: Edward Elgar.

Tavlas, G. (1993a). 'The theory of optimum currency areas revisited', *Finance and Development*, June, pp. 32–35.

Tavlas, G. (1993b). 'The "new" theory of optimum currency areas', *The World Economy*, pp. 663–685.

Thirsk, W. (1985). 'Should taxes be included in trade agreements?' in *Canadian Trade at a Crossroads: Options for New International Agreements* (eds D. Conklin and T. Courchene). Toronto: Ontario Economic Council, pp. 138–52.

Thomsen, S. and P. Nicolaides (1991). *The Evolution of Japanese Direct Investment in Europe*. New York: Harvester Wheatsheaf.

Thygesen, N. (1987). 'Is the EEC an optimal currency area?' in *The ECU Market* (eds R. Levics and A. Sommariva). Toronto: D.C. Heath, Lexington Books, pp. 163–189.

Tinbergen, J. (1954). *International Economic Integration*. Amsterdam: Elsevier.

Tironi, E. (1982). 'Customs union theory in the presence of foreign firms', *Oxford Economic Papers*, pp. 150–171.

Tovias, A. (1982). 'Testing factor price equalization in the EEC', *Journal of Common Market Studies*, pp. 375–388.

Tovias, A. (1990). 'The impact of liberalizing government procurement policies of individual EC countries on trade with nonmembers', *Weltwirschaftliches Archiv*, pp. 722–736.

Trebilcock, M. (1986). *The Political Economy of Economic Adjustment*. Toronto: University of Toronto Press.

Tsoukalis, T. (1993). *The New European Economy*. Oxford. Oxford University Press.

Tyson, L. (1987). 'Comments on Brander's "Shaping comparative advantage": creating advantage, an industrial policy perspective', in *Shaping Comparative Advantage* (eds R. G. Lipsey and W. Dobson). Toronto: C.D. Howe Institute, pp. 65–82.

Tyson, L. (1991). 'They are not us. Why American ownership still matters', *The American Prospect*, (Winter), pp. 37–49.

Tyson, L. (1992). *Who's Bashing Whom?* Washington: Institute for International Economics.

Tyson, L. and J. Zysman (1987a). 'American industry in international competition', in *American industry in International Competition* (eds J. Zysman and L. Tyson). Ithaca: Cornell University Press, pp. 15–59.

Tyson, L. and J. Zysman (1987b). 'Conclusion: what to do now?', in *American Industry in International Competition* (eds J. Zysman and L. Tyson). Ithaca: Cornell University Press, pp. 422–427.

UNCTAD (1983). *The Role of Transnational Enterprises in Latin American Economic Integration Efforts: Who Integrates with Whom, How and for Whose Benefit?* New York: United Nations.

UNCTAD (1993). *World Investment Report: Transnational Corporations and Integrated International Production*. New York: United Nations.

UNCTAD (1994). *World Investment Report: Transnational Corporations, Employment and the Workforce.* New York: United Nations.

UNCTAD (1995a). 'Incentives and foreign direct investment', TD/B/ITNC/Misc. 1, 6 April 1995.

UNCTAD (1995b). *World Investment Report: Transnational Corporations and Competitiveness.* New York: United Nations.

UNCTAD (1996). *World Investment Report: Investment, Trade and International Policy Arrangements.* New York: United Nations.

UNCTAD (1997). *World Investment Report: Transnational Corporations, Market Structure and Competition Policy.* New York: United Nations.

UNCTC (1988). *Transnational Corporations in World Development.* New York: United Nations.

UNCTC (1989). *Transnational Corporations and International Economic Relations: Recent Developments and Selected Issues.* New York: United Nations.

UNCTC (1990). *Regional Economic Integration and Transnational Corporations in the 1990s: Europe 1992, North America and Developing Countries.* New York: United Nations.

UNCTC (1991a). *The Impact of Trade-related Investment Measures on Trade and Development.* New York: United Nations.

UNCTC (1991b). *World Investment Report: The Triad in Foreign Direct Investment.* New York: United Nations.

UN/ECE (1994). *Economic Survey of Europe 1993–1994.* New York: United Nations.

Ungerer, H., O. Evans, T. Mayer and P. Young (1986). *The European Monetary System: Recent Development.* Washington: IMF.

Utton, M. (1986). 'Developments in British industrial and competition policies', in *European Industrial Policy* (ed. G. Hall). London: Croom Helm, pp. 59–83.

van Aarle, B. (1996). 'The impact of the single market on trade and foreign direct investment in the European Union', *Journal of World Trade*, pp. 121–138.

van Brabant, J. (1980). *Socialist Economic Integration.* Cambridge: Cambridge University Press.

van Brabant, J. (1988). 'Product specialisation in the CMEA-concepts and empirical evidence', *Journal of Common Market Studies*, pp. 287–315.

van Brabant, J. (1996). 'Remaking Europe – the accession of transition economies', *Economia Internazionale*, pp. 507–531.

Vanek, J. (1962). *International Trade.* Homewood: Richard D. Irwin.

Vanek, J. (1965). *General Equilibrium of International Discrimination.* Cambridge, MA: Harvard University Press.

Vanhove, N. and L. Klaassen (1987). *Regional Policy: A European Approach.* Aldershot: Avebury.

van Meerhaeghe, M. (1985). *International Economic Institutions.* Dordrecht: Martinus Nijhoff.

van Mourik, A. (1987). 'Testing the factor price equalisation theorem in the EC: an alternative approach', *Journal of Common Market Studies*, pp. 79–86.

Varian, H. (1984). *Microeconomic Analysis.* New York: Norton.

Vaubel, R. (1978). 'Real exchange rate changes in the European Community', *Journal of International Economics*, pp. 319–339.

Vaubel, R. (1990). 'Currency competition and European monetary integration', *Economic Journal*, pp. 936–946.

Venables, A. (1995). 'Economic integration and the location of firms', *American Economic Review* (Papers and Proceedings), pp. 296–300.

Verboven, F. (1996). 'International price discrimination in the European car market', *RAND Journal of Economics*, pp. 240–268.

Verdoorn, P. and C. van Bochove (1972). 'Measuring integration effects: a survey', *European Economic Review*, pp. 337–349.

Viner, J. (1950). *The Customs Union Issue*. London: Stevens and Sons Limited for the Carnegie Endowment for International Peace.

Viner, J. (1976). 'A letter to W.M. Corden', *Journal of International Economics*, pp. 107–108.

Vosgerau, H. (1989). 'International capital movements and trade in an intertemporal setting', in *European Factor Mobility* (eds I. Gordon and A. Thirlwall). New York: St Martin's Press, pp. 215–232.

Wallis, K. (1968). 'The EEC and United States foreign investment: some empirical evidence re-examined', *Economic Journal*, pp. 717–719.

Weber, A. (1909). *Theory of the Location of Industries*. Chicago: University of Chicago Press.

Werner, P. (1970). *Report to the Council and the Commission on the Realization by Stages of Economic and Monetary Union in the Community*. Luxembourg: European Communities.

Wescott, R. (1983). 'US approaches to industrial policy', in *Industrial Policies for Growth and Competiveness* (eds G. Adams and L. Klein). Lexington, MA: Lexington Books, pp. 87–151.

Whalley, J. (1987). 'Brander's 'Shaping comparative advantage': remarks', in *Shaping Comparative Advantage* (eds R. G. Lipsey and W. Dobson). Toronto: C.D. Howe Institute, pp. 83–89.

Whalley, J. (1992), 'CUSTA and NAFTA: can WHFTA be far behind?', *Journal of Common Market Studies*, pp. 125–141.

Whalley, J. (ed.) (1985). *Canada–United States Free Trade*. Toronto: University of Toronto Press.

White Paper (*Completing the Internal Market*) (1985). Luxembourg: EC.

Whitman, M. (1967). *International and Interregional Payments Adjustment: A Synthetic View*. Princeton: Essays in International Finance, Princeton University.

Wilkinson, B. (1985). 'Canada/US free trade and canadian economic, cultural and political sovereignty', in *Canadian Trade at a Crossroads: Options for New International Agreements* (eds D. Conklin and T. Chourchene). Toronto: Ontario Economic Council, pp. 291–307.

Wilkinson, C. (1984). 'Trends in industrial policy in the EC: theory and practice', in *European Industry: Public Policy and Corporate Strategy* (ed. A. Jacquemin). Oxford: Clarendon Press, pp. 39–78.

Williamson, J. and A. Bottrill (1973). 'The impact of customs unions on trade in manufacturers', in *The Economics of Integration* (ed. M. Krauss). London: George Allen & Unwin, pp. 118–151.

Winters, A. (1987). 'Negotiating the abolition of non-tariff barriers', *Oxford Economic Papers*, pp. 465–480.

Winters, A. (1994). 'The EC and protection: the political economy', *European Economic Review*, pp. 596–603.

Wong, J. (1988). 'The Association of Southeast Asean Nations', in *International Economic Integration* (ed. A. El-Agraa). London: Macmillan, pp. 314–328.

Wonnacott, P. (1987). *The United States and Canada: The Quest For Free Trade*. Washington: Institute for International Economics.

Wonnacott, P. and R. Wonnacott (1981). 'Is unilateral tariff reduction preferable to a customs union? The customs union of the missing foreign tariffs', *American Economic Review*, pp. 704–713.

World Bank (1993). *The East Asian Miracle*. New York: Oxford University Press.

World Trade Organization (1995). *Regionalism and the World Trading System*. Geneva: World Trade Organization.

Wren, C. (1990). 'Regional policy in the 1980s', *National Westminster Bank Quarterly Review*, pp. 52–64.

Yamada, T. and T. Yamada (1996). 'EC integration and Japanese foreign direct investment in the EC', *Contemporary Economic Policy*, pp. 48–57.

Yamawaki, H. (1991). 'Discussion', in *European Integration: Trade and Industry* (eds A. Winters and A. Venables). Cambridge: Cambridge University Press, pp. 231–233.

Yannopoulos, G. (1988). *Customs Unions and Trade Conflicts*. London: Routledge.

Yannopoulos, G. (1990). 'Foreign direct investment and European integration: the evidence from the formative years of the European Community', *Journal of Common Market Studies*, pp. 235–259.

Young, S. (1993). 'Globalism and regionalism: complements or competitors', in *Pacific Dynamism and the International Economic System* (eds F. Bergsten and M. Noland). Washington: Institute for International Economics, pp. 111–131.

Yuill, D., K. Allen, J. Bachtler, K. Clement and F. Wishdale (1994). *European Regional Incentives, 1994–95*. London: Bowker.

Zimmermann, K. (1995). 'Tackling the European migration problem', *Economic Perspectives*, pp. 45–62.

Zysman, J. (1983). *Governments, Markets and Growth*. Ithaca: Cornell University Press.

Index